THE BOOK

# Suzuki GSX-R600, GSX-R750 and GSX-R1000
## Service and Repair Manual

## by Phil Mather

**Models covered**

*(3986-304)*

GSX-R600K1 and K2. 599cc. 2001 to 2002
GSX-R750Y, K1 and K2. 749cc. 2000 to 2002
GSX-R1000K1 and K2. 988cc. 2001 to 2002

© Haynes Publishing 2003

ABCDE
FGHIJ
KLMNO
PQRST

Printed in the USA

A book in the **Haynes Service and Repair Manual Series**

ISBN **1 85960 986 4**

**British Library Cataloguing in Publication Data**
A catalogue record for this book is available from the British Library.

**Library of Congress Control Number** 2003101250

**Haynes Publishing**
Sparkford, Yeovil, Somerset BA22 7JJ, England

**Haynes North America, Inc**
861 Lawrence Drive, Newbury Park, California 91320, USA

**Editions Haynes**
4, Rue de l'Abreuvoir
92415 COURBEVOIE CEDEX, France

**Haynes Publishing Nordiska AB**
Box 1504, 751 45 UPPSALA, Sweden

# Contents

## LIVING WITH YOUR SUZUKI GSX-R

### Introduction

### Daily (pre-ride checks)

## MAINTENANCE

### Routine maintenance and servicing

# Contents

# Suzuki
# Every Which Way

by Julian Ryder

## From Textile Machinery to Motorcycles

Suzuki were the second of Japan's Big Four motorcycle manufacturers to enter the business, and like Honda they started by bolting small two-stroke motors to bicycles. Unlike Honda, they had manufactured other products before turning to transportation in the aftermath of World War II.

In fact Suzuki has been in business since the first decade of the 20th-Century when Michio Suzuki manufactured textile machinery.

The desperate need for transport in post-war Japan saw Suzuki make their first motorised bicycle in 1952, and the fact that by 1954 the company had changed its name to Suzuki Motor Company shows how quickly the sideline took over the whole company's activities. In their first full manufacturing year,

Suzuki made nearly 4500 bikes and rapidly expanded into the world markets with a range of two-strokes.

Suzuki didn't make a four-stroke until 1977 when the GS750 double-overhead-cam across-the-frame four arrived. This was several years after Honda and Kawasaki had established the air-cooled four as the industry standard, but no motorcycle epitomises the era of what came to be known as the Universal

The T500 two-stroke twin

**One of the later GT750 'kettle' models with front disc brakes**

50 cc racer won six of the eight world titles chalked up by Suzuki during the 1960s as well as providing Mitsuo Itoh with the distinction of being the only Japanese rider to win an Isle of Man TT. Mr Itoh still works for Suzuki, he's in charge of their racing program.

Europe got the benefit of Suzuki's two-stroke expertise in a succession of air-cooled twins, the six-speed 250 cc Super Six being the most memorable, but the arrival in 1968 of the first of a series of 500 cc twins which were good looking, robust and versatile marked the start of mainstream success.

So confident were Suzuki of their two-stroke expertise that they even applied it to the burgeoning Superbike sector. The GT750 water-cooled triple arrived in 1972. It was big, fast and comfortable although the handling and stopping power did draw some comment. Whatever the drawbacks of the road bike, the engine was immensely successful in Superbike and Formula 750 racing. The roadster has its devotees, though, and is now a sought-after bike on the classic Japanese scene. Do not refer to it as the Water Buffalo in such company. Joking aside, the later disc-braked versions were quite civilised, but the audacious idea of using a big two-stroke motor in what was essentially a touring bike was a surprising success until the fuel crisis of the mid-'70s effectively killed off big strokers.

The same could be said of Suzuki's only real lemon, the RE5. This is still the only mass-produced bike to use the rotary (or Wankel) engine but never sold well. Fuel consumption in the mid-teens allied to frightening complexity and excess weight meant the RE5 was a non-starter in the sales race.

Japanese motorcycle better than the GS. So well engineered were the original fours that you can clearly see their genes in the GS500 twins that are still going strong in the mid-1990s. Suzuki's ability to prolong the life of their products this way means that they are often thought of as a conservative company. This is hardly fair if you look at some of their landmark designs, most of which have been commercial as well as critical successes.

## Two-stroke Success

Early racing efforts were bolstered by the arrival of Ernst Degner who defected from the East German MZ team at the Swedish GP of 1961, bringing with him the rotary-valve secrets of design genius Walter Kaaden. The new Suzuki 50 cc racer won its first GP on the Isle of Man the following year and winning the title easily. Only Honda and Ralph Bryans interrupted Suzuki's run of 50 cc titles from 1962 to 1968.

The arrival of the twin-cylinder 125 racer in 1963 enabled Hugh Anderson to win both 50 and 125 world titles. You may not think 50 cc racing would be exciting - until you learn that the final incarnation of the thing had 14 gears and could do well over 100 mph on fast circuits. Before pulling out of GPs in 1967 the

**Suzuki's GT250X7 was an instant hit in the popular 250 cc 'learner' sector**

The GS400 was the first in a line of four-stroke twins

## Development of the Four-stroke range

When Suzuki got round to building a four-stroke they did a very good job of it. The GS fours were built in 550, 650, 750, 850, 1000 and 1100 cc sizes in sports, custom, roadster and even shaft-driven touring forms over many years. The GS1000 was in on the start of Superbike racing in the early 1970s and the GS850 shaft-driven tourer was around nearly 15 years later. The fours spawned a line of 400, 425, 450 and 500 cc GS twins that were essentially the middle half of the four with all their reliability. If there was ever a criticism of the GS models it was that with the exception of the GS1000S of 1980, colloquially known as the ice-cream van, the range was visually uninspiring.

They nearly made the same mistake when they launched the four-valve-head GSX750 in 1979. Fortunately, the original twin-shock version was soon replaced by the 'E'-model with Full-Floater rear suspension and a full set of all the gadgets the Japanese industry was then keen on and has since forgotten about, like 16-inch front wheels and anti-dive forks. The air-cooled GSX was like the GS built in 550, 750 and 1100 cc versions with a variety of half, full and touring fairings, but the GSX that is best remembered is the Katana that first appeared in 1981. The power was provided by an 1000 or 1100 cc GSX motor, but wrapped around it was the most outrageous styling package to come out of Japan. Designed by Hans Muth of Target Design, the Katana looked like nothing seen before or since. At the time there was as much anti feeling as praise, but now it is rightly regarded as a classic, a true milestone in motorcycle design. The factory have even started making 250 and 400 cc fours for the home market with the same styling as the 1981 bike.

Just to remind us that they'd still been building two-strokes for the likes of Barry Sheene, in 1986 Suzuki marketed a road-going version of their RG500 square-four racer which had put an end to the era of the four-stroke in 500 GPs when it appeared in 1974. In 1976 Suzuki not only won their first 500 title with Sheene, they sold RG500s over the counter and won every GP with them - with the exception of the Isle of Man TT which the works riders boycotted. Ten years on, the RG500 Gamma gave road riders the nearest experience they'd ever get to riding a GP bike. The fearsome beast could top 140 mph and only weighed 340 lb - the other alleged GP replicas were pussy cats compared to the Gamma's man-eating tiger.

The RG only lasted a few years and is already firmly in the category of collector's item; its four-stroke equivalent, the GSX-R, is still with us and looks like being so for many years. You have to look back to 1985 and its launch to realise just what a revolutionary step the GSX-R750 was: quite simply it was the first race replica. Not a bike dressed up to look like a race bike, but a genuine racer with lights on, a bike that could be taken straight to the track and win.

The first GSX-R, the 750, had a completely new motor cooled by oil rather than water and an aluminium cradle frame. It was sparse, a little twitchy and very, very fast. This time Suzuki got the looks right, blue and white bodywork based on the factory's racing colours and endurance-racer lookalike twin headlights. And then came the 1100 - the big GSX-R got progressively more brutal as it chased the Yamaha EXUP for the heavyweight championship.

The GS750 led the way for a series of four cylinder models

If you want to read the full history of the 750, then go for Rob Simmonds' excellent history of the GSX-R750 in the Haynes Great Bikes Series, but this manual is for the latest generation of all three capacities of GSX-R, 600 and 1000 as well as the 750.

Like all their ancestors, these Suzukis are almost track ready. They are the lightest, sharpest handling, most rev-crazy bikes in their classes. Issues like comfort or luggage carrying are not relevant. Just how race ready are they? When the 1000 first appeared in 2001, the field at the Le Mans 24 Hour race and the Bol d'Or looked like a GSX-R1000 one-make cup except for the factory Superbikes. Running in restricted 'Super-production' form, GSX-R1000s won every race in the World Endurance Championship except the Suzuka 8 Hours and took 17 out of a possible 24 podiums, racking up three clean-sweeps of the rostrum positions.

The 750, often overlooked as road riders now go for either 600 or 1000 cc capacity machines, holds the distinction of being the last ever 750 cc four-cylinder-engined bike to win a round of the World Superbike Championship, the rider was Pierfrancesco Chili and the place was Donington Park on 27 May 2001. In the States, the slightly freer Superbike regulations helped Mat Mladdin to win three consecutive AMA titles, the last one on the fuel-injected Y model and Akira Ryo won the 2001 All-Japan Superbike title.

In the Supersport class the 600 won the first ever World title for that category back in 1999 and the new fuel-injected bikes have carried all before them in domestic championships all over the world. Go to any trackday and the chances are that the fast guys will be on GSX-R600s. It's just about the most uncompromising motorcycle you could buy for road use but on a track it all makes sense.

**Later four-stroke models, like this GSX1100, were fitted with 16v engines**

And alongside all these mould-breaking designs, Suzuki were also making the best looking custom bikes to come out of Japan, the Intruders; the first race replica trail bike, the DR350; the sharpest 250 Supersports, the RGV250; and a bargain-basement 600, the Bandit. The Bandit proved so popular they went on to build 1200 and 750 cc versions of it. I suppose that's predictable, a range of four-stroke fours just like the GS and GSXs. It's just like the company really, sometimes predictable, admittedly - but never boring.

## Suzuki GSX-R model history

Many bikes have been labelled as 'race replicas', that is bikes that look like their relatives that inhabit Superbike or MotoGP racing. Indeed, there are those who will tell you that the very first GSX-R750 that appeared in 1985 was the first such bike, the first 'race replica'.

I would contend that that statement is rubbish: GSX-Rs of all capacities have never been race replicas, they have always been the real thing. When the competition had to build homologation specials to make their bikes competitive in Superbike racing, Suzuki just stuck slicks on their machines and went racing. True there was a 'double-R' 750 model in '89 to enable flat-slide carburettors to be used and a 750 SP as in Sport Production model in '94, but compared to building a whole new and very expensive bike as Honda did with their RC30 and later with their SP-2,

or a limited-edition racers-only machine like the Yamaha R7, Suzuki mass-produced competitive racing bikes with lights on. This adherence to the spirit of production bike racing rather than the letter of the law meant their works teams were always struggling to be competitive but at lower levels clubmen could buy a GSX-R and, if the rider was good enough, win. Has any bike ever built won more races than the GSX-R750?

**Suzuki's GSX-R range represented their cutting edge sports bikes**

**The GSX-R600K2 MoviStar model**

**The GSX-R750Y**

**The GSX-R1000K2**

This new generation of GSX-R differs from the earlier bikes in that they all use fuel-injection and two butterfly valves in the inlet tract. The first is controlled by the twistgrip as normal but the second is under the control of the engine management system and is a major player in making the GSX's power delivery so useable. Other than that Suzuki did what they've always done with their flagship sportsters, they made them lighter and more powerful than the opposition. Which sounds simple and probably is if you're building a one-off MotoGP bike – but as any engineer will tell you, adding lightness is a very difficult trick and mass-producing it is even trickier.

# Acknowledgements

Our thanks are due to GT Motorcycles of Yeovil who supplied the machines featured in the illustrations throughout this manual. We would also like to thank NGK Spark Plugs (UK) Ltd for supplying the colour spark plug condition photographs, the Avon Rubber Company for supplying information on tyre fitting and Draper Tools Ltd for some of the workshop tools shown.

Thanks are also due to Julian Ryder who wrote the introduction 'Every Which Way', to Suzuki (GB) Ltd who supplied model photographs and to Kel Edge who supplied the photograph on the rear cover of Gregorio Lavilla riding the GSX-R750 Alstare Suzuki.

# About this Manual

The aim of this manual is to help you get the best value from your motorcycle. It can do so in several ways. It can help you decide what work must be done, even if you choose to have it done by a dealer; it provides information and procedures for routine maintenance and servicing; and it offers diagnostic and repair procedures to follow when trouble occurs.

We hope you use the manual to tackle the work yourself. For many simpler jobs, doing it yourself may be quicker than arranging an appointment to get the motorcycle into a dealer and making the trips to leave it and pick it up. More importantly, a lot of money can be saved by avoiding the expense the shop must pass on to you to cover its labour and overhead costs. An added benefit is the sense of satisfaction and accomplishment that you feel after doing the job yourself.

References to the left or right side of the motorcycle assume you are sitting on the seat, facing forward.

## GSX-R600

The GSX-R600K1 was introduced in November 2000, replacing the GSX-R600Y with a revised specification for engine and chassis resulting in an increase in power output and an overall weight saving of 11 kg.

The engine was a liquid cooled four-cylinder with double overhead camshafts driven by chain off the right-hand end of the crankshaft. Drive was transmitted to the six-speed gearbox via a conventional wet multi-plate clutch, and to the rear wheel by chain and sprockets.

Compared with the carburetted GSX-R600, this model featured a newly designed cylinder head with larger valves, slimmer valve stems and revised porting for greater airflow efficiency in conjunction with a larger air filter housing, and the SDTV (Suzuki Dual Throttle Valve) fuel injection system. The crankshaft was narrower, reducing the machine's overall width, and the crankshaft bearing areas made smaller to reduced friction. Engine covers were made from magnesium and the cylinder block was integral with the upper crankcase. The crankcases were a three-piece 'cassette' design resulting in a shorter overall engine unit length.

The chassis comprised a compact, twin-spar aluminium alloy frame with a bolt-on rear subframe and box-section swingarm, lighter in weight than that on the previous GSX-R600 but with enhanced torsional rigidity. Front suspension was by conventional, three-way adjustable telescopic forks and rear suspension was by a rising rate, three-way adjustable aluminium-bodied mono-shock.

Braking was by twin discs with four piston calipers at the front and a single disc with a two-piston caliper at the rear.

The GSX-R600K1 was available in pearl white and deep blue, pearl yellow and metallic black, or candy blue and black.

The GSX-R600K2 was introduced in November 2001. Minor detail changes included modifications to the sprocket cover, fuel pump, horn mounting and luggage hooks. The exhaust system was made from stainless steel and the candy blue and black colour option was replaced by candy blue and metallic silver. A limited edition model was available in Telefonica Movistar livery.

## GSX-R750

The GSX-R750Y was introduced in March 2000, replacing the GSX-R750X with a revised specification for engine and chassis resulting in an increase in power output and an overall weight saving of 13 kg.

The engine was a liquid cooled four-cylinder with double overhead camshafts driven by chain off the right-hand end of the crankshaft. Drive was transmitted to the six-speed gearbox via a conventional wet multi-plate clutch, and to the rear wheel by chain and sprockets.

Compared with the GSX-R750X, this model featured a newly designed cylinder head with revised porting and slimmer valve stems for greater airflow efficiency, and the earlier fuel injection system was replaced by the SDTV(Suzuki Dual Throttle Valve) system. New, lighter camshafts, valve springs, pistons, connecting rods and crankshaft were fitted. Engine covers were made from magnesium and the cylinder block was integral with the upper crankcase. The crankcases were a three-piece 'cassette' design resulting in a shorter overall engine unit length. The radiator was increased in size to improve cooling.

The chassis comprised a compact, twin-spar aluminium alloy frame with a bolt-on rear subframe and braced, box-section swingarm. Front suspension was by upside-down, three-way adjustable forks and rear suspension was by a rising rate, three-way adjustable aluminium-bodied mono-shock.

Braking was by twin discs with four piston calipers at the front and a single disc with a two-piston caliper at the rear. The brake calipers were made from aluminium.

The GSX-R750Y was available in pearl white and deep blue, pearl yellow and metallic black, or candy blue and black.

The GSX-R750K1 was introduced in January 2001. The remote idle speed adjuster was deleted. Minor detail changes included modifications to the clutch friction plates and fuel rail. The candy blue and black colour option was replaced by pearl red and metallic silver.

The GSX-R750K2 was introduced in November 2001. The remotely mounted STV (secondary throttle valve) servo with cable operated throttle valve was replaced with a servo mounted directly onto the No. 4 throttle body. Renewable swingarm pivot bosses

were fitted to the frame. Minor detail changes included modifications to the sprocket cover, fuel pump, front brake caliper and luggage hooks. The exhaust system was now made from stainless steel. The colour options were unchanged.

## GSX-R1000

The GSX-R1000K1 was introduced in November 2000.

The engine was a liquid cooled four-cylinder with double overhead camshafts driven by chain off the right-hand end of the crankshaft. It was based on the GSX-R750 unit with increased dimensions where necessary in view of the increased capacity and mechanical loads. The crankcases were of the three-piece 'cassette' design, although physically larger to accommodate the increase in piston stroke as well as wider transmission gear pinions, a larger clutch, a new oil cooler system and a balancer shaft to counteract secondary vibration.

Drive was transmitted to the six-speed gearbox via a conventional multi-plate clutch, and to the rear wheel by chain and sprockets.

The fuel system was the SDTV (Suzuki Dual Throttle Valve) fuel injection system and a digitally-controlled valve was placed in the exhaust system to optimise back-pressure according to engine speed. The exhaust system and silencer core were made from titanium.

The chassis comprised a twin-spar aluminium alloy frame with increased outside wall thickness, a bolt-on rear subframe and braced, box-section swingarm. Front suspension was by upside-down, three-way adjustable forks and rear suspension was by a rising rate, three-way adjustable aluminium-bodied mono-shock.

Braking was by twin discs with six piston calipers at the front and a single disc with a two-piston caliper at the rear. The brake calipers were made from aluminium.

The GSX-R1000K1 was available in pearl white and deep blue, pearl black and metallic silver, or pearl red and metallic black.

The GSX-R1000K2 was introduced in January 2002. Minor detail changes included modifications to the fuel pump and luggage hooks. The manual fast idle (choke) operation was replaced by an automatic system. The pearl black and metallic silver colour option was replaced by candy blue and pearl black.

Performance data

## Maximum power
GSX-R600 . . . . . . . . . . . . . . . . . . . . . . . . . . . . . . . . . . . . . . . . . . . . . .   101 bhp (75.3 kW) @ 12,800 rpm
GSX-R750 . . . . . . . . . . . . . . . . . . . . . . . . . . . . . . . . . . . . . . . . . . . . . .   139 bhp (103.7 kW) @ 12,500 rpm
GSX-R1000 . . . . . . . . . . . . . . . . . . . . . . . . . . . . . . . . . . . . . . . . . . . . .   150 bhp (111.0 kW) @ 10,500 rpm

## Maximum torque
GSX-R600 . . . . . . . . . . . . . . . . . . . . . . . . . . . . . . . . . . . . . . . . . . . . . .   47 lbf ft (64 Nm) @ 10,100 rpm
GSX-R750 . . . . . . . . . . . . . . . . . . . . . . . . . . . . . . . . . . . . . . . . . . . . . .   62 lbf ft (84 Nm) @ 10,000 rpm
GSX-R1000 . . . . . . . . . . . . . . . . . . . . . . . . . . . . . . . . . . . . . . . . . . . . .   80 lbf ft (108 Nm) @ 8000 rpm

## Power-to-weight ratio (approximate)
GSX-R600 . . . . . . . . . . . . . . . . . . . . . . . . . . . . . . . . . . . . . . . . . . . . . .   0.70 bhp per kg
GSX-R750 . . . . . . . . . . . . . . . . . . . . . . . . . . . . . . . . . . . . . . . . . . . . . .   0.84 bhp per kg
GSX-R1000 . . . . . . . . . . . . . . . . . . . . . . . . . . . . . . . . . . . . . . . . . . . . .   0.94 bhp per kg

## Top speed
GSX-R600 . . . . . . . . . . . . . . . . . . . . . . . . . . . . . . . . . . . . . . . . . . . . . .   160 mph (257 km/h)
GSX-R750 . . . . . . . . . . . . . . . . . . . . . . . . . . . . . . . . . . . . . . . . . . . . . .   169 mph (272 km/h)
GSX-R1000 . . . . . . . . . . . . . . . . . . . . . . . . . . . . . . . . . . . . . . . . . . . . .   182 mph (293 km/h)

## Acceleration
GSX-R600
   Time taken to cover a ¼ mile from a standing start . . . . . . . . . . . . .   11.0 secs
   Terminal speed after ¼ mile . . . . . . . . . . . . . . . . . . . . . . . . . . . . . .   125 mph (201 km/h)
GSX-R750
   Time taken to cover a ¼ mile from a standing start . . . . . . . . . . . . .   10.5 secs
   Terminal speed after ¼ mile . . . . . . . . . . . . . . . . . . . . . . . . . . . . . .   134 mph (215 km/h)
GSX-R1000
   Time taken to cover a ¼ mile from a standing start . . . . . . . . . . . . .   10.3 secs
   Terminal speed after ¼ mile . . . . . . . . . . . . . . . . . . . . . . . . . . . . . .   147 mph (236 km/h)

## Average fuel consumption
*Miles per Imp gal, miles per litre, litres per 100 km*
GSX-R600 . . . . . . . . . . . . . . . . . . . . . . . . . . . . . . . . . . . . . . . . . . . . . .   36 mpg, 7.9 mpl, 7.8 l/100 km
GSX-R750 . . . . . . . . . . . . . . . . . . . . . . . . . . . . . . . . . . . . . . . . . . . . . .   38 mpg, 8.4 mpl, 7.4 l/100 km
GSX-R1000 . . . . . . . . . . . . . . . . . . . . . . . . . . . . . . . . . . . . . . . . . . . . .   30 mpg, 6.6 mpl, 9.4 l/100 km
Fuel tank capacity (all models) . . . . . . . . . . . . . . . . . . . . . . . . . . . . .   18 litres (3.96 Imp gal)

## Fuel tank range
GSX-R600 . . . . . . . . . . . . . . . . . . . . . . . . . . . . . . . . . . . . . . . . . . . . . .   140 miles (225 km)
GSX-R750 . . . . . . . . . . . . . . . . . . . . . . . . . . . . . . . . . . . . . . . . . . . . . .   150 miles (241 km)
GSX-R1000 . . . . . . . . . . . . . . . . . . . . . . . . . . . . . . . . . . . . . . . . . . . . .   120 miles (193 km)

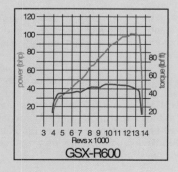

GSX-R600

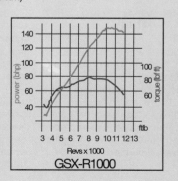

GSX-R1000

Performance data sourced from Motor Cycle News road test features. See the MCN website for up-to-date biking news.

MCN www.motorcyclenews.com

## Weights and dimensions

Wheelbase
    GSX-R600 . . . . . . . . . . . . . . . . . . . . . . . . . . . . . . . . . . . . . . .   1400 mm
    GSX-R750 and GSX-R1000 . . . . . . . . . . . . . . . . . . . . . . . . . . . .   1410 mm
Overall length
    GSX-R600 and GSX-R750 . . . . . . . . . . . . . . . . . . . . . . . . . . . . .   2040 mm
    GSX-R1000 . . . . . . . . . . . . . . . . . . . . . . . . . . . . . . . . . . . . . . . .   2045 mm
Overall height
    GSX-R600 and GSX-R1000 . . . . . . . . . . . . . . . . . . . . . . . . . . . .   1135 mm
    GSX-R750 . . . . . . . . . . . . . . . . . . . . . . . . . . . . . . . . . . . . . . . .   1134 mm
Overall width
    GSX-R600 and GSX-R1000 . . . . . . . . . . . . . . . . . . . . . . . . . . . .   715 mm
    GSX-R750 . . . . . . . . . . . . . . . . . . . . . . . . . . . . . . . . . . . . . . . .   717 mm
Seat height
    GSX-R600 and GSX-R1000 . . . . . . . . . . . . . . . . . . . . . . . . . . . .   830 mm
    GSX-R750 . . . . . . . . . . . . . . . . . . . . . . . . . . . . . . . . . . . . . . . .   829 mm
Ground clearance (all models) . . . . . . . . . . . . . . . . . . . . . . . . . . . .   130 mm
Dry weight
    GSX-R600 . . . . . . . . . . . . . . . . . . . . . . . . . . . . . . . . . . . . . . . .   163 kg
    GSX-R750 . . . . . . . . . . . . . . . . . . . . . . . . . . . . . . . . . . . . . . . .   166 kg
    GSX-R1000 . . . . . . . . . . . . . . . . . . . . . . . . . . . . . . . . . . . . . . .   170 kg

## Engine

Type . . . . . . . . . . . . . . . . . . . . . . . . . . . . . . . . . . . . . . . . . . . . . . . . . . . . . . . . Liquid cooled, in-line 4-cylinder
Capacity
  GSX-R600 . . . . . . . . . . . . . . . . . . . . . . . . . . . . . . . . . . . . . . . . . . . . . . 599 cc
  GSX-R750 . . . . . . . . . . . . . . . . . . . . . . . . . . . . . . . . . . . . . . . . . . . . . . 749 cc
  GSX-R1000 . . . . . . . . . . . . . . . . . . . . . . . . . . . . . . . . . . . . . . . . . . . . . 988 cc
Bore
  GSX-R600 . . . . . . . . . . . . . . . . . . . . . . . . . . . . . . . . . . . . . . . . . . . . . . 67 mm
  GSX-R750 . . . . . . . . . . . . . . . . . . . . . . . . . . . . . . . . . . . . . . . . . . . . . . 72 mm
  GSX-R1000 . . . . . . . . . . . . . . . . . . . . . . . . . . . . . . . . . . . . . . . . . . . . . 73 mm
Stroke
  GSX-R600 . . . . . . . . . . . . . . . . . . . . . . . . . . . . . . . . . . . . . . . . . . . . . . 42.5 mm
  GSX-R750 . . . . . . . . . . . . . . . . . . . . . . . . . . . . . . . . . . . . . . . . . . . . . . 46.0 mm
  GSX-R1000 . . . . . . . . . . . . . . . . . . . . . . . . . . . . . . . . . . . . . . . . . . . . . 59.0 mm
Compression ratio
  GSX-R600 . . . . . . . . . . . . . . . . . . . . . . . . . . . . . . . . . . . . . . . . . . . . . . 12.2:1
  GSX-R750 and GSX-R1000 . . . . . . . . . . . . . . . . . . . . . . . . . . . . . . . . 12.0:1
Camshafts . . . . . . . . . . . . . . . . . . . . . . . . . . . . . . . . . . . . . . . . . . . . . . . . . DOHC, chain driven
Valves . . . . . . . . . . . . . . . . . . . . . . . . . . . . . . . . . . . . . . . . . . . . . . . . . . . . . 4 valves per cylinder
Fuel system . . . . . . . . . . . . . . . . . . . . . . . . . . . . . . . . . . . . . . . . . . . . . . . . Fuel injection
Clutch . . . . . . . . . . . . . . . . . . . . . . . . . . . . . . . . . . . . . . . . . . . . . . . . . . . . . Wet multi-plate, hydraulically operated
Transmission . . . . . . . . . . . . . . . . . . . . . . . . . . . . . . . . . . . . . . . . . . . . . . . 6 speed constant mesh
Final drive
  Chain
    GSX-R600 . . . . . . . . . . . . . . . . . . . . . . . . . . . . . . . . . . . . . . . . . . . . RK 525SMOZ6 (110 links)
    GSX-R750 . . . . . . . . . . . . . . . . . . . . . . . . . . . . . . . . . . . . . . . . . . . . RK 525ROZ4 (110 links)
    GSX-R1000 . . . . . . . . . . . . . . . . . . . . . . . . . . . . . . . . . . . . . . . . . . . DID50V4 (110 links)
  Sprockets
    GSX-R600 . . . . . . . . . . . . . . . . . . . . . . . . . . . . . . . . . . . . . . . . . . . . 16 tooth front, 45 tooth rear
    GSX-R750 and GSX-R1000 . . . . . . . . . . . . . . . . . . . . . . . . . . . . . . 17 tooth front, 42 tooth rear

## Chassis

Type . . . . . . . . . . . . . . . . . . . . . . . . . . . . . . . . . . . . . . . . . . . . . . . . . . . . . . . . Twin spar, aluminium alloy
Rake
  GSX-R600 and GSX-R1000 . . . . . . . . . . . . . . . . . . . . . . . . . . . . . . . . 24.0°
  GSX-R750 . . . . . . . . . . . . . . . . . . . . . . . . . . . . . . . . . . . . . . . . . . . . . . 24.1°
Trail
  GSX-R600 and GSX-R1000 . . . . . . . . . . . . . . . . . . . . . . . . . . . . . . . . 96.0 mm
  GSX-R750 . . . . . . . . . . . . . . . . . . . . . . . . . . . . . . . . . . . . . . . . . . . . . . 94.1 mm
Front suspension
  GSX-R600 . . . . . . . . . . . . . . . . . . . . . . . . . . . . . . . . . . . . . . . . . . . . . . 45 mm diameter telescopic forks
  GSX-R750 and GSX-R1000 . . . . . . . . . . . . . . . . . . . . . . . . . . . . . . . . 43 mm diameter upside down forks
  Travel
    GSX-R600 and GSX-R750 . . . . . . . . . . . . . . . . . . . . . . . . . . . . . . . 125 mm
    GSX-R1000 . . . . . . . . . . . . . . . . . . . . . . . . . . . . . . . . . . . . . . . . . . . 120 mm
  Adjustments . . . . . . . . . . . . . . . . . . . . . . . . . . . . . . . . . . . . . . . . . . . . . Spring pre-load, compression and rebound damping
Rear suspension
  Type . . . . . . . . . . . . . . . . . . . . . . . . . . . . . . . . . . . . . . . . . . . . . . . . . . . Rising rate with monoshock
  Stroke . . . . . . . . . . . . . . . . . . . . . . . . . . . . . . . . . . . . . . . . . . . . . . . . . . 75 mm
  Wheel travel . . . . . . . . . . . . . . . . . . . . . . . . . . . . . . . . . . . . . . . . . . . . . 130 mm
  Adjustments . . . . . . . . . . . . . . . . . . . . . . . . . . . . . . . . . . . . . . . . . . . . . Spring pre-load, compression and rebound damping
Tyre sizes
  Front (all models) . . . . . . . . . . . . . . . . . . . . . . . . . . . . . . . . . . . . . . . . 120/70 ZR 17 58W
  Rear
    GSX-R600 and GSX-R750 . . . . . . . . . . . . . . . . . . . . . . . . . . . . . . . 180/55 ZR 17 73W
    GSX-R1000 . . . . . . . . . . . . . . . . . . . . . . . . . . . . . . . . . . . . . . . . . . . 190/50 ZR 17
Brakes
  Front
    GSX-R600 and GSX-R750 . . . . . . . . . . . . . . . . . . . . . . . . . . . . . . . Twin 320 mm discs with Tokico four-piston calipers
    GSX-R1000 . . . . . . . . . . . . . . . . . . . . . . . . . . . . . . . . . . . . . . . . . . . Twin 320 mm discs with Tokico six-piston calipers
  Rear . . . . . . . . . . . . . . . . . . . . . . . . . . . . . . . . . . . . . . . . . . . . . . . . . . . . Single 220 mm disc with two-piston caliper

## Frame and engine numbers

The frame serial number is stamped into the right-hand side of the steering head and is also repeated on the VIN plate. The engine number is stamped into the back of the crankcase. Both of these numbers should be recorded and kept in a safe place so they can be furnished to law enforcement officials in the event of a theft. The throttle bodies also have an identification number stamped into them.

The frame serial number and engine serial number should also be kept in a handy place (such as with your driving licence) so they are always available when purchasing or ordering parts for your machine.

The engine number is stamped into the back of the crankcase

The throttle body ID number location

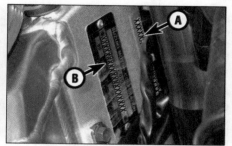

The frame number (A) and VIN plate (B) can be found on the steering head

## Identifying model codes

The procedures in this manual identify the bikes by engine size (e.g. GSX-R600), then if further clarification is required also by the model code (e.g. GSX-R600K1). The model code corresponds to the production year (which may not necessarily be the same as the year of first registration) and can also be determined from the frame number as follows:

### UK models

| Model code | Prod. yr. | Frame number |
| --- | --- | --- |
| GSX-R600K1 | 2001 | JS1BG111100100001-on |
| GSX-R600K2 | 2002 | JS1BG111100103068-on |
| GSX-R750Y | 2000 | JS1BD111100100001-on |
| GSX-R750K1 | 2001 | JS1BD111100101827-on |
| GSX-R750K2 | 2002 | JS1BD111100102127-on |
| GSX-R1000K1 | 2001 | JS1BL111100100001-on |
| GSX-R1000K2 | 2002 | JS1BL111100102548-on |

### European models

| Model code | Prod. yr. | Frame number |
| --- | --- | --- |
| GSX-R600K1 | 2001 | JS1BG111200100001-on |
| GSX-R600K2 | 2002 | JS1BG111200110601-on |
| GSX-R750Y | 2000 | JS1BD111200100001-on |
| GSX-R750K1 | 2001 | JS1BD111200104709-on |
| GSX-R750K2 | 2002 | JS1BD111200109343-on |
| GSX-R1000K1 | 2001 | JS1BL111200100001-on |
| GSX-R1000K2 | 2002 | JS1BL111200108731-on |

### US models

| Model code | Prod. yr. | Frame number |
| --- | --- | --- |
| GSX-R600K1 | 2001 | not available |
| GSX-R600K2 | 2002 | not available |
| GSX-R750Y | 2000 | JS1GR7HAY2100001-on |
| GSX-R750K1 | 2001 | JS1GR7HA12100001-on |
| GSX-R750K2 | 2002 | JS1GR7HA22100001-on |
| GSX-R1000K1 | 2001 | JS1GT74A12100001-on |
| GSX-R1000K2 | 2002 | JS1GT74A22100001-on |

## Buying spare parts

Once you have found all the identification numbers, record them for reference when buying parts. Since the manufacturers change specifications, parts and vendors (companies that manufacture various components on the machine), providing the ID numbers is the only way to be reasonably sure that you are buying the correct parts.

Whenever possible, take the worn part to the dealer so direct comparison with the new component can be made. Along the trail from the manufacturer to the parts shelf, there are numerous places that the part can end up with the wrong number or be listed incorrectly.

The two places to purchase new parts for your motorcycle – the accessory store and the franchised dealer – differ in the type of parts they carry. While dealers can obtain virtually every part for your motorcycle, the accessory dealer is usually limited to normal high wear items such as shock absorbers, tune-up parts, various engine gaskets, cables, chains, brake parts, etc. Rarely will an accessory outlet have major suspension components, cylinders, transmission gears, or cases.

Used parts can be obtained for roughly half the price of new ones, but you can't always be sure of what you're getting. Once again, take your worn part to the breaker (wrecking yard) for direct comparison.

Whether buying new, used or rebuilt parts, the best course is to deal directly with someone who specialises in parts for your particular make.

Professional mechanics are trained in safe working procedures. However enthusiastic you may be about getting on with the job at hand, take the time to ensure that your safety is not put at risk. A moment's lack of attention can result in an accident, as can failure to observe simple precautions.

There will always be new ways of having accidents, and the following is not a comprehensive list of all dangers; it is intended rather to make you aware of the risks and to encourage a safe approach to all work you carry out on your bike.

## Asbestos

● Certain friction, insulating, sealing and other products - such as brake pads, clutch linings, gaskets, etc. - contain asbestos. Extreme care must be taken to avoid inhalation of dust from such products since it is hazardous to health. If in doubt, assume that they do contain asbestos.

## Fire

● Remember at all times that petrol is highly flammable. Never smoke or have any kind of naked flame around, when working on the vehicle. But the risk does not end there - a spark caused by an electrical short-circuit, by two metal surfaces contacting each other, by careless use of tools, or even by static electricity built up in your body under certain conditions, can ignite petrol vapour, which in a confined space is highly explosive. Never use petrol as a cleaning solvent. Use an approved safety solvent.

● Always disconnect the battery earth terminal before working on any part of the fuel or electrical system, and never risk spilling fuel on to a hot engine or exhaust.

● It is recommended that a fire extinguisher of a type suitable for fuel and electrical fires is kept handy in the garage or workplace at all times. Never try to extinguish a fuel or electrical fire with water.

## Fumes

● Certain fumes are highly toxic and can quickly cause unconsciousness and even death if inhaled to any extent. Petrol vapour comes into this category, as do the vapours from certain solvents such as trichloro-ethylene. Any draining or pouring of such volatile fluids should be done in a well ventilated area.

● When using cleaning fluids and solvents, read the instructions carefully. Never use materials from unmarked containers - they may give off poisonous vapours.

● Never run the engine of a motor vehicle in an enclosed space such as a garage. Exhaust fumes contain carbon monoxide which is extremely poisonous; if you need to run the engine, always do so in the open air or at least have the rear of the vehicle outside the workplace.

## The battery

● Never cause a spark, or allow a naked light near the vehicle's battery. It will normally be giving off a certain amount of hydrogen gas, which is highly explosive.

● Always disconnect the battery ground (earth) terminal before working on the fuel or electrical systems (except where noted).

● If possible, loosen the filler plugs or cover when charging the battery from an external source. Do not charge at an excessive rate or the battery may burst.

● Take care when topping up, cleaning or carrying the battery. The acid electrolyte, evenwhen diluted, is very corrosive and should not be allowed to contact the eyes or skin. Always wear rubber gloves and goggles or a face shield. If you ever need to prepare electrolyte yourself, always add the acid slowly to the water; never add the water to the acid.

## Electricity

● When using an electric power tool, inspection light etc., always ensure that the appliance is correctly connected to its plug and that, where necessary, it is properly grounded (earthed). Do not use such appliances in damp conditions and, again, beware of creating a spark or applying excessive heat in the vicinity of fuel or fuel vapour. Also ensure that the appliances meet national safety standards.

● A severe electric shock can result from touching certain parts of the electrical system, such as the spark plug wires (HT leads), when the engine is running or being cranked, particularly if components are damp or the insulation is defective. Where an electronic ignition system is used, the secondary (HT) voltage is much higher and could prove fatal.

# Remember...

✗ **Don't** start the engine without first ascertaining that the transmission is in neutral.

✗ **Don't** suddenly remove the pressure cap from a hot cooling system - cover it with a cloth and release the pressure gradually first, or you may get scalded by escaping coolant.

✗ **Don't** attempt to drain oil until you are sure it has cooled sufficiently to avoid scalding you.

✗ **Don't** grasp any part of the engine or exhaust system without first ascertaining that it is cool enough not to burn you.

✗ **Don't** allow brake fluid or antifreeze to contact the machine's paintwork or plastic components.

✗ **Don't** siphon toxic liquids such as fuel, hydraulic fluid or antifreeze by mouth, or allow them to remain on your skin.

✗ **Don't** inhale dust - it may be injurious to health (see Asbestos heading).

✗ **Don't** allow any spilled oil or grease to remain on the floor - wipe it up right away, before someone slips on it.

✗ **Don't** use ill-fitting spanners or other tools which may slip and cause injury.

✗ **Don't** lift a heavy component which may be beyond your capability - get assistance.

✗ **Don't** rush to finish a job or take unverified short cuts.

✗ **Don't** allow children or animals in or around an unattended vehicle.

✗ **Don't** inflate a tyre above the recommended pressure. Apart from overstressing the carcass, in extreme cases the tyre may blow off forcibly.

✔ **Do** ensure that the machine is supported securely at all times. This is especially important when the machine is blocked up to aid wheel or fork removal.

✔ **Do** take care when attempting to loosen a stubborn nut or bolt. It is generally better to pull on a spanner, rather than push, so that if you slip, you fall away from the machine rather than onto it.

✔ **Do** wear eye protection when using power tools such as drill, sander, bench grinder etc.

✔ **Do** use a barrier cream on your hands prior to undertaking dirty jobs - it will protect your skin from infection as well as making the dirt easier to remove afterwards; but make sure your hands aren't left slippery. Note that long-term contact with used engine oil can be a health hazard.

✔ **Do** keep loose clothing (cuffs, ties etc. and long hair) well out of the way of moving mechanical parts.

✔ **Do** remove rings, wristwatch etc., before working on the vehicle - especially the electrical system.

✔ **Do** keep your work area tidy - it is only too easy to fall over articles left lying around.

✔ **Do** exercise caution when compressing springs for removal or installation. Ensure that the tension is applied and released in a controlled manner, using suitable tools which preclude the possibility of the spring escaping violently.

✔ **Do** ensure that any lifting tackle used has a safe working load rating adequate for the job.

✔ **Do** get someone to check periodically that all is well, when working alone on the vehicle.

✔ **Do** carry out work in a logical sequence and check that everything is correctly assembled and tightened afterwards.

✔ **Do** remember that your vehicle's safety affects that of yourself and others. If in doubt on any point, get professional advice.

● If in spite of following these precautions, you are unfortunate enough to injure yourself, seek medical attention as soon as possible.

**Note:** *The daily (pre-ride) checks outlined in the owner's manual covers those items which should be inspected on a daily basis.*

# Engine/transmission oil level

## Before you start:

✔ Start the engine and allow it to reach normal operating temperature.

*Caution: Do not run the engine in an enclosed space such as a garage or workshop.*

✔ Stop the engine and allow the motorcycle to stand undisturbed for a few minutes to allow the oil level to stabilise. Make sure the motorcycle is on level ground and held upright whilst the oil level is checked.

## Bike care:

● If you have to add oil frequently, you should check whether you have any oil leaks. If there is no sign of oil leakage from the joints and gaskets the engine could be burning oil (see *Fault Finding*).

## The correct oil

● Modern, high-revving engines place great demands on their oil. It is very important that the correct oil for your bike is used.

● Always top up with a good quality motorcycle oil of the specified type and viscosity and do not overfill the engine. A different viscosity oil can be used if required (see oil viscosity chart).

| Oil type | API grade SF or SG |
|---|---|
| Oil viscosity | SAE 10W40 |

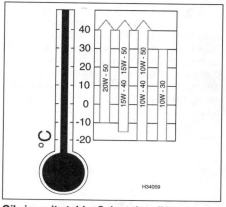

Oil viscosity table: Select the oil best suited to your conditions

**1** Wipe the oil level window in the clutch cover so that it is clean.

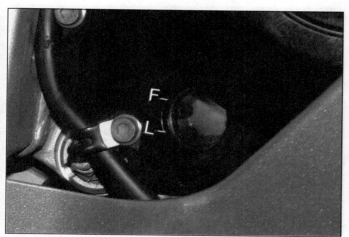

**2** With the motorcycle held upright, the oil level should lie between the 'F' and 'L' lines.

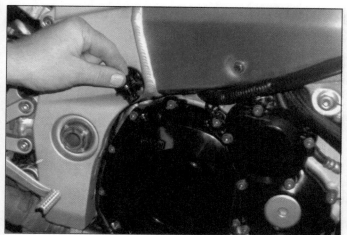

**3** If the level is below the 'L' line, remove the filler cap from the top of the clutch cover.

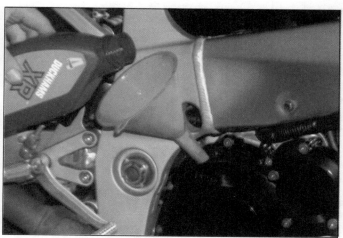

**4** Top the engine up with the recommended grade and type of oil, to bring the level up to the 'F' line on the window. Do not overfill. Refit the filler cap.

# Brake fluid level checks

> ⚠ **Warning: Brake hydraulic fluid can harm your eyes and damage painted surfaces, so use extreme caution when handling and pouring it and cover surrounding surfaces with rag. Do not use fluid that has been standing open for some time, as it absorbs moisture from the air which can cause a dangerous loss of braking effectiveness.**

## Before you start:

✔ Support the motorcycle in an upright position and turn the handlebars until the top of the front brake master cylinder is as level as possible.

✔ The rear master cylinder reservoir is located below the seat cowling on the right-hand side of the machine.

✔ If topping up is necessary, make sure you have the correct hydraulic fluid. DOT 4 is recommended.

✔ Wrap a rag around the reservoir being worked on to ensure that any spillage does not come into contact with painted surfaces.

✔ Access to the rear reservoir cap screws is restricted by the seat cowling. Remove the cowling to access the screws (see Chapter 8).

## Bike care:

● The fluid level in the front and rear brake master cylinder reservoirs will drop slightly as the brake pads wear down.

● If any fluid reservoir requires repeated topping-up this is an indication of an hydraulic leak somewhere in the system, which should be investigated immediately.

● Check for signs of fluid leakage from the hydraulic hoses and components – if found, rectify immediately..

● Check the operation of both brakes before taking the machine on the road; if there is evidence of air in the system (spongy feel to lever or pedal), it must be bled as described in Chapter 7.

# FRONT BRAKE

**1** The front brake fluid level is visible through the reservoir body – it must be between the UPPER and LOWER level lines.

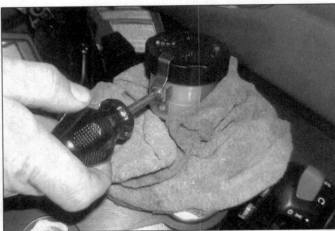

**2** If the level is below the LOWER level line, remove the reservoir cap clamp screw, then unscrew the cap and remove the diaphragm plate and the diaphragm.

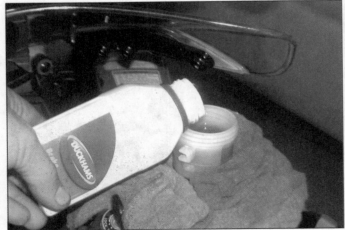

**3** Top up with new clean DOT 4 brake fluid, until the level is just below the UPPER level line. Do not overfill the reservoir, and take care to avoid spills (see **Warning** above).

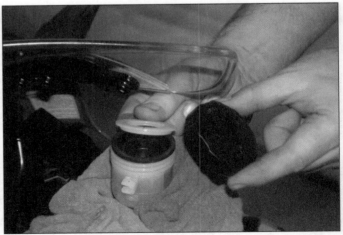

**4** Ensure that the diaphragm is correctly seated before installing the plate and cap. Tighten the cap and the clamp screw securely.

# REAR BRAKE

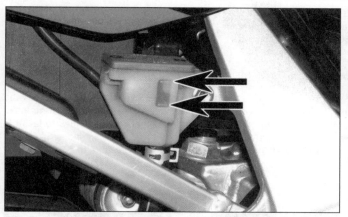

1 The rear brake fluid level is visible by looking through the translucent body of the reservoir – the fluid level must be between the UPPER and LOWER level lines.

2 If the level is below the LOWER level line, undo the reservoir mounting bolt and displace the reservoir.

3 Unscrew the reservoir cover screws and remove the cover and diaphragm.

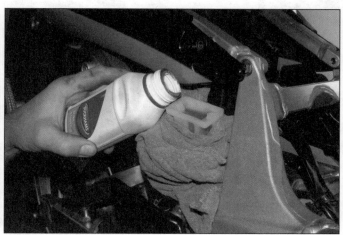

4 Top up with new clean DOT 4 brake fluid, until the level is just below the UPPER level line. Do not overfill the reservoir, and take care to avoid spills (see **Warning** above).

5 Ensure that the diaphragm is correctly seated before installing the cover. Tighten the cover screws securely, then install the reservoir.

# Coolant level check

⚠️ **Warning: DO NOT remove the radiator pressure cap to add coolant. Topping up is done via the coolant reservoir tank filler. DO NOT leave open containers of coolant about, as it is poisonous.**

## Before you start:
✔ Make sure you have a supply of coolant available (a mixture of 50% distilled water and 50% corrosion inhibited ethylene glycol anti-freeze is needed).
✔ Make sure the motorcycle is on level ground.

## Bike care:
● Use only the specified coolant mixture. It is important that anti-freeze is used in the system all year round, and not just in the winter. Do not top the system up using only water, as the system will become too diluted.
● Do not overfill the reservoir tank. If the coolant is significantly above the 'F' level line at any time, the surplus should be siphoned or drained off to prevent the possibility of it being expelled out of the overflow hose.
● If the coolant level falls steadily, check the system for leaks (see Chapter 1). If no leaks are found and the level continues to fall, it is recommended that the machine is taken to a Suzuki dealer for a pressure test.

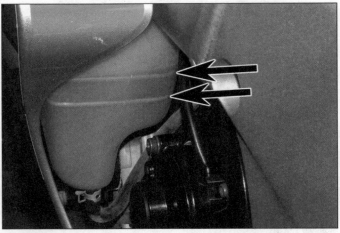

1 The coolant reservoir is located on the inside of the left-hand fairing side panel. The coolant level should be between the 'F' and 'L' level lines (arrowed) on the back of the reservoir.

2 To access the filler cap for topping up, remove the three (GSX-R600 and GSX-R750) fairing side panel screws . . .

3 . . . or two (GSX-R1000) fairing side panel screws and ease the panel out to gain access to the reservoir filler cap.

4 Remove the reservoir cap and top the coolant level up with the recommended coolant mixture, using a funnel to avoid spillage. Fit the cap securely, then install the side panel.

# Tyres

### The correct pressures:
● The tyres must be checked when **cold**, not immediately after riding. Note that low tyre pressures may cause the tyre to slip on the rim or come off. High tyre pressures will cause abnormal tread wear and unsafe handling.

● Use an accurate pressure gauge.

● Proper air pressure will increase tyre life and provide maximum stability and ride comfort.

| Tyre pressures (cold) | |
| --- | --- |
| Front | 36 psi (2.50 Bar) |
| Rear | 36 psi (2.50 Bar) |

### Tyre care:
● Check the tyres carefully for cuts, tears, embedded nails or other sharp objects and excessive wear. Operation of the motorcycle with excessively worn tyres is extremely hazardous, as traction and handling are directly affected.
● Check the condition of the tyre valve and ensure the dust cap is in place.
● Pick out any stones or nails which may have become embedded in the tyre tread. If left, they will eventually penetrate through the casing and cause a puncture.
● If tyre damage is apparent, or unexplained loss of pressure is experienced, seek the advice of a tyre fitting specialist without delay.

### Tyre tread depth:
● At the time of writing UK law requires that tread depth must be at least 1 mm over 3/4 of the tread breadth all the way around the tyre, with no bald patches. Many riders, however, consider 2 mm tread depth minimum to be a safer limit. The manufacturer's recommended minimum tread depth is given below.
● Many tyres now incorporate wear indicators in the tread. Identify the triangular pointer or 'TWI' mark on the tyre sidewall to locate the indicator bar and renew the tyre if the tread has worn down to the bar.

| Minimum tyre tread depths | |
| --- | --- |
| Front | 1.6 mm |
| Rear | 2.0 mm |

1 Check the tyre pressures when the tyres are cold and keep them properly inflated.

2 Measure tread depth at the centre of the tyre using a tread depth gauge.

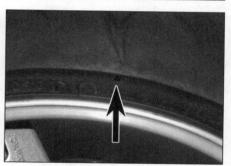

3 Tyre tread wear indicator bar location marking (usually either an arrow, a triangle or the letters TWI) on the sidewall (arrowed).

# Suspension, steering and drive chain

### Suspension and steering:
● Check that the front and rear suspension operates smoothly without binding.
● Check that the suspension is adjusted as required.

● Check that the steering moves smoothly from lock-to-lock .

### Drive chain:
● Check that the drive chain slack isn't excessive, and adjust if necessary (see Chapter 1).
● If the chain looks dry, lubricate it (see Chapter 1).

# Legal and safety checks

### Lighting and signalling:
● Take a minute to check that the headlight, tail light, brake light, instrument lights and turn signals all work correctly.
● Check that the horn sounds when the switch is operated.
● A working speedometer graduated in mph is a statutory requirement in the UK.

### Safety:
● Check that the throttle grip rotates smoothly and snaps shut when released, in all steering positions. Also check for the correct amount of freeplay (see Chapter 1).
● Check that the engine shuts off when the kill switch is operated.
● Check that sidestand return spring holds the stand securely up when retracted.

### Fuel:
● This may seem obvious, but check that you have enough fuel to complete your journey. If you notice signs of fuel leakage – rectify the cause immediately.
● Ensure you use the correct grade unleaded fuel – see Chapter 4 Specifications.

# Chapter 1
# Routine maintenance and Servicing

## Contents

## Degrees of difficulty

| | | | | |
|---|---|---|---|---|
| **Easy,** suitable for novice with little experience  | **Fairly easy,** suitable for beginner with some experience  | **Fairly difficult,** suitable for competent DIY mechanic  | **Difficult,** suitable for experienced DIY mechanic  | **Very difficult,** suitable for expert DIY or professional |

## Specifications

**Engine/transmission**

| | |
|---|---|
| Valve clearances (COLD engine) | |
| Intake valves | 0.10 to 0.20 mm |
| Exhaust valves | 0.20 to 0.30 mm |
| Spark plugs | |
| Type | |
| Standard | NGK CR9E or Nippondenso U27ESR-N |
| For cold climate (below 5°C) | NGK CR8E or Nippondenso U24ESR-N |
| For extended high speed riding | NGK CR10E or Nippondenso U31ESR-N |
| Electrode gap | 0.7 to 0.8 mm |
| Engine idle speed | |
| GSX-R600 | 1300 ± 100 rpm |
| GSX-R750 | 1200 ± 100 rpm |
| GSX-R1000 | 1150 ± 100 rpm |
| Clutch release mechanism screw (see text) | ¼ turn out |
| Cylinder compression | |
| Standard | 156 to 213 psi (11 to 15 Bar)* |
| Minimum | 128 psi (9 Bar)* |
| Maximum difference between cylinders | 28 psi (2 Bar)* |

*Note: If all cylinders record less than the standard (even if they are above the minimum), or if the difference between any two cylinders is greater than the maximum, or if any one cylinder is less than the minimum, the engine should be overhauled.*

| | |
|---|---|
| Oil pressure (with engine warm) | |
| GSX-R600 and GSX-R750 | 28 to 71 psi (2.0 to 5.0 Bar) at 3000 rpm, oil at 60°C |
| GSX-R1000 | 14 to 57 psi (1.0 to 4.0 Bar) at 3000 rpm, oil at 60°C |

1

## Frame and cycle parts

Drive chain
  Freeplay .................................................. 20 to 30 mm
  Stretch limit (21 pin length – see text) ...................... 319.4 mm
Freeplay adjustments
  Clutch cable ............................................. 10 to 15 mm
  Throttle cables
    Accelerator cable ...................................... 2 to 4 mm
    Decelerator cable ...................................... zero freeplay (see text)
Rear brake pedal height ...................................... 50 to 60 mm
Tyre pressures (cold) and tread depth ........................ see *Daily (pre-ride) checks*

## Recommended lubricants and fluids

Drive chain lubricant ........................................ Aerosol chain lubricant suitable for O-ring chains
Engine/transmission oil type ................................. API grade SF or SG motorcycle oil
Engine/transmission oil viscosity ............................ SAE 10W40
Engine/transmission oil capacity
  GSX-R600 and GSX-R750
    Oil change ............................................. 2.8 litres
    Oil and filter change .................................. 3.1 litres
    Following engine overhaul – dry engine, new filter ..... 3.4 litres
  GSX-R1000
    Oil change ............................................. 3.0 litres
    Oil and filter change .................................. 3.3 litres
    Following engine overhaul – dry engine, new filter ..... 3.6 litres
Coolant type ................................................. 50% distilled water, 50% corrosion inhibited ethylene glycol anti-freeze
Coolant capacity ............................................. 2.4 litres
Brake fluid .................................................. DOT 4

## Miscellaneous

Steering head bearings ....................................... Lithium-based multi-purpose grease
Wheel bearings (unsealed) .................................... Lithium-based multi-purpose grease
Swingarm pivot bearings ...................................... Lithium-based multi-purpose grease
Suspension linkage bearings .................................. Lithium-based multi-purpose grease
Bearing seal lips ............................................ Lithium-based multi-purpose grease
Gearchange lever/rear brake pedal/footrest pivots ............ Lithium-based multi-purpose grease
Front brake lever and clutch lever pivots .................... 10W40 motor oil
Cables ....................................................... Cable lubricant or 10W40 motor oil
Sidestand pivot and spring hook .............................. Lithium-based multi-purpose grease
Throttle grip ................................................ Multi-purpose grease or dry film lubricant

## Torque settings

Brake hose banjo bolts ....................................... 23 Nm
Engine/transmission oil drain plug ........................... 23 Nm
Exhaust downpipe clamp bolts ................................. 23 Nm
Exhaust control valve pipe clamp bolt (GSX-R1000) ............ 23 Nm
Exhaust system mounting bolt ................................. 23 Nm
Fork clamp bolts ............................................. 23 Nm
Handlebar clamp bolts ........................................ 23 Nm
Main oil gallery plug ........................................ 35 Nm
PAIR reed valve cover bolt ................................... 10 Nm
Rear axle nut
  GSX-R600 and GSX-R750
    US and Canada .......................................... 110 Nm
    All others ............................................. 120 Nm
  GSX-R1000 .............................................. 100 Nm
Rear brake torque arm nut .................................... 34 Nm
Silencer mounting bolt ....................................... 23 Nm
Silencer to exhaust system mounting nuts ..................... 25 Nm
Spark plugs .................................................. 11 Nm
Steering stem nut ............................................ 90 Nm
Thermostat housing air bleed bolt ............................ 5.5 Nm
Timing inspection cap ........................................ 11 Nm

**Note:** *Always perform the pre-ride inspection at every maintenance interval (in addition to the procedures listed). The intervals listed below are the intervals recommended by the manufacturer for each particular operation during the model years covered in this manual. Your owner's manual may have different intervals for your model.*

## Daily (pre-ride)
☐ See 'Daily (pre-ride) checks' at the beginning of this manual.

## After the initial 600 miles (1000 km)
**Note:** *This check is usually performed by a Suzuki dealer after the first 600 miles (1000 km) from new. Thereafter, maintenance is carried out according to the following intervals of the schedule.*

## Every 600 miles (1000 km)
☐ Clean and lubricate the drive chain (Section 1)

## Every 4000 miles (6000 km) or 6 months
*Carry out all the items under the Daily (pre-ride) checks and the 600 mile (1000 km) check, plus the following:*
☐ Clean the air filter element (Section 2)
☐ Check the spark plugs (Section 3)
☐ Check the fuel hoses, EVAP hoses (California models), and fuel system components (Section 4)
☐ Change the engine oil (Section 5)
☐ Check and adjust the engine idle speed (Section 6)
☐ Check throttle cable operation and freeplay (Section 7)
☐ Check the operation of the clutch release mechanism (Section 8)
☐ Check the cooling system (Section 9)
☐ Check and adjust the drive chain (Section 10)
☐ Check the brake pads for wear (Section 11)
☐ Check the operation of the brakes, and for fluid leakage (Section 12)
☐ Check the tyre and wheel condition, and the tyre tread depth (Section 13)
☐ Check the tightness of all nuts and bolts (Section 14)
☐ Check and lubricate the sidestand, lever pivots and cables (Section 15)

## Every 7500 miles (12,000 km) or 12 months
*Carry out all the items under the 4000 mile (6000 km) check, plus the following:*
☐ Renew the spark plugs (Section 16)
☐ Check throttle valve synchronisation (Section 17)
☐ Check the operation of the PAIR system (Section 18)
☐ Check the steering head bearing freeplay (Section 19)
☐ Check the front and rear suspension (Section 20)
☐ Check the tightness of the exhaust system bolts (Section 21)
☐ Check the operation of the exhaust control valve – GSX-R1000 (Section 22)

## Every 11,000 miles (18,000 km) or 18 months
*Carry out all the items under the 4000 mile (6000 km) check, plus the following:*
☐ Renew the air filter element (Section 23)
☐ Change the engine oil and renew the oil filter (Section 24)

## Every 15,000 miles (24,000 km) or 24 months
*Carry out all the items under the 7500 mile (12,000 km) check, plus the following:*
☐ Check the valve clearances (Section 25)

## Every two years
☐ Change the brake fluid (Section 26)
☐ Change the coolant (Section 27)

## Every four years
☐ Renew the brake hoses (Section 28)
☐ Renew the fuel hoses and EVAP hoses (California models) (Section 29)

## Non-scheduled maintenance
☐ Check the headlight aim (Section 30)
☐ Check the wheel bearings (Section 31)
☐ Change the front fork oil (Section 32)
☐ Check the cylinder compression (Section 33)
☐ Check the engine oil pressure (Section 34)
☐ Re-grease the steering head bearings (Section 35)
☐ Re-grease the swingarm and suspension linkage bearings (Section 36)
☐ Renew the brake master cylinder and caliper seals (Section 37)

1

## Component locations on the right-hand side

1  Rear brake fluid reservoir
2  Engine/transmission oil filler cap
3  Air filter
4  Front brake fluid reservoir
5  Throttle cable adjusters
6  Radiator pressure cap

7  Engine/transmission oil filter
8  Engine/transmission oil drain plug
9  Engine/transmission oil level window
10 Rear brake light switch
11 Rear brake pedal height adjuster

Component locations on the left-hand side

1    Clutch cable upper adjuster
2    Steering head bearing adjuster
3    Coolant reservoir
4    Idle speed adjuster
5    Battery

6    Drive chain adjusters
7    Clutch release mechanism cap
8    Clutch cable lower adjuster
9    Coolant drain hose for system draining

# Introduction

1 This Chapter is designed to help the home mechanic maintain his/her motorcycle for safety, economy, long life and peak performance.

2 Deciding where to start or plug into the routine maintenance schedule depends on several factors. If the warranty period on your motorcycle has just expired, and if it has been maintained according to the warranty standards, you may want to pick up routine maintenance as it coincides with the next mileage or calendar interval. If you have owned the machine for some time but have never performed any maintenance on it, then you may want to start at the nearest interval and include some additional procedures to ensure that nothing important is overlooked. If you have just had a major engine overhaul, then you may want to start the maintenance routine from the beginning. If you have a used machine and have no knowledge of its history or maintenance record, you may desire to combine all the checks into one large service initially and then settle into the maintenance schedule prescribed.

3 Before beginning any maintenance or repair, the machine should be cleaned thoroughly. Cleaning will help ensure that dirt does not contaminate the engine and will allow you to detect wear and damage that could otherwise easily go unnoticed.

4 Certain maintenance information is sometimes printed on decals attached to the motorcycle. If the information on the decals differs from that included here, use the information on the decal.

# Every 600 miles (1000 km)

### 1 Drive chain – cleaning and lubrication

## Cleaning

1 A neglected drive chain won't last long and can quickly damage the sprockets. Routine chain cleaning and lubrication isn't difficult and will ensure maximum chain and sprocket life.

**1.4 Apply lubricant to the overlap between the chain sideplates**

2 To clean the chain, support the bike upright on an auxiliary stand with the rear wheel off the ground and shift the transmission into neutral. Wipe the chain with a rag soaked in paraffin (kerosene) while slowly rotating the wheel, or alternatively apply the paraffin with a spray bottle to remove dirt and old lubricant. Cover the wheel and tyre to avoid splashing them with paraffin during the cleaning process.

3 Wipe the chain off with a clean rag and allow it to dry, using compressed air if available. If the chain is excessively dirty, remove the rear wheel (see Chapter 7), then soak the chain in a paraffin bath for a few minutes and scrub it clean with a stiff brush.
*Caution: Don't use petrol (gasoline), solvents or other cleaning fluids which might damage the sealing properties of the chain O-rings. Don't use high-pressure water.*

## Lubrication

4 Once the chain is clean and dry, apply the lubricant to the area where the side plates overlap – not the middle of the rollers **(see illustration).** Note: *Use an aerosol drive chain lubricant suitable for O-ring chains only; do not use a chain lube which may contain solvents that could damage the O-rings.*

 *Apply the lubricant to the top of the lower chain run, so centrifugal force will work the oil into the chain when the bike is moving. After applying the lubricant, let it soak in a few minutes before wiping off any excess.*

5 For routine lubrication, the best time to lubricate the chain is after the motorcycle has been ridden. When the chain is warm, the lubricant will penetrate the joints between the side plates better than when cold.

6 Ensure any lubrication is cleaned off the wheel and tyre before riding the motorcycle.

7 Suzuki specify inspecting the drive chain every 4000 miles (6000 km). It is, however, good practice to check the chain during the cleaning/lubricating process and make adjustments if required (see Section 10).

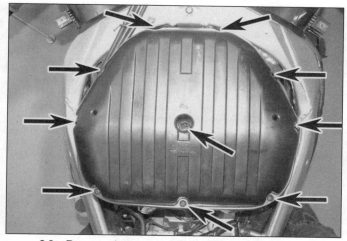

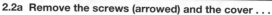

2.2a Remove the screws (arrowed) and the cover . . .

2.2b . . . and lift out the filter

# Every 4000 miles (6000 km) or 12 months

## 2 Air filter –
cleaning

**Caution: If the machine is continually ridden in dusty conditions, the filter should be cleaned more frequently.**

**1** Raise the front of the fuel tank (see Chapter 4).

**2** Remove the air filter cover screws and lift off the cover **(see illustration)**. Note the position of the gasket around the edge of the

2.4 Clean the crankcase filter element

cover. Withdraw the filter from the housing **(see illustration)**. Note the position of the filter gasket.

**3** Tap the filter on a hard surface to dislodge any dirt. If compressed air is available, use it to clean the filter element, directing the air from the outside. If the element is damaged or extremely dirty, fit a new one.

**4** Ensure the inside of the filter housing is clean. Lift out the crankcase breather filter element **(see illustration)**. If lightly soiled, the element should be washed in warm soapy water and dried thoroughly before installation. If the element is heavily soiled or has deteriorated, fit a new one. Excessive oil in the element is an indication of high crankcase pressure caused by worn piston rings or cylinders.

**5** Release the clip and remove the plug from the bottom of the filter housing to allow any fluid to drain, then install the plug and secure it with the clip **(see illustration)**.

**6** Ensure the filter gasket is correctly located in the housing, then install the filter. Make sure the gasket is properly seated around the edge of the cover and fit the cover. Install the cover screws and tighten them securely. Fit the remaining components in the reverse order of removal.

## 3 Spark plug gaps –
check and adjustment

**Note:** *The spark plug caps are integral with the ignition coils. To avoid damaging the wiring, always disconnect the connectors before removing the coil/caps. Do not attempt to lever the coil/caps off the plugs or pull them off with pliers. Do not drop the coils.*

**1** Make sure your spark plug socket is the correct size before attempting to remove the plugs – a suitable one is supplied in the motorcycle's tool kit which is stored under the passenger seat. Make sure the ignition is switched OFF.

**2** To access the spark plugs, remove the air filter housing (see Chapter 4).

**3** Check that the cylinder location is marked on each coil/cap wiring connector and mark them accordingly if not, then disconnect the connectors **(see illustration)**

**4** Clean the area around the coil/caps to prevent any dirt falling into the spark plug channels, then pull the coil/cap off each spark plug **(see illustration)**.

**5** Clean the area around the base of the plugs

2.5 Filter housing drain plug

3.3 Disconnect the wiring connector . . .

3.4 . . . then pull the coil/cap off the spark plug

**3.5 Removing a spark plug using the socket supplied in the toolkit**

to prevent any dirt falling into the engine when the plugs are removed. Using either the plug socket supplied in the bike's toolkit or a deep socket type wrench, unscrew the plugs from the cylinder head **(see illustration)**. Lay each plug out in relation to its cylinder; if any plug shows up a problem it will then be easy to identify the troublesome cylinder.

**6** Look for excessive deposits and evidence of a cracked or chipped insulator around the centre electrode. Compare your spark plugs to the colour spark plug reading chart at the end of this manual. Check the threads, the washer and the ceramic insulator body for cracks and other damage. If in doubt concerning the condition of the plugs, install new ones – the expense is minimal.

**7** Inspect the electrodes for wear. Both the centre and side electrodes should have square edges and the side electrode should be of uniform thickness. If the electrodes are not excessively worn, and if the deposits can be easily removed with a wire brush, the plugs can be re-gapped and re-used.

**8** Before installing the plugs, make sure they are the correct type and heat range and measure the gap between the electrodes **(see illustrations)**. Compare the gap to that specified and adjust as necessary. If the gap must be adjusted, bend the side electrode only and be very careful not to chip or crack the insulator nose **(see illustration)**. Make sure the washer is in place before installing each plug.

**9** Since the cylinder head is made of aluminium, which is soft and easily damaged, thread each plug into the head turning the tool

by hand. Once the plug is finger-tight, tighten it to the torque setting specified at the beginning of this Chapter. If a torque wrench is not available, tighten it an extra ¼ to ½ turn – do not over-tighten the spark plugs.

*As the plugs are quite recessed, slip a short length of hose over the end of the plug to use as a tool to thread it into place. The hose will grip the plug well enough to turn it, but will start to slip if the plug begins to cross-thread in the hole – this will prevent damaged threads.*

**10** Install the spark plug coil/caps, then connect the coil/cap wiring connectors.
**11** Install the air filter housing (see Chapter 4).

*Stripped plug threads in the cylinder head can be repaired with a thread insert – see 'Tools and Workshop Tips' in the Reference section.*

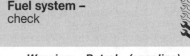
**4   Fuel system –**
check

⚠ *Warning: Petrol (gasoline) is extremely flammable, so take extra precautions when you work on any part of the fuel system. Don't smoke or allow open flames or bare light bulbs near the work area, and don't work in a garage where a natural gas-type appliance is present. If you spill any fuel on your skin, rinse it off immediately with soap and water. When you perform any kind of work on the fuel system, wear safety glasses and have a fire extinguisher suitable for a Class B type fire (flammable liquids) on hand.*

**Check**

**1** Raise the fuel tank (see Chapter 4) and check the tank, the fuel hose, the vacuum hoses and, on California models, the EVAP system hoses (see Chapter 4), for signs of leaks, deterioration or damage. In particular

check that there are no leaks from the fuel hose or hose unions. Renew any hose that is cracked or deteriorated.

**2** If the joint between the fuel pump mounting plate and the tank is leaking, ensure the mounting bolts are tightened to the specified torque setting (see Chapter 4); if the leak persists, remove the pump and fit a new gasket (see Chapter 4).

**3** Inspect the joints between the fuel rail, the injectors and the throttle body. If there are any leaks, remove the fuel rail and fit new seals and O-rings to the injectors (see Chapter 4).

**Filter renewal**

**4** Cleaning and/or renewal of the fuel filter is advised after a particularly high mileage has been covered, although no interval is specified by Suzuki. It is also necessary if fuel starvation is suspected.

**5** The filter is integral with the fuel pump. Remove the pump from the fuel tank and disassemble the unit to access the filter (see Chapter 4).

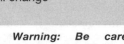
**5   Engine/transmission –**
oil change

⚠ *Warning: Be careful when draining the oil, as the exhaust pipes, the engine, and the oil itself can cause severe burns.*

**1** Regular oil and filter changes are the single most important maintenance procedure you can perform on a motorcycle. The oil not only lubricates the internal parts of the engine, transmission and clutch, but it also acts as a coolant, a cleaner, a sealant, and a protector. Because of these demands, the oil takes a terrific amount of abuse and should be drained and the engine/transmission refilled with new oil of the correct type and grade at the specified service interval. The oil filter should be changed with every third oil change (see Section 24).

**2** Before changing the oil, warm up the engine so the oil will drain easily.

**3** Support the bike upright on an auxiliary stand on level ground, and position a drain tray below the engine. Unscrew the oil filler

**3.8a  Using a wire gauge to measure the spark plug electrode gap**

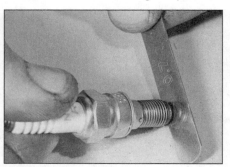
**3.8b  Using a feeler gauge to measure the spark plug electrode gap**

**3.8c  Adjust the electrode gap by bending the side electrode only**

**5.3 Unscrew the oil filler cap . . .**

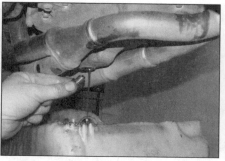

**5.4 . . . then unscrew the drain plug**

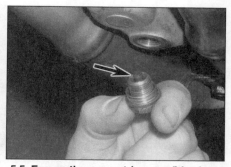

**5.5 Ensure the magnet (arrowed) is clean before installing the sump plug**

cap from the clutch cover to vent the crankcase and to act as a reminder that there is no oil in the engine **(see illustration)**.

**4** Next, unscrew the oil drain plug from the sump on the bottom of the engine and allow the oil to flow into the drain tray **(see illustration)**. Note the magnet inside the plug and clean off any metal swarf. Check the condition of the sealing washer on the drain plug and fit a new one if it is damaged or worn. It is good practice to fit a new washer whenever the drain plug is removed.

 *To help determine whether any abnormal or excessive engine wear is occurring, place a strainer between the engine and the drain tray so that any debris in the oil is filtered out and can be examined. If there are flakes or chips of metal in the oil or on the drain plug magnet, then something is drastically wrong internally and the engine will have to be disassembled for inspection and repair. If there are pieces of fibre-like material in the oil, the clutch is wearing excessively and should be checked.*

**5** When the oil has completely drained, fit the plug into the sump, using a new sealing washer if necessary, and tighten it to the torque setting specified at the beginning of this Chapter **(see illustration)**. Avoid overtightening, as damage to the sump will result.

**6** Refill the engine with the correct amount

and type of oil (see Specifications). With the motorcycle held upright on level ground, the oil level should lie between the 'F' and 'L' lines on the inspection window (see *Daily (pre-ride) checks*). Install the filler cap. Start the engine and let it run for two or three minutes (make sure that the oil pressure warning display and the warning light extinguish after a few seconds). Shut it off, wait a few minutes, then recheck the oil level. If necessary, add more oil to bring the level up to the 'F' line on the window. Check that there are no leaks from around the drain plug.

 *Saving a little money on the difference between good and cheap oils won't pay off if the engine is damaged as a result.*

**7** The oil drained from the engine should be disposed of properly. Check with your local refuse disposal company, disposal facility or environmental agency to see whether they will accept the used oil for recycling. Don't pour used oil into drains or onto the ground.

**OIL CARE**
FOLLOW THE CODE

O I L   B A N K   L I N E
**0800 66 33 66**
www.oilbankline.org.uk

*Note: It is antisocial and illegal to dump oil down the drain. To find the location of your local oil recycling bank, call this number free. In the USA, note that any oil supplier must accept used oil for recycling*

## 6   Idle speed –
### check and adjustment

**1** The idle speed should be checked and adjusted before and after the throttle valves are synchronised (balanced) and when it is obviously too high or too low. Before adjusting the idle speed, turn the handlebars back-and-forth and see if the idle speed changes as this is done. If it does, the throttle cables may not be adjusted or routed correctly, or may be worn out. This is a dangerous condition that can cause loss of control of the bike. Be sure to correct this problem before proceeding (see Section 7).

**2** The engine should be at normal operating temperature, which is usually reached after 10 to 15 minutes of stop/start riding. Place the motorcycle on its sidestand, and make sure the transmission is in neutral. On all GSX-R600 and 750 models and the GSX-R1000K1 model, make sure the fast idle (choke) lever is in the OFF (forward) position.

**3** On GSX-R750Y models, the idle speed adjuster is located inside the left-hand fairing side panel **(see illustration)**. On GSX-R600, GSX-R750K1/K2 and GSX-R1000 models, raise the fuel tank (see Chapter 4) to access the idle speed adjuster on the throttle cable pulley backplate **(see illustrations)**. With the engine idling, turn the adjuster until the idle speed listed in this Chapter's Specifications is obtained. Turn the screw clockwise to increase idle speed, and anti-clockwise to

**1**

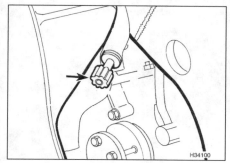

**6.3a  Idle speed adjuster (arrowed) on GSX-R750Y models**

H34100

**6.3b  Idle speed adjuster (arrowed) on GSX-R600 models**

**6.3c  Idle speed adjuster on GSX-R750K1/K2 and GSX-R1000 models**

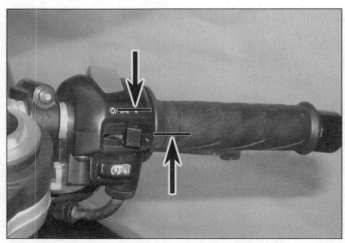

7.4 Throttle cable freeplay is measured in terms of twistgrip rotation

7.5a Decelerator (A) and accelerator (B) throttle cables

decrease it. **Note:** *On GSX-R1000K2 models the fast idle mechanism is actuated automatically by the STV servo when the engine is cold and should cancel when engine coolant temperature reaches 40 to 50°C. If the idle speed cannot be adjusted correctly, check for a possible fault in the coolant temperature sensor or sensor wiring (see Chapter 4, Section 11). Details on adjusting the fast idle speed are given in Chapter 4, Section 16.*

**4** Snap the throttle open and shut a few times, then recheck the idle speed. If necessary, repeat the adjustment procedure.

**5** If a smooth, steady idle can't be achieved, the throttle valves may need synchronising (see Section 17).

### 7  Throttle cables – check and adjustment

**1** Make sure the throttle twistgrip rotates easily from fully closed to fully open with the front wheel turned at various angles. The twistgrip should return automatically from fully open to fully closed when released.

**2** If the throttle sticks, this is probably due to a cable fault. Remove the cables (see Chapter 4) and lubricate them (see Section 15). If the inner cables still do not run smoothly in the outer cables, renew the cables.

**3** With the cables removed, check that the twistgrip turns smoothly around the handlebar– dirt combined with a lack of lubrication can cause the action to be stiff. Clean and lightly grease the twistgrip pulley and the inside of the twistgrip housing. Install the lubricated or new cables, making sure they are correctly routed (see Chapter 4). If this fails to improve the operation of the throttle, the fault could lie in the throttle bodies. Remove the air filter housing and check the action of the throttle pulley (see Chapter 4).

**4** With the throttle operating smoothly, check for a small amount of freeplay in the cables, measured in terms of the amount of twistgrip rotation before the throttle opens, and compare the amount to that listed in this Chapter's Specifications **(see illustration)**. If it is incorrect, adjust the cables.

**5** Minor adjustment can be made at the twistgrip end of the cables. Loosen the lockring on the decelerator (throttle closing) cable adjuster and turn the adjuster fully in **(see illustrations)**. Now loosen the lockring on the accelerator (throttle opening) cable and turn the adjuster until the specified amount of freeplay is obtained, then retighten the lockring. Hold the twistgrip in the fully closed position and turn the decelerator cable adjuster out until resistance can just be felt in the cable – at this point all the freeplay has been taken up. Tighten the lockring.

**6** If the adjusters have reached their limit, or if major adjustment is required, raise the fuel tank and adjust the cables at the throttle body end. Loosen the locknut on the decelerator cable adjuster and turn the adjuster until all freeplay has been taken up in the cable **(see illustration)**. Now loosen the locknut on the

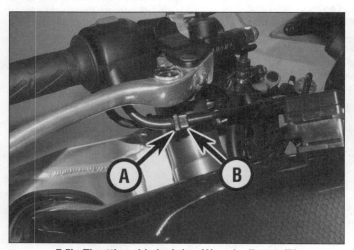

7.5b Throttle cable lockring (A) and adjuster (B)

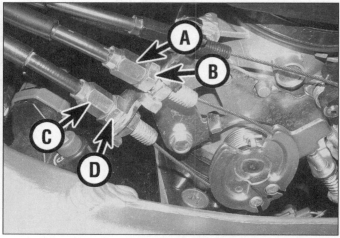

7.6a Accelerator cable adjuster (A) and locknut (B). Decelerator cable adjuster (C) and locknut (D)

accelerator cable and turn the adjuster until the specified amount of freeplay is obtained, then retighten the locknut. Hold the twistgrip in the fully closed position and slowly turn the decelerator cable adjuster to obtain 1 mm deflection in the inner cable, then tighten the locknut **(see illustration)**.

**7** If the cables cannot be adjusted as specified, install new ones (see Chapter 4).

 ***Warning: Turn the handlebars all the way through their travel with the engine idling. Idle speed should not change. If it does, the cables may be routed incorrectly. Correct this condition before riding the bike.***

**8** Check that the throttle twistgrip operates smoothly and snaps shut quickly when released.

## 8 Clutch – check and adjustment

### Cable adjustment

**1** Check that the clutch lever operates smoothly and easily.

**2** If the lever action is heavy or stiff, remove the cable (see Chapter 2) and lubricate it (see Section 15). If the inner cable still does not run smoothly in the outer cable, fit a new cable. Install the lubricated or new cable (see Chapter 2).

**3** If the lever itself is stiff, remove the lever from its bracket (see Chapter 6) and check for damage or distortion, or any other cause, and remedy as necessary. Clean and lubricate the pivot bolt and contact areas (see Section 15).

**4** Adjustment of the clutch cable is necessary to compensate for stretch in the cable. Check that the clutch lever freeplay is within the specifications listed at the beginning of this Chapter **(see illustration)**.

**5** If adjustment is required, turn the handlebar lever adjuster in or out until the correct amount of freeplay is obtained. The adjuster spring should hold the adjuster in place once adjustment has been made **(see illustration)**.

### Release mechanism adjustment

**6** Periodic adjustment of the clutch release

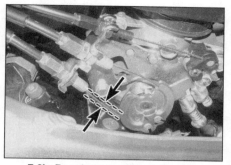

**7.6b Decelerator cable deflection measurement**

mechanism is necessary to compensate for wear of the clutch plates and ensure smooth operation of the clutch and transmission.

**7** Turn the cable adjuster at the handlebar lever fully in **(see illustration 8.5)**. **Note:** *There should be no tension in the clutch cable while the release mechanism is being adjusted. If necessary, turn the adjuster in at the lower end of the cable as well.*

**8** Remove the left-hand fairing side panel (see Chapter 8) and remove the clutch release mechanism cover from the engine sprocket cover **(see illustration)**.

**9** Loosen the release mechanism adjuster locknut and turn the adjuster out two or three turns, then turn the adjuster in until resistance can just be felt **(see illustration)**. Now turn the adjuster out 1/4 turn and hold the adjuster to prevent it turning while the locknut is tightened.

**10** Loosen the locknut on the adjuster at the

**8.4 Measuring clutch lever freeplay**

lower end of the cable and turn the adjuster until the specified amount of freeplay is obtained at the clutch lever **(see illustration)**. Tighten the locknut. Subsequent adjustments can be made using the lever adjuster only (see Step 5). If the specified amount of freeplay cannot be obtained at the clutch lever, fit a new cable.

**11** Install the clutch release mechanism cover and the fairing side panel (see Chapter 8).

## 9 Cooling system – check

 ***Warning: The engine must be cool before beginning this procedure.***

**1** Check the coolant level (see *Daily (pre-ride) checks*).

**2** Remove the fairing side panels (see Chapter 8) and check the cooling system for evidence of leaks. Examine each coolant hose along its entire length. Look for cracks, abrasions and other damage. Squeeze each hose at various points. They should feel firm, yet pliable, and return to their original shape when released. If they are cracked or hard, fit new ones (see Chapter 3).

**3** Check for evidence of leaks at each cooling system joint and ensure the hose clips are tightened securely. On GSX-R600 and 750 models, check the hoses to the oil cooler at the front of the engine. Check around the bottom of the water pump, which is on the

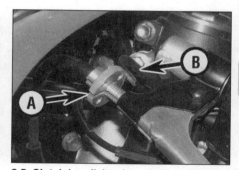

**8.5 Clutch handlebar lever adjuster (A) and spring (B)**

**1**

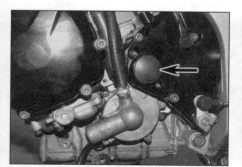

**8.8 Prise off the cover (arrowed) . . .**

**8.9 . . . then loosen the locknut and turn the adjuster screw as described**

**8.10 Adjuster on the lower end of the clutch cable**

**9.6 Turn the cap slowly anticlockwise to release pressure in the system**

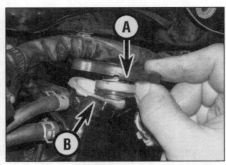

**9.9 Align tabs (A) with cut-outs (B) when installing the pressure cap**

left-hand side of the engine. If the pump cover is leaking, fit a new cover O-ring. If coolant is leaking from the back of the pump, the internal mechanical seal has probably failed and should be renewed (see Chapter 3).

**4** Check the radiator for leaks and other damage. Leaks in the radiator leave tell-tale scale deposits or coolant stains on the outside of the core below the leak. If leaks are noted, remove the radiator (see Chapter 3) and have it repaired by a specialist.

*Caution: Do not use a liquid leak stopping compound to try to repair leaks.*

**5** Check the radiator fins for mud, dirt and insects, which may impede the flow of air through the radiator. If the fins are dirty, remove the radiator (see Chapter 3) and clean it using water or low pressure compressed air directed through the fins from the back. If the fins are bent or distorted, straighten them carefully with a screwdriver. Where there is

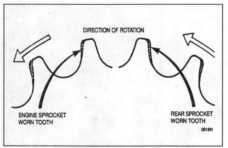

**10.2 Check the sprockets in the areas indicated to see if they are worn excessively**

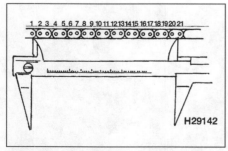

**10.4 Measure the distance between the 1st and 21st pins to determine chain stretch**

substantial damage to the radiator's surface area, renew the radiator.

⚠️ *Warning: Do not remove the pressure cap when the engine is hot. It is good practice to cover the cap with a heavy cloth and turn the cap slowly anti-clockwise. If you hear a hissing sound (indicating that there is still pressure in the system), wait until it stops, then continue turning the cap until it can be removed.*

**6** Remove the pressure cap from the radiator filler neck by turning it anti-clockwise until it reaches the stop. Now press down on the cap and continue turning it until it can be removed **(see illustration)**.

**7** Check the condition of the coolant in the system. If it is rust-coloured or if accumulations of scale are visible, drain, flush and refill the system with new coolant (See Section 27). Check the cap seal for cracks and other damage. If in doubt about the pressure cap's condition, have it tested by a Suzuki dealer or fit a new one.

**8** Check the antifreeze content of the coolant with an antifreeze hydrometer. If the system has not been topped-up with the correct coolant mixture (see *Daily (pre-ride) checks*) the coolant will be too weak to offer adequate protection. If the hydrometer indicates a weak mixture, drain, flush and refill the system (see Section 27).

**9** Install the pressure cap – align the tabs on the cap with the cut-outs in the filler neck, then press the cap down and turn it clockwise until it is tight **(see illustration)**.

**10** Start the engine and let it reach normal

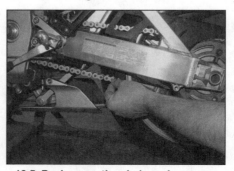

**10.5 Push up on the chain and measure the slack**

operating temperature, then check that here are no leaks. As the coolant temperature increases, the fan should come on automatically and the temperature should begin to drop. If it does not, refer to Chapter 3 and check the fan, the fan switch and fan circuit carefully.

**11** If the coolant level is consistently low, and no evidence of leaks can be found, have the entire system pressure checked by a Suzuki dealer.

## 10 Drive chain – check and adjustment

### Check

**1** Support the bike upright on an auxiliary stand with the rear wheel off the ground and shift the transmission into neutral. Check the entire length of the chain for damaged rollers, loose links and pins, and missing O-rings. In some cases, where lubrication has been neglected, corrosion and galling may cause the links to bind and kink. If any damage is found, it's time to fit a new chain (see Chapter 6).

**2** Remove the front sprocket cover (see Chapter 6). Check the teeth on the front and rear sprockets for wear **(see illustration)**. If the sprockets are worn they must be renewed (see Chapter 6). **Note:** *Never install a new chain on old sprockets, and never use the old chain if you install new sprockets – renew the chain and sprockets as a set.*

**3** Inspect the drive chain slider on the swingarm for excessive wear and renew it if worn (see Chapter 6).

**4** To check chain stretch, first remove the chainguard. Ensure the rear wheel is off the ground, then press down on the chain bottom run to tension the top run, and measure the distance between 21 chain pins on the top run, midway between the sprockets **(see illustration)**. Rotate the wheel and take three measurements in different places on the chain. If the chain has stretched beyond the limit in the Specifications at the beginning of this Chapter, replace it with a new one (see Chapter 6).

*Caution: If the machine is ridden with excessive slack in the drive chain, the chain could contact the frame and swingarm, causing severe damage.*

### Adjustment

**5** With the bike on its side stand, push up on the bottom run of the chain and measure the total up and down slack at a point midway between the two sprockets, then compare your measurement to that listed in this Chapter's Specifications **(see illustration)**. Since the chain will rarely wear evenly, roll the bike forwards so that another section of chain can be checked; do this several times to check the entire length of chain. Any adjustment should be based upon the measurement taken at the tightest point. **Note:** *If you find a tight spot, mark it with felt*

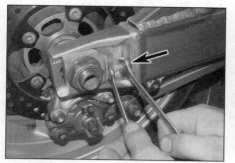

10.9a Loosen the adjuster locknut . . .

10.9b . . . then turn the adjuster bolt as required

10.9c Adjuster blocks must align with same marks (arrowed) on both sides of the swingarm

pen or paint, and repeat the check after the bike has been ridden. If the chain's still tight in the same area, it may be damaged or worn. Because a tight or kinked chain can damage the transmission output shaft bearing, it's a good idea to fit a new one.

**6** Rotate the rear wheel until the chain is positioned with the tightest point at the centre of its bottom run.

**7** On all US and Canadian models remove the split pin from the rear axle nut.

**8** Loosen the rear axle nut and the brake torque arm nut.

**9** Loosen the adjuster locknut on each side of the swingarm, then turn the adjuster bolts evenly until the specified amount of slack is obtained at the centre of the bottom run of the chain (see illustrations). Ensure that the back of each chain adjuster block is in the same position in relation to the marks on the swingarm (see illustration); if not, the rear

wheel will be out of alignment with the front. If there is a discrepancy in the position of the blocks, correct it with the adjusters and then check the chain slack again.

**10** Tighten the axle nut to the torque setting specified at the beginning of this Chapter. On all US and Canadian models fit a new split pin through the axle nut and bend the ends of the pin securely.

**11** Tighten the chain adjuster locknuts securely and tighten the brake torque arm nut to the specified torque setting.

## 11 Brake pads – wear check

**1** Each brake pad has a wear indicator that can be viewed without removing the pads from the caliper (see illustration).

**2** On the front caliper, unscrew the bolts securing the pad spring and remove the spring – the pad wear indicator cutouts are visible by looking at the top edge of the pads (see illustrations).

**3** On the rear caliper, the pad wear indicator groove is visible by looking up at the bottom edge of the pads from underneath the caliper (see illustrations). On GSX-R600 and 750 models, first remove the caliper cover by levering it off with a screwdriver.

**4** If the pads are dirty or if you are in doubt as to the amount of friction material remaining, remove them for inspection (see Chapter 7). **Note:** Some after-market pads may use different indicators to those on the original equipment as shown.

**5** Renew the pads if they are worn level with the wear indicator cutouts (front) or groove (rear). Always renew brake pads in sets and renew the pads in the both front brake calipers at the same time. If the pads appear to be wearing unevenly, remove the caliper and check the operation of the pistons (see Chapter 7).

## 12 Brake system – check

**1** A routine general check of the brake system will ensure that any problems are discovered and remedied before the rider's safety is jeopardised.

**2** Check the brake lever and pedal for loose fixings, improper or rough action, excessive

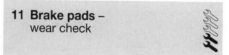

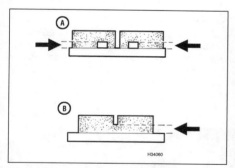

11.1 Front (A) and rear (B) brake pad wear limit indicator lines

11.2a Remove the pad spring . . .

11.2b . . . to check the front pads for wear

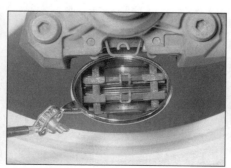

11.3a Using a mirror to check rear brake pad wear

11.3b On GSX-R600 and 750 models, remove the rear caliper cover

1

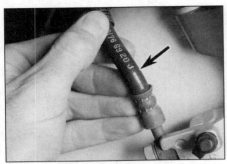

12.3 Flex the brake hoses and check for cracks, bulges and leaking fluid

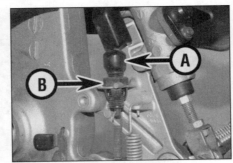

12.5 Brake light switch (A) and adjuster nut (B)

12.6 Front brake lever span adjuster

play, bends, and other damage. Renew any damaged parts (see Chapter 6). Clean and lubricate the lever and pedal pivots if their action is stiff or rough (see Section 15).

3 Make sure all brake fasteners are tight. Check the brake pads for wear (see Section 11) and make sure the fluid level in the reservoirs is correct (see *Daily (pre-ride) checks*). Look for leaks at the hose connections and check for cracks in the hoses (see illustration). If the lever or pedal is spongy, bleed the brakes (see Chapter 7). The brake fluid should be changed every two years (see Section 26) and the hoses renewed if they deteriorate, or every four years irrespective of their condition (see Section 28). The master cylinder and caliper seals should be renewed if leaks are evident (see Chapter 7).

4 Make sure the brake light operates when the front brake lever is pulled in. The front brake light switch is not adjustable. If it fails to operate properly, check it (see Chapter 9).

5 Make sure the brake light is activated just before the rear brake takes effect. The switch is mounted behind the right-hand footrest bracket. If adjustment is necessary, hold the switch and turn the adjuster nut on the switch body (see illustration). If the brake light comes on too late, turn the ring clockwise. If

the brake light comes on too soon or is permanently on, turn the ring anti-clockwise. If the switch doesn't operate the brake light, check it (see Chapter 9).

6 The front brake lever has a span adjuster which alters the distance of the lever from the handlebar. Each setting is identified by a number on the adjuster which aligns with the arrow on the lever bracket (see illustration). Pull the lever away from the handlebar and turn the adjuster dial until the setting which best suits the rider is obtained. There are six settings – setting 1 gives the largest span, and setting 6 the smallest. When making adjustment ensure that the pin set in the lever bracket is engaged in its detent in the adjuster.

7 Check the position of the rear brake pedal. The distance between the top edge of the brake pedal and the top of the rider's footrest should be as specified at the beginning of this Chapter (see illustration). To adjust the pedal height, loosen the (upper) locknut on the master cylinder pushrod clevis, then turn the pushrod until the pedal is at the correct height. Tighten the locknut securely and check the adjustment of the brake light switch (see Step 5).

## 13 Wheels and tyres – general check

### *Wheels*

1 Cast wheels are virtually maintenance free, but they should be kept clean and checked periodically for cracks and other damage. Also check the wheel runout and alignment (see Chapter 7). Never attempt to repair damaged cast wheels; they must be renewed if damaged. Check that the wheel balance weights are fixed firmly to the wheel rim (see illustration). If you suspect that a weight has fallen off, have the wheel rebalanced by a motorcycle tyre specialist.

### *Tyres*

2 Check the tyre condition and tread depth thoroughly – see *Daily (pre-ride) checks*. Check the valve rubber for signs of damage or deterioration and have it renewed if necessary by a tyre fitting specialist. Also, make sure the valve stem cap is in place and tight.

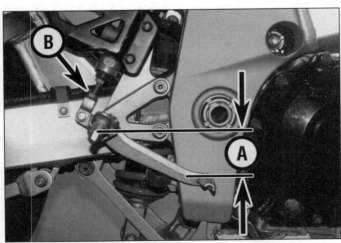

12.7 Brake pedal height (A) can be adjusted after loosening locknut (B)

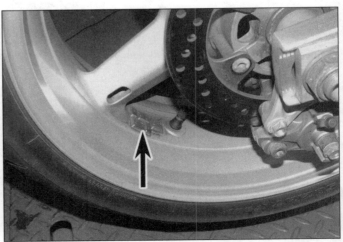

13.1 Check that the wheel balance weights are firmly attached

**15.3a Lubricating a cable with a cable oiler clamp**

## 14 Nuts and bolts –
### tightness check

1 Since vibration of the machine tends to loosen fasteners, all nuts, bolts, screws, etc. should be periodically checked for proper tightness.
2 Pay particular attention to the following:
  *Gearchange lever, brake and clutch lever, and brake pedal mounting bolts*
  *Footrest, footrest bracket and stand bolts*
  *Shock absorber mounting bolts and suspension linkage bolts*
  *Handlebar clamp and set bolts*
  *Front axle and clamp bolts*
  *Front fork clamp bolts (top and bottom yoke)*
  *Front fork cap bolts*
  *Steering stem nut*
  *Steering damper bolt/nut*
  *Rear axle nut*

*Swingarm pivot nut and locknut*
*Brake caliper mounting bolts*
*Brake hose banjo bolts and caliper bleed valves*
*Brake disc bolts and rear sprocket nuts*
*Brake master cylinder mounting bolts*
*Brake torque arm bolt and nut at each end*
3 If a torque wrench is available, use it along with the torque specifications at the beginning of this and other Chapters.

## 15 Stand, lever pivots
### and cables –
### lubrication

### Pivot points

1 Since the controls, cables and various other components of a motorcycle are exposed to the elements, they should be lubricated periodically to ensure safe and trouble-free operation.
2 The footrest pivots, clutch and brake lever pivots, brake pedal and gearchange lever pivots and linkage and sidestand pivot should be lubricated frequently. In order for the lubricant to be applied where it will do the most good, the component should be disassembled (see Chapter 6). However, lubricant applied to the pivot joint will usually work its way into the areas where friction occurs. If motor oil or light grease is being used, apply it sparingly as it may attract dirt (which could cause the controls to bind or wear at an accelerated rate). **Note:** *One of the best lubricants for the control lever pivots is a dry-film lubricant.*

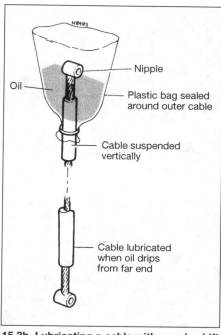

**15.3b Lubricating a cable with a makeshift funnel and motor oil**

### Cables

3 To lubricate the cables, disconnect the relevant cable at its upper end, then lubricate it with a pressure clamp, or if one is not available, using the set-up shown **(see illustrations)**. See Chapter 4 for the choke and throttle cable removal procedures, and Chapter 2 for the clutch cable.

# Every 7500 miles (12,000 km) or 12 months

*Carry out all the items under the 4000 mile (6000 km) check, plus the following:*

## 16 Spark plugs –
### renewal

1 Remove the old spark plugs as described in Section 3 and install new ones.

## 17 Throttle valves –
### synchronisation

⚠ **Warning: Petrol (gasoline) is extremely flammable, so take extra precautions when you work on any part of the fuel system. Don't smoke or allow open flames or bare light bulbs near the work area, and don't work in a garage where a natural gas-type appliance is present. If you spill any fuel on your skin, rinse it off immediately with soap and water. When you perform any kind of work on the fuel system, wear safety glasses and have a**

*fire extinguisher suitable for a Class B type fire (flammable liquids) on hand.*

⚠ **Warning: Take great care not to burn your hand on the hot engine unit when accessing the gauge take-off points on the throttle bodies. Do not allow exhaust gases to build up in the work area; either perform the check outside or use an exhaust gas extraction system.**
1 Throttle valves that are out of synchronisation will result in increased fuel consumption, increased engine temperature, less than ideal throttle response and higher vibration levels. Synchronisation is the process of adjusting the throttle valves so they each pass the same amount of fuel/air mixture to their respective cylinders. This is done by measuring the vacuum produced in each intake tract as the piston descends on its induction stroke and adjusting the throttle valves accordingly.
2 To synchronise the throttle valves you will need a set of vacuum gauges or calibrated tubes to measure engine vacuum. The equipment used should be suitable for a four cylinder engine and come complete with the necessary adapters and hoses to fit the take

off points on the throttle bodies. **Note:** *Because of the nature of the synchronisation procedure and the need for special instruments, most owners leave the task to a Suzuki dealer.*
3 Start the engine and let it run until it reaches normal operating temperature, then shut it off.
4 Raise the front of the fuel tank and support it on its prop, then undo the screw securing the inlet air pressure (IAP) sensor to the housing and displace the sensor **(see illustration)**.

**17.4a Undo the screw (arrowed) and displace the inlet air pressure (IAP) sensor**

1

17.4b The inlet air temperature sensor (arrowed) . . .

17.4c . . . screws into the front of the air filter housing

17.7 Throttle valve synchronisation gauge set-up

Remove the air filter housing (see Chapter 4). Remove the inlet air temperature (IAT) sensor from the housing and reconnect it to its wiring connector on the bike **(see illustrations)**.

5 Disconnect the PAIR vacuum hose from the take-off stub on No. 3 throttle body (GSX-R600), No. 4 throttle body (GSX-R750 and 1000), and remove the blanking caps from the take-off stubs on the remaining throttle bodies (see Chapter 4, Section 12). Connect the vacuum gauge hoses to the take-off stubs. Make sure they are a good fit because any air leaks will result in false readings.
*Caution: Take great care to avoid the possibility of drawing dirt into the engine. If available, secure a fine mesh over the throttle body inlets to act as a temporary filter.*
6 Start the engine and increase the idle speed to the level specified at the beginning of this Chapter using the idle speed adjuster screw

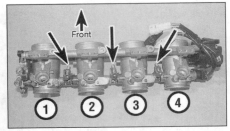

17.8 Throttle valve synchronising screws (arrowed)

*Throttle body shown removed for clarity. Numbers indicate cylinder identity.*

**(see illustration 6.3a, b or c)**. If using vacuum gauges fitted with damping adjustment, set this so that the needle flutter is just eliminated but so that they can still respond to small changes in pressure.
7 The vacuum readings for all of the cylinders should be the same **(see illustration)**. If the vacuum readings vary, turn the adjusting screws situated in the throttle linkage in-between each throttle body as follows.
8 First synchronise No. 1 and No. 2 throttle valves using the left-hand synchronising screw. Next synchronise No. 3 and No. 4 throttle valves using the right-hand screw **(see illustration)**. Finally synchronise throttle valves Nos. 1 and 2 to Nos. 3 and 4 using the centre screw. **Note:** *Do not press on the screws whilst adjusting them, otherwise a false reading will be obtained. Ensure the idle speed remains at the specified level throughout the procedure and adjust it if necessary.*

9 When all the throttle valves are synchronised, open and close the throttle twistgrip quickly to settle the linkage, and recheck the gauge readings, readjusting if necessary.
10 When the adjustment is complete, turn the engine OFF. Disconnect the vacuum gauge hoses and install the blanking caps and the PAIR vacuum hose (see Step 5).
11 If fitted, remove any temporary filter from the throttle body inlets. Install the IAT sensor in the air filter housing, then install the air filter housing (see Chapter 4). Install the IAP sensor.
12 Start the engine and re-check the idle speed; use the adjuster screw to correct it if necessary.
13 Install the remaining components in the reverse order of removal.

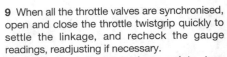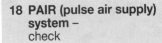

## 18 PAIR (pulse air supply) system – check

1 The system draws fresh air into the exhaust ports where it promotes the burning of unburnt gases, thereby reducing the emission of harmful hydrocarbons into the atmosphere. An air control valve is opened and closed by pressure changes in the intake manifold of No. 3 or No. 4 cylinder (whichever throttle body the hose connects to) and reed valves prevent exhaust gases flowing back into the system.
2 Remove the air filter housing (see Chapter 4). Release the clip securing the vacuum hose to the small union on the front of the control valve, then release the clip securing the air filter housing hose to the union on the rear of the valve and disconnect the hoses **(see illustration)**.
3 Undo the bolts that secure the PAIR assembly to the valve cover and lift off the assembly **(see illustration)**. The reed valves should remain inside their covers; carefully prise them out, noting how they fit. If the reed valves remain in the valve cover, note how they fit then carefully lift them off **(see illustration)**.
4 If required, release the clips securing the hoses to the control valve and separate the valve from the rest of the assembly.

18.2 Disconnect the vacuum hose (A) and air filter housing hose (B)

18.3a Undo the bolts (arrowed) to remove the PAIR assembly

18.3b Remove the reed valves noting how they fit

**18.5 Clean the reeds with solvent**

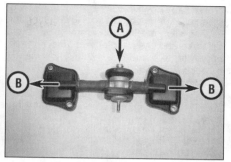

**18.6a Air blown into union (A) should flow out a side unions (B)**

**18.6b Using a vacuum pump to test the PAIR valve**

5 Inspect the reed valves for damage and deterioration. Clean the reeds carefully with a suitable solvent to remove any gum **(see illustration)**. Take care not to damage the sealing surfaces of the valves as no gaskets are fitted. Suzuki give no specifications for the valves but if there is any doubt about their condition, have them checked by a Suzuki dealer. **Note:** *Carbon deposits on the reed valves are an indication that the cut-off valve is faulty.*

6 To test the control valve, first blow air into the inlet union on the rear of the valve and check that it flows out the side unions **(see illustration)**. Next, connect a hand operated vacuum pump to the small union on the front of the valve and slowly draw vacuum of 491 mmHg **(see illustration)**. Again blow air into the inlet union and check that this time it does not flow out the side unions. If the valve fails either of these tests, it is faulty and should be replaced with a new one. If there is any doubt about the performance of the valve, have it tested by a Suzuki dealer.

7 Inspect the hoses and clips securing the reed valve covers to the cut-off valve. Inspect the air filter housing and vacuum hoses and clips. Renew any components that are damaged or deteriorated.

8 Installation is the reverse of removal, noting the following:

● Install the reed valves reed side down.
● Tighten the reed valve cover bolts to the specified torque setting.
● Secure the hoses on their unions with the clips.
● Ensure the vacuum hose is firmly connected to the appropriate throttle body

## 19 Steering head bearings –
check and adjustment

1 Steering head bearings can become dented, rough or loose during normal use of the machine. In extreme cases, worn or loose steering head bearings can cause steering wobble – a condition that is potentially dangerous.

### Check

2 Remove the steering damper to allow free movement of the steering (see Chapter 6). Support the motorcycle in an upright position using an auxiliary stand, then raise the front wheel off the ground by placing a support under the engine.

3 Point the front wheel straight ahead and slowly turn the handlebars from lock to lock. Any indents or roughness in the bearing races will be felt and if the bearings are too tight the bars will not move smoothly and freely. If the bearings are damaged they should be renewed (see Chapter 6). If the bearings are too tight, adjust them as described below.

4 Next, grasp the fork sliders and try to move them forwards and backwards **(see illustration)**. Any looseness in the steering head bearings will be felt as front to back movement of the forks. **Note:** *Freeplay in the*

**19.4 Checking for play in the steering head bearings**

**19.6b . . . the handlebar clamp bolts . . .**

*fork due to worn fork bushes can be misinterpreted as steering head bearing play. If play is felt in the steering head bearings, adjust them as follows.*

### Adjustment

5 Although not essential, it is wise to raise the front of the fuel tank and support it on its prop to avoid the possibility of damage should a tool slip while adjustment is being made (see Chapter 4).

6 Loosen the fork clamp bolts in the top yoke, the handlebar clamp bolts and the steering stem nut **(see illustrations)**.

7 Using a slim C-spanner or a suitable drift located in one of the notches, loosen the adjuster locknut; now, loosen the adjuster nut slightly, then tighten it until all front to back freeplay in the bearings is removed, yet the

**19.6a Loosen the clamp bolts on both sides in the top yoke . . .**

**19.6c . . . and the steering stem nut**

1

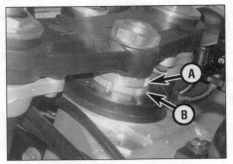

**19.7 Adjuster locknut (A) and adjuster nut (B)**

steering is able to move freely from lock to lock (see illustration). The object is to set the adjuster nut so that the bearings are under a very light loading, just enough to remove any front to back freeplay.

*Caution: Take great care not to overtighten the adjuster nut – excessive pressure will cause premature failure of the bearings.*

8 If available, the loading can be checked with a spring balance. Attach one end of the balance to the end of a handlebar and set the front wheel in the straight ahead position. Now pull on the balance (see illustration). If the bearing is adjusted correctly, the steering should start to turn when between 200 and 500 grams register on the balance scale. Connect the balance to the other handlebar and check the loading again – the result should be the same.

9 With the bearings correctly adjusted, tighten the locknut securely against the

adjuster nut, making sure the adjuster nut does not turn as you do so. Now tighten the steering stem nut, the fork clamp bolts in the top yoke and the handlebar clamp bolts, in that order, to the torque settings specified at the beginning of this Chapter.

10 Check the bearing adjustment as described above and re-adjust if necessary. Install the remaining components in the reverse order of removal.

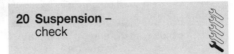

**20 Suspension –**
check

1 The suspension components must be maintained in top operating condition to ensure rider safety. Loose, worn or damaged suspension parts decrease the motorcycle's stability and control.

### Front suspension

2 While standing alongside the motorcycle, apply the front brake and push on the handlebars to compress the forks several times. They should move up-and-down smoothly without binding. If binding is felt, the forks should be disassembled and inspected (see Chapter 6).

3 Inspect the fork tubes for scratches, corrosion and pitting which will cause premature seal failure – if the damage is excessive, new tubes should be installed (see Chapter 6).

4 Inspect the area above (GSX-R600) or below (GSX-R750 and GSX-R1000) the dust

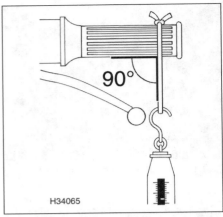

H34065

**19.8 Checking the bearing loading with a spring balance**

seal for signs of oil leaks, then carefully lever off the dust seal using a flat-bladed screwdriver and inspect the area around the fork seal (see illustrations). If leaks are evident, the seals must be renewed (see Chapter 6).

5 The forks are adjustable for spring pre-load, rebound damping and compression damping and it is essential that both fork legs are adjusted equally (see Chapter 6).

6 Check the tightness of all suspension nuts and bolts to be sure none have worked loose, referring to the torque settings specified at the beginning of Chapter 6.

### Rear suspension

7 Inspect the rear shock for fluid leaks and tightness of its mountings. If leaks are found, a new shock must be installed or advice sought from a suspension specialist on overhauling the shock (see Chapter 6).

8 With the aid of an assistant to support the bike, compress the rear suspension several times. It should move up and down freely without binding. If binding is felt, the worn or faulty component must be identified and renewed. The problem could be caused by the shock absorber, the suspension linkage components or the swingarm components.

9 Support the motorcycle using an auxiliary stand so that the rear wheel is off the ground. Grasp the swingarm and rock it from side to side – there should be no discernible movement at the rear (see illustration). If there's a little movement or a clicking can be heard, check the tightness of all the rear suspension mounting bolts and nuts, referring to the torque settings specified at the beginning of Chapter 6, and re-check for movement.

10 Grasp the top of the rear wheel and pull it upwards – there should be no discernible freeplay before the shock absorber begins to compress (see illustration). Any freeplay indicates worn bearings in the suspension linkage or swingarm, or worn shock absorber mountings. The worn components must be renewed (see Chapter 6).

**20.4a Check for oil leaks around the dust seals . . .**

**20.4b . . . and underneath the seals**

**20.9 Checking for play in the swingarm bearings**

**20.10 Checking for play in the shock mountings and suspension linkage**

**20.11 Check here (arrowed) for movement between the frame and swingarm**

**21.2a Check the tightness of the exhaust downpipe clamp bolts . . .**

**21.2b . . . the exhaust system mounting bolt . . .**

**11** To make a more accurate assessment of the swingarm bearings, remove the rear wheel (see Chapter 7) and the bolt securing the suspension linkage rods to the swingarm (see Chapter 6). Grasp the rear of the swingarm with one hand and place your other hand at the junction of the swingarm and the frame. Try to move the rear of the swingarm from side-to-side. Any wear in the bearings will be felt as movement between the swingarm and the frame at the front **(see illustration)**. If there is any wear, the swingarm will be felt to move forwards and backwards at the front (not from side-to-side). Next, move the swingarm up and down through its full travel. It should move freely, without any binding or rough spots. If the swingarm bearings are worn or if the swingarm does not move freely, new bearings must be fitted (see Chapter 6).

**21.2c . . . and the silencer mounting bolt**

beginning of this Chapter **(see illustrations)**. **Note:** *On GSX-R600 and GSX-R750 models the exhaust system is a one-piece unit which bolts directly onto the silencer. On GSX-R1000 models, the front section of the exhaust system is connected to the silencer via a single pipe section incorporating the exhaust control valve (see Section 22). Ensure that the pipe clamp bolt is tightened securely.*

## 21 Exhaust system bolts – tightness check

**1** Remove the fairing side panels (see Chapter 8). If required, remove the radiator mounting bolts and displace the radiator to improve access to the exhaust downpipe bolts (see Chapter 3).
**2** Using a torque wrench, check that the exhaust downpipe clamp bolts, the silencer to exhaust system nuts, and the exhaust system and the silencer mounting bolts are tightened to the torque settings specified at the

## 22 Exhaust control valve – check (GSX-R1000)

**1** The exhaust control valve is located inside a single pipe section of the exhaust system below the swingarm. The valve is connected by two cables to a servo located on the inside

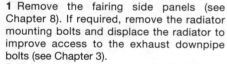

**22.2 Check the operation of the servo pulley**

of the right-hand main frame spar. The servo is actuated by the engine control module (ECM).
**2** To check the operation of the control valve, raise the front of the fuel tank and support it on its prop. Turn the ignition ON and observe the movement of the servo pulley and cables (this is a self-cleaning function which occurs each time the ignition is turned on) **(see illustration)**. If the pulley does not move, check the operation of the servo (see Chapter 4).
**3** If the cable action is stiff, remove the valve section of the exhaust system and check the condition of the cables and the operation of the valve (see Chapter 4). **Note:** *Before the cables are disconnected the servo pulley should be set in the adjustment position with the use of a Suzuki mode select switch, service tool Pt. No. 09930-82710.*

1

---

# Every 11,000 miles (18,000 km) or 18 months

*Carry out all the items under the 4000 mile (6000 km) check:*

## 23 Air filter – renewal

**1** Remove the old air filter as described in Section 2 and install a new one.

## 24 Engine/transmission – oil and oil filter change

 *Warning: Be careful when draining the oil, as the exhaust pipes, the engine, and the oil itself can cause severe burns.*

**1** Remove the right-hand fairing side panel (see Chapter 8).
**2** Drain the engine oil as described in Section 5, Steps 2 to 5.
**3** Now place the drain tray below the oil filter, which is on the front, right-hand side of the engine. Clean the crankcase around the filter, then unscrew the filter using a filter adapter (Suzuki service tool Pt. No. 09915-40610 or an aftermarket alternative) or strap wrench

and tip any residual oil into the drain tray **(see illustration)**.

**4** Smear clean engine oil onto the seal of the new filter, then screw it onto the engine by hand until the seal just seats **(see illustration)**. Using the filter adapter, tighten the filter a further two whole turns. **Note:** *Although Suzuki specify two whole turns, on the machine photographed the filter became very tight well before this, and tightening it further would possibly have damaged the seal or the filter. It is best to use your own judgement should the filter become very tight – the most important consideration is that the filter does not leak.*

**5** Wipe any oil off the exhaust pipes to prevent smoking when the engine is started and refill the engine with oil as described in Section 5, Step 6.

24.3  Removing the oil filter with an adapter

24.4  Installing the new oil filter

# Every 15,000 miles (24,000 km) or 24 months

*Carry out all the items under the 7500 mile (12,000 km) check:*

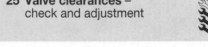

## 25  Valve clearances –
check and adjustment

### Check

**1** The engine must be completely cool for this maintenance procedure, so let the machine sit overnight before beginning.

**2** Remove the right-hand fairing side panel (see Chapter 8), the spark plugs (see Section 3) and the valve cover (see Chapter 2). The cylinders are numbered 1 to 4 from left to right, viewed as normally seated on the bike.

**3** Make a chart or sketch of all valve positions so that a note of each clearance can be made against the relevant valve.

**4** Unscrew the timing inspection cap from the starter clutch cover on the right-hand side of the engine **(see illustration)**. Discard the cap O-ring as new one should be fitted on

reassembly. The engine can be turned using a 14 mm socket on the starter clutch bolt, turning it in a clockwise direction only **(see illustration)**. Alternatively, to turn the engine in either direction, place the motorcycle on an auxiliary stand so that the rear wheel is off the ground, select a high gear and rotate the rear wheel by hand.

**5** Turn the engine in the normal direction of

rotation (clockwise) until the scribe line on the starter clutch aligns with the notch in the timing inspection hole and the cutout in the left-hand end of the exhaust camshaft is at 2 o'clock and the cutout in the end of the intake camshaft is at 12 o'clock **(see illustrations)**.

**6** Check the clearances on the No. 2 and No. 4 intake valves and the No. 3 and No. 4 exhaust valves as follows. Insert a feeler gauge of the

25.4a  Remove the timing inspection cap

25.4b  Turn the crankshaft in a clockwise direction

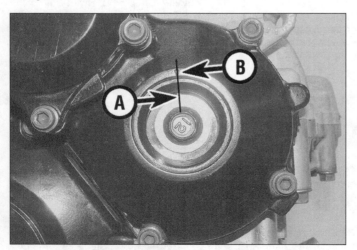

25.5a  Align the scribe line (A) with the notch (B)

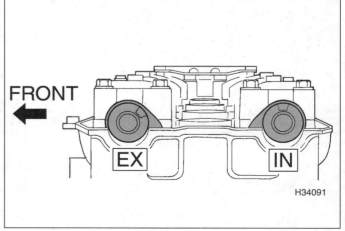

25.5b  Exhaust and intake camshaft cutouts for checking Nos. 2 and 4 intake valves and Nos. 3 and 4 exhaust valves

25.6 Checking the valve clearance with a feeler gauge

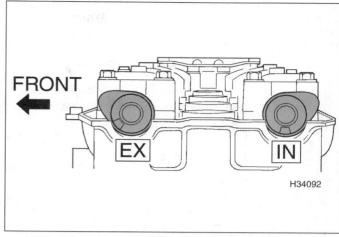

25.7 Exhaust and intake camshaft cutouts for checking Nos. 1 and 3 intake valves and Nos. 1 and 2 exhaust valves

25.11a Lift out the cam follower . . .

25.11b . . . and retrieve the shim from inside the follower . . .

25.11c . . . or from on the top of the valve

same thickness as the correct valve clearance (see Specifications at the beginning of this Chapter) between the camshaft lobe and the cam follower of each valve in turn. The gauge should be a firm sliding fit – you should feel a slight drag when the you pull the gauge out **(see illustration)**. If not, use the feeler gauges to obtain the exact clearance. Record the measured clearances on your chart. **Note:** *The intake and exhaust valve clearances are different.*

7 Now turn the engine clockwise through 360° so that the scribe line on the starter clutch again aligns with the notch in the timing inspection hole. The cutout in the exhaust camshaft should now be at 8 o'clock and the cutout in the intake camshaft should be at six o'clock **(see illustration)**.

8 Check the clearances on the No. 1 and No. 3 intake valves and the No. 1 and No. 2 exhaust valves as described in Step 6. Record the measured clearances on your chart.

### Adjustment

9 When all clearances have been measured and recorded, identify whether the clearance on any valve falls outside that specified. If it does, the shim between the follower and the valve must be replaced with one of a thickness which will restore the correct clearance.

10 Changing the shims requires removal of the camshafts (see Chapter 2). There is no need to remove both camshafts if shims from only intake or exhaust valves need changing. Place rags over the spark plug holes and the cam chain tunnel to prevent a shim dropping into the engine on removal.

11 With the camshaft removed, lift out the cam follower of the valve in question **(see illustration)**. Retrieve the shim from either the inside of the follower or pick it out of the top of the valve using a magnet, a small screwdriver with a dab of grease on it (the shim will stick to the grease), or a pair of pliers **(see illustrations)**. Do not allow the shim to fall into the engine.

12 The shim size should be marked on its upper face – a shim marked 170 is 1.70 mm thick – but the shim should be measured with a micrometer to check that it has not worn **(see illustration)**. If the shim has worn undersize, this must be taken into account and the valve clearance adjusted accordingly.

13 Using the appropriate shim selection chart, find where the measured valve clearance and existing shim thickness values intersect and read off the shim size required **(see illustrations overleaf)**.

14 New shims are available in 0.05 mm increments from 1.200 to 2.200 mm and can

be obtained from a Suzuki dealer. **Note:** *If the required replacement shim is greater than 2.20 mm (the largest available), the valve is probably not seating correctly due to a build-up of carbon deposits or valve damage. Remove the valve for checking (see Chapter 2).*

15 When replacing a shim, lubricate it with engine oil or molybdenum disulphide oil (a 50/50 mixture of molybdenum disulphide grease and engine oil) and fit it into its recess in the top of the valve with the size marking facing up. Check that the shim is correctly seated, then lubricate the follower with engine oil or molybdenum disulphide oil and install it

**1**

25.12 Measuring the shim thickness with a micrometer

onto the valve. Repeat the process for any other valves as required, then install the camshafts (see Chapter 2).

16 Rotate the crankshaft several turns to seat the new shim(s), then check the clearances again.

17 Install the remaining components in the reverse order of removal. Fit a new O-ring on the timing inspection cap and smear it with engine oil before tightening it to the specified torque setting.

PRESENT SHIM SIZE (mm)

| MEASURED TAPPET CLEARANCE (mm) | 1.20 | 1.25 | 1.30 | 1.35 | 1.40 | 1.45 | 1.50 | 1.55 | 1.60 | 1.65 | 1.70 | 1.75 | 1.80 | 1.85 | 1.90 | 1.95 | 2.00 | 2.05 | 2.10 | 2.15 | 2.20 |
|---|---|---|---|---|---|---|---|---|---|---|---|---|---|---|---|---|---|---|---|---|---|
| 0.00-0.04 |  |  | 1.20 | 1.25 | 1.30 | 1.35 | 1.40 | 1.45 | 1.50 | 1.55 | 1.60 | 1.65 | 1.70 | 1.75 | 1.80 | 1.85 | 1.90 | 1.95 | 2.00 | 2.05 | 2.10 |
| 0.05-0.09 |  | 1.20 | 1.25 | 1.30 | 1.35 | 1.40 | 1.45 | 1.50 | 1.55 | 1.60 | 1.65 | 1.70 | 1.75 | 1.80 | 1.85 | 1.90 | 1.95 | 2.00 | 2.05 | 2.10 | 2.15 |
| 0.10-0.20 | SPECIFIED CLEARANCE/NO ADJUSTMENT REQUIRED |  |  |  |  |  |  |  |  |  |  |  |  |  |  |  |  |  |  |  |  |
| 0.21-0.25 | 1.30 | 1.35 | 1.40 | 1.45 | 1.50 | 1.55 | 1.60 | 1.65 | 1.70 | 1.75 | 1.80 | 1.85 | 1.90 | 1.95 | 2.00 | 2.05 | 2.10 | 2.15 | 2.20 | 2.20 |  |
| 0.26-0.30 | 1.35 | 1.40 | 1.45 | 1.50 | 1.55 | 1.60 | 1.65 | 1.70 | 1.75 | 1.80 | 1.85 | 1.90 | 1.95 | 2.00 | 2.05 | 2.10 | 2.15 | 2.20 |  |  |  |
| 0.31-0.35 | 1.40 | 1.45 | 1.50 | 1.55 | 1.60 | 1.65 | 1.70 | 1.75 | 1.80 | 1.85 | 1.90 | 1.95 | 2.00 | 2.05 | 2.10 | 2.15 | 2.20 |  |  |  |  |
| 0.36-0.40 | 1.45 | 1.50 | 1.55 | 1.60 | 1.65 | 1.70 | 1.75 | 1.80 | 1.85 | 1.90 | 1.95 | 2.00 | 2.05 | 2.10 | 2.15 | 2.20 |  |  |  |  |  |
| 0.41-0.45 | 1.50 | 1.55 | 1.60 | 1.65 | 1.70 | 1.75 | 1.80 | 1.85 | 1.90 | 1.95 | 2.00 | 2.05 | 2.10 | 2.15 | 2.20 |  |  |  |  |  |  |
| 0.46-0.50 | 1.55 | 1.60 | 1.65 | 1.70 | 1.75 | 1.80 | 1.85 | 1.90 | 1.95 | 2.00 | 2.05 | 2.10 | 2.15 | 2.20 |  |  |  |  |  |  |  |
| 0.51-0.55 | 1.60 | 1.65 | 1.70 | 1.75 | 1.80 | 1.85 | 1.90 | 1.95 | 2.00 | 2.05 | 2.10 | 2.15 | 2.20 |  |  |  |  |  |  |  |  |
| 0.56-0.60 | 1.65 | 1.70 | 1.75 | 1.80 | 1.85 | 1.90 | 1.95 | 2.00 | 2.05 | 2.10 | 2.15 | 2.20 |  |  |  |  |  |  |  |  |  |
| 0.61-0.65 | 1.70 | 1.75 | 1.80 | 1.85 | 1.90 | 1.95 | 2.00 | 2.05 | 2.10 | 2.15 | 2.20 |  |  |  |  |  |  |  |  |  |  |
| 0.66-0.70 | 1.75 | 1.80 | 1.85 | 1.90 | 1.95 | 2.00 | 2.05 | 2.10 | 2.15 | 2.20 |  |  |  |  |  |  |  |  |  |  |  |
| 0.71-0.75 | 1.80 | 1.85 | 1.90 | 1.95 | 2.00 | 2.05 | 2.10 | 2.15 | 2.20 |  |  |  |  |  |  |  |  |  |  |  |  |
| 0.76-0.80 | 1.85 | 1.90 | 1.95 | 2.00 | 2.05 | 2.10 | 2.15 | 2.20 |  |  |  |  |  |  |  |  |  |  |  |  |  |
| 0.81-0.85 | 1.90 | 1.95 | 2.00 | 2.05 | 2.10 | 2.15 | 2.20 |  |  |  |  |  |  |  |  |  |  |  |  |  |  |
| 0.86-0.90 | 1.95 | 2.00 | 2.05 | 2.10 | 2.15 | 2.20 |  |  |  |  |  |  |  |  |  |  |  |  |  |  |  |
| 0.91-0.95 | 2.00 | 2.05 | 2.10 | 2.15 | 2.20 |  |  |  |  |  |  |  |  |  |  |  |  |  |  |  |  |
| 0.96-1.00 | 2.05 | 2.10 | 2.15 | 2.20 |  |  |  |  |  |  |  |  |  |  |  |  |  |  |  |  |  |
| 1.01-1.05 | 2.10 | 2.15 | 2.20 |  |  |  |  |  |  |  |  |  |  |  |  |  |  |  |  |  |  |
| 1.06-1.10 | 2.15 | 2.20 |  |  |  |  |  |  |  |  |  |  |  |  |  |  |  |  |  |  |  |
| 1.11-1.15 | 2.20 |  |  |  |  |  |  |  |  |  |  |  |  |  |  |  |  |  |  |  |  |

25.13a Shim selection chart – intake valves

H31236

PRESENT SHIM SIZE (mm)

| MEASURED TAPPET CLEARANCE (mm) | 1.20 | 1.25 | 1.30 | 1.35 | 1.40 | 1.45 | 1.50 | 1.55 | 1.60 | 1.65 | 1.70 | 1.75 | 1.80 | 1.85 | 1.90 | 1.95 | 2.00 | 2.05 | 2.10 | 2.15 | 2.20 |
|---|---|---|---|---|---|---|---|---|---|---|---|---|---|---|---|---|---|---|---|---|---|
| 0.05-0.09 |  |  |  | 1.20 | 1.25 | 1.30 | 1.35 | 1.40 | 1.45 | 1.50 | 1.55 | 1.60 | 1.65 | 1.70 | 1.75 | 1.80 | 1.85 | 1.90 | 1.95 | 2.00 | 2.05 |
| 0.10-0.14 |  |  | 1.20 | 1.25 | 1.30 | 1.35 | 1.40 | 1.45 | 1.50 | 1.55 | 1.60 | 1.65 | 1.70 | 1.75 | 1.80 | 1.85 | 1.90 | 1.95 | 2.00 | 2.05 | 2.10 |
| 0.15-0.19 |  | 1.20 | 1.25 | 1.30 | 1.35 | 1.40 | 1.45 | 1.50 | 1.55 | 1.60 | 1.65 | 1.70 | 1.75 | 1.80 | 1.85 | 1.90 | 1.95 | 2.00 | 2.05 | 2.10 | 2.15 |
| 0.20-0.30 | SPECIFIED CLEARANCE/NO ADJUSTMENT REQUIRED |  |  |  |  |  |  |  |  |  |  |  |  |  |  |  |  |  |  |  |  |
| 0.31-0.35 | 1.30 | 1.35 | 1.40 | 1.45 | 1.50 | 1.55 | 1.60 | 1.65 | 1.70 | 1.75 | 1.80 | 1.85 | 1.90 | 1.95 | 2.00 | 2.05 | 2.10 | 2.15 | 2.20 | 2.20 |  |
| 0.36-0.40 | 1.35 | 1.40 | 1.45 | 1.50 | 1.55 | 1.60 | 1.65 | 1.70 | 1.75 | 1.80 | 1.85 | 1.90 | 1.95 | 2.00 | 2.05 | 2.10 | 2.15 | 2.20 |  |  |  |
| 0.41-0.45 | 1.40 | 1.45 | 1.50 | 1.55 | 1.60 | 1.65 | 1.70 | 1.75 | 1.80 | 1.85 | 1.90 | 1.95 | 2.00 | 2.05 | 2.10 | 2.15 | 2.20 |  |  |  |  |
| 0.46-0.50 | 1.45 | 1.50 | 1.55 | 1.60 | 1.65 | 1.70 | 1.75 | 1.80 | 1.85 | 1.90 | 1.95 | 2.00 | 2.05 | 2.10 | 2.15 | 2.20 |  |  |  |  |  |
| 0.51-0.55 | 1.50 | 1.55 | 1.60 | 1.65 | 1.70 | 1.75 | 1.80 | 1.85 | 1.90 | 1.95 | 2.00 | 2.05 | 2.10 | 2.15 | 2.20 |  |  |  |  |  |  |
| 0.56-0.60 | 1.55 | 1.60 | 1.65 | 1.70 | 1.75 | 1.80 | 1.85 | 1.90 | 1.95 | 2.00 | 2.05 | 2.10 | 2.15 | 2.20 |  |  |  |  |  |  |  |
| 0.61-0.65 | 1.60 | 1.65 | 1.70 | 1.75 | 1.80 | 1.85 | 1.90 | 1.95 | 2.00 | 2.05 | 2.10 | 2.15 | 2.20 |  |  |  |  |  |  |  |  |
| 0.66-0.70 | 1.65 | 1.70 | 1.75 | 1.80 | 1.85 | 1.90 | 1.95 | 2.00 | 2.05 | 2.10 | 2.15 | 2.20 |  |  |  |  |  |  |  |  |  |
| 0.71-0.75 | 1.70 | 1.75 | 1.80 | 1.85 | 1.90 | 1.95 | 2.00 | 2.05 | 2.10 | 2.15 | 2.20 |  |  |  |  |  |  |  |  |  |  |
| 0.76-0.80 | 1.75 | 1.80 | 1.85 | 1.90 | 1.95 | 2.00 | 2.05 | 2.10 | 2.15 | 2.20 |  |  |  |  |  |  |  |  |  |  |  |
| 0.81-0.85 | 1.80 | 1.85 | 1.90 | 1.95 | 2.00 | 2.05 | 2.10 | 2.15 | 2.20 |  |  |  |  |  |  |  |  |  |  |  |  |
| 0.86-0.90 | 1.85 | 1.90 | 1.95 | 2.00 | 2.05 | 2.10 | 2.15 | 2.20 |  |  |  |  |  |  |  |  |  |  |  |  |  |
| 0.91-0.95 | 1.90 | 1.95 | 2.00 | 2.05 | 2.10 | 2.15 | 2.20 |  |  |  |  |  |  |  |  |  |  |  |  |  |  |
| 0.96-1.00 | 1.95 | 2.00 | 2.05 | 2.10 | 2.15 | 2.20 |  |  |  |  |  |  |  |  |  |  |  |  |  |  |  |
| 1.01-1.05 | 2.00 | 2.05 | 2.10 | 2.15 | 2.20 |  |  |  |  |  |  |  |  |  |  |  |  |  |  |  |  |
| 1.06-1.10 | 2.05 | 2.10 | 2.15 | 2.20 |  |  |  |  |  |  |  |  |  |  |  |  |  |  |  |  |  |
| 1.11-1.15 | 2.10 | 2.15 | 2.20 |  |  |  |  |  |  |  |  |  |  |  |  |  |  |  |  |  |  |
| 1.16-1.20 | 2.15 | 2.20 |  |  |  |  |  |  |  |  |  |  |  |  |  |  |  |  |  |  |  |
| 1.21-1.25 | 2.20 |  |  |  |  |  |  |  |  |  |  |  |  |  |  |  |  |  |  |  |  |

25.13b Shim selection chart – exhaust valves

H31237

27.3 Allow the coolant to drain completely

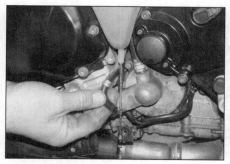

27.4 Draining the coolant reservoir

27.15 Refill the system slowly to avoid trapping air

# Every two years

## 26 Brakes –
### fluid change

1 The brake fluid should be changed at the prescribed interval or whenever a master cylinder or caliper overhaul is carried out. Refer to Chapter 7, Section 11 for details. Ensure that all the old fluid is be pumped from the hydraulic system and that the level in the fluid reservoir is checked and the brakes tested before riding the motorcycle.

 **HAYNES HiNT** *Old brake fluid is invariably much darker in colour than new fluid, making it easy to see when all old fluid has been expelled from the system.*

## 27 Cooling system –
### draining, flushing and refilling

⚠ *Warning: Allow the engine to cool completely before performing this maintenance operation. Also, don't allow antifreeze to come into contact with your skin or the painted surfaces of the motorcycle. Rinse off spills immediately with plenty of water. Antifreeze is highly toxic if ingested. Never leave antifreeze lying around in an open container or in puddles on the floor; children and pets are attracted by its sweet smell and may drink it. Check with local authorities (councils) about disposing of antifreeze. Many communities have collection centres which will see that antifreeze is disposed of safely. Antifreeze is also combustible, so don't store it near open flames.*

### Draining

1 Support the motorcycle upright on a level surface using an auxiliary stand. Remove the fairing side panels (see Chapter 8). Cover the radiator pressure cap with a heavy cloth then remove it by turning it anti-clockwise until it reaches a stop. If you hear a hissing sound (indicating there is still pressure in the system), wait until it stops. Now press down on the cap and continue turning the cap until it can be removed **(see illustration 9.6)**.

2 On GSX-R600 and 750 models, release the cable tie securing the coolant hoses together on the lower, left-hand side of the bike.

3 Position a suitable container beneath the water pump on the left-hand side of the engine. Loosen the clip securing the radiator hose to the pump cover, then pull the hose off its union and allow the coolant to drain completely from the system **(see illustration)**.

4 Remove the reservoir cap, then detach the overflow hose from the bottom of the reservoir and drain the coolant **(see illustration)**. Rinse the inside of the reservoir with clean water and reconnect the overflow hose.

### Flushing

5 Flush the radiator with clean water by inserting a garden hose in the filler neck. Allow the water to run through until it is clear. If there is a lot of rust in the water, remove the radiator and have it cleaned professionally (see Chapter 3).

6 Reconnect the radiator hose to the water pump and tighten the clip securely.

7 Fill the cooling system via the radiator with clean water mixed with a flushing compound.

27.16 Fill the coolant reservoir to the F level line

Make sure the flushing compound is compatible with aluminium components, and follow the manufacturer's instructions carefully. Rock the machine from side to side to bleed any trapped air from the system and top up as necessary. When the system is full (all the way up to the top of the radiator filler neck), fit the pressure cap.

8 Fill the coolant reservoir to the F level line with clean water and fit the cap.

9 Start the engine and allow it to reach normal operating temperature. Let it run for about ten minutes.

10 Stop the engine and let it cool for a while. Cover the pressure cap with a heavy rag and turn it anti-clockwise to the stop. If you hear a hissing sound (indicating there is pressure in the system), wait until it stops. Now press down on the cap and continue turning it until it can be removed.

11 Drain the system once again.

12 Refill the system with clean water, fit the radiator cap and repeat the procedure in Steps 8 to 11.

13 Drain the coolant reservoir, then ensure the overflow hose is properly fitted and secured with its clip (see Step 4).

### Refilling

14 Fit the radiator hose onto the water pump and tighten the clip securely. If required, fit the cable tie (see Step 2).

15 Fill the system with the proper coolant mixture (see this Chapter's Specifications) **(see illustration)**. *Note: Pour the coolant in to the radiator slowly to minimise the amount of air entering the system.* Rock the machine from side to side to bleed any trapped air from the system and top up as necessary.

16 Fill the coolant reservoir to the F level line with coolant mixture and fit the cap **(see illustration)**.

17 Start the engine and allow it to idle for 2 to 3 minutes. Flick the throttle twistgrip part open 3 or 4 times, so that the engine speed rises to approximately 4000 – 5000 rpm, then stop the engine. Any air trapped in the system should bleed back to the radiator filler neck.

18 Carefully loosen the air bleed bolt on the top of the thermostat housing and allow any

**1**

**27.18 Bleeding air out of the system from the top of the thermostat housing (arrowed)**

trapped air to escape, then tighten the bolt to the specified torque setting **(see illustration)**.
**19** Top the coolant level up to the radiator filler neck as necessary, then fit the pressure cap.
**20** Check the system for leaks.
**21** Install the remaining components in the reverse order of removal.

**22** Do not dispose of the old coolant by pouring it down the drain. Instead pour it into a heavy plastic container, cap it tightly and take it into an authorised disposal site or service station – see **Warning** at the beginning of this Section.

# Every four years

### 28 Brake hoses – renewal

**1** The hoses will deteriorate with age and should be renewed regardless of their apparent condition (see Chapter 7).
**2** Always renew the banjo union sealing washers when fitting new hoses. Refill the system with new brake fluid and bleed the system as described in Chapter 7.

### 29 Fuel hoses and EVAP hoses – renewal

⚠️ *Warning: Petrol (gasoline) is extremely flammable, so take extra precautions when you work on any part of the fuel system. Don't smoke or allow open flames or bare light bulbs near the work area, and don't work in a garage where a natural gas-type appliance is present. If you spill any fuel on your skin, rinse it off immediately with soap and water. When you perform any kind of work on the fuel system, wear safety glasses and have a fire extinguisher*

*suitable for a Class B type fire (flammable liquids) on hand.*

**1** The fuel delivery, intake air pressure system and PAIR system hoses should be renewed regardless of their condition. On California models, also renew the EVAP emission control system hoses (see Chapter 4).
**2** Remove the fuel tank and the air filter housing. Disconnect the various hoses, noting the routing of each one and how it is secured. **Note:** *It is advisable to make a sketch of the hoses before removing them to ensure they are correctly installed.*
**3** Where appropriate, secure each new hose to its unions using new clips. Run the engine and check that the fuel system is working correctly before taking the machine out on the road.

# Non-scheduled maintenance

### 30 Headlight aim – check and adjustment

**Note:** *An improperly adjusted headlight may cause problems for oncoming traffic or provide poor, unsafe illumination of the road ahead. Before adjusting the headlight aim, be sure to consult with local traffic laws and regulations –*

*for UK models refer to MOT Test Checks in the Reference section at the back of this manual.*
**1** The headlight beam can adjusted both horizontally and vertically. Before making any adjustment, check that the tyre pressures are correct and the suspension is adjusted as required. Make any adjustments to the headlight aim with the machine on level ground, with the fuel tank half full and with an assistant sitting on the seat. If the bike is

usually ridden with a passenger, have a second assistant to do this. Remove the six trim clips securing the lower inner panel to the underside of the fairing and remove the panel **(see illustration)**. Refer to Chapter 8, Section 5 for details of how to release the trim clips.
**2** Horizontal adjustment is made by turning the adjuster screw on the top left-hand corner of the headlight unit **(see illustration)**. Turn it clockwise to move the beam to the left, and anti-clockwise to move it to the right.
**3** Vertical adjustment is made by turning the adjuster in the middle of the headlight unit **(see illustration 30.2)**. Turn the adjuster clockwise to move the beam down, and anti-clockwise to move it up.

### 31 Wheel bearings – check

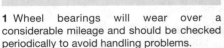

**1** Wheel bearings will wear over a considerable mileage and should be checked periodically to avoid handling problems.
**2** Support the motorcycle upright using an auxiliary stand so that the wheel being

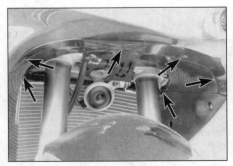

**30.1 Remove the fairing lower inner panel to access to the adjusters – it is retained by six trim clips (arrowed)**

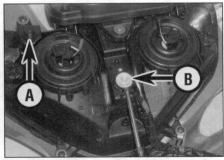

**30.2 Headlight horizontal adjuster (A) and vertical adjuster (B)**

examined is off the ground. Check for any play in the bearings by pushing and pulling the wheel against the hub **(see illustration)**. Also rotate the wheel and check that it turns smoothly.

**3** If any play is detected in the hub, or if the wheel does not rotate smoothly (and this is not due to brake or transmission drag), the wheel should be removed and the bearings inspected for wear or damage (see Chapter 7).

## 32 Front forks – oil change
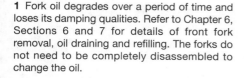

**1** Fork oil degrades over a period of time and loses its damping qualities. Refer to Chapter 6, Sections 6 and 7 for details of front fork removal, oil draining and refilling. The forks do not need to be completely disassembled to change the oil.

## 33 Cylinder compression – check

**1** Poor engine performance may be caused by leaking valves, incorrect valve clearances, a leaking head gasket, or worn pistons, piston rings or cylinder walls. A cylinder compression check will highlight these conditions and can also indicate the presence of excessive carbon deposits in the cylinder head.

**2** The only tools required are a compression gauge (with a threaded adapter to suit the spark plug hole in the cylinder head) and a spark plug socket. Depending on the outcome of the initial test, a squirt-type oil can may also be needed.

**3** Make sure the valve clearances are correctly set (see Section 25) and that the cylinder head bolts are tightened to the correct torque setting (see Chapter 2).

**4** Refer to *Fault Finding Equipment* in the Reference section for details of the compression test, and to the Specifications at the beginning of this Chapter for the test data.

## 34 Engine – oil pressure check

**1** The oil pressure 'oil can' symbol and the warning light should illuminate when the ignition (main) switch is turned ON, and they should extinguish when the engine is started – this serves as a check that the LED is sound. If the oil pressure light comes on whilst the engine is running, low oil pressure is indicated – stop the engine immediately and carry out an oil level check (see *Daily (pre-ride) checks*).

**31.2 Checking for play in the wheel bearings**

**2** An oil pressure check must be carried out if the warning light comes on when the engine is running yet the oil level is good (Step 1). It can also provide useful information about the condition of the engine's lubrication system.

**3** To check the oil pressure, a suitable gauge, hose and adapter (which screws into the crankcase) will be needed. Suzuki produce service tools Pt. Nos 09915-77330, 09915-74520 and 09915-74540 for this purpose.

**4** Remove the right-hand fairing side-panel (see Chapter 8).

**5** Position a suitable container below the main oil gallery plug on the right-hand side of the engine to catch any residual oil. Unscrew the plug and swiftly screw the gauge adapter into the crankcase threads **(see illustration)**. Connect the hose and gauge to the adapter. If much oil is lost, replenish it to the correct level before proceeding (see *Daily (pre-ride) checks*).

**6** Warm the engine up to normal operating temperature (between 10 and 20 minutes running at 2000 rpm) then increase the engine speed to 3000 rpm whilst watching the gauge reading. The oil pressure should be similar to that given in the Specifications at the beginning of this Chapter.

**7** If the pressure is significantly lower than the standard, either the pressure regulator is stuck open, the oil pump is faulty, the oil strainer or filter is blocked, or there is other engine damage. Begin diagnosis by checking the oil filter, strainer and regulator, then the oil pump (see Chapter 2). If these items are good, it is likely the bearing oil clearances are excessive and the engine needs to be overhauled.

**8** If the pressure is too high, either an oil passage is clogged, the regulator is stuck closed, or the wrong grade of oil is being used.

**9** Turn the engine OFF. Disconnect the hose and gauge from the adapter and unscrew the adapter from the crankcase.

 **Warning: Be careful when removing the pressure gauge adapter as the exhaust pipes, the**

**34.5 Main oil gallery plug (arrowed)**

*engine and the oil itself can cause severe burns.*

**10** Fit a new O-ring to the oil gallery plug, install the plug and tighten it to the torque setting specified at the beginning of this Chapter. Check the engine oil level (see *Daily (pre-ride) checks*) then install the remaining components in the reverse order of removal.

## 35 Steering head bearings – lubrication

**1** Over a considerable time the grease in the bearings will be dispersed or will harden allowing the ingress of dirt and water.

**2** The steering head should be disassembled periodically and the bearings cleaned and re-greased (see Chapter 6, Section 10).

## 36 Rear suspension bearings – lubrication

**1** Over a considerable mileage the grease in the bearings will be washed out or will harden allowing the ingress of dirt and water.

**2** The suspension linkage and the swingarm should be disassembled periodically and the bearings cleaned and re-greased as necessary (see Chapter 6, Sections 13 and 16).

## 37 Brake caliper and master cylinder seals – renewal

**1** Brake seals will deteriorate over a period of time and lose their effectiveness, leading to sticky operation of the brake master cylinders or the pistons in the brake calipers, or fluid loss.

**2** Renew all the caliper seals as a set; master cylinder seals are supplied as a kit with the piston (see Chapter 7).

**1**

# Chapter 2
# Engine, clutch and transmission

## Contents

2

## Degrees of difficulty

| Easy, suitable for novice with little experience  | Fairly easy, suitable for beginner with some experience  | Fairly difficult, suitable for competent DIY mechanic | Difficult, suitable for experienced DIY mechanic  | Very difficult, suitable for expert DIY or professional |

# Specifications – GSX-R600 models

## General

| | |
|---|---|
| Type | Four-stroke in-line four |
| Capacity | 599 cc |
| Bore | 67.0 mm |
| Stroke | 42.5 mm |
| Compression ratio | 12.2 to 1 |
| Clutch | Wet multi-plate |
| Transmission | 6-speed constant mesh |
| Final drive | Chain |

## Camshafts

| | |
|---|---|
| Intake lobe height | |
|   Standard | 36.58 to 36.62 mm |
|   Service limit (min) | 36.28 mm |
| Exhaust lobe height | |
|   Standard | 35.28 to 35.32 mm |
|   Service limit (min) | 34.98 mm |
| Journal diameter | 23.959 to 23.980 mm |
| Camshaft holder journal diameter | 24.012 to 24.025 mm |
| Journal oil clearance | |
|   Standard | 0.032 to 0.066 mm |
|   Service limit (max) | 0.15 mm |
| Runout (max) | 0.10 mm |

## Cylinder head

| | |
|---|---|
| Warpage (max) | 0.20 mm |

## Valves, guides and springs

| | |
|---|---|
| Valve clearances | see Chapter 1 |
| Intake valves | |
|   Head diameter | 27.2 mm |
|   Stem diameter | 3.975 to 3.990 mm |
|   Guide bore diameter | 4.000 to 4.012 mm |
|   Stem-to-guide clearance | 0.010 to 0.037 mm |
|   Side clearance, wobble (max) – see text | 0.35 mm |
|   Margin thickness (min) | 0.5 mm |
|   Seat width | 0.9 to 1.1 mm |
|   Head runout (max) | 0.03 mm |
|   Stem runout (max) | 0.05 mm |
| Exhaust valves | |
|   Head diameter | 22.0 mm |
|   Stem diameter | 3.955 to 3.970 mm |
|   Guide bore diameter | 4.000 to 4.012 mm |
|   Stem-to-guide clearance | 0.030 to 0.057 mm |
|   Side clearance, wobble (max) – see text | 0.35 mm |
|   Margin thickness (min) | 0.5 mm |
|   Seat width | 0.9 to 1.1 mm |
|   Head runout (max) | 0.03 mm |
|   Stem runout (max) | 0.05 mm |
| Valve springs (intake and exhaust) | |
|   Free length limit (min) | 37.8 mm |
|   Spring tension | |
|     GSX-R600K1 | 32.85 mm with 17.6 to 20.3 kg load |
|     GSX-R600K2 | 32.85 mm with 18.2 to 20.3 kg load |

## Transmission

| | |
|---|---|
| Gear ratios (no. of teeth) | |
|   Primary reduction | 1.926 to 1 (79/41T) |
|   Final reduction | 2.812 to 1 (45/16T) |
|   1st gear | 2.785 to 1 (39/14T) |
|   2nd gear | 2.000 to 1 (32/16T) |
|   3rd gear | 1.600 to 1 (32/20T) |
|   4th gear | 1.363 to 1 (30/20T) |
|   5th gear | 1.208 to 1 (29/24T) |
|   6th gear | 1.086 to 1 (25/23T) |

## Selector drum and forks

Selector fork-to-groove clearance
    Standard . . . . . . . . . . . . . . . . . . . . . . . . . . . . . . . . . . . . . . . . . . . . . . . . . . . . 0.1 to 0.3 mm
    Service limit (max) . . . . . . . . . . . . . . . . . . . . . . . . . . . . . . . . . . . . . . . . . . . . . 0.5 mm
Selector fork end thickness . . . . . . . . . . . . . . . . . . . . . . . . . . . . . . . . . . . . . . 4.8 to 4.9 mm
Selector fork groove width . . . . . . . . . . . . . . . . . . . . . . . . . . . . . . . . . . . . . . . . 5.0 to 5.1 mm

## Clutch

Friction plate
    Quantity . . . . . . . . . . . . . . . . . . . . . . . . . . . . . . . . . . . . . . . . . . . . . . . . . . . . . . . 9
    Thickness . . . . . . . . . . . . . . . . . . . . . . . . . . . . . . . . . . . . . . . . . . . . . . . . . . . . . 2.92 to 3.08 mm
    Tab width
        Standard . . . . . . . . . . . . . . . . . . . . . . . . . . . . . . . . . . . . . . . . . . . . . . . . . . 13.7 to 13.8 mm
        Service limit (min) . . . . . . . . . . . . . . . . . . . . . . . . . . . . . . . . . . . . . . . . . . 12.9 mm
Plain plate
    Quantity . . . . . . . . . . . . . . . . . . . . . . . . . . . . . . . . . . . . . . . . . . . . . . . . . . . . . . . 8 (see text)
    Warpage (max) . . . . . . . . . . . . . . . . . . . . . . . . . . . . . . . . . . . . . . . . . . . . . . . . 0.1 mm
Spring free length
    Standard . . . . . . . . . . . . . . . . . . . . . . . . . . . . . . . . . . . . . . . . . . . . . . . . . . . . . . 47.8 mm
    Service limit . . . . . . . . . . . . . . . . . . . . . . . . . . . . . . . . . . . . . . . . . . . . . . . . . . . 45.4 mm

## Lubrication system

Oil pressure . . . . . . . . . . . . . . . . . . . . . . . . . . . . . . . . . . . . . . . . . . . . . . . . . . . . . . see Chapter 1

## Cylinders

Bore standard dimension . . . . . . . . . . . . . . . . . . . . . . . . . . . . . . . . . . . . . . . . . 67.000 to 67.015 mm
Warpage of gasket face (max) . . . . . . . . . . . . . . . . . . . . . . . . . . . . . . . . . . . . 0.20 mm
Cylinder compression . . . . . . . . . . . . . . . . . . . . . . . . . . . . . . . . . . . . . . . . . . . . see Chapter 1

## Pistons

Piston diameter (measured 15.0 mm up from skirt, at 90° to piston pin axis)
    Standard . . . . . . . . . . . . . . . . . . . . . . . . . . . . . . . . . . . . . . . . . . . . . . . . . . . . . . 66.970 to 66.985 mm
    Service limit (min) . . . . . . . . . . . . . . . . . . . . . . . . . . . . . . . . . . . . . . . . . . . . . . 66.880 mm
Piston-to-bore clearance
    Standard . . . . . . . . . . . . . . . . . . . . . . . . . . . . . . . . . . . . . . . . . . . . . . . . . . . . . . 0.010 to 0.035 mm
    Service limit (min) . . . . . . . . . . . . . . . . . . . . . . . . . . . . . . . . . . . . . . . . . . . . . . 0.120 mm
Piston pin diameter
    Standard . . . . . . . . . . . . . . . . . . . . . . . . . . . . . . . . . . . . . . . . . . . . . . . . . . . . . . 13.995 to 14.000 mm
    Service limit (min) . . . . . . . . . . . . . . . . . . . . . . . . . . . . . . . . . . . . . . . . . . . . . . 13.980 mm
Piston pin bore diameter in piston
    Standard . . . . . . . . . . . . . . . . . . . . . . . . . . . . . . . . . . . . . . . . . . . . . . . . . . . . . . 14.002 to 14.008 mm
    Service limit (max) . . . . . . . . . . . . . . . . . . . . . . . . . . . . . . . . . . . . . . . . . . . . . 14.030 mm

## Piston rings

Ring end gap (free)
    Top ring
        Standard . . . . . . . . . . . . . . . . . . . . . . . . . . . . . . . . . . . . . . . . . . . . . . . . . . 7.3 mm (approx.)
        Service limit (min) . . . . . . . . . . . . . . . . . . . . . . . . . . . . . . . . . . . . . . . . . . 5.8 mm
    2nd ring
        Standard . . . . . . . . . . . . . . . . . . . . . . . . . . . . . . . . . . . . . . . . . . . . . . . . . . 9.2 mm
        Service limit (min) . . . . . . . . . . . . . . . . . . . . . . . . . . . . . . . . . . . . . . . . . . 7.4 mm
Ring end gap (installed)
    Top ring
        Standard . . . . . . . . . . . . . . . . . . . . . . . . . . . . . . . . . . . . . . . . . . . . . . . . . . 0.06 to 0.18 mm
        Service limit (max) . . . . . . . . . . . . . . . . . . . . . . . . . . . . . . . . . . . . . . . . . 0.50 mm
    2nd ring
        Standard . . . . . . . . . . . . . . . . . . . . . . . . . . . . . . . . . . . . . . . . . . . . . . . . . . 0.06 to 0.18 mm
        Service limit (max) . . . . . . . . . . . . . . . . . . . . . . . . . . . . . . . . . . . . . . . . . 0.50 mm
Ring thickness
    Top ring . . . . . . . . . . . . . . . . . . . . . . . . . . . . . . . . . . . . . . . . . . . . . . . . . . . . . . . 0.97 to 0.99 mm
    2nd ring . . . . . . . . . . . . . . . . . . . . . . . . . . . . . . . . . . . . . . . . . . . . . . . . . . . . . . 0.77 to 0.79 mm
Ring groove width in piston
    Top ring . . . . . . . . . . . . . . . . . . . . . . . . . . . . . . . . . . . . . . . . . . . . . . . . . . . . . . . 1.01 to 1.03 mm
    2nd ring . . . . . . . . . . . . . . . . . . . . . . . . . . . . . . . . . . . . . . . . . . . . . . . . . . . . . . 0.81 to 0.83 mm
    Oil ring . . . . . . . . . . . . . . . . . . . . . . . . . . . . . . . . . . . . . . . . . . . . . . . . . . . . . . . . 1.51 to 1.53 mm
Ring-to-groove clearance
    Top ring (max) . . . . . . . . . . . . . . . . . . . . . . . . . . . . . . . . . . . . . . . . . . . . . . . . . 0.18 mm
    2nd ring (max) . . . . . . . . . . . . . . . . . . . . . . . . . . . . . . . . . . . . . . . . . . . . . . . . . 0.15 mm

**2**

# GSX-R600 models (continued)

## Connecting rods

Small-end internal diameter
  Standard . . . . . . . . . . . . . . . . . . . . . . . . . . . . . . . . . . . . . . . . . . . .  14.010 to 14.018 mm
  Service limit (max) . . . . . . . . . . . . . . . . . . . . . . . . . . . . . . . . . . . . .  14.040 mm
Big-end side clearance
  Standard . . . . . . . . . . . . . . . . . . . . . . . . . . . . . . . . . . . . . . . . . . . .  0.1 to 0.2 mm
  Service limit (max) . . . . . . . . . . . . . . . . . . . . . . . . . . . . . . . . . . . . .  0.3 mm
Big-end width . . . . . . . . . . . . . . . . . . . . . . . . . . . . . . . . . . . . . . . . . .  19.95 to 20.00 mm
Crankpin width . . . . . . . . . . . . . . . . . . . . . . . . . . . . . . . . . . . . . . . . .  20.10 to 20.15 mm
Big-end ID
  Code 1 . . . . . . . . . . . . . . . . . . . . . . . . . . . . . . . . . . . . . . . . . . . . . .  35.000 to 35.008 mm
  Code 2 . . . . . . . . . . . . . . . . . . . . . . . . . . . . . . . . . . . . . . . . . . . . . .  35.008 to 35.016 mm
Crankpin OD
  Code 1 . . . . . . . . . . . . . . . . . . . . . . . . . . . . . . . . . . . . . . . . . . . . . .  30.992 to 31.000 mm
  Code 2 . . . . . . . . . . . . . . . . . . . . . . . . . . . . . . . . . . . . . . . . . . . . . .  30.984 to 30.992 mm
  Code 3 . . . . . . . . . . . . . . . . . . . . . . . . . . . . . . . . . . . . . . . . . . . . . .  30.976 to 30.984 mm
Big-end oil clearance
  Standard . . . . . . . . . . . . . . . . . . . . . . . . . . . . . . . . . . . . . . . . . . . .  0.032 to 0.056 mm
  Service limit (max) . . . . . . . . . . . . . . . . . . . . . . . . . . . . . . . . . . . . .  0.08 mm

## Crankshaft and bearings

Main bearing journal OD
  Code A . . . . . . . . . . . . . . . . . . . . . . . . . . . . . . . . . . . . . . . . . . . . . .  31.992 to 32.000 mm
  Code B . . . . . . . . . . . . . . . . . . . . . . . . . . . . . . . . . . . . . . . . . . . . . .  31.984 to 31.992 mm
  Code C . . . . . . . . . . . . . . . . . . . . . . . . . . . . . . . . . . . . . . . . . . . . . .  31.976 to 31.984 mm
Crankcase seat ID
  Code A . . . . . . . . . . . . . . . . . . . . . . . . . . . . . . . . . . . . . . . . . . . . . .  35.000 to 35.008 mm
  Code B . . . . . . . . . . . . . . . . . . . . . . . . . . . . . . . . . . . . . . . . . . . . . .  35.008 to 35.016 mm
Main bearing oil clearance
  Standard . . . . . . . . . . . . . . . . . . . . . . . . . . . . . . . . . . . . . . . . . . . .  0.016 to 0.040 mm
  Service limit (max) . . . . . . . . . . . . . . . . . . . . . . . . . . . . . . . . . . . . .  0.080 mm
Runout (max) . . . . . . . . . . . . . . . . . . . . . . . . . . . . . . . . . . . . . . . . . .  0.05 mm
Thrust bearing clearance . . . . . . . . . . . . . . . . . . . . . . . . . . . . . . . . .  0.055 to 0.110 mm
Thrust bearing thickness
  Right-hand side . . . . . . . . . . . . . . . . . . . . . . . . . . . . . . . . . . . . . . .  2.425 to 2.450 mm
  Left-hand side . . . . . . . . . . . . . . . . . . . . . . . . . . . . . . . . . . . . . . . .  Selective fit

**Torque wrench settings – see end of Specifications on page 2•10**

# Specifications – GSX-R750 models

## General

Type . . . . . . . . . . . . . . . . . . . . . . . . . . . . . . . . . . . . . . . . . . . . . . . . .  Four-stroke in-line four
Capacity . . . . . . . . . . . . . . . . . . . . . . . . . . . . . . . . . . . . . . . . . . . . . .  749 cc
Bore . . . . . . . . . . . . . . . . . . . . . . . . . . . . . . . . . . . . . . . . . . . . . . . . .  72.0 mm
Stroke . . . . . . . . . . . . . . . . . . . . . . . . . . . . . . . . . . . . . . . . . . . . . . . .  46.0 mm
Compression ratio . . . . . . . . . . . . . . . . . . . . . . . . . . . . . . . . . . . . . . .  12.0 to 1
Clutch . . . . . . . . . . . . . . . . . . . . . . . . . . . . . . . . . . . . . . . . . . . . . . . .  Wet multi-plate
Transmission . . . . . . . . . . . . . . . . . . . . . . . . . . . . . . . . . . . . . . . . . . .  6-speed constant mesh
Final drive . . . . . . . . . . . . . . . . . . . . . . . . . . . . . . . . . . . . . . . . . . . . .  Chain

## Camshafts

Intake lobe height
  Standard . . . . . . . . . . . . . . . . . . . . . . . . . . . . . . . . . . . . . . . . . . . .  36.69 to 36.73 mm
  Service limit (min) . . . . . . . . . . . . . . . . . . . . . . . . . . . . . . . . . . . . . .  36.39 mm
Exhaust lobe height
  Standard . . . . . . . . . . . . . . . . . . . . . . . . . . . . . . . . . . . . . . . . . . . .  35.28 to 35.32 mm
  Service limit (min) . . . . . . . . . . . . . . . . . . . . . . . . . . . . . . . . . . . . . .  34.98 mm
Journal diameter . . . . . . . . . . . . . . . . . . . . . . . . . . . . . . . . . . . . . . . .  23.959 to 23.980 mm
Journal holder diameter . . . . . . . . . . . . . . . . . . . . . . . . . . . . . . . . . . .  24.012 to 24.025 mm
Journal oil clearance
  Standard . . . . . . . . . . . . . . . . . . . . . . . . . . . . . . . . . . . . . . . . . . . .  0.032 to 0.066 mm
  Service limit (max) . . . . . . . . . . . . . . . . . . . . . . . . . . . . . . . . . . . . .  0.15 mm
Runout (max) . . . . . . . . . . . . . . . . . . . . . . . . . . . . . . . . . . . . . . . . . .  0.10 mm

## Cylinder head

Warpage (max) . . . . . . . . . . . . . . . . . . . . . . . . . . . . . . . . . . . . . . . . . . . . . 0.20 mm

## Valves, guides and springs

Valve clearances . . . . . . . . . . . . . . . . . . . . . . . . . . . . . . . . . . . . . . . . . . see Chapter 1
Intake valve
  Head diameter . . . . . . . . . . . . . . . . . . . . . . . . . . . . . . . . . . . . . . . . . . 29.0 mm
  Stem diameter . . . . . . . . . . . . . . . . . . . . . . . . . . . . . . . . . . . . . . . . . . 3.975 to 3.990 mm
  Guide bore diameter . . . . . . . . . . . . . . . . . . . . . . . . . . . . . . . . . . . . . 4.000 to 4.012 mm
  Stem-to-guide clearance . . . . . . . . . . . . . . . . . . . . . . . . . . . . . . . . . . 0.010 to 0.037 mm
  Side clearance, wobble (max) – see text . . . . . . . . . . . . . . . . . . . . . 0.35 mm
  Margin thickness (min) . . . . . . . . . . . . . . . . . . . . . . . . . . . . . . . . . . . 0.5 mm
  Seat width . . . . . . . . . . . . . . . . . . . . . . . . . . . . . . . . . . . . . . . . . . . . . 0.9 to 1.1 mm
  Head runout (max) . . . . . . . . . . . . . . . . . . . . . . . . . . . . . . . . . . . . . . 0.03 mm
  Stem runout (max) . . . . . . . . . . . . . . . . . . . . . . . . . . . . . . . . . . . . . . 0.05 mm
Exhaust valve
  Head diameter . . . . . . . . . . . . . . . . . . . . . . . . . . . . . . . . . . . . . . . . . . 24.0 mm
  Stem diameter . . . . . . . . . . . . . . . . . . . . . . . . . . . . . . . . . . . . . . . . . . 3.955 to 3.970 mm
  Guide bore diameter . . . . . . . . . . . . . . . . . . . . . . . . . . . . . . . . . . . . . 4.000 to 4.012 mm
  Stem-to-guide clearance . . . . . . . . . . . . . . . . . . . . . . . . . . . . . . . . . . 0.030 to 0.057 mm
  Side clearance, wobble (max) – see text . . . . . . . . . . . . . . . . . . . . . 0.35 mm
  Margin thickness (min) . . . . . . . . . . . . . . . . . . . . . . . . . . . . . . . . . . . 0.5 mm
  Seat width . . . . . . . . . . . . . . . . . . . . . . . . . . . . . . . . . . . . . . . . . . . . . 0.9 to 1.1 mm
  Head runout (max) . . . . . . . . . . . . . . . . . . . . . . . . . . . . . . . . . . . . . . 0.03 mm
  Stem runout (max) . . . . . . . . . . . . . . . . . . . . . . . . . . . . . . . . . . . . . . 0.05 mm
Valve springs (intake and exhaust)
  Free length
    Standard . . . . . . . . . . . . . . . . . . . . . . . . . . . . . . . . . . . . . . . . . . . 39.3 mm
    Service limit (min) . . . . . . . . . . . . . . . . . . . . . . . . . . . . . . . . . . . . 37.8 mm
  Spring tension . . . . . . . . . . . . . . . . . . . . . . . . . . . . . . . . . . . . . . . . . . 32.85 mm with 19.0 kg load

## Transmission

Gear ratios (no. of teeth)
  Primary reduction . . . . . . . . . . . . . . . . . . . . . . . . . . . . . . . . . . . . . . . 1.857 to 1 (78/42T)
  Final reduction . . . . . . . . . . . . . . . . . . . . . . . . . . . . . . . . . . . . . . . . . 2.470 to 1 (42/17T)
  1st gear . . . . . . . . . . . . . . . . . . . . . . . . . . . . . . . . . . . . . . . . . . . . . . 2.785 to 1 (39/14T)
  2nd gear . . . . . . . . . . . . . . . . . . . . . . . . . . . . . . . . . . . . . . . . . . . . . 2.052 to 1 (39/19T)
  3rd gear . . . . . . . . . . . . . . . . . . . . . . . . . . . . . . . . . . . . . . . . . . . . . . 1.681 to 1 (37/22T)
  4th gear . . . . . . . . . . . . . . . . . . . . . . . . . . . . . . . . . . . . . . . . . . . . . . 1.450 to 1 (29/20T)
  5th gear . . . . . . . . . . . . . . . . . . . . . . . . . . . . . . . . . . . . . . . . . . . . . . 1.304 to 1 (30/23T)
  6th gear . . . . . . . . . . . . . . . . . . . . . . . . . . . . . . . . . . . . . . . . . . . . . . 1.181 to 1 (26/22T)

## Selector drum and forks

Selector fork-to-gear groove clearance
  Standard . . . . . . . . . . . . . . . . . . . . . . . . . . . . . . . . . . . . . . . . . . . . . . 0.1 to 0.3 mm
  Service limit (max) . . . . . . . . . . . . . . . . . . . . . . . . . . . . . . . . . . . . . . 0.5 mm
Selector fork end thickness . . . . . . . . . . . . . . . . . . . . . . . . . . . . . . . . . 4.8 to 4.9 mm
Selector fork groove width in gears . . . . . . . . . . . . . . . . . . . . . . . . . . . 5.0 to 5.1 mm

## Clutch

Friction plate
  Quantity . . . . . . . . . . . . . . . . . . . . . . . . . . . . . . . . . . . . . . . . . . . . . . 10
  Thickness
    Standard . . . . . . . . . . . . . . . . . . . . . . . . . . . . . . . . . . . . . . . . . . . 2.92 to 3.08 mm
    Service limit (min) . . . . . . . . . . . . . . . . . . . . . . . . . . . . . . . . . . . . 2.72 mm
  Tab width
    Standard . . . . . . . . . . . . . . . . . . . . . . . . . . . . . . . . . . . . . . . . . . . 13.7 to 13.8 mm
    Service limit (min) . . . . . . . . . . . . . . . . . . . . . . . . . . . . . . . . . . . . 12.9 mm
Plain plate
  Quantity . . . . . . . . . . . . . . . . . . . . . . . . . . . . . . . . . . . . . . . . . . . . . . 9
  Warpage (max) . . . . . . . . . . . . . . . . . . . . . . . . . . . . . . . . . . . . . . . . . 0.1 mm
Spring free length
  Standard . . . . . . . . . . . . . . . . . . . . . . . . . . . . . . . . . . . . . . . . . . . . . . 54.15 mm
  Service limit (min) . . . . . . . . . . . . . . . . . . . . . . . . . . . . . . . . . . . . . . 51.50 mm

## Lubrication system

Oil pressure . . . . . . . . . . . . . . . . . . . . . . . . . . . . . . . . . . . . . . . . . . . . . . see Chapter 1

**2**

# GSX-R750 models (continued)

## Cylinders

Bore standard dimension . . . . . . . . . . . . . . . . . . . . . . . . . . . . . . . . . . .   72.000 to 72.015 mm
Warpage of gasket face (max) . . . . . . . . . . . . . . . . . . . . . . . . . . . . . . .   0.20 mm
Cylinder compression . . . . . . . . . . . . . . . . . . . . . . . . . . . . . . . . . . . . . .   see Chapter 1

## Pistons

Piston diameter (measured 15.0 mm up from skirt, at 90° to piston pin axis)
   Standard . . . . . . . . . . . . . . . . . . . . . . . . . . . . . . . . . . . . . . . . . . . .   71.965 to 71.980 mm
   Service limit (min) . . . . . . . . . . . . . . . . . . . . . . . . . . . . . . . . . . . . .   71.880 mm
Piston-to-bore clearance
   Standard . . . . . . . . . . . . . . . . . . . . . . . . . . . . . . . . . . . . . . . . . . . .   0.030 to 0.040 mm
   Service limit (max) . . . . . . . . . . . . . . . . . . . . . . . . . . . . . . . . . . . .   0.120 mm
Piston pin diameter
   Standard . . . . . . . . . . . . . . . . . . . . . . . . . . . . . . . . . . . . . . . . . . . .   14.995 to 15.000 mm
   Service limit (min) . . . . . . . . . . . . . . . . . . . . . . . . . . . . . . . . . . . . .   14.980 mm
Piston pin bore diameter in piston
   Standard . . . . . . . . . . . . . . . . . . . . . . . . . . . . . . . . . . . . . . . . . . . .   15.002 to 15.008 mm
   Service limit (max) . . . . . . . . . . . . . . . . . . . . . . . . . . . . . . . . . . . .   15.030 mm

## Piston rings

Ring end gap (free)
   Top ring
      Standard . . . . . . . . . . . . . . . . . . . . . . . . . . . . . . . . . . . . . . . . .   7.0 mm (approx.)
      Service limit (min) . . . . . . . . . . . . . . . . . . . . . . . . . . . . . . . . . . .   5.6 mm
   2nd ring
      Standard . . . . . . . . . . . . . . . . . . . . . . . . . . . . . . . . . . . . . . . . .   7.8 mm (approx.)
      Service limit (min) . . . . . . . . . . . . . . . . . . . . . . . . . . . . . . . . . . .   6.2 mm
Ring end gap (installed)
   Top ring
      Standard . . . . . . . . . . . . . . . . . . . . . . . . . . . . . . . . . . . . . . . . .   0.06 to 0.18 mm
      Service limit (max) . . . . . . . . . . . . . . . . . . . . . . . . . . . . . . . . . .   0.50 mm
   2nd ring
      Standard . . . . . . . . . . . . . . . . . . . . . . . . . . . . . . . . . . . . . . . . .   0.06 to 0.18 mm
      Service limit (max) . . . . . . . . . . . . . . . . . . . . . . . . . . . . . . . . . .   0.50 mm
Ring thickness
   Top ring . . . . . . . . . . . . . . . . . . . . . . . . . . . . . . . . . . . . . . . . . . . .   0.97 to 0.99 mm
   2nd ring . . . . . . . . . . . . . . . . . . . . . . . . . . . . . . . . . . . . . . . . . . . .   0.77 to 0.79 mm
Ring groove width in piston
   Top ring . . . . . . . . . . . . . . . . . . . . . . . . . . . . . . . . . . . . . . . . . . . .   1.01 to 1.03 mm
   2nd ring . . . . . . . . . . . . . . . . . . . . . . . . . . . . . . . . . . . . . . . . . . . .   0.81 to 0.83 mm
   Oil ring . . . . . . . . . . . . . . . . . . . . . . . . . . . . . . . . . . . . . . . . . . . . .   1.51 to 1.53 mm
Ring-to-groove clearance
   Top ring (max) . . . . . . . . . . . . . . . . . . . . . . . . . . . . . . . . . . . . . . .   0.18 mm
   2nd ring (max) . . . . . . . . . . . . . . . . . . . . . . . . . . . . . . . . . . . . . . .   0.15 mm

## Connecting rods

Small-end internal diameter
   Standard . . . . . . . . . . . . . . . . . . . . . . . . . . . . . . . . . . . . . . . . . . . .   15.010 to 15.018 mm
   Service limit (max) . . . . . . . . . . . . . . . . . . . . . . . . . . . . . . . . . . . .   15.040 mm
Big-end side clearance
   Standard . . . . . . . . . . . . . . . . . . . . . . . . . . . . . . . . . . . . . . . . . . . .   0.1 to 0.2 mm
   Service limit (max) . . . . . . . . . . . . . . . . . . . . . . . . . . . . . . . . . . . .   0.3 mm
Big-end width . . . . . . . . . . . . . . . . . . . . . . . . . . . . . . . . . . . . . . . . . . .   19.95 to 20.00 mm
Crankpin width . . . . . . . . . . . . . . . . . . . . . . . . . . . . . . . . . . . . . . . . . . .   20.10 to 20.15 mm
Big-end ID
   Code 1 . . . . . . . . . . . . . . . . . . . . . . . . . . . . . . . . . . . . . . . . . . . . . .   36.000 to 36.008 mm
   Code 2 . . . . . . . . . . . . . . . . . . . . . . . . . . . . . . . . . . . . . . . . . . . . . .   36.008 to 36.016 mm
Crankpin OD
   Code 1 . . . . . . . . . . . . . . . . . . . . . . . . . . . . . . . . . . . . . . . . . . . . . .   32.992 to 33.000 mm
   Code 2 . . . . . . . . . . . . . . . . . . . . . . . . . . . . . . . . . . . . . . . . . . . . . .   32.984 to 32.992 mm
   Code 3 . . . . . . . . . . . . . . . . . . . . . . . . . . . . . . . . . . . . . . . . . . . . . .   32.976 to 32.984 mm
Big-end oil clearance
   Standard . . . . . . . . . . . . . . . . . . . . . . . . . . . . . . . . . . . . . . . . . . . .   0.032 to 0.056 mm
   Service limit (max) . . . . . . . . . . . . . . . . . . . . . . . . . . . . . . . . . . . .   0.08 mm

## Crankshaft and bearings

Main bearing journal OD
  Code A . . . . . . . . . . . . . . . . . . . . . . . . . . . . . . . . . . . . . . . . . . . . . . . 31.992 to 32.000 mm
  Code B . . . . . . . . . . . . . . . . . . . . . . . . . . . . . . . . . . . . . . . . . . . . . . . 31.984 to 31.992 mm
  Code C . . . . . . . . . . . . . . . . . . . . . . . . . . . . . . . . . . . . . . . . . . . . . . . 31.976 to 31.984 mm
Crankcase seat ID
  Code A . . . . . . . . . . . . . . . . . . . . . . . . . . . . . . . . . . . . . . . . . . . . . . . 35.000 to 35.008 mm
  Code B . . . . . . . . . . . . . . . . . . . . . . . . . . . . . . . . . . . . . . . . . . . . . . . 35.008 to 35.016 mm
Main bearing oil clearance
  Standard . . . . . . . . . . . . . . . . . . . . . . . . . . . . . . . . . . . . . . . . . . . . . . 0.016 to 0.040 mm
  Service limit (max) . . . . . . . . . . . . . . . . . . . . . . . . . . . . . . . . . . . . . . . . 0.080 mm
Runout (max) . . . . . . . . . . . . . . . . . . . . . . . . . . . . . . . . . . . . . . . . . . . . . . 0.05 mm
Thrust bearing clearance . . . . . . . . . . . . . . . . . . . . . . . . . . . . . . . . . . . 0.055 to 0.110 mm
Thrust bearing thickness
  Right-hand side . . . . . . . . . . . . . . . . . . . . . . . . . . . . . . . . . . . . . . . . . . 2.425 to 2.450 mm
  Left-hand side . . . . . . . . . . . . . . . . . . . . . . . . . . . . . . . . . . . . . . . . . . . Selective fit

**Torque wrench settings – see end of Specifications on page 2•10**

# Specifications – GSX-R1000 models

## General

Type . . . . . . . . . . . . . . . . . . . . . . . . . . . . . . . . . . . . . . . . . . . . . . . . . . . Four-stroke in-line four
Capacity . . . . . . . . . . . . . . . . . . . . . . . . . . . . . . . . . . . . . . . . . . . . . . . . . 988 cc
Bore . . . . . . . . . . . . . . . . . . . . . . . . . . . . . . . . . . . . . . . . . . . . . . . . . . . . 73.0 mm
Stroke . . . . . . . . . . . . . . . . . . . . . . . . . . . . . . . . . . . . . . . . . . . . . . . . . . 59.0 mm
Compression ratio . . . . . . . . . . . . . . . . . . . . . . . . . . . . . . . . . . . . . . . . . 12.0 to 1
Clutch . . . . . . . . . . . . . . . . . . . . . . . . . . . . . . . . . . . . . . . . . . . . . . . . . . Wet multi-plate
Transmission . . . . . . . . . . . . . . . . . . . . . . . . . . . . . . . . . . . . . . . . . . . . . 6-speed constant mesh
Final drive . . . . . . . . . . . . . . . . . . . . . . . . . . . . . . . . . . . . . . . . . . . . . . . Chain

## Camshafts

Intake lobe height
  Standard . . . . . . . . . . . . . . . . . . . . . . . . . . . . . . . . . . . . . . . . . . . . . . . 37.01 to 37.05 mm
  Service limit (min) . . . . . . . . . . . . . . . . . . . . . . . . . . . . . . . . . . . . . . . . . 36.71 mm
Exhaust lobe height
  Standard . . . . . . . . . . . . . . . . . . . . . . . . . . . . . . . . . . . . . . . . . . . . . . . 35.98 to 36.02 mm
  Service limit (min) . . . . . . . . . . . . . . . . . . . . . . . . . . . . . . . . . . . . . . . . . 35.68 mm
Journal diameter . . . . . . . . . . . . . . . . . . . . . . . . . . . . . . . . . . . . . . . . . . 23.959 to 23.980 mm
Journal holder diameter . . . . . . . . . . . . . . . . . . . . . . . . . . . . . . . . . . . . 24.012 to 24.025 mm
Journal oil clearance
  Standard . . . . . . . . . . . . . . . . . . . . . . . . . . . . . . . . . . . . . . . . . . . . . . . 0.032 to 0.066 mm
  Service limit (max) . . . . . . . . . . . . . . . . . . . . . . . . . . . . . . . . . . . . . . . . 0.15 mm
Runout (max) . . . . . . . . . . . . . . . . . . . . . . . . . . . . . . . . . . . . . . . . . . . . . 0.10 mm

## Cylinder head

Warpage (max) . . . . . . . . . . . . . . . . . . . . . . . . . . . . . . . . . . . . . . . . . . . 0.20 mm

## Valves, guides and springs

Valve clearances . . . . . . . . . . . . . . . . . . . . . . . . . . . . . . . . . . . . . . . . . . see Chapter 1
Intake valve
  Head diameter . . . . . . . . . . . . . . . . . . . . . . . . . . . . . . . . . . . . . . . . . . . 29.0 mm
  Stem diameter . . . . . . . . . . . . . . . . . . . . . . . . . . . . . . . . . . . . . . . . . . . 3.975 to 3.990 mm
  Guide bore diameter . . . . . . . . . . . . . . . . . . . . . . . . . . . . . . . . . . . . . . 4.000 to 4.012 mm
  Stem-to-guide clearance . . . . . . . . . . . . . . . . . . . . . . . . . . . . . . . . . . . 0.010 to 0.037 mm
  Side clearance, wobble (max) – see text . . . . . . . . . . . . . . . . . . . . . . . . 0.35 mm
  Margin thickness (min) . . . . . . . . . . . . . . . . . . . . . . . . . . . . . . . . . . . . 0.5 mm
  Seat width . . . . . . . . . . . . . . . . . . . . . . . . . . . . . . . . . . . . . . . . . . . . . 0.9 to 1.1 mm
  Head runout (max) . . . . . . . . . . . . . . . . . . . . . . . . . . . . . . . . . . . . . . . 0.03 mm
  Stem runout (max) . . . . . . . . . . . . . . . . . . . . . . . . . . . . . . . . . . . . . . . 0.05 mm
Exhaust valve
  Head diameter . . . . . . . . . . . . . . . . . . . . . . . . . . . . . . . . . . . . . . . . . . . 24.0 mm
  Stem diameter . . . . . . . . . . . . . . . . . . . . . . . . . . . . . . . . . . . . . . . . . . . 3.955 to 3.970 mm
  Guide bore diameter . . . . . . . . . . . . . . . . . . . . . . . . . . . . . . . . . . . . . . 4.000 to 4.012 mm
  Stem-to-guide clearance . . . . . . . . . . . . . . . . . . . . . . . . . . . . . . . . . . . 0.030 to 0.057 mm
  Side clearance, wobble (max) – see text . . . . . . . . . . . . . . . . . . . . . . . . 0.35 mm
  Margin thickness (min) . . . . . . . . . . . . . . . . . . . . . . . . . . . . . . . . . . . . 0.5 mm

2

# GSX-R1000 models (continued)

## Valves, guides and springs (continued)

Exhaust valve (continued)

Seat width . . . . . . . . . . . . . . . . . . . . . . . . . . . . . . . . . . . . . . . 0.9 to 1.1 mm

Head runout (max) . . . . . . . . . . . . . . . . . . . . . . . . . . . . . . . . 0.03 mm

Stem runout (max) . . . . . . . . . . . . . . . . . . . . . . . . . . . . . . . . 0.05 mm

Valve springs (intake and exhaust)

Free length limit (min) . . . . . . . . . . . . . . . . . . . . . . . . . . . . . 37.0 mm

Spring tension . . . . . . . . . . . . . . . . . . . . . . . . . . . . . . . . . . . . . 32.5 mm with 13.0 kg load

## Transmission

Gear ratios (no. of teeth)

Primary reduction . . . . . . . . . . . . . . . . . . . . . . . . . . . . . . . . . 1.553 to 1 (73/47T)

Final reduction . . . . . . . . . . . . . . . . . . . . . . . . . . . . . . . . . . . . 2.470 to 1 (42/17T)

1st gear . . . . . . . . . . . . . . . . . . . . . . . . . . . . . . . . . . . . . . . . . . . 2.687 to 1 (43/16T)

2nd gear . . . . . . . . . . . . . . . . . . . . . . . . . . . . . . . . . . . . . . . . . 2.052 to 1 (39/19T)

3rd gear . . . . . . . . . . . . . . . . . . . . . . . . . . . . . . . . . . . . . . . . . 1.681 to 1 (37/22T)

4th gear . . . . . . . . . . . . . . . . . . . . . . . . . . . . . . . . . . . . . . . . . 1.450 to 1 (29/20T)

5th gear . . . . . . . . . . . . . . . . . . . . . . . . . . . . . . . . . . . . . . . . . 1.304 to 1 (30/23T)

6th gear . . . . . . . . . . . . . . . . . . . . . . . . . . . . . . . . . . . . . . . . . 1.208 to 1 (29/24T)

## Selector drum and forks

Selector fork-to-gear groove clearance

Standard . . . . . . . . . . . . . . . . . . . . . . . . . . . . . . . . . . . . . . . . 0.1 to 0.3 mm

Service limit (max) . . . . . . . . . . . . . . . . . . . . . . . . . . . . . . . . 0.5 mm

Selector fork end thickness . . . . . . . . . . . . . . . . . . . . . . . . . 4.8 to 4.9 mm

Selector fork groove width in gears . . . . . . . . . . . . . . . . . . 5.0 to 5.1 mm

## Clutch

Friction plate

Quantity . . . . . . . . . . . . . . . . . . . . . . . . . . . . . . . . . . . . . . . . . 10

Thickness

Standard . . . . . . . . . . . . . . . . . . . . . . . . . . . . . . . . . . . . . . 2.72 to 2.88 mm

Service limit (min) . . . . . . . . . . . . . . . . . . . . . . . . . . . . . . 2.42 mm

Tab width

Standard . . . . . . . . . . . . . . . . . . . . . . . . . . . . . . . . . . . . . . 13.85 to 13.96 mm

Service limit (min) . . . . . . . . . . . . . . . . . . . . . . . . . . . . . . 13.05 mm

Plain plate

Quantity . . . . . . . . . . . . . . . . . . . . . . . . . . . . . . . . . . . . . . . . . 9

Warpage (max) . . . . . . . . . . . . . . . . . . . . . . . . . . . . . . . . . . . 0.1 mm

Spring free length

Standard . . . . . . . . . . . . . . . . . . . . . . . . . . . . . . . . . . . . . . . . 77.77 mm

Service limit (min) . . . . . . . . . . . . . . . . . . . . . . . . . . . . . . . . 73.90 mm

## Lubrication system

Oil pressure . . . . . . . . . . . . . . . . . . . . . . . . . . . . . . . . . . . . . . . see Chapter 1

## Cylinders

Bore standard dimension . . . . . . . . . . . . . . . . . . . . . . . . . . . 73.000 to 73.015 mm

Warpage of gasket face (max) . . . . . . . . . . . . . . . . . . . . . . . 0.20 mm

Cylinder compression . . . . . . . . . . . . . . . . . . . . . . . . . . . . . . see Chapter 1

## Pistons

Piston diameter (measured 15.0 mm up from skirt, at 90° to piston pin axis)

Standard . . . . . . . . . . . . . . . . . . . . . . . . . . . . . . . . . . . . . . . . 72.965 to 72.980 mm

Service limit (min) . . . . . . . . . . . . . . . . . . . . . . . . . . . . . . . . 72.880 mm

Piston-to-bore clearance

Standard . . . . . . . . . . . . . . . . . . . . . . . . . . . . . . . . . . . . . . . . 0.030 to 0.040 mm

Service limit (max) . . . . . . . . . . . . . . . . . . . . . . . . . . . . . . . . 0.120 mm

Piston pin diameter

Standard . . . . . . . . . . . . . . . . . . . . . . . . . . . . . . . . . . . . . . . . 15.995 to 16.000 mm

Service limit (min) . . . . . . . . . . . . . . . . . . . . . . . . . . . . . . . . 15.980 mm

Piston pin bore diameter in piston

Standard . . . . . . . . . . . . . . . . . . . . . . . . . . . . . . . . . . . . . . . . 16.002 to 16.008 mm

Service limit (max) . . . . . . . . . . . . . . . . . . . . . . . . . . . . . . . . 16.030 mm

## Piston rings

Ring end gap (free)
  Top ring
    Standard . . . . . . . . . . . . . . . . . . . . . . . . . . . . . . . . . . . . . . . . . . . . . . 7.2 mm (approx.)
    Service limit (min) . . . . . . . . . . . . . . . . . . . . . . . . . . . . . . . . . . . . 5.8 mm
  2nd ring
    Standard . . . . . . . . . . . . . . . . . . . . . . . . . . . . . . . . . . . . . . . . . . . . . . 10.2 mm (approx.)
    Service limit (min) . . . . . . . . . . . . . . . . . . . . . . . . . . . . . . . . . . . . 8.2 mm
Ring end gap (installed)
  Top ring
    Standard . . . . . . . . . . . . . . . . . . . . . . . . . . . . . . . . . . . . . . . . . . . . . . 0.06 to 0.18 mm
    Service limit (max) . . . . . . . . . . . . . . . . . . . . . . . . . . . . . . . . . . . 0.50 mm
  2nd ring
    Standard . . . . . . . . . . . . . . . . . . . . . . . . . . . . . . . . . . . . . . . . . . . . . . 0.06 to 0.18 mm
    Service limit (max) . . . . . . . . . . . . . . . . . . . . . . . . . . . . . . . . . . . 0.50 mm
Ring thickness
  Top ring . . . . . . . . . . . . . . . . . . . . . . . . . . . . . . . . . . . . . . . . . . . . . . . . . 0.97 to 0.99 mm
  2nd ring . . . . . . . . . . . . . . . . . . . . . . . . . . . . . . . . . . . . . . . . . . . . . . . . . 0.77 to 0.79 mm
Ring groove width in piston
  Top ring . . . . . . . . . . . . . . . . . . . . . . . . . . . . . . . . . . . . . . . . . . . . . . . . . 1.01 to 1.03 mm
  2nd ring . . . . . . . . . . . . . . . . . . . . . . . . . . . . . . . . . . . . . . . . . . . . . . . . . 0.81 to 0.83 mm
  Oil ring . . . . . . . . . . . . . . . . . . . . . . . . . . . . . . . . . . . . . . . . . . . . . . . . . . 1.51 to 1.53 mm
Ring-to-groove clearance
  Top ring (max) . . . . . . . . . . . . . . . . . . . . . . . . . . . . . . . . . . . . . . . . . 0.18 mm
  2nd ring (max) . . . . . . . . . . . . . . . . . . . . . . . . . . . . . . . . . . . . . . . . . 0.15 mm

## Connecting rods

Small-end internal diameter
  Standard . . . . . . . . . . . . . . . . . . . . . . . . . . . . . . . . . . . . . . . . . . . . . . 16.010 to 16.018 mm
  Service limit (max) . . . . . . . . . . . . . . . . . . . . . . . . . . . . . . . . . . . . 16.040 mm
Big-end side clearance
  Standard . . . . . . . . . . . . . . . . . . . . . . . . . . . . . . . . . . . . . . . . . . . . . . 0.1 to 0.2 mm
  Service limit (max) . . . . . . . . . . . . . . . . . . . . . . . . . . . . . . . . . . . . 0.3 mm
Big-end width . . . . . . . . . . . . . . . . . . . . . . . . . . . . . . . . . . . . . . . . . . . . . 19.95 to 20.00 mm
Crankpin width . . . . . . . . . . . . . . . . . . . . . . . . . . . . . . . . . . . . . . . . . . . . 20.10 to 20.15 mm
Big-end ID
  Code 1 . . . . . . . . . . . . . . . . . . . . . . . . . . . . . . . . . . . . . . . . . . . . . . . . . 38.000 to 38.008 mm
  Code 2 . . . . . . . . . . . . . . . . . . . . . . . . . . . . . . . . . . . . . . . . . . . . . . . . . 38.008 to 38.016 mm
Crankpin OD
  Code 1 . . . . . . . . . . . . . . . . . . . . . . . . . . . . . . . . . . . . . . . . . . . . . . . . . 34.992 to 35.000 mm
  Code 2 . . . . . . . . . . . . . . . . . . . . . . . . . . . . . . . . . . . . . . . . . . . . . . . . . 34.984 to 34.992 mm
  Code 3 . . . . . . . . . . . . . . . . . . . . . . . . . . . . . . . . . . . . . . . . . . . . . . . . . 34.976 to 34.984 mm
Big-end oil clearance
  Standard . . . . . . . . . . . . . . . . . . . . . . . . . . . . . . . . . . . . . . . . . . . . . . 0.032 to 0.056 mm
  Service limit (max) . . . . . . . . . . . . . . . . . . . . . . . . . . . . . . . . . . . . 0.08 mm

## Crankshaft and bearings

Main bearing journal OD
  Code A . . . . . . . . . . . . . . . . . . . . . . . . . . . . . . . . . . . . . . . . . . . . . . . . 34.992 to 35.000 mm
  Code B . . . . . . . . . . . . . . . . . . . . . . . . . . . . . . . . . . . . . . . . . . . . . . . . 34.984 to 34.992 mm
  Code C . . . . . . . . . . . . . . . . . . . . . . . . . . . . . . . . . . . . . . . . . . . . . . . . 34.976 to 34.984 mm
Crankcase seat ID
  Code A . . . . . . . . . . . . . . . . . . . . . . . . . . . . . . . . . . . . . . . . . . . . . . . . 38.000 to 38.008 mm
  Code B . . . . . . . . . . . . . . . . . . . . . . . . . . . . . . . . . . . . . . . . . . . . . . . . 38.008 to 38.016 mm
Main bearing oil clearance
  Standard . . . . . . . . . . . . . . . . . . . . . . . . . . . . . . . . . . . . . . . . . . . . . . 0.016 to 0.040 mm
  Service limit (max) . . . . . . . . . . . . . . . . . . . . . . . . . . . . . . . . . . . . 0.080 mm
Runout (max) . . . . . . . . . . . . . . . . . . . . . . . . . . . . . . . . . . . . . . . . . . . . . 0.05 mm
Thrust bearing clearance . . . . . . . . . . . . . . . . . . . . . . . . . . . . . . . . . 0.070 to 0.110 mm
Thrust bearing thickness
  Right-hand side . . . . . . . . . . . . . . . . . . . . . . . . . . . . . . . . . . . . . . . . 2.420 to 2.440 mm
  Left-hand side . . . . . . . . . . . . . . . . . . . . . . . . . . . . . . . . . . . . . . . . . Selective fit

## Balancer shaft and bearings

Balancer shaft oil clearance
  Standard . . . . . . . . . . . . . . . . . . . . . . . . . . . . . . . . . . . . . . . . . . . . . . 0.020 to 0.044 mm
  Service limit (max) . . . . . . . . . . . . . . . . . . . . . . . . . . . . . . . . . . . . 0.080 mm

**2**

# GSX-R1000 models (continued)

## Balancer shaft and bearings (continued)
Shaft bearing journal OD
 Code A .................................................. 22.992 to 23.000 mm
 Code B .................................................. 22.984 to 22.992 mm
Crankcase seat ID
 Code A .................................................. 26.000 to 26.008 mm
 Code B .................................................. 26.008 to 26.016 mm

# Torque wrench settings – all models

| | |
|---|---|
| Cam chain guide bolt ........................................ | 10 Nm |
| Cam chain stopper bolt ...................................... | 14 Nm |
| Cam chain tensioner blade bolt ............................ | 10 Nm |
| Cam chain tensioner cap bolt | |
|   GSX-R600K1, GSX-R750Y and K1, GSX-R1000K1 .............. | 23 Nm |
|   GSX-R600K2, GSX-R750K2, GSX-R1000K2 ................... | 35 Nm |
| Cam chain tensioner mounting bolts ........................ | 10 Nm |
| Camshaft holder bolts ...................................... | 10 Nm |
| Clutch centre nut .......................................... | 150 Nm |
| Clutch spring bolts ........................................ | 10 Nm |
| Connecting rod cap bolts | |
|   Initial setting | |
|     GSX-R600 and GSX-R750 .............................. | 15 Nm |
|     GSX-R1000 ......................................... | 21 Nm |
|   Final setting ............................................ | + 90° |
| Crankcase bolts – lower-to-middle crankcase | |
|   Lower crankcase 8 mm bolts | |
|     Initial setting .................................... | 15 Nm |
|     Final setting ...................................... | 26 Nm |
|   Lower crankcase 6 mm bolts | |
|     Initial setting .................................... | 6 Nm |
|     Final setting ...................................... | 11 Nm |
| Crankcase bolts – middle-to-upper crankcase | |
|   Middle-to-upper crankcase 9 mm bolts (crankshaft journal bolts) | |
|     Initial setting .................................... | 18 Nm |
|     Final setting | |
|       GSX-R600 and GSX-R1000 .......................... | + 50° |
|       GSX-R750 ........................................ | 32 Nm |
|   Middle-to-upper crankcase bolts (8 mm) – GSX-R1000 | |
|     Initial setting .................................... | 15 Nm |
|     Final setting ...................................... | 26 Nm |
|   Middle-to-upper crankcase bolts (6 mm) | |
|     Initial setting .................................... | 6 Nm |
|     Final setting ...................................... | 11 Nm |
| Crankcase breather cover bolts ............................ | 10 Nm |
| Crankcase oil hose union bolt ............................. | 12 Nm |
| Crankcase water jacket plug ............................... | 9.5 Nm |
| Cylinder head 6 mm bolts .................................. | 10 Nm |
| Cylinder head 10 mm bolts | |
|   Initial setting .......................................... | 25 Nm |
|   Final setting | |
|     GSX-R600 and GSX-R750 .............................. | 46 Nm |
|     GSX-R1000 ......................................... | 51 Nm |
| Engine mountings | |
|   Upper rear adjuster bolt | |
|     GSX-R750Y ......................................... | 10 Nm |
|     GSX-R600, GSX-R750K1, K2 and GSX-R1000 .............. | 23 Nm |
|   Lower rear adjuster bolt | |
|     GSX-R750Y ......................................... | 10 Nm |
|     GSX-R600, GSX-R750K1, K2 and GSX-R1000 .............. | 23 Nm |
|   Rear adjuster bolt locknuts ............................. | 45 Nm |
|   Rear mounting bolt nuts ................................. | 75 Nm |
|   Front mounting bolts .................................... | 55 Nm |
|   Front mounting lug pinch bolt(s) ........................ | 23 Nm |

| | |
|---|---|
| Gearchange selector drum bearing retainer bolt ................. | 10 Nm |
| Gearchange selector drum centre bolt ......................... | 10 Nm |
| Gearchange stopper arm bolt ................................. | 10 Nm |
| Oil cooler bolts (GSX-R600 and GSX-R750) ..................... | 10 Nm |
| Oil cooler pipe union bolts (GSX-R1000) ...................... | 10 Nm |
| Oil gallery plug | |
|    Cylinder head – GSX-R1000 ............................ | 11 Nm |
|    Upper crankcase – GSX-R1000 ......................... | 11 Nm |
|    Lower crankcase – all models ......................... | 35 Nm |
| Oil pressure switch ........................................ | 14 Nm |
| Oil pump mounting bolts .................................... | 10 Nm |
| Oil strainer bolts ......................................... | 10 Nm |
| Oil sump bolts ............................................ | 10 Nm |
| Piston oil jet bolts ........................................ | 10 Nm |
| Selector fork shaft retainer bolt ............................. | 19 Nm |
| Starter clutch bolt ........................................ | 55 Nm |
| Timing inspection cap ...................................... | 11 Nm |
| Valve cover bolts .......................................... | 14 Nm |

## 1  General information

The engine/transmission unit is a water-cooled, four cylinder in-line design fitted transversely across the frame. The valves are operated by double overhead camshafts which are chain driven off the crankshaft. The engine/transmission unit is constructed from aluminium alloy with the crankcase divided horizontally into three sections. On GSX-R1000 models a balancer shaft is gear driven off the crankshaft.

The crankcase incorporates a wet sump, pressure-fed lubrication system which uses a gear-driven, dual-rotor oil pump. On GSX-R600 and GSX-R750 models a crankcase mounted oil cooler works in conjunction with the engine cooling system; on GSX-R1000 models the oil cooler is of the radiator type.

Power from the crankshaft is transferred via a wet, multi-plate type clutch to a six-speed, constant-mesh transmission unit. Final drive to the rear wheel is by chain and sprockets.

## 2  Operations possible with the engine in the frame

The components and assemblies listed below can be removed without having to remove the engine/transmission assembly from the frame. If however, a number of areas require attention at the same time, removal of the engine is recommended.

*Valve cover*
*Cam chain tensioner*
*Camshafts*
*Starter motor*
*Starter clutch and idle gear*
*Ignition rotor and crankshaft position sensor*
*Clutch*
*Gearchange mechanism (external components)*
*Alternator*
*Oil sump, oil strainer and pressure relief valve*
*Oil cooler*
*Oil pump*

## 3  Operations requiring engine removal

It is necessary to remove the engine/transmission assembly from the frame to gain access to the following components.

*Cylinder head*
*Cam chain, tensioner blade and guides*
*Pistons/connecting rod assemblies*
*Crankshaft and bearings*
*Transmission shafts*
*Selector drum and forks*

## 4  Major engine repair – general note

1  It is not always easy to determine when or if an engine should be completely overhauled, as a number of factors must be considered.

2  High mileage is not necessarily an indication that an overhaul is needed, while low mileage, on the other hand, does not preclude the need for an overhaul. Frequency of servicing is probably the single most important consideration. An engine that has regular and frequent oil and filter changes, as well as other required maintenance, will most likely give many miles of reliable service. Conversely, a neglected engine, or one which has not been run in properly, may require an overhaul very early in its life.

3  Exhaust smoke and excessive oil consumption are both indications that piston rings and/or valve guides are in need of attention, although make sure that the fault is not due to oil leakage.

4  If the engine is making obvious knocking or rumbling noises, the connecting rod and/or main bearings are probably at fault.

5  Loss of power, rough running, excessive valve train noise and high fuel consumption rates may also point to the need for an overhaul, especially if they are all present at the same time. If a complete tune-up does not remedy the situation, major mechanical work is the only solution.

6  An engine overhaul generally involves restoring the internal parts to the specifications of a new engine. The piston rings and main and connecting rod bearings are usually renewed during a major overhaul. The valve seats are re-ground and, if necessary, re-cut by a specialist engineer, since they are usually in less than perfect condition at this point. The end result should be a like new engine that will give as many trouble-free miles as the original.

7  Before beginning the engine overhaul, read through the related procedures to familiarise yourself with the scope and requirements of the job. Overhauling an engine is not all that difficult, but it is time consuming. Plan on the motorcycle being tied up for a minimum of two weeks. Check on the availability of parts and make sure that any necessary special tools, equipment and supplies are obtained in advance.

8  Most work can be done with typical workshop hand tools, although a number of precision measuring tools are required for inspecting parts to determine if they must be renewed. Often a dealer will handle the inspection of parts and offer advice concerning reconditioning and renewal. As a general rule, time is the primary cost of an overhaul so it does not pay to install worn or substandard parts.

9  As a final note, to ensure maximum life and minimum trouble from a rebuilt engine, everything must be assembled with care in a spotlessly clean environment.

**2**

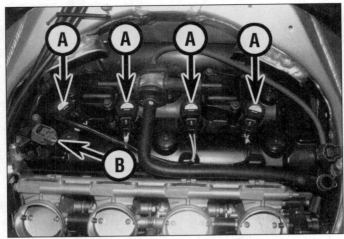

5.8 Disconnect the coil/plug caps (A) and camshaft position sensor (B) wiring connectors

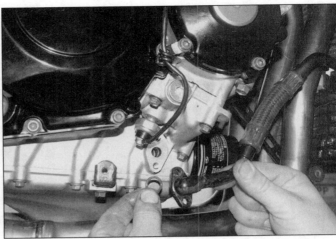

5.9a Disconnect the oil cooler pipes on GSX-R1000 models . . .

## 5 Engine – removal and installation

> ⚠ **Warning: The engine is very heavy. Removal and installation should be carried out with the aid of at least one assistant; personal injury or damage could occur if the engine falls or is dropped. If available, an hydraulic or mechanical floor jack should be used to support and lower or raise the engine.**

**Note:** *A peg spanner is required to loosen and*

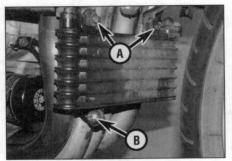

5.9b . . . then undo the upper (A) and lower (B) mounting bolts

5.12b . . . and remove the brackets

*tighten the locknuts on the engine rear mounting bolt adjusters and, on GSX-R600 and GSX-R750 models, the adjusters themselves. If the Suzuki service tool (Pt .No. 09940-14990) is not available, a suitable peg spanner will have to be obtained or fabricated (see* **Tool Tip***).*

### Removal

**1** Support the bike in an upright position using an auxiliary stand. Work can be made easier by raising the machine to a suitable working height on an hydraulic ramp or a suitable platform. Make sure the motorcycle is secure and will not topple over (see *Tools and Workshop Tips* in the Reference section).

5.12a Undo the bolts . . .

5.14a Unclip the wiring loom guide . . .

**2** If the engine is dirty, particularly around its mountings, wash it thoroughly before starting any major dismantling work. This will make work much easier and rule out the possibility of dirt falling into some vital component.
**3** Remove the seats and the fairing side panels (see Chapter 8).
**4** Disconnect the negative (-ve) lead from the battery (see Chapter 9).
**5** Drain the engine oil and the coolant (see Chapter 1).
**6** Remove the fuel tank and the air filter housing (see Chapter 4).
**7** Remove the throttle bodies (see Chapter 4). Plug the engine intake manifolds with clean rag to prevent debris falling into the engine.
**8** Disconnect the ignition coil/plug cap wiring connectors and remove the coil caps (see Chapter 5). Disconnect the camshaft position sensor wiring connector **(see illustration)**. Secure the wiring clear of the engine.
**9** On GSX-R1000 models, undo the bolts securing the oil cooler pipes to each side of the crankcase and disconnect the pipes **(see illustration)**. Discard the O-rings as new ones must be fitted on reassembly. Undo the bolt securing the oil cooler to its lower mounting bracket, then support the cooler and undo the bolts securing it to the radiator **(see illustration)**. **Note:** *Be prepared to catch any residual oil left in the cooler.*
**10** Remove the radiator and the coolant reservoir (see Chapter 3).
**11** Remove the exhaust system (see Chapter 4).
**12** Undo the bolts securing the radiator lower bracket and the oil cooler lower bracket (GSX-R1000) to the crankcase and remove the brackets, noting how they fit **(see illustrations)**.
**13** If required, remove the oil filter (see Chapter 1).
**14** Remove the fairing front inner panel (see Chapter 8). Unclip the wiring loom guide from the engine front cover, then undo the screws securing the cover and remove it **(see illustrations)**.

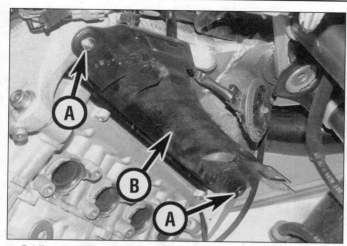

5.14b ... then undo the screws (A) and remove the cover (B)

5.15 Disconnect the wire from the oil pressure switch

**15** Undo the nut on the oil pressure switch and disconnect the wire **(see illustration)**. Release the wire from the clips on the crankcase cover bolts and secure it clear of the engine.

**16** Pull back the boot on the starter motor terminal, then undo the terminal nut (GSX-R600 and 750 models) or terminal bolt (GSX-R1000) and disconnect the lead **(see illustration)**. Unscrew the crankcase bolt that secures the earth (ground) lead and disconnect the lead **(see illustration)**. Temporarily install the bolt.

**17** Trace the wiring from the crankshaft position sensor below the starter motor and the gear position sensor on the lower left-hand side of the crankcase and disconnect it at the connectors. On GSX-R750 models, trace the wiring from the sidestand switch and disconnect it at the connector. Disconnect the coolant temperature sensor wiring connector **(see illustration)**.

**18** Trace the alternator wiring back from the top of the alternator cover on the left-hand side of the engine and disconnect it at the connector.

**19** Release the wiring from any clips or ties, noting its routing, and secure it clear of the engine.

**20** Remove the front sprocket cover and the sprocket (see Chapter 6). Remove the clutch pushrod for safekeeping **(see illustration)**.

**21** At this point, position an hydraulic or mechanical jack under the engine with a block of wood between the jack head and sump. Make sure the jack is centrally positioned so the engine will not topple in any direction when the last mounting bolt is removed. Take the weight of the engine on the jack **(see illustration)**.

**22** Undo the engine front left-hand mounting bolts and remove them **(see illustration)**.

**23** Loosen the engine front right-hand mounting pinch bolt(s). **Note:** *On GSX-R1000 models there are two front right-hand*

5.16a Displace the boot (A) and disconnect the terminal lead (B)

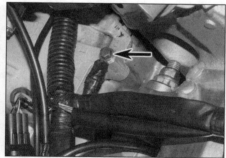

5.16b Disconnect the crankcase earth (ground) terminal

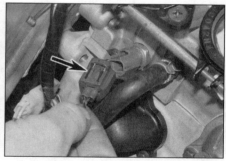

5.17 Disconnect the coolant temperature sensor wiring connector

**2**

5.20 Remove the clutch pushrod

5.21 Support the weight of the engine on a jack

5.22 Undo the front left-hand mounting bolts

5.23a Loosen the pinch bolt(s) . . .

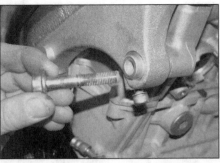

5.23b . . . then undo the front right-hand mounting bolt(s)

5.24 Leave the lower rear engine mounting bolt temporarily in place

5.25a Undo the locknut on the lower bolt adjuster

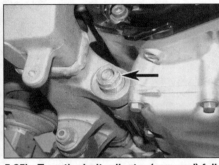

5.25b Turn the bolt adjuster (arrowed) fully anti-clockwise

*For the locknut, a peg spanner can be made by cutting an old 22 mm socket as shown – measure the width and depth of the slots in the locknut to determine the size of the castellations on the socket. If an old socket is not available, castellations can be welded onto a suitable nut. If required, a similar tool can be made for the adjuster bolt. It is important to use a tool to which a torque wrench can be applied on installation, rather than using a drift to knock the nut and bolt loose.*

*mounting bolts.* Undo and remove the front right-hand mounting bolt(s) **(see illustrations)**. **Note:** *The front left-hand and right-hand bolts are different lengths – do not mix them up.*
24 Undo the nut on the engine lower rear

mounting bolt but do not remove the bolt **(see illustration)**. **Note:** *The rear mounting bolt nuts are self-locking, and Suzuki advise that they should only be used once. Obtain new nuts before installing the engine.*

25 Using either the Suzuki service tool *(Pt. No. 09940-14990)* or a suitable peg spanner (see **Tool Tip**), undo the locknut on the lower adjuster bolt fitted in the right-hand side of the frame **(see illustration)**. Now use the service tool or a suitable socket as applicable and turn the adjuster bolt anti-clockwise to loosen it fully **(see illustration)**.
26 Undo the nut on the upper rear engine mounting bolt but do not remove the bolt. Follow Step 25 and undo the locknut on the upper adjuster bolt, then turn the adjuster bolt anti-clockwise to loosen it fully **(see illustration)**.
27 Make sure the engine is properly supported on the jack and have an assistant support it as well. Withdraw the upper and lower rear mounting bolts **(see illustration)**.
28 Check that all wiring, cables and hoses are disconnected and clear of the engine. Carefully lower the engine, remembering to lift the drive chain off the gearbox output shaft, then manoeuvre the engine out of the frame **(see illustration)**.

5.26 Use the peg spanner to undo the bolt adjuster locknut

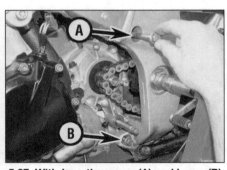

5.27 Withdraw the upper (A) and lower (B) rear mounting bolts

5.28 Lift the chain off the output shaft as the engine is removed

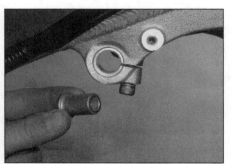

5.29a If required, remove the front right-hand mounting bolt spacer(s) . . .

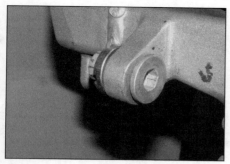

5.29b . . . and the rear mounting adjuster bolts

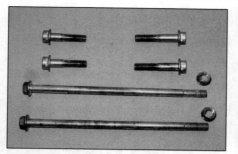

5.30a Engine mounting bolts (there are two front right-hand bolts on GSX-R1000 models) . . .

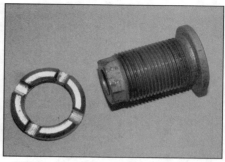

5.30b . . . and rear engine adjuster bolt and locknut

**29** If required, remove the spacer(s) for the front right-hand mounting bolt(s), noting how they fit **(see illustration)**. If required, thread the adjuster bolts for the rear mountings out of the frame **(see illustration)**.

### Installation

**30** Clean the threads of the engine mounting bolts and, if removed, the rear mounting adjuster bolts **(see illustrations)**.

**31** If removed, thread the adjuster bolts for the rear engine mountings all the way into the frame from the inside **(see illustration 5.29b)**. If removed, install the spacer(s) for the front right-hand mounting bolt(s); make sure the shouldered end faces the inside **(see illustration 5.29a)**.

**32** With the aid of an assistant place the engine unit on top of the jack and block of wood and carefully raise it into position in the frame, remembering to lift the drive chain over the gearbox output shaft. Ensure no wires, cables or hoses become trapped between the engine and the frame.

**33** Align the bolt holes and slide the rear mounting bolts through from the left-hand side.

**34** Install the front mounting bolts and tighten them finger-tight. **Note:** *The right-hand bolt(s) are longer than the left-hand bolts.*

**35** Turn the adjuster bolts clockwise and tighten them to the torque setting specified at the beginning of this Chapter, using the same tool as on removal.

**36** Fit the adjuster locknuts and tighten them to the specified torque setting.

**37** Fit the new self-locking nuts onto the rear mounting bolts and tighten them finger-tight.

**38** Ensure that the front mounting bolts are still finger-tight, then tighten the nuts on the rear mounting bolts, then the left-hand front bolts, and the right-hand front bolt(s), to the torque settings specified at the beginning of this Chapter. Finally tighten the pinch bolts on the mounting lugs for the right-hand front mounting bolt(s) to the specified torque setting.

**39** The remainder of the installation procedure is the reverse of removal, noting the following points.

● Make sure all wires, cables and hoses are correctly routed and connected, and secured by the relevant clips or ties.

● Tighten all bolts to the specified torque settings.

● On GSX-R1000 models, apply a suitable non-permanent thread locking compound to the oil cooler pipe bolt threads.

● Adjust the throttle and clutch cable freeplay (see Chapter 1).

● Adjust the drive chain (see Chapter 1).

● Refill the engine with oil and coolant (see Chapter 1 and *Daily (pre-ride) checks*).

● Prior to installing the fairing side panels start the engine and check that there is no coolant or oil leakage.

---

### 6  Engine disassembly and reassembly – general information

#### Disassembly

**1** Before disassembling the engine, the external surfaces of the unit should be thoroughly cleaned and degreased. This will prevent contamination of the engine internals, and will also make working a lot easier and cleaner. A high flash-point solvent, such as paraffin (kerosene) can be used, or better still, a proprietary engine degreaser such as Gunk. Use a paraffin brush or old paintbrush to work the solvent into the recesses of the engine casings. Take care to exclude solvent or water from the electrical components and intake and exhaust ports.

 **Warning: The use of petrol (gasoline) as a cleaning agent should be avoided because of the risk of fire.**

**2** When clean and dry, arrange the unit on the workbench, leaving a suitable clear area for working. Gather a selection of small containers and plastic bags so that parts can be grouped together in an easily identifiable manner. Some paper and a pen should be on hand to permit notes to be made and labels attached where necessary. A supply of clean rag is also required.

**3** Before commencing work, read through the appropriate section so that some idea of the necessary procedure can be gained. When removing components it should be noted that great force is seldom required. In many cases, a

component's reluctance to be removed is indicative of an incorrect approach or removal method – if in any doubt, re-check with the text. In cases where fasteners have corroded, apply penetrating oil or WD40 before disassembly.

**4** When disassembling the engine, keep 'mated' parts together (e.g. valve assemblies, pistons and connecting rods, clutch plates etc. that have been in contact with each other during engine operation). These 'mated' parts must be reused or renewed as assemblies.

**5** Engine/transmission disassembly should be done in the following general order with reference to the appropriate Sections.

> *Remove the valve cover*
> *Remove the cam chain tensioner and cam chain guide blades*
> *Remove the camshafts*
> *Remove the cylinder head*
> *Remove the starter clutch*
> *Remove the crankshaft position sensor (see Chapter 5)*
> *Remove the clutch*
> *Remove the oil pump*
> *Remove the gearchange mechanism*
> *Remove the starter motor and alternator (see Chapter 9)*
> *Remove the oil sump*
> *Separate the lower crankcase from the middle crankcase*
> *Remove the transmission shafts/gears*
> *Remove the selector drum and forks*
> *Separate the middle and upper crankcases*
> *Remove the crankshaft and connecting rod assemblies*

#### Reassembly

**6** Reassembly is accomplished by reversing the general disassembly sequence.

---

### 7  Valve cover – removal and installation

**Note:** *This procedure can be carried out with the engine in the frame. If the engine has been removed, ignore the steps which do not apply.*

#### Removal

**1** Remove the fairing side panels (see Chapter 8).

2

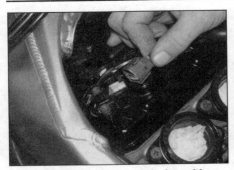

7.4 Disconnect the camshaft position sensor connector

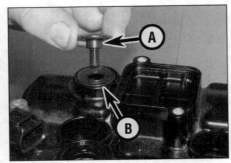

7.5 Remove the cover bolts (A) and washers (B)

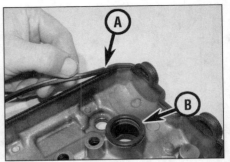

7.6 Discard the gasket (A) and O-rings (B)

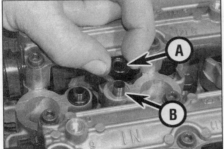

7.7 Remove the O-rings (A) from the dowels (B)

7.9 Apply sealant to the corners of the end caps

**2** Remove the fuel tank and air filter housing (see Chapter 4).

**3** Disconnect the vacuum hose from the small union on the front of the PAIR valve; if required, remove the PAIR valve assembly (see Chapter 1, Section 18).

**4** Disconnect the ignition coil/plug cap wiring connectors and remove the coil caps (see Chapter 5). Disconnect the camshaft position sensor wiring connector **(see illustration)**.

**5** Unscrew the valve cover bolts and remove them along with their sealing washers **(see illustration)**. Discard the washers as new ones must be fitted on reassembly.

**6** Lift the valve cover off the cylinder head. If it is stuck, do not try to lever it off with a screwdriver. Tap around the joint with a soft-faced mallet to dislodge it. Discard the cover gasket and O-rings as a new ones must be fitted on reassembly **(see illustration)**.

**7** Remove the dowels from the cylinder

head or cover if they are loose and discard the O-rings **(see illustration)**.

### Installation

**8** Clean the mating surfaces of the cylinder head and cover with a suitable solvent to remove all traces of old sealant and gasket.

**9** If removed, fit the dowels into the cylinder head and fit new O-rings over the dowels. Lay the new gasket and O-rings onto the valve cover, making sure they fit correctly into the grooves. Apply a suitable, non-permanent sealant to the corners of the camshaft end caps **(see illustration)**.

**10** Position the cover on the cylinder head, making sure the gasket and O-rings stay in place and the cover locates correctly onto the dowels. Install the cover bolts with new sealing washers and tighten the bolts to torque setting specified at the beginning of this Chapter.

**11** Install the remaining components in the reverse order of removal.

### 8 Cam chain tensioner – removal, inspection and installation

**Note:** *This procedure can be carried out with the engine in the frame. If the engine has been removed, ignore the steps which do not apply.*

### Removal

**1** Remove the right-hand fairing side panel (see Chapter 8).

**2** Remove the fuel tank, air filter housing and, if required for access, displace the throttle bodies (see Chapter 4).

**3** Unscrew the timing inspection cap from the starter clutch cover on the right-hand side of the engine (see Chapter 1, Section 25). Discard the O-ring as a new one must be fitted on reassembly. Remove the valve cover (see Section 7). Using a socket on the starter clutch bolt, turn the engine in a clockwise direction until the scribe line on the starter clutch aligns with the notch in the inspection hole and the number 1 arrow on the exhaust camshaft sprocket points forwards and is level with the top surface on the cylinder head **(see illustrations 9.3a and 9.3b)**.

**4** Place a rag under the cam chain tensioner to catch any residual oil, then unscrew the tensioner cap bolt. Withdraw the bolt from the tensioner, and discard the sealing washers from each side of the oil hose banjo union **(see illustration)**.

**5** Undo the tensioner mounting bolts and withdraw the tensioner body from the back of the cylinder head **(see illustration)**. Discard the gasket as a new one must be fitted on reassembly. Withdraw the spring and ball from inside the tensioner body.

*Caution: Do not rotate the engine with the cam chain tensioner removed.*

### Inspection

**6** Examine the tensioner components for signs of wear or damage. Install the ball and spring and check that the tensioner push rod extends under spring pressure and that the teeth on the top edge of the push rod are not

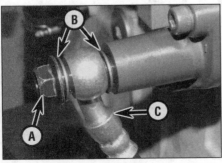

8.4 Cap bolt (A), sealing washers (B) and banjo union (C)

8.5 Withdraw the tensioner body and discard the gasket (arrowed)

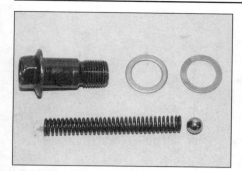

8.6a Check the condition of the ball and spring

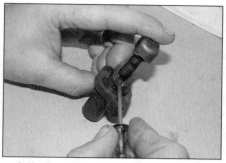

8.6b Depress the catch to retract the tensioner pushrod

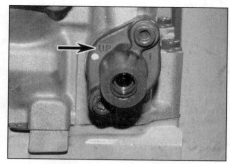

8.8 Note the UP mark on the tensioner body

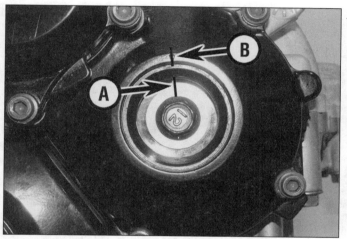

9.3a Align the scribe line (A) with the notch (B) . . .

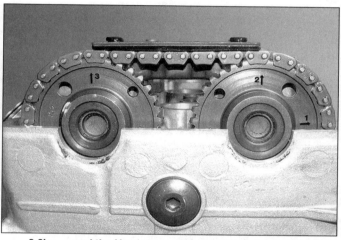

9.3b . . . and the No. 1 arrow with the top surface of the cylinder head

worn or damaged. Depress the catch and retract the push rod into the tensioner body **(see illustrations)**.

**7** If any components are worn or damaged replace them with new ones.

### Installation

**8** Ensure the push rod is fully retracted into the tensioner body and install the ball. Fit a new gasket onto the body and install it on the cylinder head with the UP mark facing up **(see illustration)**. Tighten the mounting bolts to the torque setting specified at the beginning of this Chapter.

**9** Install the spring. Fit the oil hose banjo union onto the cap bolt with new sealing washers on both sides of the union, and install the cap bolt finger-tight. **Note:** GSX-R600K1, GSX-R750Y, K1 and GSX-R1000K1 models use aluminium sealing washers; all later models use steel/rubber composite washers. Where aluminium sealing washers are fitted, lubricate the washers and the threads of the cap bolt with clean engine oil before reassembly. Note that a clicking noise will be heard as the cap bolt is installed.

**10** Align the neck of the banjo union with the centreline of the lower tensioner body mounting bolt, then tighten the cap bolt to the specified torque setting.

**11** Check that the sprocket markings are still correctly aligned as described in Step 3, and that the cam chain is tensioned. Rotate the engine a couple of times and recheck that the sprocket markings and starter clutch/notch markings are in alignment.

**12** Fit the timing inspection cap into the starter clutch cover using a new O-ring, and smear it and the threads with clean engine oil. Install the remaining components in the reverse order of removal.

### 9 Camshafts and followers – removal, inspection and installation

**Note:** This procedure can be carried out with the engine in the frame. If the engine has been removed, ignore the steps which do not apply.

### Removal

**1** Remove the valve cover (see Section 7). If required for access, remove the throttle bodies (see Chapter 4).

**2** Unscrew the timing inspection cap from the starter clutch cover on the right-hand side of the engine (see Chapter 1, Section 25). Discard the cap O-ring as a new one must be fitted on reassembly.

**3** Using a socket on the starter clutch bolt, turn the engine in a clockwise direction until the scribe line on the starter clutch aligns with the notch in the inspection hole and the number 1 arrow on the exhaust camshaft sprocket points forwards and is level with the top surface on the cylinder head **(see illustrations)**.

**4** Remove the cam chain tensioner (see Section 8).

**5** Before disturbing the camshaft holders, check for identification markings. The intake camshaft holder is marked IN, and the exhaust camshaft holder is marked EX **(see illustration)**. These markings ensure that the

**2**

9.5 Note camshaft holder identification

9.7a Lift off the camshaft holder and remove the dowels (arrowed)

9.7b Note the camshaft identification marks

9.10 Inspect the camshaft journals for wear and damage

holders can be matched up to their original camshafts on installation. If no markings are visible, make your own using a felt pen.

6 Working on one camshaft at a time, unscrew the holder bolts evenly and a little at a time in the **reverse** of the numerical sequence marked on each holder **(see illustration 9.31b)**. While loosening the bolts make sure that the holder is lifting squarely away from the cylinder head and is not sticking on the locating dowels.

*Caution: If the bolts are loosened carelessly and the holder does not come away from the head squarely, the holder is likely to break. If this happens the complete cylinder head assembly must be renewed; the holders are matched to the cylinder head and cannot be renewed separately. Also, a camshaft could be damaged if the holder bolts are not loosened evenly and the pressure from a depressed valve causes the shaft to bend.*

7 Remove the bolts and the cam chain top guide, noting how it fits. Lift off the camshaft holders and remove the camshaft holder dowels for safekeeping if they are loose **(see illustration)**. Slip the cam chain off the intake camshaft sprocket and lift the camshaft out of the head, then remove the exhaust camshaft. **Note:** *Secure the cam chain to some convenient point with wire or a cable tie to prevent it falling into the engine.* The camshafts are marked for identification. The intake camshaft is marked 'IN' and the exhaust camshaft is marked 'EX' **(see illustration)**.

8 If the cam followers and shims are being removed, obtain a container which is divided into sixteen compartments, and label each compartment with the location of its corresponding valve in the cylinder head. If a container is not available, use labelled plastic bags. **Note:** *It is essential that the followers*

*and shims are only fitted to their corresponding valves.* Lift each cam follower out of the cylinder head using either a magnet or a pair of pliers (see Chapter 1, Section 25). Retrieve the shim from either the inside of the follower or pick it out of the top of the valve, using a magnet or a small screwdriver with a dab of grease on it (the shim will stick to the grease). Do not allow the shim to fall into the engine. Store each shim with its respective follower.

9 Cover the cylinder head to prevent anything falling into the engine.

## Inspection

10 Inspect the bearing surfaces of the head and the holders and the corresponding journals on the camshaft. Look for score marks, deep scratches and evidence of spalling (a pitted appearance) **(see illustration)**.

11 Check the camshaft lobes for heat discoloration (blue appearance), score marks, chipped areas, flat spots and spalling **(see illustrations)**. Measure the height of each lobe with a micrometer and compare the results to the Specifications at the beginning of this Chapter **(see illustration)**. If damage is noted or wear is excessive, the camshaft must be renewed.

12 Check camshaft runout by supporting each end of the camshaft on V-blocks, and measuring any runout at the journals using a dial gauge (see *Tools and Workshop Tips* in the *Reference* section). If the runout exceeds the specified limit the camshaft must be renewed.

13 If removed, inspect the outer surfaces of the cam followers for evidence of wear, scoring or other damage **(see illustration)**. If the surface of a follower is in poor condition, it is probable that the bore in which it works is also damaged. Remove the valves (see Section 12) and measure the internal diameter of the follower bore in the cylinder head. If the bore is seriously out-of-round the cylinder head will have to be renewed.

9.11a Inspect the camshaft lobes for wear . . .

9.11b . . . here's an example of spalling requiring repair or renewal

9.11c Measuring the camshaft lobes with a micrometer

9.13 Inspect the outer surface of the cam followers

**HAYNES HiNT** *Refer to Tools and Workshop Tips in the Reference section for details of how to read a micrometer and dial gauge.*

9.19 Lay a strip of Plastigauge across each journal, along the camshaft centreline

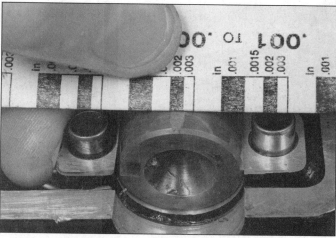

9.21 Compare the width of the crushed Plastigauge with the scale provided

**14** The camshaft journal oil clearance should now be checked. There are two possible ways of doing this, either by direct measurement (see Steps 15 to 17) or by the use of a product known as Plastigauge (see Steps 18 to 21). If Plastigauge is used and the oil clearance is excessive, use direct measurement to determine whether it is the camshaft or the holder that is worn.

**15** If direct measurement is to be used, make sure the camshaft holder dowels are in position then fit the holders, making sure they are in their correct location **(see illustration 9.5)**. Tighten the holder bolts evenly and a little at a time in the correct numerical sequence as marked on the holder to the specified torque setting **(see illustration 9.31b)**.

**16** Make a chart or sketch of the cylinder head so that a note of each measurement can be made against the appropriate bearing surface. Using telescoping gauges and a micrometer (see *Tools and Workshop Tips*), measure the internal diameter of each holder journal and record it on the chart. Now measure the diameter of the corresponding camshaft journals with a micrometer.

**17** To determine the journal oil clearance, subtract the camshaft journal diameter from the internal holder journal diameter. Compare the result to the clearance specified. If the clearance is greater than specified, compare the individual measurements of the camshaft journal and the holder to those specified and renew whichever component is beyond its service limit.

**18** If the Plastigauge method is to be used, clean the camshafts and the bearing surfaces in the cylinder head and camshaft holder with a clean, lint-free cloth. Lay the camshafts in place in the cylinder head. **Note:** *Check that the valve timing marks are correctly aligned when installing the camshaft to avoid valve damage.*

**19** Cut strips of Plastigauge and lay one piece on each camshaft journal, along the camshaft centreline **(see illustration)**. Make

sure the camshaft holder dowels are in position then fit the holder, making sure it is in its correct location **(see illustration 9.5)**. Tighten the holder bolts evenly and a little at a time in the correct numerical sequence as marked on the holder to the specified torque setting **(see illustration 9.31b)**. **Note:** *The camshaft must not rotate during this procedure.*

**20** Now unscrew the bolts evenly and a little at a time in the reverse of the numerical sequence and carefully lift off the camshaft holder.

**21** To determine the oil clearance, compare the crushed Plastigauge (at its widest point) on each journal to the scale printed on the Plastigauge container **(see illustration)**. Compare the results to this Chapter's Specifications. If the oil clearance is greater than specified, follow Steps 15 and 16 to determine which component is worn beyond its service limit.

> **HAYNES HiNT**
> *Before renewing camshafts or the cylinder head and journal holders because of damage, check with local machine shops specialising in motorcycle engine work. In the case of the camshafts, it may be possible for cam lobes to be welded, reground and hardened, at a cost far lower than that of a new camshaft. If the bearing surfaces in the cylinder head are damaged, it may be possible for them to be bored out to accept bearing inserts. Due to the cost of a new cylinder head it is recommended that all options be explored!*

**22** Check the camshaft sprockets for wear, chipped teeth and other damage **(see illustration)**. The camshaft sprockets are integral with the camshafts, the crankshaft sprocket is integral with the ignition timing rotor.

**23** If the sprockets are worn, the chain and the sprocket on the crankshaft are probably worn as well and should be checked (see Section 13).

### Installation

**24** Make sure the bearing surfaces in the cylinder head, on the camshafts and in the holders are clean, then liberally apply molybdenum disulphide oil (a 50/50 mixture of molybdenum disulphide grease and engine oil) to each of them. Also apply oil to the camshaft lobes and the followers.

**25** If removed, lubricate each shim and fit it into its recess in the top of the valve, with the size marking on each shim facing up. Check that the shim is correctly seated, then install the follower (see Chapter 1, Section 25). **Note:** *It is most important that the shims and followers are returned to their original valves otherwise the valve clearances will be inaccurate.*

**26** Ensure that the scribe line on the starter clutch still aligns with the notch in the inspection hole **(see illustration 9.3a)**. If it is necessary to turn the crankshaft to restore the alignment, hold the cam chain up to prevent it jamming between the crankcase and the crankshaft sprocket.

**27** Keeping the front run of the cam chain taut, lay the exhaust camshaft (identified by EX) into

9.22 Inspect he camshaft sprockets for wear and chipped teeth

**2**

9.28 Lock the cam chain in position on the exhaust camshaft sprocket with a cable tie

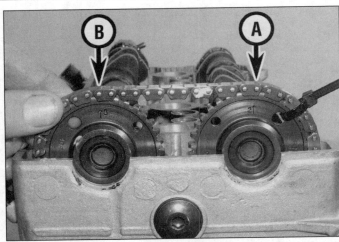

9.29 Engage the 14th cam chain pin from the No. 2 arrow (A) with the No. 3 arrow (B)

the cylinder head. The number 1 arrow on the exhaust camshaft sprocket should point forwards and be level with the top surface on the cylinder head (see illustration 9.3b).

28 Engage the chain on the sprocket and lock it in position with a cable tie (see illustration).

29 The number 2 arrow on the exhaust camshaft sprocket should point upwards. Starting from the cam chain pin that is directly above the number 2 arrow, count 14 pins along the chain towards the intake side. Lay the intake camshaft (identified by IN) into the cylinder head and engage the intake camshaft

sprocket with the chain so that the 14th pin is directly above the arrow marked 3 on the sprocket (see illustration).

30 Before proceeding further, check that everything aligns as described in Steps 26, 27 and 29, and make adjustments as necessary, then lock the chain and the intake camshaft sprocket in position with a cable tie (see illustration).

31 Make sure the camshaft holder dowels are in position then fit the holders, making sure they are in their correct locations (see illustration 9.5). Install the cam chain top guide and the holder bolts, then tighten the

bolts evenly and a little at a time in the numerical sequence marked on each holder to the specified torque setting (see illustrations). Note: The camshaft holder bolts are of the high tensile type, indicated by a 9 mark on the bolt head. Don't use any other type of bolt.

Caution: The camshaft is likely to break if it is tightened down onto the closed valves before the open valves. The holders are likely to break if they are not tightened down evenly and squarely.

32 Install the cam chain tensioner (see Section 8). Cut the cable ties on the cam chain sprockets. Turn the engine in a clockwise direction two complete revolutions and ensure that everything still aligns (see Steps 26, 27 and 29) and that the camshafts are not pinched by the holders.

33 Install the remaining components in the reverse order of removal, noting the following:
● Fit a new O-ring on the timing inspection cap and smear the O-ring and plug threads with clean engine oil.
● Check the valve clearances and adjust them if necessary (see Chapter 1).

9.30 Lock the cam chain in position on the inlet camshaft sprocket with a cable tie

9.31a Install the cam chain top guide

## 10 Cylinder head – removal and installation

Note: To remove the cylinder head the engine must be removed from the frame.

### Removal

1 Remove the throttle bodies (see Chapter 4). Remove the engine from the frame (see Section 5). Remove the camshafts, cam followers and shims (see Section 9).

2 Loosen the clip securing the coolant hose to the back of the cylinder head and disconnect the hose (see illustration). If not already done, loosen the clip securing the hose to the thermostat housing and remove the hose.

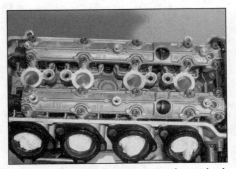

9.31b Bolt tightening sequence is marked on each camshaft holder

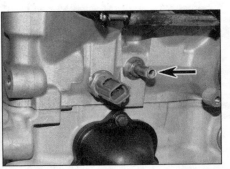

10.2 Disconnect the coolant hose from the union on the back of the head

**3** Undo the cam chain stopper bolt and remove the bolt (see illustration 10.15). Discard the sealing washer as a new one must be fitted on reassembly.

**4** The cylinder head is secured by two 6 mm bolts and ten 10 mm bolts. First unscrew and remove the 6 mm bolts (see illustration).

**5** Working from the outside to the centre in a criss-cross pattern, loosen the 10 mm bolts evenly and a little at a time until they are all slack, then remove the bolts and their washers (see illustration).

**6** Lift the head off the upper crankcase, passing the cam chain down through the tunnel as you do. If the head is stuck, tap around the joint with a soft-faced mallet to free it. Do not attempt to free the head by levering it off – you'll damage the sealing surfaces.

**7** Secure the cam chain to prevent it falling into the engine and stuff a clean rag into the cam chain tunnel to prevent any debris falling in. Remove the old cylinder head gasket.

**8** If they are loose, remove the two dowels from the rear edge of the upper crankcase for safekeeping. If either appears to be missing it is probably stuck in the underside of the cylinder head.

**9** Inspect the cylinder head gasket and the mating surfaces on the cylinder head and upper crankcase for signs of leakage, which could indicate that the head is distorted. If necessary, check the cylinder head with a straight-edge (see Section 12). Discard the old head gasket as a new one must be fitted on reassembly.

**10** If required, undo the screws securing the intake rubber and remove the rubbers, noting how they fit (see illustration). Discard the O-rings as new ones must be fitted on reassembly (see illustration).

### Installation

**11** Clean the mating surfaces of the cylinder head and upper crankcase with a suitable solvent to remove all traces of old gasket. If a scraper is used, take care not to scratch or gouge the soft aluminium. Ensure none of the old gasket material falls into the crankcase, the cylinder bores or the oil and coolant passages.

> **HAYNES HINT** *Refer to Tools and Workshop Tips for details of gasket removal methods.*

**12** If removed, fit new O-rings into the grooves in the intake rubbers, then install them. Apply a suitable non-permanent thread

**10.3  Remove the stopper bolt and washer**

locking compound to the mounting screws and tighten them securely.

**13** If removed, install the two dowels in the upper crankcase and fit the new head gasket. Check that the gasket locates over the dowels and that all the holes are correctly aligned (see illustration).

**14** Remove any rag from the cam chain tunnel. With the help of an assistant, keep the cam chain taught and pass it up through the tunnel while the head is lowered onto the upper crankcase (see illustration). Secure the cam chain.

**10.4  Undo and remove the 6 mm bolts . . .**

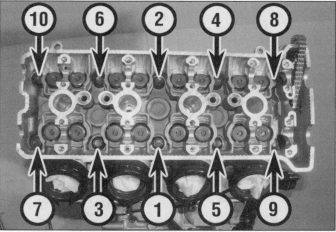

**10.5  . . . then loosen the 10 mm bolts in the *reverse* of the tightening sequence shown**

**10.10a  The top edge of the intake rubber is marked UP**

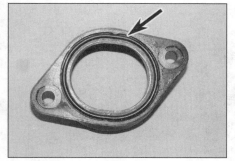

**10.10b  Fit new O-rings into the grooves in the back of the intake rubbers**

**10.13  Fit the new gasket making sure it locates over the dowels (arrowed)**

2

**10.14 Install the head, passing the cam chain up through the tunnel**

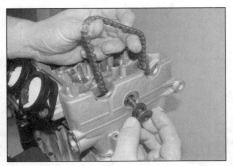

**10.15 Install the stopper bolt between the front and rear runs of the cam chain**

**15** Fit a new sealing washer to the cam chain stopper bolt with the metal side of the washer facing the bolt. Install the bolt, ensuring it passes between the front and rear runs of the cam chain, and tighten it to the torque setting specified at the beginning of this Chapter **(see illustration)**.

**16** The washers fitted to the 10 mm cylinder head bolts have rounded edges on their upper surface. Ensure the washers are fitted onto the bolts with the rounded edges facing the bolt heads. Apply clean engine oil to the washers and the bolt threads, then install the bolts and tighten them finger-tight **(see illustration)**.

**17** Working from the centre to the outside in a criss-cross pattern, tighten the 10 mm bolts evenly and a little at a time to the initial torque setting specified at the beginning of this Chapter, then tighten them in the same sequence to the final torque setting **(see illustration 10.5)**.

**18** Install the 6 mm bolts and tighten them to the specified torque setting **(see illustration 10.4)**.

**19** Install the remaining components in the reverse order of removal.

## 11 Valves/valve seats/ valve guides – servicing

**1** Because of the complex nature of this job and the special tools and equipment required, most owners leave servicing of the valves, valve seats and valve guides to a professional. However, you can make an initial assessment of whether the valves are seating, and therefore sealing, correctly by pouring a small amount of solvent into each of the valve ports. If the solvent leaks past any valve into the combustion chamber the valve is not seating and sealing correctly.

**2** You can also remove the valves from the cylinder head, clean the components and check them for wear to assess the extent of the work needed. The head can then be reassembled.

**3** The dealer service department will remove the valves and springs, renew the valves and guides, recut the valve seats, check and renew the valve springs, spring retainers and collets (as necessary), fit new valve stem seals and reassemble the valve components.

**4** After the valve service has been performed, the head will be in like-new condition. When the head is returned, be sure to clean it again very thoroughly before installation on the engine, to remove any metal particles or abrasive grit that may still be present from the valve service operations. Use compressed air, if available, to blow out all the holes and passages.

## 12 Cylinder head and valves – disassembly, inspection and reassembly

**1** As mentioned in the previous section, valve overhaul should be left to a Suzuki dealer. However, disassembly, cleaning and inspection of the valves and related components can be done by the home mechanic. This way no expense is incurred if the inspection reveals that overhaul is not required at this time.

**2** To disassemble the valve components without the risk of damaging them, a valve spring compressor is essential. Make sure the valve spring compressor is suitable for motorcycle work.

### Disassembly

**3** Before proceeding, arrange to label and store the valves along with their related components in such a way that they can be returned to their original locations without getting mixed up **(see illustration)**. Either use the same container as the cam followers and shims are stored in (see Section 9), or obtain a separate container and label each compartment accordingly. Alternatively, labelled plastic bags will do just as well.

**4** Compress the valve spring on the first valve with a spring compressor, making sure it is

**10.16 Lubricate the washers and threads of the 10 mm head bolts**

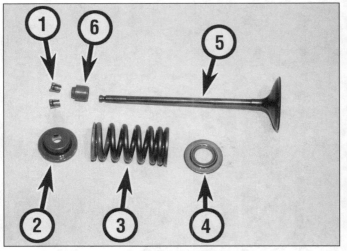

**12.3 Valve components**

| | | |
|---|---|---|
| 1  Collets | 3  Spring | 5  Valve |
| 2  Spring retainer | 4  Spring seat | 6  Valve stem seal |

**12.4a Make sure the spring compressor is a good fit on the top . . .**

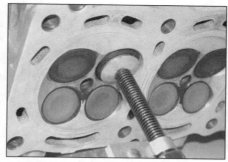

**12.4b . . . and the bottom of the valve assembly**

**12.5a Remove the collets . . .**

**12.5b . . . then the spring retainer . . .**

**12.5c . . . valve spring . . .**

**12.5d . . . and the valve**

correctly located onto each end of the valve assembly **(see illustrations)**. On the underside of the head make sure the plate on the compressor only contacts the valve and not the soft aluminium of the head – if the plate is too big for the valve, use a spacer between them. Do not compress the springs any more than is absolutely necessary.

*Caution: Take great care not to mark the cam follower bore with the spring compressor.*

**5** Remove the collets, using either needle-nose pliers, tweezers, a magnet or a screwdriver with a dab of grease on it **(see illustration)**. Carefully release the valve spring compressor and remove the spring retainer,

noting which way up it fits, the spring and the valve **(see illustrations)**. If the valve binds in the guide and won't pull through, push it back into the head and deburr the area around the collet groove with a very fine file or whetstone **(see illustration)**.

**6** Pull the valve stem seal off the top of the valve guide with pliers and discard it (the old seals should never be reused), then remove the spring seat noting which way up, it fits – using a magnet is the easiest way to remove the seat from the head **(see illustrations)**.

**7** Repeat the procedure for the remaining valves. Remember to keep the parts for each valve together so they can be reinstalled in the same location.

**8** Clean the cylinder head with solvent and dry it thoroughly. Compressed air will speed the drying process and ensure that all holes and recessed areas are clean. **Note:** *Do not use a wire brush mounted in a drill motor to*

*clean the combustion chambers as the head material is soft and may be scratched or eroded away by the wire brush.*

**9** Clean all of the valve springs, collets, retainers and spring seats with solvent and dry them thoroughly. Do the parts from one valve at a time so that no mixing of parts between valves occurs.

**10** Scrape off any deposits that may have formed on the valve, then use a motorised wire brush to remove deposits from the valve heads and stems. Again, make sure the valves do not get mixed up.

### Inspection

**11** Inspect the cylinder head very carefully for cracks and other damage. If cracks are found, a new head will be required. Check the cam bearing surfaces for wear and evidence of seizure. Check the camshafts for wear as well (see Section 9).

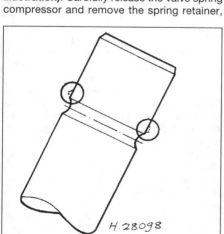

**12.5e If necessary, deburr the area above the collet groove**

**12.6a Pull the stem seal off with pliers . . .**

**12.6b .. then remove the spring seat**

**2**

**12.13 Examine the valve seat (arrowed) and measure its width**

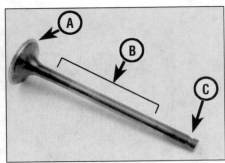

**12.14a Examine the valve face (A), stem (B) and collet groove (C)**

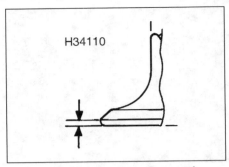

**12.14b Measure the valve margin thickness**

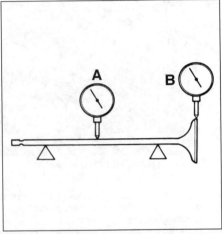

**12.16 Measure the valve stem runout (A) and valve head runout (B)**

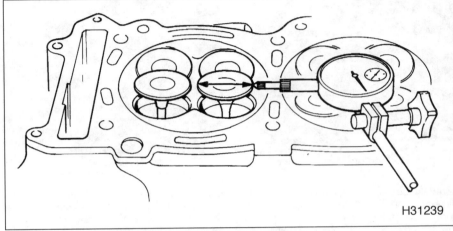

**12.17 Measure the amount of 'wobble' as shown**

**12** Using a precision straight-edge and a feeler gauge, check the head gasket mating surface for warpage. Refer to *Tools and Workshop Tips* in the Reference section for details of how to use the straight-edge. If the head is warped beyond the limit specified at the beginning of this Chapter, consult your Suzuki dealer or take it to a specialist repair shop for rectification.

**13** Examine the valve seats in the combustion chamber **(see illustration)**. If they are pitted, cracked or burned, the head will require work beyond the scope of the home mechanic. Measure the valve seat width and compare it to this Chapter's Specifications. If

it exceeds the service limit, or if it varies around its circumference, consult your Suzuki dealer or take the head to a specialist repair shop for rectification.

**14** Examine each valve face for cracks, pits and burned spots. Measure the valve margin thickness and compare it to this Chapter's Specifications **(see illustrations)**. If it exceeds the service limit, or if it varies around its circumference, replace the valve with a new one.

**15** Check the valve stem and the collet groove area for wear and damage **(see illustration 12.14a)**. Rotate the valve and check for any obvious indication that it is

bent. Check the end of the stem for pitting and excessive wear.

**16** Using V-blocks and a dial gauge, measure the valve stem runout and the valve head runout and compare the results to the Specifications **(see illustration)**. If either measurement exceeds the service limit, a new valve must be fitted.

**17** Clean the valve guides to remove any carbon build-up, then install each valve in its guide in turn so that its face is 10 mm above the seat. Mount a dial gauge against the side of the valve face and measure the amount of side clearance (wobble) between the valve stem and its guide in two directions **(see illustration)**.

**18** If the side clearance exceeds the limit specified, remove the valve and measure the valve stem diameter **(see illustration)**. Also measure the inside diameter of the guide with a small hole gauge and micrometer **(see illustration)**. Measure the guides at each end and at the centre to determine if they are worn unevenly. Subtract the stem diameter from the valve guide inside diameter to obtain the valve stem-to-guide clearance. If the stem-to-guide clearance is greater than specified, renew whichever of the components is worn beyond its specifications. If the valve guide is within specifications, but is worn unevenly, it should be renewed.

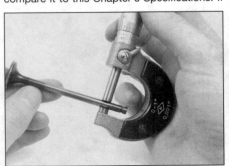

**12.18a Measuring the valve stem diameter with a micrometer**

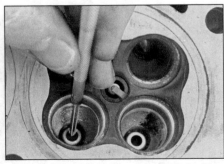

**12.18b Measuring the valve guide inside diameter with a small hole gauge**

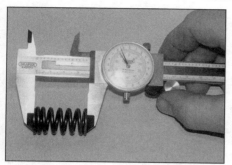

12.19 Measuring valve spring free length

12.20 Check that the springs are not bent

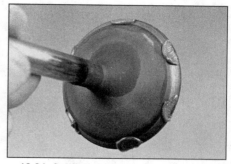

12.24 Apply the grinding compound in small dabs to the valve face only

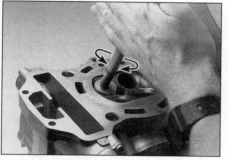

12.25a Rotate the grinding tool back-and-forth between the palms of your hands

12.25b The grinding process should leave the valve face (arrowed) . . .

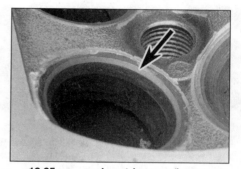

12.25c . . . and seat (arrowed) as an unbroken ring of uniform width

19 Check the end of each valve spring for wear. Measure the spring free length and compare it to that listed in the specifications (see illustration). If any spring is shorter than specified it has sagged and must be renewed.
20 Place each spring upright on a flat surface and check it for bend with a set square (see illustration). If the bend in any spring is excessive, it must be renewed. The spring tension should also be checked by measuring the amount of weight needed to compress each spring to the specified length. If the weight required to compress the spring to the specified length is greater or less than the weight specified, the spring must be renewed.
21 Check the spring retainers and collets for wear and damage. Any questionable parts should not be reused, as extensive damage will occur in the event of failure during engine operation.
22 If the inspection indicates that no overhaul work is required, the valve components can be reinstalled in the head.

### Reassembly

23 Unless a valve service has been performed, before installing the valves in the head they should be ground in (lapped) to ensure a positive seal between the valves and seats. Note: Suzuki advise against grinding in the valves after the seats have been recut. The valve seat must be soft and unpolished for final seating to occur when the engine is first run. Valve grinding requires coarse and fine grinding compound and a valve grinding tool.

If a grinding tool is not available, a piece of rubber or plastic hose can be slipped over the valve stem (after the valve has been installed in the guide) and used to turn the valve.
24 Apply a small amount of coarse grinding compound to the valve face, then slip the valve into the guide (see illustration). Note: Make sure each valve is installed in its correct guide and be careful not to get any grinding compound on the valve stem.
25 Attach the grinding tool (or hose) to the valve and rotate the tool between the palms of your hands. Use a back-and-forth motion (as though rubbing your hands together) rather than a circular motion so that the valve rotates alternately clockwise and anti-clockwise rather than in one direction only (see illustration). Lift the valve off the seat and turn it at regular intervals to distribute the grinding compound properly. Continue the grinding procedure until the valve face and

seat contact area is of uniform width and unbroken around the entire circumference of the valve face and seat (see illustrations).
26 Carefully remove the valve from the guide and wipe off all traces of grinding compound. Use solvent to clean the valve and wipe the seat area thoroughly with a solvent soaked cloth.
27 Repeat the procedure with fine valve grinding compound, then repeat the entire procedure for the remaining valves.
28 Working on one valve at a time, lay the spring seat in place in the cylinder head with its shouldered side facing up so that it fits into the base of the spring (see illustration). Lubricate the new valve stem seal with molybdenum disulphide oil and fit it onto the valve guide. Use an appropriate size deep socket to push the seal squarely over the end of the guide until it is felt to clip into place (see illustration).

**2**

12.28a Install the valve seat shouldered side up

12.28b Press the stem seal into place with a suitably sized socket

**12.32 Tap each valve stem lightly to seat the collets**

29 Coat the valve stem with molybdenum disulphide oil, then install it into its guide, rotating it slowly to avoid damaging the seal. Check that the valve moves up and down freely in the guide. Next, install the valve spring, with its closer-wound coils facing down into the cylinder head, followed by the spring retainer, with its shouldered side facing down into the top of the spring (**see illustration 12.3**).

30 Apply a small amount of grease to the collets to help hold them in place. Compress the spring with the valve spring compressor and install the collets (**see illustration 12.5a**). When compressing the spring, depress it only as far as is absolutely necessary to slip the collets into place. Make certain that the collets are securely located in the collet groove and release the spring compressor.

31 Repeat the procedure for the remaining valves. Remember to keep the parts for each valve together and separate from the other valves so they can be reinstalled in the same location.

32 Support the cylinder head on blocks so the valves can't contact the work surface, then tap the end of each valve stem lightly to seat the collets in their grooves (**see illustrations**).

 *Check for proper sealing of the valves by pouring a small amount of solvent into each of the valve ports. If the solvent leaks past any valve into the combustion chamber the valve grinding operation on that valve should be repeated.*

## 13 Cam chain, tensioner blade and guides – removal, inspection and installation

**Note:** *To remove the cam chain and associated components the engine must be removed from the frame.*

1 Except in cases of oil starvation, the cam chain wears very little. If the chain has stretched excessively and can no longer be correctly tensioned by the cam chain tensioner, it is likely that the chain guides and tensioner blade will be worn and in need of renewal as well. Also check the condition of the camshaft sprockets (see Section 9) and crankshaft sprocket (see Step 10). **Note:** *Check the*

*operation of the cam chain tensioner if the chain is slack but appears to be in good condition.*

### Removal

2 Remove the cylinder head (see Section 10). The cam chain top guide is secured by two of the camshaft holder bolts (**see illustration 9.31a**).

3 Remove the starter clutch and the washer behind the starter clutch (see Section 14).

4 Undo the pivot bolt securing the cam chain front guide in the crankcase (**see illustration**). Pull the cam chain back against the tensioner blade, then turn the front guide through 180° and lift it out of the cam chain tunnel (**see illustration**).

5 Undo the pivot bolt securing the tensioner blade, then remove the bolt and the washer fitted behind the blade (**see illustration**). Lift the tensioner blade out of the cam chain tunnel.

6 Disengage the cam chain from the crankshaft sprocket and lift the chain out (**see illustration**).

7 Note the alignment marks on the crankshaft and the crankshaft sprocket, then slide the sprocket off the shaft (**see illustration**).

### Inspection

8 Examine the sliding surface of the guides and tensioner blade for signs of wear or damage (**see illustration**). Check them carefully for cracks in the surface and along the edges. Install new components if necessary.

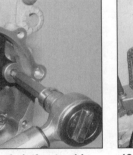

**13.4a Undo the cam chain front guide pivot bolt . . .**

**13.4b . . . then turn the guide and lift it out**

**13.5 Remove the tensioner blade pivot bolt and washer (arrowed)**

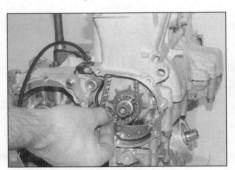

**13.6 Disengage the chain from the sprocket . . .**

**13.7 . . . then remove the sprocket, noting the alignment marks (arrowed)**

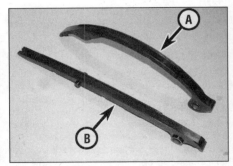

**13.8 Examine the tensioner blade (A) and guide (B) for wear and damage**

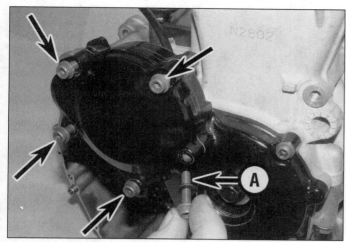
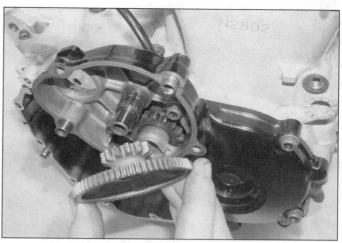

**14.2 Reduction gear cover bolts – note the sealing washer (A)**

**14.3 Remove the reduction gear, noting how it fits**

**9** Lay the chain on the work surface and pull it taught. Check all round the chain; if there is any discernible slack between the links, or if there is any doubt about its condition, fit a new chain.
**10** Inspect the teeth of the crankshaft sprocket. If there are any signs of wear or damage, fit a new sprocket. It is good practice to renew the chain and sprocket at the same time.

### Installation

**11** Installation is the reverse of removal, noting the following:
● Align the marks on the crankshaft and crankshaft sprocket and install the sprocket.
● Install the cam chain and secure its upper end with wire or a cable tie.
● Fit the washer on the tensioner blade pivot bolt behind the blade.
● Apply a suitable, non-permanent locking compound to the threads of the pivot bolts.
● Tighten the pivot bolts to the specified torque setting.

### 14 Starter clutch and gears – removal, inspection and installation

**Note:** *This procedure can be carried out with the engine in the frame. If the engine has been removed, ignore the steps which do not apply.*

### Removal

**1** Remove the fairing right-hand side panel (see Chapter 8).
**2** Undo the bolts securing the reduction gear cover, noting the sealing washer fitted on the lower front bolt, and remove the cover **(see illustration)**. Remove the gasket and discard it as a new one must be fitted on reassembly. Note the position of the locating dowels and remove them for safe-keeping if loose.
**3** Remove the wave washer and outer thrust washer from the reduction gear shaft, then

remove the gear noting which way round it fits **(see illustration)**.
**4** Remove the bearing, the inner thrust washer and the shaft **(see illustration)**.
**5** Release the oil pressure switch wiring from the guide retained by the lower starter clutch cover bolt. Undo the cover bolts, noting the sealing washer fitted on the upper front bolt, and remove the cover **(see illustration)**. Remove the gasket and discard it. Note the position of the dowels and remove them for safe-keeping if loose.
**6** Remove the wave washer from the idle gear shaft, then remove the gear, noting which way round it fits, and withdraw the shaft **(see illustrations)**.
**7** Before proceeding further, the operation of the starter clutch can be checked while it is in situ. Check that the driven gear on the back of the starter clutch is able to rotate freely anti-clockwise as you look at it, but locks when rotated clockwise.

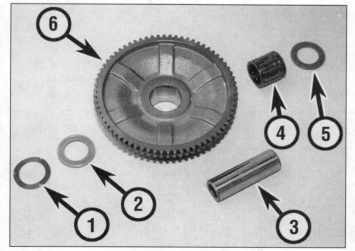
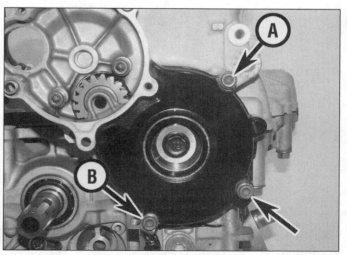

**14.4 Reduction gear components**

1 Wave washer  3 Shaft  5 Inner thrust washer
2 Outer thrust washer  4 Bearing  6 Reduction gear

**14.5 Starter clutch cover bolts – note the sealing washer (A) and wiring guide (B)**

14.6a Remove the wave washer and idle gear . . .

14.6b . . . then withdraw the gear shaft

**8** To undo the starter clutch bolt it is necessary to stop the crankshaft from turning. If the engine is in the frame, engage 1st gear and have an assistant hold the rear brake on hard with the rear tyre in firm contact with the ground. If the engine has been removed from the frame, use a suitable peg spanner to hold the starter clutch while undoing the bolt. Suzuki produces a service tool for this purpose (Pt. No. 09920-34830) or a suitable tool can be made from two strips of steel bolted together **(see illustration)** **(see Tool Tip)**.

**9** Remove the bolt and washer and slide the starter clutch and its thrust washer off the end of the crankshaft, noting how it fits **(see illustrations)**.

### Inspection

**10** With the starter clutch face down, check that the driven gear rotates freely in a clockwise direction and locks against the rotor in an anti-clockwise direction **(see illustration)**. If it doesn't, renew the starter clutch.
**11** Withdraw the driven gear from the starter

clutch. If it appears stuck, rotate the gear clockwise as you withdraw it to free it from the clutch sprags. Lift the needle bearing for the gear off the starter clutch assembly **(see illustration)**.
**12** Check the bearing surface on the hub of the starter clutch, the condition of the sprags inside the clutch body and the condition of the clutch needle bearing **(see illustration)**. If there are signs of excessive wear, or the sprags or bearing rollers are damaged, marked or pitted, the starter clutch assembly should be renewed.

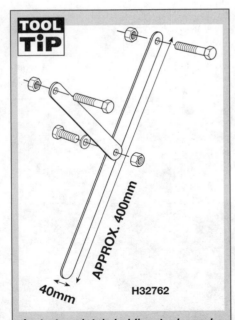

**TOOL TiP**

APPROX. 400mm

40mm          H32762

*A starter clutch holding tool can be made from strips of steel pivoted as shown. Use bolts secured with nuts in each end, which are long enough to engage the holes in the clutch body.*

14.8 Undoing the starter clutch bolt using the home-made tool

14.9b . . . then slide off the starter clutch and thrust washer (arrowed)

14.9a Remove the bolt and washer . . .

14.10 Driven gear should rotate freely clockwise

14.11 Starter clutch (A), driven gear bearing (B) and driven gear (C)

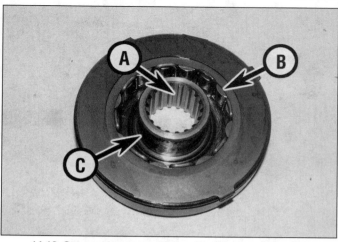

14.12 Starter clutch needle bearing (A), sprags (B) and hub bearing surface (C)

13 Check the condition of the needle roller bearings for the driven gear and the reduction gear. Check the condition of the rollers and the cages and renew the bearing if any wear or damage is found, or if any roughness or stiffness is detected when the components are assembled and turned (see *Tools and Workshop Tips (Section 5)* in the Reference Section).

14 Examine the teeth of the starter gears and the corresponding teeth of the starter motor drive shaft. Renew the gears and/or starter motor if worn or chipped teeth are discovered on related gears. Also check the gear shafts for damage, and check that the gears are not a loose fit on the shafts. Renew the shafts if necessary.

## Installation

15 Clean all old gasket and sealant from the covers and crankcase.

16 Lubricate the needle bearing and the hub of the starter driven gear with clean engine oil, then install the bearing and the gear into the clutch, rotating the gear clockwise as you do so to spread the sprags and allow the hub of the gear to enter (see illustration 14.10).

17 Slide the thrust washer and the starter clutch assembly onto the crankshaft, aligning the scribe line on the clutch with the punch mark on the crankshaft (see illustration). Install the bolt and washer, then using the method employed on removal to stop the crankshaft from turning, tighten the bolt to the torque setting specified at the beginning of this Chapter.

18 Lubricate the idle gear shaft with clean engine oil and slide it through the gear. Install the idle gear, making sure the inner pinion meshes with the teeth of the starter driven gear, and press the gear shaft into its bore in the crankcase. Fit the wave washer onto the end of the shaft (see illustration 14.6a).

19 If removed, install the starter clutch cover dowels. Apply a smear of suitable, non-permanent sealant across the crankcase joints, then fit the new cover gasket, making sure it locates correctly onto the dowels, and install the cover (see illustration). Tighten the cover bolts securely, ensuring a new sealing washer is installed on the upper front bolt and the wiring guide is on the lower cover bolt (see illustration 14.5). Secure the oil pressure switch wiring with the guide.

20 Lubricate the reduction gear shaft with clean engine oil and fit it into its bore in the crankcase, then slide on the inner thrust washer (see illustration 14.4). Lubricate the needle bearing and slide it into the gear, then slide the gear onto the shaft. Ensure the smaller

pinion faces inwards and meshes correctly with the teeth of the idle gear outer pinion, and the larger pinion meshes with the starter motor drive shaft (see illustration 14.3). Fit the outer thrust washer followed by the wave washer onto the end of the shaft.

21 If removed, install the reduction gear cover dowels then fit the new cover gasket, making sure it locates correctly onto the dowels, and install the cover (see illustration). Tighten the cover bolts securely, ensuring a new sealing washer is installed on the lower front bolt (see illustration 14.2).

22 Check the engine/transmission oil level and top up if necessary (see *Daily (pre-ride) checks*).

23 Install the fairing right-hand side panel (see Chapter 8).

## 15 Clutch –
### removal, inspection and installation

**Note:** *This procedure can be carried out with the engine in the frame. If the engine has been removed, ignore the steps which do not apply.*

### Removal

1 Remove the fairing right-hand side panel (see Chapter 8).

14.17 Align the scribe line with the punch mark on the crankshaft

14.19 Install the starter clutch cover dowels (arrowed) and gasket

14.21 Install the reduction gear cover dowels (arrowed) and gasket

2

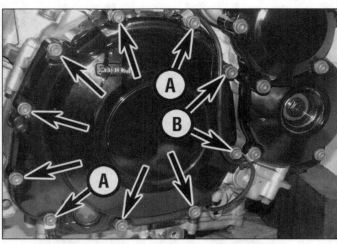

15.3 Clutch cover bolts – note the guides (A) and sealing washers (B)

15.4 Remove the bolts, spring cups and springs

2 Drain the engine/transmission oil (see Chapter 1). Release the oil pressure switch wiring from the guide retained by the upper clutch cover bolt. Release the fuel tank water drain hose from the guide retained by the lower clutch cover bolt. Position a suitable receptacle underneath the clutch cover to catch any residual oil when the cover is removed.

3 Undo the cover bolts, noting the sealing washers fitted on the two front bolts, and remove the cover **(see illustration)**. Remove the gasket and discard it. Note the position of the locating dowels and remove them for safe-keeping if loose.

4 Undo the clutch spring bolts a little at a time in a criss-cross pattern, then remove the bolts, the spring cups and the springs **(see illustration)**.

5 Remove the clutch pressure plate, then remove the thrust washer, release bearing and clutch lifter, and withdraw the right-hand pushrod from the centre of the gearbox input shaft **(see illustrations)**.

6 Note the location of the outer friction plate tabs, then withdraw the clutch plates from the clutch housing **(see illustration)**. Unless the plates are being renewed, keep them in their original order.

7 On all GSX-R600 models, GSX-R750K2 and GSX-R1000K2 models, withdraw the anti-judder spring and the spring seat **(see illustration)**.

8 The clutch nut is staked onto the input shaft **(see illustration)**. Unstake the nut using a hammer and small chisel, taking care not to damage the shaft.

9 To loosen the clutch nut the input shaft must be locked using one of the following methods:

● If the engine is in the frame, engage 1st gear and have an assistant hold the rear brake on hard with the rear tyre in firm contact with the ground.

● Use the Suzuki service tool (Pt. No. 09920-53740) to engage the clutch centre splines.

15.5a Remove the clutch pressure plate . . .

15.5b . . . the thrust washer (A), release bearing (B) and clutch lifter (C) . . .

15.5c . . . and the right-hand clutch pushrod

15.6 Outer friction plate tabs locate in shallow slots in the clutch housing

15.7 Withdraw the anti-judder spring and spring seat

15.8 The clutch nut is staked onto the input shaft

15.9a Remove the clutch nut . . .

15.9b . . . then the dished washer and plain washer (arrowed)

15.10a Remove the clutch centre . . .

15.10b . . . then the outer thrust washer

15.11a Withdraw the sleeve and needle bearing . . .

15.11b . . . then manoeuvre out the clutch housing . . .

● Use a proprietary clutch holding tool which will engage the clutch centre splines. The type shown in illustration 15.29a is of the self-locking type.

● If the engine is out of the frame, fit a suitable ring spanner around the transmission output shaft end (where the front sprocket fits), shift the transmission into gear and counter-hold the shaft while slackening the nut.

*Caution: The clutch nut is extremely tight. If a clutch holding tool is used, ensure it does not slip and damage the clutch.*

Unscrew the nut and remove the dished washer and plain washer from the input shaft, noting which way round the dished washer fits **(see illustrations). Note:** *If the nut has been reused several times or if it was damaged when it was unstaked, discard it and fit a new one on reassembly.*

**10** Remove the clutch centre from the shaft, then remove the outer thrust washer **(see illustrations)**.

**11** Withdraw the sleeve and needle bearing from the centre of the clutch housing and manoeuvre the housing out of the crankcase **(see illustrations). Note:** *The primary driven gear on the back of the clutch housing may bind on the crankshaft. Rotate the crankshaft until it is clear of the gear, then remove the housing.*

**12** Remove the inner thrust washer from the shaft, noting which way round it fits **(see illustration)**.

**13** Remove the oil pump drive gear from the back of the clutch housing **(see illustration)**.

## Inspection

**14** After an extended period of service the

clutch friction plates will wear and promote clutch slip. Measure the thickness of each friction plate and the width of their tabs using a vernier caliper **(see illustrations)**. If any plate has worn to or beyond the service limits given in the Specifications at the beginning of

this Chapter, the friction plates must be renewed as a set. Also, if any of the plates smell burnt or are glazed, they must be renewed as a set. **Note:** *On GSX-R600 and GSX-R750 models the inner friction plate has dampers fitted to the tabs.*

15.12 . . . and remove the inner thrust washer

15.13 Remove the oil pump drive gear from the back of the clutch housing

15.14a Measure the thickness of the friction plates . . .

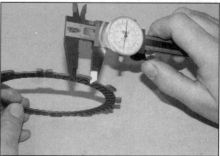

15.14b . . . and the width of the tabs

2

**15.15 Check the plain plates for warpage**

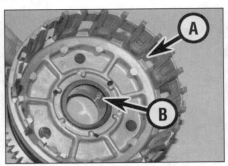

**15.16a Inspect the slots in the housing (A) and the bearing surface (B)**

**15.16b Inspect the slots in the clutch centre (A) and the spring bolt threads (B)**

**15** The plain plates should not show any signs of excess heating (bluing). Check for warpage using a surface plate and feeler gauges **(see illustration)**. If any plate exceeds the maximum permissible warpage, or shows signs of bluing, all plain plates must be renewed as a set. The total number of friction and plain plates for each model are given in the Specifications at the beginning of this Chapter.

*On GSX-R600 models 2.3 mm and 2.6 mm thick plain plates are fitted; only one to two of the thinner plates will be fitted and they should be located at the pressure plate end of the clutch.*

*On GSX-R750Y models two 1.6 mm and seven 2.0 mm plain plates are fitted; the two thinner plates should be fitted at the pressure plate end of the clutch.*

*On GSX-R750K1/K2 models, 1.6 mm and 2.0 mm plain plates are fitted; the thinner plates,*

*up to a maximum of three, being fitted towards the pressure plate end of the clutch. On GSX-R1000 models all plain plates supplied as new parts will be 2.3 mm thick. Note however that single 2.0 mm and 2.6 mm plates may have been fitted with the 2.3 mm plates from new.*

**16** Inspect the clutch assembly for burrs and indentations on the tabs of the friction plates and/or the slots in the housing with which they engage **(see illustration)**. Similarly check for wear between the inner tongues of the plain plates and the slots in the clutch centre **(see illustration)**. Wear of this nature will cause clutch drag and slow disengagement during gear changes, since the plates will snag when the pressure plate is lifted. With care, a small amount of wear can be corrected by dressing with a fine file, but if this is excessive the worn components should be renewed.

**17** Ensure the threads for the spring bolts in the clutch centre are in good condition.

**18** On all GSX-R600 models, GSX-R750K2 and GSX-R1000K2 models, inspect the anti-judder spring and the spring seat for signs of wear or distortion and renew if necessary.

**19** Check the pressure plate, thrust washer, release bearing, clutch lifter and right-hand pushrod for signs of roughness, wear or damage, and renew any parts necessary as necessary **(see illustration 15.5b)**. Check that the pushrod is straight by rolling it on a flat surface. **Note:** *The left-hand clutch pushrod can be removed for inspection after the front sprocket cover has been removed (see Chapter 6). The pushrod/input shaft oil seal is retained by a lip in the crankcase and can only be renewed when the lower crankcase is removed.*

**20** Inspect the bearing surfaces of the clutch housing and the input shaft sleeve for wear **(see illustration)**. Check the cage and the rollers in the needle bearing for damage or roughness (see *Tools and Workshop Tips (Section 5)* in the Reference Section).

**21** The clutch housing incorporates a cush-drive mechanism; check that the springs are not loose or broken and that there is no backlash between the housing and the primary driven gear, otherwise renew the housing **(see illustration)**.

**22** Check the teeth of the primary driven gear on the back of the clutch housing and the corresponding teeth of the primary drive gear on the crankshaft **(see illustration)**. Renew the clutch housing if any teeth are worn or chipped. The primary drive gear is an integral part of the crankshaft; if the gear is damaged take the crankshaft to a Suzuki dealer or specialist engineer for assessment (see Section 30 for removal of the crankshaft).

**23** Measure the free length of each clutch spring **(see illustration)**. If any spring is shorter than the specified service limit, the clutch springs must be renewed as a set.

### Installation

**24** Remove all traces of old gasket from the crankcase and clutch cover surfaces.

**25** Slide the inner thrust washer, with its flat surface facing out, onto the transmission input shaft **(see illustration 15.12)**.

**15.20 Inspect the input shaft sleeve and needle bearing**

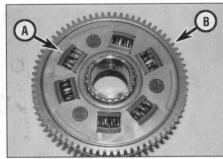

**15.21 Check the cush-drive springs (A) and primary driven gear teeth (B)**

**15.22 Inspect the teeth on the crankshaft primary drive gear**

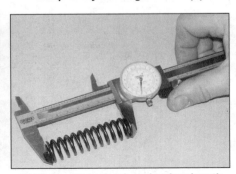

**15.23 Measure clutch spring free length**

**15.27  Ensure the oil pump driven gear (arrowed) is engaged**

**15.29a  Tighten the clutch nut . . .**

**15.29b  . . . then stake it to the input shaft**

26  Fit the oil pump drive gear onto the back of the clutch housing, making sure the shouldered inner section faces the housing and the flat side faces the engine **(see illustration 15.13)**.

27  Lubricate the needle roller bearing and sleeve with clean engine oil. Slide the clutch housing onto the input shaft, making sure the primary drive gears and the oil pump drive gears engage. Hold the housing in position and slide the sleeve and needle roller bearing into the middle of the housing. Rock the clutch housing back and forth to ensure the oil pump drive gears are correctly engaged **(see illustration)**.

28  Install the outer thrust washer and the clutch centre **(see illustrations 15.10b and 15.10a)**.

29  Install the plain washer and the dished washer with its raised inner edge facing out. Install the clutch nut with the shoulder facing out. Using the method employed on removal to lock the input shaft, tighten the nut to the torque setting specified at the beginning of this Chapter **(see illustration)**. Stake the nut to secure it on the shaft using a punch **(see illustration)**.

30  Coat each clutch plate with clean engine, then build up the plates in the clutch housing, starting with a friction plate, then a plain plate and alternating friction and plain plates until all are installed **(see illustrations)**. Fit the plates in the order described below, according to model:

**GSX-R600:** There are seven friction plates with 48 friction faces, one with 40 friction faces and one with dampers on its tabs, one to three 2.3 mm plain plates with the remaining plain plates being 2.6 mm. Fit the spring seat and anti-judder spring; the anti-judder spring must be fitted the correct way round, with its outer edge raised off the spring seat. Fit the friction plate with the dampers on its tabs over the anti-judder spring and its seat. Now alternate plain and friction plates to build up the clutch, placing any thinner (2.3 mm) plain plates at the end of the pack. Finish with the friction plate which has 40 friction faces, and locate its tabs in the shallow slots in the housing.

**GSX-R750Y:** There are two friction plates with a green marking and eight with a purple marking, and two 1.6 mm plain plates and seven 2.0 mm plain plates. Start with a green friction plate, then a 2.0 mm plain plate, then alternate purple friction plates and 2.0 mm plain plates until the last two plain plates are of the 1.6 mm type and the last friction plate is the green marked plate.

**GSX-R750K1:** There are eight friction plates with a purple marking, one with a green marking and one with dampers fitted to its tabs, and one to three 1.6 mm plain plates with the rest being 2.0 mm thick. Start with the friction plate with the dampers on its tabs, then fit a 2.0 mm plain plate, then alternate purple friction plates and 2.0 mm plain plates until the last plain plates are of the 1.6 mm type and the last friction plate is the one with green marking. Note that the tabs of this last friction plate must fit into the shallow slots in the clutch housing.

**GSX-R750K2:** There are eight friction plates with a purple marking, one with a green marking, and one with dampers fitted to its tabs, and one to three 1.6 mm plain plates with the rest being 2.0 mm thick. Fit the spring seat and anti-judder spring; the anti-judder spring must be fitted the correct way round, with its outer edge raised off the spring seat. Fit the friction plate with the dampers on its tabs over the anti-judder spring and its seat. Fit a 2.0 mm plain plate, then alternate purple friction plates and 2.0 mm plain plates until the last plain plates are of the 1.6 mm type and the last friction plate is the one with green marking. Note that the tabs of this last friction plate must fit into the shallow slots in the clutch housing.

**GSX-R1000K1:** There are eight friction plates with a green marking and two with a brown marking. There are nine plain plates in total, either all 2.3 mm thick, or seven 2.3 mm, one 2.0 mm and one 2.6 mm (see Note in Step 15). Start with a brown friction plate, then a 2.3 mm plain plate, then alternate green friction plates and 2.3 mm plain plates until, where applicable, the last plain plates are the 2.0 mm and 2.6 mm types and the last friction plate is a brown marked plate. Fit the tabs of this last friction plate into the shallow slots of the clutch housing.

**GSX-R1000K2:** There are eight friction plates with a green marking and two with a brown marking. There are nine plain plates in total, either all 2.3 mm thick, or seven 2.3 mm, one 2.0 mm and one 2.6 mm (see Note in Step 15). Fit the spring seat and anti-judder spring; the anti-judder spring must be fitted the correct

**2**

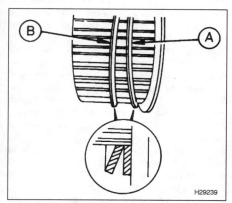

**15.30a  Correct fitting of spring seat (A) and anti-judder spring (B)**

H29239

**15.30b  Build up the clutch, starting with a friction plate . . .**

**15.30c  . . . and then a plain plate and so on**

**15.32 Install the cover dowels (arrowed) and the gasket**

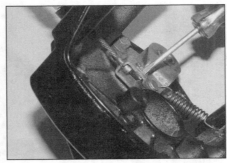

**16.4a Bend the tab to release the cable end . . .**

**31** Install the right-hand pushrod, the clutch lifter, release bearing and thrust washer **(see illustrations 15.5c and 15.5b)**. Fit the pressure plate and install the springs, spring cups and bolts, then tighten the bolts evenly in a criss-cross pattern to the specified torque setting.

**32** If removed, install the clutch cover dowels. Apply a smear of suitable, non-permanent sealant across the crankcase joints then fit the new cover gasket, making sure it locates correctly onto the dowels, and install the cover **(see illustration)**. Tighten the cover bolts securely, ensuring new sealing washers are installed on the two front bolts and the guides are installed on the upper and lower cover bolts **(see illustration 15.3)**. Secure the oil pressure switch wiring and the fuel tank water drain hose with the guides.

**33** Replenish the engine/transmission oil and check the level (see *Daily (pre-ride) checks*)

**34** Check the clutch release mechanism adjustment (see Chapter 1).

**35** Install the fairing side panels (see Chapter 8).

---

way round, with its outer edge raised off the spring seat. Fit one of the brown marked friction plates over the anti-judder spring and seat. Fit a 2.3 mm plain plate, then alternate green friction plates and 2.3 mm plain plates

until, where applicable, the last plain plates are the 2.0 mm and 2.6 mm types and the last friction plate is a brown marked plate. Fit the tabs of this last friction plate into the shallow slots of the clutch housing.

**16.4b . . . then unscrew the adjuster from the sprocket cover**

**16.5a With the slots in the adjuster and the bracket aligned, pull the outer cable out of the adjuster . . .**

## 16 Clutch cable – removal and installation

### Removal

**1** Remove the fairing left-hand side panel (see Chapter 8) and displace the coolant reservoir (see Chapter 3).

**2** Remove the front sprocket cover (see Chapter 6).

**3** Turn the handlebar lever adjuster fully in so there is no tension in the cable (see Chapter 1).

**4** Bend out the tab in the cable retainer on the end of the clutch release mechanism arm, then slip the cable end out of the retainer, noting how it fits **(see illustration)**. Loosen the cable adjuster locknut on the top of the sprocket cover, then unscrew the adjuster and withdraw the cable from the cover **(see illustration)**.

**5** Align the slot in the cable adjuster at the lever end with the slot in the lever bracket, then pull the outer cable end from the socket in the adjuster and release the inner cable from the lever **(see illustrations)**. Release the cable from the guide on the left-hand side of the steering head, then remove the cable from the machine, noting its routing **(see illustration)**.

**6** Inspect the clutch release mechanism in the front sprocket cover **(see illustration)**. Check the mechanism for smooth operation and any signs of wear or damage. If required, unscrew the two bolts securing the mechanism to the cover, then disconnect the return spring and remove the mechanism for cleaning and re-greasing **(see illustration)**.

**7** If required, withdraw the left-hand clutch pushrod. Clean the pushrod and lubricate it with a smear of grease before installing it **(see illustration 5.20)**.

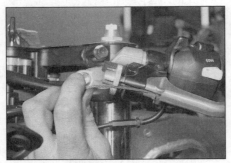

**16.5b . . . the inner cable out of the bracket . . .**

**16.5c . . . and the cable end out of the lever**

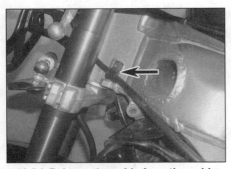

**16.5d Release the cable from the guide (arrowed)**

**16.6a Inspect the clutch release mechanism**

## Installation

**8** Installation is the reverse of removal, noting the following:
● Ensure the cable is correctly secured by the tab in the cable retainer (see Step 4).
● Ensure the cable is correctly routed.
● Check the clutch release mechanism adjustment and cable adjustment (see Chapter 1).

## 17 Gearchange mechanism –
removal, inspection and installation

**Note:** *This procedure can be carried out with the engine in the frame. If the engine has been removed, ignore the steps which do not apply.*

### Removal

**1** Remove the clutch (see Section 15). Make sure the transmission is in neutral and remove the front sprocket cover (see Chapter 6).
**2** Remove the circlip from the left-hand end of the gearchange shaft and slide off the washer **(see illustration)**.
**3** Working on the right-hand side of the engine, note how the gearchange shaft return spring ends fit on each side of the locating pin in the crankcase, and how the selector arm

**16.6b Clutch release mechanism is secured by two bolts**

pawls engage with the pins on the gearchange cam **(see illustration)**. Withdraw the gearchange shaft from the crankcase, noting the thrust washer on the shaft **(see illustration)**.
**4** Note how the stopper arm roller locates in the neutral detent on the gearchange cam **(see illustration)**. Undo the stopper arm pivot bolt and remove the bolt, stopper arm, washer and return spring in that order **(see illustration)**.
**5** If required, unscrew the selector drum centre bolt and remove the gearchange cam. *Note the position of the cam as the selector*

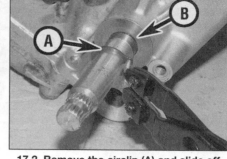

**17.2 Remove the circlip (A) and slide off the washer (B)**

*drum is likely to rotate when the centre bolt is undone.* Remove the locating pin from the end of the selector drum and store it with the cam for safekeeping (see Section 25).
**6** If required, undo the bolts securing the gear position sensor on the lower left-hand side of the crankcase and withdraw the sensor **(see illustration)**. Release the wiring from the guide on the water pump mounting bolt and disconnect it at the connector. Discard the sensor O-ring as a new one must be fitted on reassembly. Withdraw the sensor plungers and their springs from the end of the selector drum for safekeeping **(see illustration)**.

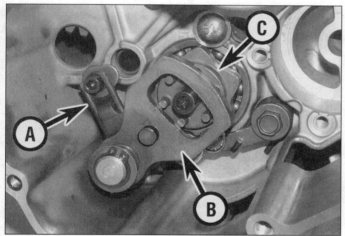

**17.3a Note the arrangement of the return spring (A), the selector arm (B) and the gearchange cam (C)**

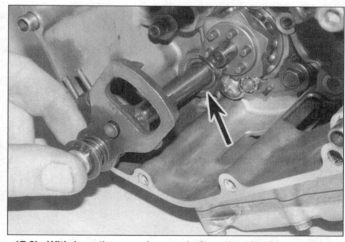

**17.3b Withdraw the gearchange shaft, noting the thrust washer**

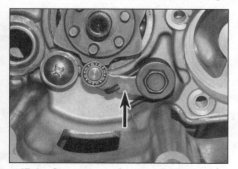

**17.4a Stopper arm (arrowed) locates in neutral detent**

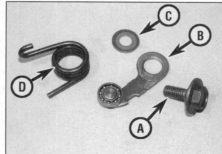

**17.4b Pivot bolt (A), stopper arm (B), washer (C) and return spring (D)**

**17.6a Undo the bolts to remove the gear position sensor**

2

17.6b Remove the plungers and springs for safekeeping

17.7 Gearchange shaft return spring is retained by a circlip (arrowed)

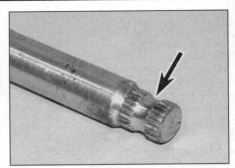

17.9 Check the splines (arrowed) on the end of the shaft

## Inspection

7 Inspect the stopper arm return spring and the gearchange shaft return spring. If they are fatigued, worn or damaged they must be renewed. The shaft return spring is retained by a circlip. To remove the circlip, slide it down the length of the shaft, do not stretch it over the shaft (see illustration). Note which way round the spring is fitted and how it locates on the tab on the selector arm. Ensure the circlip is correctly located in its groove.

8 The gearchange shaft return spring ends locate each side of the selector fork shaft retainer bolt. Check that the bolt is tight; if loose, remove it and apply a suitable non-permanent thread-locking compound, then tighten it to the torque specified at the beginning of this Chapter.

9 Check the gearchange shaft for straightness and damage to the splines (see illustration). If the shaft is bent you can attempt to straighten it, but if the splines are damaged the shaft must be renewed.

10 Check the condition of the shaft oil seal in the left-hand side of the crankcase. If it is damaged or deteriorated it must be renewed. Lever out the old seal and press or drive the new one in squarely, with its lip facing inward, using a seal driver or suitable socket (see illustrations).

11 Check that the gearchange shaft needle bearings rotate freely and have no sign of freeplay between them and the crankcase. To renew the bearings, draw them out of the crankcase with a bearing puller, noting that once removed they cannot be re-used. Drive the new bearings into place, making sure they enter squarely. Refer to Tools and Workshop Tips in the Reference Section for more information on bearings and how to remove and install them.

12 Check the selector arm pawls for wear (see illustration). The outer arm can be renewed separately by removing the circlip, washer and spring and drawing the arm off the shaft (see illustration). Note that the arm is fitted with the pawls facing inwards. The inner arm is integral with the gearchange shaft.

13 Inspect the lobes and the pins on the gearchange cam and check that the stopper arm roller turns freely. The stopper arm should be a light fit on the pivot bolt with no appreciable freeplay between them. Renew any worn or damaged parts as necessary.

14 If removed, inspect the contacts on the back of the gear position sensor for wear (see illustration). Check the plungers and springs for wear and damage and renew any parts as necessary.

## Installation

15 If removed, fit the pin in the end of the selector drum, then install the gearchange cam, locating the pin in the recess in the back of the cam. Clean the threads of the centre bolt, then apply a suitable non-permanent thread-locking compound. Install the bolt and tighten it to the torque setting specified at the beginning of this Chapter (see Section 25).

16 Ensure the gearchange cam is in the neutral position. Slide the stopper arm and its washer onto the pivot bolt, and apply a suitable non-permanent thread locking compound to the bolt threads. Fit the return

17.10a Lever out the old seal . . .

17.10b . . . and press the new one into place

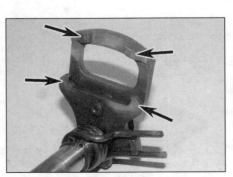

17.12a Check the selector arm pawls (arrowed) for wear

17.12b The outer arm is retained by a circlip (arrowed)

17.14 Check the gear position sensor contacts

17.16 Fit the return spring into the crankcase first

17.20a Fit the new O-ring . . .

17.20b . . . then install the gear position sensor

spring over the lug in the crankcase, then install the stopper arm and tighten the pivot bolt to the specified torque setting (see illustration). Ensure the spring locates against the cutout in the arm and the roller is in the neutral detent on the cam (see illustration 17.4a).

17 Check that the gearchange shaft return spring is properly positioned and that the circlip is in its groove, then slide the thrust washer onto the shaft. Lightly grease the inside of the gearchange shaft oil seal and slide the shaft into place from the right-hand side (see illustration 17.3b).

18 Locate the selector arm pawls onto the pins on the selector cam and the ends of the return spring onto each side of the selector fork shaft retaining bolt (see illustration 17.3a).

19 Install the washer and circlip onto the left-hand end of the gearchange shaft (see illustration 17.2).

20 If removed, install the gear position sensor springs and plungers. Smear the new O-ring with grease and fit it into the crankcase, then install the gear position sensor and secure it with the bolts (see illustrations). Feed the wiring underneath the water pump and secure it with the guide, then connect the wiring connector.

21 Install the remaining components in the reverse order of removal.

## 18 Oil pump – removal, inspection and installation

**Note:** This procedure can be carried out with the engine in the frame. If the engine has been removed, ignore the steps which do not apply. For details of how to check the oil pressure see Chapter 1.

### Removal

1 Remove the clutch (see Section 15).

2 Turn the oil pump driven gear so that its drive pin is horizontal; this will prevent the pin dropping out when the gear is removed (see illustration).

3 Remove the circlip from the pump drive shaft, then remove the gear, the pin and the washer (see illustrations).

4 Unscrew the three bolts securing the pump to the crankcase and withdraw the pump (see illustration). Note how the flat on the inner end of the pump drive shaft engages with the fork on the water pump shaft. Remove the gasket from the back of the pump body and discard it as a new one must be fitted on reassembly (see illustration).

### Inspection

5 Inspect the pump body for any obvious damage such as cracks or distortion, and check that the shaft rotates freely and without any side-to-side play or excessive endfloat.

6 If required, undo the screw on the back of the pump cover and remove the cover (see illustration). Note: The internal components of the pump are not available separately and Suzuki provides no specifications for checking the pump components for wear. However, if there is a problem with low oil pressure, examination of the internal components will confirm if the pump is damaged or not.

**2**

18.2 Position the oil pump driven gear with the pin (arrowed) horizontal

18.3a Remove the circlip and the gear . . .

18.3b . . . then remove the pin and the washer (arrowed)

18.4a Undo the pump mounting bolts

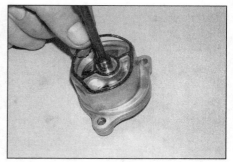

18.4b Discard the gasket on the back of the pump

18.6 Pump cover is retained by single screw

18.7 Oil pump components

1  Circlip
2  Driven gear
3  Gear drive pin
4  Washer
5  Inner rotor
6  Rotor drive pin
7  Drive shaft
8  Pump body
9  Cover screw
10 Outer rotor
11 Cover

**7** Lay the pump components on a clean work surface in the exact order of disassembly **(see illustration)**. Withdraw the drive shaft from the pump body and lift the inner rotor off the shaft, noting which way round it fits. Note how the pin locates through the shaft and in the notches in the inner rotor. **Note:** *Always install the pump rotors the same way round so that mated surfaces continue to run together.*

**8** Remove the outer rotor from the pump body. Clean all the components in solvent.

**9** Inspect the pump body and rotors for scoring and wear. If any damage, scoring or uneven or excessive wear is evident, renew the pump.

**10** Check the pump drive gear on the back of the clutch and the driven gear for wear or damage, and renew them as a set if necessary.

**11** If the pump is good, make sure all the components are clean, then lubricate them with clean engine oil and reassemble the pump in the reverse order of disassembly. Check that the shaft rotates freely before and after tightening the cover screw securely.

### Installation

**12** Fit a new gasket to the back of the pump body and smear it with general purpose grease, then install the pump, ensuring that the drive shaft engages with the water pump. Press the pump fully into the crankcase.

**13** Install the pump mounting bolts and tighten them to the specified torque setting.

**14** Position the drive shaft so that the hole for the drive pin is horizontal, then fit the washer, drive pin, gear and circlip **(see illustration 18.3b and 18.3a)**. Make sure the circlip is properly seated in its groove.

**15** Install the clutch (see Section 15).

## 19 Oil cooler –
removal and installation

**Note:** *This procedure can be carried out with the engine in the frame. If the engine has been removed, ignore the steps which do not apply.*

### GSX-R1000

#### Removal

**1** To remove the oil cooler refer to Section 5, Step 9.

**2** Check the oil cooler for damage and clear any dirt or debris that might obstruct air flow and inhibit cooling **(see illustration)**. If necessary, use water or low pressure compressed air directed through the fins from the back. If the fins are bent or distorted, straighten them carefully with a screwdriver. Where there is substantial damage to the oil cooler's surface area, renew the oil cooler.

**3** Remove the spacers from the mounting bushes **(see illustration)**. Inspect the bushes and fit new ones if they are damaged or deteriorated.

**4** Check for leakage at the pipe unions **(see illustration)**. If necessary, undo the union bolts and detach the union, then fit new O-rings on reassembly **(see illustration)**.

#### Installation

**5** Installation is the reverse of removal.

### GSX-R600 and GSX-R750

#### Removal

**6** Remove the fairing side panels (see Chapter 8). Drain the engine oil and the coolant (see Chapter 1).

**7** To gain access to the cooler, loosen the

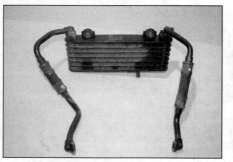

19.2 Clean the oil cooler assembly and check for damage

19.3 Remove the spacers from the mounting bushes

19.4a Check the unions for leaks

19.4b An O-ring (arrowed) is fitted inside each union

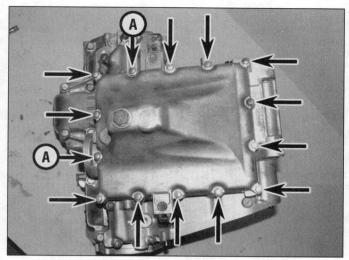
20.3 Sump bolts (arrowed) – note the bolts with sealing washers (A)

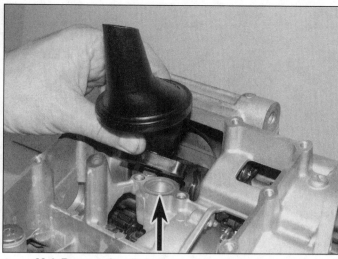
20.4 Remove the oil strainer and the O-ring (arrowed)

clips securing the coolant hose between the union on the lower, left-hand side of the radiator and the water pump, and detach the hose.

8 Loosen the clips securing the coolant hoses to the unions on the oil cooler and detach the hoses.

9 Unscrew the cooler mounting bolts and remove the cooler. Discard the O-ring as a new one must be fitted on reassembly.

## Installation

10 Installation is the reverse of removal, noting the following:

● Smear the new O-ring with general purpose grease and make sure it seats in the groove in the cooler body.

● Tighten the mounting bolts to the specified torque setting.

● Replenish the engine oil and refill the cooling system (see Chapter 1 and *Daily (pre-ride) checks*).

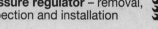
## 20 Oil sump, strainer and pressure regulator – removal, inspection and installation

**Note:** *This procedure can be carried out with*

*the engine in the frame. If the engine has been removed, ignore the steps which do not apply.*

### Removal

1 Remove the exhaust system (see Chapter 4).
2 Drain the engine oil (see Chapter 1).
3 Unscrew the sump bolts, loosening them evenly in a criss-cross pattern to prevent distortion, and remove the sump noting the position of the bolts with the sealing washers **(see illustration)**. Discard the gasket and washers as new ones must be fitted on reassembly. If they are loose, remove the locating dowels from either the sump or the crankcase for safekeeping. Note the position of the fairing brackets and remove them if required.
4 Undo the bolts securing the oil strainer and remove the strainer **(see illustration)**. Discard the O-ring as a new one must be fitted.
5 If required, pull the pressure regulator out of its socket in the crankcase **(see illustration)**. **Note:** *Suzuki do not list a replacement O-ring for the pressure regulator so do not remove it unless it is obviously damaged. Check with your Suzuki dealer as to the availability of a suitable replacement O-ring.*
6 Remove all traces of old gasket from the

sump and crankcase mating surfaces with a suitable solvent. If a scraper is used, take care not to scratch or gouge the soft aluminium.

### Inspection

7 Clean the sump thoroughly.
8 Wash the oil strainer with a suitable solvent and remove any debris caught in the mesh, using compressed air if available. Inspect the strainer for any signs of wear or damage and renew it if necessary.
9 Clean the pressure regulator. Push the plunger into the regulator body and check that it moves freely against the spring pressure **(see illustration)**.

### Installation

10 Smear the pressure regulator O-ring with general purpose grease and press the regulator firmly into its recess in the sump.
11 Smear the new oil strainer O-ring with grease and install it in the recess in the sump **(see illustration)**. Install the strainer, making sure it is fitted the correct way round, and tighten the retaining bolts to the specified torque setting.
12 If removed, fit the locating dowels into the crankcase (if the engine has been removed

20.5 Pressure regulator is a press fit in crankcase

20.9 Checking the operation of the pressure regulator

20.11 Fit a new O-ring for the oil strainer

**2**

20.12 Align the new gasket with the bolt holes . . .

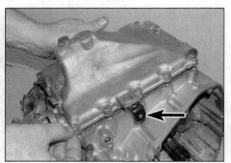

20.13 . . . and install the sump. Note the fairing bracket (arrowed)

and is positioned upside down on the work surface) or into the sump (if the engine is in the frame). Lay a new gasket onto the crankcase or sump, making sure the holes in the gasket align correctly with the bolt holes, and that the gasket locates correctly onto the dowels **(see illustration)**.

**13** Position the sump on the crankcase **(see illustration)**. Install the bolts, using new sealing washers as applicable. Tighten the bolts evenly in a criss-cross pattern to the specified torque setting.

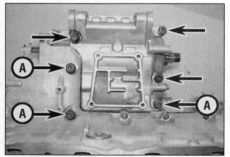

21.5 Unscrew the 8 mm bolts in the top of the crankcase – note the copper washers fitted (A)

**14** If removed, fit the fairing brackets and tighten their retaining bolts securely.
**15** Install the exhaust system (see Chapter 4), but do not fit the fairing side panels.
**16** Replenish the engine with oil and check the level (see Chapter 1 and *Daily (pre-ride) checks*). Start the engine and check that there are no leaks around the sump, then install the fairing side panels (see Chapter 8).

## 21 Crankcases – separation and reassembly

### Separation

**1** To gain access to the transmission shafts and selector drum and forks, the lower crankcase must be separated from the middle crankcase. To gain access to the crankshaft, connecting rods and bearings, the lower crankcase must first be separated from the middle crankcase and the transmission shafts removed, then the middle crankcase must be separated from the upper crankcase.
**2** To enable the crankcases to be separated, the engine must be removed from the frame (see Section 5).

### Lower crankcase

**3** Before the lower crankcase can be separated from the middle crankcase, remove the oil sump, the oil strainer and pressure regulator (see Section 20) and the clutch (see Section 15). If the selector drum and forks are being removed, also remove the gearchange mechanism (see Section 17). The selector drum and forks can be removed after separation of the lower crankcase (see Section 25).
**4** If the lower crankcase is being separated as part of a complete engine overhaul, also remove the following components:
● Oil pump (Section 18).
● Water pump (Chapter 3).
● Oil cooler – GSX-R600 and GSX-R750 models (Section 19).
With all the relevant components removed, proceed as follows.
**5** Unscrew the 8 mm bolts in the top of the crankcase, noting the positions of the bolts with copper washers **(see illustration)**. **Note:** *As each bolt is removed, store it in its relative position in a cardboard template of the crankcases. This will ensure all bolts are installed in the correct location on reassembly. Also note the washers fitted with certain bolts, and keep them with their bolts as different washers are used in different places.*
**6** Turn the engine upside down. Support it on wood blocks if required. Unscrew the 6 mm lower crankcase bolts, noting the positions of the bolts with sealing washers **(see illustrations)**.
**7** Carefully lift the lower crankcase off the middle crankcase **(see illustration)**. If it is stuck, do not try to lever it off with a screwdriver. Tap around the joint with a soft-faced mallet to dislodge it. **Note:** *If the halves do not separate easily, make sure all fasteners have been removed.*
**8** The lower crankcase will come away

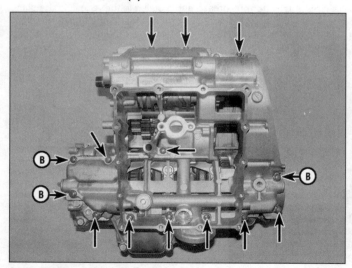

21.6a Unscrew the bolts in the lower crankcase – note the sealing washers (B) on GSX-R600 and 750 models . . .

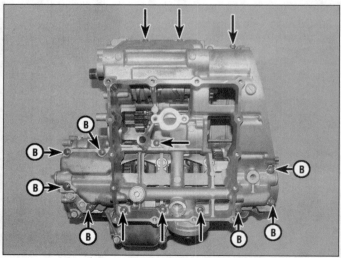

21.6b . . . and sealing washers (B) on GSX-R1000 models

21.7 Lift the lower crankcase off the middle crankcase . . .

21.8 . . . leaving the transmission shafts in the middle crankcase

21.9a Remove the dowels, if loose . . .

21.9b . . . and the oil passage O-rings

21.12 Unscrew the bolts in the top of the crankcase – note the sealing washer (A)

21.13 Unscrew the bolts on the front edge of the crankcase (GSX-R1000 shown)

leaving the transmission shafts in the middle crankcase (see illustration).

9 Note the location of the dowels and remove them for safekeeping if they are loose (see illustration). Also remove the oil passage O-rings from the middle crankcase and discard them as new ones must be fitted on reassembly (see illustration).

**Middle crankcase**

10 Before the middle crankcase can be separated from the upper crankcase, first remove the following:
- Cylinder head (Section 10).
- Cam chain, tensioner blade and guides (Section 13).
- Starter clutch and gears (Section 14).
- Crankshaft position sensor (Chapter 5)
- Alternator and starter motor (Chapter 9).

11 Remove the lower crankcase (Steps 3 to 9) and the transmission shafts (see Section 23).

12 With the engine the right way up, unscrew the 6 mm bolts in the top of the crankcase (see illustration). Note the sealing washer on the right-hand bolt. **Note:** *As each bolt is removed, store it in its relative position in a cardboard template of the crankcases. This will ensure all bolts are installed in the correct location on reassembly. Also note the washers fitted with certain bolts, and keep them with their bolts as different washers are used in different places.*

13 Turn the engine upside down. Support it on wood blocks if required. On GSX-R600 and GSX-R750 models, unscrew the 6 mm bolts along the front edge of the crankcase and remove the bolts, noting the hose guide. On GSX-R1000 engines, unscrew the 8 mm bolts along the front edge of the crankcase and remove the bolts (see illustration).

14 Now unscrew the 9 mm crankshaft journal bolts a little at a time in the **reverse** order of

the tightening sequence marked in the crankcase until they are all finger-tight, then remove the bolts (see illustration).

15 Carefully lift the middle crankcase off the upper crankcase, using a soft-faced mallet to tap around the joint to initially separate the halves if necessary (see illustration). **Note:** *If the halves do not separate easily, make sure all fasteners have been removed.*

16 The middle crankcase will come away leaving the crankshaft in the upper crankcase (see illustration). Take care not to dislodge the lower main bearing shells which should remain in their seats in the middle crankcase (see illustration). Remove the shells if they are loose, but keep them in order. On GSX-R1000 models, the balancer shaft will remain in the upper crankcase and the lower balancer shaft shells should remain in their seats in the middle crankcase; note the position of the balancer shaft seal (see Section 31).

**2**

21.14 Unscrew the crankshaft journal bolts

21.15 Lift the middle crankcase off the upper crankcase . . .

21.16a . . . leaving the crankshaft in the upper crankcase. Note the dowels (arrowed)

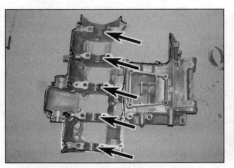

**21.16b The lower main bearing shells should remain in the middle crankcase**

**21.17 Remove the oil passage O-ring**

17 Note the location of the dowels and remove them for safekeeping if they are loose **(see illustration 21.16a)**. Also remove the oil passage O-ring from the upper crankcase and discard it as a new one must be fitted on reassembly **(see illustration)**.

18 Refer to Sections 27 and 30 for the removal and installation of the components housed in the upper crankcase.

### Reassembly

#### Middle crankcase

19 Remove all traces of old sealant from the middle and upper crankcase mating surfaces with a suitable solvent and clean the threads of all the crankcase bolts.

20 Ensure that all components and their bearings are in place in the upper crankcase. Check that the crankshaft thrust bearings are correctly located in the upper crankcase (see Section 30). Lubricate the crankshaft bearings with clean engine oil.

21 If removed, fit the locating dowels into the upper crankcase and install a new oil passage O-ring **(see illustrations 21.16a and 21.17)**.

22 Check that the lower main bearing shells are correctly located in the middle crankcase. On GSX-R1000 models, ensure that the lower balancer shaft shells are correctly located in the middle crankcase and that the balancer shaft seal is installed in the upper crankcase (see Section 31).

23 Apply a thin coating of suitable sealant to the mating surface of the middle crankcase **(see illustrations)**.

*Caution: Do not apply an excessive amount of sealant as it will ooze out when the case halves are assembled and may obstruct oil passages. Do not apply the sealant on or too close to any of the bearing shells or surfaces.*

24 Carefully fit the middle crankcase onto the upper crankcase, making sure the dowels all locate correctly into the middle crankcase.

25 Check that the middle crankcase is correctly seated. **Note:** *The crankcases should fit together without being forced. If the casings are not correctly seated, remove the middle crankcase and investigate the problem. Do not attempt to pull the casings*

*together using the crankcase bolts as they will crack and be ruined.*

26 Install the ten 9 mm crankshaft journal bolts in their original locations **(see illustration 21.14)**. Secure all the bolts finger-tight, then tighten them a little at a time in the numerical sequence marked in the crankcase, to the initial torque setting specified at the beginning of this Chapter.

27 On GSX-R600 and GSX-R1000 models, now tighten each bolt in sequence and in one continuous movement to the final torque setting specified using a torque angle gauge. If tightening is paused between the initial and final settings, slacken the bolt to below the initial setting and repeat the procedure. **Note:** *If a torque angle gauge is not available, paint a small reference mark on the top of each bolt after tightening them to the initial torque setting. Then, using a ring spanner so that you can see the mark, tighten the bolts to the final setting.*

28 On GSX-R750 models, now tighten the bolts in sequence to the final torque setting specified.

29 On GSX-R600 and GSX-R750 models, install the six 6 mm bolts along the front edge of the crankcase, noting the hose guide. On GSX-R1000 engines, install the seven 8 mm bolts along the front edge of the crankcase **(see illustration 21.13)**. First tighten the bolts a little at a time in a criss-cross pattern to the initial torque setting specified, then tighten them to the final torque setting.

30 Turn the engine the right way up. Install the five 6 mm bolts in the top of the crankcase, not forgetting the sealing washer with the right-hand front bolt **(see illustration 21.12)**. First tighten the bolts a little at a time in a criss-cross pattern to the initial torque setting specified, then tighten them to the final torque setting.

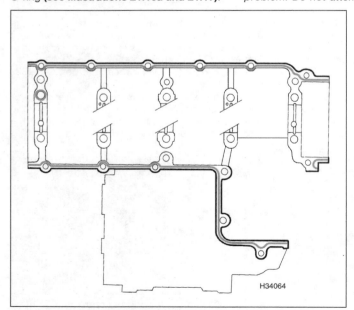

**21.23a Apply sealant to the shaded areas (GSX-R600 and 750 models)**

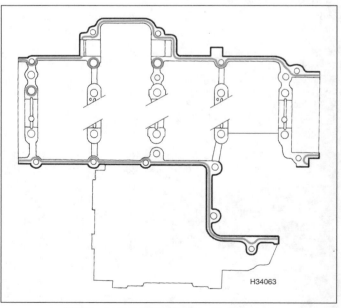

**21.23b Apply sealant to the shaded areas (GSX-R1000 models)**

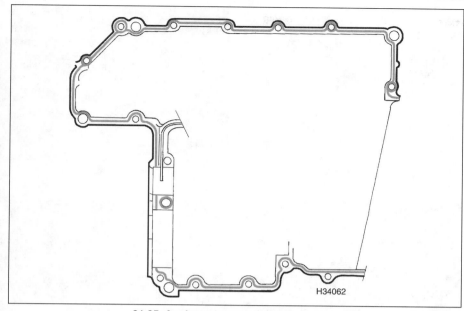

21.35 Apply sealant to the shaded areas

**31** With all the crankcase bolts tightened, check that the crankshaft rotates smoothly and easily. If there are any signs of undue stiffness, tight or rough spots, or any other problem, the fault must be rectified before proceeding further.

### Lower crankcase

**32** Remove all traces of old sealant from the lower and middle crankcase mating surfaces with a suitable solvent and clean the threads of all the crankcase bolts.

**33** Ensure that all components and their bearings are in place in the middle and lower crankcases. Check that the transmission bearing locating pins and half-ring retainers are correctly located and ensure the new oil seals are installed on the transmission input and output shafts (see Section 23). Lubricate the transmission shafts and the gearchange selector drum and forks, particularly around the bearings, with clean engine oil. Make sure that the selector drum is in the neutral position (see illustration 17.4a).

**34** If removed, fit the locating dowels into the middle crankcase and install new O-rings into the oil passage holes (see illustrations 21.9a and 21.9b).

**35** Apply a thin coating of suitable sealant to the mating surface of the lower crankcase (see illustration).
*Caution: Do not apply an excessive amount of sealant as it will ooze out when the case halves are assembled and may obstruct oil passages. Do not apply the sealant on or too close to any of the bearing shells or surfaces.*

**36** Carefully fit the lower crankcase onto the middle crankcase, making sure selector forks locate correctly into their grooves in the transmission gears. Make sure the dowels all locate correctly into the lower crankcase.

**37** Check that the lower crankcase is correctly seated. **Note:** *The crankcases should fit together without being forced. If the casings are not correctly seated, remove the lower crankcase and investigate the problem. Do not attempt to pull the casings together using the crankcase bolts as they will crack and be ruined.*

**38** Check that the transmission shafts rotate freely and independently in neutral.

**39** Install the fourteen 6 mm lower crankcase bolts in their original locations with new sealing washers as applicable **(see illustration 21.6a or 21.6b).** Tighten the bolts a little at a time in a criss-cross pattern to the initial torque setting specified.

**40** Turn the engine the right way up and install the six upper crankcase bolts in their original locations with new copper washers as applicable **(see illustration 21.5).** First tighten the bolts a little at a time in a criss-cross pattern to the initial torque setting specified, then tighten them to the final torque setting.

**41** Now tighten the lower crankcase bolts to the final torque setting specified.

**42** With all crankcase bolts tightened, check that the crankshaft and transmission shafts rotate smoothly and easily. Rotate the selector drum by hand and select each gear in turn whilst rotating the input shaft. Check that all gears can be selected and that the shafts rotate freely in every gear. If there are any signs of undue stiffness, tight or rough spots, or of any other problem, the fault must be rectified before proceeding further.

**43** Install the remaining components in the reverse order of removal.

## 22 Crankcases and cylinder bores – inspection and servicing

### Crankcases

**1** After the crankcases have been separated, remove the gear selector drum and forks (see Section 25) and the crankshaft and connecting rod assemblies (see Sections 27 and 30).

**2** Unscrew the oil pressure switch (see Chapter 9). Undo the bolts securing the coolant union to the back of the cylinder block and remove the union; discard the O-ring as a new one must be fitted on reassembly **(see illustrations).** Undo the bolts securing the crankcase breather cover to the middle crankcase and remove the cover; discard the gasket as a new one must be fitted **(see illustration).**

**2**

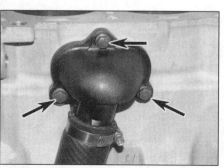

22.2a Undo the bolts to remove the coolant union . . .

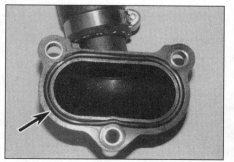

22.2b . . . and fit a new O-ring on reassembly

22.2c Remove the crankcase breather and discard the gasket (arrowed)

22.3a Remove the piston oil jets . . .

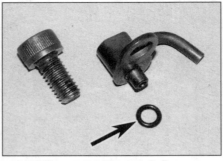

22.3b . . . and fit a new O-ring on reassembly

22.3c Unscrew the transmission oil jet

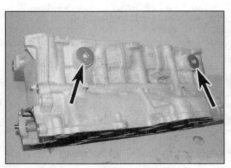

22.4a Unscrew the water jacket plugs . . .

22.4b . . . and the internal . . .

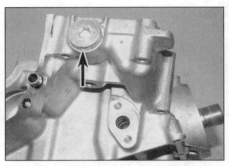

22.4c . . . and external oil gallery plugs

**3** Undo the bolts securing the piston oil jets in the upper crankcase and remove the jets, noting how they fit. Remove the O-rings and discard them as new ones must be fitted **(see illustrations)**. Unscrew the transmission oil jet **(see illustration)**.

**4** Unscrew the water jacket plugs from the front of the cylinder block and the oil galley plugs from the lower crankcase **(see illustrations)**. Discard the sealing washers as new ones must be fitted.

**5** The crankcases should be cleaned thoroughly with clean solvent and dried with compressed air. All oil passages, oil jets and coolant passages should be blown out with compressed air.

**6** Remove all traces of old sealant from the mating surfaces with a suitable solvent. Minor damage to the surfaces can be cleaned up with a fine file or sharpening stone.

*Caution: Be very careful not to nick or*

22.15 Check the head gasket mating surface with a straight-edge as shown

*gouge the crankcase mating surfaces or oil leaks will result. Check the crankcases very carefully for cracks and other damage.*

**7** Small cracks or holes in aluminium castings may be repaired with an epoxy resin adhesive as a temporary measure. Permanent repairs can only be effected by argon-arc welding, and only a specialist in this process is in a position to advise on the economy or practical aspect of such a repair. If any damage is found that can't be repaired, renew the crankcase halves as a set.

**8** Damaged threads can be economically reclaimed by using a diamond section wire insert, of the Heli-Coil type, which is easily fitted after drilling and re-tapping the affected thread.

**9** Sheared studs or screws can usually be removed with stud extractors, which consist of a tapered, left-thread screw of very hard steel. These are inserted into a pre-drilled hole in the stud, and usually succeed in dislodging the most stubborn stud or screw.

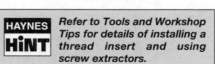

**HAYNES HiNT** *Refer to Tools and Workshop Tips for details of installing a thread insert and using screw extractors.*

**10** Always clean the crankcases thoroughly after any repair work to ensure no dirt or metal swarf is trapped inside when the engine is rebuilt.

**11** Fit a new O-ring onto the base of each piston oil jet and smear it with clean engine oil **(see illustration 22.3b)**. Push each jet into its

bore in the upper crankcase, making sure the oil nozzle points up into the cylinder. Apply a suitable non-permanent thread locking compound to the jet bolts and tighten them to the specified torque setting. Install the transmission oil jet **(see illustration 22.3c)**.

**12** Fit new sealing washers to the water jacket and oil gallery plugs and install the plugs, then tighten them to the specified torque settings.

**13** Fit a new crankcase breather cover gasket onto the middle crankcase and install the cover, then tighten the cover bolts to the specified torque setting **(see illustration 22.2c)**. Fit a new O-ring into the groove in the cylinder block coolant union. Lubricate the O-ring with coolant, then install the union and tighten the union bolts to the specified torque setting **(see illustration 22.2b)**.

**14** Install the remaining components in the reverse order of removal.

*Cylinder bores*

**15** Using a precision straight-edge and a feeler gauge, check the head gasket mating surface for warpage **(see illustration)**. Refer to *Tools and Workshop Tips* in the Reference section for details of how to use the straight-edge. If the block is warped beyond the limit specified at the beginning of this Chapter, consult your Suzuki dealer or take it to a specialist repair shop for rectification.

**16** Check the cylinder walls carefully for scratches and score marks. The cylinders are electro-plated with Suzuki's SCEM (Suzuki Composite Electrochemical Material), a highly wear resistant nickel-phosphorus-silicon-

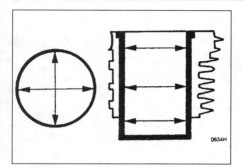

**22.17 Measure the cylinder bore in the directions shown with a telescoping gauge**

carbide coating which should last the life of the engine. If the cylinders are badly scratched, scuffed or scored, the crankcase set must be renewed. The cylinder bores should not be honed.

**17** The standard bore diameter range is given in the specifications. Suzuki do not specify a service limit for bore wear, but you can use telescoping gauges and a micrometer (see *Tools and Workshop Tips*) to check the dimensions of each cylinder to assess the amount of wear, taper and ovality. Measure near the top (but below the level of the top piston ring at TDC), centre and bottom (but above the level of the oil ring at BDC) of the bore, both parallel to and across the crankshaft axis **(see illustration)**. Compare the results to the standard bore diameter range in the specifications at the beginning of this Chapter.

**18** If the precision measuring tools are not

available, take the upper crankcase to a Suzuki dealer or specialist motorcycle repair shop for assessment.

## 23 Transmission shafts – removal and installation

**Note:** *To remove the transmission shafts the engine must be removed from the frame.*

### Removal

**1** Separate the lower crankcase from the middle crankcase (see Section 21).
**2** Lift the output shaft and input shaft out of the crankcase, noting their relative positions in the case and how they fit together **(see illustration)**. If they are stuck, use a soft-faced hammer and gently tap on the ends of the shafts to free them.
**3** Remove the input shaft left-hand oil seal **(see illustration)**. Remove the oil seal from the left-hand end of the output shaft, noting how it fits **(see illustration)**.
**4** Remove the bearing half-ring retainers and the bearing dowel pins from the middle crankcase, noting how they fit **(see illustrations)**. If they are not in their slots or holes in the crankcase, remove them from the bearings themselves on the shafts.
**5** If required, the shafts can be disassembled and inspected for wear or damage (see Section 24).

### Installation

**6** Install the bearing half-ring retainers into

**23.2 Note the relative position of the input (A) and output (B) transmission shafts**

their slots in the upper crankcase half, and install the bearing dowels into their holes.
**7** Lower the input shaft into position in the middle crankcase. Ensure the hole in the needle bearing engages correctly on the dowel, the ball bearing locating pin faces forward and locates in its recess, and the groove in the bearing engages correctly with the half-ring retainer **(see illustrations)**.
**8** Grease the lips of the new output shaft oil seal and fit the seal onto the left-hand end of the shaft. Lower the output shaft into position, making sure the hole in the needle bearing engages correctly on the dowel, the ball bearing locating pin faces back and locates in its recess, and the groove in the bearing engages correctly with the half-ring retainer.
**9** Fit the new input shaft oil seal against the left-hand end of the shaft.
**10** Make sure both transmission shafts are correctly seated and rotate freely.

**23.3a Remove the input shaft oil seal**

**23.3b Remove the output shaft oil seal**

**23.4a Remove the bearing half-ring retainers . . .**

**23.4b . . . and the dowel pins**

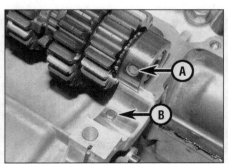

**23.7a Hole in bearing (A) fits on dowel (B)**

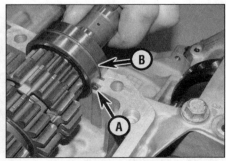

**23.7b Locating pin (A) fits into recess and groove (B) fits onto half-ring retainer**

2

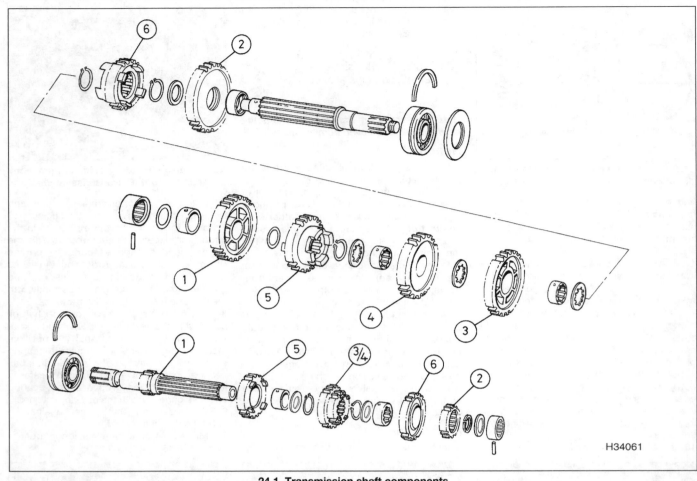

**24.1 Transmission shaft components**

*Numbers indicate gears*

**Caution: If any of the bearing locating pins, half-ring retainers or dowel pins are not properly installed, the crankcase halves will not seat correctly.**

**11** Position the gears in the neutral position and check the shafts are free to rotate independently (i.e. the input shaft can turn whilst the output shaft is held stationary) before proceeding further.

**12** Install the lower crankcase (see Section 21).

**24 Transmission shafts –** disassembly, inspection and reassembly

**Note:** *References to the right- and left-hand ends of the transmission shafts are made as though they are installed in the engine and the engine is the correct way up.*

**1** Remove the transmission shafts from the middle crankcase (see Section 23). Always disassemble the transmission shafts separately to avoid mixing up the components **(see illustration)**.

## Input shaft disassembly

 **HAYNES HiNT** *When disassembling the transmission shafts, place the parts on a long rod or thread a wire through them to keep them in order and facing the proper direction.*

**2** Remove the needle bearing and dished oil seal (where fitted) from the left-hand end of the shaft **(see illustration 24.22)**.

**3** Locate the circlip behind the 6th gear pinion. Use circlip pliers to spread the circlip and slide it toward the 3rd/4th gear pinion **(see illustration)**. Slide the 6th and 2nd gear pinions towards the 3rd/4th gear pinion to expose the snap-ring on the end of the shaft and remove the snap ring **(see illustrations)**.

**24.3a Slide the circlip towards the 3rd/4th gear pinion**

**24.3b Slide the gears back to expose the snap-ring (A) . . .**

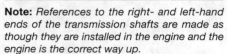

24.3c . . . and remove the snap-ring

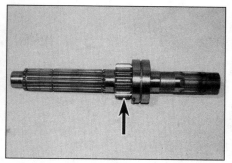

24.7 The 1st gear pinion is integral with the shaft

24.14 Protect the end of the shaft with a piece of soft metal (arrowed) when removing the bearing

**4** Slide the 2nd gear pinion and the 6th gear pinion and bush off the shaft (see illustrations 24.21a, 24.20c and b).

**5** Slide off the splined washer, then remove the circlip securing the combined 3rd/4th gear pinion and slide the pinion off the shaft (see illustrations 24.20a, 24.19b and 19a).

**6** Remove the circlip securing the 5th gear pinion, then slide the thrust washer, 5th gear pinion and its bush off the shaft (see illustrations 24.18d, c, b and a).

**7** The 1st gear pinion is integral with the shaft (see illustration).

### Input shaft inspection

**8** Wash all the components in clean solvent and dry them off.

**9** Check the gear teeth for cracking, chipping, pitting and other obvious wear or damage. Any pinion that is damaged must be renewed. Inspect the dogs and the dog holes in the pinions for cracks, chips, and excessive wear especially in the form of rounded edges. Make sure mating gears engage properly. Renew the paired gears as a set if necessary.

**10** Measure the selector fork groove width and the fork to groove clearance (see Section 25).

**11** Check for signs of scoring or bluing on the pinions, bushes and shaft. This could be caused by overheating due to inadequate lubrication. Check that all the oil holes and passages are clear. Renew any damaged pinions or bushes.

**12** Check that each pinion moves freely on the shaft or bush but without undue freeplay. Check that each bush moves freely on the shaft but without undue freeplay.

**13** The shaft is unlikely to sustain damage unless the engine has seized, placing an unusually high loading on the transmission, or the machine has covered a very high mileage. Check the surface of the shaft, especially where a pinion turns on it, and renew the shaft if it has scored or picked up, or if there is any wear.

**14** Refer to *Tools and Workshop Tips* in the *Reference* Section and check the bearings. The ball bearing should be a tight fit on the shaft. Renew the bearing if it is worn, loose or damaged; use a bearing puller to remove it and protect the end of the shaft with a piece

of soft metal (brass or aluminium) (see illustration). Install the new bearing using a press and a length of tubing which bears only on the bearing's inner race. Install the needle roller bearing on the shaft and check it for play or roughness. Renew the bearing if it is worn or damaged.

**15** Check the needle bearing oil seal and renew it if it is damaged or deteriorated.

**16** Check the washers and renew any that are bent or worn. Discard the circlips and the snap-ring as new ones must be fitted on reassembly.

### Input shaft reassembly

**17** During reassembly, apply clean engine oil to the mating surfaces of the shaft, pinions and bushes. When installing the circlips and snap-ring, do not expand their ends any further than is necessary. Install the stamped

circlips so that the chamfered side faces the pinion it secures (see *Correct fitting of a stamped circlip* illustration in *Tools and Workshop Tips* of the *Reference* Section).

**18** Slide the 5th gear bush all the way onto the shaft, then slide the 5th gear pinion onto the bush, with its dogs facing away from the integral 1st gear (see illustrations). Slide on the washer, then install the circlip, making sure it is properly seated in its groove (see illustrations).

**19** Slide the combined 3rd/4th gear pinion onto the shaft, so that the larger (4th gear) pinion faces the 5th gear pinion dogs (see illustration). Fit the circlip onto the shaft but do not locate it in its groove – slide it past the groove and as far towards the 3rd/4th gear pinion as possible (see illustration).

**20** Slide on the splined washer, then the 6th gear pinion splined bush; align the oil hole in

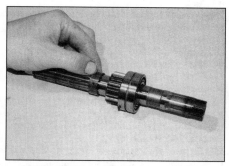

24.18a Slide on the 5th gear bush . . .

24.18b . . . the 5th gear pinion . . .

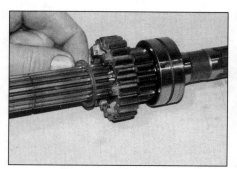

24.18c . . . and the washer . . .

24.18d . . . and secure them with the circlip

**2**

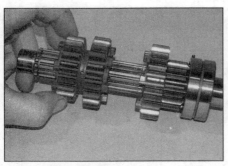

24.19a Slide on the 3rd /4th gear pinion

24.19b Slide the circlip past its groove (arrowed)

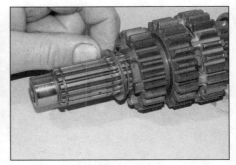

24.20a Slide on the splined washer . . .

24.20b . . . then align the hole in the splined bush (A) with the hole in the shaft (B) and fit the bush

24.20c Fit the 6th gear pinion onto the bush

24.21a Slide on the 2nd gear pinion and secure it with the snap-ring

the bush with the hole in the shaft **(see illustrations)**. Fit the 6th gear pinion onto the bush, with its dogs facing the dogs on the 3rd gear pinion **(see illustration)**.

**21** Slide the 2nd gear pinion onto the shaft **(see illustration)**. Secure the pinion with the snap-ring, making sure it is properly seated in its groove **(see illustration 24.3c)**. Now slide the 6th and 2nd gear pinions up to the snap ring to expose the groove for the 3rd/4th gear pinion circlip, then move the circlip along the shaft and fit it into the groove **(see illustration)**.

**22** Fit the dished oil seal (where fitted) and needle bearing onto the end of the shaft **(see illustration)**.

**23** Check that all components have been correctly installed **(see illustration)**.

### Output shaft disassembly

**24** Remove the needle bearing and the thrust washer from the right-hand end of the shaft **(see illustrations 24.39 and 24.38c)**.

**25** Slide the 1st gear pinion and its bush off the shaft, followed by the thrust washer and the 5th gear pinion **(see illustrations 24.38b and a, 24.37b and a)**.

**26** Remove the circlip securing the 4th gear pinion, then slide the splined washer, 4th gear pinion and its bush off the shaft **(see illustrations 24.36b and a, 24.35c and b)**.

**27** Slide off the splined washer, followed by the 3rd gear pinion and its bush **(see illustrations 24.35a, 24.34c and b)**.

**28** Remove the splined washer, then the circlip securing the 6th gear pinion, and slide the pinion off the shaft **(see illustrations 24.34a, 24.33b and a)**.

**29** Remove the circlip securing the 2nd gear pinion, then slide the thrust washer, the 2nd gear pinion and its bush off the shaft **(see illustrations 24.32d, c, b and a)**.

### Output shaft inspection

**30** Refer to Steps 8 to 16 above.

### Output shaft reassembly

**31** During reassembly, apply clean engine oil to the mating surfaces of the shaft, pinions and bushes. When installing the circlips, do not expand their ends any further than is necessary. Install the stamped circlips so that their chamfered side faces the pinion it secures (see *Correct fitting of a stamped circlip* illustration in *Tools and Workshop Tips* in the *Reference* Section).

**32** Slide the 2nd gear bush all the way onto the shaft, then slide the 2nd gear pinion (flat faces towards the bearing) onto the bush, followed by the thrust washer **(see illustrations)**. Secure them in place with the circlip, making sure it is properly seated in its groove **(see illustration)**.

24.21b Slide the circlip into its groove

24.22 Install the bearing

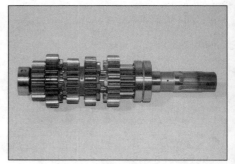

24.23 The completed input shaft should look like this

24.32a  Slide on the 2nd gear bush . . .

24.32b  . . . the 2nd gear pinion . . .

24.32c  . . . and the washer . . .

24.32d  . . . and secure them with the
circlip

24.33a  Slide on the 6th gear pinion . . .

24.33b  . . . and secure it with the circlip

**33** Slide the 6th gear pinion onto the shaft
with its selector fork groove facing away from
the 2nd gear pinion, and secure it in place
with the circlip, making sure it is properly
seated in its groove **(see illustrations)**.
**34** Slide on the splined washer and the 3rd

gear pinion bush; align the oil hole in the bush
with the hole in the shaft **(see illustration)**.
Install the 3rd gear pinion on the bush so that
its open side faces the 6th gear pinion **(see
illustrations)**.
**35** Slide on the splined washer and the 4th

gear pinion bush; align the oil hole in the bush
with the hole in the shaft **(see illustration)**.
Install the 4th gear pinion on the bush so that
its open side faces away from the 3rd gear
pinion **(see illustrations)**.
**36** Slide on the splined washer, then install

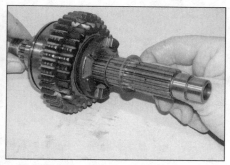

24.34a  Slide on the splined washer . . .

24.34b  . . . then align the hole in the
splined bush (A) with the hole in the
shaft (B) and fit the bush

24.34c  Fit the 3rd gear pinion onto the
bush

24.35a  Slide on the splined washer . . .

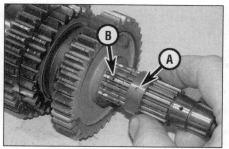

24.35b  . . . then align the hole in the
splined bush (A) with the hole in the
shaft (B) and fit the bush

24.35c  Fit the 4th gear pinion onto the
bush

**2**

24.36a Slide on the splined washer . . .

24.36b . . . and secure it with the circlip

24.37a Slide on the 5th gear pinion . . .

24.37b . . . and the thrust washer

24.38a Slide on the bush . . .

24.38b . . . the 1st gear pinion . . .

24.38c . . . and the thrust washer

24.39 Install the bearing

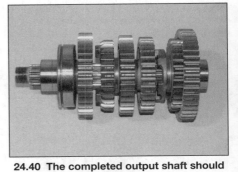

24.40 The completed output shaft should look like this

the circlip making sure it is properly seated in its groove (see illustrations).

**37** Slide the 5th gear pinion onto the shaft with its selector fork groove facing the 4th gear pinion, followed by the thrust washer (see illustrations).

25.3 Note the position of the selector forks (arrowed) and mark them as an aid to installation

**38** Slide on the 1st gear pinion bush and pinion (with its open side facing the 5th gear pinion), followed by the thrust washer (see illustrations).

**39** Fit the needle bearing onto the end of the shaft (see illustration).

**40** Check that all components have been correctly installed (see illustration).

## 25 Selector drum and forks – removal, inspection and installation

**Note:** *To remove the selector drum and forks the engine must be removed from the frame.*

### Removal

**1** The selector drum and forks are housed inside the lower crankcase. Separate the

lower crankcase from the middle crankcase (see Section 21).

**2** If not already done, remove the gear position sensor, the sensor plungers and springs (see Section 17).

**3** Before removing the selector forks, mark each fork for identification using a felt pen and note which way round they fit, as an aid to installation (see illustration). Note how the guide pin on each fork locates in the groove in the selector drum.

**4** Unscrew the retaining bolt and remove the selector fork shaft retainer, noting how it fits. Unscrew the gearchange selector drum bearing retaining bolts and remove them (see illustration).

**5** Support the selector forks and withdraw the fork shafts from the right-hand side of the crankcase (see illustration). Once removed from the crankcase, slide the forks back onto the shafts in their correct order.

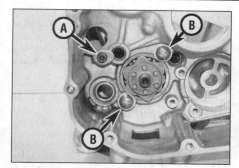

**25.4 Unscrew the bolt (A) and the bearing retaining screws (B)**

**25.5 Support the selector forks and withdraw the shafts**

**25.6a Withdraw the selector drum**

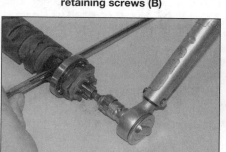

**25.6b Unscrew the centre bolt . . .**

**25.6c . . . and remove the gearchange cam. Note the pin (arrowed)**

**25.7 Pull the bearing off the selector drum**

**6** Withdraw the selector drum from the crankcase **(see illustration)**. To remove the gearchange cam from the end of the selector drum, pass a steel rod through the drum to hold it while unscrewing the centre bolt **(see illustrations)**. The cam locates on a pin in the end of the selector drum. Remove the pin for safekeeping.

**7** If necessary, pull the caged ball bearing off the end of the selector drum **(see illustration)**.

### Inspection

**8** Inspect the selector forks for any signs of wear or damage, especially around the fork ends where they engage with the groove in the pinion. Check the guide pins and internal bearing surface for wear and pitting **(see illustration)**. Check closely to see if the forks are bent. If the forks are in any way damaged they must be renewed.

**9** Check that the forks fit correctly on their shafts. They should move freely with a light fit but no appreciable freeplay **(see illustration)**. Check that the fork shaft holes in the crankcases are not worn or damaged.

**10** Check each selector fork shaft for trueness by rolling it on a flat surface. A bent shaft will cause difficulty in selecting gears and make the gearchange action heavy. Renew the shafts if bent.

**11** With the fork engaged with its gear pinion groove, measure the fork-to-groove clearance using a feeler gauge, and compare the result to the specifications at the beginning of this Chapter **(see illustration)**. If the clearance exceeds the service limit specified, measure

the thickness of the fork ends and the width of the groove and compare the results with the specifications **(see illustrations)**. Renew whichever components are worn beyond their specifications.

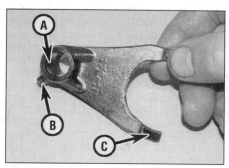

**25.8 Inspect the bearing surfaces (A), the guide pins (B) and the fork ends (C)**

**25.11a Measuring fork-to-groove clearance**

**12** Inspect the grooves in the selector drum for signs of wear or damage.

**13** Check that the selector drum bearings rotate freely and have no sign of freeplay between them and the crankcase. A needle

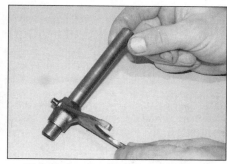

**25.9 Forks should slide freely on the shafts**

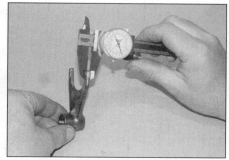

**25.11b Measuring the thickness of the fork ends . . .**

**2**

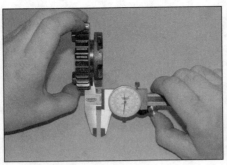

**25.11c . . . and the width of the gear pinion groove**

bearing is on the left-hand end in the crank-case **(see illustration)**. A caged ball bearing is on the right-hand end of the selector drum. Refer to *Tools and Workshop Tips* in the Reference Section for information on bearings and how to remove and install them.

**14** If required, check the condition of the gearchange shaft bearings, the gear position sensor contacts, springs and plungers (see Section 17).

### Installation

**15** If removed, fit the caged ball bearing onto the selector drum with the marked side facing out. Install the pin in the end of the drum and fit the gearchange cam ensuring it locates onto the pin **(see illustration 25.6c)**. Apply a suitable non-permanent thread locking compound to the centre bolt threads, then hold the drum as on disassembly and tighten the bolt to the specified torque setting.

**16** Install the drum in the crankcase **(see illustration 25.6a)**. Rotate the drum so that the neutral detent in the gearchange cam is positioned to align with the stopper arm when it is installed (see Section 17).

**17** Lubricate the selector fork shafts with clean engine oil and slide them into the bores in the crankcase. As each shaft is installed, fit each selector fork in turn, making sure it is in its correct location and the right way round (see Step 3), and that its guide pin locates in its groove in the selector drum **(see illustrations)**.

**18** Apply a suitable non-permanent thread locking compound to the threads of the gearchange selector drum bearing retaining

**25.17a  Fit the selector forks onto the shafts . . .**

**25.13  Selector drum needle bearing**

bolts, then install them and tighten them to the specified torque settings **(see illustration 25.4)**.

**19** Apply a suitable non-permanent thread locking compound to the threads of the selector fork shaft retainer bolt. Install the retainer, making sure its tab locates correctly against the crankcase, then install the bolt and tighten it to the specified torque **(see illustration 25.4)**.

**20** Install the lower crankcase (see Section 21). Install the gear position sensor assembly (see Section 17).

## 26 Connecting rod and main bearings – general information

**1** Even though new main and connecting rod bearings are generally fitted during engine overhaul, the old bearings should be retained for close examination as they may reveal valuable information about the condition of the engine.

**2** Bearing failure occurs mainly because of lack of lubrication, the presence of dirt or other foreign particles, overloading the engine and/or corrosion. Regardless of the cause of bearing failure, it must be corrected before the engine is reassembled to prevent it from happening again.

**3** When examining the bearings, lay them out on a clean surface in the same general position as their location on the crankshaft journals. This will enable you to match any noted bearing problems with the corresponding crankshaft journal.

**25.17b  . . . and ensure the guide pins engage the drum**

**4** Dirt and other foreign particles get into the engine in a variety of ways. They may be left in the engine during assembly or they may pass through filters or breathers, then get into the oil and from there into the bearings. Metal chips from machining operations and normal engine wear are often present. Abrasives are sometimes left in engine components after reconditioning operations, especially when parts are not thoroughly cleaned using the proper cleaning methods. Whatever the source, foreign objects often end up imbedded in the soft bearing material and are easily recognised. Large particles will not imbed in the bearing and will score or gouge the bearing and journal. The best prevention for this cause of bearing failure is to clean all parts thoroughly and keep everything spotlessly clean during engine reassembly. Regular oil and filter changes are also recommended.

**5** Lack of lubrication or lubrication breakdown has a number of interrelated causes. Excessive heat (which thins the oil), overloading (which squeezes the oil from the bearing face) and oil leakage or throw off (from excessive bearing clearances, worn oil pump or high engine speeds) all contribute to lubrication breakdown. Blocked oil passages will starve a bearing of lubrication and destroy it. When lack of lubrication is the cause of bearing failure, the bearing material is wiped or extruded from the steel backing of the bearing. Temperatures may increase to the point where the steel backing and the journal turn blue from overheating.

**HAYNES HINT**  *Refer to Tools and Workshop Tips for bearing fault finding.*

**6** Riding habits can have a definite effect on bearing life. Full throttle low, speed operation, or labouring the engine, puts very high loads on bearings, which tend to squeeze out the oil film. These loads cause the bearings to flex, which produces fine cracks in the bearing face (fatigue failure). Eventually the bearing material will loosen in pieces and tear away from the steel backing. Short trip riding leads to corrosion of bearings, as insufficient engine heat is produced to drive off the condensed water and corrosive gases produced. These products collect in the engine oil, forming acid and sludge. As the oil is carried to the engine bearings, the acid attacks and corrodes the bearing material.

**7** Incorrect bearing installation during engine assembly will lead to bearing failure as well. Tight fitting bearings which leave insufficient bearing oil clearances result in oil starvation. Dirt or foreign particles trapped behind a bearing insert result in high spots on the bearing which lead to failure.

**8** To avoid bearing problems, clean all parts thoroughly before reassembly, double check all bearing clearance measurements and lubricate the new bearings with clean engine oil during installation.

## 27 Connecting rods and bearings – removal, inspection and installation

**Note:** *To remove the connecting rods the engine must be removed from the frame.*

### Removal

**1** Separate the middle crankcase from the upper crankcase (see Section 21).

**2** Before detaching the piston/connecting rod assemblies from the crankshaft, measure the big-end side clearance on each rod with a feeler gauge **(see illustration)**. If the clearance on any rod is greater than the service limit listed in the Specifications at the beginning of this Chapter, measure the big-end and crankpin widths as described in Step 11.

**3** Using paint or a felt marker pen, mark the relevant cylinder identity on each connecting rod and cap. Mark across the cap-to-connecting rod join and note which side of the rod faces the front of the engine so that the cap and rod are fitted the correct way around on reassembly. Cylinders are numbered 1 to 4, from the left to right side of the engine. **Note:** *The number already across the rod and cap indicates rod bearing size, not cylinder number. This number faces the rear of the engine.*

**4** Working on one connecting rod at a time, unscrew the connecting rod cap bolts and remove the cap, complete with the lower bearing shell, from the crankpin **(see illustration)**. If the cap appears stuck, tap it on one end with a hammer while pulling it. Detach the rod, complete with the upper bearing shell, from the crankpin. **Note:** *If you are only removing one connecting rod, the crankshaft can be left in place and the rod/piston manoeuvred out the top of the bore as described in Step 6. If, however, all rods require attention, it is advisable to remove the crankshaft.*

**5** Lift the crankshaft out of the upper crankcase half, taking care not to dislodge the upper main bearing shells (see Section 30). Remove the upper bearing shells if they are loose but keep them in order **(see illustration 30.2)**. Note the position of the crankshaft thrust bearings in the upper crankcase. Note

**27.2 Measuring big-end side clearance with a feeler gauge**

**27.5 Note the position of the crankshaft thrust bearings (arrowed)**

**27.4 Remove the cap and bearing shell from the crankpin**

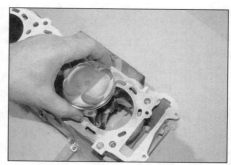
**27.6 Lift the piston/connecting rod assembly out of the top of the cylinder**

which side of the centre main bearing housing each thrust bearing fits – they are colour coded for size and must be fitted in their original locations **(see illustration)**. Remove the thrust bearings for safekeeping (see Section 30). On GSX-R1000 models, remove the balancer shaft and shaft seal from the front of the crankcase (see Section 31).

**6** Push each piston/connecting rod assembly to the top end of the cylinder bore and remove it, making sure the rod does not mark the bore **(see illustration)**. Note the indent on the top of each piston which should face the front (exhaust side).

*Caution: Do not try to remove the piston/connecting rod from the bottom of the cylinder bore. The piston will not pass the crankcase main bearing webs.*

**7** Fit the related bearing shells (if removed), bearing cap and bolts on each connecting rod assembly so that they are all kept together as

a matched set **(see illustration)**. Note how the locating pins in the cap fit into the rod. **Note:** *It is not necessary to renew the big end bolts when the connecting rods are removed, only if they should signs of damage.*

**8** Remove the pistons from the connecting rods (see Section 28).

### Inspection

**9** Check the connecting rods for cracks and other obvious damage.

**10** Apply clean engine oil to the piston pin, insert it into its connecting rod small-end and check for any freeplay between the two **(see illustration)**. If there is freeplay, measure the pin external diameter and the small-end bore diameter and compare the measurements to the specifications at the beginning of this Chapter **(see illustrations)**. Renew components that are worn beyond the service limit.

**2**

**27.7 Keep the bearing shells and piston/connecting rod assemblies together**

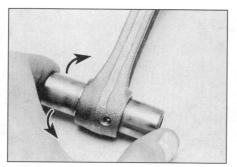
**27.10a Check for freeplay between the piston pin and connecting rod**

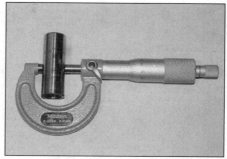
**27.10b Measuring the external diameter of the piston pin . . .**

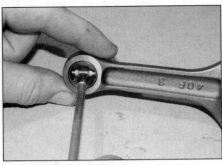

27.10c ... and the small-end bore

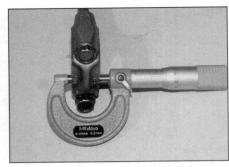

27.11a Measure the width of the connecting rod ...

27.11b ... and the corresponding crankpin

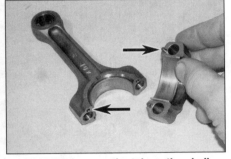

27.16 Make sure the tab on the shell locates in the notch

11 If the side clearance measured in Step 2 exceeds the service limit, measure the width of the connecting rod big-end and the width of the crankpin (see illustrations). Compare the results to the specifications at the beginning of this Chapter, and renew whichever component exceeds those specifications.

12 Refer to Section 26 and examine the connecting rod bearing shells. If they are scored, badly scuffed or appear to have seized, new shells must be installed. Always renew the shells in the connecting rods as a set. If any are badly damaged, check the corresponding crankpin. Evidence of extreme heat, such as discoloration, indicates that lubrication failure has occurred. Be sure to check the oil pump, pressure regulator and all oil holes and passages thoroughly before reassembling the engine.

13 Have the rods checked by a Suzuki dealer if you are in doubt about their straightness.

## Oil clearance check

14 Whether new bearing shells are being fitted or the original ones are being re-used, the connecting rod big-end bearing oil clearance should be checked prior to reassembly. Bearing oil clearance is measured with a product known as Plastigauge.

15 Remove the bearing shells from the rods and caps, keeping them in order. Clean the backs of the bearing shells, the bearing locations in both the connecting rod and cap, and the crankpin journal with a suitable solvent.

16 Press the bearing shells into their locations, ensuring that the tab on each shell engages the notch in the connecting rod or cap (see illustration). Make sure the bearings are fitted in the correct locations and take care not to touch any shell's bearing surface with your fingers.

17 Support the crankshaft. Cut an appropriate size length of Plastigauge (it should be slightly shorter than the width of the crankpin) and place it on the crankpin journal to be checked (see illustration 30.15). Do not place Plastigauge over the oil holes in the journal.

18 Fit the connecting rod and cap onto the crankpin, ensuring that the rod is fitted the correct way round and that the previously made markings and the cap locating pins align.

19 Lubricate the threads of the cap bolts with clean engine oil, then install the bolts and tighten them to the initial torque setting specified. Now tighten each bolt in one continuous movement to the final torque setting specified using a torque angle gauge (see illustration 27.36b). If tightening is paused between the initial and final settings, slacken the bolt to below the initial setting and repeat the procedure. Note: If a torque angle gauge is not available, paint a small reference mark on the top of each bolt after tightening it to the initial torque setting. Then, using a ring spanner so that you can see the mark, tighten the bolt to the final setting. It is essential that, throughout this procedure, the connecting rod does not rotate on the crankshaft.

20 Undo the cap bolts and remove the cap and connecting rod from the crankshaft, again taking great care that the rod does not rotate on the crankshaft.

21 Compare the width of the crushed Plastigauge on the crankpin to the scale printed on the Plastigauge envelope to obtain the connecting rod bearing oil clearance (see illustration 30.19). Compare the reading to the specifications at the beginning of this Chapter. If the clearance is within the range specified and the bearings are in perfect condition, they can be reused

22 Carefully scrape away all traces of the Plastigauge from the crankpin journal and bearing shells using a fingernail or other object which will not score the bearing surfaces.

23 If the oil clearance is beyond the service limit, first check the crankpin journal size code. The crankpin journal size code is stamped on the inner left-hand crankshaft web and will be either a 1, 2 or 3 (see illustration). Measure the actual diameter of the crankpin journal with a micrometer and compare the result with the Specifications at the beginning of this Chapter (see illustration). For example, on GSX-R600 models, if the journal being measured is code 1, the Specifications indicate that the service limit for that journal is 30.992 mm. If the journal diameter is larger than the service limit, new bearing shells can be fitted (see Steps 26 and 27). If the journal diameter is smaller than the service limit, the crankshaft must be renewed.

24 Repeat the oil clearance check for the remaining connecting rods. Always renew all of the shells (on all four rods) at the same time.

25 Install the new shells and check the oil clearance once again.

27.23a Crankpin journal size codes

27.23b Measuring the crankpins

## Bearing shell selection

**26** New shells for the big-end bearings are supplied on a selected fit basis. Size codes for the crankpin journals are stamped on the inner left-hand crankshaft web and will be either a 1, 2 or 3 (**see illustration 27.23a**). The first number is for the left-hand (No. 1 cylinder) journal, and so on. Each connecting rod size code is marked on the flat face of the connecting rod and cap and will be either a 1 or 2 (**see illustration**).

**27** A corresponding range of bearing shells is available. To select the correct shells, use the table to cross-refer the crankpin journal size code with the connecting rod size code to determine the colour code for the shells required. For example, if the connecting rod size code is 2, and the crankpin size code is 3, then the bearing required is Yellow. The colour is marked on the side of the shell (**see illustration**).

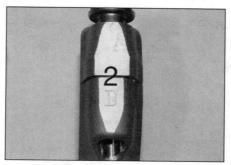
27.26 Connecting rod size code

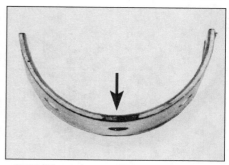
27.27 The colour code is marked on the side of the shell

| Connecting rod code | Crankpin code | | |
|---|---|---|---|
| | 1 | 2 | 3 |
| 1 | Green | Black | Brown |
| 2 | Black | Brown | Yellow |

## Installation

**28** Fit the pistons onto the connecting rods if they were removed (see Section 28).

**29** Ensure that the backs of the bearing shells, the bearing seats in the caps and rods and the crankpin journals are clean. If new shells are being fitted, ensure that all traces of protective grease are removed using paraffin (kerosene). Dry the shells, caps, rods and journals with a clean, lint-free cloth. Install the shells, making sure the tab on each shell engages the notch in the cap or rod (**see illustration 27.16**).

**30** Make sure the bearings are fitted in their correct locations and take care not to touch any bearing surfaces with your fingers.

**31** Lubricate the pistons, rings and cylinder bore with clean engine oil. Stagger the piston

27.32 Insert the piston/connecting rod assembly into the top of the cylinder . . .

27.33 . . . and carefully feed in each piston ring

ring end gaps (see Section 29). If available, use a piston ring compressor to aid installation.

**32** Insert the piston/connecting rod assembly into the top of its cylinder, taking care not to allow the connecting rod to mark the bore (**see illustration**). Make sure the indent on the top of the piston faces the front (exhaust side) of the engine. Press the piston carefully into the cylinder until the piston crown is flush with the top of the bore.

**33** If a ring compressor is not available, carefully compress and feed each piston ring into the bore as the piston is inserted (**see illustration**).

**34** Make sure the connecting rod assemblies are correctly installed (see Step 3). Position the rods for the No. 1 and No. 4 cylinders against the back of the crankcase, and the No. 2 and No. 3 cylinders against the front of the crankcase (**see illustration**). Make sure all the bearing shells and the crankshaft thrust bearings are in place (**see illustration**). Lubricate the shells with molybdenum disulphide oil (a 50/50 mixture of molybdenum disulphide grease and clean engine oil).

**35** If the crankshaft was removed, lower it into position in the upper crankcase (see Section 30) and on GSX-R1000 models install the balancer shaft (see Section 31). Working

**2**

27.34a Position the connecting rods as shown

27.34b Ensure the main bearing shells (A), the connecting rod shells (B) and the thrust bearings (C) are in place

**27.35 Lubricate the cap bolt threads**

**27.36a Tighten the cap bolts to the initial torque setting . . .**

**27.36b . . . then to the final setting with an angle gauge**

on one connecting rod at a time, pull the rod onto the crankpin and fit the cap onto the rod, making sure it is the right way round and that the previously made markings and the cap locating pins align. Lubricate the threads of the cap bolts with clean engine oil, then install the bolts and tighten them finger-tight at this stage **(see illustration)**. Check to make sure that all components have been returned to their original locations using the marks made on disassembly.

**36** Tighten the bearing cap bolts in two stages as described in Step 19, first to the initial torque setting specified, and then to the final torque setting specified **(see illustrations)**.

**37** Check that the rods rotate smoothly and freely on the crankpin. If there are any signs of roughness or tightness, remove the rods and re-check the bearing clearance. Sometimes tapping the connecting rod cap bolts will relieve tightness.

**38** Install the remaining components in the reverse order of disassembly.

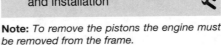

**28 Pistons –**
removal, inspection and installation

**Note:** *To remove the pistons the engine must be removed from the frame.*

## Removal

**1** Remove the connecting rod/piston(s) (see Section 27).

**2** Before removing the piston from the connecting rod, ensure it is marked with its cylinder identity. Cylinders are numbered 1 to 4, from the left to right side of the engine. If the piston is going to be cleaned, scratch the identity lightly on the inside of the piston skirt. Each piston must be installed in its original cylinder on reassembly. Note the indent on the top of each piston which faces the front (exhaust side) of the engine **(see illustration)**; if this is not visible, mark the piston accordingly so that it can be installed the correct way round.

**3** Carefully prise out the circlip on one side of the piston using needle-nose pliers or a small flat-bladed screwdriver inserted into the notch **(see illustration)**. Push the piston pin out from the other side with a suitably sized socket to free the piston from the connecting rod **(see illustration)**. Remove the other circlip and discard them as new ones must be used. When the piston has been removed, install its pin back into its bore so that related parts do not get mixed up.

> **HAYNES HiNT** *If a piston pin is a tight fit in the piston bosses, heat the piston gently with a hot air gun – this will expand the alloy piston sufficiently to release its grip on the pin. If the piston pin is particularly stubborn, extract it using a drawbolt tool, but be careful to protect the piston's working surfaces – see Tools and Workshop Tips in the Reference section.*

**4** Using your thumbs or a piston ring removal and installation tool, carefully remove the rings from the pistons, working on one piston at a time **(see illustration)**. Do not nick or gouge the pistons in the process. Carefully note which way up each ring fits and in which groove as they must be installed in their original positions if being re-used. The upper surface of the top two rings should have a manufacturer's mark or letter at one end – if the mark on each ring is different, note which mark is for the top ring and which is for the second **(see illustration)**. The rings can also be identified by their different cross-section. **Note:** *It is good practice to renew the piston rings when an engine is being overhauled.*

**5** Clean all traces of carbon from the tops of the pistons. A hand-held wire brush or a piece of fine emery cloth can be used once most of the deposits have been scraped away. Do not, under any circumstances, use a wire brush mounted in a drill motor; the piston

**28.2 Indent faces the front (exhaust side) of the engine**

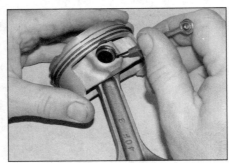

**28.3a Prise out the circlip . . .**

**28.3b . . . then push out the piston pin**

**28.4a Removing the piston rings with a ring removal and installation tool**

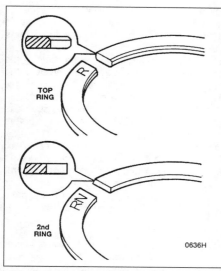

**28.4b Letters should face UP – note the different cross section**

material is soft and will be eroded away by the wire brush.

**6** Use a piston ring groove cleaning tool to remove any carbon deposits from the ring grooves. If a tool is not available, a piece broken off an old ring will do the job. Be very careful to remove only the carbon deposits. Do not remove any metal and do not nick or gouge the sides of the ring grooves.

**7** Once the carbon has been removed, clean the pistons with a suitable solvent and dry them thoroughly. If the identification previously marked on the piston is cleaned off, be sure to re-mark it with the correct identity. Make sure the oil return holes at the back of the oil ring groove are clear.

## Inspection

**8** Carefully inspect each piston for cracks around the skirt, at the pin bosses and at the ring lands. Normal piston wear appears as even, vertical wear on the thrust surfaces of the piston and slight looseness of the top ring in its groove. If the skirt is scored or scuffed, the engine may have been suffering from overheating and/or abnormal combustion, which caused excessively high operating temperatures. The oil pump should be checked thoroughly.

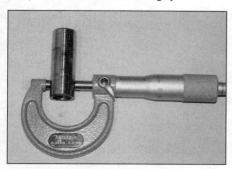

**28.12b Measuring the external diameter of the pin . . .**

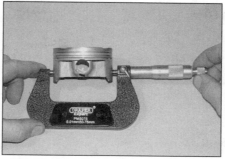

**28.10 Measuring the piston diameter**

**9** A hole in the top of the piston, in one extreme, or burned areas around the edge of the piston crown, indicate that pre-ignition or knocking under load have occurred. If you find evidence of any problems the cause must be corrected or the damage will occur again (see *Fault Finding* in the *Reference* section).

**10** Check the piston-to-bore clearance by measuring the bore (see Section 22) and the piston diameter. Make sure each piston is matched to its correct cylinder. Measure the piston 15 mm up from the bottom of the skirt and at 90° to the piston pin axis **(see illustration)**. Subtract the piston diameter from the bore diameter to obtain the clearance. If it is greater than the figure specified at the beginning of this Chapter, check whether it is the bore or piston that is worn. If the piston diameter is less that the service limit, new pistons and rings should be fitted. Note that the bore is electro-plated and its surface is unlikely to wear.

**11** Measure the piston ring-to-groove clearance by fitting each ring in its groove and slipping a feeler gauge in beside it **(see illustration)**. Make sure you have the correct ring for the groove (see Step 4). Check the clearance at three or four locations around the groove. If the clearance is greater than specified, renew both the piston and rings as a set. If new rings are being used, measure the clearance using the new rings. If the clearance is greater than that specified, the piston is worn and must be renewed.

**12** Apply clean engine oil to the piston pin, insert it into the piston and check for any freeplay between the two **(see illustration)**.

**28.12c . . . and the internal diameter of the pin bore**

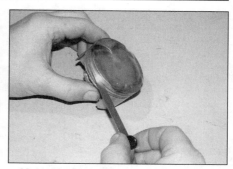

**28.11 Measuring piston ring-to-groove clearance**

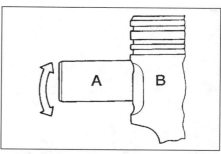

**28.12a Slip the pin (A) into the piston (B) and try to rock it back and forth. If its loose, renew the piston and pin**

Measure the pin external diameter and the pin bore in the piston and compare the results to the Specifications at the beginning of this Chapter **(see illustrations)**. Repeat the measurements between the pin and the connecting rod small-end (see Section 27, Step 10). Renew components that are worn beyond the specified limits.

## Installation

**13** Inspect and install the piston rings (see Section 29).

**14** Install a **new** circlip into one side of the piston (never re-use old circlips), then lubricate the piston pin, the piston pin bore and the connecting rod small-end bore with clean engine oil.

**15** Install the piston on its correct connecting rod, making sure the indent on the top of the piston faces forwards **(see illustration)**. Insert the piston pin from the side without the circlip.

**2**

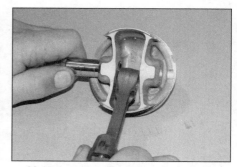

**28.15 Install the piston on its rod and insert the piston pin**

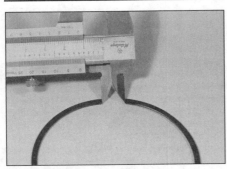

29.3 Measuring piston ring free end gap

29.4 Measuring piston ring installed end gap

29.7a Install the oil ring expander . . .

29.7b . . . then fit the side rails

Secure the pin with the other **new** circlip. When installing the circlips, compress them only just enough to fit them in the piston, and make sure they are properly seated in their grooves with the open end away from the removal notch.

16 Install the piston/connecting rod assembly (see Section 27).

## 29 Piston rings – inspection and installation

### Inspection

1 It is good practice to renew the piston rings when an engine is being overhauled. Before

installing the new piston rings, the compression ring (top and 2nd rings) end gaps must be checked, both free and installed.

2 Lay out each piston with its ring set so the rings will be matched with the same piston and cylinder during the measurement procedure. The upper surface of the top two rings should have a manufacturer's mark or letter at one end – if the mark on each ring is different, note which mark is for the top ring and which is for the second **(see illustration 28.4b)**.

3 To measure the free end gap, lay the ring on a flat surface and measure the gap between the ends using a vernier caliper **(see illustration)**. Compare the results to the specifications at the beginning of this Chapter and renew any ring that is outside its service limit.

4 To measure the installed end gap, insert the

ring into the top of the cylinder and square it up with the cylinder walls by pushing it in with the top of the piston. The ring should be about 20 mm below the top edge of the cylinder. Slip a feeler gauge between the ends of the ring to measure the gap and compare the result to the Specifications at the beginning of this Chapter **(see illustration)**.

5 If the gap is larger or smaller than specified, check that you have the correct rings before proceeding. Excess end gap is not critical unless it exceeds the service limit. Again, check that you have the correct rings for your engine.

6 Repeat the procedure for the other compression ring and then the compression rings in the other cylinders. Remember to keep the rings together with their matched pistons.

### Installation

7 The oil control ring (lowest on the piston) is installed first. It is composed of three separate components; the expander and the upper and lower side rails. Slip the expander into the groove, positioning its ends so that they touch yet do not overlap **(see illustration)**. Install the lower side rail **(see illustration)**. Do not use a piston ring installation tool on the oil ring side rails as they may be damaged. Instead, place one end of the side rail into the groove between the expander and the ring land. Hold it firmly in place and slide a finger or thin blade around the piston while pushing the rail into the groove. Next, install the upper side rail in the same manner.

8 After the oil control ring been installed, check that both its upper and lower side rails can be turned smoothly in the ring groove.

9 Fit the second compression ring into the middle groove in the piston with its mark or letter facing up (see Step 2). Do not expand the ring any more than is necessary to slide it into place. To avoid breaking the ring, use a piston ring installation tool **(see illustration 28.4a)** or old pieces of feeler gauge blade **(see illustration)**.

10 Install the top compression ring in the same manner into the top groove in the piston.

11 Once the rings are correctly installed, check they move freely without snagging and stagger their end gaps as shown **(see illustration)**.

## 30 Crankshaft and main bearings – removal, inspection and installation

**Note:** *To remove the crankshaft the engine must be removed from the frame.*

### Removal

1 Separate the middle crankcase from the upper crankcase (see Section 21) and disconnect the piston/connecting rod assemblies from the crankshaft (see Section 27). Unless required, there is no need to remove the assemblies from the cylinders; push the pistons up the bores so that the connecting rod ends

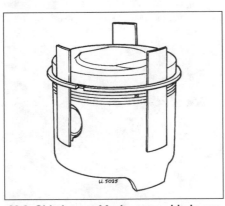

29.9 Old pieces of feeler gauge blade can be used to guide the rings over the piston

29.11 Stagger the ring end gaps as shown

**30.2  Remove the bearing shells if they are loose**

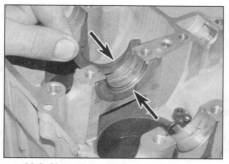

**30.3  Note the position of the thrust bearings (arrowed) before removing them**

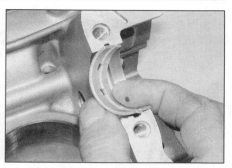

**30.10  Push the centre of the shell sideways to remove it**

are clear of the crankshaft and wrap clean rag around the rods to prevent damage to the bores.
2  Lift the crankshaft out of the upper crankcase, taking care not to dislodge the upper main bearing shells. Remove the bearing shells if they are loose but keep them in order **(see illustration)**.
3  The thrust bearings are located in the upper crankcase on each side of the centre main bearing housing. Note which side of the main bearing housing each thrust bearing fits – they are colour coded for size and must be fitted in their original locations **(see illustration)**. Remove the thrust bearings for safekeeping.
4  On GSX-R1000 models, remove the balancer shaft and shaft seal from the front of the crankcase (see Section 31).

### Inspection

5  Clean the crankshaft with a suitable solvent, paying particular attention to flush out the oil passages. If available, blow the crank dry with compressed air, and also blow through the oil passages.
6  Inspect the primary drive gear for wear or damage. If any of the gear teeth are excessively worn, chipped or broken, the crankshaft must be renewed. On GSX-R1000 models, inspect the balancer shaft gear.
7  Refer to Section 26 and examine the main bearing shells. If they are scored, badly scuffed or appear to have been seized, new shells must be installed. Always renew the main bearing shells as a set. If any are badly damaged, check the corresponding crankshaft journal. Evidence of extreme heat, such as discoloration, indicates that

lubrication failure has occurred. Be sure to check the oil pump, pressure regulator and all oil holes and passages thoroughly before reassembling the engine.
8  The crankshaft journals should be given a close visual examination, paying particular attention where damaged bearings have been discovered. If the journals are scored or pitted in any way a new crankshaft will be required. Note that undersize bearing shells are not available, precluding the option of re-grinding the crankshaft.
9  Place the crankshaft on V-blocks and check the runout at the main bearing journals using a dial gauge (see *Tools and Workshop Tips* in the *Reference* Section). Compare the reading to the maximum specified at the beginning of this Chapter. If the runout exceeds the limit, a new crankshaft must be installed.
10  If required, remove the bearing shells from the crankcases by pushing their centres to the side, then lifting them out **(see illustration)**. Keep the shells in order so that they can be fitted in their original locations for the oil clearance check.

### Oil clearance check

11  Whether new bearing shells are being fitted or the original ones are being re-used, the main bearing oil clearance should be checked before the engine is reassembled. Main bearing oil clearance is measured with a product known as Plastigauge. **Note:** *On GSX-R1000 models, the balancer shaft bearing oil clearance can be checked at the same time if required (see Section 31).*
12  If not already done, remove the bearing

shells from the crankcases. Use a suitable solvent to clean the backs of the bearing shells and the bearing seats in both crankcases, and the main bearing journals on the crankshaft. Remove all traces of old sealant from the middle and upper crankcase mating surfaces with a suitable solvent
13  Press the bearing shells into their seats, ensuring that the tab on each shell engages in the notch in the crankcase **(see illustration)**. Make sure the bearings are fitted in the correct locations and take care not to touch bearing surfaces with your fingers.
14  Lay the crankshaft in position in the upper crankcase. If removed, fit the dowels into the crankcase **(see illustration 21.16a)**.
15  Cut five appropriate size lengths of Plastigauge (they should be slightly shorter than the width of the crankshaft journals). Place a strip of Plastigauge along the centreline of each journal **(see illustration)**. Do not place Plastigauge over the oil holes in the crankshaft. **Note:** *It is essential that, throughout this procedure, the crankshaft does not rotate in the crankcase.*
16  Carefully fit the middle crankcase onto the upper crankcase, ensuring that the Plastigauge is not disturbed. Make sure the dowels locate correctly and that the middle crankcase half is correctly seated. **Note:** *Do not tighten the crankcase bolts if the casing is not correctly seated.*
17  Clean the threads of the 9 mm crankshaft journal bolts and install them in their original locations. Tighten the bolts a little at a time in the numerical sequence marked in the crankcase **(see illustration)**, to the torque

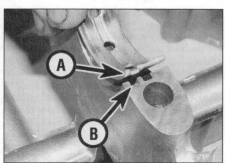

**30.13  Ensure tab (A) locates in notch (B)**

**30.15  Lay a strip of Plastigauge along the centreline of each journal**

**30.17  Tighten the crankshaft journal bolts to the specified torque setting**

**2**

30.19 Compare the width of the crushed Plastigauge with the scale provided

30.21a Crankshaft journal size codes

30.21b Measuring the crankshaft journals

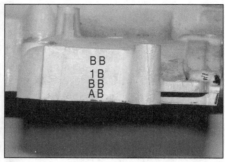

30.23 Crankshaft bearing seat size codes (GSX-R1000 shown)

## Bearing shell selection

23 New shells for the main bearings are supplied on a selected fit basis. Size codes for the crankshaft journals are stamped on the outer left-hand crankshaft web and will be either an A, B or C **(see illustration 30.21a)**. The first letter is for the outer left-hand journal, and so on. The corresponding bearing seat size codes are stamped into the rear of the upper crankcase and will be either an A or B **(see illustration)**. **Note:** *The numeral 1 is stamped immediately before the five main bearing code letters. On GSX-R1000 models, the top two code letters are for the balancer shaft bearings.*

24 A corresponding range of bearing shells is available. To select the correct shells, use the table to cross-refer the crankshaft journal size code with the crankcase seat size code to determine the colour code for the shells required. For example, if the crankcase seat size code is B, and the crankshaft journal size code is C, then the bearing required is Yellow. The colour is marked on the side of the shell **(see illustration 27.27)**.

| Crankcase seat code | Crankshaft journal code | | |
|---|---|---|---|
| | A | B | C |
| A | Green | Black | Brown |
| B | Black | Brown | Yellow |

## Thrust bearing check and selection

25 The thrust bearings are located in the upper crankcase between the crank webs and the centre main bearing housing. The thrust bearing clearance should be checked before the engine is reassembled.

26 Lay the crankshaft in position in the upper crankcase and slide the thrust bearings into place (see Step 3). Push the crankshaft as far as it will go toward the left-hand (alternator) side of the crankcase so that there is no clearance between the crank and the right-hand thrust bearing. Insert a feeler gauge between the crank and the left-hand thrust bearing and measure the thrust bearing clearance **(see illustration)**. Compare the result with the Specifications at the beginning of this Chapter. If the clearance is excessive, adjust it as follows.

27 Remove the right-hand thrust bearing, then measure its thickness with a micrometer and compare the result with the Specifications at the beginning of this Chapter **(see illustration)**. If the bearing is within the specifications, install it in its location, then follow Step 28. If the bearing is thinner than the specified size, fit a new bearing, then measure the thrust bearing clearance again (see Step 26). If the clearance is still excessive, follow Step 28. **Note:** *There is only one size thickness for the right-hand thrust bearing.*

28 Remove the left-hand thrust bearing, then push the crankshaft as far as it will go toward the left-hand (alternator) side of the crankcase so that there is no clearance between the

setting specified at the beginning of this Chapter (see Section 21, Steps 26 to 28).

18 Unscrew the crankshaft journal bolts a little at a time in the **reverse** order of the tightening sequence marked in the crankcase until they are all finger-tight, then remove the bolts. Carefully lift off the middle crankcase, making sure the Plastigauge is not disturbed.

19 Compare the width of the crushed Plastigauge on each crankshaft journal to the scale printed on the Plastigauge envelope to obtain the main bearing oil clearance **(see illustration)**. Compare the reading to the specifications at the beginning of this Chapter. If the clearance is within the range specified and the bearings are in perfect condition, they can be reused

20 Carefully scrape away all traces of the Plastigauge from the crankshaft journals and bearing shells using a fingernail or other object which will not score the bearing surfaces.

21 If the clearance is beyond the service limit, first check the crankshaft journal size code. The crankshaft journal size code is stamped on the outer left-hand crankshaft web and will be either an A, B or C **(see illustration)**. Measure the actual diameter of the crankshaft journal with a micrometer and compare the result with the Specifications at the beginning of this Chapter **(see illustration)**. For example, on GSX-R600 models, if the journal being measured is code A, the Specifications indicate that the service limit for that journal is 31.992 mm. If the journal diameter is larger than the service limit, new bearing shells can be fitted (see Steps 23 and 24). If the journal diameter is smaller than the service limit, the crankshaft must be renewed. Always renew all of the shells (on all five journals) at the same time.

22 Install the new shells and check the oil clearance once again.

30.26 Measuring the clearance between the crank and the left-hand thrust bearing

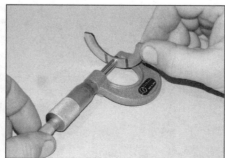

30.27 Measuring the thickness of the right-hand thrust bearing

| Thrust bearing selection table GSX-R600 and GSX-R750 | |
|---|---|
| Left-hand bearing clearance (bearing removed) | Bearing colour-code required |
| 2.430 to 2.460 mm | Red |
| 2.460 to 2.485 mm | Black |
| 2.485 to 2.510 mm | Blue |
| 2.510 to 2.535 mm | Green |
| 2.535 to 2.560 mm | Yellow |
| 2.560 to 2.585 mm | White |

| Thrust bearing selection table GSX-R1000 | |
|---|---|
| Left-hand bearing clearance (bearing removed) | Bearing colour-code required |
| 2.440 to 2.470 mm | Black |
| 2.470 to 2.490 mm | Orange |
| 2.490 to 2.510 mm | Blue |
| 2.510 to 2.530 mm | Green |
| 2.530 to 2.550 mm | Yellow |
| 2.550 to 2.570 mm | Red |
| 2.570 to 2.590 mm | Brown |

crank and the right-hand thrust bearing. Insert a feeler gauge between the crank and the main bearing housing where the left-hand bearing fits, and measure the clearance. Using the tables above, select a new left-hand thrust bearing according to the clearance measured. For example, on GSX-R600 models, if the clearance with the bearing removed is 2.495 mm, the bearing required is colour-coded Blue. Re-check the clearance with the new bearings (see Step 26).

### Installation

29 If removed, install the piston/connecting rod assemblies in the cylinders (see Section 27).
30 Ensure that the backs of the bearing shells, the bearing seats in the crankcases and the crankpin journals are clean. If new shells are being fitted, ensure that all traces of the protective grease are cleaned off using paraffin (kerosene). Dry the shells, seats and journals with a clean, lint-free cloth. Install the shells, making sure the tab on each shell engages the notch in the bearing seat (see illustration 30.13).
31 Make sure the bearings are fitted in their correct locations and take care not to touch any bearing surfaces with your fingers.
32 Lubricate the shells, preferably with molybdenum disulphide oil (a 50/50 mixture of molybdenum disulphide grease and clean engine oil) or clean engine oil.
33 Install the thrust bearings in their correct locations on each side of the centre main bearing housing. Make sure the oil grooves face out (see illustration 30.3).
34 Lower the crankshaft into position in the upper crankcase and connect the piston/connecting rod assemblies to the crankshaft (see Section 27). On GSX-R1000 models, install the balancer shaft and shaft seal, ensuring that the balancer shaft is correctly timed to the crankshaft (see Section 31).

35 Install the middle crankcase onto the upper crankcase (see Section 21).

### 31 Balancer shaft – removal, inspection and installation (GSX-R1000)

### Removal

1 Separate the middle crankcase from the upper crankcase (see Section 21).
2 Remove the shaft oil seal from the crankcase (see illustration).
3 Note how the punch mark on the balancer shaft pinion aligns with the index mark on the crankshaft gear, then lift the balancer shaft out of the upper crankcase, taking care not to dislodge the upper balancer shaft shells (see illustration).
4 Remove the thrust washers from each end of the shaft (see illustration).
5 Note how the punch mark on the balancer pinion aligns with the index mark on the balancer shaft (see illustration). Carefully pull the pinion off the shaft, noting how the shaft locates between the dampers on the inside of the pinion (see illustration).

### Inspection

6 Clean the balancer shaft with a suitable solvent, paying particular attention to flush out the oil passage. If available, blow through the oil passage with compressed air.
7 Inspect the pinion for wear or damage. If any of the gear teeth are excessively worn, chipped or broken, the pinion must be renewed. Inspect the crankshaft gear.

**2**

31.2 Remove the balancer shaft oil seal

31.3 Note how the index mark on the crankshaft gear aligns with the punch mark on the pinion

31.4 Remove the thrust washers

31.5a Note how the punch mark on the pinion aligns with the index mark on the balancer shaft

31.5b Note how the shaft locates between the pinion dampers

**31.8 Inspect the dampers, noting how they fit**

**31.14a Balancer shaft journal size codes**

table to cross-refer the balancer shaft journal size code with the crankcase seat size code to determine the colour code for the shells required. For example, if the crankcase seat size code is A, and the crankshaft size code is B, then the bearing required is Black. The colour is marked on the side of the shell **(see illustration 27.27).**

| Crankcase seat code | Balancer shaft journal code | |
|---|---|---|
| | A | B |
| A | Green | Black |
| B | Black | Brown |

**8** Check the dampers for signs of wear or deterioration and renew them as a set if necessary **(see illustration).**
**9** Examine the balancer shaft bearing shells. If they are scored, badly scuffed or appear to have been seized, new shells must be installed. Always renew the bearing shells as a set. If any are badly damaged, check the corresponding balancer shaft journal.
**10** Examine the balancer shaft journals, paying particular attention where damaged bearings have been discovered. If the journals are scored or pitted in any way a new balancer shaft should be fitted.
**11** Reassemble the shaft assembly ensuring that the punch mark on the pinion aligns with the index mark on the shaft (see Step 5).

### Oil clearance check

**12** Whether new bearing shells are being fitted or the original ones are being re-used, the balancer shaft bearing oil clearance should be checked before the engine is reassembled. Bearing oil clearance is measured with a product known as Plastigauge.
**13** Follow Steps 12 to 20 in Section 30, and apply the same procedure for checking the crankshaft oil clearance to the balancer shaft. **Note:** *The balancer shaft oil clearance can be checked separately or at the same time as the crankshaft oil clearance if required.* Fit the thrust washers on the balancer shaft and the shaft oil seal in the crankcase, then install the shaft in the crankcase. Install the 9 mm crankshaft journal bolts and tighten them to the specified torque, then install the four 8 mm

crankcase bolts on the balancer shaft housing and tighten them to the specified torque (see Section 21, Step 29).
**14** If the clearance is beyond the service limit, first check the balancer shaft journal size code. The journal size code is stamped on the shaft and will be either an A or B **(see illustration).** Measure the actual diameter of the shaft journal with a micrometer and compare the result with the Specifications at the beginning of this Chapter **(see illustration).** For example, if the journal being measured is code A, the Specifications indicate that the service limit for that journal is 22.992 mm. If the journal diameter is larger than the service limit, new bearing shells can be fitted (see Steps 16 and 17). If the journal diameter is smaller than the service limit, the shaft must be renewed. Always renew all of the shells (on both journals) at the same time.
**15** Install the new shells and check the oil clearance once again.

### Bearing shell selection

**16** New shells for the balancer shaft bearings are supplied on a selected fit basis. Size codes for the shaft journals are stamped on the shaft and will be either an A or B **(see illustration 31.14).** The left-hand letter is for the left-hand journal, the right-hand letter is for the right-hand journal. The corresponding bearing seat size codes are stamped into the rear of the upper crankcase above the main bearing size codes and will be either an A or B **(see illustration 30.23).**
**17** A corresponding range of bearing shells is available. To select the correct shells, use the

### Installation

**18** Ensure that the backs of the bearing shells, the bearing seats in the crankcases and the balancer shaft journals are clean. If new shells are being fitted, ensure that all traces of the protective grease are cleaned off using paraffin (kerosene). Dry the shells, seats and journals with a clean, lint-free cloth. Install the shells, making sure the tab on each shell engages the notch in the bearing seat **(see illustration 30.13).**
**19** Make sure the bearings are fitted in their correct locations and take care not to touch any bearing surfaces with your fingers.
**20** Lubricate the shells with molybdenum disulphide oil.
**21** Fit the thrust washers on the balancer shaft and the shaft oil seal in the crankcase.
**22** With the crankshaft installed, align the punch mark on the balancer shaft pinion with the index mark on the crankshaft gear, then install the balancer shaft **(see illustration).**
**23** Install the remaining components in the reverse order of disassembly.

### 32 Initial start-up after overhaul

**1** Make sure the engine oil level and coolant level are correct (see *Daily (pre-ride) checks).*
**2** Pull the coil/plug caps off the spark plugs and insert a spare spark plug into each cap. Position the spare plugs so that their bodies are earthed (grounded) against the engine. *Caution: Do not lay the plugs against the magnesium engine covers as they could be damaged.* Turn the ignition switch ON and crank the engine over with the starter until the oil pressure warning LED goes off (which indicates that oil pressure exists). Turn the ignition OFF. Remove the spare spark plugs and reconnect the coil/plug caps.
**3** Make sure there is fuel in the tank, then operate the choke.
**4** Start the engine and allow it to run at a moderately fast idle until it reaches operating temperature.

 *Warning: If the oil pressure warning LED doesn't go off, or it comes on while the engine is running, stop the engine immediately.*

**31.14b Measuring the balancer shaft journals**

**31.22 Align the marks and install the balancer shaft**

| GSX-R600 and GSX-R750 models | | |
|---|---|---|
| Up to 500 miles (800 km) | 7000 rpm max | Vary throttle position/speed |
| 500 to 1000 miles (800 to 1600 km) | 10,500 rpm max | Vary throttle position/speed. Use full throttle for short bursts |
| Over 1000 miles (1600 km) | 14,000 rpm max | Do not exceed tachometer red line |

| GSX-R1000 models | | |
|---|---|---|
| Up to 500 miles (800 km) | 6000 rpm max | Vary throttle position/speed |
| 500 to 1000 miles (800 to 1600 km) | 9000 rpm max | Vary throttle position/speed. Use full throttle for short bursts |
| Over 1000 miles (1600 km) | 12,000 rpm max | Do not exceed tachometer red line |

5 Check carefully that there are no oil and coolant leaks and make sure the transmission and controls, especially the throttle and brakes, function properly before road testing the machine. Refer to Section 33 for the recommended running-in procedure.

6 Upon completion of the road test, and after the engine has cooled down completely, recheck the valve clearances (Chapter 1) and check the engine oil level and coolant level (see *Daily (pre-ride) checks*).

## 33 Recommended running-in procedure

1 Treat the machine gently for the first few miles to make sure oil has circulated throughout the engine and any new parts installed have started to seat.

2 Even greater care is necessary if a major engine overhaul has been undertaken. In the case of a new crankshaft or piston and connecting rod assemblies, the bike will have to be run in as when new. This means greater use of the transmission and a restraining hand on the throttle until at least 1000 miles (1600 km) have been covered. There's no point in keeping to any set speed limit – the main idea is to keep from labouring the engine and to gradually increase performance up to the 1000 mile (1600 km) mark. These recommendations can be lessened to an extent when only a top end overhaul has been undertaken. Experience is the best guide, since it's easy to tell when an engine is running freely. The following maximum engine speed limitations (above), which Suzuki provide for new motorcycles, can be used as a guide.

3 If a lubrication failure is suspected, stop the engine immediately and try to find the cause. If an engine is run without oil, even for a short period of time, severe damage will occur.

2

# Chapter 3
# Cooling system

## Contents

## Degrees of difficulty

| | | | | |
|---|---|---|---|---|
| **Easy,** suitable for novice with little experience  | **Fairly easy,** suitable for beginner with some experience  | **Fairly difficult,** suitable for competent DIY mechanic  | **Difficult,** suitable for experienced DIY mechanic  | **Very difficult,** suitable for expert DIY or professional |

## Specifications

### Coolant
Mixture type and capacity . . . . . . . . . . . . . . . . . . . . . . . . . . . . . . . . . .   see Chapter 1

### Pressure cap
Cap valve opening pressure . . . . . . . . . . . . . . . . . . . . . . . . . . . . . . . .   13.5 to 17.8 psi (0.95 to 1.25 Bar)

### Fan switch
Cooling fan cut-in temperature . . . . . . . . . . . . . . . . . . . . . . . . . . . . .   105°C approx.
Cooling fan cut-out temperature . . . . . . . . . . . . . . . . . . . . . . . . . . . .   100°C approx.

### Coolant temperature sensor
Resistance
  @ 20°C . . . . . . . . . . . . . . . . . . . . . . . . . . . . . . . . . . . . . . . . . . . . .   2.450 K-ohms approx.
  @ 50°C . . . . . . . . . . . . . . . . . . . . . . . . . . . . . . . . . . . . . . . . . . . . .   0.811 K-ohms approx.
  @ 80°C . . . . . . . . . . . . . . . . . . . . . . . . . . . . . . . . . . . . . . . . . . . . .   0.318 K-ohms approx.
  @ 110°C . . . . . . . . . . . . . . . . . . . . . . . . . . . . . . . . . . . . . . . . . . . .   0.142 K-ohms approx.
  @ 130°C . . . . . . . . . . . . . . . . . . . . . . . . . . . . . . . . . . . . . . . . . . . .   0.088 K-ohms approx.

### Thermostat
Opening temperature . . . . . . . . . . . . . . . . . . . . . . . . . . . . . . . . . . . . .   82°C
Valve lift . . . . . . . . . . . . . . . . . . . . . . . . . . . . . . . . . . . . . . . . . . . . . . .   8 mm (min) @ 95°C

### Torque settings
Coolant union to cylinder block bolts . . . . . . . . . . . . . . . . . . . . . . . .   10 Nm
Cooling fan switch . . . . . . . . . . . . . . . . . . . . . . . . . . . . . . . . . . . . . . .   17 Nm
Engine coolant temperature (ECT) sensor . . . . . . . . . . . . . . . . . . . .   18 Nm
Thermostat cover bolts . . . . . . . . . . . . . . . . . . . . . . . . . . . . . . . . . . .   10 Nm
Water pump cover screws . . . . . . . . . . . . . . . . . . . . . . . . . . . . . . . . .   6 Nm
Water pump impeller bolt . . . . . . . . . . . . . . . . . . . . . . . . . . . . . . . . . .   8 Nm
Water pump mounting bolts . . . . . . . . . . . . . . . . . . . . . . . . . . . . . . . .   10 Nm

**3**

## 1  General information

The cooling system uses a water/antifreeze coolant to carry excess energy away from the engine in the form of heat. The cylinders are surrounded by a water jacket through which the coolant is circulated by thermo-syphonic action in conjunction with a water pump. The pump is mounted on the lower, left-hand side of the engine. Hot coolant flows upwards to the thermostat and then to the radiator, where it is cooled by the passing air. It then flows through the water pump and back to the engine where the cycle is repeated.

On GSX-R600 and GSX-R750 models coolant from the pump also flows through the oil cooler which is mounted on the front of the engine crankcases.

A thermostat is fitted in the system to prevent the coolant flowing through the radiator when the engine is cold, thus allowing the engine to reach normal operating temperature quickly. An electrically-controlled cooling fan is fitted behind the radiator to aid cooling in extreme conditions.

Coolant temperature information is supplied to the engine control module (ECM) and the instrument cluster display by a sensor mounted in the rear of the cylinder head.

The complete cooling system is partially sealed and pressurised, the pressure being controlled by a spring-loaded valve in the radiator cap. By pressurising the coolant the boiling point is raised, preventing premature boiling in adverse conditions. The overflow pipe from the radiator is connected to a reservoir into which excess coolant is expelled under pressure. The discharged coolant automatically returns to the radiator when the engine cools.

⚠ *Warning: Do not remove the pressure cap from the radiator when the engine is hot. Scalding hot coolant and steam may be blown out under pressure, which could cause serious injury. When the engine has cooled, place a thick rag, like a towel over the pressure cap; slowly rotate the cap anti-clockwise to allow any residual pressure to escape before removing the cap completely.*

⚠ *Warning: Do not allow antifreeze to come in contact with your skin or painted surfaces of the motorcycle. Rinse off any spills immediately with plenty of water. Antifreeze is highly toxic if ingested. Never leave antifreeze lying around in an open container or in puddles on the floor; children and pets are attracted by its sweet smell and may drink it. Check with the local authorities about disposing of used antifreeze. Many communities will have collection centres for the safe disposal of antifreeze.*

*Caution: At all times use the specified type of antifreeze, and always mix it with distilled water in the correct proportion. Antifreeze contains corrosion inhibitors which are essential to avoid damage to the cooling system. A lack of these inhibitors could lead to a build-up of corrosion which would block the coolant passages, resulting in overheating and severe engine damage. Distilled water must be used as opposed to tap water to avoid a build-up of scale which would also block the passages.*

## 2  Radiator pressure cap – check

1  If problems such as overheating or loss of coolant occur, check the entire system as described in Chapter 1. The operation of the radiator cap pressure valve should be checked by a Suzuki dealer with the special tester required to do the job. If the cap is defective, renew it.

## 3  Coolant reservoir – removal and installation

### Removal

1  The coolant reservoir is located on the inside of the fairing left-hand side panel. Remove the panel for access (see Chapter 8).
2  Place a suitable container underneath the reservoir, then release the clip securing the radiator overflow hose to the base of the reservoir. Detach the hose and allow the coolant to drain into the container **(see illustration)**.
3  Unscrew the reservoir mounting bolts and remove the reservoir **(see illustration 3.2)**. Note the routing of the reservoir breather hose over the back of the engine unit.

### Installation

4  Installation is the reverse of removal. Make sure the breather hose is correctly routed before installing the reservoir mounting bolts, and secure the radiator overflow hose with its clip. On completion refill the reservoir as described in *Daily (pre-ride) checks*.

## 4  Cooling fan switch, cooling fan and fan relay – check and renewal

### Cooling fan switch

#### Check

1  If the engine is overheating and the cooling fan isn't coming on, first check the coolant level (see *Daily (pre-ride) checks*). If the level is correct, check the cooling fan circuit fuse (see Chapter 9). If the fuse is blown, check the fan circuit for a short to earth (see *Wiring diagrams* at the end of Chapter 9). On GSX-R1000 models, check the fan relay as described below.

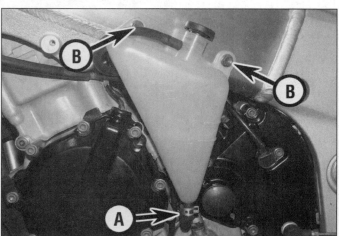

**3.2  Detach the hose (A) and undo the mounting bolts (B)**

**4.2  Cooling fan switch wiring connector**

**2** If the fuse is good, remove the fairing left-hand side panel (see Chapter 8), and disconnect the wiring connector from the fan switch on the left-hand side of the radiator **(see illustration)**.

**3** Using a jumper wire, connect the black/white wire terminal in the wiring connector to earth (ground) and turn the ignition ON. If the fan comes on, the switch connection or the switch is defective and must be renewed (see Steps 7 to 10). If it does not come on, the fan motor should be tested (see Steps 11 and 12).

**4** If the fan stays on all the time the ignition is ON, disconnect the fan switch wiring connector. The fan should stop. If it does, the switch is defective and must be renewed. If it doesn't, check the wiring between the switch and the fan motor for a short to earth.

**5** If the fan works but is suspected of cutting in at the wrong temperature, a more comprehensive test of the switch can be made as follows. Remove the switch (see Steps 7 to 10). Fill a small heatproof container with oil and place it on a stove. Connect the probes of an ohmmeter or continuity tester to the switch terminals, and using some wire or other support, suspend the switch in the oil so that just the sensing portion and the threads are submerged **(see illustration 5.3)**. Also place a thermometer capable of reading temperatures up to 110°C in the oil so that its bulb is close to the switch. **Note:** *None of the components should be allowed to touch the container directly.*

**6** Initially there should be no continuity (infinite resistance) indicating that the switch is open (OFF). Heat the oil slowly, stirring it gently.

 *Warning: This must be done very carefully to avoid the risk of personal injury.*

When the temperature reaches around 105°C there should be continuity (zero resistance), indicating that the switch has closed (ON). Now turn the heat off. As the temperature falls below 100°C there should again be no continuity (infinite resistance), indicating that the switch is open (OFF). If the test results are different, or they are obtained at different temperatures, then the switch is faulty and must be renewed.

**Renewal**

 *Warning: The engine must be completely cool before carrying out this procedure.*

**7** Drain the cooling system (see Chapter 1).

**8** Disconnect the wiring connector from the fan switch, then unscrew the switch and withdraw it from the radiator. Discard the O-ring as a new one must be fitted on reassembly.

**9** Apply a smear of grease to the new O-ring and fit it on the switch. Install the switch and tighten it to the torque setting specified at the beginning of the Chapter. Take care not to overtighten the switch.

**4.12 Disconnect the fan motor wiring connector**

**10** Reconnect the switch wiring and refill the cooling system (see Chapter 1 and *Daily (pre-ride) checks*). Install the remaining components in the reverse order of removal.

## Cooling fan

### Check

**11** If the engine is overheating and the fan does not come on (and the fan switch is good, and on the GSX-R1000 models the relay is good), the fault lies in either the cooling fan motor or the relevant wiring. Test all the wiring and connections as described in Chapter 9.

**12** To test the fan motor, remove the fairing right-hand side panel (see Chapter 8). Trace the wiring from the fan motor and disconnect it at the connector **(see illustration)**. Using a 12 volt battery and two jumper wires, connect the battery positive (+ve) terminal to the blue wire terminal on the fan side of the wiring connector and the battery negative (-ve) terminal to the black wire terminal. Once connected the fan should operate. If it does not, and the wiring is all good, then the fan motor is faulty.

### Renewal

 *Warning: The engine must be completely cool before carrying out this procedure.*

**13** Remove the radiator (see Section 7).

**14** Unscrew the three bolts securing the fan assembly to the radiator and remove the fan **(see illustration)**.

**15** Installation is the reverse of removal. Ensure the motor wiring is not trapped

**4.17a Displace the cooling fan relay and disconnect the wiring connector**

**4.14 Cooling fan is secured by three bolts**

between the fan and the radiator and tighten the mounting bolts securely, then install the radiator (see Section 7).

## Cooling fan relay – GSX-R1000 models

**16** The relay is mounted on the front of the battery carrier. To access the relay, remove the rider's seat (see Chapter 8). If necessary, remove the fuel tank (see Chapter 4).

**17** The fan relay is on the right-hand side of the fuel pump relay; pull the relay off its mounting lugs and disconnect the wiring connector **(see illustration)**. Using a multimeter or test light, check for continuity between terminals 1 and 2 on the relay **(see illustration)**. There should be no continuity. Now use jumper wires to connect the positive (+ve) terminal of a fully charged 12 volt battery to terminal 3 on the relay and the negative (-ve) battery terminal to relay terminal 4. There should now be continuity between terminals 1 and 2. If the relay fails either of the checks it must be renewed.

---

**5  Engine coolant temperature (ECT) sensor –** check and renewal

---

### Check

**1** The engine coolant temperature (ECT) sensor is located in the rear of the cylinder head on the left-hand side **(see illustration)**. If a sensor fault is indicated by the fuel injection

**3**

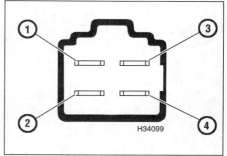

**4.17b Cooling fan relay terminal identification**

**5.1 Engine coolant temperature (ECT) wiring connector**

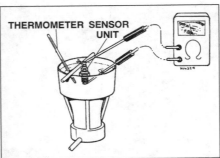

**5.3 Coolant temperature sensor testing set-up**

**5.6 Disconnect the wiring connector from the sensor (arrowed)**

system diagnostic process (see Chapter 4), carry out the preliminary checks as described in Chapter 4, Section 11.

**2** To check the sensor resistance remove it from the cylinder head (see Steps 5 to 7).

**3** Fill a small heatproof container with oil and place it on a stove. Using an ohmmeter set to the K-ohms scale, connect the meter probes to the sensor terminals, and using some wire or other support, suspend the sensor in the oil so that just the sensing portion and the threads are submerged **(see illustration)**. Also place a thermometer capable of reading temperatures up to 140°C in the oil so that its bulb is close to the switch. **Note:** *None of the components should be allowed to touch the container directly.*

**4** Check the meter reading and compare the result with the specifications at the beginning of this Chapter, then heat the oil slowly, stirring it gently.

 *Warning: This must be done very carefully to avoid the risk of personal injury.*

As the temperature of the oil rises, the sensor resistance should fall. Check that the specified resistance is obtained at the correct temperature (see Specifications at the beginning of this Chapter). If the readings obtained are different, or are obtained at different temperatures, the sensor is faulty and must be renewed. If the readings are as specified, the fault could lie in the coolant temperature display circuit in the instrument cluster (see Chapter 9).

## Renewal

 *Warning: The engine must be completely cool before carrying out this procedure.*

**5** Remove the fuel tank (see Chapter 4). Depending on the tools available, it may be necessary to disconnect the fuel hose from the fuel rail to gain access to the sensor.

**6** Disconnect the sensor wiring connector **(see illustration)**.

**7** If required, drain the cooling system (see Chapter 1), otherwise place a rag on the crankcase underneath the sensor and unscrew the sensor from the cylinder head. Discard the sealing washer as a new one must be fitted on reassembly.

**8** Installation is the reverse of removal, noting the following:

● Fit a new sealing washer to the sensor.
● Tighten the sensor to the torque setting specified at the beginning of this Chapter.
● Top-up or refill the cooling system as necessary (see Chapter 1 and *Daily (pre-ride) checks*).

## 6 Thermostat – removal, check and installation

## Removal

 *Warning: The engine must be completely cool before carrying out this procedure.*

**1** The thermostat is automatic in operation and should give many years service without requiring attention. In the event of a failure, the valve will probably jam open, in which case the engine will take much longer than normal to warm up. Conversely, if the valve jams shut, the coolant will be unable to circulate and the engine will overheat. Neither condition is acceptable, and the fault must be investigated promptly.

**2** Drain the cooling system (see Chapter 1). Remove the fuel tank (see Chapter 4).

**3** The thermostat is located in the thermostat housing, which is on the back of the cylinder head below the throttle body assembly.

**4** Release the radiator overflow hose from the guide secured by the lower thermostat housing bolt, then undo the housing bolts and ease the housing off the cylinder head **(see illustration)**.

**5** If required, release the clips securing the coolant hoses to the thermostat housing and disconnect the hoses. Remove the thermostat housing.

**6** Withdraw the thermostat, noting how it fits **(see illustration)**.

## Check

**7** Examine the thermostat visually before carrying out the test. If it remains in the open position at room temperature, it should be renewed **(see illustration)**.

**8** Fill a small, heatproof container with cold water and place it on a stove. Using a piece of wire, suspend the thermostat in the water.

**6.4 Undo the bolts to detach the housing . . .**

**6.6 . . . and remove the thermostat**

**6.7 Thermostat should be closed at room temperature**

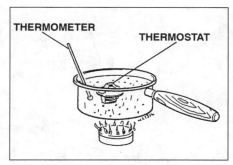
6.8 Thermostat testing set-up

6.11a Fit the thermostat with the hole at the top

6.11b Fit the hose guide (arrowed) to the lower bolt

Place a thermometer in the water so that its bulb is close to the thermostat **(see illustration)**. **Note:** *None of the components should be allowed to touch the container directly.*

9 Heat the water, noting the temperature when the thermostat opens, and compare the result with the specifications given at the beginning of this Chapter. Also check the amount the valve opens after it has been heated at 95°C for a few minutes and compare the measurement to the specifications. If the readings obtained differ from those given, the thermostat is faulty and must be renewed.

10 In the event of thermostat failure, as an emergency measure only, it can be removed and the machine used without it. **Note:** *Take care when starting the engine from cold as it will take much longer than usual to warm up.* Ensure that a new unit is installed as soon as possible.

## Installation

11 Installation is the reverse of removal, noting the following:
● Apply a smear of grease to the rubber seal on the thermostat.
● Install the thermostat with the bleed hole at the top **(see illustration)**.
● Fit the overflow hose guide and tighten the housing bolts to the specified torque setting **(see illustration)**.
● Install the coolant hoses (see Section 9).

## 7 Radiator – removal and installation

### Removal

> **Warning: The engine must be completely cool before carrying out this procedure.**

1 Remove the fairing side panels (see Chapter 8) and drain the cooling system (see Chapter 1).
2 Loosen the clips securing the coolant hoses to the radiator and detach the hoses noting where they fit **(see illustrations)**. Disconnect the fan switch wiring connector and the fan motor wiring connector **(see illustrations 4.2 and 4.12)**.
3 On GSX-R1000 models, undo the bolts securing the oil cooler to the brackets on the bottom of the radiator.
4 On all models, undo the radiator lower mounting bolt and remove the bolt and washer **(see illustration)**.
5 Support the radiator, then undo the upper mounting bolts and remove the bolts and washers and lift off the radiator **(see illustration)**. **Note:** *When removing components of the cooling system, be prepared to catch any residual fluids.*
6 If required, separate the cooling fan from the radiator (see Section 4). Note the spacers inside the bushes on the radiator mounting brackets and remove them for safekeeping. If required, undo the bolt that secures the lower bracket to the crankcase and remove the bracket.
7 Check the radiator for damage and clear any dirt or debris that might obstruct air flow and inhibit cooling (see Chapter 1). Check the mounting bushes and fit new ones if they are damaged or deteriorated.

**3**

7.2a Loosen the clips . . .

7.2b . . . and detach the hoses . . .

7.2c . . . noting where they fit

7.4 Undo the lower . . .

7.5 . . . then the upper radiator mounting bolts

## Installation

**8** Installation is the reverse of removal, noting the following:

● Ensure the bushes and spacers are correctly installed in the mounting brackets **(see illustration)**.

● Ensure the fan and fan switch wiring is securely connected.

● Check the condition of the coolant hoses and the hose clips (see Chapter 1).

● On completion, refill the cooling system (see Chapter 1).

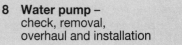

| 8 | Water pump – |
|---|---|
|   | check, removal, |
|   | overhaul and installation |

## Check

**1** The water pump is located on the lower left-hand side of the engine. Check the area around the pump for signs of leakage.

**2** To prevent leakage of water from the cooling system into the lubrication system a mechanical seal is fitted on the pump shaft behind the impeller. If the seal fails, a drain hole in the underside of the pump body allows the coolant to escape **(see illustration)**. Look for telltale signs of leakage around the drain hole. To prevent oil entering the cooling system, an oil seal is installed on the shaft behind the mechanical seal.

**7.8  Ensure each bush and spacer is correctly installed**

**3** The pump shaft runs in two bearings. To check the bearings, first remove the pump and the pump cover (see Steps 4 to 9). Rock the impeller back-and-forth and spin it by hand. If there is excessive movement in the shaft or the bearings are noisy or rough when turned, new bearings must be fitted.

## Removal

**4** Drain the coolant and the engine oil (see Chapter 1).

**5** Remove the coolant reservoir (see Section 3), and the front sprocket cover (see Chapter 6). **Note:** *On GSX-R600 and GSX-R750 models, one of the front sprocket cover bolts also secures the water pump to the crankcase.*

**6** To displace the pump cover, undo the bolt(s) securing the pump to the crankcase

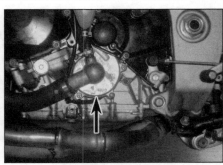

**8.2  Check the underside of the water pump for signs of leakage**

and undo the cover screws **(see illustration)**. There is no need to detach the hoses unless you want to remove the cover from the bike. Discard the cover O-ring as a new one must be fitted on reassembly. Note the guide for the gear position sensor wiring.

**7** Withdraw the pump body from the crankcase and discard the body O-ring as a new one must be fitted on reassembly.

**8** To remove the pump as an assembly, first loosen the clips securing the coolant hoses to the pump cover and detach the hoses, noting which fits where.

**9** Undo the bolt(s) securing the pump to the crankcase **(see illustration 8.6)** and withdraw the pump **(see illustration)**. Discard the body O-ring. If required, undo the cover screws and remove the cover. Discard the cover O-ring.

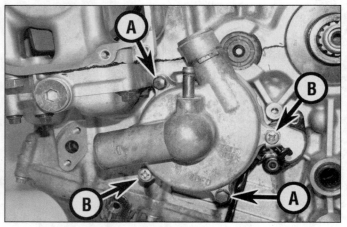

**8.6  Water pump mounting bolts (A) and cover screws (B)**

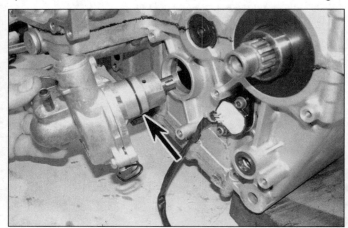

**8.9  Withdraw the pump and discard the O-ring**

**8.10a  Hold the impeller with grips . . .**

**8.10b  . . . then remove the bolt, lock washer and sealing washer . . .**

**8.10c  . . . and lift off the impeller**

## Overhaul

**10** Hold the impeller with some suitable grips, then unscrew the impeller bolt, noting the sealing washer and lock washer, and remove the impeller (see illustrations). Inspect the sealing washer and renew it if necessary

**11** Remove the seal ring from the back of the impeller, and withdraw the pump shaft from the rear of the pump body, noting the E-clip on the shaft (see illustrations).

**12** To renew the seals without disturbing the bearings, first pull the mechanical seal out of the pump body with a knife-edged bearing puller (see *Tools and Workshop Tips* in the reference Section) (see illustration). Next, lever out the oil seal using a small flat-bladed screwdriver, noting how it fits. Take care not to damage or scratch the inside of the pump body.

**13** Lubricate the new oil seal with multi-purpose grease and install it in the pump body. The marked side of the seal should face the bearings. Carefully press the seal into its seat with a suitable sized socket. Now carefully press the new mechanical seal into place making sure the socket presses on the body of the seal, not the sprung seal itself.

**14** If the bearings and seals are being renewed at the same time, use a knife-edged bearing puller (see *Tools and Workshop Tips* in the reference Section) and draw out the first bearing from the rear of the body (see illustration). Use the same technique to draw the second bearing out of the body. Note that once disturbed, the bearings should not be reused. Follow Step 12 and remove the seals.

**15** Press each new bearing into its seat in the pump body with a suitable sized socket, installing the smaller diameter bearing first. Follow Step 13 and install the new seals.

**16** Ensure the E-clip is securely fitted in the groove in the pump shaft, then smear the shaft with grease and install the shaft. Fit the new seal ring onto the back of the impeller then fit the impeller onto the shaft.

**8.11a Remove the seal ring from the impeller . . .**

**8.12 If required, remove the seals (arrowed) from the front of the pump . . .**

**17** Install the convex side of the lock washer and the metal side of the sealing washer towards the head of the impeller bolt, then apply a suitable, non permanent thread locking compound to the bolt threads and install the bolt. Hold the impeller as before and tighten the bolt to the specified torque.

## Installation

**18** Installation is the reverse of removal, noting the following:

● Lubricate the pump cover O-ring with coolant before fitting it (see illustration).

**8.11b . . . and withdraw the pump shaft – note the E-clip (arrowed)**

**8.14 . . . and the bearings from the rear of the pump body**

● Apply a smear of grease to the new pump body O-ring before fitting it (see illustration).
● Ensure the fork in the water pump shaft is engaged with the tab on the oil pump shaft.
● Ensure the guide for the gear position wiring is fitted to the forward facing pump cover screw.
● Tighten the cover screws and pump mounting bolts to the specified torque settings.
● If removed, install the coolant hoses fully onto their unions and secure them with the clips.
● Replenish the coolant and the engine oil (see Chapter 1 and *Daily (pre-ride) checks*).

**3**

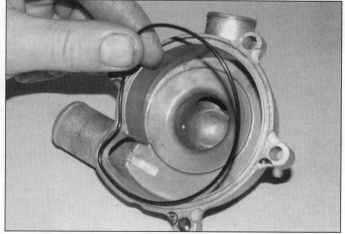

**8.18a Install the new O-ring inside the lip around the pump body**

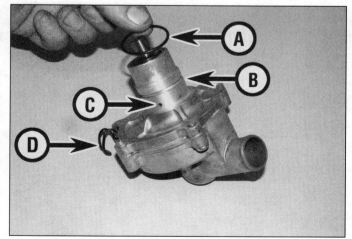

**8.18b Install the new O-ring (A) in the groove (B). Note the drain hole (C) and the wiring guide (D)**

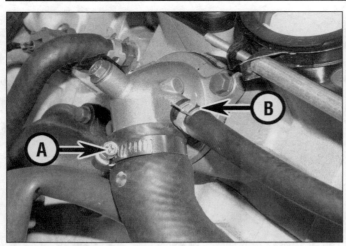

9.2 Large bore hoses are secured with hose clips (A). Small bore hoses are secures by spring clips (B)

9.5 Work the hose on all the way to the index mark

## 9  Coolant hoses –
### removal and installation

### Removal

**1** Before removing a hose, drain the coolant (see Chapter 1). **Note:** *When removing components of the cooling system, be prepared to catch any residual coolant.*

**2** Use a screwdriver or small socket to loosen the larger-bore hose clips, then slide them back along the hose and clear of the union spigot. The smaller-bore hoses are secured by spring clips which can be expanded by squeezing their ends together with pliers **(see illustration)**.

*Caution: The radiator unions are fragile. Do not use excessive force when attempting to remove the hoses.*

**3** If a hose proves stubborn, release it by rotating it on its union before working it off. If all else fails, cut the hose with a sharp knife then slit it lengthways at the union so that it can be peeled off (see *Tools and Workshop Tips* in the reference Section). Whilst this means renewing the hose, it is preferable to buying a new radiator.

**4** The coolant union on the back of the cylinder block can be removed by unscrewing its bolts (see Chapter 2, Section 22). If the union is removed, the O-ring must be renewed.

### Installation

**5** Slide the clip onto the hose first and then work the hose all the way onto its union as far as the shoulder or index mark **(see illustration)**.

> **HAYNES HiNT**
> *If the hose is difficult to push on its union, it can be softened by soaking it in very hot water, or alternatively a little soapy water can be used as a lubricant.*

**6** Rotate the hose on its unions to settle it in position before sliding the clips into place and tightening them securely.

**7** If removed, tighten the coolant union bolts to the specified torque setting.

# Chapter 4
# Fuel and exhaust systems

## Contents

## Degrees of difficulty

| Easy, suitable for novice with little experience 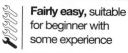 | Fairly easy, suitable for beginner with some experience 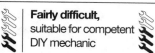 | Fairly difficult, suitable for competent DIY mechanic | Difficult, suitable for experienced DIY mechanic | Very difficult, suitable for expert DIY or professional |
|---|---|---|---|---|

## Specifications

### Fuel
Grade
GSX-R600 European models . . . . . . . . . . . . . . . . . . . . . . . . . . . Unleaded, minimum 91 RON (Research Octane Number)
GSX-R600 US model . . . . . . . . . . . . . . . . . . . . . . . . . . . . . . . . . Unleaded, minimum 87 ((R+M) /2 method)
GSX-R750 and GSX-R1000 European models . . . . . . . . . . . . . . . Premium unleaded, minimum 95 RON (Research Octane Number)
GSX-R750 and GSX-R1000 US models . . . . . . . . . . . . . . . . . . . . Premium unleaded, minimum 90 ((R+M) /2 method)
Fuel tank capacity (including reserve) . . . . . . . . . . . . . . . . . . . . . . 18 litres

### Fuel supply system
Operating pressure . . . . . . . . . . . . . . . . . . . . . . . . . . . . . . . . . . . 43 psi (2.97 Bar)
Pump flow rate . . . . . . . . . . . . . . . . . . . . . . . . . . . . . . . . . . . . . . 1.2 litre per 30 secs.

### Throttle body
Identification marking
GSX-R600 – California . . . . . . . . . . . . . . . . . . . . . . . . . . . . . . . . 39 F1
GSX-R600 – all other markets . . . . . . . . . . . . . . . . . . . . . . . . . . . 39 F0
GSX-R750 Y and K1 – California . . . . . . . . . . . . . . . . . . . . . . . . . 35 F1
GSX-R750 Y and K1 – all other markets . . . . . . . . . . . . . . . . . . . 35 F0
GSX-R750 K2 – California . . . . . . . . . . . . . . . . . . . . . . . . . . . . . . 35 F3
GSX-R750 K2 – all other markets . . . . . . . . . . . . . . . . . . . . . . . . 35 F2
GSX-R1000 K1 – California . . . . . . . . . . . . . . . . . . . . . . . . . . . . . 40 F1
GSX-R1000 K1 – all other markets . . . . . . . . . . . . . . . . . . . . . . . 40 F0
GSX-R1000 K2 – California . . . . . . . . . . . . . . . . . . . . . . . . . . . . . 40 F3
GSX-R1000 K2 – all other markets . . . . . . . . . . . . . . . . . . . . . . . 40 F2
Bore diameter
GSX-R600 . . . . . . . . . . . . . . . . . . . . . . . . . . . . . . . . . . . . . . . . . 38 mm
GSX-R750 . . . . . . . . . . . . . . . . . . . . . . . . . . . . . . . . . . . . . . . . . 42 mm
GSX-R1000 K1 . . . . . . . . . . . . . . . . . . . . . . . . . . . . . . . . . . . . . . 38 mm
GSX-R1000 K2 . . . . . . . . . . . . . . . . . . . . . . . . . . . . . . . . . . . . . . 42 mm
Idle speed . . . . . . . . . . . . . . . . . . . . . . . . . . . . . . . . . . . . . . . . . see Chapter 1
Fast idle speed
GSX-R600 . . . . . . . . . . . . . . . . . . . . . . . . . . . . . . . . . . . . . . . . . 3000 rpm
GSX-R750 . . . . . . . . . . . . . . . . . . . . . . . . . . . . . . . . . . . . . . . . . 3500 rpm
GSX-R1000K1 . . . . . . . . . . . . . . . . . . . . . . . . . . . . . . . . . . . . . . 2200 rpm
GSX-R1000K2 . . . . . . . . . . . . . . . . . . . . . . . . . . . . . . . . . . . . . . 1800 +200 rpm/–300 rpm

**4**

## Component test data

Air pressure (AP) sensor
Input voltage .................................................... 4.5 to 5.5 V
Output voltage ................................................ 3.6 V @ 760 mmHg
Camshaft position (CMP) sensor
Resistance
GSX-R600 K2 and GSX-R750 K2 ........................ 0.9 to 2.0 K-ohms
All other models ......................................... 0.9 to 1.7 K-ohms
Peak voltage .................................................. above 0.7 V
Crankshaft position (CKP) sensor
Resistance ..................................................... 70 to 220 ohms
Peak voltage .................................................. above 0.5 V
Engine coolant temperature (ECT) sensor
Input voltage .................................................. 4.5 to 5.5 V
Resistance ..................................................... 2.3 to 2.6 K-ohms @ 20°C
Exhaust control valve servo position sensor – GSX-R1000
Input voltage .................................................. 4.5 to 5.5 V
Output voltage
Closed ....................................................... above 0.2 V
Open ......................................................... below 4.8 V
Resistance ..................................................... 3.1 K-ohms
Gear position (GP) sensor voltage ......................... above 0.6 V
Injector voltage ................................................. Battery voltage (12 V approx)
Injector resistance ............................................ 11 to 16 ohms @ 20°C
Intake air pressure (IAP) sensor
Input voltage .................................................. 4.5 to 5.5 V
Output voltage
GSX-R600 ................................................... 1.32 V approx at idle
GSX-R750 ................................................... 2.70 V approx at idle
GSX-R1000 .................................................. 2.64 V approx at idle
Intake air temperature (IAT) sensor
Input voltage .................................................. 4.5 to 5.5 V
Resistance ..................................................... 2.2 to 2.7 K-ohms @ 20°C
Secondary throttle position (STP) sensor – GSX-R600, GSX-R750K2 and GSX-R1000
Input voltage .................................................. 4.5 to 5.5 V
Output voltage
GSX-R600
Closed ................................................... 0.8 V approx
Open ..................................................... 4.0 V approx
GSX-R750K2 and GSX-R1000
Closed ................................................... 0.5 V approx
Open ..................................................... 3.7 V approx
Resistance
GSX-R600
Closed ................................................... 0.8 K-ohms approx
Open ..................................................... 3.9 K-ohms approx
GSX-R750K2 and GSX-R1000
Closed ................................................... 0.5 K-ohms approx
Open ..................................................... 3.9 K-ohms approx
Secondary throttle valve (STV) servo resistance
GSX-R600 ................................................... 5.6 ohms approx
GSX-R750K2, GSX-R1000 ................................ 6.5 ohms approx
Secondary throttle valve servo position sensor – GSX-R750Y, K1
Input voltage .................................................. 4.5 to 5.5 V
Output voltage
Closed ....................................................... 0.2 to 0.8 V
Open ......................................................... 4.2 to 4.8 V
Resistance ..................................................... 3.1 K-ohms approx
Throttle position (TP) sensor
Input voltage .................................................. 4.5 to 5.5 V
Output voltage
Closed ....................................................... 1.1 V approx
Open ......................................................... 4.3 V approx
Resistance
Closed ....................................................... 1.1 K-ohms approx
Open ......................................................... 4.3 K-ohms approx
Tip over (TO) sensor
Resistance ..................................................... 60 to 64 K-ohms
Voltage ......................................................... 2.5 V approx

## Torque settings

| | |
|---|---|
| Camshaft position (CMP) sensor mounting bolt . . . . . . . . . . . . . . . . . . | 8 Nm |
| Exhaust system | |
|    Downpipe clamp bolts . . . . . . . . . . . . . . . . . . . . . . . . . . . . . | 23 Nm |
|    System-to-frame mounting bolt . . . . . . . . . . . . . . . . . . . . . . . . | 23 Nm |
|    Silencer-to-downpipe nuts . . . . . . . . . . . . . . . . . . . . . . . . . . | 25 Nm |
|    Silencer-to-passenger footrest bolt nut . . . . . . . . . . . . . . . . . . . | 23 Nm |
| Exhaust control valve – GSX-R1000 | |
|    Servo mounting bolts . . . . . . . . . . . . . . . . . . . . . . . . . . . . | 5 Nm |
|    Servo pulley bolt . . . . . . . . . . . . . . . . . . . . . . . . . . . . . . | 5 Nm |
| Fuel rail mounting screws | |
|    GSX-R600 and GSX-R750Y, K1 . . . . . . . . . . . . . . . . . . . . . . . | 5 Nm |
|    GSX-R750K2 and GSX-R1000 . . . . . . . . . . . . . . . . . . . . . . . | 3.5 Nm |
| Fuel pressure check bolt – GSX-R750Y . . . . . . . . . . . . . . . . . . . . | 5 Nm |
| Fuel pump mounting bolts . . . . . . . . . . . . . . . . . . . . . . . . . . . . | 10 Nm |
| Intake air temperature (IAT) sensor . . . . . . . . . . . . . . . . . . . . . . . | 18 Nm |
| PAIR reed valve cover bolt . . . . . . . . . . . . . . . . . . . . . . . . . . . | 10 Nm |
| Secondary throttle position (STP) sensor Torx screw(s) . . . . . . . . . . . | 3.5 Nm |
| Secondary throttle valve (STV) servo mounting bolts – GSX-R750K2 | |
|    and GSX-R1000 . . . . . . . . . . . . . . . . . . . . . . . . . . . . . . . | 3.5 Nm |
| Secondary throttle valve (STV) servo mounting bolts – | |
|    GSX-R750Y, K1 . . . . . . . . . . . . . . . . . . . . . . . . . . . . . . . | 5 Nm |
| Secondary throttle valve (STV) servo pulley bolt – GSX-R750Y, K1 . . . | 5 Nm |
| Secondary throttle valve (STV) servo mounting studs – GSX-R600 . . . . | 3.5 Nm |
| Secondary throttle valve (STV) servo cover nuts – GSX-R600 . . . . . . . | 2 Nm |
| Throttle body connecting bolts . . . . . . . . . . . . . . . . . . . . . . . . . | 6 Nm |
| Throttle position (TP) sensor screws . . . . . . . . . . . . . . . . . . . . . . | 3.5 Nm |

## 1  General information and precautions

### General information

The fuel system consists of the fuel tank, incorporating the fuel pump and filter, the fuel hose to the fuel rail on the throttle bodies, and the injectors that are located in each throttle body – one for each cylinder. The fuel pump is activated initially by the ignition switch and continues to deliver fuel so long as the engine is running. Fuel pressure is controlled within the pump by a pressure regulator. In the event of the machine falling over, a tip-over sensor cuts power to the fuel pump, injectors and ignition coils.

The entire fuel injection system is controlled by the engine control module (ECM) which monitors data sent from the various system sensors and adjusts fuel delivery to the engine accordingly. If a fault develops in the injection system, the FI warning LED illuminates on the instrument cluster and an LCD code is displayed. In the case of a minor fault the engine will continue to run enabling the machine to be ridden, although performance will be significantly reduced. For comprehensive fault diagnosis and certain service procedures, a Suzuki mode select switch (Pt. No. 09930-82710) is required.

The SDTV (Suzuki Dual Throttle Valve) fuel injection system uses two throttle valves in each throttle body. The main valve is actuated by the throttle cables from the handlebar twistgrip, the secondary valve is actuated by a servo controlled by the ECM for the purpose of smoothing air flow into the throttle body.

Suzuki's SRAD (Suzuki Ram Air Direct) system consists of large ducts in the nose of the fairing which feed the airbox. Air is drawn into the throttle bodies via the airbox which is housed under the fuel tank. For running the engine from cold, a fast idle lever is incorporated in the left-handlebar switch housing and is connected to the throttle body assembly by a cable. GSX-R1000K2 models are fitted with a wax element fast idle unit which does away with the need for a choke cable.

The exhaust system is a four-into-one design. The GSX-R1000 models are fitted with a SET (Suzuki Exhaust Tuning) exhaust control valve; the butterfly type valve is operated by a servomotor. All models feature a PAIR system which introduces filtered air into the exhaust ports to promote the burning of excess fuel in the exhaust gases, and on California models an EVAP emission control system prevents fuel vapour escaping into the atmosphere from the fuel tank.

### Precautions

⚠️ Warning: Petrol (gasoline) is extremely flammable, so take extra precautions when you work on any part of the fuel system. Don't smoke or allow open flames or bare light bulbs near the work area, and don't work in a garage where a natural gas-type appliance is present. If you spill any fuel on your skin, rinse it off immediately with soap and water. When you perform any kind of work on the fuel system, wear safety glasses and have a fire extinguisher suitable for a class B type fire (flammable liquids) on hand.

Always perform service procedures in a well-ventilated area to prevent a build-up of fumes.

Never work in a building containing a gas appliance with a pilot light, or any other form of naked flame. Ensure that there are no naked light bulbs or any sources of flame or sparks nearby.

Do not smoke (or allow anyone else to smoke) while in the vicinity of petrol (gasoline) or of components containing it. Remember the possible presence of vapour from these sources and move well clear before smoking.

Check all electrical equipment belonging to the house, garage or workshop where work is being undertaken (see the Safety first! section of this manual). Remember that certain electrical appliances such as drills, cutters etc. create sparks in the normal course of operation and must not be used near petrol (gasoline) or any component containing it. Again, remember the possible presence of fumes before using electrical equipment.

Always mop up any spilt fuel and safely dispose of the rag used.

Any stored fuel that is drained off during servicing work must be kept in sealed containers that are suitable for holding petrol (gasoline), and clearly marked as such; the containers themselves should be kept in a safe place. Note that this last point applies equally to the fuel tank if it is removed from the machine; also remember to keep its filler cap closed at all times.

Read the Safety first! section of this manual carefully before starting work.

Owners of machines used in the US, particularly California, should note that their machines must comply at all times with

**4**

**2.2a Undo the tank front mounting bolts (arrowed)**

**2.2b Support the front of the tank with the prop**

## Removal

**3** Follow steps 1 and 2. Ensure the ignition switch is OFF, then disconnect the fuel pump wiring connector **(see illustration)**.

**4** Place a rag underneath the fuel hose to catch any residual fuel, then release the clip on the fuel hose connector and disconnect the hose from the union on the bottom of the fuel pump **(see illustration)**. Pull the breather hose off the union on the underside of the tank **(see illustration)**.

**5** Undo the bolts securing the tank rear bracket to the frame, then remove the prop and lift off the tank **(see illustration)**. Note the location of the fuel tank mounting rubbers on the lower edge of the tank and the frame **(see illustrations)**. Inspect the mounting rubbers for signs of damage or deterioration and renew them if necessary. Note the location of the heat shield, if fitted, on the underside of the tank.

## Installation

**6** Check that the tank mounting rubbers and heat shield are fitted, then carefully lower the fuel tank into position on the frame. Install the bolts in the tank rear bracket and tighten them finger-tight.

**7** Raise the front of the tank and support it with the prop. Align the fuel hose connector with the union on the bottom of the fuel pump and push it on fully so that the clip engages **(see illustration 2.4a)**. Push the breather hose fully onto the union on the bottom of the tank **(see illustration 2.4b)**.

**8** Ensure the ignition switch is OFF, then connect the fuel pump wiring connector **(see illustration 2.3)**.

**9** Ensure the grommet and sleeve are in place on both the front tank mounting lugs, then remove the prop and lower the tank. Align the lugs with the threaded holes in the frame, then install the washers and bolts and tighten the bolts securely. Tighten the tank rear bracket bolts.

**10** Start the engine and check that there is no sign of fuel leakage, then turn it OFF.

**11** Clip the fuel tank prop in the storage space underneath the passenger's seat, then install the remaining components in the reverse order of removal.

**2.3 Disconnect the fuel pump wiring connector . . .**

**2.4a . . . and the fuel hose connector. Note the mounting rubber (arrowed)**

Federal or State legislation governing the permissible levels of noise and of pollutants such as unburnt hydrocarbons, carbon monoxide etc. that can be emitted by those machines. All vehicles offered for sale must comply with legislation in force at the date of manufacture and must not subsequently be altered in any way which will affect their emission of noise or of pollutants.

In practice, this means that adjustments may not be made to any part of the fuel, ignition or exhaust systems by anyone who is not authorised or mechanically qualified to do so, or who does not have the tools, equipment and data necessary to properly carry out the task. Also if any part of these systems is to be renewed it must be renewed with only genuine Suzuki components or by components which are approved under the relevant legislation. The machine must never be used with any part of these systems removed, modified or damaged.

## 2 Fuel tank –
raise, removal and installation

⚠️ *Warning: Refer to the precautions given in Section 1 before starting work.*

### Raise

**1** Make sure the fuel cap is secure, then remove the rider's and passenger's seats (see Chapter 8). Remove the fuel tank prop from the storage space underneath the passenger's seat.

**2** Undo the bolts securing the front of the fuel tank to the frame **(see illustration)**. Note the location of the washer, grommet and sleeve on each tank mounting lug. Raise the front of the tank and support it with the prop **(see illustration)**.

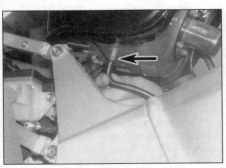

**2.4b Disconnect the breather hose**

**2.5a Unscrew the tank bracket bolts**

**2.5b Tank rubbers locate in brackets on both sides of the frame**

## 3 Fuel tank –
cleaning and repair

1 All repairs to the fuel tank should be carried out by a professional who has experience in this critical and potentially dangerous work. Even after cleaning and flushing the fuel system, explosive fumes can remain and ignite during repair of the tank.
2 If the fuel tank is removed from the bike, it should not be placed in an area where sparks or open flames could ignite the fumes coming out of the tank. Be especially careful inside garages where a natural gas-type appliance is located, because the pilot light could cause an explosion.

## 4 Fuel pump –
pressure and
fuel delivery check

**Warning: Refer to the precautions given in Section 1 before starting work.**

1 The fuel pump is located inside the fuel tank. When the ignition is switched ON, it should be possible to hear the pump run for a few seconds until the system is up to pressure. If you can't hear anything, first check the fuse (see Chapter 9), then check the relay (see Section 5). If they are good, check the wiring and terminals for physical damage or loose or corroded connections and rectify as necessary (see the *Wiring Diagrams* at the end of Chapter 9). If the pump still will not run, fit a new pump assembly.

### Pressure check

2 To check the fuel pressure, a suitable gauge, gauge hose and adapters will be needed to connect. Suzuki provides service tools (Pt. Nos. 09915-77330, 09915-74520, 09940-40211 and 09940-40220) for this purpose.
3 On GSX-R750Y models raise the fuel tank, then place some rag and a suitable container underneath the fuel pressure check bolt on the fuel rail between Nos. 3 and 4 injectors. Carefully undo the bolt and catch any residual fuel in the container. Discard the bolt washer as a new one must be fitted on reassembly. Use the adapter (Pt. No. 09940-40211) to connect the gauge and hose to the fuel rail.
4 On all other models raise the fuel tank, then disconnect the fuel hose from the fuel pump (see Section 2). Use the adapters to connect the gauge between the fuel tank and the fuel rail.
5 Turn the ignition switch ON and check the pressure reading on the gauge. The pressure should be as specified at the beginning of this Chapter.
6 Turn the ignition OFF and disconnect the gauge and adapters. Use a rag to catch any residual fuel as before. On GSX-R750Y models fit a new washer to the pressure check bolt and tighten the bolt to the torque

5.2a Displace the fuel pump relay and disconnect the wiring connector

setting specified at the beginning of this Chapter. On all other models connect the fuel hose to the pump (see Section 2).
7 If the pressure is too low, check for a leak in the fuel supply system, a blocked fuel filter (see Section 7), a faulty pressure regulator or a faulty fuel pump.
8 If the pressure is too high, either the pressure regulator or the fuel pump check valve is faulty.
9 Suzuki provides no test procedure for the pressure regulator. Disassemble the pump to inspect the regulator (see Section 7). A new regulator is only available as an integral part of the pump filter cartridge. The fuel check valve is an integral part of the pump and is not available separately.

### Fuel delivery check

10 Raise the fuel tank, then disconnect the fuel hose from the fuel pump **(see illustration 2.4a)**.
11 Attach a length of fuel hose to the pump union, then place the open end of the hose in a calibrated container suitable for holding at least 2 litres of fuel.
12 Ensure the ignition is OFF, then disconnect the fuel pump wiring connector **(see illustration 2.3)**. Using a fully charged 12 volt battery and two insulated jumper wires, connect the battery positive (+ve) terminal to the pump's yellow/red wire terminal, and the battery negative (-ve) terminal to the pump's black/white wire terminal. Let fuel flow from the pump into the container for 30 seconds, then disconnect the battery.
13 Measure the amount of fuel that has flowed into the container and compare it to

6.2a Undo the bolts (arrowed) . . .

the amount specified at the beginning of this Chapter. If the flow rate recorded is below the minimum required, either the fuel filter is blocked or the pump is defective and must be renewed.

## 5 Fuel pump relay –
check

1 The relay is mounted on the front of the battery carrier. To access the relay, remove the rider's seat (see Chapter 8). If necessary, remove the fuel tank (see Step 2). **Note:** *On GSX-R1000 models, the fuel pump relay is on the left-hand side of the fan motor relay.*
2 Pull the relay off its mounting lugs and disconnect the wiring connector **(see illustration)**. Using a multimeter or test light, check for continuity between terminals 1 and 2 on the relay **(see illustration)**. There should be no continuity. Now use jumper wires to connect the positive (+ve) terminal of a fully charged 12 volt battery to terminal 3 on the relay and the negative (-ve) battery terminal to relay terminal 4. There should be continuity shown across terminals 1 and 2. If the relay fails either of the checks, renew it.

## 6 Fuel pump –
removal and installation

**Warning: Refer to the precautions given in Section 1 before starting work.**

### Removal

1 The fuel pump is located inside the fuel tank. Remove the tank and drain it (see Section 2).
2 Turn the tank upside down and rest it on some clean rag to protect the paintwork. Undo the bolts securing the pump base to the underside of the tank and lift out the pump **(see illustrations)**. Discard the O-ring as a new one must be fitted on reassembly.
3 If required, disassemble the pump assembly to clean the filter and check the operation of the level sensor (see Section 7).

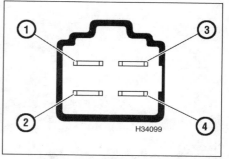
5.2b Fuel pump relay terminal identification

**4**

6.2b ... and lift out the pump

6.4 Ensure the wiring terminals (arrowed) are tight

6.5 Clip secures the fuel pressure regulator

6.6 Fit a new O-ring into the recess around the tank aperture

**4** Check that the wiring terminals for the fuel pump and the level sensor are tight **(see illustration)**.

**5** If required, release the clip securing the fuel pressure regulator to the filter cartridge and pull off the regulator **(see illustration)**. Discard the O-ring as a new one must be fitted on reassembly. On reassembly, install the new O-ring on the regulator and smear it with engine oil, then press the regulator into place and secure it with the clip.

### Installation

**6** Fit a new O-ring into the recess around the aperture on the underside of the fuel tank and smear the O-ring lightly with grease **(see illustration)**.

**7** Install the pump and align the holes in the pump base with the threaded holes in the tank. Apply a suitable thread locking compound to the bolts and install them finger-tight, then tighten them gradually in a criss-

cross pattern to the torque setting specified at the beginning of this Chapter.

**8** Install the fuel tank (see Section 2) and refill it. Ensure there are no signs of fuel leakage around the pump base.

## 7 Fuel filter, filter cartridge and fuel level sensor – removal, check and installation

> **Warning: Refer to the precautions given in Section 1 before starting work.**

### Fuel filter and filter cartridge

**1** Remove the fuel pump assembly (see Section 6).

**2** Undo the nuts securing the pump and level sensor terminals and detach the wires, noting their position, then undo the screws securing the pump assembly to the pump base **(see illustrations)**. Note the fuel pump wire terminal secured by the assembly screw.

**3** Pull the pump assembly out of the base and discard the O-ring on the base fuel union as a

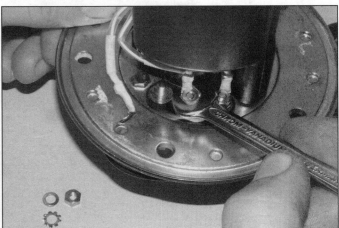

7.2a Disconnect the pump and level sensor terminals ...

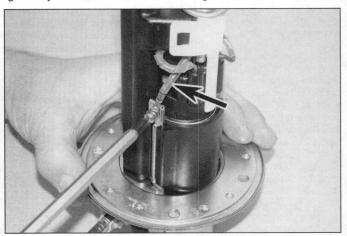

7.2b ... then undo the screws securing the assembly to the base. Note the terminal (arrowed)

7.3a  Pull off the pump assembly and discard the O-ring (arrowed)

7.3b  Slide off the filter shield

7.4a  Clean any sediment out of the pump base . . .

7.4b  . . . and off the filter element

7.5a  Detach the clip . . .

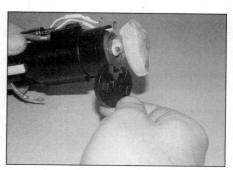

7.5b  . . . then pull off the cover . . .

new one must be fitted on reassembly (see illustration). Slide the filter shield off the filter element (see illustration).

4 Clean any sediment out of the pump base (see illustration). Once the filter element is dry, clean any sediment off the gauze with a soft brush or low pressure compressed air (see illustration). If the element is damaged, or if there is sediment inside the element, a new filter should be fitted.

5 If there is sediment inside the fuel filter, a new filter cartridge should also be fitted. Detach the clip and cover from the bottom of the pump and pull off the filter (see illustrations). If required, pull the pump out of the pump case/filter cartridge.

6 Install the components in the reverse order of disassembly, noting the following:
● Fit a new O-ring to the pump base fuel union and smear it with engine oil (see illustration 7.3a).

● Ensure the clips are in place on both brackets for the pump retaining screws (see illustration).

### Fuel level sensor

Note: On GSX-R600K1, GSX-R750Y, K1 and GSX-R1000K1 models, the fuel warning LED will flicker when the volume of fuel in the tank drops to 4 litres; when it drops to 2 litres the warning LED will remain on. On all K2 models onwards, the fuel warning LED will come on when the volume of fuel in the tank drops to 4 litres.

7 Remove the fuel pump assembly (see Section 6).

8 Trace the wires from the sensor to their terminals on the pump base, noting their position, then undo the nuts securing the wires and detach them (see illustration).

9 Connect a self-powered test light or battery and bulb test circuit to the sensor earth

(ground) terminal and to the sensor wires in turn (see illustration, part A shown overleaf). Note that K2 models onward, only have one sensor wire. The bulb should come on after a few seconds in each case if the sensor is good.

10 Undo the screw securing the sensor to the fuel pump and unclip the sensor from the pump case/filter cartridge, noting how it fits.

11 Connect a test light as in Step 9 and immerse the sensor in water as shown in part B of illustration 7.9, noting the different water levels. The bulb should come on after a few seconds in each case if the sensor is good.

12 If the tests show the lever sensor to be good, check the wiring circuit and fuel level resistor (see Chapter 9, Section 16). Take care to wipe all water off the sensor before installing it in the fuel tank and ensure the sensor terminals are connected in the correct order. If the sensor is faulty, renew it.

**4**

7.5c  . . . and the filter

7.6  Ensure the clips (arrowed) are in place on the pump brackets

7.8  Sensor earth (A), high level (B) and low level (C) terminals

Single level terminal on K2 models onwards

PART A

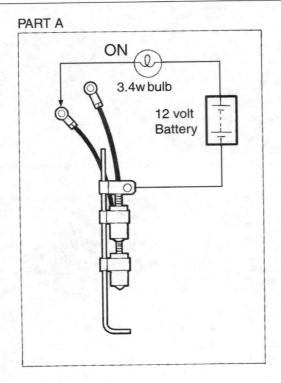

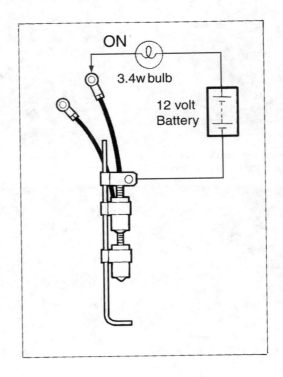

PART B

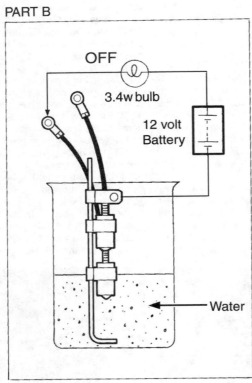

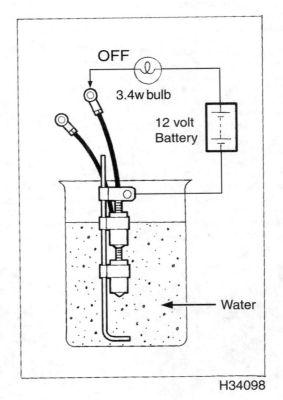

H34098

**7.9 Fuel level sensor test set-ups (see text)**

*Two-wire type sensor shown as fitted to GSX-R600K1, GSX-R750Y, K1 and GSX-R1000K1 models*

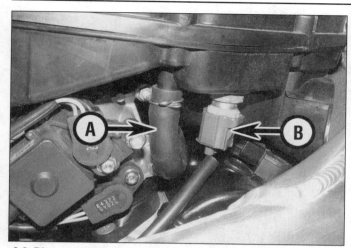

8.2 Disconnect the PAIR hose (A) and the intake air temperature (IAT) sensor wiring connector (B)

8.3a Disconnect the crankcase breather hose . . .

13 Installation is the reverse of removal ensuring the sensor wires are correctly connected.

## 8 Air filter housing – removal and installation

### Removal

1 Raise the fuel tank and support it with the prop (see Section 2).
2 Release the clip and disconnect the PAIR hose, then disconnect the intake air tempera-ture (IAT) sensor wiring connector from the right-hand side of the housing (see illustration).
3 Release the clip and disconnect the crankcase breather hose from the back of the housing, then disconnect the vacuum hose and the intake air pressure (IAP) sensor wiring connector (see illustrations).
4 Loosen the clamp screws securing the housing to the throttle bodies and undo the bolt securing the front of the housing to the frame, then lift off the housing (see illustrations). Note the foam seals between the housing inlets and the ducts in the frame.

### Installation

5 Installation is the reverse of removal. Make sure the inlet seals locate correctly against the ducts in the frame – there should be no gaps between them (see illustration).

## 9 Fuel injection system – general description

1 The fuel injection system consists of two main component groups, the fuel supply circuit and the electronic control circuit.

8.3b . . . and the vacuum hose (arrowed) . . .

8.3c . . . and wiring connector from the intake air pressure (IAP) sensor

8.4a Loosen the clamp screws (arrowed) . . .

8.4b . . . then undo the front mounting bolt . . .

8.4c . . . and lift off the housing

8.5 Check the position of the inlet seals (arrowed)

4

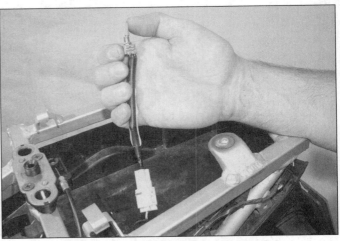

**10.2a Remove the cover from the connector . . .**          **10.2b . . . and install the mode select switch**

2 The fuel supply circuit consists of the tank, pump and filter, pressure regulator and injectors. Fuel is pumped under pressure from the tank to the fuel rail, from which the individual injectors are fed. Operating pressure is maintained initially by the pump check valve and, once the engine is running, by the pressure regulator. The injectors spray pressurised fuel into the throttle body where it mixes with air and vaporises, before entering the cylinder where it is compressed and ignited.

3 The electronic control circuit consists of the engine control module (ECM), which operates and co-ordinates both the fuel injection and ignition systems, and the various sensors which provide the ECM with information on engine operating conditions.

4 The ECM monitors signals from the following sensors:

● *Intake air temperature (IAT) sensor*
● *Intake air pressure (IAP) sensor*
● *Throttle position (TP) sensor*
● *Secondary throttle position (STP) sensor (GSX-R600 and GSX-R1000 models)*
● *Camshaft position (CMP) sensor*
● *Crankshaft position (CKP) sensor*
● *Coolant temperature (ECT) sensor*
● *Atmospheric pressure (AP) sensor*
● *Gear position (GP) sensor*

5 Based on the information it receives, the ECM calculates the appropriate ignition and fuel requirements of the engine. By varying the length of the electronic pulse it sends to each injector, the ECM controls the length of time the injectors are held open and thereby the amount of fuel that is supplied to the engine. Fuel supply varies according to the engine's needs for starting, warming-up, idling, cruising and acceleration.

6 In the event of an abnormality in any of the sensor signals, the ECM will determine whether the engine can still be run safely. If it can, a back-up mode replaces the sensor signal with a fixed signal, restricting performance but allowing the bike to be ridden home or to a dealer. When this occurs,

the LCD display in the instrument cluster will indicate the letters FI every two seconds (alternating with the coolant temperature reading), and the FI LED will come on. If the unit decides that the fault is too serious, the appropriate system will be shut down and the engine will not run. When this occurs, the LCD display in the instrument cluster will indicate the letters FI continuously, and the FI LED will flash. See Section 10 for fault finding.

7 The system incorporates two safety circuits. When the ignition is switched ON, the fuel pump runs for three seconds and pressurises the system. Thereafter the pump automatically switches off until the engine is started. The second circuit incorporates a tip-over sensor, which automatically switches off the fuel pump and cuts the ignition and injection circuits if the motorcycle falls over.

## 10 Fuel injection system – fault finding

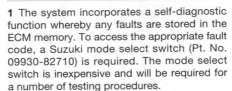

1 The system incorporates a self-diagnostic function whereby any faults are stored in the ECM memory. To access the appropriate fault code, a Suzuki mode select switch (Pt. No. 09930-82710) is required. The mode select switch is inexpensive and will be required for a number of testing procedures.

2 Remove the passenger seat (see Chapter 8) and locate the mode select switch wiring connector which is secured to the left-hand side of the seat sub-frame. Remove the connector cover, ensure the ignition and select switch are OFF, then connect the select switch **(see illustrations)**.

3 Start the engine, or if it will not start, crank the engine on the electric starter for at least 4 seconds. Turn the mode select switch ON. The fault codes will be displayed on the LCD panel on the instrument cluster in ascending order. Note the codes and identify the faults from the table opposite. **Note:** *Do not disconnect the ECM wiring connectors before*

*recording the fault codes. The ECM memory is erased when the connectors are disconnected.*

4 To check the fuel injection system components see Section 11.

5 Once the fault has been corrected, turn the ignition switch ON. If the fault has been cleared, the instrument display with indicate the code C00. Turn the mode select switch OFF and ignition switch OFF and disconnect the mode select switch. Refit the wiring connector cover and install the passenger seat (see Chapter 8).

## 11 Fuel injection system components – check, removal and installation

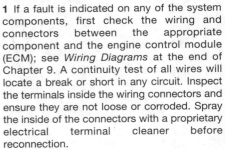

1 If a fault is indicated on any of the system components, first check the wiring and connectors between the appropriate component and the engine control module (ECM); see *Wiring Diagrams* at the end of Chapter 9. A continuity test of all wires will locate a break or short in any circuit. Inspect the terminals inside the wiring connectors and ensure they are not loose or corroded. Spray the inside of the connectors with a proprietary electrical terminal cleaner before reconnection.

2 It is possible to undertake some checks on system components using a multimeter and comparing the results with the specifications at the beginning of this Chapter. **Note:** *Different meters may give slightly different results to those specified even though the component being tested is not faulty – do not consign a component to the bin before having it double-checked.* However, some faults will only become evident when a component is tested with a peak voltage tester, in which case the checks should be undertaken by a Suzuki dealer.

3 If after a thorough check the source of a fault has not been identified, it is possible that the ECM itself is faulty. Suzuki provides no

| Fault code | Faulty component – symptoms | Possible causes |
|---|---|---|
| CHEC | No ECM signal – engine will not run | Kill switch OFF<br>Faulty wiring or wiring connector<br>Faulty ignition safety interlock system (clutch switch, sidestand switch, diode or gear position switch)<br>Damaged ignition fuse |
| C00 | No fault | System clear |
| C11 | Camshaft position sensor – engine will continue to run but will not restart once turned OFF | Faulty wiring or wiring connector<br>Damaged sensor or intake cam pin |
| C12 | Crankshaft position sensor – engine will not run | Faulty wiring or wiring connector<br>Damaged sensor or timing rotor |
| C13 | Intake air pressure sensor – engine will run, air pressure signal fixed at 760 mmHg | Faulty wiring or wiring connector<br>Damaged sensor |
| C14 | Throttle position sensor – engine will run, throttle position and ignition timing fixed | Faulty wiring or wiring connector<br>Damaged sensor |
| C15 | Engine coolant temperature sensor – engine will run, coolant temperature signal fixed at 80°C | Faulty wiring or wiring connector<br>Damaged sensor |
| C21 | Intake air temperature sensor – engine will run, air temperature signal fixed at 40°C | Faulty wiring or wiring connector<br>Damaged sensor |
| C22 | Atmospheric pressure sensor – engine will run, atmospheric pressure signal fixed at 760 mmHg | Faulty wiring or wiring connector<br>Damaged sensor |
| C23 | Tip-over sensor – engine will not run | Faulty wiring or wiring connector<br>Damaged sensor |
| C24* | No. 1 cylinder ignition coil – engine will run on other 3 cylinders, fuel supply to No. 1 cylinder cut | Faulty wiring or wiring connector<br>Damaged ignition coil<br>Faulty power supply for the ignition system (see Chapter 5 for details) |
| C25* | No. 2 cylinder ignition coil – engine will run on other 3 cylinders, fuel supply to No. 2 cylinder cut | Faulty wiring or wiring connector<br>Damaged ignition coil<br>Faulty power supply for the ignition system (see Chapter 5 for details) |
| C26* | No. 3 cylinder ignition coil – engine will run on other 3 cylinders, fuel supply to No. 3 cylinder cut | Faulty wiring or wiring connector<br>Damaged ignition coil<br>Faulty power supply for the ignition system (see Chapter 5 for details) |
| C27* | No. 4 cylinder ignition coil – engine will run on other 3 cylinders, fuel supply to No. 4 cylinder cut | Faulty wiring or wiring connector<br>Damaged ignition coil<br>Faulty power supply for the ignition system (see Chapter 5 for details) |
| C28 | Secondary throttle valve servo – engine will run, GSX-R600 model valve fixed in half open position, GSX-R750 model valve fixed in fully open position, GSX-R1000 model valve fixed in closed position | Faulty wiring or wiring connector<br>Damaged servo motor |
| C29<br>GSX-R600 and GSX-R1000 only | Secondary throttle position sensor – engine will run, GSX-R600 model valve fixed in fully open position, GSX-R1000 model valve fixed in closed position | Faulty wiring or wiring connector<br>Damaged sensor |
| C30<br>GSX-R600K1 only | Secondary throttle control unit – engine will run, valve fixed in fully open position | Faulty wiring or wiring connector<br>Damaged control unit |
| C31 | Gear position sensor – engine will run, signal fixed in 6th gear | Faulty wiring or wiring connector<br>Damaged sensor<br>Faulty gearchange mechanism |
| C32* | No. 1 fuel injector – engine will run on other 3 cylinders | Faulty wiring or wiring connector<br>Damaged fuel injector |
| C33* | No. 2 fuel injector – engine will run on other 3 cylinders | Faulty wiring or wiring connector<br>Damaged fuel injector |
| C34* | No. 3 fuel injector – engine will run on other 3 cylinders | Faulty wiring or wiring connector<br>Damaged fuel injector |
| C35* | No. 4 fuel injector – engine will run on other 3 cylinders | Faulty wiring or wiring connector<br>Damaged fuel injector |
| C41 | Fuel pump control system – engine will not run | Faulty wiring or wiring connector to pump and/or pump relay<br>Faulty pump relay (see Section 5)<br>Damaged fuel pump (see Section 6) |
| C42 | Ignition switch – engine will not run | Faulty wiring or wiring connector<br>Damaged switch (see Chapter 9 for details) |
| C46<br>GSX-R1000 only | Exhaust control valve servo – engine will run, valve fixed in fully open position | Faulty wiring or wiring connector<br>Faulty control valve cable adjustment<br>Damaged servo (see Section 17 for details) |

*The engine will not run when two or more ignition coils or fuel injectors fail

**4**

**11.4 Location of the camshaft position (CMP) sensor**

test specifications for the ECM. In order to determine conclusively that the unit is defective, it should be substituted with a known good one. If the problem is then rectified, the original unit is faulty.

### Camshaft position (CMP) sensor

**4** Make sure the ignition is OFF. Remove the air filter housing (see Section 8). The CMP sensor is on the left-hand end of the valve cover **(see illustration)**. Disconnect the wiring connector. Using an ohmmeter or multimeter set to the K-ohms scale, measure the resistance between the sensor terminals. If the result is as specified, check that there is no continuity between each terminal and earth (ground).
**5** If the results are good, have the sensor peak voltage tested by a Suzuki dealer.
**6** To inspect the sensor and intake cam pin, remove the valve cover (see Chapter 2).

### Crankshaft position (CKP) sensor

**7** Make sure the ignition is OFF. Raise the fuel tank (see Section 2). The CKP sensor is on the right-hand end of the crankshaft. Trace the wiring from behind the right-hand crankcase cover, just forward of the starter motor, and disconnect it at the wiring connector **(see illustration)**. Using an ohmmeter or multimeter set to the ohms scale, measure the resistance between the terminals on the sensor side of the connector. If the result is as specified, check that there is no continuity between each terminal and earth (ground).
**8** If the results are good, have the sensor peak voltage tested by a Suzuki dealer.

**11.10 Location of the intake air pressure (IAP) sensor**

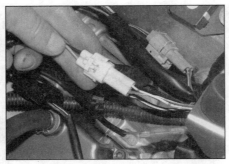

**11.7 Trace the crankshaft position (CKP) sensor wiring to the connector**

**9** To remove the sensor and the timing rotor, see Chapter 5.

### Intake air pressure (IAP) sensor

**10** Make sure the ignition is OFF. Raise the fuel tank (see Section 2). The IAP sensor is on the back of the air filter housing **(see illustration)**. Check the condition of the vacuum hose between the sensor and the throttle bodies. If the hose is cracked or perished renew it. Ensure the hose is a tight fit on the sensor union, the hose connectors and the throttle bodies.
**11** Disconnect the sensor wiring connector and turn the ignition ON. Connect the positive (+ve) probe of a voltmeter to the red wire terminal on the loom side of the wiring connector and the negative (-ve) probe first to earth (ground), then to the black/brown wire terminal to check the input voltage. Turn the ignition OFF. If the input voltage is not as specified, check the wiring to the ECM and the ECM connector terminals.
**12** If the input voltage is good, reconnect the wiring to the sensor, then start the engine and allow it idle. Insert the positive (+ve) probe of a voltmeter into the green/black wire terminal in the connector and the negative (-ve) probe into the black/brown wire terminal to check the output voltage. If the result is as specified, take the sensor to a Suzuki dealer for vacuum testing.
**13** To remove the IAP sensor, first disconnect the vacuum hose and the wiring connector. Undo the screw securing the sensor to the air filter housing and withdraw the sensor. On installation, ensure the wiring

**11.14 Location of the throttle position (TP) sensor (GSX-R1000 shown)**

connector terminals are clean and that the vacuum hose is a tight fit on the sensor union.

### Throttle position (TP) sensor

**Note:** *The colour coding for the TP sensor wiring changes at the black wiring connector.*
**14** Make sure the ignition is OFF. Remove the fuel tank (see Section 2). The TP sensor is located on the right-hand end of the throttle bodies **(see illustration)**; on GSX-R600, GSX-R750K2 and GSX-R1000 models it is the lower of the two sensors. Trace the wiring from the sensor to the black wiring connector which is secured to the fuel rail by a cable tie. If necessary, cut the tie to release the connector, then disconnect it. Turn the ignition ON and connect the positive (+ve) probe of a voltmeter to the red wire terminal on the loom side of the wiring connector and the negative (-ve) probe first to earth (ground), then to the black/brown wire terminal to check the input voltage. Turn the ignition OFF. If the input voltage is not as specified, check the wiring to the ECM, the multi-pin wiring connector for the injector loom and the ECM connector terminals.
**15** If the input voltage is good, check for continuity between the yellow wire terminal on the sensor side of the wiring connector and earth (ground). There should be no continuity.
**16** Using an ohmmeter set to the K-ohms scale, measure the resistance between the yellow and black wire terminals on the sensor side of the wiring connector, first with the throttle closed, then turn the twistgrip so that the throttle is fully open. If the results are as specified, reconnect the wiring connector.
**17** Turn the ignition ON and connect the probes of a voltmeter between the yellow and black wire terminals in the connector to check the output voltage, first with the throttle closed, then turn the twistgrip so that the throttle is fully open. Turn the ignition OFF. If the results are not as specified, the sensor is faulty.
**18** To remove the TP sensor, first disconnect the black wiring connector (see Step 14). Mark the position of the sensor to aid installation, then undo the Torx bolt securing the sensor to the No. 4 throttle body and remove the sensor. Note how the end of the throttle shaft engages the slot in the sensor.
**19** Installation is the reverse of removal. Ensure that the throttle shaft engages correctly in the slot in the sensor and align any register marks before tightening the Torx bolt to the torque setting specified at the beginning of this Chapter. Ensure the black wiring connector terminals are clean and secure the sensor wiring to the fuel rail with a cable tie.
**20** To adjust the position of the TP sensor, first check the engine idle speed and adjust it if necessary (see Chapter 1). Turn the engine OFF and connect the mode select switch to the wiring connector (see Section 10).
**21** Turn the select switch ON. A code C00 will be displayed on the LCD panel on the

instrument cluster with a line in front of it. If the line is in the mid-way position i.e. -C00, the TP sensor is adjusted correctly. If the line is above or below the mid-way position (_C00 or -C00), loosen the Torx bolts securing the sensor to the No. 4 throttle body and carefully move the sensor up or down until the line is in the mid-way position. Tighten the Torx bolts to the specified torque setting.

### Engine coolant temperature (ECT) sensor

**22** Make sure the ignition is OFF. Remove the fuel tank (see Section 2). The ECT sensor is located in the rear of the cylinder head on the left-hand side **(see illustration)**. Disconnect the sensor wiring connector and turn the ignition ON. Connect the positive (+ve) probe of a voltmeter to the black/blue wire terminal on the loom side of the connector and the negative (-ve) probe first to earth (ground), then to the black/brown wire terminal to check the input voltage. Turn the ignition OFF. If the input voltage is not as specified, check the wiring to the ECM and the ECM connector terminals.

**23** Using an ohmmeter or multimeter set to the K-ohms scale, measure the resistance between the terminals on the sensor itself with the engine cold. If the result is not as specified, the sensor is faulty.

**24** If the sensor is working correctly, the resistance should drop as the engine warms up. A check for sensor performance is described in Chapter 3.

### Intake air temperature (IAT) sensor

**25** Make sure the ignition is OFF. Raise the fuel tank (see Section 2). The IAT sensor is on the right-hand side of the air filter housing **(see illustration)**. Disconnect the sensor wiring connector and turn the ignition ON. Connect the positive (+ve) probe of a voltmeter to the dark green wire terminal on the loom side of the wiring connector and the negative (-ve) probe first to earth (ground), then to the black/brown wire terminal to check the input voltage. Turn the ignition OFF. If the input voltage is not as specified, check the wiring to the ECM and the ECM connector terminals.

**26** Using an ohmmeter or multimeter set to the K-ohms scale, measure the resistance between the terminals on the sensor itself. If the result is not as specified, the sensor is faulty.

**27** The sensor screws into an insert in the bottom of the air filter housing. To remove the sensor, first disconnect the wiring connector, then unscrew the sensor. Note the O-ring on the sensor body and renew it on installation if it is damaged.

### Atmospheric pressure (AP) sensor

**28** Make sure the ignition is OFF. On GSX-R750Y models remove the seat cowling (see

**11.22 Location of the engine coolant temperature (ECT) sensor**

Chapter 8); the AP sensor is on the left-hand side of the sub frame to the rear of the regulator/rectifier. On all other models remove the rider's seat (see Chapter 8); the AP sensor is on the right-hand side of the starter solenoid above the ECM **(see illustration)**.

**29** Disconnect the sensor wiring connector and turn the ignition ON. Connect the positive (+ve) probe of a voltmeter to the red wire terminal on the loom side of the wiring connector and the negative (-ve) probe first to earth (ground), then to the black/brown wire terminal to check the input voltage. Turn the ignition OFF. If the input voltage is not as specified, check the wiring to the ECM and the ECM connector terminals.

**30** If the input voltage is good, reconnect the wiring to the sensor, then turn the ignition ON. Insert the positive (+ve) probe of a voltmeter into the green/yellow wire terminal in the connector and the negative (-ve) probe into the black/brown wire terminal to check the output voltage. Turn the ignition OFF.

**31** If the output voltage is not as specified, the AP sensor air passage may be clogged with dirt. Disconnect the wiring connector and undo the nut(s) securing the sensor. Clean the outside of the sensor with a damp cloth and check the air passage for any obstruction, then retest the output voltage (see Step 29).

**32** If the output voltage is as specified, take the sensor to a Suzuki dealer for vacuum testing.

### Tip-over (TO) sensor

**33** Make sure the ignition is OFF. Remove the rider's seat (see Chapter 8). The TO

**11.28 Location of the atmospheric pressure (AP) sensor (GSX-R600/1000 shown)**

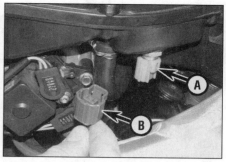

**11.25 Intake air temperature (IAT) sensor (A) and wiring connector (B)**

sensor is on the left-hand side in front of the battery. Note the TO sensor holder is marked UPPER on the top edge **(see illustration)**.

**34** Trace the wiring from the sensor and disconnect it at the connector. Using an ohmmeter or multimeter set to the K-ohms scale, measure the resistance between the black and black/white wire terminals on the sensor side of the connector. Compare the result to that given in the Specifications at the beginning of this Chapter; if the result is good, reconnect the wiring connector.

**35** With the connector reconnected, turn the ignition ON and insert the probes of a voltmeter into the black and black/brown wire terminals on the loom side of the wiring connector to check the voltage. If the result is good, carefully unclip the sensor from its bracket and check the voltage reading when the sensor is leaned 43° to one side and then to the other, this simulates the cut-off point reached if the motorcycle falls over – at each point the voltage should drop to zero. If not the sensor is faulty.

**36** To remove the sensor, first disconnect the wiring connector. Unclip the sensor holder from its bracket and remove the sensor from the holder, noting which way round it fits. Installation is the reverse of removal.

### Secondary throttle valve (STV) servo

#### GSX-R600

**37** Make sure the ignition is OFF. Remove the air filter element (see Chapter 1) in order to view the secondary throttle valves. The STV

**11.33 Tip-over (TO) sensor – note the marking on the holder**

**11.37 Location of the secondary throttle valve (STV) servo**

servo is on the right-hand side of the No. 4 throttle body **(see illustration)**.

**38** Turn the ignition ON and check the operation of the secondary throttle valves in start-up mode. From half-open the valves should first close, then open fully and then return to the half-open position. Turn the ignition OFF. If the valves do not move as described, trace the wiring from the servo to the secondary throttle control (STC) unit and check that the connectors are clean and tight.

**39** Trace the wiring from the servo to the wiring connector which is secured by a cable tie. If necessary, cut the tie to release the connector, then disconnect it. Check that there is no continuity between the red wire terminal on the servo side of the connector and earth (ground).

**40** Using an ohmmeter or multimeter set to the ohms scale, connect the positive (+ve) probe to the red wire terminal on the sensor side of the connector and the negative (-ve) probe to the black wire terminal and measure the servo resistance. If the result is as specified, check the STC unit (see Steps 78 to 80).

**41** To remove the servo, first note the position of the secondary throttle valves. Undo the nuts securing the servo motor cover and remove them, then lift off the cover. The secondary throttle position (STP) sensor is mounted on the cover. Note how the tab on the STP sensor engages the slot in the throttle shaft. **Note:** *It is not necessary to remove the STP sensor from the cover.*

**42** Undo the screw securing the servo wiring connector and disconnect the connector. Undo the studs securing the servo motor and remove the motor and the gasket between the motor and the throttle body. Note how the motor drive locates on the throttle shaft. **Note:** *The STV adjuster is pre-set by the factory and should not be removed.*

**43** Installation is the reverse of removal. **Note:** *Ensure the secondary throttle valves are correctly positioned before installing any of the STV servo components.* If the motor gasket is damaged fit a new one. Apply a small quantity of grease to the slot in the throttle shaft and align the tab on the STP sensor with the slot before installing the motor cover. Tighten the fixing studs and nuts to the

torque settings specified at the beginning of this Chapter.

## GSX-R750Y and GSX-R750K1

**Note:** *The STV servo unit incorporates the servo motor and secondary throttle position (STP) sensor. If either function is faulty the complete unit will have to be renewed.*

**44** Make sure the ignition is OFF. Raise the fuel tank (see Section 2). The STV servo assembly mounts on a bracket on the right-hand side of the No. 4 throttle body.

**45** Turn the ignition ON and check the operation of the servo in start-up mode. The servo pulley should rotate backwards and forwards one time. Turn the ignition OFF. If the pulley does not move as described, disconnect the servo motor wiring connector. Use jumper wires to connect the positive (+ve) terminal of a 12v battery to the pink wire terminal on the servo side of the connector and the negative (-ve) battery terminal to the grey wire terminal. The servo pulley should rotate in one direction. Now reverse the wire connections and ensure the pulley rotates in the other direction. If the pulley does not rotate, or only rotates in one direction, renew the servo. **Note:** *Disconnect the jumper wires as soon as the test is complete to avoid damaging the servo.*

**46** If the pulley moves correctly when connected to the battery with jumper wires, check the wiring to the ECM and the ECM connector terminals.

**47** If the pulley moves correctly when the ignition is turned ON, ensure the STV cables are correctly adjusted (see Section 13).

**48** If the fault code is still displayed after checking the servo and cable adjustment, make sure the ignition is OFF and disconnect the STP sensor wiring connector. Turn the ignition ON, then connect the positive (+ve) probe of a voltmeter to the red wire terminal on the loom side of the wiring connector and the negative (-ve) probe first to earth (ground), then to the black/brown wire terminal to check the input voltage. Turn the ignition OFF. If the input voltage is not as specified, check the wiring to the ECM and the ECM connector terminals.

**49** If the input voltage is good, check for continuity between the yellow wire terminal on the servo side of the wiring connector and earth (ground). There should be no continuity.

**50** Reconnect the STP sensor wiring connector. Connect the mode select switch (see Section 10). Turn the select switch ON and turn the ignition ON; the servo will move to the adjustment position. With the ignition still ON, disconnect the STP sensor wiring connector, then using an ohmmeter set to the K-ohms scale, measure the resistance between the yellow and white wire terminals on the servo side of the wiring connector. Turn the ignition OFF. If the result is not as specified, the sensor is faulty.

**51** If the result is as specified, it is likely a fault exists in the output voltage of the STP sensor indicating either a fault in the ECM or

the sensor itself. Further tests and adjustments are best undertaken by a Suzuki dealer as incorrect adjustment of the output voltage can damage the STV servo.

**52** To remove the servo see Section 13.

## GSX-R750K2

**53** Make sure the ignition is OFF. Remove the air filter element (see Chapter 1) in order to view the throttle valves. The STV servo is on the right-hand side of the No. 4 throttle body **(see illustration 11.37)**.

**54** Turn the ignition ON and check the operation of the secondary throttle valves in start-up mode. From 20% open the valves should first close, then open fully and then return to the 20% open position. Turn the ignition OFF. If the valves do not move as described, check the wiring from the servo to the ECM and check the ECM connector terminals.

**55** Disconnect the STV servo wiring connector and check that there is no continuity between the terminals on the servo side of the connector an earth (ground).

**56** Using an ohmmeter or multimeter set to the ohms scale, measure the resistance first between the pink and black wire terminals on the servo side of the connector, then between the white/black and green wire terminals. If the result is not as specified, the STV servo is faulty. If the result is as specified, have the ECM checked by a Suzuki dealer.

**57** To remove the servo, first note the position of the secondary throttle valves. Undo the bolts securing the servo to the No. 4 throttle body and remove the servo. Note how the motor drive locates on the throttle shaft. The secondary throttle position (STP) sensor is mounted on the servo. Note how the tab on the STP sensor engages the slot in the throttle shaft. **Note:** *It is not necessary to remove the STP sensor from the servo.*

**58** Installation is the reverse of removal. **Note:** *Ensure the secondary throttle valves are correctly positioned before installing any of the STV servo components.* Apply a small quantity of grease to the slot in the throttle shaft and align the tab on the STP sensor with the slot before installing the servo. Tighten the fixing bolts to the torque settings specified at the beginning of this Chapter.

## GSX-R1000

**59** Make sure the ignition is OFF. Remove the air filter element (see Chapter 1) in order to view the throttle valves. The STV servo is on the right-hand side of the No. 4 throttle body **(see illustration 11.37)**.

**60** Turn the ignition ON and check the operation of the secondary throttle valves in start-up mode as described in Step 54. If the valves do not move as described, check the wiring from the servo to the ECM and check the ECM connector terminals.

**61** Disconnect the STV servo wiring connector and check that there is no continuity between the terminals on the servo side of the connector and earth (ground).

Measure the resistance first between the pink and black wire terminals on the servo side of the connector, then between the white/black and green wire terminals (see Step 56). If the result is not as specified, the STV servo is faulty. If the result is as specified, have the ECM checked by a Suzuki dealer.

62 To remove and install the servo see Steps 57 and 58.

### Secondary throttle position (STP) sensor

#### GSX-R600

63 Make sure the ignition is OFF. Raise the fuel tank (see Section 2). The STP sensor is mounted on the STV servo on the right-hand side of the No. 4 throttle body (see illustration 11.72).

64 Trace the wiring from the sensor and disconnect it at the connector, the turn the ignition ON. Connect the positive (+ve) probe of a voltmeter to the blue wire terminal on the loom side of the wiring connector and the negative (-ve) probe first to earth (ground), then to the black wire terminal to check the input voltage. Turn the ignition OFF. If the input voltage is not as specified, check the wiring to the ECM and the ECM connector terminals.

65 If the input voltage is good, check for continuity between the yellow wire terminal on the sensor side of the wiring connector and earth (ground). There should be no continuity.

66 Remove the air filter element (see Chapter 1) and close the secondary throttle valves by finger pressure. Using an ohmmeter or multimeter set to the K-ohms scale, connect the positive (+ve) probe to the yellow wire terminal on the sensor side of the connector and the negative (-ve) probe to the black wire terminal and measure the sensor resistance. Now turn the ignition ON and measure the resistance as the valves open in start-up mode. Turn the ignition OFF.

67 If the results are not as specified, first check the sensor adjustment as follows. Close the secondary throttle valves and loosen the sensor Torx screws. Connect the ohmmeter or multimeter to the yellow and black wire terminals (see Step 66) then adjust the position of the sensor until the resistance reading is within specification (valves closed); tighten the sensor screws. If the specified resistance cannot be obtained, have the STV adjuster reset by a Suzuki dealer.

68 If the specified resistance still cannot be obtained the STP sensor is faulty.

69 If the results are as specified, reconnect the sensor wiring connector and turn the ignition ON. Insert the probes of a voltmeter into the yellow and black wire terminals on the loom side of the connector to check the output voltage while carefully closing and opening the throttle valves by finger pressure. If the output voltage is not as specified the STP sensor is faulty. If the output voltage is good, have the STC unit and the ECM checked by a Suzuki dealer.

70 To remove the sensor, first disconnect the wiring connector. Mark the position of the sensor to aid installation, then undo the Torx screws securing the sensor to the STV servo and remove the sensor. Note how the end of the throttle shaft engages the slot in the sensor.

71 Installation is the reverse of removal. Apply a small quantity of grease to the slot in the throttle shaft and align the tab on the sensor with the slot before installing the motor cover. Tighten the Torx screws to the torque settings specified at the beginning of this Chapter.

#### GSX-R750K2 and GSX-R1000

72 Make sure the ignition is OFF. Raise the fuel tank (see Section 2). The STP sensor is mounted on the STV servo on the right-hand side of the No. 4 throttle body (see illustration).

73 Trace the wiring from the sensor and disconnect it at the connector, the turn the ignition ON. Connect the positive (+ve) probe of a voltmeter to the red wire terminal on the loom side of the wiring connector and the negative (-ve) probe first to earth (ground), then to the black/brown wire terminal to check the input voltage. Turn the ignition OFF. If the input voltage is not as specified, check the wiring to the ECM and the ECM connector terminals.

74 If the input voltage is good, check for continuity between the yellow wire terminal on the sensor side of the wiring connector and earth (ground). There should be no continuity.

75 Remove the air filter element (see Chapter 1) and close the secondary throttle valves by finger pressure. Using an ohmmeter or multimeter set to the K-ohms scale, connect the positive (+ve) probe to the yellow wire terminal on the sensor side of the connector and the negative (-ve) probe to the black wire terminal and measure the sensor resistance. Now open the secondary throttle valves by finger pressure and measure the sensor resistance.

76 If the results are not as specified, first check the sensor adjustment as follows. Close the secondary throttle valves and loosen the sensor Torx mounting screw. Connect the ohmmeter or multimeter to the yellow and black wire terminals (see Step 75) then adjust the position of the sensor until the resistance reading is within specification (valves closed); tighten the Torx screw. If the specified resistance cannot be obtained, the STP sensor is faulty.

77 If the results are as specified, reconnect the sensor wiring connector and turn the ignition ON. Insert the probes of a voltmeter into the yellow and black wire terminals on the loom side of the connector to check the output voltage while carefully closing and opening the throttle valves by finger pressure. If the output voltage is not as specified the STP sensor is faulty. If the output voltage is good, have the ECM checked by a Suzuki dealer.

**11.72 Location of the secondary throttle position (STP) sensor (GSX-R1000 shown)**

### Secondary throttle control (STC) unit – GSX-R600K1 only

78 Remove the seat cowling (see Chapter 8); the STC unit is on the left-hand side of the sub frame to the front of the regulator/rectifier.

79 Turn the ignition ON. Insert the positive (+ve) probe of a voltmeter into the orange/white wire terminal on the loom side of the unit wiring connector and connect the negative (-ve) probe first to earth (ground), then into the black/white wire terminal to check the input voltage. Turn the ignition OFF. Battery voltage should be shown. If the input voltage is not as specified, check the wiring to the ECM and the ECM connector terminals.

80 It is possible to test the internal circuitry of the STC unit, but this requires the use of a specific test meter. If you suspect that the STC unit is faulty, have it tested by a Suzuki dealer.

### Gear position (GP) sensor

81 Support the bike on an auxiliary stand and raise the sidestand. Raise the fuel tank (see Section 2). Ensure the engine kill switch is in the RUN position. The GP sensor is located on the left-hand side of the engine unit behind the water pump (see Chapter 2, Section 17).

82 Trace the wiring from the sensor to the connector. Turn the ignition switch ON and insert the positive (+ve) probe of a voltmeter into the pink wire terminal in the connector and connect the negative (-ve) probe to earth (ground) to check the output voltage. Select each gear in turn and check that the voltage is above the specified minimum in each gear. Turn the ignition OFF.

83 If the output voltage is not as specified, either the pink wire to the GP switch or the GP switch itself is faulty.

84 If the output voltage is as specified check the wiring from the sensor to the ECM and check the ECM connector terminals.

85 To remove the GP sensor see Chapter 2, Section 17.

### Fuel injectors

86 Make sure the ignition is OFF. Remove the fuel tank (see Section 2). Identify the faulty injector by the fault code and disconnect the injector wiring connector (see Section 14). **Note:** *The injectors are numbered 1 to 4 from the left-hand to right-hand side of the engine.*

**4**

Using an ohmmeter or multimeter set to the ohms scale, measure the resistance between the terminals on the injector. If the result is as specified, check that there is no continuity between each terminal and earth (ground).

87 Turn the ignition ON. Connect the positive (+ve) probe of a voltmeter to the yellow/red wire terminal on the loom side of the wiring connector and the negative (-ve) probe to earth (ground) to check the input voltage. **Note:** *Injector voltage can only be detected for 3 seconds after the ignition has been turned ON.* Turn the ignition OFF. If the input voltage is not as specified, refer to the Wiring Diagrams at the end of Chapter 9 and check for a fault in the yellow/red wire.

88 If the input voltage is as specified check, refer to the Wiring Diagrams at the end of Chapter 9 and check for a fault in the individual injector wiring.

### 12 Throttle bodies – removal and installation

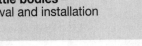

> ⚠ **Warning: Refer to the precautions given in Section 1 before starting work.**

### Removal

1 On GSX-R750Y and GSX-R750K1 models, connect the mode select switch (see Section 10). Turn the select switch ON and turn the ignition ON to position the STV servo in the adjustment position. In this position, the cable slots should be facing downwards, i.e. opposite the cable adjusters **(see illustration)**.

2 Remove the air filter housing (see Section 8).

3 On GSX-R600, GSX-R750 and GSX-R1000K1 models, disconnect the fast idle (choke) cable from the backplate on the No. 1 throttle body and the fast idle cam (see Section 16).

4 Disconnect the throttle cables from the backplate on the No. 1 throttle body and the throttle pulley (see Section 15).

5 On GSX-R750Y models, detach the idle speed adjuster from its bracket.

6 Disconnect the vacuum hose from the PAIR valve **(see illustration)**.

7 Disconnect the multi-pin wiring connector for the throttle body assembly loom **(see illustration)**.

8 Using a long screwdriver inserted through the hole in each side of the frame, loosen the clamp screws securing the throttle bodies to the inlet stubs – one screw on each side secures both bodies for that side **(see illustration)**. Ease the bodies up off the stubs and remove them. **Note:** *On GSX-R750Y and GSX-R750K1 models, the STV servo assembly remains attached to the No. 4 throttle body (see Section 13).*

### Installation

9 Installation is the reverse of removal, noting the following:
● Ensure the throttle bodies are fully engaged with the inlet stubs on the cylinder head before tightening the clamps.
● Ensure the terminals in the multi-pin connector are clean and reconnect it firmly.
● Check the operation of the fast idle (except GSX-R1000K2) and throttle cables and adjust them as necessary (see Chapter 1).
● On GSX-R750Y and GSX-R750K1 models, check the operation of the STV servo (see Section 13).
● Check the engine idle speed and adjust as necessary (see Chapter 1).

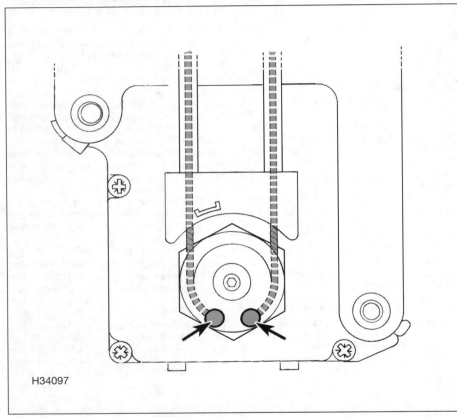

H34097

**12.1 In the adjustment position the cable slots (arrowed) must be facing downwards (GSX-R750Y and K1)**

**12.6 Disconnect the PAIR valve vacuum hose (arrowed)**

**12.7 Disconnect the throttle body assembly wiring connector**

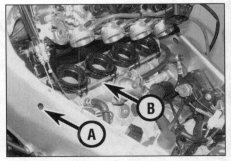

**12.8 Insert a long screwdriver through hole (A) to loosen clamp screw (B)**

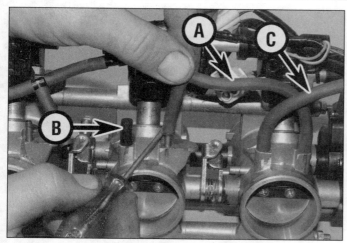

**13.2  Disconnect the intake air pressure (IAP) hose assembly (A), the blanking plugs (B) and the PAIR hose (C)**

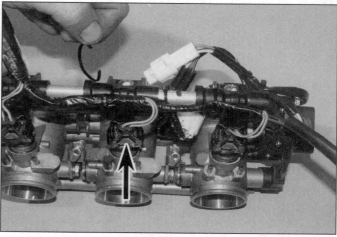

**13.3a  Cut the cable ties and disconnect the fuel injector wiring connectors (arrowed) . . .**

## 13 Throttle bodies – overhaul

**Warning: Refer to the precautions given in Section 1 before starting work.**

### Disassembly

**Note:** *In the fully open position, the secondary throttle valves protrude outside the throttle bodies. Take care not to damage the valves when laying the throttle bodies on the work surface.*

**1** On GSX-R750Y and GSX-R750K1 models remove the STV servo assembly (see Steps 22 to 25).
**2** Disconnect the intake air pressure (IAP) hoses from the unions on each throttle body and remove the IAP hose assembly, then remove the blanking plugs from the unions on each throttle body and the PAIR vacuum hose **(see illustration)**.
**3** Cut the cable ties which secure the wiring loom to the fuel rail. Disconnect the wiring connectors to the fuel injectors, disconnect the wiring connector for the throttle position (TP) sensor, secondary throttle position (STP) sensor and secondary throttle valve (STV) servo as applicable, then remove the throttle body assembly wiring loom **(see illustrations)**.
**4** Remove the fuel injectors (see Section 14).
**5** If required, remove the STV servo (GSX-R600, GSX-R750K2, GSX-R1000) and TP sensor and (see Section 11).
**6** The linkage for the fast idle mechanism and the throttle pulley adjuster screws are mounted on the backplate on the No. 1 throttle body. The backplate is retained by two of the three bolts which hold the throttle body assembly together **(see illustration)**. To remove the backplate, undo the two bolts and withdraw them carefully from the throttle body assembly to avoid disturbing the throttle body

alignment. Remove the backplate from the bolts, noting how it fits.
**7** On GSX-R750 and GSX-R1000 models the throttle pulley is a press fit on the valve shaft and should not be removed. On GSX-R600 models the throttle pulley is retained by a nut and washer; only remove the pulley if the pulley spring or the pulley itself is damaged.
**8** The throttle bodies on GSX-R750Y and GSX-R750K1 models are not designed to be separated. The throttle bodies on all other models are designed to be separated into left and right-hand pairs between the No. 2 and No. 3 bodies. First note the arrangement of

the throttle valve and secondary throttle valve synchronising screws, levers and springs between the No. 2 and No. 3 bodies **(see illustration)**. Undo the third throttle body connecting bolt, then withdraw it carefully and separate the throttle bodies.
*Caution: The throttle valves and secondary throttle valves must not be removed from the valve shafts.*

### Cleaning

*Caution: Use only a petroleum based solvent or dedicated injector cleaner for throttle body cleaning. Don't use caustic cleaners.*

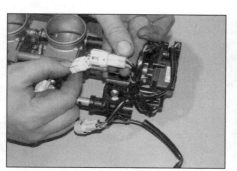

**13.3b  . . . then disconnect the sensor and servo connectors . . .**

**13.3c  . . . and remove the throttle body assembly wiring loom**

**13.6  Throttle body backplate is retained by two bolts (arrowed)**

**13.8  Note the arrangement of the synchronising components for the secondary throttle (A) and throttle (B) valves**

**4**

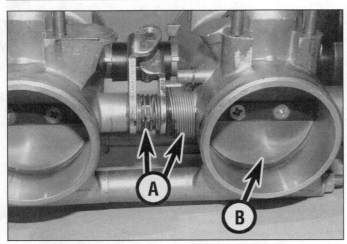

**13.13 Check the condition of the shaft springs (A) and the movement of the throttle valves (B)**

**13.14 Check the condition of the fast idle and throttle pulley components**

**9** Ensure that only metal components are submerged in cleaning solvent and always follow manufacturers recommendations as to cleaning time. If a spray cleaner is used, direct the spray into all passages.

**10** After the cleaner has loosened and dissolved most of the varnish and other deposits, use a nylon-bristled brush to remove the stubborn deposits. Rinse the throttle bodies again, then dry them with compressed air.

**11** Use compressed air to blow out all of the fuel and air passages.

*Caution: Never clean the jets or passages with a piece of wire or a drill bit, as they will be enlarged, causing the fuel and air metering rates to be upset.*

### Inspection

**12** Check the throttle bodies for cracks or any other damage which may result in air getting in.

**13** Check that the throttle valves move smoothly and freely in the bodies. Inspect the valve shafts and throttle bodies for wear. Check the condition of the valve shaft springs **(see illustration)**.

**14** Check the components on the throttle body backplate **(see illustration)**. All the springs, levers and screws are available as separate items and should be renewed if they are worn, corroded or damaged.

### Reassembly

**15** Align the two pairs of throttle bodies and ensure that the throttle valve synchronising mechanism is correctly positioned. Fit the throttle body backplate onto the connecting bolts before inserting the bolts into the throttle bodies, then tighten the bolts to the torque setting specified at the beginning of this Chapter. Install the synchronisation springs after the injectors are joined together.

**16** Check the operation of the throttle pulley.

**17** If removed, install the TP sensor and STV servo (see Section 11). **Note:** *Where fitted, the*

*TP sensor and STP sensors are very similar in appearance. To avoid confusion, the TP sensor wiring connector is black and the STP sensor connector is white.*

**18** Install the fuel injectors (see Section 14).

**19** Connect the TP sensor, STP sensor and STV servo as applicable to the throttle body assembly wiring loom. Connect the fuel injector wiring connectors. **Note:** *The multi-pin wiring connector should be at the left-hand end of the assembly.* Secure the wiring loom to the fuel rail with cable ties.

**20** Install the remaining components in the reverse order of disassembly.

**21** On GSX-R750Y and GSX-R750K1 models install the STV servo assembly (see Steps 26 to 33).

### STV servo assembly – GSX-R750Y and GSX-R750K1 models

#### Removal

**22** To remove the servo assembly, first set the servo in the adjustment position and remove the throttle bodies (see Section 12). Disconnect the servo motor and STV position sensor wiring connectors. Loosen the servo cable adjuster locknuts.

**23** Hold the servo pulley to prevent it turning and undo the pulley centre bolt, then remove the pulley with the cables attached. Note how the slot in the pulley aligns with the motor shaft. Detach the cables from the stop on the motor body and note how they locate in the inner track on the pulley.

**24** Detach the cable adjusters from the mounting bracket, then disconnect the cable ends from the STV pulley, noting how they fit – the upper cable should be identified with the code 2-35F 9K02 and is slightly longer than the lower cable code 1-35F 9I28.

**25** Undo the bolts securing the servo motor to the mounting bracket and, if required, undo the bolts securing the bracket to the throttle body, taking note of the wiring clamp location.

The STV pulley is a press fit on the valve shaft and should not be removed.

#### Installation

**26** Install the bracket and the servo motor in the reverse order of removal and tighten the servo motor mounting bolts to the specified torque setting.

**27** Loosen the cable adjuster locknuts fully. Connect the cable ends to the STV pulley and install the adjusters loosely in the mounting bracket. Make sure the cables are fitted in the correct order (see Step 24).

**28** Fit the cables into the inner track on the servo pulley, then install the pulley on the motor shaft and install the cables in the stop on the motor body. Hold the servo pulley to prevent it turning and tighten the centre bolt to the specified torque setting.

**29** Connect the servo motor and STV position sensor wiring connectors, then install the throttle bodies (see Section 12).

#### Adjustment

**30** To adjust the STV cables, first set the servo in the adjustment position (see Section 12).

**31** Make sure the cables are pulled firmly against the stop on the motor body. Turn the upper cable adjuster until all the freeplay is taken out of the cable, then turn the lower cable adjuster to set the specified freeplay in the cable.

**32** Ensure the mode select switch is OFF, then turn the ignition ON and check the operation of the STV servo (see Section 11, Step 45).

**33** Turn the mode select switch ON. If the STV servo fault code is not displayed on the LCD panel in the instrument cluster the adjustment is correct. If the fault code is displayed on the LCD panel, check the cable adjustment again (see Steps 30 and 31) then adjust the settings of the secondary throttle valves as follows.

**34** Make sure the ignition is OFF. Disconnect the servo motor wiring connector and use jumper wires to connect the positive (+ve) terminal of a 12V battery to the pink wire terminal on the servo side of the connector and the negative (-ve) battery terminal to the grey wire terminal. The servo should move the valves into the fully closed position.

*Caution: Disconnect the jumper wires as soon as each step is complete to avoid damaging the servo.*

**35** Turn the ignition ON and insert the positive (+ve) probe of a voltmeter into the yellow wire terminal on the loom side of the STP sensor wiring connector and the negative (-ve) probe into the black/brown wire terminal to check the output voltage with the valves fully closed. Turn the ignition OFF. If the voltage is less than specified, set the servo in the adjustment position (see Section 12) and turn the upper STV cable adjuster out a _ turn, then recheck the output voltage. Continue this process until the output voltage is within specification. **Note:** *Adjusting the valve settings is a gradual process. Do not attempt to adjust the cable with the valves in the fully closed position as this can damage the servo.*

**36** Now check the output voltage with the valves fully open. Make sure the ignition is OFF. Use the jumper wires to connect the positive (+ve) battery terminal to the grey wire terminal on the servo side of the motor connector and the negative (-ve) battery terminal to the pink wire terminal. The servo should move the valves into the fully open position. Turn the ignition ON and check the output voltage (see Step 35). Turn the ignition OFF. If the voltage is more than specified, set the servo in the adjustment position (see Section 12) and turn the lower STV cable adjuster out a _ turn, then recheck the output voltage. Continue this process until the output voltage is within specification.

## 14 Fuel injectors – removal and installation

 **Warning: Refer to the precautions given in Section 1 before starting work.**

### Removal

**Note:** *The fuel injectors can be removed with the throttle bodies in place. If the bodies have been removed, ignore the Steps which do not apply.*

**1** Remove the air filter housing (see Section 8). Disconnect the battery negative terminal (see Chapter 9).

**2** Cut the cable ties securing the throttle body assembly wiring loom to the fuel rail and disconnect the individual fuel injector wiring connectors.

**3** Unscrew the screws securing the fuel rail to the throttle bodies and remove the bolts and washers if fitted. On GSX-R600 models, remove the spacers between the fuel rail and the throttle bodies. Carefully lift the fuel rail off the throttle bodies – the injectors will come away with the rail **(see illustrations)**.

14.3a Unscrew the bolts . . .

14.3b . . . then lift off the fuel rail assembly

**4** Pull each injector out of the fuel rail, noting how it fits **(see illustration)**. Discard the injector seals and O-ring as new ones must be fitted on reassembly **(see illustration)**.

**5** If required, disconnect the fuel hose from the fuel rail **(see illustration)**. On GSX-R750 and GSX-R1000 models, the fuel rail comprises individual injector holders and joining pieces pressed together with an O-ring in each joint **(see illustration)**. If required, disconnect the rail components, taking care to keep them in the correct order for reassembly. Discard the O-rings as new ones must be used on reassembly.

**6** Modern fuels contain detergents which should keep the injectors clean and free of gum or varnish from fuel residue. If an injector is suspected of being blocked, clean it through with injector cleaner. If the injector is clean but its performance is suspect, take it to a Suzuki dealer for assessment.

### Installation

**Note:** *Apply a smear of clean engine oil to all new seals and O-rings before reassembly.*

**7** On GSX-R750 and GSX-R1000 models, if required, fit new O-rings onto the unions of the fuel rail components and assemble the fuel rail. If removed, connect the fuel hose to the rail.

**8** Fit new seals and an O-ring onto each injector, then press the injectors into the fuel rail carefully. **Note:** *Avoid twisting the injectors as this may damage the O-ring seals..*

**9** Fit the fuel rail and injectors onto the throttle bodies, making sure each injector is correctly aligned before pressing the assembly into place. On GSX-R600 models, install the spacers between the fuel rail and the throttle bodies.

**10** Install the fuel rail screws and washers (where fitted), and tighten them to the specified torque setting.

14.4a Pull each injector out of the fuel rail . . .

14.4b . . . discard the injector seal (A) and O-ring (B)

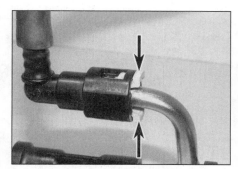

14.5a Press the tabs (arrowed) to disconnect the fuel hose

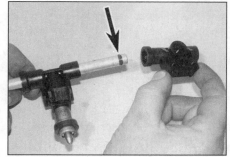

14.5b Pull off the injector holder and discard the O-ring (arrowed)

**4**

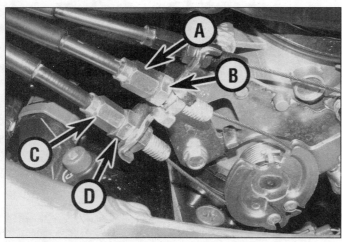

**15.2a Accelerator cable (A) and locknut (B). Decelerator cable (C) and locknut (D)**

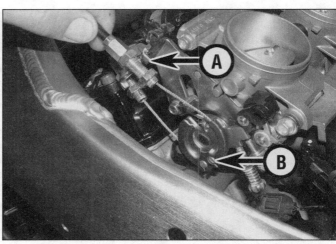

**15.2b Disconnect the cable from the backplate (A) and the pulley (B)**

11 Connect the individual injector wiring connectors and secure the wiring loom to the fuel rail with cable ties. Install the remaining components in the reverse order of removal. On completion, start the engine and check carefully that there are no fuel leaks.

## 15 Throttle cables – removal and installation

### Removal

1 Raise the fuel tank (see Section 2).

2 Loosen the locknuts securing the throttle cable adjusters to the backplate on the No. 1 throttle body and detach the cables, noting how they fit – the upper cable is the accelerator (throttle opening) cable, the lower cable is the decelerator (throttle closing) cable **(see illustration)**. Disconnect the cables from the throttle pulley **(see illustration)**.

3 Remove the screw securing the accelerator (front) cable retaining plate to the handlebar switch/throttle twistgrip housing, and unscrew the decelerator (rear) cable retaining ring **(see illustration)**.

4 Remove the handlebar housing screws and separate the halves **(see illustration)**. Note

how the pin on the upper half of the housing locates in the hole in the handlebar. Detach the cable ends from the twistgrip pulley, noting how they fit, then pull the cables out of the lower half of the housing **(see illustrations)**.

5 Thread the cables through the guide on the front, left-hand side of the frame and remove them from the machine, noting the correct routing of each cable **(see illustration)**.

### Installation

6 Thread the cables through the guide on the frame, making sure they are correctly routed – they must not interfere with any other component and should not be kinked or bent sharply.

7 Install the accelerator cable elbow in the lower half of the handlebar housing, and secure the cable retaining plate with the screw **(see illustration)**. Install the decelerator cable elbow in the lower half of the housing, and secure the cable with the retaining ring.

8 Lubricate the end of each cable with multi-purpose grease. Fit the lower half of the handlebar housing onto the twistgrip pulley and attach the cable ends to the pulley.

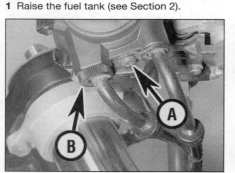

**15.3 Remove the retainer plate screw (A) and unscrew the ring (B)**

**15.4a Remove the housing screws (arrowed) and separate the halves**

**15.4b Detach the cable ends from the pulley . . .**

**15.4c . . . and pull the cables out of the housing**

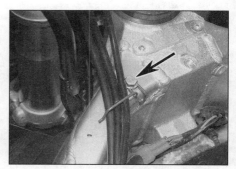

**15.5 Loosen the bolt (arrowed) and free the cables from the guide**

**15.7  Secure the accelerator cable elbow with the retaining plate**

**15.8  Locate the pin (A) in the hole (B)**

**15.10  Install the locknuts (arrowed) each side of the backplate**

Ensure the cables are correctly aligned on the pulley, then fit the upper half of the housing **(see illustration)**. Install the retaining screws, and tighten them securely. Check that the twistgrip pulley turns freely.

9 Fit the lower end of each cable onto the throttle pulley; the accelerator cable goes around the top of the pulley, the decelerator cable goes around the bottom **(see illustration 15.2a)**.

10 Install the cable adjusters onto the backplate, ensuring the adjuster locknuts are located on each side of the plate **(see illustration)**. Adjust the cables as described in Chapter 1.

11 Install the fuel tank (see Section 2).

12 Start the engine and check that the idle speed does not rise as the handlebars are turned. If it does, correct the problem before riding the motorcycle.

## 16  Fast idle system – removal, installation and adjustment

### GSX-R600, GSX-R750 and GSX-R1000K1

#### Removal

1 Raise the fuel tank (see Section 2).

2 Loosen the locknuts on the fast idle cable adjuster, then detach the adjuster from the backplate on the No. 1 throttle body and disconnect the cable from the fast idle cam **(see illustration)**.

3 Loosen the fast idle handlebar lever clamp screw, then remove the two switch/lever housing screws, one of which secures the choke cable elbow retainer plate **(see illustration)**. Note how the pin on the upper half of the housing locates in the hole in the handlebar. Pull the lever fully open and detach the cable end from the lever, noting how it fits. Pull the cable elbow out of the lower half of the housing **(see illustrations)**.

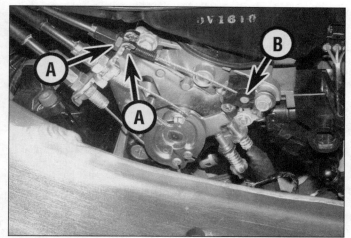

**16.2  Loosen the locknuts (A) and detach the cable from the fast idle cam (B)**

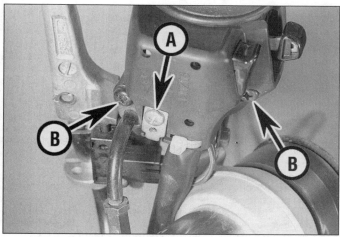

**16.3a  Loosen the clamp screw (A) then remove the housing screws (B)**

**16.3b  Push the lever fully open . . .**

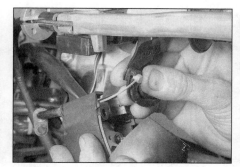

**16.3c  . . . and detach the cable end from the lever . . .**

**16.3d  . . . and pull the cable out of the housing**

**4**

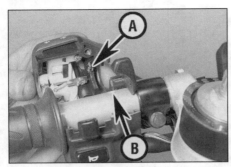

**16.6 Locate the pin (A) in the hole (B)**

**16.7 Adjuster locknuts must be located on each side of backplate**

**16.8 In-line adjuster at cable elbow (arrowed)**

**16.12 Fast idle speed adjuster screw – GSX-R750/1000**

**4** Thread the cable through the guide on the front, left-hand side of the frame and remove it from the machine, noting its routing **(see illustration 15.5)**.

### Installation

**5** Thread the cable through the guide on the frame, making sure it is correctly routed – it must not interfere with any other component and should not be kinked or bent sharply.

**6** Install the cable elbow in the lower half of the housing and lubricate the end of the cable with multi-purpose grease. Attach the cable end to the lever. Fit the two halves of the housing onto the handlebar **(see illustration)**. Install the retaining screws and tighten them securely, then tighten the lever clamp screw (see Step 3). Check that the lever turns freely.

**7** Fit the lower end of the cable onto the fast idle cam and install the cable adjuster onto the backplate, ensuring the adjuster locknuts

are located on each side of the plate **(see illustration)**.

**8** Make sure the fast idle handlebar lever is in the OFF (forward) position, then turn the adjuster until there is a small amount of freeplay left in the cable and tighten the locknuts. Fine adjustment of cable freeplay can be made using the in-line adjuster at the cable elbow near the fast idle operating lever **(see illustration)**. **Note:** *Suzuki gives no specifications for fast idle cable freeplay. Ensure that with the handlebar lever in the OFF position the fast idle cam does not engage the throttle valve mechanism.*

### Adjustment

**9** Check the cable freeplay (see Step 8).

**10** The engine should be at normal operating temperature, which is usually reached after 10 to 15 minutes of stop/start riding. Make sure that the idle speed is correctly adjusted (see Chapter 1).

**11** With the engine running, pull the handlebar lever back to the ON position and check that the idle speed increases to the specified fast idle speed.

**12** To adjust the fast idle speed, raise the fuel tank, if not already done, to access the fast idle adjuster. On GSX-R600 models the adjuster is on the back of the throttle pulley; on all other models the adjuster is on the throttle cable pulley backplate **(see illustration)**. With the engine idling and the handlebar lever in the ON position, turn the adjuster until the specified fast idle speed is obtained. Turn the screw clockwise to increase idle speed, and anti-clockwise to decrease it.

**13** Return the handlebar lever to the OFF position and check that the idle speed returns to normal. If necessary, adjust the idle speed (see Chapter 1) then install the fuel tank (see Section 2).

### GSX-R1000K2

**Note:** *The fast idle mechanism is actuated by the STV servo when the engine is cold and should cancel automatically when engine coolant temperature reaches 40 to 50°C. If the idle speed cannot be adjusted correctly (see Chapter 1), check for a possible fault in the coolant temperature sensor or sensor wiring (see Chapter 4, Section 11).*

**14** The engine should be cold. Start the engine and check the fast idle speed. If the fast idle speed is not within the specifications, raise the fuel tank to access the fast idle adjuster which is on the throttle cable pulley backplate **(see illustration 16.12)**. With the engine idling, turn the adjuster until the specified fast idle speed is obtained. Turn the screw clockwise to increase idle speed, and anti-clockwise to decrease it.

**15** Leave the engine running and check that the fast idle setting cancels automatically when the engine coolant temperature reaches 40 to 50°C. At that point the idle speed should fall to the normal (warm engine) specification. If necessary, adjust the idle speed (see Chapter 1) then install the fuel tank (see Section 2).

## 17 Exhaust system –
removal and installation

⚠ *Warning: If the engine has been running the exhaust system will be very hot. Allow the system to cool before carrying out any work.*

### Silencer – all models

#### Removal

**1** Undo the nuts and remove the washers securing the silencer to the exhaust pipe flange **(see illustration)**.

**2** Unscrew the nut from the bolt securing the silencer to the passenger footrest bracket, then support the silencer and withdraw the bolt **(see illustration)**. Note the large washers each side of the bush in the footrest bracket.

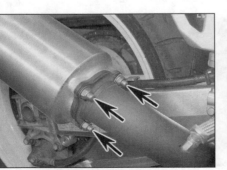

**17.1 Silencer to exhaust pipe nuts (arrowed)**

**17.2 Silencer to passenger footrest bracket bolt (arrowed)**

Lift the silencer off the flange on the exhaust pipe.

**3** Discard the silencer gasket as a new one must be fitted on reassembly. Note the O-rings fitted to the studs on the silencer to exhaust pipe flange joint.

### Installation

**4** If required, fit new O-rings to the silencer studs. Apply a smear of grease to the new silencer gasket to keep it in place, then install the gasket and fit the silencer onto the exhaust pipe flange.

**5** Ensure the large washers are fitted each side of the bush in the footrest bracket, then align the silencer mounting bracket with the footrest bracket and install the nut and bolt finger-tight.

**6** Install the washers and nuts on the silencer studs and tighten the nuts to the torque setting specified at the beginning of this Chapter. Tighten the silencer mounting bolt nut to the specified torque.

**7** Run the engine and check that there are no exhaust gas leaks.

### *Complete system – GSX-R600 and GSX-R750 models*

#### Removal

**8** Remove the fairing side panels (see Chapter 8). Remove the radiator (see Chapter 3).

**9** Unscrew the nut from the bolt securing the silencer to the passenger footrest bracket but leave the bolt in place **(see illustration)**.

**10** Undo and remove the bolt securing the exhaust system to the frame **(see illustration 17.9)**. Note the spacer fitted inside the bush in the frame bracket.

**11** Unscrew the downpipe clamp retaining bolts from the cylinder head and remove the bolts **(see illustration)**.

**12** Support the system, then withdraw the silencer mounting bolt and lower the system from the machine.

**13** Remove the gaskets from the cylinder head exhaust ports and discard them as new ones must be fitted on reassembly. Note the spacer inside the bush on the exhaust system to frame bracket.

#### Installation

**14** If removed, fit the spacer into the bush in the frame bracket from the left-hand side.

**15** Apply a smear of grease to the new exhaust port gaskets to keep it in place, then install the gaskets in the ports **(see illustration)**.

**16** Manoeuvre the exhaust system into position so that the downpipes are located in the cylinder head, then align the silencer mounting bracket with the passenger footrest bracket and install the nut and bolt finger-tight. Ensure the large washers are fitted each side of the bush in the footrest bracket. Install the bolt securing the exhaust system to the frame and tighten it finger-tight.

**17** Install the downpipe clamp bolts and tighten them evenly to the torque setting specified at the beginning of this Chapter. Now

17.9 Silencer mounting (A) and exhaust system to frame mounting (B)

17.15 Fit a new gasket into each exhaust port

tighten the other bolts to the specified torque.

**18** Run the engine and check that there are no exhaust gas leaks.

### *Exhaust downpipes – GSX-R1000 models*

**19** Remove the fairing side panels (see Chapter 8). Remove the oil cooler (see Chapter 2). Remove the radiator (see Chapter 3).

**20** Loosen the clamp securing the exhaust control valve housing to the downpipes **(see illustration)**.

**21** Follow Step 11, then lower the downpipes from the machine, leaving the exhaust control valve housing and silencer in place. Discard the seal fitted between the downpipes and control valve as a new one must be fitted on reassembly. If required, remove the silencer (see Steps 1 to 3).

**22** Installation is the reverse of removal (see Steps 15 to 18).

18.1 Exhaust control valve servo is mounted inside the right-hand frame spar

17.11 Unscrew the downpipe clamp bolts

17.20 Loosen the bolt (A) on the exhaust control valve housing clamp (B)

**23** Refer to Section 18 for removal of the exhaust control valve housing.

### 18 Exhaust control valve components (GSX-R1000) – check, removal and installation

⚠️ *Warning: If the engine has been running the exhaust system will be very hot. Allow the system to cool before carrying out any work.*

**Note:** *These procedures require the use of the Suzuki mode select switch (Pt. No. 09930-82710).*

### *Servo check*

**1** Make sure the ignition is OFF. Raise the fuel tank (see Section 2). Turn the ignition ON and observe the movement of the servo pulley and cables **(see illustration)**. Turn the ignition OFF. If the pulley does not move, disconnect the servo motor wiring connector. Use jumper wires to connect the terminals of a 12V battery to the wire terminals on the servo side of the connector. The servo pulley should rotate in one direction. Now reverse the wire connections and ensure the pulley rotates in the other direction. If the pulley does not rotate, or only rotates in one direction, renew the servo. **Note:** *Disconnect the jumper wires as soon as the test is complete to avoid damaging the servo.*

**2** If the pulley moves correctly when connected to the battery with jumper wires, check the wiring to the ECM and the ECM connector terminals.

**4**

18.11 Lower control valve cable adjuster position

18.12a Hold the pulley and undo the centre bolt

## Servo removal and installation

**Note:** *For ease of identification the upper control valve cable adjuster is black and the lower cable adjuster is silver.*

### Removal

**9** Make sure the ignition is OFF. Remove the seats (see Chapter 8) and raise the fuel tank (see Section 2).
**10** Connect the mode select switch (see Section 10). Turn the select switch ON and turn the ignition ON to position the control valve servo in the adjustment position **(see illustration 12.1)**. Turn the ignition OFF.
**11** Check the position of the adjuster on the lower control valve cable; from new there should be 13.5 mm of thread exposed. Note the position of the adjuster **(see illustration)**.
**12** Hold the servo pulley to prevent it turning and undo the pulley centre bolt **(see illustration)**. Loosen the locknut on the lower cable adjuster and turn the adjuster in to slacken the cable, then remove the pulley from the servo motor with the cables attached **(see illustrations)**. Note how the slot in the pulley aligns with the motor shaft. Detach the cables from the stop on the motor body and note how they locate in the inner track on the pulley.
**13** Disconnect the servo motor and valve position sensor wiring connectors, then undo the bolts securing the servo to the right-hand side of the frame and remove the servo **(see illustration)**. Note how the bolts fit and the position of the spacers between the servo and the frame.

### Installation

**14** Installation is the reverse of removal. Ensure the spacers are correctly positioned behind the servo and tighten the mounting bolts to the specified torque setting.
**15** Connect the servo motor and valve position sensor wiring connectors. Make sure the servo is in the adjustment position (see Step 10).
**16** Ensure the cables are correctly fitted into the inner track on the servo pulley, then install the pulley on the motor shaft and install the cables in the stop on the motor body **(see illustration)**. Hold the servo pulley to prevent it turning and tighten the centre bolt to the specified torque setting.
**17** Turn the adjuster on the lower cable out to expose 13.5 mm of thread and tighten the adjuster locknut (see Step 11).
**18** Install the remaining components in the reverse order of removal.

## Control valve removal, inspection and installation

### Removal

**19** Make sure the ignition is OFF. Remove the seats and the fairing right-hand side panel (see Chapter 8). Raise the fuel tank (see Section 2).
**20** Remove the silencer (see Section 17).
**21** Detach the cables from the servo pulley (see Steps 10 to 12).

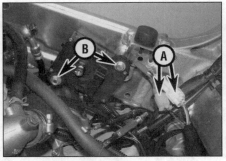

18.12b Slacken the lower (silver) cable adjuster (arrowed) . . .

18.12c . . . and pull the pulley off the servo motor

**3** If a code displayed on the LCD panel on the instrument cluster indicates a fault with the servo, but the servo motor is good, first adjust the control valve cables (see Steps 34 to 37). If the fault code is still displayed after adjusting the cables, make sure the ignition is OFF and disconnect the valve position sensor wiring connector.
**4** Turn the ignition ON and connect the positive (+ve) probe of a voltmeter to the red wire terminal on the loom side of the wiring connector and the negative (-ve) probe first to earth (ground), then to the black/brown wire terminal to check the input voltage. Turn the ignition OFF. If the input voltage is not as specified, check the wiring to the ECM and the ECM connector terminals.
**5** If the input voltage is good, check for continuity between the yellow wire terminal on the sensor side of the wiring connector and earth (ground). There should be no continuity.

**6** Reconnect the position sensor wiring connector. Connect the mode select switch (see Section 10). Turn the select switch ON and turn the ignition ON to position the servo in the adjustment position. Turn the ignition OFF. Disconnect the sensor wiring connector.
**7** Using an ohmmeter or multimeter set to the K-ohms scale, connect the positive (+ve) probe to the yellow wire terminal on the sensor side of the connector and the negative (-ve) probe to the white wire terminal and measure the sensor resistance. If the result is not as specified with the servo in the adjustment position, the servo is faulty.
**8** If the result is as specified, it is likely a fault exists in the position sensor output voltage indicating either a fault in the ECM or the sensor itself. Further tests and adjustments are best undertaken by a Suzuki dealer as incorrect adjustment of the output voltage can damage the servo.

18.13 Disconnect wiring connectors (A) and unscrew the mounting bolts (B)

18.16 Ensure both cables are pushed fully into the stop

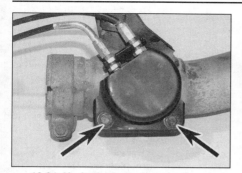

**18.24  Undo the bolts (arrowed) and remove the cover**

**18.25  Note the position of the cables and cable adjusters**

**18.26  Scrape any carbon off the valve inside the pipe**

**18.28  Position the cable adjusters so that there is a 3 mm gap between the adjuster and the pulley**

**18.29  Fit a new control valve to exhaust system seal**

22  Remove the bolt securing the control valve housing to the frame (see illustration 17.9, item B). Loosen the clamp securing the control valve housing to the downpipes, then pull the control valve housing off the end of the downpipes (see illustration 17.20). Note the spacer fitted inside the bush in the frame bracket. Discard the seal fitted between the downpipes and control valve housing as a new one must be fitted on reassembly.

23  Feed the cables out of the guide on the inside of the frame behind the swingarm pivot and remove the control valve housing from the bike.

24  Undo the bolts securing the control valve pulley cover and remove the cover (see illustration).

25  Note the position of the cables and cable adjusters (see illustration). If required, loosen the locknuts securing the adjusters to the bracket on the control valve, then disconnect the cable ends from the pulley and remove the cables.

### Inspection

26  Check the operation of the control valve; it should turn smoothly and be held in the fully closed position by the return spring. Scrape any carbon off the valve and the inside of the pipe (see illustration). Individual components are not available for the valve; if it is damaged or corroded it must be renewed.

### Installation

27  Installation is the reverse of removal. Fit the cable ends into the pulley, ensuring the cable with the elbow goes around the underside of the pulley. Note: The cable with the elbow on its lower end has the black adjuster on its upper end.

28  Fit the adjusters into the bracket on the control valve. Turn the locknuts to allow 3 mm clearance between the adjuster ends and the valve pulley, then tighten the locknuts (see illustration). Smear the threads of the cover bolts with a suitable copper-based grease, then install the cover and tighten the bolts securely.

29  If removed, fit the spacer into the bush in the frame bracket from the left-hand side. Fit a new seal into the control valve housing and ensure the clamp is in place on the end of the housing (see illustration). Feed the cables

through the guide on the inside of the frame and install the housing on the end of the downpipes. Fit the mounting bolt and tighten it to the specified torque, then tighten the clamp securely.

30  Make sure the servo is in the adjustment position (see Step 10), then install the cables on the servo pulley (see Steps 16 and 17).

31  Install the silencer (see Section 17).

## Cable removal and installation

### Removal

32  Disconnect the cables from the servo pulley (see Steps 9 to 12).

33  Remove the silencer (see Section 17) then remove the control valve housing and disconnect the cables from the valve pulley (see Steps 22 to 25).

### Installation and adjustment

34  Install the new cables on the valve pulley (see Steps 27 and 28). Pull the cable with the black adjuster straight, then turn the black

adjuster to set the length of the exposed inner cable (servo motor end) to 28 to 29 mm (see illustration). Tighten the black adjuster locknut.

35  Pull the cable with the silver adjuster straight, then turn the silver adjuster all the way in. Now adjust the cable length with the adjuster at the control valve end. Loosen the adjuster locknuts on the control valve bracket and turn the adjuster to set the length of the exposed inner cable (servo motor end) to 52 to 53 mm (see illustration overleaf). Tighten the locknuts on the control valve bracket and fit the cover, then install the control valve housing (see Step 29).

36  Make sure the servo is in the adjustment position (see Step 10), then install the cables on the servo pulley (see Steps 16 and 17).

37  Make sure the mode select switch is OFF. Turn the ignition ON and check the movement of the servo pulley and cables. Turn the mode select switch ON and check the LCD display on the instrument cluster. If no fault code is displayed the cable adjustment is correct. If

**4**

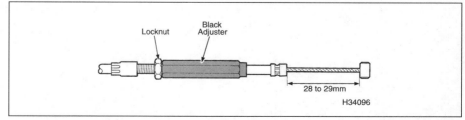

**18.34  Exposed length of inner cable (28 to 29 mm) on cable with black adjuster**

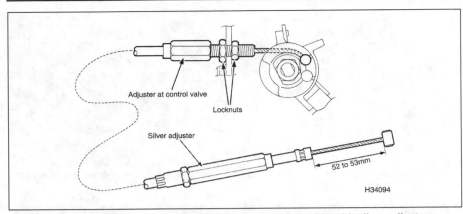

**18.35 Exposed inner cable length (52 to 53 mm) on cable with silver adjuster**

fault code C46 is displayed, have the cables readjusted by a Suzuki dealer to correct the output voltage of the exhaust control valve position sensor.

*Caution: Incorrect adjustment of the output voltage can damage the servo.*

## 19 EVAP system
(California models)

### General information

1 This system prevents the escape of fuel vapour into the atmosphere by storing it in a charcoal-filled canister **(see illustration)**.
2 When the engine is not running, excess fuel vapour from the tank passes, via the breather hose, through a pressure control valve into the canister. When the engine is started, intake manifold depression draws the vapour back from the canister into the throttle bodies to be burned during the normal combustion process.
3 The canister has a one way valve which allows air to be drawn into the system as the volume of fuel decreases in the tank. The system also has a shut-off valve which prevents any fuel escaping through it in the event of the bike falling over.

4 The system is not adjustable and can only be properly tested by a Suzuki dealer. However the owner can check that all the hoses are in good condition and are securely connected at each end. Renew any hoses that are cracked, split or generally deteriorated.
5 The pressure control valve can be checked by disconnecting the hoses from the valve and blowing through it. Note which way round the valve fits. Air should pass through the valve easily when blowing into it from the canister side, but it should be harder to blow through from the fuel tank side. If the performance of the control valve is suspect have it checked by a Suzuki dealer.

*Caution: Fuel vapour is toxic. A small amount of vapour will be present in the valve when it is removed from the bike. Take care not to inhale the vapour when checking the valve.*

### Removal and installation

6 To access the canister remove the seat cowling (see Chapter 8). The canister is mounted on the right-hand side of the rear sub- frame. Label and disconnect the hoses, then remove the clamp screw and take the canister out. Make sure the hoses are correctly reconnected on installation.
7 The pressure control valve is located in the breather hose mid-way between the canister and the fuel tank. The shut-off valve is located under the fuel tank.

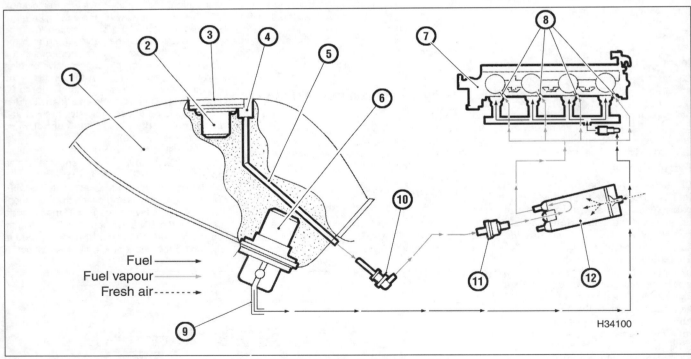

**19.1 EVAP system – California models**

| | | | |
|---|---|---|---|
| 1 Fuel tank | 4 Vapour separator | 7 Throttle bodies | 10 Fuel shut-off valve |
| 2 Fuel filler neck | 5 Breather tube | 8 Purge ports | 11 Fuel pressure control valve |
| 3 Fuel filler cap | 6 Fuel pump | 9 Fuel feed hose | 12 Canister |

# Chapter 5
# Ignition system

## Contents

## Degrees of difficulty

| Easy, suitable for novice with little experience |  | Fairly easy, suitable for beginner with some experience |  | Fairly difficult, suitable for competent DIY mechanic |  | Difficult, suitable for experienced DIY mechanic | | Very difficult, suitable for expert DIY or professional |  |

## Specifications

### General information

| | |
|---|---|
| Firing order . . . . . . . . . . . . . . . . . . . . . . . . . . . . . . . . . . . . . . . . . . . . . . . . . . . | 1–2–4–3 |
| Cylinder identification (from left to right-hand side of the bike) . . . . . . . | 1–2–3–4 |
| Spark plugs . . . . . . . . . . . . . . . . . . . . . . . . . . . . . . . . . . . . . . . . . . . . . . . | see Chapter 1 |
| Ignition rev limiter | |
| GSX-R600 . . . . . . . . . . . . . . . . . . . . . . . . . . . . . . . . . . . . . . . . . . . . . . . . . | 14,000 rpm |
| GSX-R750 . . . . . . . . . . . . . . . . . . . . . . . . . . . . . . . . . . . . . . . . . . . . . . . . . | 13,700 rpm |
| GSX-R1000 . . . . . . . . . . . . . . . . . . . . . . . . . . . . . . . . . . . . . . . . . . . . . . . . | 12,300 rpm |

### Ignition coils

| | |
|---|---|
| **GSX-R750** | |
| Primary winding resistance . . . . . . . . . . . . . . . . . . . . . . . . . . . . . . . . . . | 0.8 to 1.2 ohms |
| Secondary winding resistance (with plug lead and cap) . . . . . . . . . | 8 to 15 K-ohms |
| **GSX-R600 and GSX-R1000 models** | |
| Primary winding resistance . . . . . . . . . . . . . . . . . . . . . . . . . . . . . . . . . . | 0.8 to 2.0 ohms |
| Secondary winding resistance . . . . . . . . . . . . . . . . . . . . . . . . . . . . . . . | 8 to 15 K-ohms |

**5**

2.4 Check for battery input voltage at the ECM (arrowed)

2.5a Disconnect the wiring connector . . .

2.5b . . . then pull the coil/cap off the spark plug

## 1 General information

The transistorised electronic ignition system is combined with the fuel injection system, both being controlled by the ECM (engine control module). The ignition system comprises a rotor, crankshaft position sensor (CKP sensor), engine control module (ECM) and ignition coils.

The triggers on the rotor, which is fitted to the right-hand end of the crankshaft, generate a signal in the CKP sensor as the crankshaft rotates. The CKP sensor sends that signal to the ECM which, in conjunction with information received from the throttle position, gear position and engine coolant temperature sensors, calculates the ignition timing and supplies the ignition coils with the power necessary to produce a spark at the plugs. There is no provision for checking or adjusting the ignition timing on these models.

On all models the ignition coil for each spark plug is incorporated in the spark plug cap.

The system incorporates a safety interlock circuit which will cut the ignition if the sidestand is put down whilst the engine is running and in gear, or if a gear is selected whilst the engine is running and the sidestand is down (see Chapter 9).

Maximum engine speed is restricted by the ECM to prevent engine damage (see Specifications).

Because of the inter-relation between the ignition and fuel injection systems, and the comprehensive fault diagnosis procedure incorporated in the Suzuki fuel injection system, details of all system sensor checks are provided in Chapter 4.

**Note:** *Individual ignition system components can be checked but not repaired. If ignition system troubles occur, and the faulty component can be isolated, the only cure for the problem is to renew the part. Keep in mind that most electronic parts, once purchased, cannot be returned. To avoid unnecessary expense, make very sure the faulty component has been positively identified before buying a new part.*

## 2 Ignition system –
check

⚠️ *Warning: The energy levels in electronic systems can be very high. On no account should the ignition be switched on whilst the plugs or plug caps are being held. Shocks from the HT circuit can be most unpleasant. Secondly, it is vital that the engine is not turned over or run with any of the plug caps removed, and that the plugs are soundly earthed (grounded) when the system is checked for sparking. The system components can be seriously damaged if the HT circuit becomes isolated.*

1 As no means of adjustment is available, any failure of the system can be traced to failure of a system component or a simple wiring fault. Of the two possibilities, the latter is by far the most likely. In the event of failure, check the system in a logical fashion, as described below.

2 Remove the air filter housing (see Chapter 4). Refer to Chapter 4 and trace the wiring from the cam position (CMP), crankshaft position (CKP), throttle position (TPS), engine coolant temperature (ECT) and gear position (GP) sensors to their respective wiring connectors and then to the ECM. Ensure that the connector terminals are clean and that the connectors are secure.

3 Check the battery condition and the ignition circuit fuse (see Chapter 9).

4 Disconnect the ECM multi-pin wiring connector and turn the ignition ON (see illustration). Connect the probes of a voltmeter between the orange/white and black/white wire terminals on the loom side of the wiring connector and check for battery input voltage (12V approx). Turn the ignition OFF. If the input voltage is not as specified, check the ignition (main) switch, side stand relay and engine stop switch (see Chapter 9).

5 Check that the cylinder location is marked on each ignition coil/plug cap wiring connector and mark them accordingly if not, then disconnect the connectors (see illustration). Pull the coil/caps off the spark plugs and reconnect the wiring connectors (see illustration). **Note:** *To avoid damaging the wiring, always disconnect the connectors before removing the coil/caps. Do not attempt to lever the coil/caps off the plugs or pull them off with pliers. Do not drop the coils.*

6 Connect each coil/cap to a known good spark plug and lay each plug on the engine with the threads earthed (grounded). If necessary, secure each spark plug with an insulated tool.

*Caution: Do not lay the plugs against the magnesium engine covers as they could be damaged.*

⚠️ *Warning: Do not remove any of the spark plugs from the engine to perform this check – atomised fuel being pumped out of the open spark plug hole could ignite, causing severe injury!*

7 Having observed the above precautions, check that the kill switch is in the RUN position and the transmission is in neutral, then turn the ignition switch ON and turn the engine over on the starter motor. If the system is in good condition a regular, fat blue spark should be evident at each plug electrode. If the spark appears thin or yellowish, or is non-existent, further investigation will be necessary.

8 The ignition system must be able to produce a spark at each coil/cap which is capable of jumping a particular size gap. Suzuki specify that a healthy system should produce a spark capable of jumping 8 mm. Use an adjustable ignition spark gap test tool to check the strength of the spark (see illustration).

2.8 An adjustable spark gap tester

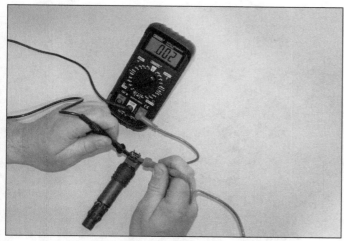

3.4 Measuring the coil/cap primary resistance

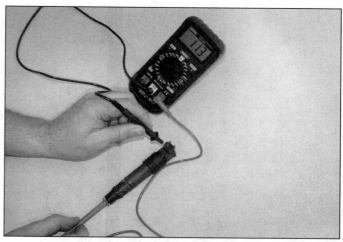

3.5 Measuring the coil/cap secondary resistance

9 Connect one of the coil/caps to the protruding electrode on the test tool, and clip the tool to a good earth (ground) on the engine or frame. Check that the kill switch is in the RUN position, turn the ignition switch ON and turn the engine over on the starter motor. If the system is in good condition a regular, fat blue spark should be seen to jump the gap between the test tool electrodes. Repeat the test on the other coil/caps. If the test results are good the entire ignition system can be considered good. If one or more of the sparks appears thin or yellowish, or is non-existent, further investigation will be necessary. Before proceeding further, turn the ignition OFF and remove the key as a safety measure.

10 Ignition faults can be divided into two categories, namely those where the ignition system has failed completely, and those which are due to a partial failure. The likely faults are listed below, starting with the most probable source of failure. Work through the list systematically, referring to the relevant sections for details of the necessary checks and tests.

● Loose, corroded or damaged wiring connections, broken or shorted wiring between any of the component parts of the ignition system (see Chapter 9).

● Faulty spark plug, dirty or damaged plug electrodes, incorrect gap between electrodes, incorrect spark plug (see Chapter 1).

● Faulty ignition (main) switch or engine stop switch (see Chapter 9).

● Faulty clutch, neutral or sidestand switch (see Chapter 9).

● Faulty crankshaft position sensor or damaged rotor (see Chapter 4).

● Faulty ignition coil/plug cap.

● Faulty engine control module.

11 If the above checks don't reveal the cause of the problem, have the ignition system tested by a Suzuki dealer.

## 3 Ignition coil/plug cap – removal, check and installation

**Note:** Refer to Chapter 4, Section 10 for fault finding details.

### Removal

1 Remove the air filter housing (see Chapter 4). Disconnect the battery negative (-ve) lead.
2 Check that the cylinder location is marked on each coil/plug cap wiring connector and mark them accordingly if not, then disconnect the connectors **(see illustration 2.5a)**. Pull the coil/caps off the spark plugs and mark their cylinder location also **(see illustration 2.5b)**.
**Note:** To avoid damaging the wiring, always disconnect the connectors before removing the coil/caps. Do not attempt to lever the coil/caps off the plugs or pull them off with pliers. Do not drop the coils.

### Check

3 Ensure the primary circuit terminals in the top of the coil/cap and the spark plug terminal inside the cap are undamaged and free from corrosion.
4 Using an ohmmeter or multimeter set to the ohms scale, measure the coil/cap primary

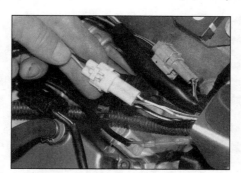

4.2 Disconnect the crankshaft position (CKP) sensor wiring at the connector

resistance between the primary circuit terminals **(see illustration)**. Compare the result with the specifications at the beginning of this Chapter.
5 Now set the meter to the K-ohms scale and measure the coil/cap secondary resistance between the negative (-ve) primary circuit terminal and the spark plug terminal **(see illustration)**. Compare the result with the specifications at the beginning of this Chapter.
6 If either of the results are not as specified the coil/cap is probably faulty. Have the coil/cap peak voltage tested by a Suzuki dealer to confirm this.

### Installation

7 Ensure the spark plug channels are free from any obstructions and press the coil/caps fully home onto the spark plugs.
8 Ensure the connectors are reconnected in the correct order (see Step 2).
9 Connect the battery negative (-ve) lead and install the remaining components in the reverse order of removal.

## 4 Crankshaft position (CKP) sensor – removal and installation

**Note:** Refer to Chapter 4, Sections 10 and 11 for fault finding and testing details.

### Removal

1 Remove the seat cowling (see Chapter 8) and disconnect the battery negative (-ve) lead.
2 Trace the CKP sensor wiring back from the top of the right-hand side crankcase cover and disconnect it at the 2-pin connector with the black and green wires **(see illustration)**. Free the wiring from any clips or ties and feed it through to the cover.
3 Remove the starter clutch (see Chapter 2).
4 Remove the screws securing the CKP sensor mounting plate to the crankcase and

4.4a Remove the wiring clamp (A) and CKP sensor mounting plate (B) screws

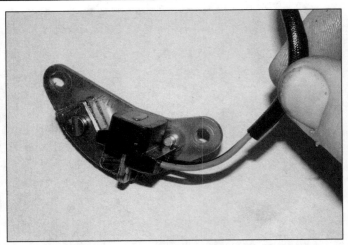

4.4b The CKP sensor is on the inside of the mounting plate

the screw securing the wiring clamp **(see illustration)**. Remove the rubber wiring grommet from its recess, then remove the sensor assembly, noting how it fits **(see illustration)**.
**5** Examine the rotor for signs of damage and install a new one if necessary (see Chapter 2, Section 13). **Note:** *The rotor is integral with the cam chain sprocket on the crankshaft.*

### Installation

**6** Install the sensor assembly onto the crankcase and tighten its screws securely.
**7** Apply a smear of sealant to the rubber wiring seal and fit the grommet in its recess in the crankcase. Locate the wiring under its clamp and tighten the clamp screw.
**8** Install the starter clutch (see Chapter 2).
**9** Route the wiring up to the connector and reconnect it. Secure the wiring in its clips or ties.

**10** Reconnect the battery negative (-ve) lead and install the seat cowling (see Chapter 8).

## 5 Engine control module (ECM) – check, removal and installation

**1** If the testing procedures described in this Chapter and Chapter 4, Sections 10 and 11 indicate that all ignition and fuel injection system components are functioning correctly, yet a fault exists, take the machine to a Suzuki dealer for testing. No details are available for checking the ECM on home workshop equipment.
**2** To remove the ECM, first remove the rider's seat (see Chapter 8) and disconnect the battery negative (-ve) lead.
**3** The ECM is located to the rear of the battery **(see illustration 2.4)**. Disconnect the

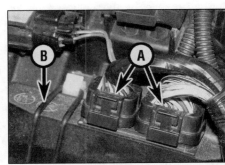

5.3 ECM multi-pin wiring connectors (A) and fixing strap (B)

multi-pin wiring connectors from the unit, then unclip its mounting strap and remove it **(see illustration)**.
**4** Installation is the reverse of removal. Make sure the wiring connectors are clean and secure.

# Chapter 6
# Frame, suspension and final drive

## Contents

## Degrees of difficulty

| | | | | |
|---|---|---|---|---|
| **Easy,** suitable for novice with little experience  | **Fairly easy,** suitable for beginner with some experience  | **Fairly difficult,** suitable for competent DIY mechanic  | **Difficult,** suitable for experienced DIY mechanic | **Very difficult,** suitable for expert DIY or professional |

## Specifications

### Front forks

Fork oil type
  GSX-R600 and GSX-R750 . . . . . . . . . . . . . . . . . . . . . . . . . . . . . . SAE 10W fork oil
  GSX-R1000 . . . . . . . . . . . . . . . . . . . . . . . . . . . . . . Suzuki L01 fork oil
Fork oil capacity
  GSX-R600 . . . . . . . . . . . . . . . . . . . . . . . . . . . . . . 528 cc
  GSX-R750 . . . . . . . . . . . . . . . . . . . . . . . . . . . . . . 473 cc
  GSX-R1000 . . . . . . . . . . . . . . . . . . . . . . . . . . . . . . 517 cc
Fork oil level*
  GSX-R600 . . . . . . . . . . . . . . . . . . . . . . . . . . . . . . 102 mm
  GSX-R750 . . . . . . . . . . . . . . . . . . . . . . . . . . . . . . 103 mm
  GSX-R1000 . . . . . . . . . . . . . . . . . . . . . . . . . . . . . . 90 mm
Fork spring free length service limit
  GSX-R600 . . . . . . . . . . . . . . . . . . . . . . . . . . . . . . 243.0 mm
  GSX-R750 . . . . . . . . . . . . . . . . . . . . . . . . . . . . . . 244.0 mm
  GSX-R1000 . . . . . . . . . . . . . . . . . . . . . . . . . . . . . . 231.0 mm
Fork tube protrusion above top yoke (not inc. top bolt)
  GSX-R600 . . . . . . . . . . . . . . . . . . . . . . . . . . . . . . 6.3 mm
  GSX-R750 . . . . . . . . . . . . . . . . . . . . . . . . . . . . . . 4.0 mm
  GSX-R1000 . . . . . . . . . . . . . . . . . . . . . . . . . . . . . . 6.0 mm
*Oil level is measured from the top of the tube with the fork spring removed and the leg fully compressed.

### Rear suspension

Spring pre-load adjustment
  GSX-R600 and GSX-R750
    Min pre-load . . . . . . . . . . . . . . . . . . . . . . . . . . . . . . 196.5 mm
    Max pre-load . . . . . . . . . . . . . . . . . . . . . . . . . . . . . . 186.5 mm
    Standard pre-load . . . . . . . . . . . . . . . . . . . . . . . . . . . . . . 191.5 mm
  GSX-R1000
    Min pre-load . . . . . . . . . . . . . . . . . . . . . . . . . . . . . . 182.0 mm
    Max pre-load . . . . . . . . . . . . . . . . . . . . . . . . . . . . . . 172.0 mm
    Standard pre-load . . . . . . . . . . . . . . . . . . . . . . . . . . . . . . 177.0 mm
Swingarm pivot bolt runout (max) . . . . . . . . . . . . . . . . . . . . . . . . . . 0.3 mm

6

## Final drive

| | |
|---|---|
| Drive chain slack and lubricant | see Chapter 1 |
| Drive chain type | |
| GSX-R600 | RK525SMOZ6 (110 links) |
| GSX-R750 | RK525ROZ4 (110 links) |
| GSX-R1000 | DID50V4 (110 links) |
| Sprocket sizes | |
| Front (engine) sprocket | 16T |
| Rear (wheel) sprocket | 45T |

## Torque settings

| | |
|---|---|
| Clutch lever clamp bolt | 10 Nm |
| Rider's footrest bracket bolts | 23 Nm |
| Sidestand mounting bracket bolt | 50 Nm |
| Handlebar clamp bolts | 23 Nm |
| Handlebar set bolts | 10 Nm |
| Front brake master cylinder clamp bolts | 10 Nm |
| Fork clamp bolts (top and bottom yoke) | 23 Nm |
| Fork compression damping adjuster – GSX-R600 and GSX-R750 | 18 Nm |
| Fork damper cartridge bolt | |
| GSX-R600 and GSX-R750 | 35 Nm |
| GSX-R1000 | 40 Nm |
| Fork damper rod locknut | |
| GSX-R600 and GSX-R750 | 20 Nm |
| GSX-R1000 | 29 Nm |
| Fork tube top bolt | |
| GSX-R600 and GSX-R750 | 35 Nm |
| GSX-R1000 | 23 Nm |
| Front sprocket nut | 115 Nm |
| Rear shock absorber nut/bolt | 50 Nm |
| Rear shock absorber upper mounting bracket nut | 115 Nm |
| Rear sprocket nuts | 60 Nm |
| Rear suspension linkage arm and linkage rod nuts | 78 Nm |
| Speed sensor rotor bolt | |
| GSX-R600 and GSX-R750 | 20 Nm |
| GSX-R1000 | 23 Nm |
| Steering damper mounting bolt and nut | 23 Nm |
| Steering head bearing adjuster nut initial setting (see text) | 45 Nm |
| Steering head bearing locknut | 80 Nm |
| Steering stem nut | 90 Nm |
| Swingarm pivot bolt | 15 Nm |
| Swingarm pivot nut | 100 Nm |
| Swingarm pivot bolt locknut | 90 Nm |
| Swingarm pivot height adjustment boss nut – GSX-R750K2 only | 65 Nm |

## 1 General information

All models have a twin spar, box-section aluminium frame which uses the engine as a stressed member.

Front suspension on GSX-R600 models is by conventional telescopic forks. GSX-R750 and GSX-R1000 models are fitted with upside-down forks. Front suspension on all models is adjustable for spring pre-load, rebound and compression damping. All models are fitted with an hydraulic steering damper.

At the rear, an alloy swingarm acts on a single shock absorber via a three-way linkage. The shock absorber is adjustable for spring pre-load, rebound and compression damping on all models.

The drive to the rear wheel is by chain and sprockets.

## 2 Frame – inspection and repair

1 The frame should not require attention unless accident damage has occurred. In most cases, frame renewal is the only satisfactory remedy for such damage. A few frame specialists have the jigs and other equipment necessary for straightening frames to the required standard of accuracy, but even then there is no simple way of assessing to what extent the frame may have been over stressed.
2 After a high mileage, the frame should be examined closely for signs of cracking or splitting at the welded joints. Loose engine mounting bolts can cause ovaling or fracturing of the mounting points. Minor damage can often be repaired by specialised welding, depending on the extent and nature of the damage.

3 Remember that a frame which is out of alignment will cause handling problems. If, as the result of an accident, misalignment is suspected, it will be necessary to strip the machine completely so the frame can be thoroughly checked.

## 3 Footrests, brake pedal and gearchange lever – removal and installation

### Rider's footrests

#### Removal

1 Remove the split pin from the bottom of the footrest pivot pin, then withdraw the pivot pin and remove the footrest, noting the fitting of the return spring and spacer **(see illustration)**.
2 If required, remove the footrest bracket to access the footrest holder bolt (see Steps 6 to 8 and 10 to 11). **Note:** *The rear brake lever and*

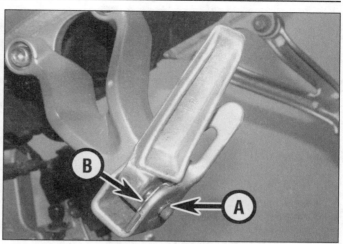

3.1 Remove the split pin (A) and withdraw the pivot pin. Note the position of the return spring (B)

3.4 Remove the E-clip (A) and withdraw the pivot pin. Note the position of the detent plate, ball and spring (B)

the gearchange lever are supported by the footrest holders.

### Installation

3 Installation is the reverse of removal, noting the following:
● If removed, align the lugs on the footrest holder with the footrest bracket.
● Apply a small amount of copper-based grease to the pivot pin.
● Use a new split pin and bend its ends securely.

## Passenger footrests

### Removal

4 Remove the E-clip from the bottom of the footrest pivot pin, then withdraw the pivot pin and remove the footrest, noting the position of the detent plate, ball and spring (see illustration). Discard the E-clip if it is damaged and fit a new one on reassembly.

### Installation

5 Installation is the reverse of removal. Apply

a small amount of copper-based grease to the pivot pin and ball. Ensure the E-clip is properly located in the groove in the pivot pin.

## Brake pedal

### Removal

6 Unhook the brake pedal return spring and brake light spring from the bracket on the back of the brake pedal (see illustration).
7 Remove the split pin and washer from the clevis pin securing the brake pedal to the master cylinder pushrod (see illustration 3.6). Remove the clevis pin and separate the pedal from the pushrod.
8 Unscrew the two bolts securing the footrest bracket to the frame, then turn the bracket round to access the footrest holder bolt (see illustration). Take care not to strain the brake hoses or the brake light switch wiring. Undo the footrest holder bolt, then remove the footrest and pedal. Slide the pedal off the holder.

### Installation

9 Installation is the reverse of removal, noting the following:
● Apply copper-based grease to the brake pedal pivot.
● Align the lugs on the footrest holder with the bracket.
● Tighten the footrest bracket bolts to the torque setting specified at the beginning of this Chapter.
● Use a new split pin on the clevis pin securing the brake pedal to the master cylinder pushrod and bend the split pin ends securely.
● Check the operation of the rear brake light switch (see Chapter 1).

## Gearchange lever

### Removal

10 Loosen the gearchange linkage rod locknuts, then unscrew the rod and separate it from the lever and the gearchange arm (the

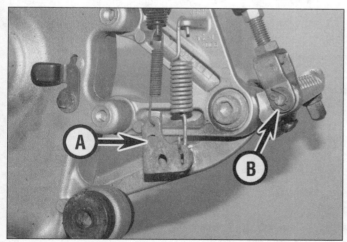

3.6 Unhook the springs from the bracket (A). Note the split pin and washer (B) on the brake pedal clevis pin

3.8 Unscrew the bolts (arrowed) and displace the bracket

6

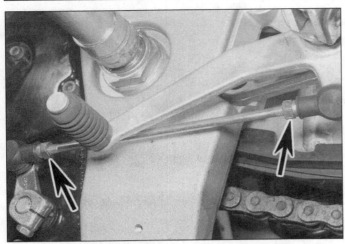

3.10 Loosen the locknuts (arrowed) and unscrew the rod

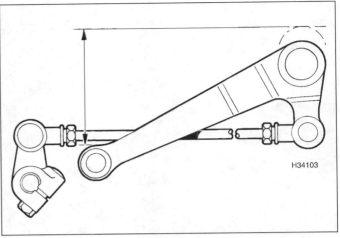

3.12 Standard gearchange lever tip position below top surface of footrest

rod is reverse-threaded on one end and so will simultaneously unscrew from both lever and arm) (see illustration). Note the how far the rod is threaded into the lever and arm as this determines the height of the lever relative to the footrest.

11 Unscrew the two bolts securing the footrest bracket to the frame, then turn the bracket round to access the footrest holder bolt. Undo the footrest holder bolt, then remove the footrest and lever. Slide the lever off the holder. Refer to Section 18 for removal of the gearchange linkage arm.

### Installation

12 Installation is the reverse of removal, noting the following:

● Apply copper-based grease to the gearchange lever pivot.

● Align the lugs on the footrest holder with the bracket.

● Tighten the footrest bracket bolts to the torque setting specified at the beginning of this Chapter.

● Adjust the gearchange lever height as

required by screwing the rod in or out of the lever and arm, then tighten the locknuts securely. Note that Suzuki specify a standard position of 52 to 62 mm, this being the distance of the gearchange lever tip below the top surface of the rider's footrest (see illustration).

### 4 Sidestand –
removal and installation

#### Removal

1 The sidestand pivots on a bracket which is attached to a lug on the underside of the frame. Springs between the bracket and the stand ensure that it is held in the retracted or extended position.

2 Support the bike using an auxiliary stand. To remove the stand only, first undo the pivot bolt nut, then undo the pivot bolt and remove the stand, releasing the springs as you do (see illustrations).

3 To remove the sidestand and bracket, first trace the wiring from the sidestand switch and disconnect it at the connector, then undo the bolts securing the sidestand bracket to the frame and remove the stand (see illustrations).

#### Installation

4 If the sidestand bracket was removed, tighten its mounting bolts to the specified torque setting.

5 On installation, apply grease to the pivot bolt shank and tighten the nut securely. Check that the sidestand springs are correctly located and hold the stand securely up when not in use – an accident is almost certain to occur if the stand extends while the machine is in motion.

6 Check the operation of the sidestand switch (see Chapter 1).

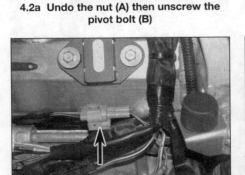

4.2a Undo the nut (A) then unscrew the pivot bolt (B)

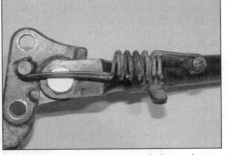

4.2b Note which way round the springs are fitted

4.3a Disconnect the sidestand switch wiring connector . . .

4.3b . . . then undo the bolts from the underside of the bike

5.2 Disconnect the brake light switch wires (arrowed)

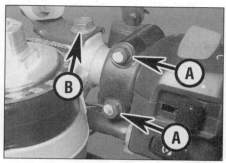

5.4 Undo the clamp bolts (A) and the reservoir bolt (B)

5.5a Undo the handlebar set bolt (arrowed) . . .

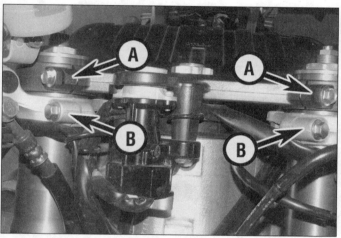

5.5b . . . and the top yoke clamp bolts (A). Note the handlebar clamp bolts (B)

5.6 Remove the steering stem nut and washer

## 5  Handlebars and levers – removal and installation

### Right handlebar removal

**Note:** *Unless the handlebar is being renewed the bar end weight and twistgrip can be left in place.*

**1** If required, raise or remove the fuel tank to avoid damaging the paintwork (see Chapter 4). Place the motorcycle on an auxiliary stand.
**2** Disconnect the brake light switch wires from the switch on the underside of the master cylinder **(see illustration)**. Release the throttle cables from the twistgrip pulley (see Chapter 4). Free the handlebar switch wiring from its guide under the top yoke and position the switch/twistgrip housing away from the handlebar.
**3** Undo the screw retaining bar end weight and remove the weight, then pull the twistgrip off the handlebar.
**4** Undo the front brake master cylinder clamp bolts and remove the back of the clamp, noting how it fits **(see illustration)**. Undo the bolt securing the hydraulic reservoir to the handlebar bracket, then position the master cylinder and reservoir

assembly clear of the handlebar. Ensure no strain is placed on the hydraulic hose. Keep the hydraulic reservoir upright to prevent air entering the system.
**5** Undo the set bolt securing the handlebar to the top yoke and loosen the fork clamp bolts in the top yoke **(see illustrations)**.
**6** Undo the steering stem nut and remove the washer, then carefully ease the top yoke up off the fork tubes **(see illustration)**. Ensure no strain is placed on the wiring loom.
**7** Loosen the handlebar clamp bolt, then ease the handlebar up and off the fork **(see illustration 5.5b)**.

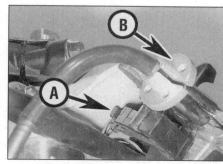

5.9 Clutch switch wiring connector (A), clutch cable adjuster (B)

### Left handlebar removal

**Note:** *Unless the handlebar is being renewed the bar end weight, grip and clutch lever/lever bracket can be left in place.*

**8** If required, raise or remove the fuel tank to avoid damaging the paintwork (see Chapter 4). Place the motorcycle on an auxiliary stand.
**9** Disconnect the clutch switch wiring connector from the switch on the underside of the clutch lever bracket **(see illustration)**. On all models except the GSX-R1000K2, release the choke cable from the handlebar lever (see Chapter 4). Free the handlebar switch wiring from its guide under the top yoke and position the switch housing away from the handlebar.
**10** Screw the clutch cable adjuster fully into the lever bracket **(see illustration 5.9)**. Align the slots in the adjuster and the bracket, then pull the outer cable end out of the adjuster and release the inner cable from the lever. If there is not enough slack in the cable to free it from the adjuster, remove the clutch lever (see Step 14).
**11** Undo the screw retaining the bar end weight and remove the weight, then pull the grip off the handlebar. **Note:** *The grip will probably be stuck in place - it may be necessary to slit the grip with a sharp knife in*

**6**

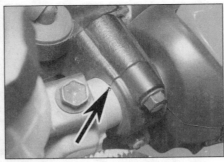

5.11 Loosen the bracket bolt (arrowed)

5.13 Align the clamp joint with the punch mark (arrowed)

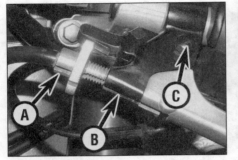

5.14 Clutch cable adjuster (A), lever bracket (B) and pivot bolt (C)

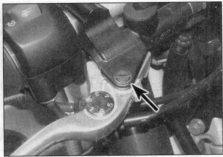

5.15 Front brake lever pivot bolt (arrowed)

cable **(see illustration)**. Align the slots in the adjuster and the bracket. Unscrew the lever pivot bolt locknut on the underside of the lever, then unscrew the pivot bolt and remove the lever, detaching the cable as you do.

**15** To remove the front brake lever, unscrew the lever pivot bolt locknut on the underside of the lever, then unscrew the pivot bolt and remove the lever **(see illustration)**.

**16** Installation is the reverse of removal. Apply grease to the pivot bolt shaft and the contact areas between the lever and its bracket. Grease the exposed end of the clutch cable and the cable socket in the lever. Adjust the clutch cable freeplay (see Chapter 1). Check the operation of the front brake lever span adjuster.

## 6 Forks –
### removal and installation

### Removal

**1** Remove the fairing and the fairing side panels (see Chapter 8).
**2** Remove the front wheel (see Chapter 7) and the mudguard (see Chapter 8).
**3** Work on each fork leg individually. Note the routing of the various cables and hoses around the forks. If both fork legs are being removed, note which side they fit and mark them accordingly.
**4** Loosen but do not remove the fork clamp bolt in the top yoke and the handlebar clamp bolt **(see illustration)**. Depending on the tools available, access to the right-hand fork clamp bolt may be restricted by the front brake reservoir bracket. If required, undo the bracket bolt and displace the reservoir **(see illustration 5.4)**.
**5** If the forks are to be disassembled, or if the fork oil is being changed, loosen the fork top bolt while the leg is still clamped in the bottom yoke **(see illustration 6.4)**.
**6** Support the fork leg, then loosen but do not remove the clamp bolts in the bottom yoke. Remove the fork by twisting it and pulling it downwards **(see illustrations)**. Make sure the handlebar clamp does not bind on the fork tube as it is withdrawn.

*order to remove it.* Loosen the clutch lever bracket bolt and slide the bracket off the handlebar **(see illustration)**.
**12** Follow Steps 5 to 7 and remove the top yoke and handlebar.

### Handlebar installation

**13** Installation is the reverse of removal, noting the following:
● Ensure the top yoke is correctly positioned on the fork tubes (see Section 6) and install the handlebar set bolt before tightening the handlebar clamp bolt.
● Refer to the Specifications at the beginning of this Chapter and tighten the steering stem nut, the fork clamp bolts, the handlebar set bolt and the handlebar clamp bolt, in that order.
● Ensure the back of the front brake master cylinder clamp is installed with the UP mark

facing up, and align the clamp joint with the punch mark on the top of the handlebar **(see illustration)**. Tighten the top clamp bolt first. Tighten the clamp bolts to the specified torque.
● Refer to Chapter 4 for installation of the throttle cables and, where fitted, the choke cable.
● If removed, apply a suitable non-permanent locking compound to the handlebar end-weight retaining screws. If new grips are being fitted, secure them using a suitable adhesive.
● Check the operation of the front brake light switch and clutch switch before riding the motorcycle.

### Handlebar levers

**14** To remove the clutch lever, first screw the clutch cable adjuster fully into the lever bracket to provide maximum freeplay in the

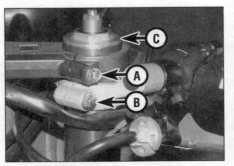

6.4 Fork clamp bolt (A), handlebar clamp bolt (B) and fork top bolt (C)

6.6a Loosen the fork clamp bolts (arrowed) in the bottom yoke . . .

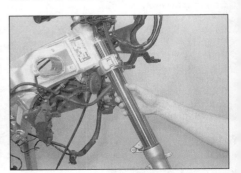

6.6b . . . and remove the fork

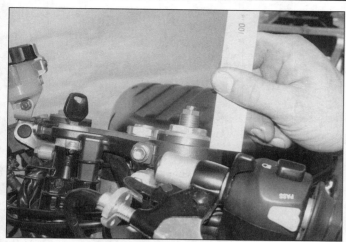

6.7 Set the fork to the correct height

7.6 Pour the oil into the top of the tube

 **HAYNES HiNT** *If the fork legs are seized in the yokes, spray the area with penetrating oil and allow time for it to soak in before trying again.*

## Installation

**7** Remove all traces of corrosion from the fork tubes and the yokes. Slide the fork leg up through the bottom yoke and handlebar clamp and into the top yoke. Set the fork tube the correct distance above the top yoke as specified at the beginning of this Chapter **(see illustration)**.
**8** Tighten the clamp bolts in the bottom yoke to the specified torque setting **(see illustration 6.6a)**. If the fork has been dismantled or if the fork oil has been changed, tighten the fork top bolt to the specified torque setting. Tighten the fork clamp bolt in the top yoke and the handlebar clamp bolt to the specified torque setting **(see illustration 6.4)**.
**9** If displaced, install the front brake reservoir and tighten the bracket bolt securely.
**10** Install the remaining components in the reverse order of removal.
**11** Check the operation of the front forks and brakes before taking the machine on the road.

## 7 Forks – oil change

**1** After a high mileage the fork oil will deteriorate and its damping and lubrication qualities will be impaired. Always change the oil in both fork legs at the same time.
**2** Remove the fork leg; ensure that the top bolt is loosened while the leg is still clamped in the bottom yoke (see Section 6).
**3** Refer to Section 8 to remove the fork top bolt. Follow Steps 3 to 8 for GSX-R600

models, Steps 39 to 42 on GSX-R750 models and Steps 75 to 78 on GSX-R1000 models.
**4** Invert the fork leg over a suitable container and pump the fork and damper rod to expel as much oil as possible.
**5** Support the leg and allow it to drain for several minutes. Wipe any excess oil off the spring and spacer. If the fork oil contains metal particles inspect the fork components for signs of wear (see Section 8).
**6** Slowly pour in the correct quantity and type of fork oil as specified at the beginning of this Chapter **(see illustration)**. Pump the fork and damper rod at least ten times each to distribute the oil evenly and expel any trapped air. Secure the fork leg upright and allow it to stand for several minutes to allow all the air to escape. Take great care to ensure that all air is expelled from the damper cartridge at this stage. **Note:** *On GSX-R1000 models it is essential that oil to the exact manufacturer's specification is used otherwise the performance of the fork will be seriously impaired.*
**7** Fully compress the fork tube and damper rod into the slider and measure the oil level from the top of the tube **(see illustration)**. Add or subtract oil until it is at the level specified at the beginning of this Chapter.

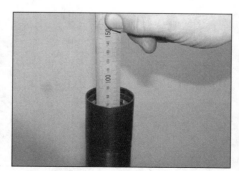

7.7 Measure the oil level with the fork held vertical

**8** Install the remaining components in the reverse order of removal, noting the following:
● Ensure the fork spring is fitted the correct way round (see Section 8).
● Fit a new O-ring to the fork top bolt.
● Tighten the fork top bolt to the specified torque setting once the fork is clamped in the bottom yoke.
● Check the fork adjustment settings and ensure that each fork is set the same adjustment setting (see Section 14).

## 8 Forks – disassembly, inspection and reassembly

### GSX-R600 models

**Note:** *The fork bushes must be disturbed in order to renew the dust and oil seals. New fork bushes must be fitted on reassembly.*

#### Disassembly

**1** Always dismantle the fork legs separately to avoid interchanging parts. Store all components in separate, clearly marked containers **(see illustration)**.
**2** Before dismantling the fork leg, it is advisable to loosen the damper cartridge bolt in the bottom of the fork slider. Turn the leg upside down and compress the fork tube in the slider so that the spring exerts maximum pressure on the damper cartridge, then loosen the bolt **(see illustration)**.
**3** If the fork top bolt was not loosened with the fork on the motorcycle, clamp the fork tube between the padded jaws of a vice, taking care not to overtighten the vice or score the tube's surface, and loosen the top bolt.
**4** Support the fork leg in an upright position and unscrew the fork top bolt from the top of the fork tube **(see illustration)**. Slide the fork tube down into the slider.

 **6**

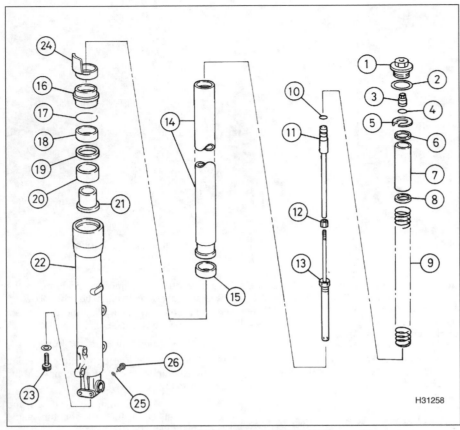

**8.2 Loosen the damper cartridge bolt**

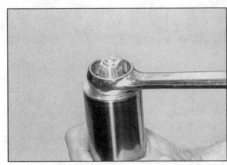

**8.4 Unscrew the fork top bolt**

**8.1 Front fork components – GSX-R600**

| | | |
|---|---|---|
| 1  Top bolt | 11 Rebound damping | 20 Top bush |
| 2  O-ring |     adjuster | 21 Damper cartridge |
| 3  Pre-load adjuster | 12 Locknut |     seat |
| 4  O-ring | 13 Damper cartridge | 22 Fork slider |
| 5  Slotted collar | 14 Fork tube | 23 Damper rod bolt and |
| 6  Washer | 15 Bottom bush |     washer |
| 7  Spacer | 16 Dust seal | 24 Fork protector |
| 8  Spring seat | 17 Retaining clip | 25 O-ring |
| 9  Spring | 18 Oil seal | 26 Compression damping |
| 10 O-ring | 19 Washer |     adjuster |

**5** With the aid of an assistant, pull up on the fork top bolt, then grasp the spacer and press down on it to compress the spring and expose the locknut on the bottom of the preload adjuster **(see illustration)**. Slip a

spanner onto the locknut, then counter-hold the pre-load adjuster and loosen the locknut **(see illustration)**.

**6** Carefully release the pressure on the spacer and allow the slotted collar to rest

against the underside of the locknut under spring pressure. Unscrew the top bolt assembly from the damper rod and remove it **(see illustration)**.

**7** The top bolt/preload adjuster/rebound damping adjuster assembly should only be disassembled if it is damaged or if the internal O-ring seals have failed. Thread the top bolt off the top of the pre-load adjuster, then hold the pre-load adjuster and screw the damping adjuster rod through and out of the bottom of the pre-load adjuster. Discard the O-rings as new ones must be fitted on reassembly.

**8** Grasp the spacer and compress the spring and remove the slotted collar, noting how it fits, then remove the washer, the spacer and the spring seat **(see illustrations)**. Withdraw the spring, noting which way up it fits **(see illustration)**.

**8.5a Push the spacer down to expose the locknut (arrowed)**

**8.5b Counter-hold the pre-load adjuster and loosen the locknut**

**8.6 Draw the top bolt assembly out of the fork**

8.8a Remove the slotted collar . . .

8.8b . . . the washer . . .

8.8c . . . the spacer . . .

8.8d . . . and the spring seat

8.8e Withdraw the spring

8.10 Remove the damper cartridge bolt

**9** Invert the fork leg over a suitable container and pump the fork and damper rod to expel as much fork oil as possible.

**10** Remove the previously loosened damper cartridge bolt and its sealing washer from the bottom of the slider **(see illustration)**. Discard the washer as a new one must be fitted on reassembly.

**11** Withdraw the damper cartridge from inside the fork tube.

**12** Remove the fork protector from the top of the slider, then carefully prise the dust seal from the top of the slider to gain access to the oil seal retaining clip **(see illustration)**. Discard the dust seal as a new one must be fitted on reassembly.

**13** Carefully remove the retaining clip, taking care not to scratch the surface of the tube **(see illustration)**.

**14** To separate the tube from the slider it is necessary to displace the top bush and oil seal. The bottom bush should not pass through the top bush, and this can be used to good effect. Push the tube gently inwards until it stops against the damper cartridge seat. Take care not to do this forcibly or the seat may be damaged. Then pull the tube sharply outwards until the bottom bush strikes the top bush **(see illustration)**. Repeat this operation until the top bush and seal are tapped out of the slider and the tube can be removed.

**15** With the tube removed, slide off the oil seal, washer and top bush, noting which way up they fit **(see illustration)**. Discard the oil seal as a new one must be fitted on reassembly. Note that Suzuki advise that both

bushes are renewed when the fork is dismantled (see Step 21 for removal of the bottom bush).

**16** If the damper cartridge seat did not come

8.12 Prise off the dust seal . . .

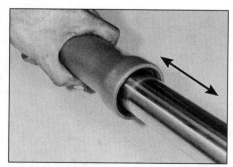

8.14 Separate the tube from the slider by pulling them apart firmly several times

out with the tube, tip it out of the slider, noting which way up it fits. If required, unscrew the compression damping adjuster from the bottom of the slider. Discard the O-ring as a

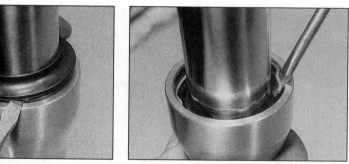

8.13 . . . and remove the retaining clip

8.15 The oil seal (1), washer (2), top bush (3) and bottom bush (4) will come out with the fork tube

**6**

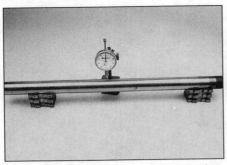

**8.18 Check the fork tube for runout using V-blocks and a dial gauge**

new one must be fitted on reassembly. **Note:** *The compression damping adjuster should not be disassembled.*

### Inspection

**17** Clean all parts in a suitable solvent and blow them dry with compressed air, if available. Check the surface of the fork tube for score marks, scratches, flaking of the finish and excessive or abnormal wear. Look for dents in the tube and renew the tube in both forks if any are found.

**18** Check the fork tube for runout using V-blocks and a dial gauge **(see illustration)**. If the condition of the fork tube is suspect have it checked by a Suzuki dealer or suspension specialist. Suzuki provides no specifications for fork tube runout.

⚠️ *Warning: If the tube is bent it should not be straightened; renew it.*

**8.25a Install the top bush . . .**

**8.26 Install the oil seal . . .**

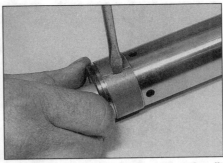

**8.21 Prise the bottom bush apart at the slit with a flat-bladed screwdriver**

**19** Inspect the inside surface of the slider for score marks, scratches and signs of excessive wear. Check the fork seal seat for nicks, gouges and scratches. If damage is evident, leaks will occur. Also check the oil seal washer for damage or distortion and renew it if necessary.

**20** Check the spring for cracks and other damage. Measure the spring free length and compare the result to the specifications at the beginning of this Chapter. If the spring is defective or has sagged below the service limit, fit new springs in both forks. Never renew only one spring.

**21** Suzuki advise that the fork bushes be renewed every time the fork is dismantled. Wear of their Teflon coated surfaces will occur over a period of time and they are likely to be damaged during the separation of the fork tube and slider. To remove the bottom bush from the fork tube, prise it apart at the slit

**8.25b . . . and the washer**

**8.27 . . . and secure it with the retaining clip**

using a flat-bladed screwdriver and slide it off **(see illustration)**. Ensure the seat for the bush in the fork tube is clean, then install the new bush over the end of the fork tube by hand.

**22** Check the damper cartridge assembly for damage and wear. Hold the cartridge and gently pump the damper rod in and out. If the rod does not move smoothly the assembly must be renewed.

### Reassembly

**23** If removed, fit a new O-ring to the compression damping adjuster and install it in the fork slider. Tighten the adjuster to the torque setting specified at the beginning of this Chapter.

**24** Install the damper cartridge seat into the lower end of the fork tube. Lubricate the fork tube and bottom bush with the specified fork oil and insert the assembly into the slider.

**25** Push the fork tube fully into the slider, then lubricate the new top bush and slide it down over the tube. Press the bush squarely into its recess in the slider as far as possible, then install the oil seal washer with its flat side facing up **(see illustrations)**. Either use the service tool (Pt. No. 09940-52861) or a suitable piece of tubing to tap the bush fully into place; the tubing must be slightly larger in diameter than the fork tube and slightly smaller in diameter than the bush recess in the slider. **Note:** *Take care not to scratch the fork tube during reassembly; if the fork tube is pushed fully into the slider any accidental scratching is confined to the area above the oil seal.*

**26** Lubricate the inside of the new oil seal with fork oil and slide it over the tube so that its markings face upwards. Press the seal squarely into the slider and tap it lightly into place as described in Step 25, until the retaining clip groove is visible above the seal **(see illustration)**.

> **HAYNES HINT** *Place the old oil seal on top of the new one to protect it when driving the seal into place.*

**27** Once the seal is seated, fit the retaining clip, making sure it is correctly located in its groove **(see illustration)**.

**28** Lubricate the inside of the new dust seal, then slide it down the fork tube and press it into position. Fit the fork protector to the top of the slider, engaging its tab with the cutout in the slider.

**29** Insert the damper cartridge assembly into the fork tube and slide it fully down so that it engages the damper cartridge seat. Fit a new sealing washer to the damper cartridge bolt and apply a few drops of a suitable non-permanent thread locking compound, then install the bolt into the bottom of the slider **(see illustration 8.10)**. Tighten the bolt to the specified torque setting. If the damper cartridge assembly rotates inside the tube, temporarily install the spring, spacer and fork top bolt and compress the fork leg to hold the assembly in place, then remove them when the bolt has been tightened. **Note:** *To enable the damper rod to be kept extended out of the slider later on, it is worth securing a length of wire around the base of the locknut on the top of the rod to use as a holder* **(see illustration).**

**30** Pour in the correct quantity and type of fork oil (see Section 7).

**31** Pull the fork tube and damper rod out of the slider as far as possible then install the spring with its tapered end downwards **(see illustration 8.8e)**. Install the spring seat, the spacer and the washer **(see illustrations 8.8d, 8.8c and 8.8b)**.

**32** Keeping the damper rod fully extended, grasp the spacer and compress the spring. If used, remove the length of wire, then slide the slotted collar into position between the washer and the locknut on the damper rod **(see illustration 8.8a)**. Carefully release the spring pressure.

**33** If the top bolt/preload adjuster/rebound damping adjuster assembly was disassembled, fit a new O-ring onto the damping adjuster and thread it into the pre-load adjuster until it protrudes 1.5 mm above the top. Fit a new O-ring onto the pre-load adjuster and thread the fork top bolt onto it. Fit a new O-ring onto the fork top bolt. **Note:** *Smear the O-rings with fork oil to avoid damaging them during reassembly.*

**34** Thread the top bolt assembly on the damper rod and screw it all the way down onto the rod. Follow Step 5 to put a spanner on the locknut, then counter-hold the pre-load adjuster and tighten the locknut securely against it, to the specified torque if the correct tools are available **(see illustration 8.5b)**.

**35** Pull the fork tube fully out of the slider and carefully screw the top bolt into the fork tube making sure it is not cross-threaded. **Note:** *The top bolt can be tightened to the specified torque setting at this stage if the tube is held between the padded jaws of a vice. However, to avoid the risk of damaging the tube, a better method is to tighten the top bolt when the fork leg has been installed and is securely clamped in the bottom yoke (see Section 6).*

**36** Install the fork leg (see Section 6). Adjust the fork settings as required (see Section 14).

## GSX-R750 models

**Note:** *The fork bushes must be disturbed in order to renew the dust and oil seals. New fork bushes must be fitted on reassembly.*

### Disassembly

**37** Always dismantle the fork legs separately to avoid interchanging parts. Store all components in separate, clearly marked containers **(see illustration)**.

**38** Before dismantling the fork leg, it is advisable to loosen the damper cartridge bolt in the bottom of the fork slider. Turn the leg upside down and compress the fork slider in the tube so that the spring exerts maximum

**8.29 Use a length of wire to keep the damper rod extended**

pressure on the damper cartridge assembly, then loosen the bolt **(see illustration 8.2)**.

**39** If the fork top bolt was not loosened with

the fork on the motorcycle, clamp the fork tube between the padded jaws of a vice, taking care not to overtighten the vice or score the tube's surface, and loosen the top bolt **(see illustration 8.4)**.

**40** Support the fork leg in an upright position and unscrew the fork top bolt from the top of the fork tube. Slide the fork tube down onto the slider.

**41** With the aid of an assistant, pull up on the fork top bolt, then press down on the spacer to compress the spring and expose the locknut on the bottom of the damping adjuster. Insert a suitably sized washer with a slot cut in it under the locknut **(see illustration)**. Carefully release the pressure on the spacer and allow the slotted washer to rest against the underside of the locknut under spring pressure. **Note:** *Suzuki produces service tools*

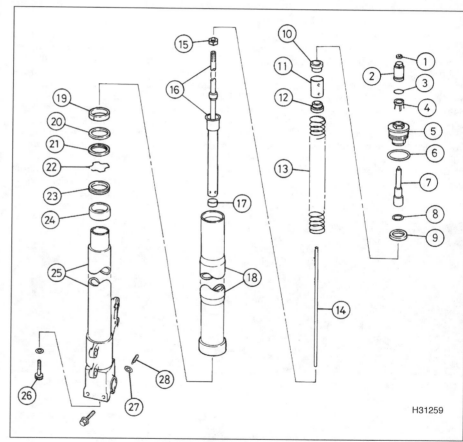

**8.37 Front fork components – GSX-R750**

| | | |
|---|---|---|
| 1 Snap ring | 10 Spacer seat | 20 Washer |
| 2 Pre-load adjuster | 11 Spacer | 21 Oil seal |
| 3 O-ring | 12 Spring seat | 22 Retaining clip |
| 4 Adjuster tripod | 13 Spring | 23 Dust seal |
| 5 Top bolt | 14 Adjuster rod | 24 Top bush |
| 6 O-ring | 15 Locknut | 25 Fork slider |
| 7 Rebound damping adjuster | 16 Damper rod/cartridge | 26 Damper rod bolt and washer |
| 8 Washer | 17 Damper rod/cartridge seat | 27 O-ring |
| 9 Top bolt rubber seat | 18 Fork tube | 28 Compression damping adjuster |
| | 19 Bottom bush | |

**6**

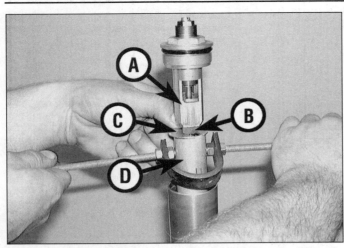

8.41a Damping adjuster (A), locknut (B), slotted washer (C) and spacer (D)

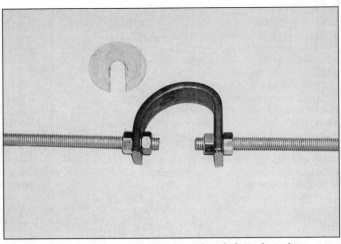

8.41b A home-made spacer tool and slotted washer

*(spacer holder Pt. No. 09940-94930 and stopper plate Pt. No. 09940-94922) to do this. Alternatively, use the set-up shown (see illustration).*

**42** Using two spanners, one on the locknut and one on the flats on the base of the damping adjuster, loosen the locknut. Unscrew the top bolt assembly from the damper rod, then withdraw the adjuster rod from inside the damper rod **(see illustrations)**.

**43** The top bolt/preload adjuster/rebound damping adjuster assembly should only be disassembled if it is damaged or if the internal O-ring seals have failed. Remove the snap-ring from the top of the damping adjuster,

then unscrew and remove the pre-load adjuster and withdraw the adjuster tripod. Unscrew the damping adjuster from the top bolt. Note the rubber seat on the base of the top bolt. Discard the O-rings as new ones must be fitted on reassembly.

**44** Compress the spacer and remove the slotted washer, then remove the washer, the spacer seat, the spacer and the spring seat **(see illustration 8.37)**. Withdraw the spring from the tube, noting which way up it fits.

**45** Invert the fork leg over a suitable container and pump the fork and damper rod to expel as much fork oil as possible.

**46** Remove the previously loosened damper

cartridge bolt and its sealing washer from the bottom of the slider **(see illustration 8.10)**. Discard the washer as a new one must be fitted on reassembly. If the damper cartridge bolt was impossible to slacken as described in Step 38, note that a Suzuki service tool (Pt. No. 09940-30221) is available to hold the damper cartridge in place while the bolt is unscrewed; the tool passes down the fork tube, over the damper rod and engages the top of the cartridge body.

**47** Withdraw the damper cartridge assembly and its seat from inside the fork tube.

**48** Carefully prise the dust seal from the bottom of the tube to gain access to the oil seal retaining clip. Discard the dust seal as a new one must be fitted on reassembly.

**49** Carefully remove the retaining clip, taking care not to scratch the surface of the slider **(see illustration)**.

**50** To separate the slider from the tube it is necessary to displace the bottom bush and oil seal. The top bush should not pass through the bottom bush, and this can be used to good effect. Push the slider gently inwards until it stops, then pull the slider sharply outwards until the top bush strikes the bottom bush **(see illustration 8.14)**. Repeat this operation until the bottom bush and seal are tapped out of the tube and the slider can be removed.

**51** With the slider removed, remove the top bush by carefully levering its ends apart using a screwdriver **(see illustration)**. Slide the bottom bush, the oil seal washer, the oil seal, the retaining clip and the dust seal off the slider, noting which way round they fit **(see illustration)**. Discard the seals and bushes as new ones must be fitted on reassembly.

**52** If required, unscrew the compression damping adjuster from the bottom of the slider. Discard the O-ring as a new one must be fitted on reassembly. **Note:** *The compression damping adjuster should not be disassembled.*

## Inspection

**53** Clean all parts in a suitable solvent and

8.42a Unscrew the top bolt assembly . . .

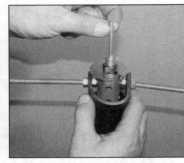

8.42b . . . and withdraw the damping adjuster rod

8.49 Remove the retaining clip from the bottom of the fork tube

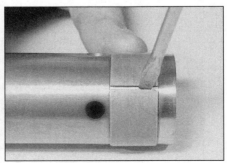

8.51a Prise the top bush apart at the slit with a flat-bladed screwdriver

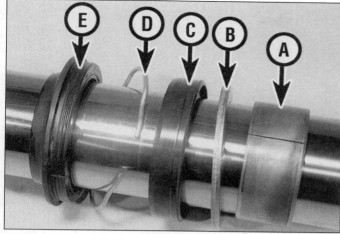

8.51b  Bottom bush (A), oil seal washer (B), oil seal (C), retaining clip (D) and dust seal (E)

8.61  Make sure the top bush seats properly in its recess

blow them dry with compressed air, if available. Check the surface of the fork slider for score marks, scratches, flaking of the finish and excessive or abnormal wear. Look for dents in the slider and renew the slider in both forks if any are found.

54  Check the fork slider for runout using V-blocks and a dial gauge. If the condition of the fork slider is suspect have it checked by a Suzuki dealer or suspension specialist. Suzuki provides no specifications for runout.

⚠ **Warning: If the slider is bent or exceeds the runout limit, it should not be straightened; renew it.**

55  Inspect the inside surface of the fork tube for score marks, scratches and signs of excessive wear. Check the fork seal seat for nicks, gouges and scratches. If damage is evident, leaks will occur. Also check the oil seal washer for damage or distortion and renew it if necessary.

56  Check the spring for cracks and other damage. Measure the spring free length and compare the measurement to the specifications at the beginning of this Chapter. If the spring is defective or has sagged below the service limit, fit new springs in both forks. Never renew only one spring.

57  Check the damper cartridge assembly for damage and wear. Hold the cartridge and gently pump the rod in and out. If the rod does not move smoothly the assembly must be renewed.

## Reassembly

58  If removed, fit a new O-ring to the compression damping adjuster and install it in the fork slider. Tighten the adjuster to the torque setting specified at the beginning of this Chapter.

59  Wrap some insulating tape over the ridges on the end of the fork slider to protect the lips of the new oil seal as it is installed. Lubricate the inner surfaces of the new seals and bushes with the specified fork oil.

60  Slide the new dust seal onto the slider,

making sure it is fitted the right way up, then slide on the retaining clip and the new oil seal with the marked side of the oil seal facing the dust seal. Remove the insulating tape and fit the oil seal washer and new bottom bush **(see illustration 8.51b)**.

61  Fit the new top bush into its recess in the slider **(see illustration)**. Lubricate the slider and bushes with fork oil, then carefully insert the slider fully into the fork tube.

62  Press the bottom bush squarely into its recess in the fork tube as far as possible, then slide the oil seal washer on top of the bush **(see illustration)**. Using either the special service tool (Pt. No. 09940-52861) or a

suitable drift, carefully drive the bottom bush fully into its recess using the oil seal washer to prevent damaging the edges of the bush. **Note:** *Take care not to scratch the slider during reassembly; if the slider is fully extended from the fork tube any accidental scratching is confined to the area above the oil seal. If necessary, tape the oil seal, retaining clip and dust seal out of the way while the bush is being installed.*

63  Press the oil seal into the fork tube until the retaining clip groove is visible, then fit the retaining clip, making sure it is correctly located in its groove **(see illustrations)**. Press the dust seal into position **(see illustration)**.

8.62  Make sure the bottom bush enters the fork tube squarely

8.63a  Press the oil seal into the fork tube . . .

8.63b  . . . then install the retaining clip . . .

8.63c  . . . and the dust seal

**6**

**8.66 Install the spring tapered end upwards**

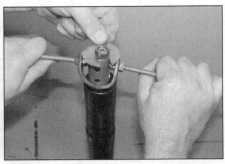

**8.67 Insert the slotted washer under the locknut**

64 Lay the fork leg flat. Fit the seat onto the bottom of the damper cartridge, then insert the damper cartridge assembly into the fork leg until it contacts the bottom of the slider. Fit a new sealing washer onto the damper cartridge bolt and apply a few drops of a suitable non-permanent thread locking compound, then install the bolt into the bottom of the slider and tighten it to the

torque setting specified at the beginning of this Chapter **(see illustration 8.10)**. **Note:** *If the damper cartridge assembly rotates inside the slider, the Suzuki service tool described in Step 46 can be used or hold the head of the cartridge body, or a suitable tool can be fabricated from a piece of tubing which will achieve the same result. To enable the damper rod to be kept extended out of the*

*fork tube later on, it is worth securing a length of wire around the base of the locknut on the top of the rod to use as a holder* **(see illustration 8.29)**.

65 Pour in the correct quantity and type of fork oil (see Section 7).

66 Extend the slider and pull the damper rod out of the fork tube as far as possible. Install the spring with its tapered end upwards, the spring seat, spacer, spacer seat and washer **(see illustration)**.

67 Keeping the damper rod fully extended, press down on the spacer to compress the spring (see Step 41). If used, remove the length of wire, then insert the slotted washer under the locknut **(see illustration)**. Fit the adjuster rod inside the damper rod **(see illustration 8.42b)**.

68 If the top bolt/preload adjuster/rebound damping adjuster assembly was disassembled, set the damping adjuster so that it protrudes approximately 1.5 mm from the top of the adjuster housing, then install the adjuster in the top bolt. Install the adjuster tripod, then fit a new O-ring onto the pre-load adjuster and thread it into the top bolt. Fit the snap ring into the groove in the damping adjuster. Fit a new O-ring onto the fork top bolt and install the rubber seat on the base of the bolt. **Note:** *Smear the O-rings with fork oil to avoid damaging them during reassembly.*

69 Thread the top bolt assembly onto the damper rod and screw it all the way down onto the rod. Counter-hold the flats on the base of the damping adjuster and tighten the locknut securely against it, to the specified torque if the correct tools are available.

70 Press down on the spacer to compress the spring and remove the slotted washer, then carefully release the spring pressure. Remove the spring compressor.

71 Pull the slider all the way out of the fork tube and carefully screw the top bolt into the fork tube making sure it is not cross-threaded. **Note:** *The top bolt can be tightened to the specified torque setting at this stage if the tube is held between the padded jaws of a vice. However, to avoid the risk of damaging the tube, a better method is to tighten the top bolt when the fork leg has been installed and is securely clamped in the bottom yoke (see Section 6).*

72 Install the fork leg (see Section 6). Adjust the fork settings as required (see Section 14).

## GSX-R1000 models

**Note:** *The fork bushes on GSX-R1000 models cannot be renewed separately. If, upon inspection, the bushes are found to be worn, new fork tubes will have to be fitted.*

### Disassembly

73 Always dismantle the fork legs separately to avoid interchanging parts. Store all components in separate, clearly marked containers **(see illustration)**.

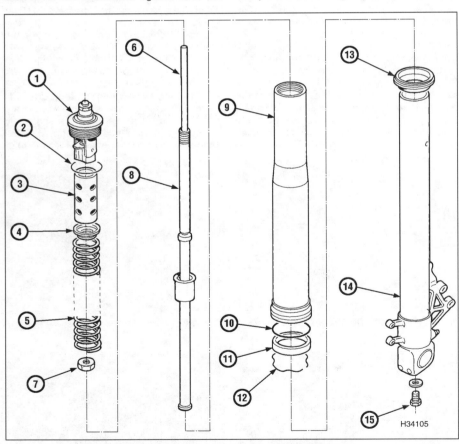

H34105

**8.73 Front fork components – GSX-R1000**

| | | |
|---|---|---|
| 1  Top bolt | 7  Locknut | 12 Retaining clip |
| 2  O-ring | 8  Damper rod/ | 13 Dust seal |
| 3  Spacer |     cartridge | 14 Fork slider |
| 4  Spring seat | 9  Fork tube | 15 Damper rod bolt and |
| 5  Spring | 10 Washer |     washer |
| 6  Adjuster rod | 11 Oil seal | |

8.80a Remove the spacer . . .

8.80b . . . and the spring seat

8.82a Withdraw the damper cartridge assembly . . .

**74** Before dismantling the fork leg, it is advisable to loosen the damper cartridge bolt in the bottom of the fork slider. Turn the leg upside down and compress the fork tube in the slider so that the spring exerts maximum pressure on the damper cartridge assembly, then loosen the bolt (see illustration 8.2).

**75** If the fork top bolt was not loosened with the fork on the motorcycle, clamp the fork tube between the padded jaws of a vice, taking care not to overtighten the vice or score the tube's surface, and loosen the top bolt (see illustration 8.4).

**76** Support the fork leg in an upright position and unscrew the fork top bolt from the top of the fork tube. Slide the fork tube down onto the slider.

**77** Follow Step 41 to expose the locknut on the bottom of the damping adjuster and insert a suitably sized washer with a slot cut in it under the locknut (see illustration 8.41a).

**78** Counter-hold the top bolt and loosen the locknut, then unscrew the top bolt assembly from the damper rod and remove it (see illustration 8.42a). **Note:** *The top bolt assembly should not be disassembled.*

**79** Withdraw the damping adjuster rod from inside the damper rod (see illustration 8.42b).

**80** Compress the spacer and remove the slotted washer (see illustration 8.67). Remove the spacer and spring seat (see illustrations). Withdraw the spring from the tube, noting which way up it fits.

**81** Invert the fork leg over a suitable container and pump the fork and damper rod to expel as much fork oil as possible.

**82** Follow Steps 46 and 47 to remove the damper cartridge assembly, then pull the slider out of the fork tube (see illustrations).

**83** Carefully prise the dust seal from the bottom of the tube to gain access to the oil seal retaining clip, then remove the retaining

clip. Carefully prise out the oil seal, then remove the oil seal washer (see illustrations). Discard the seals as new ones must be fitted on reassembly.

### Inspection

**Note:** *Although compression damper adjusters are fitted to GSX-R1000 models, Suzuki do not recommend their removal and the adjusters are not listed as replacement parts.*

**84** Follow Steps 53 to 57 to clean and inspect the fork components. Both fork bushes are fitted inside the fork tube; if the bushes are worn or scuffed, the fork tube must be renewed (see illustration). Do not attempt removal of the fork bushes.

### Reassembly

**85** Lubricate the inner surfaces of the new seals with the specified fork oil. Slide the new

8.82b . . . and pull the slider out from the tube

8.83a Prise off the dust seal . . .

8.83b . . . and remove the retaining clip

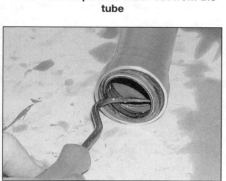

8.83c Prise out the oil seal . . .

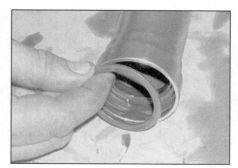

8.83d . . . and remove the washer

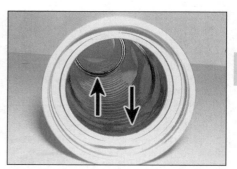

8.84 The bushes (arrowed) are inside the fork tube

**6**

**8.93a Measure the damper rod above the locknut**

**8.93b Set the rebound damping adjuster (arrowed) on the softest setting**

**8.94 Counter-hold the top bolt and tighten the locknut**

dust seal onto the slider, making sure it is fitted the right way up, then slide on the retaining clip, the new oil seal with the marked side of the oil seal facing the dust seal, and the oil seal washer.

86 Lubricate the slider and bushes inside the fork tube with fork oil, then carefully insert the slider fully into the fork tube.

87 Install the oil seal washer in its recess in the fork tube, then press the oil seal in, using either the special service tool (Pt. No. 09940-52861) or a suitable drift. **Note:** *Take care not to scratch the slider during reassembly; extend the slider and fork tube so that any accidental scratching is confined to the area above the oil seal. If necessary, tape the retaining clip and dust seal out of the way while the oil seal is being installed.*

88 Press the oil seal into the fork tube until the retaining clip groove is visible, then fit the retaining clip, making sure it is correctly located in its groove **(see illustrations 8.63a and b)**. Press the dust seal into position **(see illustration 8.63c)**.

89 Insert the damper cartridge assembly into the fork leg until it contacts the bottom of the slider. Fit a new sealing washer onto the damper cartridge bolt and apply a few drops of a suitable non-permanent thread locking compound, then install the bolt into the bottom of the slider and tighten it to the torque setting specified at the beginning of this Chapter **(see illustration 8.10)**. **Note:** *If the damper cartridge assembly rotates inside the slider, the Suzuki service tool described in Step 46 can be used or hold the head of the cartridge body, or a suitable tool can be fabricated from a piece of tubing which will achieve the same result. To enable the damper rod to be kept extended out of the fork tube later on, it is worth securing a length of wire around the base of the locknut on the top of the rod to use as a holder (see illustration 8.29).*

90 Pour in the correct quantity and type of fork oil (see Section 7).

91 Extend the slider and pull the damper rod out of the fork tube as far as possible. Install the spring with its tapered end upwards, the spring seat and spacer **(see illustrations 8.66, 8.80b and a)**.

92 Keeping the damper rod fully extended,

press down on the spacer to compress the spring (see Step 41). If used, remove the length of wire, then insert the slotted washer under the locknut. Fit the damping adjuster rod inside the damper rod **(see illustration 8.42b)**.

93 Check the position of the locknut on the damper rod; the top edge of the locknut should be 11 mm below the top of the rod **(see illustration)**. Turn the top bolt rebound damping adjuster fully anti-clockwise to set it on the softest setting **(see illustration)**.

94 Thread the top bolt onto the damper rod and screw it all the way down to the locknut **(see illustration 8.42a)**. Counter-hold the top bolt and tighten the locknut securely against it, to the specified torque if the correct tools are available **(see illustration)**.

95 Press down on the spacer to compress the spring and remove the slotted washer, then carefully release the spring pressure. Remove the spring compressor.

96 Pull the slider all the way out of the fork tube and carefully screw the top bolt into the fork tube making sure it is not cross-threaded. **Note:** *The top bolt can be tightened to the specified torque setting at this stage if the tube is held between the padded jaws of a vice. However, to avoid the risk of damaging the tube, a better method is to tighten the top bolt when the fork leg has been installed and is securely clamped in the bottom yoke (see Section 6).*

97 Install the fork leg (see Section 6). Adjust the fork settings as required (see Section 14).

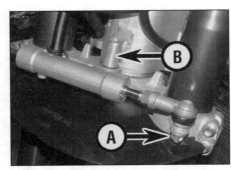

**9.3 Steering damper is secured to the lower fork yoke (A) and steering head (B)**

## 9 Steering damper – removal and installation

### Removal

1 Remove the fairing and the fairing side panels (see Chapter 8).

2 The damper requires no maintenance other than cleaning of the damper rod.

3 Undo the nut securing the damper rod to the lower fork yoke and remove the nut and washer **(see illustration)**.

4 Undo the bolt securing the damper body to the frame steering head, then remove the bolt and the steering damper. Note the seals fitted each side of the bearing in the damper body.

5 Inspect the damper rod for wear, score marks and corrosion. Damage to the surface of the rod will lead to oil loss and lack of damping. Pump the rod all the way in and out of the damper body. Movement should be slow and progressive and the rod should move smoothly. If the rod binds, or there is no resistance, fit a new damper.

6 Inspect the bearing in the damper body. If the centre is loose, press the bearing out and fit a new one.

### Installation

7 Installation is the reverse of removal, noting the following:
● Lubricate the damper body bearing with grease.
● Tighten the mounting nut and bolt to the specified torque setting.

## 10 Steering stem – removal and installation

### Removal

1 Remove the front forks (see Section 6) and the steering damper (see Section 9).

2 Raise, or if required, remove the fuel tank to avoid damaging the paintwork (see Chapter 4).

3 Free the handlebar switch wiring from its guide under the top yoke **(see illustration)**.

**10.3 Free the wiring from the guide**

Remove the set bolt securing each handlebar to the top yoke and support the handlebars so they are out of the way **(see illustration 5.5a)**. Ensure no strain is placed on the brake hose or the wiring. Keep the brake fluid reservoir upright to prevent air entering the system.

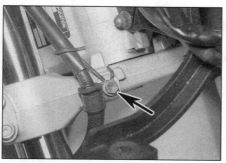

**10.4 Unscrew the bolt (arrowed) and detach the brake hose**

**4** Unscrew the bolt securing the front brake hose clamp to the bottom yoke **(see illustration)**.
**5** Remove the air filter housing (see Chapter 4). Disconnect the ignition switch wiring connector and free the wiring from its guide.

**6** Unscrew and remove the steering stem nut and remove the washer **(see illustration 5.6)**. Gently ease the top yoke upwards off the steering stem. Feed the ignition switch wiring through to the front of the frame, noting its routing, and remove the top yoke.
**7** Unscrew the locknut using either a C-spanner, a peg spanner or a suitable drift located in one of the notches, then remove the washer, noting how it fits **(see illustrations)**.
**8** Support the bottom yoke and unscrew the adjuster nut, then lower the steering stem out of the steering head **(see illustration)**.
**9** Remove the bearing cover, the upper bearing inner race and the upper bearing from the top of the steering head **(see illustration)**. **Note:** *Do not attempt to remove the outer races from the frame or the lower bearing from the steering stem unless new bearings are being installed.*

**10.7a Remove the locknut . . .**

**10.7b . . . and washer . . .**

**10.8 . . . then support the bottom yoke and remove the adjuster nut**

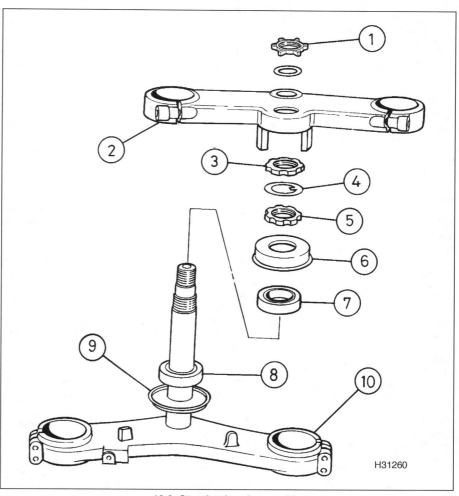

**10.9 Steering head assembly**

| | | |
|---|---|---|
| 1 Steering stem nut and washer | 4 Lockwasher | 8 Lower bearing |
| 2 Top yoke | 5 Adjuster nut | 9 Dust seal |
| 3 Locknut | 6 Bearing cover | 10 Bottom yoke and steering stem |
| | 7 Upper bearing | |

H31260

**6**

10.12a Fit the upper bearing . . .

10.12b . . . the upper bearing inner race . . .

10.12c . . . and the bearing cover

10.13 Tighten the adjuster nut as described

**10** Remove all traces of old grease from the bearings and races and check them for wear or damage (see Section 11).

### Installation

**11** Apply general purpose grease to the bearing outer races in the steering head and the inner race, and work grease well into both the upper and lower bearings.

**12** Carefully lift the steering stem up through the steering head. Install the upper bearing in the top of the steering head, then install the inner race and the bearing cover **(see illustrations)**.

**13** Thread the adjuster nut onto the steering stem. If the correct tools are available, tighten the nut to the initial torque setting specified at the beginning of this Chapter, then turn the steering stem from lock to lock five or six times to settle the bearings. Loosen the adjuster nut by 1/4 to 1/2 a turn, so that the steering is able to move freely from lock to lock but without any front to back freeplay. If the tools are not available, tighten the adjuster nut carefully until all front to back freeplay is removed, then tighten it 1/2 a turn further **(see illustration)**. Turn the steering stem from lock to lock five or six times to settle the bearings. Loosen the adjuster nut by 1/4 to 1/2 a turn, so that the steering is able to move freely from lock to lock but without any front to back freeplay.
*Caution: Take great care not to apply excessive pressure to the bearings as this will cause their premature failure. If new bearings have been fitted you may need to carry out the adjustment procedure several*

*times to allow them to settle properly. The object is to set the adjuster nut so that the bearings are under a very light loading, just enough to remove any front to back freeplay.*

**14** Fit the washer onto the steering stem, aligning the tab on its inside with the groove in the stem. Fit the locknut and tighten it to the specified torque setting, making sure the adjuster nut does not turn as you do so **(see illustration 10.7b and a)**.

**15** Fit the top yoke onto the steering stem and feed the ignition switch wiring through to the connector making sure it is correctly routed. Connect the wiring and secure it with the guide. Install the air filter housing (see Chapter 4).

**16** Install the steering stem nut and its washer and tighten it finger-tight. Temporarily

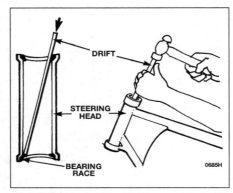

11.4 Drive the bearing outer races out with a brass drift as shown

install one of the fork legs to align the top and bottom yokes, and secure it by tightening the bottom yoke clamp bolts only. Tighten the steering stem nut to the specified torque setting, then remove the fork leg.

**17** Attach the front brake hose clamp to the bottom yoke **(see illustration 10.4)**. Install the steering damper **(see illustration 9.3)**.

**18** Locate the handlebars onto the underside of the top yoke and secure them with the set bolts, but leave the bolts finger-tight at this stage. Feed the handlebar switch wiring into its guide under the top yoke.

**19** Install the remaining components in the reverse order of removal and then tighten the handlebar set bolts to the specified torque setting.

**20** Carry out a check of the steering head bearing adjustment as described in Chapter 1, and if necessary re-adjust.

## 11 Steering head bearings – inspection and renewal

### Inspection

**1** Remove the steering stem (see Section 10).

**2** Remove all traces of old grease from the bearings and races and check them for wear or damage.

**3** The outer races and the upper bearing inner race should be polished and free from indentations. Inspect the bearing balls for signs of wear, pitting or discoloration, and examine the ball cages for signs of cracks or splits. Spin the bearings by hand. They should spin freely and smoothly. If there are any signs of wear on any of the above components, both upper and lower bearing assemblies must be renewed as a set. **Note:** *Do not attempt to remove the outer races from the frame or the lower bearing from the steering stem unless new bearings are being installed.*

### Renewal

**4** The outer races are an interference fit in the frame steering head and can be tapped out with a suitable drift **(see illustration)**. Tap firmly and evenly around each race to ensure that it is driven out squarely. It may prove advantageous to curve the end of the drift slightly to improve access.

**5** Alternatively, the outer races can be removed using a slide-hammer type bearing extractor – these can often be hired from tool shops.

**6** The new outer races can be installed in the steering head using a drawbolt arrangement **(see illustration)**, or by using a large diameter bearing driver. Ensure that the drawbolt washer or driver (as applicable) bears only on the outer edge of the race and does not contact the bearing seat. Alternatively, have the races installed by a Suzuki dealer equipped with the bearing race installing tools.

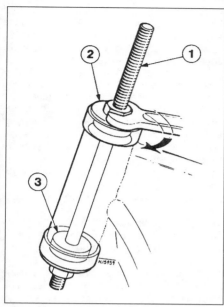

**11.6 Drawbolt arrangement for fitting steering head bearing outer races**

1  Long bolt or threaded bar
2  Thick washer
3  Guide for lower outer race

 *Installation of new bearing outer races is made much easier if the races are left overnight in the freezer. This causes them to contract slightly making them a looser fit.*

**7** To remove the lower bearing from the steering stem, carefully tap it free with a chisel, then use two screwdrivers placed on opposite sides of the race to work it free. If the bearing is firmly in place it will be necessary to use a bearing puller **(see illustrations)**. Take the steering stem to a Suzuki dealer if required. Check the condition of the dust seal and fit a new one if necessary.

**8** Install the dust seal, then fit the new lower bearing onto the steering stem. A length of tubing with an internal diameter slightly larger than the steering stem will be needed to tap the bearing into position **(see illustration)**.

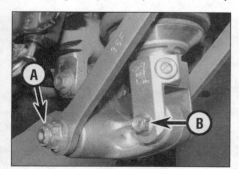

**12.3 Linkage rods to linkage arm bolt (A) and shock to linkage arm bolt (B)**

**11.7a Work the lower bearing free carefully . . .**

Ensure that the drift bears only on the inner edge of the bearing and does not contact the balls or cage.
**9** Install the steering stem (see Section 10).

 **12 Rear shock absorber –** removal, inspection and installation

### Removal

**1** Support the bike using an auxiliary stand. Position a support under the rear wheel so that it does not drop when the shock absorber is removed, but ensure that the weight of the machine is off the rear suspension so that the shock is not compressed.
**2** Remove the fairing side panels (see Chapter 8).
**3** Unscrew the nut and remove the bolt securing the lower ends of the linkage rods to the linkage arm **(see illustration)**.
**4** Unscrew the nut and remove the bolt securing the bottom of the shock to the suspension linkage arm **(see illustration 12.3)**.
**5** Unscrew the nut from the bolt securing the top of the shock to the upper mounting bracket, then support the shock and withdraw the bolt **(see illustration)**. On GSX-R600 and GSX-R750 models, lower the shock down through the swingarm and remove it from the bike. On GSX-R1000 models, remove the shock from the left-hand side of the frame.

**12.5 Shock upper mounting bolt (arrowed)**

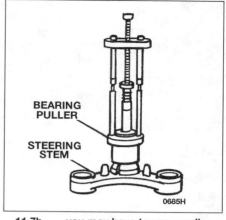

**11.7b . . . you may have to use a puller**

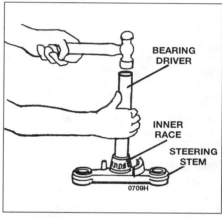

**11.8 Install the lower bearing using a suitable driver or length of tubing**

### Inspection

**6** Inspect the body of the shock absorber for physical damage and the coil spring for looseness, cracks or signs of fatigue **(see illustration)**.
**7** Inspect the shock for signs of oil leakage.
**8** Ensure the spring pre-load adjuster threads are clean and the adjusters are free to rotate **(see illustration)**.
**9** Check the bush in the mounting at the upper end of the shock for wear and deterioration **(see illustration 12.8)**.

**12.6 Check the shock body and spring for damage**

**6**

mounting bolts and to the bearings in the linkage arm.
● Install the upper mounting bolt first, but do not tighten the nut until the lower mounting bolt is installed.
● Tighten the mounting bolts to the torque settings specified at the beginning of this Chapter.
● Adjust the suspension as required (see Section 14).

## 13 Rear suspension linkage – removal, inspection and installation

### Removal

1 Support the bike using an auxiliary stand. Position a support under the rear wheel so that it does not drop when the suspension linkage is disconnected, but ensure that the weight of the machine is off the rear suspension so that the shock is not compressed.
2 Remove the fairing side panels (see Chapter 8). Remove the sidestand (see Section 4).
3 Unscrew the nut and remove the bolt securing the lower ends of the linkage rods to the linkage arm (see illustration 12.3).
4 Unscrew the nut and remove the bolt securing the upper ends of the linkage rods to the swingarm and remove the linkage rods, noting how they fit (see illustration).
5 Unscrew the nut and remove the bolt securing the bottom of the shock to the linkage arm (see illustration 12.3).

6 Unscrew the nut and withdraw the bolt securing the linkage arm to the frame, then remove the arm, noting the washers fitted between the arm and the frame (see illustration).

### Inspection

7 Withdraw the spacers from the linkage arm, noting their different sizes, and clean all the components thoroughly with a suitable solvent to remove all traces of dirt and grease (see illustration). Remove any corrosion from the spacers with steel wool and dry the needle roller bearings in the linkage arm with compressed air, if available.
8 Inspect the components closely, looking for obvious signs of wear such as scoring and pitting, and for elongation of the bolt holes in the linkage rods. Apply clean oil to the spacers, then slip each one back into its bearing in the linkage arm and check that there is not an excessive amount of freeplay between the two (see illustration). Ensure the bearings turn smoothly without binding or grating. **Note:** *The long middle spacer in the linkage arm is supported by two needle roller bearings.* Don't forget to check the condition of the linkage rod spacer and two needle roller bearings in the bottom of the swingarm (see Section 16).
9 Renew any components as required. Refer to *Tools and Workshop Tips (Section 5)* in the Reference section for more information on bearings and bearing removal. **Note:** *The needle bearings should only be removed if new bearings are going to be fitted. Note the position of the bearings before removing them. The new bearings should be pressed or drawn into place and must not be driven into position.*

### Installation

10 Installation is the reverse of removal, noting the following:
● Apply general purpose grease to the bearings, spacers and pivot bolts.
● Ensure the washers are fitted between the linkage arm and the frame (see illustration 13.6).
● Install all nuts and bolts finger-tight to begin with, then tighten them to the torque settings specified at the beginning of this Chapter.
● Check the operation of the rear suspension before taking the machine on the road.

10 If the shock absorber is in any way damaged or worn a new one must be installed. Individual components are not available from Suzuki although it is worth checking whether the shock can be rebuilt by a suspension specialist.
11 Check the tightness of the shock absorber upper mounting bracket. If the bracket is loose, raise the fuel tank (see Chapter 4) and tighten the mounting bracket nut to the torque setting specified at the beginning of this Chapter.
*Caution: If the shock is being renewed, take the old shock to a Suzuki dealer or suspension specialist for discharge of the nitrogen gas.*

### Installation

12 Installation is the reverse of removal, noting the following:
● Apply general purpose grease to the

13.4 Bolt (arrowed) secures linkage rods to swingarm

13.7 Rear suspension linkage components

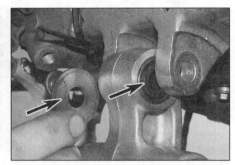
13.6 Note the washers fitted between the linkage arm and the frame

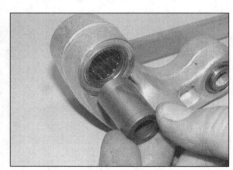
13.8 Check the bearings and spacers for freeplay

12.8 Inspect the adjusters and adjuster threads (A) and the upper mounting bush (B)

## 14 Suspension – adjustments

**Note:** *The front and rear suspension on all models is adjustable for spring pre-load, rebound and compression damping. Refer to the suspension setting table in the owner's manual supplied with your motorcycle for recommended settings for solo and pillion riding.*

## Front forks

**1** Spring pre-load is adjusted using a suitable spanner on the adjuster flats **(see illustration)**. The adjuster is located in the fork top bolt; turn the adjuster clockwise to increase pre-load and anti-clockwise to decrease it. The amount of pre-load is indicated by lines on the adjuster which extend from the top bolt hex. The standard preload setting is with four lines shown. Maximum to minimum preload settings range from 1 to 7 on GSX-R600 models, from 0 to 7 on GSX-R750 models, and from 0 to 5 on GSX-R1000 models.

**2** Rebound and compression damping are adjusted using a flat-bladed screwdriver in the slot in the damping adjusters. The rebound adjusters are located in the fork top bolts **(see illustration 14.1)**. The compression adjusters are located in the bottom of the forks **(see illustration)**.

**3** On GSX-R600 and GSX-R750 models, adjust the rebound and compression damping by turning the adjuster clockwise until it stops, then turning it anti-clockwise 1 and 1/8 turn so that the punch mark aligns with the arrowhead **(see illustration)**; this is the standard setting. To increase damping turn the adjuster clockwise, and to decrease it turn the adjuster anti-clockwise. Turn the adjusters 1/8 turn at a time until a suitable setting has been found.

**4** On GSX-R1000 models, adjust the rebound and compression damping adjusters by turning the adjuster clockwise until it stops, then turning it anti-clockwise counting the clicks. The standard setting for the rebound adjuster is 6 clicks out, and for the compression adjuster it is 10 clicks out. To increase damping turn the adjuster in (clockwise) and to decrease it turn the adjuster out (anti-clockwise). Turn the adjusters 1/8 turn at a time until a suitable setting has been found.

*Caution: Always make sure the adjusters in both fork legs are set in corresponding positions.*

## Rear shock absorber

**5** Spring pre-load is adjusted by turning the adjuster nut on the shock absorber body **(see illustration)**. Position the motorcycle upright on an auxiliary stand and measure the spring length (from the top to bottom spring coils), then compare this to the standard pre-load figure given in the specifications **(see illustration)**. If adjustment is required, use a slim C-spanner to loosen the locknut, then turn the adjuster nut clockwise to increase pre-load or anti-clockwise to decrease it. Tighten the locknut securely after adjustment. **Note:** *Do not set the spring length beyond the minimum and maximum pre-load settings* (see Specifications at the beginning of this Chapter).

**6** Rebound and compression damping are adjusted using a screwdriver in the slot in the damping adjusters. The rebound adjuster is located in the bottom of the shock, the compression adjuster is located in the top of the shock **(see illustrations)**.

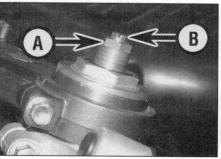

**14.1  Spring pre-load adjuster (A) and rebound damping adjuster (B)**

**14.2  Compression damping adjuster (arrowed)**

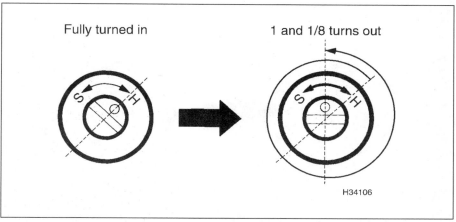

**14.3  Front fork rebound and compression damping adjuster standard setting – GSX-R600 and GSX-R750 models**

**14.5a  Rear shock spring pre-load adjuster and locknut (arrowed)**

**14.5b  Rear shock spring pre-load measurement**

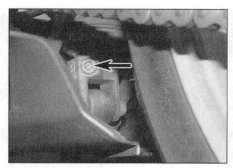

**14.6a  Rear shock rebound damping adjuster**

**14.6b  Rear shock compression damping adjuster**

**6**

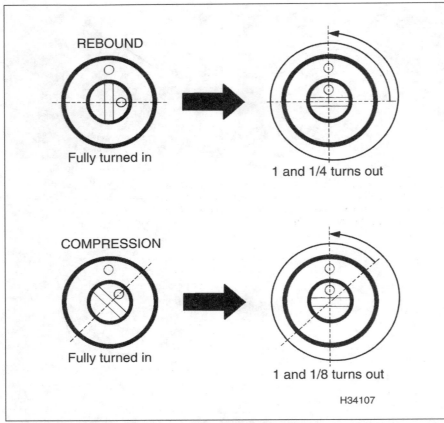

REBOUND

Fully turned in

1 and 1/4 turns out

COMPRESSION

Fully turned in

1 and 1/8 turns out

H34107

**14.7 Rear shock rebound and compression damping adjuster standard setting – GSX-R600 and GSX-R750 models**

**7** On GSX-R600 and GSX-R750 models, adjust the rebound damping by turning the adjuster clockwise until it stops, then turning it anti-clockwise 1 and 1/8 turns so that the punch marks align **(see illustration)**. Adjust the compression damping by turning the adjuster clockwise until it stops, then turning it anti-clockwise 1 and 1/8 turns so that the punch marks align. Turn the adjusters 1/8 turn at a time until a suitable setting has been found.

**8** On GSX-R1000 models, adjust the rebound and compression damping adjusters by turning the adjuster clockwise until it stops, then turning it anti-clockwise, counting the number of clicks. The standard position for rebound damping is 7 clicks out, and the standard position for compression damping is 8 clicks out. To increase damping turn the adjuster clockwise, and to decrease damping turn the adjuster anti-clockwise. Turn the adjusters 1/8 turn at a time until a suitable setting has been found.

## 15 Swingarm – removal and installation

### Removal

**1** Remove the fairing side panels (see Chapter 8).

**2** Undo the screws securing the chainguard and remove the chainguard **(see illustration)**.

**3** Remove the rear wheel (see Chapter 7).

**4** Remove the rear shock absorber (see Section 12).

**5** On GSX-R750 and GSX-R1000 models, remove the front sprocket (see Section 18). Rest the drive chain over the gearbox output shaft **(see illustration)**. **Note:** *On GSX-R750 and GSX-R1000 models the chain will come off with the swingarm. To remove the chain from the swingarm the chain must be split (see Section 17). Only split the chain if a new chain or new swingarm are to be fitted.*

**6** Disconnect the hydraulic hose from the rear brake caliper following the procedure in Chapter 7. Release the hose from the guides on the swingarm **(see illustrations)**. **Note:** *On GSX-R600 and GSX-R1000 models undo the bolts securing the guides to release the hose.*

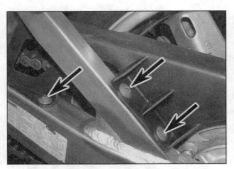

**15.2 Remove the chainguard screws (arrowed)**

**15.5 Remove the front sprocket and rest the chain on the gearbox shaft – GSX-R750 and GSX-R1000 models**

**15.6a Release the brake hose from the guides on the top of the swingarm – GSX-R750 . . .**

**15.6b . . . and GSX-R600 and GSX-R1000 . . .**

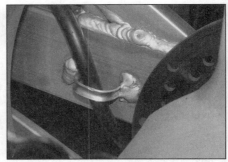

**15.6c . . . and from the closed guide on the back of the swingarm**

15.8 Undo the swingarm pivot bolt locknut

A peg 'socket' can be made by cutting a 32 mm socket as shown – measure the width and depth of the slots in the locknut to determine the size of the castellations on the socket (left). If an old socket is not available, a nut can be used and suitable pegs can be brazed or welded onto it (right).

Feed the hose through the closed guide on the swingarm and secure it in an upright position to minimise fluid loss.

7 Undo the nut and remove the bolt securing the brake torque arm to the caliper bracket and remove the caliper.

8 Undo the locknut on the right-hand end of the swingarm pivot bolt (see illustration). Suzuki provides a service tool to do this (Pt. No. 09940-14970). Alternatively a similar tool can be made (see Tool Tip).

9 Counter-hold the pivot bolt, then undo the nut on the left-hand end of the bolt and remove the nut and washer (see illustrations).

10 Support the swingarm, then unscrew the pivot bolt and remove it, then ease the swingarm out of the back of the frame (see illustration). On GSX-R750 and GSX-R1000 models, ease the chain out between the gearbox output shaft and the frame (see illustration). On all models, note the position

of the dust covers and washers fitted to each end of the swingarm pivot and remove them for safekeeping.

11 If required, unscrew the nut and remove the bolt securing the upper ends of the linkage rods to the swingarm and remove the linkage rods, noting how they fit (see illustration 13.4).

12 If required, undo the bolts securing the chain slider and remove it (see illustration). On GSX-R600 models, remove the mud flap.

Installation

13 Clean the frame around the swingarm mountings and check that the pivot bolt is a good fit in the mountings.

14 On GSX-R750K2 models, check that the

pivot height adjustment bosses in the frame are not worn or damaged and that they are tight in the frame. Only remove the pivot bosses if new ones are to be fitted. First undo the boss nut on the inside of the frame, then undo the set screws on the outside of the frame. Fit the new boss and tighten the set screws securely, than install the nut and tighten it to the torque setting specified at the beginning of this Chapter.

15 If removed, install the chain slider, and on GSX-R600 models, install the mud flap.

16 Ensure the bearings, spacers and pivot bolt are lubricated with multi-purpose grease (see Section 16). Fit the washers and dust covers to each end of the swingarm pivot (see illustration).

15.9a Counter-hold the pivot bolt . . .

15.9b . . . and unscrew the pivot bolt nut

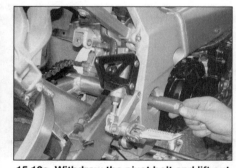

15.10a Withdraw the pivot bolt and lift out the swingarm

15.10b Ease the chain out with the swingarm – GSX-R750 and GSX-R1000 models

15.12 Chain slider is retained by three bolts

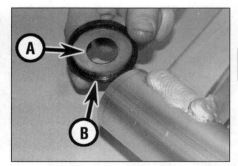

15.16 Fit the washer (A) and dust cover (B) to each end of the swingarm pivot

6

**16.2 Remove the brake torque arm (arrowed) if required**

**16.3a Inspect the chain adjuster bolts and threads**

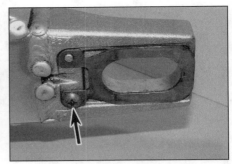

**16.3b Axle plates are retained by screws (arrowed)**

17 Offer up the swingarm, making sure the chain is correctly looped around it. On GSX-R750 and GSX-R1000 models, ease the chain between the gearbox output shaft and the frame and rest it over the gearbox output shaft (see illustration 15.10b).
18 Align the swingarm pivot with the frame mountings and install the pivot bolt from the right-hand side (see illustration 15.10a). Tighten the pivot bolt to the torque setting specified at the beginning of this Chapter.
19 Install the washer and nut on the left-hand end of the pivot bolt, then counter-hold the bolt and tighten the nut to the specified torque setting.
20 Install the locknut on the right-hand end of the pivot bolt, then tighten the locknut to the specified torque setting (see Step 8).
21 Install the remaining components in the reverse order of removal, noting the following:

● Bleed the rear brake after installing the rear wheel (see Chapter 7).
● Check the drive chain slack (see Chapter 1).
● Check the operation of the rear suspension and brake before taking the machine on the road.

### 16 Swingarm – inspection and bearing renewal

## Inspection

1 Clean the swingarm with a suitable solvent, removing all traces of dirt, corrosion and grease.
2 If required, undo the nut and remove the bolt securing the brake torque arm to the swingarm (see illustration).
3 Inspect the drive chain adjuster bolts and

the bolt threads in the swingarm (see illustration). Stripped threads in the swingarm can be repaired with a thread insert – see 'Tools and Workshop Tips' in the Reference section. Inspect the axle plates on the inside of the swingarm ends and fit new plates if they are gouged or distorted (see illustration).
4 Withdraw the spacers from the needle roller bearings in both ends of the swingarm pivot (see illustration). Remove any corrosion from the spacers with steel wool. If necessary, wash old grease out of the bearings with a suitable solvent, then dry the bearings with compressed air, if available.
5 Inspect the components closely, looking for obvious signs of wear such as scoring and pitting. Apply clean oil to the spacers, then slip each one back into its bearing and check that there is not an excessive amount of freeplay between the two. Ensure the bearings turn smoothly without binding or grating. If there is any doubt about the condition of the bearings have them checked by a Suzuki dealer or renew them.
6 Clean the swingarm pivot bolt and check the bolt for wear where it passes through the frame and the bearing spacers (see illustration). Slide the bearing spacers onto the pivot bolt and check that there is not an excessive amount of freeplay between the two.
7 If required, follow Steps 4 and 5 and check the linkage rod spacer and two needle roller bearings in the bottom of the swingarm (see illustrations).
8 Check the pivot bolt for straightness by rolling it on a flat surface such as a piece of plate glass. If available, place the bolt in V-blocks and measure the runout using a dial gauge. If the runout exceeds the limit specified, fit a new one.
9 Lay the swingarm on the work surface and support it so that the pivot end is level (check this with a spirit level). Install the chain adjuster blocks and the axle and check the level of the axle. If the axle is not level, the swingarm is out of true and must be renewed.

## Bearing renewal

**Note:** *The needle bearings should only be removed if new bearings are going to be fitted – removal of the bearings will destroy them.*

**16.4 Remove the spacers and inspect the bearings (arrowed)**

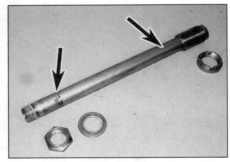

**16.6 Check the pivot bolt for wear at the pivot points (arrowed)**

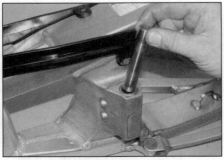

**16.7a Check the linkage rod spacer . . .**

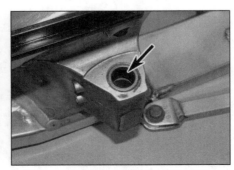

**16.7b . . . and the linkage rod bearings (arrowed)**

**10** Remove the inner sleeves from the bearings **(see illustration 16.4)**. Note the position of the bearings before removing them.

**11** Suzuki recommend the use of a knife-edged puller to extract the bearings. Locate the bearing puller tool behind the inner edge of the first bearing to be removed, note that there is only a small clearance in which to locate the puller edges. Operate the puller to draw the bearing out of the swingarm. The centre spacer can now be removed from inside the swingarm. Now use the same procedure to remove the bearing from the other side of the swingarm.

**12** If the bearings are corroded in position it may not be possible to remove them with a puller. A long rod can be inserted through the swingarm from the opposite side to drive against the outer edge of the bearing – it is not possible to make contact with the inside face of the bearing due to it being fitted tight against the seat inside the swingarm. An alternative method is to collapse the bearing, taking care not to damage the swingarm casting, enabling it to be extracted from the swingarm.

**13** The new bearings should be pressed or drawn into place so that they seat against the seat inside the swingarm – do not drive them into position. In the absence of a press, a suitable drawbolt arrangement can be made up as described in *Tools and Workshop Tips (Section 5)* in the Reference section. Do not forget to install the centre spacer between the two bearings, and fit each bearing with its marked side facing outwards.

**14** If the linkage rod bearings are being renewed note that there is no centre spacer between the bearings.

## 17 Drive chain –
removal and installation

⚠️ *Warning: NEVER install a drive chain which uses a clip-type (split) master link. ONLY use the correct tools to secure the riveted soft link – if you do not have access to such tools or do not have the skill to operate them correctly, have the chain installed by a Suzuki dealer.*

### GSX-R600 models

**Note:** *The original equipment drive chain has a riveted soft link to enable the chain to be removed without disturbing the swingarm. Refer to Tools and Workshop Tips (Section 8) in the Reference section for details of chain breaking and joining. Alternatively the chain can be removed complete as described below.*

**1** Follow Steps 1 to 4 in Section 15, then secure the brake caliper to the swingarm to avoid straining the hydraulic hose.

**2** Remove the front sprocket (see Section 18).

**3** Follow Steps 8 to 10 in Section 15, but note

it is only necessary to displace the swingarm far enough to allow the chain to be eased out between the gearbox output shaft and the frame. **Note:** *Have an assistant support the swingarm while the chain is being removed to avoid straining the rear brake hydraulic hose.* If required, temporarily install the swingarm pivot bolt to support the swingarm whilst the chain is removed.

**4** Installation is the reverse of removal. On completion, adjust and lubricate the chain (see Chapter 1).

### GSX-R750 and GSX-R1000 models

**Note:** *Due to the swingarm design it is not possible to remove the chain complete. The drive chain has a riveted soft link which must be split using either the Suzuki service tool (Pt. No. 09922-22711) or a commercially-available drive chain cutting/staking tool.*

**5** Remove the front sprocket cover (see Section 18).

**6** Slacken the drive chain (see Chapter 1).

**7** Refer to 'Tools and Workshop Tips (Section 8)' in the Reference section for details of how to identify the soft link, then split the chain at the soft link using the chain breaking tool. Note the chain's routing through the swingarm, then remove the chain from the bike.

**8** When fitting the chain, route it through the swingarm and around the front sprocket, leaving the two ends in a convenient position to work on. Assemble the new soft link and rivet it as described in Section 8 of *Tools and Workshop Tips*.

**9** If fitting the original equipment RK chain (GSX-R750) or DID chain (GSX-R1000), Suzuki specifies that the distance between the outer edges of the side plates should be 20.05 to 20.35 mm on the GSX-R750 and 21.05 to 21.35 mm on the GSX-R1000 when the sideplate is pressed into place.

**11** After the soft link pins have been riveted in place, check the staked pin ends for any signs of cracking. If either of the pins have cracked the chain must be disassembled and another new soft link and O-rings fitted. If fitting the original equipment RK chain (GSX-R750) or DID chain (GSX-R1000), Suzuki specifies that the diameter of the staked pins should be

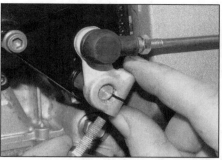

**18.1 Undo the pinch bolt and remove the gearchange arm**

5.45 to 5.85 mm on the GSX-R750 and 5.50 to 5.75 mm on the GSX-R1000.

**12** Install the sprocket cover (see Section 18). On completion, adjust and lubricate the chain (see Chapter 1).

## 18 Sprockets –
removal and installation

**Note:** *Always renew the engine and rear wheel sprockets as a set, together with the drive chain.*

### Removal

#### Front sprocket

**1** Undo the gearchange linkage arm pinch bolt and remove the arm from the shaft, noting any alignment marks **(see illustration)**. If no marks are visible, make your own before removing the arm so that it can be correctly aligned with the shaft on installation.

**2** Raise the fuel tank (see Chapter 4) and trace the wiring from the speed sensor on the sprocket cover and disconnect it at the connector **(see illustration)**.

**3** Undo the bolts securing the sprocket cover to the crankcase and displace the cover **(see illustration)**. **Note:** *On GSX-R600K1 and GSX-R750Y and K1 models remove the sprocket cover bracket with the cover. There is no need to detach the clutch cable from the cover. Note the position of the cover locating dowel and remove it for safekeeping if it is loose.*

**18.2 Disconnect the speed sensor wiring connector (arrowed)**

**18.3 Undo the bolts (arrowed) and remove the sprocket cover**

**6**

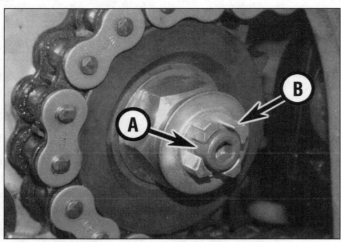

**18.4 Undo the bolt (A) and remove the speed sensor rotor (B)**

**18.5 Remove the front sprocket nut (A) and washer (B)**

**4** Have an assistant apply the rear brake, then undo the bolt securing the speed sensor rotor and remove the rotor **(see illustration)**.

**5** Apply the rear brake and slacken the front sprocket nut, then remove the nut and washer **(see illustration)**. The sprocket nut is of the self-locking type. If the locking device is no longer effective, discard the nut and fit a new one on reassembly.

**6** Slacken the drive chain (see Chapter 1). Lift the chain off the sprocket and slide the sprocket off the gearbox output shaft **(see illustration)**.

**Rear sprocket**

**7** Remove the rear wheel (see Chapter 7).
*Caution: Don't lay the wheel down on the disc as it could become warped. Lay the wheel rim on wooden blocks so that the disc is off the ground. Don't operate the brake pedal with the wheel removed.*

**8** Undo the nuts securing the sprocket to the sprocket coupling, then remove the sprocket, noting which way round it fits **(see illustration)**. If required, pull the sprocket coupling out of the hub and check the condition of the rubber dampers (see Section 19).

**9** The sprocket nuts are the self-locking type. If the locking device is no longer effective, discard the nuts and fit new ones on reassembly.

## Installation

### Front sprocket

**10** Slide the sprocket onto the gearbox shaft and lift the chain onto the sprocket; if the original sprocket is being refitted ensure it is installed the same way around as on removal. Adjust the chain (see Chapter 1).

**11** Clean the threads of the output shaft, then apply thread locking compound to the threads **(see illustration)**. Install the washer and sprocket nut. Have an assistant apply the rear brake, then tighten the nut to the torque setting specified at the beginning of this Chapter.

**12** Install the speed sensor rotor and rotor bolt. Apply the rear brake and tighten the bolt to the specified torque setting.

**13** Install the remaining components in the reverse order of removal, noting the following:
● Install the cover locating dowel.
● Lubricate the end of the clutch pushrod with general purpose grease.
● Ensure the speed sensor wiring is connected securely.
● Align the gearchange linkage arm with the shaft.

### Rear sprocket

**14** If removed, install the sprocket coupling in the hub (see Section 19).

**15** Fit the sprocket onto the coupling and install the sprocket nuts; if the original sprocket is being refitted ensure it is installed the same way around as on removal – the stamped side should face outwards. Tighten the nuts evenly to the torque setting specified at the beginning of this Chapter.

**16** Install the rear wheel (see Chapter 7).

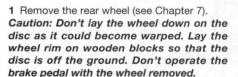

## 19 Rear sprocket coupling/rubber dampers – check and renewal

**1** Remove the rear wheel (see Chapter 7).
*Caution: Don't lay the wheel down on the disc as it could become warped. Lay the wheel rim on wooden blocks so that the disc is off the ground. Don't operate the brake pedal with the wheel removed.*

**2** Pull the spacer out of the coupling bearing seal **(see illustration)**.

**3** Pull the sprocket coupling out of the hub leaving the rubber dampers in position in the wheel **(see illustration)**. Note the spacer inside the coupling bearing and remove it if it is loose. The coupling should be a press fit between the dampers with no freeplay.

**18.6 Slide the sprocket off the gearbox shaft**

**18.8 The sprocket is secured by five nuts**

**18.11 Apply thread locking compound to the shaft threads**

19.2  Remove the spacer . . .

19.3  . . . then lift off the sprocket coupling – note the spacer (arrowed) inside the coupling

19.5  Check the condition of the rubber dampers

4  Check the coupling for cracks and damage. Also check the sprocket studs for damage and ensure they are secure in the coupling.

5  Lift the rubber dampers from the hub and check them for cracks, hardening and general deterioration **(see illustration)**. Renew the rubber dampers as a set if necessary.

6  Checking and renewal procedures for the coupling bearing are described in Chapter 7.

7  Ensure the rubber dampers are correctly located in the hub.

8  Ensure the spacer is correctly installed in the coupling bearing, then press the coupling firmly into the hub.

9  Smear the inside of the coupling bearing seal with grease then fit the spacer into the seal and install the rear wheel (see Chapter 7).

**6**

# Chapter 7
# Brakes, wheels and tyres

## Contents

## Degrees of difficulty

| | | | |
|---|---|---|---|
| **Easy,** suitable for novice with little experience  | **Fairly easy,** suitable for beginner with some experience  | **Fairly difficult,** suitable for competent DIY mechanic | **Difficult,** suitable for experienced DIY mechanic | **Very difficult,** suitable for expert DIY or professional 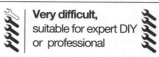 |

## Specifications

### Brakes

| | |
|---|---|
| Brake fluid type . . . . . . . . . . . . . . . . . . . . . . . . . . . . . . . . . . . | DOT 4 |
| Disc minimum thickness | |
| Standard . . . . . . . . . . . . . . . . . . . . . . . . . . . . . . . . . . . . . . | 4.8 to 5.2 mm |
| Service limit . . . . . . . . . . . . . . . . . . . . . . . . . . . . . . . . . . . . | 4.5 mm |
| Disc maximum runout (front and rear, all models) . . . . . . . . . . . . . . | 0.3 mm |
| Caliper bore ID | |
| Front | |
| GSX-R600 and GSX-R750 | |
| Lower . . . . . . . . . . . . . . . . . . . . . . . . . . . . . . . . . . . . . | 30.230 to 30.280 mm |
| Upper . . . . . . . . . . . . . . . . . . . . . . . . . . . . . . . . . . . . . | 33.960 to 34.010 mm |
| GSX-R1000 | |
| Lower . . . . . . . . . . . . . . . . . . . . . . . . . . . . . . . . . . . . . | 24.000 to 24.076 mm |
| Middle and upper . . . . . . . . . . . . . . . . . . . . . . . . . . . . . . | 27.000 to 27.076 mm |
| Rear | |
| GSX-R600 and GSX-R750 . . . . . . . . . . . . . . . . . . . . . . . . . | 38.180 to 38.256 mm |
| GSX-R1000 . . . . . . . . . . . . . . . . . . . . . . . . . . . . . . . . . . | 38.180 to 38.230 mm |
| Caliper piston OD | |
| Front | |
| GSX-R600 and GSX-R750 | |
| Lower . . . . . . . . . . . . . . . . . . . . . . . . . . . . . . . . . . . . . | 30.167 to 30.200 mm |
| Upper . . . . . . . . . . . . . . . . . . . . . . . . . . . . . . . . . . . . . | 33.901 to 33.934 mm |
| GSX-R1000 | |
| Lower . . . . . . . . . . . . . . . . . . . . . . . . . . . . . . . . . . . . . | 23.925 to 23.975 mm |
| Middle and upper . . . . . . . . . . . . . . . . . . . . . . . . . . . . . . | 26.920 to 26.970 mm |
| Rear | |
| GSX-R600 and GSX-R750 . . . . . . . . . . . . . . . . . . . . . . . . . | 38.098 to 38.148 mm |
| GSX-R1000K1 . . . . . . . . . . . . . . . . . . . . . . . . . . . . . . . . | 38.060 to 38.093 mm |
| GSX-R1000K2 . . . . . . . . . . . . . . . . . . . . . . . . . . . . . . . . | 38.080 to 38.130 mm |
| Master cylinder bore ID | |
| Front . . . . . . . . . . . . . . . . . . . . . . . . . . . . . . . . . . . . . . . | 15.870 to 15.913 mm |
| Rear . . . . . . . . . . . . . . . . . . . . . . . . . . . . . . . . . . . . . . . | 12.700 to 12.743 mm |
| Master cylinder piston OD | |
| Front . . . . . . . . . . . . . . . . . . . . . . . . . . . . . . . . . . . . . . . | 15.827 to 15.854 mm |
| Rear . . . . . . . . . . . . . . . . . . . . . . . . . . . . . . . . . . . . . . . | 12.657 to 12.684 mm |

## Wheels

Maximum wheel runout (front and rear)
  Axial (side-to-side) . . . . . . . . . . . . . . . . . . . . . . . . . . . . . . . . 2.0 mm
  Radial (out-of-round) . . . . . . . . . . . . . . . . . . . . . . . . . . . . . . . 2.0 mm
Maximum axle runout (front and rear) . . . . . . . . . . . . . . . . . . . . . . 0.25 mm

## Tyres

Tyre pressures . . . . . . . . . . . . . . . . . . . . . . . . . . . . . . . . . . . . . . . see *Daily (pre-ride) checks*
Tyre sizes*
  GSX-R600 and GSX-R750
    Front . . . . . . . . . . . . . . . . . . . . . . . . . . . . . . . . . . . . . . . . . 120/70-ZR17 (58W)
    Rear . . . . . . . . . . . . . . . . . . . . . . . . . . . . . . . . . . . . . . . . . . 180/55-ZR17 (73W)
  GSX-R1000
    Front . . . . . . . . . . . . . . . . . . . . . . . . . . . . . . . . . . . . . . . . . 120/70-ZR17 (58W)
    Rear . . . . . . . . . . . . . . . . . . . . . . . . . . . . . . . . . . . . . . . . . . 190/50-ZR17 (73W)
*Refer to the owners handbook or the tyre information label on the swingarm for approved tyre brands.

## Torque settings

Brake caliper bleed valves . . . . . . . . . . . . . . . . . . . . . . . . . . . . . . 8 Nm
Brake hose banjo bolts . . . . . . . . . . . . . . . . . . . . . . . . . . . . . . . . . 23 Nm
Front brake caliper body joining bolts . . . . . . . . . . . . . . . . . . . . . 21 Nm
Front brake caliper mounting bolts . . . . . . . . . . . . . . . . . . . . . . . . 25 Nm
Front brake disc bolts . . . . . . . . . . . . . . . . . . . . . . . . . . . . . . . . . 23 Nm
Front brake master cylinder clamp bolts . . . . . . . . . . . . . . . . . . . 10 Nm
Front brake pad pin . . . . . . . . . . . . . . . . . . . . . . . . . . . . . . . . . . . 16 Nm
Front axle . . . . . . . . . . . . . . . . . . . . . . . . . . . . . . . . . . . . . . . . . . 100 Nm
Front axle clamp bolts and axle holder clamp bolts . . . . . . . . . . . . 23 Nm
Rear axle nut
  GSX-R600 . . . . . . . . . . . . . . . . . . . . . . . . . . . . . . . . . . . . . . . 120 Nm
  GSX-R600 (US and Canada models) . . . . . . . . . . . . . . . . . . . . 110 Nm
  GSX-R750 . . . . . . . . . . . . . . . . . . . . . . . . . . . . . . . . . . . . . . . 120 Nm
  GSX-R750 (US and Canada models) . . . . . . . . . . . . . . . . . . . . 110 Nm
  GSX-R1000 . . . . . . . . . . . . . . . . . . . . . . . . . . . . . . . . . . . . . . 100 Nm
Rear brake caliper body joining bolts
  GSX-R600 and GSX-R750 . . . . . . . . . . . . . . . . . . . . . . . . . . . 30 Nm
  GSX-R1000 . . . . . . . . . . . . . . . . . . . . . . . . . . . . . . . . . . . . . . 37 Nm
Rear brake caliper mounting bolts . . . . . . . . . . . . . . . . . . . . . . . . 25 Nm
Rear brake disc bolts . . . . . . . . . . . . . . . . . . . . . . . . . . . . . . . . . . 35 Nm
Rear brake master cylinder mounting bolts . . . . . . . . . . . . . . . . . . 10 Nm
Rear brake pad pin – GSX-R1000 . . . . . . . . . . . . . . . . . . . . . . . . 17 Nm
Rear brake torque arm nut
  Front . . . . . . . . . . . . . . . . . . . . . . . . . . . . . . . . . . . . . . . . . . . 28 Nm
  Rear . . . . . . . . . . . . . . . . . . . . . . . . . . . . . . . . . . . . . . . . . . . . 34 Nm

## 1  General information

All models covered in this manual have hydraulically operated disc brakes, twin discs at the front and a single disc at the rear. On GSX-R600 and GSX-R750 models, the front brake calipers are of the four piston opposed type. On GSX-R1000 models, the front calipers are of the six piston opposed type. All models use a rear caliper of the twin piston opposed type.

All models are fitted with cast alloy wheels designed for tubeless tyres only.

*Caution: Disc brake components rarely require disassembly. Do not disassemble components unless absolutely necessary. If a hydraulic brake hose is loosened or disconnected, the union sealing washers must be renewed and the system bled upon reassembly. Do not use solvents on*

*internal brake components. Solvents will cause the seals to swell and distort. Use only clean brake fluid of the correct type for cleaning. Use care when working with brake fluid as it can injure your eyes and it will damage painted surfaces and plastic parts.*

2.1 Undo the bolts (arrowed) and remove the pad spring

## 2  Front brake pads – renewal

⚠ *Warning: The dust created by the brake system may contain asbestos, which is harmful to your health. Never blow it out with compressed air and don't inhale any of it. An approved filtering mask should be worn when working on the brakes.*

1 Undo the two bolts securing the pad spring and remove the spring **(see illustration)**.
2 On GSX-R600K1 and GSX-R750Y, K1 models, remove the R-clip from the end of the pad retaining pin, then unscrew the pad pin **(see illustrations)**. On GSX-R600K2, GSX-R750K2 and GSX-R1000 models, unscrew the pad pin from the caliper **(see illustration)**. Withdraw the pads from the caliper, noting how they fit **(see illustration)**. **Note:** *Do not operate the brake lever while the pads are out of the caliper.*

**2.2a On GSX-R600K1 and GSX-R750Y/K1, remove the R-clip (arrowed) . . .**

**2.2b . . . then unscrew the pad pin**

**2.2c On all other models, unscrew the pad pin**

**3** Inspect the surface of each pad for contamination and check that the friction material has not worn beyond its service limit (see Chapter 1, Section 11). If either pad is worn down to, or beyond, the service limit wear indicator (i.e. the wear indicator is no longer visible), is fouled with oil or grease, or heavily scored or damaged, both sets of front brake pads must be renewed together. **Note:** *It is not possible to degrease the friction material; if the pads are contaminated in any way they must be renewed.*

**4** If the pads are in good condition clean them carefully, using a fine wire brush which is completely free of oil and grease to remove all traces of road dirt and corrosion. Using a pointed instrument, dig out any embedded particles of foreign matter. Remove any areas of glazing using emery cloth. If required, spray with a dedicated brake cleaner to remove any dust.

**5** Check the condition of the brake disc (see Section 4).

**6** Remove all traces of corrosion from the pad pin. Inspect the pin and, where fitted, the R-clip, for signs of damage and renew either as necessary.

**7** If new pads are being installed, push the pistons as far back into the caliper as possible using hand pressure or a piece of wood as leverage **(see illustration)** or alternatively use a proper piston-pushing tool. This will displace brake fluid back into the hydraulic reservoir, so it may be necessary to remove the reservoir cap, diaphragm plate and diaphragm and siphon out some fluid. If the pistons are difficult to push back, attach a length of clear hose to the bleed valve and place the open end in a suitable container, then open the valve and try again. Take great care not to draw any air into the system and don't forget to tighten the valve once the pistons have been sufficiently displaced. If in doubt, bleed the brakes afterwards (see Section 11). **Note:** *Under no circumstances lever against the brake disc to push the pistons back into the caliper as damage to the disc will result.*

**8** Smear the backs of the pads and the shank of the pad pin with copper-based grease,

**2.2d Lift out the pads**

making sure that none gets on the front or sides of the pads.

**9** Insert the pads into the caliper so that the friction material of each pad faces the disc. Install the pad pin, making sure it passes through the hole in each pad.

**10** Tighten the pad pin to the torque setting specified at the beginning of this Chapter **(see illustration)**. On GSX-R600K1 and GSX-R750Y, K1 models insert the R-clip through the hole in the pad pin **(see illustration)**.

**11** Fit the pad spring and secure it with the bolts.

**12** Operate the brake lever several times to bring the pads into contact with the disc. Check the level of fluid in the hydraulic reservoir and top-up if necessary (see *Daily (pre-ride) checks*).

**13** Check the operation of the front brake before riding the motorcycle.

**2.7 Use a block of wood to press the pistons back**

## 3 Front brake calipers – removal, overhaul and installation

*Warning: If a caliper is in need of an overhaul all old brake fluid should be flushed from the system. Also, the dust created by the brake system may contain asbestos, which is harmful to your health. Never blow it out with compressed air and do not inhale any of it. An approved filtering mask should be worn when working on the brakes. Disassembly, overhaul and reassembly of the brake caliper must be done in a spotlessly clean work area to avoid contamination and possible failure of the brake hydraulic system components. Do not, under any circumstances, use*

**2.10a Tighten the pad pin to the specified torque**

**2.10b Secure the pad pin with the R-clip (where fitted)**

7

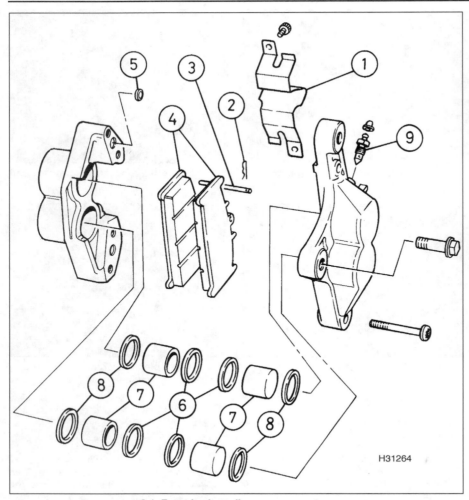

3.1 Front brake caliper components –
GSX-R600/750 models. GSX-R1000 model has six pistons

| | | | | | |
|---|---|---|---|---|---|
| 1 | Pad spring | 4 | Brake pads | 7 | Piston |
| 2 | R-clip | 5 | Caliper seal | 8 | Piston seal |
| 3 | Pad pin | 6 | Dust seal | 9 | Bleed valve |

petroleum-based solvents to clean brake parts. Use clean brake fluid of the type specified, dedicated brake cleaner or denatured alcohol only, as described. To prevent damage from spilled brake fluid, always cover paintwork when working on the braking system.

### Removal

Note: If the caliper is being overhauled (usually due to sticking pistons or fluid leaks) read through the entire procedure first and make sure that you have obtained all the new parts required, including some new DOT 4 brake fluid.

3.3a Left-hand caliper banjo bolt (arrowed)

3.3b Right-hand caliper banjo bolt (arrowed) – note the double hose arrangement

3.2a Unclip the brake hose assembly from the guides on the right-hand side . . .

3.2b . . . and back of the front mudguard

**1** If the caliper is being overhauled, remove the brake pads (see Section 2). If the caliper is just being detached from the forks as part of the fork or wheel removal procedure, the brake pads can be left in place **(see illustration)**.

**2** Unclip the brake hose assembly from the guides on the front mudguard **(see illustrations)**.

**3** If the caliper is being completely removed or overhauled, unscrew the brake hose banjo bolt and detach the banjo fitting, noting its alignment with the caliper **(see illustration)**. When working on the right-hand caliper, note the double hose arrangement **(see illustration)**. *Note: If you are planning to overhaul the caliper and do not have a source of compressed air to blow out the pistons, just loosen the banjo bolt at this stage and retighten it lightly. The hydraulic system can then be used to force the pistons out of the caliper once the pads have been removed. Disconnect the hose when the pistons have been sufficiently displaced.*

**4** Once disconnected, clamp the hose and secure it in an upright position to minimise fluid loss. Wrap a clean plastic bag tightly around the end to prevent dirt entering the system. Discard the sealing washers, as new ones must be fitted on reassembly.

**5** If the caliper body is to be split into its halves for overhaul, loosen the caliper body joining bolts at this stage and retighten them lightly **(see illustration)**.

**6** Unscrew the caliper mounting bolts and slide the caliper off the disc **(see illustration)**.

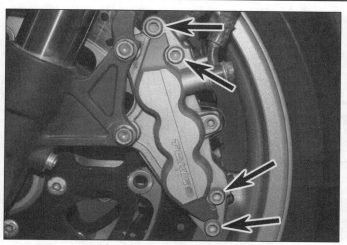

3.5 Caliper body joining bolts (arrowed)

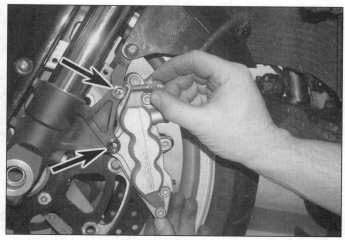

3.6 Unscrew the mounting bolts (arrowed) and slide the caliper off the disc

If the caliper is just being displaced, secure it to the motorcycle with a cable tie to avoid straining the brake hose. **Note:** *Do not operate the brake lever while either caliper is off the disc.*

### Overhaul

7 Clean the exterior of the caliper with denatured alcohol or brake system cleaner.

8 Displace the pistons from their bores as far as possible using either compressed air or by carefully operating the front brake lever to pump them out. Ensure that all the pistons are moving freely and evenly.

9 If the pistons are being displaced hydraulically, it may be necessary to top-up the hydraulic reservoir during the procedure. Also, have some clean rag ready to catch any spilled brake fluid when the pistons reach the end of their bores. **Note:** *If the compressed air method is used, direct the air into the fluid inlet on the caliper. Use only low pressure to ease the pistons out – if the air pressure is too high and the pistons are forced out, the caliper and/or pistons may be damaged.*

⚠ *Warning: Never place your fingers in front of the pistons in an attempt to catch or protect them when applying compressed air, as serious injury could result.*

3.12 Use a plastic or wooden tool to remove the seals

10 If a piston is stuck in its bore due to corrosion, and all attempts at releasing it using hydraulic pressure or compressed air have failed, the caliper should be renewed. Do not try to remove a piston by levering it out or by using pliers or other grips.

11 Unscrew the caliper body joining bolts and separate the body halves. Remove the pistons from each half. Mark each piston and the caliper body to ensure that the pistons can be matched to their original bores on reassembly. Note that two sizes of piston are used in each caliper (see Specifications at the beginning of this Chapter). On GSX-R600 and GSX-R750 models, extract the two caliper body O-rings from whichever body half they are in and discard them as new ones must be fitted on reassembly. On GSX-R1000 models only one caliper body O-ring is fitted; discard it and fit a new one on reassembly.

12 Remove the dust seals and the piston seals from the piston bores using a soft wooden or plastic tool to avoid scratching the bores **(see illustration)**. Discard the seals as new ones must be fitted on reassembly.

13 Clean the pistons and bores with clean brake fluid of the specified type. If compressed air is available, blow it through the fluid galleries in the caliper to ensure they are clear (make sure it is filtered and unlubricated).

*Caution: Do not, under any circumstances, use a petroleum-based solvent to clean brake parts.*

14 Inspect the caliper bores and pistons for signs of corrosion, nicks and burrs and loss of plating. If surface defects are present, the pistons or the caliper assembly must be renewed. If the necessary measuring equipment is available, compare the dimensions of the caliper bores and pistons to those specified at the beginning of this Chapter, and install a new caliper if necessary. If the caliper is in poor condition, the other front caliper and the master cylinder should also be checked.

15 Lubricate the new piston seals with clean brake fluid and install them in their grooves in the caliper bores, making sure the thicker side of the seal is facing the disc **(see illustration)**. Note that there are two sizes of bore in each caliper and care must therefore be taken to ensure that the correct size seals are fitted to the correct bores (see Specifications). The same applies when fitting the new dust seals and pistons.

16 Lubricate the new dust seals with clean brake fluid and install them in their grooves in the caliper bores.

17 Lubricate the pistons with clean brake fluid and install them, closed-end first, into the caliper bores, taking care not to displace the seals. Using your thumbs, push the pistons all the way in, making sure they enter the bore squarely.

18 Lubricate the new caliper body O-ring(s) with clean brake fluid and install them into one half of the caliper body (see Step 11). Join the two halves of the caliper body together, ensuring that the O-rings are not disturbed.

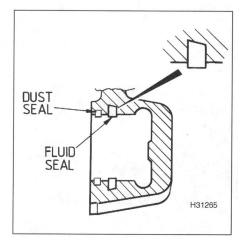

3.15 Ensure the piston seal is fitted correctly

7

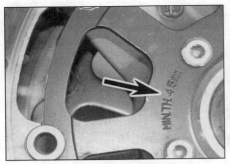

**4.2a The disc minimum thickness is marked on the disc**

Install the joining bolts and tighten them evenly to the torque setting specified at the beginning of this Chapter. If it is not possible to tighten the bolts fully at this stage, tighten them as much as possible, then tighten them fully once the caliper has been installed on the machine.

### Installation

**19** Slide the caliper onto the brake disc. If they weren't removed, make sure the pads sit squarely in the caliper before installing it.
**20** Install the caliper mounting bolts and tighten them finger-tight. If the calipers were overhauled and if not already done, tighten the caliper body joining bolts to the torque setting specified at the beginning of this Chapter **(see illustration 3.5)**. Tighten the caliper mounting bolts to the specified torque setting **(see illustration 3.6)**.
**21** If removed, connect the brake hose to the caliper, using new sealing washers on each side of the banjo fitting. Align the fitting as noted on removal **(see illustrations 3.3a and 3.3b)**. Tighten the banjo bolt to the specified torque setting.
**22** Secure the brake hose assembly in the guides on the front mudguard.
**23** If removed, install the brake pads (see Section 2).
**24** Top up the hydraulic reservoir with DOT 4 brake fluid (see *Daily (pre-ride) checks*) and bleed the system as described in Section 11. Check that there are no fluid leaks and test the operation of the brake before riding the motorcycle.

**4.3 Checking disc runout with a dial gauge**

**4.2b Measuring the disc thickness with a micrometer**

### 4 Front brake discs – inspection, removal and installation

#### Inspection

**1** Inspect the surface of the disc for score marks and other damage. Light scratches are normal after use and won't affect brake operation, but deep grooves and heavy score marks will reduce braking efficiency and accelerate pad wear. If a disc is badly grooved it must be machined or a new one fitted.
**2** The disc must not be machined or allowed to wear down to a thickness less than the service limit as listed in this Chapter's Specifications. The minimum thickness is also stamped on the disc **(see illustration)**. Check the thickness of the disc with a micrometer and renew it if necessary **(see illustration)**.
**3** To check disc runout, position the bike on an auxiliary stand with the front wheel raised off the ground. Mount a dial gauge to the fork leg, with the gauge plunger touching the surface of the disc about 10 mm from the outer edge **(see illustration)**. Rotate the wheel and watch the gauge needle, comparing the reading with the limit listed in the Specifications at the beginning of this Chapter. If the runout is greater than the service limit, check the wheel bearings for play (see Chapter 1). If the bearings are worn, install new ones (see Section 16) and repeat this check. If the disc runout is still excessive, a new pair of discs will have to be fitted, although machining by an engineer may be possible.

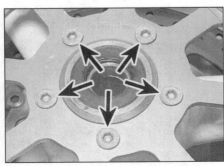

**4.5 The disc is secured by five bolts**

### Removal

**4** Remove the wheel (see Section 14).
**Caution: *Don't lay the wheel down and allow it to rest on the disc – the disc could become warped. Set the wheel on wood blocks so the wheel rim supports the weight of the wheel.***
**5** If you are not replacing the disc with a new one, mark the relationship of the disc to the wheel, so it can be installed in the same position and on the same side as originally fitted. Unscrew the disc retaining bolts, loosening them evenly and a little at a time in a criss-cross pattern to avoid distorting the disc, then remove the disc **(see illustration)**.

### Installation

**6** Before installing the disc, make sure there is no dirt or corrosion where the disc seats on the hub. If the disc does not sit flat when it is bolted down, it will appear to be warped when checked or when the front brake is used.
**7** Install the disc on the wheel with its marked side facing out, aligning the previously applied matchmarks (if you're reinstalling the original disc).
**8** Clean the threads of the disc mounting bolts, then apply a suitable non-permanent thread locking compound. Install the bolts and tighten them evenly and a little at a time in a criss-cross pattern to the torque setting specified at the beginning of this Chapter. Clean the disc using acetone or brake system cleaner. If a new disc has been installed, remove any protective coating from its working surfaces and fit new brake pads.
**9** Install the front wheel (see Section 14).
**10** Operate the brake lever several times to bring the pads into contact with the disc. Check the operation of the brake before riding the motorcycle.

### 5 Front brake master cylinder – removal, overhaul and installation

⚠️ ***Warning: If the brake master cylinder is in need of an overhaul all old brake fluid should be flushed from the system. Disassembly, overhaul and reassembly of the brake master cylinder must be done in a spotlessly clean work area to avoid contamination and possible failure of the brake hydraulic system components. Do not, under any circumstances, use petroleum-based solvents to clean brake parts. Use clean brake fluid of the type specified, dedicated brake cleaner or denatured alcohol only, as described. To prevent damage from spilled brake fluid, always cover paintwork when working on the braking system.***

### Removal

**Note:** *If the master cylinder is being overhauled (usually due to sticking or poor action, or fluid leaks) read through the entire* *procedure first and make sure that you have obtained all the new parts required, including some new DOT 4 brake fluid.*

**1** Disconnect the electrical connectors from the brake light switch **(see illustration)**.

**2** If the master cylinder is just being detached, ensure the hydraulic reservoir cover is secure. Unscrew the master cylinder clamp bolts and remove the back of the clamp, noting how it fits (see Chapter 6). Undo the bolt securing the hydraulic reservoir to the handlebar bracket, then position the master cylinder and reservoir assembly clear of the handlebar. Ensure no strain is placed on the hydraulic hose. Keep the hydraulic reservoir upright to prevent air entering the system.

**3** If the master cylinder is being overhauled, first remove the brake lever (see Chapter 6).

**4** Remove the reservoir cap clamp screw and clamp **(see illustration)**.

**5** Unscrew the brake hose banjo bolt and detach the banjo fitting, noting its alignment with the master cylinder **(see illustration)**. Once disconnected, clamp the hose and secure it in an upright position to minimise fluid loss. Wrap a clean plastic bag tightly around the end to prevent dirt entering the system. Discard the sealing washers as new ones must be fitted on reassembly.

**6** Unscrew the master cylinder clamp bolts and remove the back of the clamp, noting how it fits (see Chapter 6). Undo the bolt securing the hydraulic reservoir bracket to the handlebar, then lift the master cylinder and reservoir away from the handlebar **(see illustration)**.

**5.1 Disconnect the brake light switch wires (arrowed)**

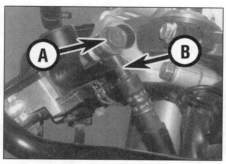

**5.5 Unscrew the banjo bolt (A) noting the alignment of the banjo fitting (B)**

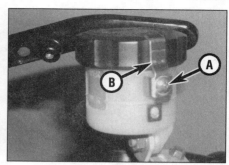

**5.4 Remove the reservoir cap clamp screw (A) and clamp (B)**

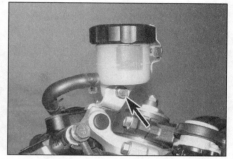

**5.6 Unscrew the bolt securing the hydraulic reservoir to the handlebar**

**7** Unscrew the reservoir cap and remove the diaphragm plate and the diaphragm **(see illustration)**. Drain the brake fluid from the

master cylinder and reservoir into a suitable container. Release the clip securing the reservoir hose to the union on the master cylinder and detach the hose. Wipe any remaining fluid out of the reservoir with a clean rag.

**8** If required, remove the screw securing the brake light switch to the bottom of the master cylinder and remove the switch (see Chapter 9).

### Overhaul

**9** Remove the cap from the fluid reservoir hose union, then remove the circlip and detach the union from the master cylinder. Discard the O-ring as a new one must be fitted on reassembly. Inspect the reservoir hose for cracks or splits and renew it if necessary.

**10** Carefully remove the dust boot from the master cylinder to reveal the piston retaining circlip **(see illustration)**.

**11** Depress the piston and use circlip pliers

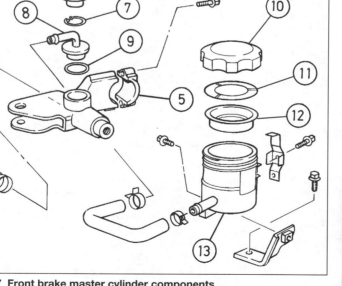

**5.7 Front brake master cylinder components**

1 Dust boot
2 Circlip
3 Piston assembly
4 Spring
5 Handlebar clamp
6 Union cap
7 Circlip
8 Reservoir hose union
9 O-ring
10 Reservoir cap
11 Diaphragm plate
12 Diaphragm
13 Reservoir

**5.10 Remove the boot from the end of the master cylinder piston . . .**

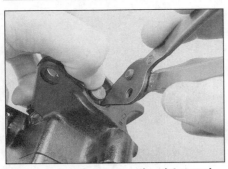

5.11a . . . then depress the piston and remove the circlip

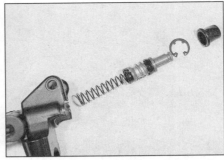

5.11b Lay out the parts in order to aid reassembly

to remove the circlip, then slide out the piston assembly and the spring, noting how they fit **(see illustrations)**. If they are difficult to remove, apply low pressure compressed air to the brake fluid outlet. Lay the parts out in the proper order to prevent confusion during reassembly.

12 Clean all parts with clean brake fluid. If compressed air is available, blow it through the fluid galleries to ensure they are clear (make sure the air is filtered and unlubricated). *Caution: Do not, under any circumstances, use a petroleum-based solvent to clean brake parts.*

13 Check the master cylinder bore for corrosion, scratches, nicks and score marks. If the necessary measuring equipment is available, compare the dimensions of the piston and bore to those given in the Specifications at the beginning of this Chapter. If damage or wear is evident, the master cylinder must be renewed. If the master cylinder is in poor condition, then the calipers should be checked as well.

14 The dust boot, circlip, piston components and spring are all included in the master cylinder rebuild kit. Use all of the new parts, regardless of the apparent condition of the old ones. If the seal and cup are not already on the piston, fit them according to the layout of the old piston assembly.

15 Install the spring in the master cylinder so that its tapered end faces out towards the piston.

16 Lubricate the piston assembly with clean brake fluid. Install the assembly into the master cylinder, making sure it is the correct way round **(see illustration 5.11b)**. Make sure the lips on the piston seals do not turn inside out when they are slipped into the bore. Depress the piston and install the new circlip, making sure it locates properly in its groove **(see illustration 5.11a)**.

17 Install the dust boot, making sure the lip is seated correctly in the groove **(see illustration 5.10)**.

18 Fit a new O-ring onto the fluid reservoir hose union, then press the union into the master cylinder and secure it with the circlip. Fit the cap over the circlip.

19 Inspect the reservoir diaphragm and fit a new one if it is damaged or deteriorated.

## Installation

20 If removed, fit the brake light switch onto the bottom of the master cylinder and tighten the screw securely (see Chapter 9).

21 Attach the master cylinder to the handlebar and fit the back of the clamp with its UP mark facing up (see Chapter 6). Align the clamp joint with the punch mark on the top of the handlebar, then tighten the upper bolt to the torque setting specified at the beginning of this Chapter, followed by the lower bolt.

22 Install the hydraulic reservoir on the handlebar and tighten its bracket bolt securely **(see illustration 5.6)**. Connect the reservoir hose to the union on the master cylinder and secure it with the clip.

23 Connect the brake hose to the master cylinder, using new sealing washers on each side of the banjo fitting. Align the hose as noted on removal **(see illustration 5.5)**. Tighten the banjo bolt to the torque setting specified at the beginning of this Chapter.

24 Install the brake lever (see Chapter 6).

25 Connect the brake light switch wiring **(see illustration 5.1)**.

26 Fill the fluid reservoir with new DOT 4 brake fluid (see *Daily (pre-ride) checks*). Refer to Section 11 and bleed the air from the system.

27 Check the operation of the brake before riding the motorcycle.

6.1 Prise off the cover . . .

6.2 . . . then remove the pad pin retaining clip

6.3 Withdraw the pad pins (arrowed) and remove the springs . . .

6.4 . . . then remove the pads and shims

## 6 Rear brake pads – renewal

⚠ *Warning: The dust created by the brake system may contain asbestos, which is harmful to your health. Never blow it out with compressed air and don't inhale any of it. An approved filtering mask should be worn when working on the brakes.*

## Removal

### GSX-R600 and GSX-R750 models

1 Prise off the brake pad cover using a flat-bladed screwdriver **(see illustration)**.

2 Remove the pad pin retaining clip, noting how the ends of the clip fit through the holes in the pad pins **(see illustration)**.

3 Note how the pad springs locate against the inside (friction material) faces of both pads and hook under the lower edges of the pads. Withdraw the pad pins from the caliper using a suitable pair of pliers and remove the springs **(see illustration)**.

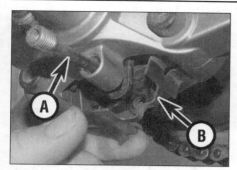

6.5a Unscrew the pad pin (A) and remove the spring (B) . . .

6.5b . . . then remove the pads

6.5c Remove the shim (A) from the back of the pad (B) noting how it fits

**4** Withdraw the pads from the caliper, noting how they fit, and remove the anti-chatter shim from the back of each pad **(see illustration)**.

### GSX-R1000 models

**5** Unscrew the pad retaining pin and withdraw the pad spring and pads from the caliper **(see illustrations)**. Remove the anti-chatter shim from the back of each pad **(see illustration)**.

*Caution: Do not operate the brake lever while the pads are out of the caliper.*

### Inspection

**6** Inspect the surface of each pad for contamination and check that the friction material has not worn beyond its service limit (see Chapter 1, Section 11). If either pad is worn down to, or beyond, the service limit wear indicator (i.e. the wear indicator is no longer visible), fouled with oil or grease, or heavily scored or damaged, both pads must be renewed as a set.

**7** If the pads are in good condition clean them carefully, using a fine wire brush which is completely free of oil and grease to remove all traces of road dirt and corrosion. Using a pointed instrument, clean out the grooves in the friction material and dig out any embedded particles of foreign matter. Remove any areas of glazing using emery cloth. If required, spray with a dedicated brake cleaner to remove any dust.

**8** Check the condition of the brake disc (see Section 8).

**9** Remove all traces of corrosion from the pad pin(s). As required, inspect the pins, pad retaining clip and pad springs for signs of damage, and renew them if necessary.

**10** If new pads are being installed, push the pistons as far back into the caliper as possible using hand pressure or a piece of wood as leverage **(see illustration 2.7)** or alternatively use a proper piston-pushing tool. This will displace brake fluid back into the hydraulic reservoir, so it may be necessary to remove the reservoir cap and diaphragm and siphon out some fluid (see *Daily (pre-ride) checks*). If the pistons are difficult to push back, attach a length of clear hose to the bleed valve and place the open end in a suitable container, then open the valve and try again. Take great care not to draw any air into the system and

don't forget to tighten the valve once the pistons have been sufficiently displaced. If in doubt, bleed the brakes afterwards (see Section 11). **Note:** *Under no circumstances lever against the brake disc to push the pistons back into the caliper as damage to the disc will result.*

**11** Smear the backs of the pads and the shank of the pad pin with copper-based grease, making sure that none gets on the front or sides of the pads.

### Installation

#### GSX-R600 and GSX-R750 models

**12** Fit the anti-chatter shim onto the back of each pad with its open end facing forward **(see illustration)**. Insert the pads into the caliper so that the friction material of each pad faces the disc, then install the first pad pin, with its holed end on the outside, making

6.12a Make sure the shims are the right way round

6.13 . . . then install the outer spring and secure it with the second pin. Install the inner spring . . .

sure the pin passes through the hole in each pad **(see illustration)**.

**13** Slide the second pin into the caliper as far as the outer pad. Install the outer pad spring against the inside (friction material) face of the outer pad. Locate one end of the spring under the first pad pin, then hook the spring onto the lower edge of the pad. Press up on the free end of the spring and slide the second pad pin under it **(see illustration)**.

**14** Install the inner pad spring against the inside (friction material) face of the inner pad and repeat the process, sliding the second pad pin all the way into the caliper **(see illustration)**.

**15** Align the holes in both pad pins and fit the retaining clip **(see illustration 6.2)**. Ensure the clip is secure in both pins, then install the pad cover.

**16** Operate the brake pedal several times to bring the pads into contact with the disc.

6.12b Install one pin through both pads . . .

6.14 . . . and slide in the second pin to secure it

**7**

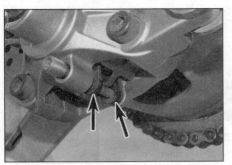

**6.17 Make sure the pin passes through both pads (arrowed)**

Check the level of fluid in the hydraulic reservoir and top-up if necessary (see *Daily (pre-ride) checks*). Check the operation of the brake before riding the motorcycle.

## GSX-R1000 models

**17** Fit the anti-chatter shim onto the back of each pad. Insert the pads into the caliper so that the friction material of each pad faces the disc, then install the spring and pad pin **(see illustration 6.5a)**. Make sure the pin passes through the hole in each pad **(see illustration)**. Tighten the pad pin to the specified torque setting.

**18** Operate the brake pedal several times to bring the pads into contact with the disc. Check the level of fluid in the hydraulic reservoir and top-up if necessary (see *Daily (pre-ride) checks*). Check the operation of the brake before riding the motorcycle.

## 7 Rear brake caliper – removal, overhaul and installation

⚠️ *Warning: If a caliper is in need of an overhaul all old brake fluid should be flushed from the system. Also, the dust created by the brake system may contain asbestos, which is harmful to your health. Never blow it out with compressed air and do not inhale any of it. An approved filtering mask should be worn when working on the brakes. Disassembly, overhaul and reassembly of the brake caliper must be done in a spotlessly clean work area to avoid contamination and possible failure of the brake hydraulic system components. Do not, under any circumstances, use petroleum-based solvents to clean brake parts. Use clean brake fluid of the type specified, dedicated brake cleaner or denatured alcohol only, as described. To prevent damage from spilled brake fluid, always cover paintwork when working on the braking system.*

## Removal

**Note:** *If the caliper is being overhauled (usually due to sticking pistons or fluid leaks) read through the entire procedure first and make sure that you have obtained all the new parts required, including some new DOT 4 brake fluid.*

**1** If the caliper is being overhauled, remove the brake pads (see Section 6). If the caliper is just being displaced, the brake pads can be left in place.

**2** If the caliper is being completely removed or overhauled, unscrew the brake hose banjo bolt and detach the banjo fitting, noting its alignment with the caliper **(see illustration)**. **Note:** *If you are planning to overhaul the caliper and do not have a source of compressed air to blow out the pistons, just loosen the banjo bolt at this stage and retighten it lightly. The hydraulic system can then be used to force the pistons out of the caliper once the pads have been removed. Disconnect the hose when the pistons have been sufficiently displaced.*

**3** Once disconnected, clamp the hose and secure it in an upright position to minimise fluid loss **(see illustration)**. Wrap a clean plastic bag tightly around the end to prevent dirt entering the system. Discard the sealing washers, as new ones must be fitted on reassembly.

**4** If the caliper body is to be split into its halves for overhaul, loosen the caliper body joining bolts at this stage and retighten them lightly **(see illustration)**.

**5** Undo the nut and bolt securing the brake torque arm to the caliper and withdraw the bolt **(see illustration)**.

**6** Loosen the caliper mounting bolts **(see illustration 7.4)**. Support the caliper, then withdraw the bolts and slide the caliper down off the disc. **Note:** *Do not operate the brake pedal while the caliper is off the disc.*

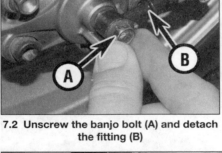

**7.2 Unscrew the banjo bolt (A) and detach the fitting (B)**

**7.3 Clamp the brake hose to minimise fluid loss**

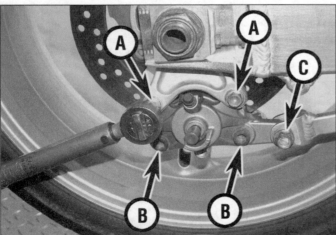

**7.4 Caliper mounting bolts (A), body joining bolts (B) and torque arm bolt (C)**

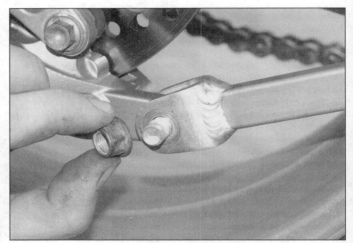

**7.5 Torque arm is secured with a nut and bolt**

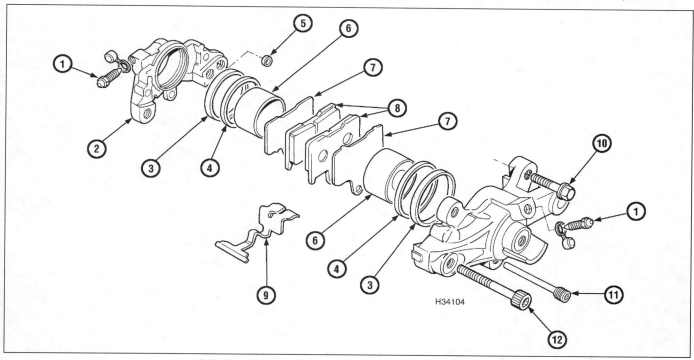

**7.8a  Rear brake caliper components – GSX-R600 and GSX-R750 models**

1  Bleed valve cap
2  Bleed valve
3  Caliper body half
4  Caliper seal
5  Piston seal
6  Dust seal
7  Piston
8  Anti-chatter shim
9  Pad pin
10 Pad spring
11 Pad pin clip
12 Pad cover
13 Caliper body half
14 Caliper joining bolt
15 Caliper mounting bolt
16 Brake pad

## Overhaul

**7** Clean the exterior of the caliper with denatured alcohol or brake system cleaner.
**8** Displace the pistons from their bores as far as possible using either compressed air or by carefully operating the brake pedal to pump them out. Ensure that both the pistons are moving freely and evenly **(see illustrations)**.
**9** If the pistons are being displaced hydraulically, it may be necessary to top-up the hydraulic reservoir during the procedure.

Also, have some clean rag ready to catch any spilled brake fluid when the pistons reach the end of their bores. **Note:** *If the compressed air method is used, direct the air into the fluid inlet on the caliper. Use only low pressure to ease the pistons out – if the air pressure is too*

**7.8b  Rear brake caliper components – GSX-R1000 models**

1  Bleed valve
2  Caliper body half
3  Piston seal
4  Dust seal
5  O-ring
6  Piston
7  Anti-chatter shim
8  Brake pad
9  Pad spring
10 Caliper mounting bolt
11 Pad pin
12 Caliper joining bolt

**7**

**7.20 Slide the caliper onto the disc and install the mounting bolts**

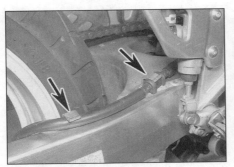

**7.22b . . . and the guides on the top of the swingarm – GSX-R750 . . .**

**7.22a Ensure the brake hose passes through the closed guide on the back of the swingarm . . .**

**7.22c . . . and GSX-R600/1000**

**8.3 Disc is secured by five bolts**

high and the pistons are forced out, the caliper and/or pistons may be damaged.

⚠️ *Warning: Never place your fingers in front of the pistons in an attempt to catch or protect them when applying compressed air, as serious injury could result.*

**10** If a piston is stuck in its bore due to corrosion, and all attempts at releasing it using hydraulic pressure or compressed air have failed, the caliper should be renewed. Do not try to remove a piston by levering it out or by using pliers or other grips.

**11** Unscrew the caliper body joining bolts and separate the body halves. Remove the piston from each half. Mark each piston and the caliper body to ensure that the pistons can be matched to their original bores on reassembly. Extract the caliper body O-ring from whichever body half it is in and discard it and fit a new one on reassembly.

**12** Remove the dust seals and the piston seals from the piston bores using a soft wooden or plastic tool to avoid scratching the bores **(see illustration 3.12)**. Discard the seals as new ones must be fitted on reassembly.

**13** Clean the pistons and bores with clean brake fluid of the specified type. If compressed air is available, blow it through the fluid galleries in the caliper to ensure they are clear (make sure it is filtered and unlubricated).

*Caution: Do not, under any circumstances, use a petroleum-based solvent to clean brake parts.*

**14** Inspect the caliper bores and pistons for signs of corrosion, nicks and burrs and loss of plating. If surface defects are present, the pistons or the caliper assembly must be renewed. If the necessary measuring equipment is available, compare the dimensions of the caliper bores and pistons to those specified at the beginning of this Chapter, and install a new caliper if necessary. If the caliper is in poor condition, the master cylinder should also be checked.

**15** Lubricate the new piston seals with clean brake fluid and install them in their grooves in the caliper bores, making sure the thicker side of the seal is facing the disc **(see illustration 3.15)**.

**16** Lubricate the new dust seals with clean brake fluid and install them in their grooves in the caliper bores.

**17** Lubricate the pistons with clean brake fluid and install them, closed-end first, into the caliper bores, taking care not to displace the seals. Using your thumbs, push the pistons all the way in, making sure they enter the bores squarely.

**18** Lubricate the new caliper body O-ring with clean brake fluid and install it into one half of the caliper body. Join the two halves of the caliper body together, making sure that the O-ring stays correctly seated in its recess. Install the joining bolts and tighten them evenly to the torque setting specified at the beginning of this Chapter. If it is not possible to tighten the bolts fully at this stage, tighten them as much as possible, then tighten them fully once the caliper has been installed on the machine.

## Installation

**19** Slide the caliper onto the brake disc. If they weren't removed, make sure the pads sit squarely in the caliper before installing it.

**20** Install the caliper mounting bolts and tighten them finger-tight **(see illustration)**. If the calipers were overhauled and if not already done, tighten the caliper body joining bolts to the torque setting specified at the beginning of this Chapter **(see illustration 7.4)**. Tighten the caliper mounting bolts to the specified torque setting.

**21** Fit the brake torque arm onto the caliper and install the bolt, then tighten the nut to the specified torque setting **(see illustration 7.5)**.

**22** If removed, connect the brake hose to the caliper, using new sealing washers on each side of the banjo fitting. Align the fitting as noted on removal. Ensure the brake hose is routed through its guides on the swingarm **(see illustrations)**. Tighten the banjo bolt to the specified torque setting.

**23** If removed, install the brake pads (see Section 6).

**24** Top up the hydraulic reservoir with DOT 4 brake fluid (see *Daily (pre-ride) checks*) and bleed the system as described in Section 11. Check for fluid leaks and test the operation of the brake before riding the motorcycle.

| 8 | Rear brake disc – inspection, removal and installation |  |
|---|---|---|

### Inspection

**1** Refer to Section 4 of this Chapter, noting that the dial gauge should be attached to the swingarm.

### Removal

**2** Remove the wheel (see Section 15).

*Caution: Don't lay the wheel down and allow it to rest on the disc or sprocket – they could become warped. Set the wheel on wood blocks so the wheel rim supports the weight of the wheel.*

**3** If you are not replacing the disc with a new one, mark the relationship of the disc to the wheel so it can be installed in the same position. Unscrew the disc retaining bolts, loosening them evenly and a little at a time in a criss-cross pattern to avoid distorting the disc, then remove the disc **(see illustration)**.

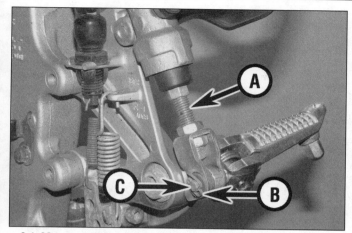

9.1 Master cylinder pushrod (A), split pin (B) and clevis pin (C)

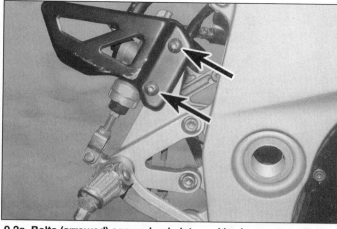

9.2a Bolts (arrowed) secure heel plate and brake master cylinder

## Installation

**4** Before installing the disc, make sure there is no dirt or corrosion where the disc seats on the hub. If the disc does not sit flat when it is bolted down, it will appear to be warped when checked or when the rear brake is used.

**5** Install the disc on the wheel with its marked side facing out, aligning the previously applied matchmarks (if you're reinstalling the original disc).

**6** Clean the threads of the disc mounting bolts, then apply a suitable non-permanent thread locking compound. Install the bolts and tighten them evenly and a little at a time in a criss-cross pattern to the torque setting specified at the beginning of this Chapter. Clean the disc using acetone or brake system cleaner. If a new disc has been installed, remove any protective coating from its working surfaces and fit new brake pads.

**7** Install the rear wheel (see Section 15).

**8** Operate the brake pedal several times to bring the pads into contact with the disc. Check the operation of the brake before riding the motorcycle.

> ## 9 Rear brake master cylinder –
> removal, overhaul and installation

> ⚠ *Warning: If the brake master cylinder is in need of an overhaul all old brake fluid should be flushed from the system. Disassembly, overhaul and reassembly of the brake master cylinder must be done in a spotlessly clean work area to avoid contamination and possible failure of the brake hydraulic system components. Do not, under any circumstances, use petroleum-based solvents to clean brake parts. Use clean brake fluid of the type specified, dedicated brake cleaner or denatured alcohol only, as described. To prevent damage from spilled brake fluid, always cover paintwork when working on the braking system.*

## Removal

**Note:** *If the master cylinder is being overhauled (usually due to sticking or poor action, or fluid leaks) read through the entire procedure first and make sure that you have obtained all the new parts required, including some new DOT 4 brake fluid.*

**1** If the master cylinder is just being displaced, remove the split pin and washer from the clevis pin securing the master cylinder pushrod to the brake pedal **(see illustration)**. Withdraw the clevis pin and separate the pushrod from the pedal. Discard the split pin as a new one must be fitted on reassembly.

**2** Loosen the bolts securing the heel plate and master cylinder to the footrest bracket, leaving them finger-tight **(see illustration)**. Undo the bolt securing the hydraulic reservoir to the frame, noting how the reservoir locates on the frame bracket **(see illustration)**. Withdraw the master cylinder bolts and displace the master cylinder and reservoir assembly. If required, release the brake hose to the rear caliper from the guides on the swingarm **(see illustrations 7.22b or 7.22c)**. **Note:** *On GSX-R600 and GSX-R1000 models undo the bolts securing the guides to release the hose.* Ensure no strain is placed on the hydraulic hose. Keep the hydraulic reservoir upright to prevent air entering the system.

9.2b Unscrew the bolt (arrowed) to remove the hydraulic reservoir

**3** If the master cylinder is being overhauled, follow Step 1 and disconnect the pushrod from the pedal. Undo the bolt securing the hydraulic reservoir to the frame, then undo the reservoir cover screws and remove the reservoir cover and diaphragm. Pour the brake fluid into a suitable container. Release the clip securing the reservoir hose to the union on the master cylinder and detach the hose **(see illustration)**. Wipe any remaining fluid out of the reservoir with a clean rag.

**4** Undo the brake hose banjo bolt and detach the banjo fitting, noting its alignment with the master cylinder **(see illustration)**. Once disconnected, clamp the hose and secure it in an upright position to minimise fluid loss **(see**

9.3 Release the clip (arrowed) to detach the hose from the master cylinder

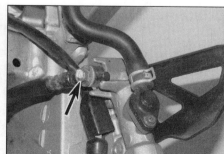

9.4 Brake hose banjo bolt (arrowed)

**7**

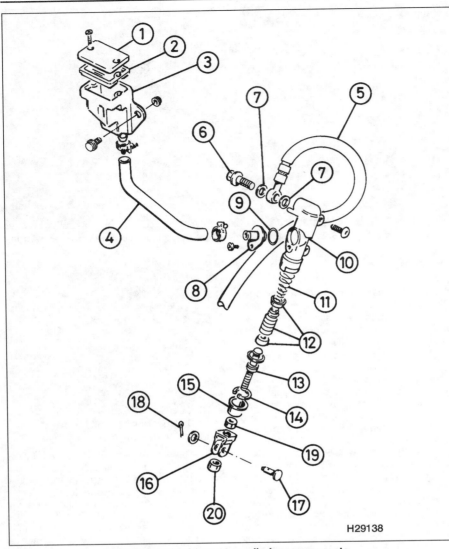

**9.6 Rear brake master cylinder components**

| | | |
|---|---|---|
| 1 Reservoir cover | 8 Reservoir hose | 14 Circlip |
| 2 Rubber diaphragm | elbow | 15 Rubber dust boot |
| 3 Reservoir | 9 O-ring | 16 Clevis |
| 4 Reservoir hose | 10 Master cylinder | 17 Clevis pin |
| 5 Brake hose | 11 Spring | 18 Split pin |
| 6 Banjo bolt | 12 Piston assembly | 19 Locknut |
| 7 Sealing washer | 13 Pushrod | 20 Clevis nut |

illustration 7.3). Wrap a clean plastic bag tightly around the end to prevent dirt entering the system. Discard the sealing washers as new ones must be fitted on reassembly.

**5** Undo the bolts securing the heel plate and master cylinder to the footrest bracket and remove the master cylinder (see illustration 9.2a).

### Overhaul

**6** Undo the screw securing the fluid reservoir hose union and detach the union from the master cylinder (see illustration). Discard the O-ring as a new one must be fitted on reassembly. Inspect the reservoir hose for cracks or splits and renew it if necessary.

**7** Mark the position of the (upper) clevis locknut on the pushrod, then loosen the locknut and thread the clevis nut, clevis and locknut off the pushrod (see illustration).

**8** Carefully remove the dust boot from the master cylinder to reveal the pushrod retaining circlip (see illustration).

**9** Depress the pushrod and use circlip pliers to remove the circlip (see illustration). Slide out the pushrod, piston assembly and spring, noting how they fit (see illustration 9.6). If they are difficult to remove, apply low pressure compressed air to the brake fluid outlet. Lay the parts out in the proper order to prevent confusion during reassembly.

**10** Clean all parts with clean brake fluid of the specified type. If compressed air is available, blow it through the fluid galleries to ensure they are clear (make sure the air is filtered and unlubricated).

*Caution: Do not, under any circumstances, use a petroleum-based solvent to clean brake parts.*

**11** Check the master cylinder bore for corrosion, scratches, nicks and score marks. If the necessary measuring equipment is available, compare the dimensions of the piston and bore to those given in the Specifications at the beginning of this Chapter. If damage or wear is evident, the master cylinder must be renewed. If the master cylinder is in poor condition, then the caliper should be checked as well.

**12** The dust boot, circlip, piston components and spring are all included in the master cylinder rebuild kit. Use all of the new parts,

9.7 Hold the clevis to loosen the locknut

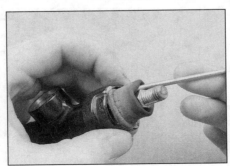
9.8 Remove the boot from the pushrod . . .

9.9 . . . then depress the piston and remove the circlip

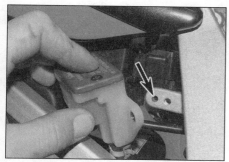

**9.22 Pin on the back of the reservoir locates in hole (arrowed)**

**10.2 Flex the brake hoses and check for cracks, bulges and leaking fluid**

**10.6 Fit a new sealing washer on each side of the banjo fitting**

regardless of the apparent condition of the old ones. If the seal and cup are not already on the piston, fit them according to the layout of the old piston assembly.

13 Install the spring in the master cylinder so that its tapered end faces out towards the piston.

14 Lubricate the piston assembly with clean brake fluid. Install the assembly into the master cylinder, making sure it is the correct way round. Make sure the lips on the piston seal do not turn inside out when they are slipped into the bore.

15 Install the pushrod, then depress the pushrod and install the new circlip, making sure it locates properly in its groove **(see illustration 9.9)**.

16 Install the dust boot, making sure the lip is seated correctly in the groove **(see illustration 9.8)**.

17 Fit a new O-ring onto the fluid reservoir hose union, then press the union into the master cylinder and secure it with the screw.

### Installation

18 Install the (upper) clevis locknut, the clevis and the clevis nut onto the master cylinder pushrod end. Position the clevis as noted on removal, but leave the locknut finger-tight.

19 Locate the master cylinder on the inside of the footrest bracket, then install the heel plate and mounting bolts and tighten the bolts to the torque setting specified at the beginning of this Chapter.

20 Align the brake pedal with the master cylinder pushrod clevis and install the clevis pin. Fit the washer and secure it with a new split pin **(see illustration 9.1)**. If the clevis position on the pushrod was disturbed during overhaul, check the brake pedal height (see Chapter 1, Section 12). Tighten the clevis locknut securely.

21 Align the brake hose as noted on removal and connect the hose to the master cylinder, using a new sealing washer on each side of the banjo fitting **(see illustration 9.4)**; bend the split pin ends securely. Tighten the banjo bolt to the torque setting specified at the beginning of this Chapter.

22 Install the fluid reservoir on the frame, making sure the pin on the back of the reservoir locates in the hole in the frame

bracket **(see illustration)**. Ensure that the hose is correctly routed behind the frame tube and install the retaining bolt finger-tight. Connect the hose to the union on the master cylinder and secure it with the clip **(see illustration 9.3)**. Check that the hose is secured with a clip at the reservoir end as well. If the clips have weakened, use new ones.

23 Fill the fluid reservoir with new DOT 4 brake fluid (see *Daily (pre-ride) checks*). Refer to Section 11 and bleed the air from the system.

24 Check the operation of the brake carefully before riding the motorcycle.

### 10 Brake hoses and fittings – inspection and renewal

### Inspection

1 Brake hose condition should be checked regularly and the hoses renewed at the specified interval (see Chapter 1).

2 Twist and flex the rubber hoses while looking for cracks, bulges and seeping hydraulic fluid **(see illustration)**. Check extra carefully around the areas where the hoses connect with the banjo fittings, as these are common areas for hose failure.

3 Inspect the banjo fittings connected to the brake hoses. If the fittings are rusted, scratched or cracked, fit new hoses.

### Renewal

4 The brake hoses have banjo fittings on each end. Cover the surrounding area with plenty of rags and unscrew the banjo bolt at each end of the hose, noting the alignment of the fitting with the master cylinder or brake caliper **(see illustrations 5.5 and 7.2)**. Free the hose from any clips or guides and remove it, noting its routing. Discard the sealing washers. **Note:** *Do not operate the brake lever or pedal while a brake hose is disconnected.*

5 Position the new hose, making sure it isn't twisted or otherwise strained, and ensure that it is correctly routed through any clips or guides and is clear of all moving components.

6 Check that the fittings align correctly, then install the banjo bolts, using new sealing

washers on both sides of the fittings **(see illustration)**. Tighten the banjo bolts to the torque setting specified at the beginning of this Chapter.

7 Flush the old brake fluid from the system, refill with new DOT 4 brake fluid (see *Daily (pre-ride) checks*) and bleed the air from the system (see Section 11).

8 Check the operation of the brakes before riding the motorcycle.

### 11 Brake system – bleeding and fluid change

### Bleeding

1 Bleeding the brakes is simply the process of removing air from the brake fluid reservoir, the hose and the brake caliper. Bleeding is necessary whenever a brake system hydraulic connection is loosened, after a component or hose is renewed, or when the master cylinder or caliper is overhauled. Leaks in the system may also allow air to enter, but leaking brake fluid will reveal their presence and warn you of the need for repair.

2 To bleed the brakes, you will need some new DOT 4 brake fluid, a length of clear vinyl or plastic hose, a small container partially filled with clean brake fluid, some rags and a spanner to fit the brake caliper bleed valve **(see illustration)**.

3 Cover the fuel tank and other painted components to prevent damage in the event that brake fluid is spilled.

**11.2 Set-up for bleeding the brakes**

**11.6 Keep the fluid level topped-up during the procedure**

4 Refer to 'Daily (pre-ride) checks' and remove the reservoir cover or cap, diaphragm plate (front brake) and diaphragm and slowly pump the brake lever (front brake) or pedal (rear brake) a few times, until no air bubbles can be seen floating up from the holes in the bottom of the reservoir. This bleeds the air from the master cylinder end of the line. Temporarily refit the reservoir cap.

5 Pull the dust cap off the bleed valve then attach one end of the clear vinyl or plastic hose to the bleed valve and submerge the other end in the clean brake fluid in the container (see illustration 11.2). When bleeding the front brakes, bleed the right-hand brake first. **Note:** To avoid damaging the bleed valve during the procedure, loosen it and then tighten it temporarily with a ring spanner before attaching the hose. With the hose attached, the valve can then be opened and closed with an open-ended spanner.

6 Check the fluid level in the reservoir. Do not allow the fluid level to drop below the lower mark during the procedure (see illustration).

7 Carefully pump the brake lever or pedal three or four times and hold it in (front) or down (rear) while opening the bleed valve. When the valve is opened, brake fluid will flow out of the caliper into the clear tubing, and the lever will move toward the handlebar, or the pedal will move down. If there is air in the system there will be air bubbles in the brake fluid coming out of the caliper.

8 Tighten the bleed valve, then release the brake lever or pedal gradually. Top-up the reservoir and repeat the process until no air bubbles are visible in the brake fluid leaving

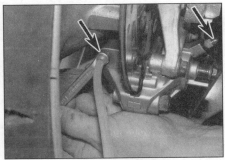

**11.8 Two bleed valves (arrowed) are fitted to the rear caliper**

the caliper, and the lever or pedal is firm when applied. On completion, disconnect the hose, then tighten the bleed valve to the torque setting specified at the beginning of this Chapter and install the dust cap. If bleeding the front brakes, start with the right-hand caliper then go on to bleed air from the left-hand caliper. If bleeding the rear brake, bleed both sides of the caliper (see illustration).

> **HAYNES HiNT**
> *If it is not possible to produce a firm feel to the lever or pedal, the fluid may be aerated. Let the brake fluid in the system stabilise for a few hours and then repeat the procedure when the tiny bubbles in the system have settled out.*

9 Top-up the reservoir, then install the diaphragm, diaphragm plate (front brake) and cap (see Daily (pre-ride) checks). Wipe up any spilled brake fluid. Check the entire system for fluid leaks.

10 Check the operation of the brakes before riding the motorcycle.

### Fluid change

11 Changing the brake fluid is a similar process to bleeding the brakes and requires the same materials plus a suitable tool for siphoning the fluid out of the reservoir. Also ensure that the container is large enough to take all the old fluid when it is flushed out of the system.

12 Follow Steps 3 and 5, then remove the reservoir cap, diaphragm plate (front brake) and diaphragm and siphon the old fluid out of the reservoir. Fill the reservoir with new brake fluid, then carefully pump the brake lever or pedal three or four times and hold it in (front) or down (rear) while opening the bleed valve. When the valve is opened, brake fluid will flow out of the caliper into the clear tubing, and the lever will move toward the handlebar, or the pedal will move down.

13 Tighten the bleed valve, then release the brake lever or pedal gradually. Keep the reservoir topped-up with new fluid to above the LOWER level at all times or air may enter the system and greatly increase the length of the task. Repeat the process until new fluid can be seen emerging from the bleed valve.

> **HAYNES HiNT**
> *Old brake fluid is invariably much darker in colour than new fluid, making it easy to see when all old fluid has been expelled from the system.*

14 Disconnect the hose, then tighten the bleed valve to the specified torque setting and install the dust cap.

15 Top-up the reservoir, then install the diaphragm, diaphragm plate (front brake) and cap (see Daily (pre-ride) checks). Wipe up any spilled brake fluid. Check the entire system for fluid leaks.

16 Check the operation of the brakes before riding the motorcycle.

## 12 Wheels – inspection and repair

1 In order to carry out a proper inspection of the wheels, it is necessary to support the bike upright so that the wheel being inspected is raised off the ground. Position the motorcycle on an auxiliary stand. Clean the wheels thoroughly to remove mud and dirt that may interfere with the inspection procedure or mask defects. Make a general check of the wheels (see Chapter 1) and tyres (see Daily (pre-ride) checks).

2 Attach a dial gauge to the fork or the swingarm and position its tip against the side of the wheel rim. Spin the wheel slowly and check the axial (side-to-side) runout of the rim (see illustration).

3 In order to accurately check radial (out of round) runout with the dial gauge, remove the wheel from the machine, and the tyre from the wheel. With the axle clamped in a vice and the dial gauge positioned on the top of the rim, the wheel can be rotated to check the runout (see illustration 12.2).

4 An easier, though slightly less accurate, method is to attach a stiff wire pointer to the fork or the swingarm and position the end a fraction of an inch from the wheel rim where the wheel and tyre join. If the wheel is true, the distance from the pointer to the rim will be constant as the wheel is rotated. **Note:** If wheel runout is excessive, check the wheel bearings very carefully before renewing the wheel.

5 The wheels should also be inspected for cracks, flat spots on the rim and other damage. Look very closely for dents in the area where the tyre bead contacts the rim. Dents in this area may prevent complete sealing of the tyre against the rim, which leads to deflation of the tyre over a period of time. If damage is evident, or if runout in either direction is excessive, the wheel will have to be renewed. Never attempt to repair a damaged cast alloy wheel.

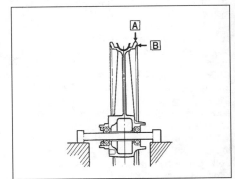

**12.2 Check the wheel for radial (out-of-round) runout (A) and axial (side-to-side) runout (B)**

## 13 Wheels – alignment check

1 Misalignment of the wheels due to a bent frame or forks can cause strange and possibly serious handling problems. If the frame or forks are at fault, repair by a frame specialist or renewal are the only options.

2 To check wheel alignment you will need an assistant, a length of string or a perfectly straight piece of wood and a ruler. A plumb bob or spirit level for checking that the wheels are vertical will also be required.

3 In order to make a proper check of the wheels it is necessary to support the bike in an upright position, using an auxiliary stand. First ensure that the chain adjuster markings coincide on each side of the swingarm (see Chapter 1, Section 10). Next, measure the

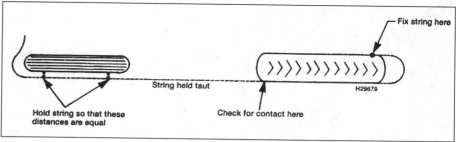

13.5 Wheel alignment check using string

width of both tyres at their widest points. Subtract the smaller measurement from the larger measurement, then divide the difference by two. The result is the amount of offset that should exist between the front and rear tyres on both sides of the machine.

4 If a string is used, have your assistant hold one end of it about halfway between the floor and the rear axle, with the string touching the back edge of the rear tyre sidewall.

5 Run the other end of the string forward and pull it tight so that it is roughly parallel to the floor (see illustration). Slowly bring the string into contact with the front edge of the rear tyre sidewall, then turn the front wheel until it is parallel with the string. Measure the distance from the front tyre sidewall to the string.

6 Repeat the procedure on the other side of the motorcycle. The distance from the front tyre sidewall to the string should be equal on both sides.

7 As previously mentioned, a perfectly straight length of wood or metal bar may be substituted for the string (see illustration).

8 If the distance between the string and tyre is greater on one side, or if the rear wheel appears to be out of alignment, have your machine checked by a Suzuki dealer or frame specialist.

9 If the front-to-back alignment is correct, the wheels still may be out of alignment vertically.

10 Using a plumb bob or spirit level, check the rear wheel to make sure it is vertical. To do this, hold the string of the plumb bob against the tyre upper sidewall and allow the weight to settle just off the floor. If the string touches both the upper and lower tyre sidewalls and is perfectly straight, the wheel is vertical. If it is not, adjust the stand until it is.

11 Once the rear wheel is vertical, check the front wheel in the same manner. If both wheels are not perfectly vertical, the frame and/or major suspension components are bent.

## 14 Front wheel – removal and installation

### Removal

Note: All K2 models require a 24 mm Allen socket to unscrew and tighten the axle.

1 Remove the fairing side panels (see Chapter 8). Using an auxiliary stand, support the motorcycle securely in an upright position with the front wheel off the ground.

2 Displace the front brake calipers (see Section 3). Note: Do not operate the brake lever while the calipers are off the disc.

3 Loosen the clamp bolts on the bottom of the right-hand fork. Support the wheel, then unscrew the axle and withdraw it from the right-hand side (see illustration). Note: Draw the wheel to the right with the axle so that it comes off the axle holder in the bottom of the left-hand fork.

4 Remove the wheel from between the forks. If required, loosen the pinch bolts on the bottom of the left-hand fork and withdraw the axle holder (see illustration).

Caution: Don't lay the wheel down and allow it to rest on the disc – the disc could become warped. Set the wheel on wood blocks so the wheel rim supports the weight of the wheel.

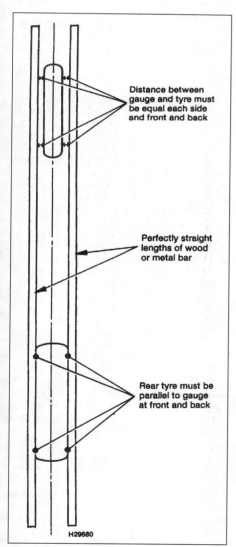

13.7 Wheel alignment check using a straight-edge

Distance between gauge and tyre must be equal each side and front and back

Perfectly straight lengths of wood or metal bar

Rear tyre must be parallel to gauge at front and back

14.3 Loosen the clamp bolts (arrowed) then unscrew the axle from the right-hand side

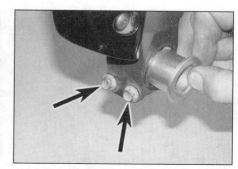

14.4 Loosen the clamp bolts and remove the axle holder on the left-hand side

7

14.10 Push the wheel to the left to locate the axle holder in the left-hand bearing seal (arrowed)

5 Clean the axle and remove any corrosion using steel wool. Check the axle for straightness by rolling it on a flat surface such as a piece of plate glass. If available, place the axle in V-blocks and check for runout using a dial gauge. If the axle is bent or the runout exceeds the limit specified at the beginning of this Chapter, renew it.

6 Wipe any old grease off the bearing seals and check the condition of the seals and the wheel bearings (see Section 16).

7 If removed, clean the axle holder and remove any corrosion with steel wool. The holder should be perfectly smooth where it locates in the fork.

### Installation

8 If removed, install the axle holder in the bottom of the left-hand fork and push it in so that its flanged rim is pressed against the fork.

15.2 Remove the axle nut and the washer (European models)

15.5 Support the wheel and withdraw the axle

Tighten the clamp bolts to the torque setting specified at the beginning of this Chapter, making sure the holder remains pressed against the fork (see illustration 14.4).

9 Apply a thin coat of grease to the axle and to the lips of the bearing seals.

10 Manoeuvre the wheel into position between the forks, making sure the directional arrow is pointing in the normal direction of rotation. Lift the wheel and slide the axle through from the right-hand side, and thread it into the axle holder (see illustration 14.3). Push the wheel to the left so that the inner end of the holder locates in the bearing seal, then tighten the axle finger-tight (see illustration).

11 Install the brake calipers (see Section 3), then tighten the axle to the specified torque setting.

12 Move the motorcycle off the stand, apply the front brake and pump the front forks a few times to settle all components in position.

13 Tighten the clamp bolts on the right-hand fork to the specified torque setting.

14 Install the fairing side panels (see Chapter 8).

15 Check the operation of the front brake before riding the motorcycle.

### 15 Rear wheel – removal and installation

### Removal

**Note:** *The following procedure describes the axle being inserted from the right-hand side of*

15.4 Remove the chain adjuster block

15.7 Remove the axle spacers from each side of the hub

*the wheel, this being the original position as supplied new. It may be found, however, 'that as shown on the machine photographed, the axle has been inserted from the opposite side.*

1 Using an auxiliary stand, support the motorcycle securely in an upright position with the rear wheel off the ground.

2 On European models, undo the axle nut and remove it, followed by the washer (see illustration).

3 On US and Canadian models, remove the split pin from the axle nut. Undo the axle nut and remove it.

4 Remove the chain adjuster block, noting how it fits (see illustration).

5 Support the wheel, then withdraw the axle and the right-hand adjuster block (see illustration). Lower the wheel out of the swingarm, making sure no strain is placed on the brake hose as the caliper lowers with it. **Note:** *Do not operate the brake pedal while the caliper is off the disc.*

6 Disengage the chain from the sprocket and draw the wheel back so the disc is clear of the caliper and remove the wheel. Note how the axle passes through the caliper mounting bracket. Secure the caliper to the swingarm with a cable tie to avoid straining the brake hose.

7 Remove the axle spacers from each side of the hub, noting how they fit (see illustration). Remove the chain adjuster block from the axle, noting how the flats on the axle head fit into the recess in the adjuster block.

**Caution: Don't lay the wheel down and allow it to rest on the disc or the sprocket – they could become warped. Set the wheel on wood blocks so the wheel rim supports the weight of the wheel. Do not operate the brake pedal with the wheel removed.**

8 Clean the axle and remove any corrosion using steel wool. Check the axle for straightness by rolling it on a flat surface such as a piece of plate glass. If available, place the axle in V-blocks and check for runout using a dial gauge. If the axle is bent or the runout exceeds the limit specified at the beginning of this Chapter, renew it.

9 Wipe all old grease off the bearing seals and check the condition of the seals and the wheel bearings (see Section 16).

### Installation

10 Ease the pistons a little way back into the brake caliper using hand pressure or a piece of wood on the pads as leverage. **Note:** *Take care not to contaminate the surface of the pads with grease.*

11 Apply a thin coat of grease to the lips of each bearing seal, to the inside and the inner faces of the axle spacers, and to the axle. Install the spacers into the hub (see illustration 15.7). Slide the right-hand chain adjuster block onto the axle, making sure it is fitted the right way round.

12 Manoeuvre the wheel into position between the ends of the swingarm and ease it forward so that the brake disc slides into the

**15.12 Check that the brake disc locates correctly in the caliper**

**15.13 Lift the chain onto the sprocket**

**15.14 Lift the wheel and install the axle**

caliper, making sure the pads sit squarely on each side of the disc **(see illustration)**.

**13** Engage the drive chain with the sprocket **(see illustration)**.

**14** Lift the wheel into position, making sure the caliper stays on the disc and the caliper bracket is correctly aligned with the wheel and the swingarm, and install the axle **(see illustration)**. Ensure the axle passes through the caliper bracket and both axle spacers. **Note:** *If you have difficulty installing the axle due to the tension of the drive chain, back off the chain adjusters (see Chapter 1).*

**15** Locate the right-hand chain adjuster block in the swingarm and the flats on the axle head in the recess in the adjuster block. Check that everything is correctly aligned, then fit the left-hand adjuster block, the washer (European models) and the axle nut. Tighten the nut finger-tight.

**16** Adjust the chain slack as described in Chapter 1.

**17** Tighten the axle nut to the torque setting specified at the beginning of this Chapter. On US and Canadian models, fit a new split pin through the nut castellations and hole in the axle and bend its ends securely.

**18** Operate the brake pedal several times to bring the pads into contact with the disc. Check the operation of the brake before riding the motorcycle.

## 16 Wheel bearings –
### inspection, removal and installation

**Caution:** *Don't lay the wheel down and allow it to rest on the disc or the sprocket – they could become warped. Set the wheel on wood blocks so the wheel rim supports the weight of the wheel, or keep the wheel upright. Don't operate the brake pedal with the wheel removed.*

**Note:** *Always renew the wheel bearings in sets, never individually. Avoid using a high pressure cleaner on the wheel bearing area.*

### Front wheel bearings

**1** Remove the wheel (see Section 14).

**2** Lever out the bearing seals from both sides of the hub using a flat-bladed screwdriver and a piece of wood. Take care not to damage the

hub **(see illustration)**. Discard the seals as new ones must be fitted on reassembly.

**3** Inspect the bearings – check that the inner race turns smoothly and that the outer race is a tight fit in the hub (see *Tools and Workshop Tips (Section 5)* in the Reference Section). **Note:** *Suzuki recommends that the bearings are not removed unless they are going to be renewed.*

**4** To remove the bearings, use a metal rod (preferably a brass punch) inserted through the centre of the bearing on one side of the hub, to tap evenly around the inner race of the bearing on the other side **(see illustrations)**. The bearing spacer will come out with the bearing.

**5** Turn the wheel over and drive out the remaining bearing using the same procedure.

**6** Thoroughly clean the hub area of the wheel with a suitable solvent and inspect the bearing seats for scoring and wear. If the seats are damaged, consult a Suzuki dealer before reassembling the wheel.

**7** Unless the new bearings are sealed, pack their open side with a suitable multi-purpose grease.

**8** The new bearings can be installed in the hub using a drawbolt arrangement or by using a bearing driver (see *Tools and Workshop Tips*). Ensure that the drawbolt washer or driver (as applicable) bears only on the outer edge of the race and does not contact the bearing seat.

**9** Install the left-hand bearing first, with the marked or sealed side facing outwards. Ensure the bearing is fitted squarely and all the way into its seat.

**10** Turn the wheel over, install the bearing spacer and then the other new bearing.

**11** Apply a smear of grease to the new seals, then press them into the hub, using a bearing driver or a suitable socket. Level the seals with the rim of the hub with a small block of wood **(see illustrations)**.

**16.2 Lever out the bearing seals**

**16.4a Drive out the wheel bearings . . .**

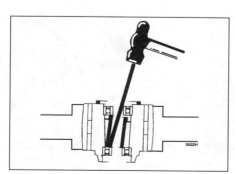

**16.4b . . . locating the drift as shown**

**16.11a Install new bearing seals . . .**

**7**

16.11b  . . . and level them in the hub

16.13  Remove the axle spacer

**12** Clean the brake discs using acetone or brake system cleaner, then install the wheel (see Section 14).

### Rear wheel bearings

**13** Remove the wheel (see Section 15) and lift the sprocket coupling out of the hub (see Chapter 6). If not already done, remove the axle spacer from the right-hand side of the hub **(see illustration)**.

**14** Lever out the bearing seal from the right-hand side of the hub using a flat-bladed screwdriver and a piece of wood. Take care not to damage the hub **(see illustration 16.2)**. Discard the seal as a new one should be fitted on reassembly.

**15** Inspect the bearings in both sides of the hub – check that the inner race turns smoothly and that the outer race is a tight fit in the hub (see *Tools and Workshop Tips (Section 5)* in the *Reference* section). **Note:** *Suzuki*

*recommends that the bearings are not removed unless they are going to be renewed.*
**16** To remove the bearings, use a metal rod (preferably a brass punch) inserted through the centre of the bearing on one side of the hub, to tap evenly around the inner race of the bearing on the other side **(see illustrations 16.4a and 16.4b)**. The bearing spacer will come out with the bearing.

**17** Turn the wheel over and drive out the remaining bearing using the same procedure.

**18** Thoroughly clean the hub area of the wheel with a suitable solvent and inspect the bearing seats for scoring and wear. If the seats are damaged, consult a Suzuki dealer before reassembling the wheel.

**19** Unless the new bearings are sealed, pack their open side with a suitable multi-purpose grease.

**20** The new bearings can be installed in the hub using a drawbolt arrangement or by using

a bearing driver (see *Tools and Workshop Tips*). Ensure that the drawbolt washer or driver (as applicable) bears only on the outer edge of the race and does not contact the bearing seat.

**21** Install the right-hand bearing first, with the marked or sealed side facing outwards. Ensure the bearing is fitted squarely and all the way into its seat.

**22** Turn the wheel over, install the bearing spacer and then the other new bearing.

**23** Apply a smear of grease to the new seal, then press it into the right-hand side of the hub, using a bearing driver or a suitable socket. Level the seal with the rim of the hub with a small block of wood **(see illustrations 16.11a and b)**.

**24** Clean the brake disc using acetone or brake system cleaner, then install the wheel (see Section 15).

### Sprocket coupling bearing

**25** Remove the wheel (see Section 15) and lift the sprocket coupling out of the hub (see Chapter 6). If not already done, remove the axle spacer from the outside of the sprocket coupling **(see illustration)**.

**26** Place the sprocket coupling on the work surface, sprocket side up, and use a suitably sized socket to drive out the bearing spacer **(see illustration)**.

**27** Lever out the bearing seal on the outside of the coupling using a flat-bladed screwdriver and a piece of wood **(see illustration)**. Take care not to damage the rim of the coupling. Discard the seal as a new one should be fitted on reassembly.

**28** Inspect the bearing – check that the inner race turns smoothly and that the outer race is a tight fit in the coupling (see *Tools and Workshop Tips (Section 5)* in the Reference Section). **Note:** *Suzuki recommends that the bearing is not removed unless it is going to be replaced with a new one.*

**29** Support the coupling on blocks of wood, sprocket side down, and drive the bearing out from the inside using a bearing driver or socket **(see illustration)**.

**30** Thoroughly clean the bearing seat with a suitable solvent and inspect the seat for scoring and wear. If the seat is damaged, consult a Suzuki dealer before reassembling the wheel.

**31** Unless the new bearing is sealed, pack it with a suitable multi-purpose grease.

**32** The new bearing can be installed in the coupling using a drawbolt arrangement or by using a bearing driver (see *Tools and Workshop Tips*). Ensure that the drawbolt washer or driver (as applicable) bears only on the outer edge of the race and does not contact the bearing seat. Ensure the bearing is fitted squarely and all the way into its seat.

**33** Apply a smear of grease to the new seal, then press it into the coupling, using a bearing driver or suitable socket. Level the seal with the rim of the coupling with a small block of wood **(see illustrations 16.11a and b)**.

16.25  Remove the axle spacer

16.26  Drive out the bearing spacer . . .

16.27  . . . then lever out the bearing seal

16.29  Drive the bearing out from the inside of the coupling

**16.34 Press the spacer into the bearing**

34 Place the coupling on the work surface, sprocket side down, and press the bearing spacer into the bearing **(see illustration)**. **Note:** *If the spacer is a tight fit in the bearing, temporarily install the left-hand axle spacer to prevent the bearing lifting off its seat.*
35 Check the sprocket coupling/rubber

dampers (see Chapter 6), then fit the sprocket coupling into the wheel and install the wheel (see Section 15).

### 17 Tyres –
general information and fitting

#### General information

1 The wheels fitted to all models are designed to take tubeless tyres only. Tyre sizes are given in the Specifications at the beginning of this chapter.
2 Refer to the *Daily (pre-ride) checks* listed at the beginning of this manual for tyre maintenance.

#### Fitting new tyres

3 When selecting new tyres, refer to the tyre information in the Owner's Handbook. Ensure

that front and rear tyre types are compatible, the correct size and correct speed rating; if necessary seek advice from a Suzuki dealer or tyre fitting specialist **(see illustration)**.
4 It is recommended that tyres are fitted by a motorcycle tyre specialist rather than attempted in the home workshop. This is particularly relevant in the case of tubeless tyres because the force required to break the seal between the wheel rim and tyre bead is substantial, and is usually beyond the capabilities of an individual working with normal tyre levers. Additionally, the specialist will be able to balance the wheels after tyre fitting.
5 Note that punctured tubeless tyres can in some cases be repaired. Repairs must be carried out by a motorcycle tyre fitting specialist. Suzuki advise that a repaired tyre should not be used at speeds above 50 mph (80 kmh) for the first 24 hours, and not above 80 mph (130 kmh) thereafter.

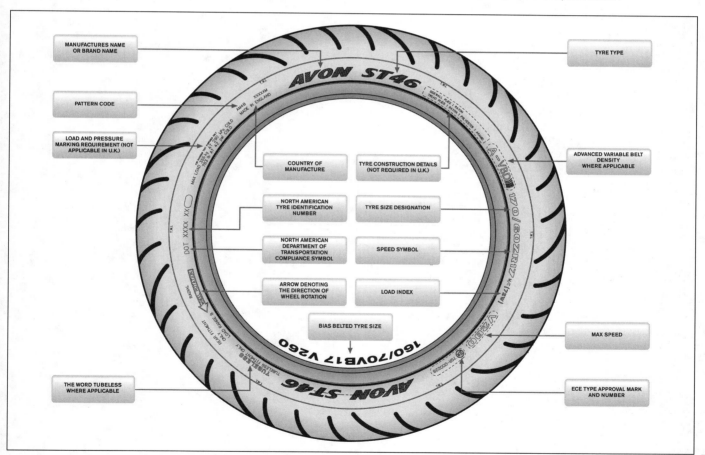

**17.3  Common tyre sidewall markings**

**7**

# Chapter 8
# Bodywork

## Contents

## Degrees of difficulty

| | | | | |
|---|---|---|---|---|
| **Easy,** suitable for novice with little experience  | **Fairly easy,** suitable for beginner with some experience  | **Fairly difficult,** suitable for competent DIY mechanic  | **Difficult,** suitable for experienced DIY mechanic  | **Very difficult,** suitable for expert DIY or professional  |

## 1 General information

This Chapter covers the procedures necessary to remove and install the bodywork. Since many service and repair operations on these motorcycles require the removal of the body panels, the procedures are grouped here and referred to from other Chapters.

In the case of damage to the bodywork, it is usually necessary to remove the broken component and replace it with a new (or used) one. The material that the body panels are composed of doesn't lend itself to conventional repair techniques. Note that there are however some companies that specialise in 'plastic welding' and there are a number of bodywork repair kits now available for motorcycles.

When attempting to remove any body panel, first study it closely, noting any fasteners and associated fittings, to be sure of returning everything to its correct place on installation. In some cases the aid of an assistant will be required when removing panels, to help avoid the risk of damage to paintwork. Once the evident fasteners have been removed, try to withdraw the panel as described but DO NOT FORCE IT – if it will not release, check that all fasteners have been removed and try again.

When installing a body panel, first study it closely, noting any fasteners and associated fittings removed with it, to be sure of returning everything to its correct place. Check that all fasteners are in good condition, including the trim clips and damping/rubber mounts; renew any faulty fasteners before the panel is reassembled. Check also that all mounting brackets are straight and repair or renew them if necessary before attempting to install the panel.

Tighten the fasteners securely, but be careful not to overtighten any of them or the panel may break (not always immediately) due to the uneven stress.

**8**

2.1a Rider's seat is retained by bolts at the front . . .

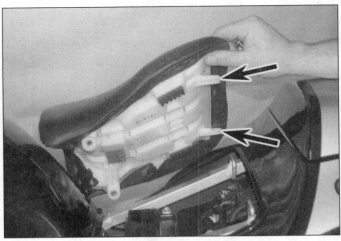

2.1b . . . and tabs (arrowed) at the back

2.2a Turn the key to unlock the seat . . .

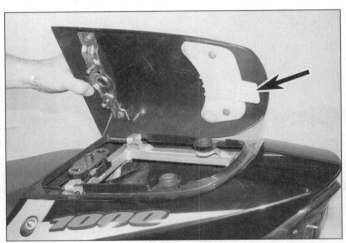

2.2b . . . then pull it forward to disengage the tab (arrowed)

## 2 Seats – removal and installation

### Removal

**1** To remove the rider's seat, first unscrew the bolts on each side at the front **(see illustration)**. Lift the front of the seat and draw it forward to disengage the tabs at the back, then remove the seat **(see illustration)**.

**2** To remove the passenger's seat, insert the ignition key into the seat lock located under the left-hand side of the seat cowling, and turn it clockwise to unlock the seat **(see illustration)**. Lift the front of the seat and draw it forward to disengage the tab at the back, then remove the seat **(see illustration)**. **Note:** A hard cover seat tail box may be fitted instead of the passenger's seat.

### Installation

**3** Installation is the reverse of removal, noting the following:
● Make sure the seat tabs are properly located.
● Press down on the front of the rider's seat to align the mounting bolt holes.
● Push down on the passenger's seat to engage the lock.

## 3 Seat cowling – removal and installation

### Removal

**1** Remove the seats (see Section 2).
**2** Undo the two screws securing each side of the seat cowling under the passenger's seat and the screw on each side at the rear of the cowling **(see illustrations)**. The front end of

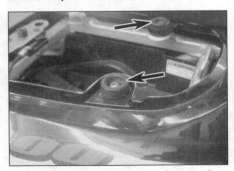

3.2a Remove the two bolts (arrowed) under the passenger's seat . . .

3.2b . . . and the bolt (arrowed) on each side at the rear

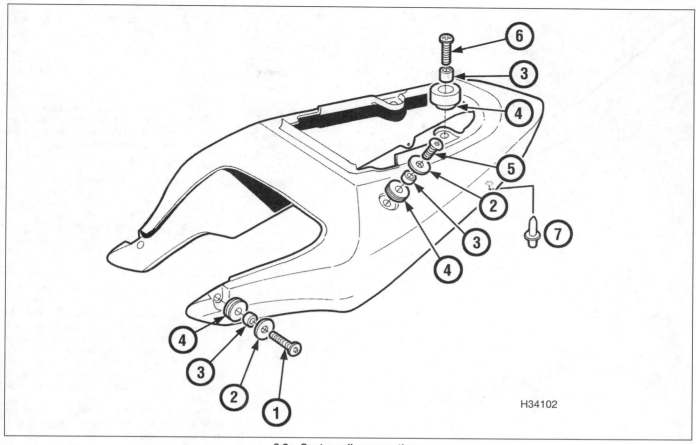

**3.2c  Seat cowling mountings**

1  Rider's seat mounting
   bolt
2  Washer

3  Collar
4  Grommet
5  Side mounting bolt

6  Rear mounting bolt
7  Trim clip or screw

the cowling on each side is secured by the rider's seat bolts which have already been removed. Take note how the seat rubbers and collars fit in the cowling **(see illustration)**.
3 Remove the two trim clips or screws which

retain the rear mudguard to the underside of the seat cowling, then draw the cowling rearwards to gain access to the tail/brake light wiring connector and disconnect it **(see illustrations)**. Lift the cowling off the bike.

### Installation

4 Installation is the reverse of removal. Check the operation of the tail/brake light before riding the motorcycle.

**3.3a  Draw the seat cowling towards the rear . . .**

**3.3b  . . . and disconnect the tail/brake light wiring connector (arrowed)**

**8**

4.1a Peel back the rubber boot . . .

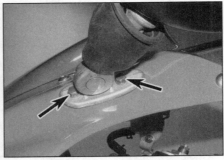

4.1b . . . to access the mounting bolts (arrowed)

## 4 Rear view mirrors – removal and installation

### Removal

**1** Peel back the rubber boot on the mirror stem to access the mounting bolts **(see illustrations)**. Undo the bolts and lift off the mirror. **Note:** *On some models the mounting bolts are fixed from the inside of the fairing panel.*

### Installation

**2** Installation is the reverse of removal.

## 5 Fairing panels – removal and installation

### Trim clips

**1** Two types of plastic trim clip are used. The most common type has a centre pin which is pushed into the body of the clip to allow it to be drawn out of the panel **(see illustration)**. To install the clip, first depress the pawls of the clip body so that the centre pin extends from the body. Now fit the clip into its hole, then push the centre pin in so that it is flush with the clip head. The clip should now be locked in place.
**2** The other type of trim clip (found on the underside of the fairing side panels) has a large circular head, with a removal slot in the body of the clip. Use a small, flat-bladed screwdriver to carefully ease the head out of the clip body, then draw the clip out of the panel. To install the clip, fit it into its hole with the head pulled out **(see illustration 5.3)**, then push the head in to lock the clip.

### Fairing side panels

#### Removal

**3** Undo the three trim clips securing the side panels together on the underside of the fairing **(see illustration)**.
**4** To remove the right-hand panel only, first remove the trim clip securing the back edge of the right inner panel to the lower inner panel **(see illustration 5.5a)**. Remove the ten

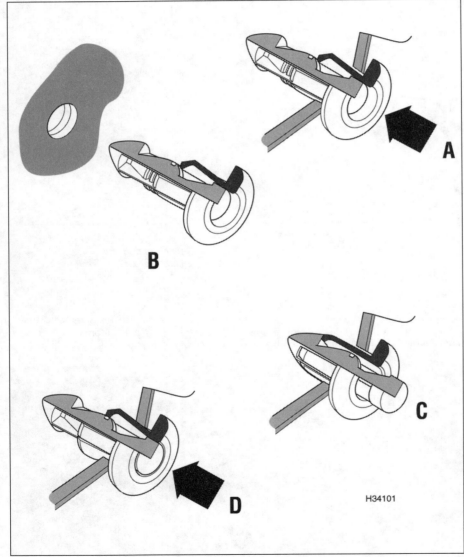

H34101

5.1 Centre pin type trim clip

*To remove, push the centre pin in (A) to allow the clip body to be withdrawn from the panel (B).*

*To install, depress the clip pawls to extend the centre pin and insert it into the panel (C), then press the centre pin in flush with the body of the clip to lock it in place (D)*

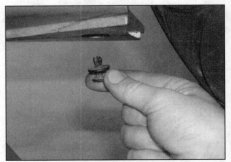

5.3 Undo the trim clips on the underside of the fairing

5.4a  Ten right-hand side panel screws (GSX-R600/750)

5.4b  Nine right-hand side panel screws (GSX-R1000)

(GSX-R600 and GSX-R750) or nine (GSX-R1000) screws securing the panel and carefully lower the panel until the turn signal wiring connector becomes accessible (see illustrations). Disconnect the connector and remove the panel, noting how it engages with

the fairing along its top edge and the other side panel along its bottom edge (see illustration).
5 To remove the left-hand panel only, first remove the trim clip securing the back edge of the left inner panel to the lower inner panel (see illustration). Remove the ten (GSX-R600

and GSX-R750) or nine (GSX-R1000) screws securing the panel and carefully lower the panel until the turn signal wiring connector becomes accessible (see illustrations). Disconnect the connector and remove the panel, noting how it engages with the fairing

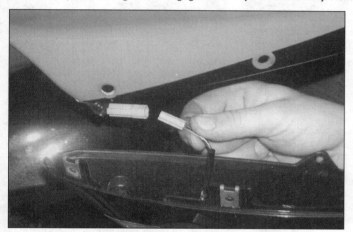

5.4c  Disconnect the turn signal wiring connector

5.5a  Detach the inner panel trim clip

5.5b  Ten left-hand side panel screws (GSX-R600/750)

5.5c  Nine left-hand side panel screws (GSX-R1000)

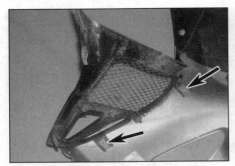

5.6 Centre panel is retained by two screws (arrowed)

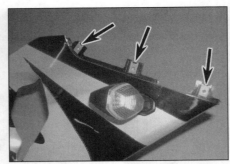

5.7a Make sure tabs (arrowed) along the top edge . . .

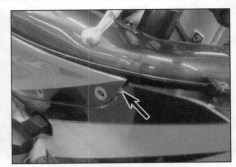

5.7b . . . and at the back of the top edge (arrowed) locate correctly

5.9 The lower inner panel is retained by six trim clips

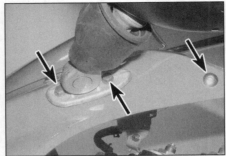

5.10 Rearmost screen screw and mirror mountings

5.11 Disconnect the headlight assembly and instrument cluster wiring connectors

along its top edge and the other side panel along its bottom edge.

6 If both panels are being removed, first remove the right-hand panel as described above. Now remove the left-hand panel, but do not remove the two lower front screws which secure the side panel to the centre panel. Remove the centre panel with the side panel **(see illustration)**.

## Installation

7 Installation is the reverse of removal. Make sure the tabs along the top edge and at the back of the top edge locate correctly with the fairing **(see illustrations)**, and the tabs on the bottom edge of the right-hand panel locate

into the slots in the bottom edge of the left-hand panel.

## *Fairing*

### Removal

8 Remove both fairing side panels (see Steps 3 to 6).

9 Remove the six trim clips securing the lower inner panel to the underside of the fairing and remove the panel **(see illustration)**.

10 Remove the rearmost screw securing the screen to the fairing on each side, then remove both rear view mirrors **(see illustration)**.

11 Trace the wiring from the headlight

assembly and the instrument cluster and disconnect it at the wiring connectors **(see illustration)**.

12 Carefully draw the fairing forward and release the pegs on the back of the headlight assembly from the grommets on the fairing bracket **(see illustration)**. Note how the air ducts locate in the fairing. Note the rubber cushions located in the rear view mirror mountings on the fairing bracket **(see illustration)**.

13 If required, undo the screws and washers securing the headlight assembly and instrument cluster inside the fairing, noting the wiring clips on the lower screws **(see illustrations)**.

14 If required, undo the remaining screws

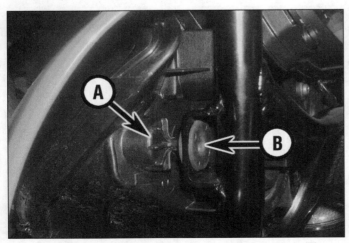

5.12a Note how the pegs (A) locate in the grommets (B)

5.12b Rubber cushion on rear view mirror mounting

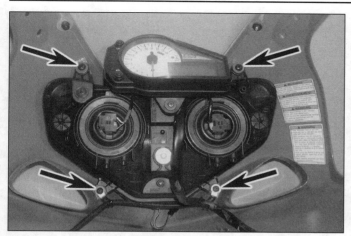

**5.13a Headlight assembly and instrument cluster is secured by four screws (arrowed)**

**5.13b Note the wiring clips on the lower screws**

securing the screen. Note the threads for the screen screws are retained in rubber wellnuts **(see illustrations)**.

**15** The fairing bracket is mounted on the steering head by two bolts **(see illustration)**. To remove the bracket, first remove the air ducts (see below).

**16** Undo any clips securing the wiring to the bracket, then undo the mounting bolts and remove the bracket.

### Installation

**17** Installation is the reverse of removal, noting the following:

● If removed, tighten the fairing bracket mounting bolts to 25 Nm.

● Ensure the lugs on the back of the headlight assembly locate correctly in the grommets on the fairing bracket.

● Ensure the wiring connectors are firmly connected and secured to the fairing bracket.

● Install the rubber cushions for the rear view mirror mountings before fitting the fairing.

### *Air ducts*

**18** Remove the fairing (see Steps 8 to 12).

**19** Release the wiring from the clips on the right hand air duct and unclip the fusebox from the top of the air duct **(see illustrations)**.

**20** Remove the trim clips securing the air ducts to the fairing bracket and remove the ducts **(see illustrations)**.

**5.14a Undo the screws (arrowed) to remove the screen**

**5.14b Screw threads are retained in rubber wellnuts**

**5.15 Fairing bracket is secured by two bolts (arrowed)**

**5.19a Release the wiring from the clips (arrowed) . . .**

**5.19b . . . and unclip the fusebox**

**5.20a Air ducts are secured by trim clips . . .**

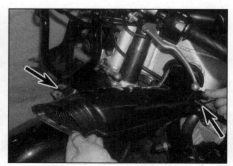

**5.20b . . . at both ends**

**8**

6.1a Unclip the brake hose assembly from the guides on the right-hand side . . .

6.1b . . . and back of the mudguard

## 6 Front mudguard – removal and installation

### Removal

1 Release the right-hand brake hose from the clip on the mudguard, then ease the clips on the left-hand hose out of the mudguard (see illustrations).
2 Unscrew the two bolts securing the mudguard to the front of each fork and remove the bolts and the washers (see illustration).
3 Unscrew the bolt securing the mudguard to the rear of each fork and remove the bolt, rubber bush and spacer (see illustration).

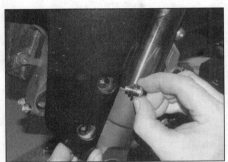

6.2 Mudguard is secured by two bolts on each side at the front . . .

4 Ease the mudguard forward and off the bike.

6.3 . . . and one bolt on each side at the rear

### Installation

5 Installation is the reverse of removal.

# Chapter 9
# Electrical system

## Contents

## Degrees of difficulty

| Easy, suitable for novice with little experience  | Fairly easy, suitable for beginner with some experience  | Fairly difficult, suitable for competent DIY mechanic  | Difficult, suitable for experienced DIY mechanic | Very difficult, suitable for expert DIY or professional |

## Specifications

### Battery
Capacity
    GSX-R600 . . . . . . . . . . . . . . . . . . . . . . . . . . . . . . . . . . . . . . . . . . 12V, 8Ah
    GSX-R750 and GSX-R1000 . . . . . . . . . . . . . . . . . . . . . . . . . . . . 12V, 10Ah
Battery voltage . . . . . . . . . . . . . . . . . . . . . . . . . . . . . . . . . . . . . . . 12.5V (min)

### Charging system
Battery current leakage . . . . . . . . . . . . . . . . . . . . . . . . . . . . . . . . . 3 mA (max)
Alternator stator coil resistance
    GSX-R600 . . . . . . . . . . . . . . . . . . . . . . . . . . . . . . . . . . . . . . . . . 0.2 to 1.5 ohms
    GSX-R750 . . . . . . . . . . . . . . . . . . . . . . . . . . . . . . . . . . . . . . . . . 0.2 to 0.5 ohms
    GSX-R1000 . . . . . . . . . . . . . . . . . . . . . . . . . . . . . . . . . . . . . . . . 0.2 to 0.9 ohms
Alternator output
    Regulated voltage output
        GSX-R600 and GSX-R1000 . . . . . . . . . . . . . . . . . . . . . . . . . 14.0 to 15.0V @ 5000 rpm
        GSX-R750 . . . . . . . . . . . . . . . . . . . . . . . . . . . . . . . . . . . . . . 13.5 to 15.0V @ 5000 rpm
    Unregulated voltage output (no-load) . . . . . . . . . . . . . . . . . . . . min. 65V AC @ 5000 rpm

### Starter motor
Starter relay resistance . . . . . . . . . . . . . . . . . . . . . . . . . . . . . . . . . 3.0 to 5.0 ohms

### Fuses
Main . . . . . . . . . . . . . . . . . . . . . . . . . . . . . . . . . . . . . . . . . . . . . . . . 30A
Headlight (high beam) . . . . . . . . . . . . . . . . . . . . . . . . . . . . . . . . . . 15A
Headlight (low beam) . . . . . . . . . . . . . . . . . . . . . . . . . . . . . . . . . . . 15A
Signal . . . . . . . . . . . . . . . . . . . . . . . . . . . . . . . . . . . . . . . . . . . . . . . 15A
Ignition . . . . . . . . . . . . . . . . . . . . . . . . . . . . . . . . . . . . . . . . . . . . . . 15A
Cooling fan . . . . . . . . . . . . . . . . . . . . . . . . . . . . . . . . . . . . . . . . . . 10A
Fuel pump . . . . . . . . . . . . . . . . . . . . . . . . . . . . . . . . . . . . . . . . . . . 10A

## Bulbs
Headlight
 Europe . . . . . . . . . . . . . . . . . . . . . . . . . . . . . . . . . . . . . . . . . 55/55W H7 halogen x 2
 US and Canada
  All Y and K1 . . . . . . . . . . . . . . . . . . . . . . . . . . . . . . . . . . . . 55/55W H7 halogen x 2
  All K2 models . . . . . . . . . . . . . . . . . . . . . . . . . . . . . . . . . . . 60/55W H4 halogen x 2
Sidelight (where applicable) . . . . . . . . . . . . . . . . . . . . . . . . . . . 5.0W
Brake/tail light . . . . . . . . . . . . . . . . . . . . . . . . . . . . . . . . . . . . . 21/5W x 2
Turn signal lights . . . . . . . . . . . . . . . . . . . . . . . . . . . . . . . . . . . 21W
Meter lights . . . . . . . . . . . . . . . . . . . . . . . . . . . . . . . . . . . . . . . LED

## Instrument panel
Fuel level resistor resistance . . . . . . . . . . . . . . . . . . . . . . . . . . . 66.5 to 73.5 ohms approx.

## Torque settings
Alternator rotor bolt
 GSX-R600 and GSX-R1000 . . . . . . . . . . . . . . . . . . . . . . . . . . 120 Nm
 GSX-R750 . . . . . . . . . . . . . . . . . . . . . . . . . . . . . . . . . . . . . . . 100 Nm
Alternator stator and wiring clamp bolts . . . . . . . . . . . . . . . . . 10 Nm
Oil pressure switch . . . . . . . . . . . . . . . . . . . . . . . . . . . . . . . . . 14 Nm

## 1 General information

All models have a 12-volt electrical system charged by a three-phase alternator with a separate regulator/rectifier.

The regulator maintains the charging system output within the specified range to prevent overcharging, and the rectifier converts the ac (alternating current) output of the alternator to dc (direct current) to power the lights and other components and to charge the battery. The alternator rotor is mounted on the left-hand end of the crankshaft.

The starter motor is mounted behind the cylinders. The starting system includes the motor, the battery, the relay, the clutch switch, gear position sensor and sidestand switch. If the engine kill switch is in the RUN position and the ignition (main) switch is ON, the starter relay allows the starter motor to operate if the transmission is in neutral (neutral light on) and the clutch lever is pulled in or, if the transmission is in gear, the side-stand is up and the clutch lever is pulled in.

**Note:** *Keep in mind that electrical parts, once purchased, cannot be returned. To avoid unnecessary expense, make very sure the faulty component has been positively identified before buying a renewal part.*

## 2 Electrical system – fault finding

⚠ *Warning: To prevent the risk of short circuits, the ignition (main) switch must always be OFF and the battery negative (-ve) terminal should be disconnected before any of the bike's other electrical components are disturbed. Don't forget to reconnect the terminal*

securely once work is finished or if battery power is needed for circuit testing.

1 A typical electrical circuit consists of an electrical component, the switches, relays, etc. related to that component and the wiring that connects the component to both the battery and the frame. To aid in locating a problem in any electrical circuit, refer to the wiring diagrams at the end of this Chapter.
2 Before tackling any troublesome electrical circuit, first study the wiring diagram (see end of Chapter) thoroughly to get a complete picture of what makes up that individual circuit. Trouble spots, for instance, can often be narrowed down by noting if other components related to that circuit are operating properly or not. If several components or circuits fail at one time, chances are the fault lies in the fuse or earth (ground) connection, as several circuits often are routed through the same fuse and earth (ground) connections.
3 Electrical problems often stem from simple causes, such as loose or corroded connections or a blown fuse. Prior to any electrical fault finding, always make a visual check of the fuse, wires and connections in the problem circuit. Intermittent failures can be especially frustrating, since you can't always duplicate the failure when it's convenient to test. In such situations, it is good practice to clean all connections in the affected circuit, whether or not they appear to be good. All the connections and wires should also be wiggled to check for looseness which can cause intermittent failure.
4 If testing instruments are going to be utilised, use the wiring diagram to plan where you will make the necessary connections in order to accurately pinpoint the trouble spot.
5 The basic tools needed for electrical fault finding include a battery and bulb test circuit, a continuity tester, a test light, and a jumper wire. A multimeter capable of reading volts, ohms and amps is also very useful as an alternative to the above, and is necessary for performing more extensive tests and checks.

 **HAYNES HiNT** *Refer to Fault Finding Equipment in the Reference Section for details of how to use electrical test equipment.*

## 3 Battery – removal, installation, inspection and maintenance

*Caution: Be extremely careful when handling or working around the battery. The electrolyte is very caustic and an explosive gas (hydrogen) is given off when the battery is charging.*

### Removal and installation

1 Remove the rider's seat (see Chapter 8).
2 Unscrew the negative (-ve) terminal bolt first and disconnect the lead from the battery **(see illustration)**. Lift up the red insulating cover to access the positive (+ve) terminal, then unscrew the bolt and disconnect the lead. Lift the battery from the bike **(see illustration)**.
3 On installation, clean the battery terminals and lead ends with a wire brush, knife or steel wool. Reconnect the leads, connecting the positive (+ve) terminal first.

3.2a Disconnect the negative lead (A) first, then the positive lead (B) . . .

3.2b . . . and lift the battery out

**Battery corrosion can be kept to a minimum by applying a layer of di-electric grease to the terminals after the leads have been connected.**

4 Install the seat (see Chapter 8).

## Inspection and maintenance

5 The battery fitted to the models covered in this manual is of the maintenance-free (sealed) type, therefore requiring no regular maintenance. However, the following checks should still be regularly performed.
6 Check the battery terminals and leads for tightness and corrosion. If corrosion is evident, clean the terminals as described in Step 3.
7 The battery case should be kept clean to prevent current leakage, which can discharge the battery over a period of time (especially when it sits unused). Wash the outside of the case with a solution of baking soda and water. Rinse the battery thoroughly, then dry it.
8 Look for cracks in the case and renew the battery if any are found. If acid has been spilled on the frame or battery box, neutralise it with a baking soda and water solution, dry it thoroughly, then touch up any damaged paint.
9 If the motorcycle sits unused for long periods of time, disconnect the leads from the battery terminals, negative (-ve) terminal first.

Refer to Section 4 and charge the battery once every month to six weeks.
10 The condition of the battery can be assessed by measuring the voltage at the battery terminals. Connect the voltmeter positive (+ve) probe to the battery positive (+ve) terminal and the negative (-ve) probe to the battery negative (-ve) terminal. When fully charged there should be more than 12.5 volts present. If the voltage falls below 12.0 volts the battery must be removed and recharged (see Section 4).

## 4 Battery – charging

**Caution: Be extremely careful when handling or working around the battery. The electrolyte is very caustic and an explosive gas (hydrogen) is given off when the battery is charging.**

1 Ensure the battery charger is suitable for charging a 12 volt battery.
2 Remove the battery (see Section 3). Connect the charger to the battery, making sure that the positive (+ve) lead on the charger is connected to the positive (+ve) terminal on the battery, and the negative (-ve) lead is connected to the negative (-ve) terminal.
3 Suzuki recommend that the battery is charged at a rate of 1.2 amps for 5 to 10 hours. Exceeding this figure can cause the battery to overheat, buckling the plates and rendering it useless. Few owners will have access to an expensive current controlled charger, so if a normal domestic charger is used check that after a possible initial peak, the charge rate falls to a safe level (**see illustration**). If the battery becomes hot during charging **stop**. Further charging will cause damage. **Note:** *In emergencies the battery can be charged at a maximum rate of 5.0 amps for a period of 1 hour. However, this is not recommended and the low amp charge is by far the safer method of charging the battery.*

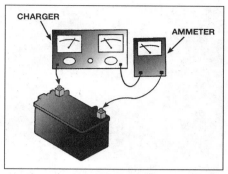

**4.3 If the charger has no built-in ammeter, connect one in series as shown. DO NOT connect the ammeter between the battery terminals or it will be ruined**

4 After charging, allow the battery to stand for 30 minutes, then measure its terminal voltage (see Section 3). If the voltage is below 12.5 volts, charge the battery again and repeat the voltage measuring process. If the voltage is still low, the battery is failing and should be renewed.
5 If the recharged battery discharges rapidly when left disconnected, it is likely that an internal short caused by physical damage or sulphation has occurred. A new battery will be required. A good battery will tend to lose its charge at about 1% per day.
6 Install the battery (see Section 3).
7 If the motorcycle is unused for long periods of time, charge the battery once every month to six weeks and leave it disconnected.

## 5 Fuses – check and renewal

1 The electrical system is protected by fuses of different ratings. The circuit fuses are housed in the fusebox, which is on the right-hand air duct in the fairing (**see illustration**). The main fuse is integral with the starter relay, which is located under the rider's seat (**see illustration**).

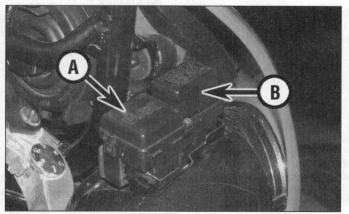

5.1a The fusebox (A) is on the right-hand air duct inside the fairing. Note the turn signal relay/side stand relay (B)

5.1b The main fuse (A) is in the starter relay (B). Note the spare fuse (C)

**5.2a  Unclip the fusebox lid to access the circuit fuses**

**2** To access the circuit fuses, unclip the fusebox lid **(see illustration)**. To access the main fuse, remove the rider's seat (see Chapter 8) and the starter relay cover **(see illustration)**.

**3** The fuses can be removed and checked visually. If you can't pull the fuse out with your fingertips, use a pair of needle-nose pliers. A blown fuse is easily identified by a break in the element **(see illustration)**. Each fuse is clearly marked with its rating and must only be renewed by a fuse of the correct rating. A spare fuse of each rating is housed in the fusebox, and a spare main fuse is housed in the bottom of the starter relay **(see illustration 5.1b)**. If a spare fuse is used, always renew it so that a spare of each rating is carried on the bike at all times.

> ⚠ **Warning: Never put in a fuse of a higher rating or bridge the terminals with any other substitute, however temporary it may be. Serious damage may be done to the circuit, or a fire may start.**

**4** If a fuse blows, be sure to check the wiring circuit very carefully for evidence of a short-circuit. Look for bare wires and chafed, melted or burned insulation. If the fuse is renewed before the cause is located, the new fuse will blow immediately.

**5** Occasionally a fuse will blow or cause an open-circuit for no obvious reason. Corrosion of the fuse ends and fusebox terminals may occur and cause poor fuse contact. If this happens, remove the corrosion with a wire brush or wire wool, then spray the fuse ends and terminals with electrical contact cleaner.

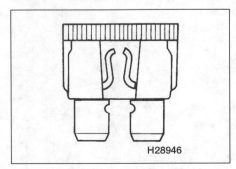

H28946

**5.3  A blown fuse can be identified by a break in the element**

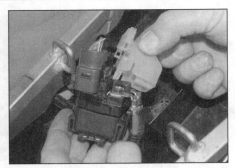

**5.2b  Remove the starter relay cover to access the main fuse**

### 6  Lighting system – check

**1** The battery provides power for operation of the headlight, tail light, brake light and instrument cluster lights. If none of the lights operate, always check battery voltage before proceeding. Low battery voltage indicates either a faulty battery or a defective charging system. Refer to Section 3 for battery checks and Section 29 for charging system tests. Also, check the condition of the fuses (see Section 5). When checking for a blown filament in a bulb, it is advisable to back up a visual check with a continuity test of the filament as it is not always apparent that a bulb has blown. When testing for continuity, remember that on tail light and turn signal bulbs it is often the metal body of the bulb that is the earth (ground). **Note:** *On US, Canadian and Australian models, the headlight and tail light are switched ON with the ignition (main) switch.*

### Headlight

**2** If the headlight fails to work, first check the bulb and the bulb terminals (see Section 7), and then the headlight high beam or low beam fuse (see Section 5). Next check for battery voltage on the supply side of the headlight wiring connector with a test light or multimeter. Refer to *Wiring Diagrams* at the end of this Chapter, then connect the negative (-ve) probe of the multimeter to earth (ground) and the positive (+ve) probe to first the high beam connector terminal (yellow wire) and then the low beam connector terminal (white wire) with the ignition switch and, where applicable, the light switch ON. Don't forget to select either high or low beam at the handlebar switch while conducting this test.

**3** If no voltage is indicated at either terminal, check the wiring between the headlight connector, light switches and the ignition switch, then check the switches themselves.

**4** If voltage is indicated, check for continuity between the white/black wiring connector terminal and earth (ground). If there is no continuity, check the earth (ground) circuit for a broken or poor connection.

### Sidelight (where applicable)

**5** If the sidelight fails to work, first check the bulb, the bulb terminals and wiring connector (see Section 7), then the signal fuse (see Section 5). Next check for voltage on the supply side of the sidelight wiring connector (brown wire), with the ignition switch and light switch ON.

**6** If no voltage is indicated, check the wiring between the connector, the light switch and the ignition switch, then check the switches themselves.

**7** If voltage is indicated, check for continuity between the white/black wiring connector terminal and earth (ground). If there is no continuity, check the earth (ground) circuit for a broken or poor connection.

### Tail light

**8** If the tail light fails to work, first check the bulb, the bulb terminals and the wiring connector (see Section 9), then the signal fuse (see Section 5). Next check for voltage on the supply side of the tail light wiring connector (brown wire) with the ignition switch and, where applicable, light switch ON.

**9** If no voltage is indicated, check the wiring between the connector, the light switch and the ignition switch, then check the switches themselves.

**10** If voltage is indicated, check for continuity between the wiring connector terminal on the tail light side of the wiring connector and the corresponding terminal in the bulbholder; no continuity indicates a break in the circuit. If continuity is present, check for continuity between the white/black wire terminal and earth (ground). If there is no continuity, check the earth (ground) circuit for a broken or poor connection.

### Brake light

**11** If the brake light fails to work, first check the bulb, the bulb terminals and the wiring connector (see Section 9), then the signal fuse (see Section 5). Next check for battery voltage on the supply side of the brake light wiring connector (white/black wire), with the brake lever pulled in or the pedal depressed.

**12** If no voltage is indicated, check the wiring between the connector, the brake light switches and the ignition switch, then check the brake light switches (see Section 14).

**13** If voltage is indicated, check for continuity between the wiring connector terminal on the brake light side of the wiring connector and the corresponding terminal in the bulbholder; no continuity indicates a break in the circuit. If continuity is present, check for continuity between the white/black wire terminal and earth (ground). If there is no continuity, check the earth (ground) circuit for a broken or poor connection

### Turn signal lights

**14** If one light fails to work, check the bulb and the bulb terminal first, then the wiring connector (see Section 11). If none of the turn signals work, first check the signal fuse.

**7.1a Disconnect the wiring connector . . .**

**7.1b . . . and remove the rubber cover**

**7.2a Release the retaining clip . . .**

15 If the fuse is good, see Section 13 for the turn signal circuit check.

### Instrument cluster and warning lights

16 The instrument cluster and warning lights are LEDs. If an LED fails, and a fault cannot be traced anywhere else in the system, a new instrument cluster will have to be fitted (see Section 15).

**7   Headlight bulb
      and sidelight bulb –
      renewal**

**Note:** *The headlight bulbs are of the quartz-halogen type. Do not touch the bulb glass as skin acids will shorten the bulb's service life. If the bulb is accidentally touched, it should be wiped carefully with a rag soaked in methylated spirit and dried before fitting.*

⚠ **Warning: Allow the bulbs time to cool before removing them if the headlight has just been on.**

### Headlight bulb

1 Disconnect the relevant wiring connector from the back of the headlight assembly and remove the rubber cover, noting how it fits **(see illustrations)**.

**7.2b . . . and withdraw the bulbholder**

2 Release the bulb retaining clip, noting how it fits, then remove the bulbholder and bulb. Pull the bulb out of the bulbholder **(see illustrations)**.
3 Fit the new bulb into the bulbholder, bearing in mind the information in the **Note** above. Make sure the tabs on the bulb fit correctly in the slots in the bulb housing, and secure the bulbholder in position with the retaining clip **(see illustration)**.
4 Install the rubber cover, making sure it is correctly seated and with the 'TOP' mark at the top, and connect the wiring connector.
5 Check the operation of the headlight bulbs.

**7.2c Pull the bulb out of the bulbholder**

**HAYNES HiNT** *Always use a paper towel or dry cloth when handling new bulbs to prevent injury if the bulb should break and to increase bulb life.*

### Sidelight bulb (where applicable)

6 Remove the six trim clips securing the lower inner panel to the underside of the fairing and remove the panel **(see illustration)**. Refer to Chapter 8, Section 5 for details of how to release the trim clips.

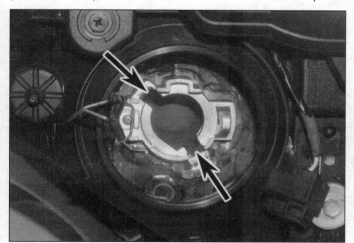

**7.3 Tabs on the bulb fit into the slots (arrowed)**

**7.6 Fairing lower inner panel is retained by six trim clips (arrowed)**

**7.7a  Twist the bulbholder and pull it out**

7  Twist the bulbholder anti-clockwise and pull it out of its socket in the base of the headlight assembly, then carefully pull the bulb out of the holder **(see illustrations)**.

8  Check that the contacts inside the bulbholder are clean and free from corrosion. Install the new bulb in the bulbholder, then press the holder into its socket in the headlight and twist it clockwise.

9  Check the operation of the sidelight, then fit the fairing lower inner panel (see Chapter 8).

## 8  Headlight assembly – removal and installation

### Removal

1  Remove the fairing (see Chapter 8).

2  Undo the screws and washers securing the headlight assembly and instrument cluster

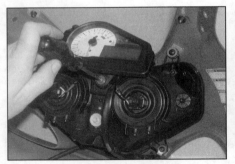

**8.3  Undo the screw to detach the instrument cluster**

**9.1b  . . . and remove the lens**

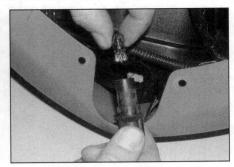

**7.7b  Pull the bulb out of the holder**

inside the fairing, noting the wiring clips on the lower screws (see Chapter 8, Section 5).

3  If required, undo the screw securing the instrument cluster to the headlight assembly, then pull the cluster off. Note how the pegs on the back of the cluster engage the grommets in brackets on the headlight assembly **(see illustration)**. Pull back the boot on the instrument cluster wiring connector and disconnect the connector (see Section 15).

### Installation

4  Installation is the reverse of removal, noting the following:

● Ensure the pegs on the instrument cluster are pressed firmly into the grommets.

● Ensure the wiring clips are installed on the headlight assembly screws.

● Check the operation of the headlight and sidelight.

● Check the headlight aim (see Chapter 1).

**9.1a  Undo the screws . . .**

**9.2  Push in and twist the bulb to remove it**

## 9  Tail/brake light bulbs – renewal

1  Remove the two screws securing the tail light lens and remove the lens, noting how it fits **(see illustrations)**.

2  Push the bulb into the holder and twist it anti-clockwise to remove it **(see illustration)**.

3  Check the socket terminals for corrosion and clean them if necessary. Line up the pins of the new bulb with the slots in the socket, then push the bulb in and turn it clockwise until it locks into place. **Note:** *The pins on the bulb are offset so it can only be installed one way. It is a good idea to use a paper towel or dry cloth when handling the new bulb to prevent injury if the bulb should break and to increase bulb life.*

4  Install the lens and tighten the screws securely, but take care not to overtighten them.

5  Check the operation of the brake/tail light bulbs.

## 10  Tail light assembly – removal and installation

### Removal

1  Remove the seat cowling (see Chapter 8).

2  Remove the screws securing the tail light assembly and carefully withdraw it from the seat cowling **(see illustration)**.

### Installation

3  Installation is the reverse of removal. Check the operation of the brake/tail light bulbs.

## 11  Turn signal bulbs – renewal

1  Remove the screw securing the turn signal lens and remove the lens, noting how it fits **(see illustration)**.

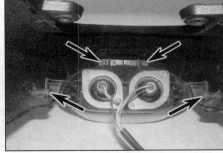

**10.2  Screws (arrowed) secure tail light assembly**

**11.1 Undo the screw (arrowed) to remove the lens**

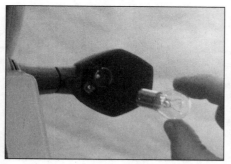

**11.2 Push in and twist the bulb anti-clockwise to remove it**

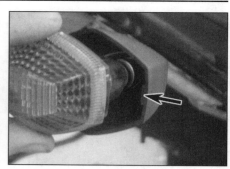

**11.4 Tab (arrowed) fits in slot in side of lens**

2  Push the bulb into the socket and twist it anti-clockwise to remove it **(see illustration)**.
3  Check the terminal inside the socket for corrosion and clean it if necessary. Line up the pins of the new bulb with the slots in the socket, then push the bulb in and turn it clockwise until it locks into place.
4  Fit the lens into the holder, locating the slot in the side of the lens on the tab in the housing, then install the screw **(see illustration)**.

*If the socket contacts are dirty or corroded, scrape them clean and spray with electrical contact cleaner before a new bulb is installed.*

### 12  Turn signal assemblies – removal and installation

#### Front

1  Remove the left or right-hand fairing side panel as required (see Chapter 8).
2  Undo the nut on the inside of the fairing panel securing the signal assembly and remove the backing plate, noting how it fits **(see illustration)**.
3  Withdraw the signal assembly from the fairing, noting how it fits. Take care not to snag the wiring as you pull it through.
4  Installation is the reverse of removal. Check the operation of the turn signals.

#### Rear

5  Remove the passenger seat (see Chapter 8). Trace the wiring back from the turn signal and disconnect it at the connector, located inside the seat cowling.
6  Unscrew the nut securing the turn signal assembly on the inside of the mudguard, and remove the backing plate, noting how it fits **(see illustration)**.
7  Withdraw the signal assembly from the mudguard, noting how it fits. Take care not to snag the wiring as you pull it through.
8  Installation is the reverse of removal. Check the operation of the turn signals.

### 13  Turn signal circuit – check

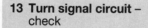

1  Most turn signal problems are the result of a burned out bulb or corroded socket. This is especially true when the turn signals function properly in one direction, but not in the other. Check the bulbs and the sockets (see Section 11) and the wiring connectors. Also, check the signal fuse (see Section 5) and the switch (see Section 19).
2  The battery provides power for operation of the turn signal lights, so if they do not operate, also check the battery voltage. Low battery voltage indicates either a faulty battery or a defective charging system. Refer to Section 3 for battery checks and Section 29 for charging system tests.
3  If the all the above are good, check the

integral turn signal/sidestand relay which is located on the right-hand air duct in the fairing, next to the fusebox **(see illustration 5.1a)**.
4  Make sure the ignition is OFF. Pull the relay off its connector **(see illustration)**. Turn the ignition ON, then connect the positive (+ve) probe of a voltmeter to the orange/green wire terminal in the relay connector and the negative (-ve) probe to a good earth (ground) and check for battery voltage. Turn the ignition OFF.
5  If there is no voltage, check the wiring from the connector to the ignition (main) switch for continuity.
6  If there is voltage, install the relay and use a test light to check the output from the light blue wire terminal on the relay. Ensure the test light is earthed and turn the ignition ON; the light should flash. If the light does not flash, renew the relay.
7  If the light flashes, check the wiring between the relay, the turn signal switch and the turn signal lights.

### 14  Brake light switches – check and renewal

#### Circuit check

1  Before checking any electrical circuit, check the bulb (see Section 9) and signal fuse (see Section 5). In the case of the rear brake, check that the problem isn't caused by incorrect adjustment (see Step 10).

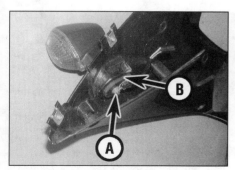

**12.2 Undo the nut (A) and remove the backing plate (B)**

**12.6 Undo the nut (arrowed) and withdraw the signal assembly**

**13.4 Pull the relay off its connector**

**14.2a Location of the front brake light switch**

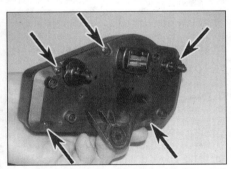

**14.2b Location of the rear brake light switch**

**2** The front brake light switch is mounted on the underside of the brake master cylinder **(see illustration)**. The rear brake light switch is mounted on the inside of the right-hand heel plate **(see illustration)**.

**3** Using a multimeter or test light connected to a good earth (ground), turn the ignition ON and check for voltage at the terminals on the brake light switch wiring connector(s). **Note:** *Do not disconnect the wiring connectors for this test.*

**4** There should be voltage on the supply wire terminal and zero on the other with the lever/pedal at rest. If there's no voltage present at either, check the wiring between the switch and the signal fuse (see the *Wiring Diagrams* at the end of this Chapter).

**5** If there is voltage at the supply wire terminal of the switch, touch the test probe to the other terminal (white/black wire), then pull the brake lever in or depress the brake pedal. If no reading is obtained or the test light doesn't

light up, renew the switch.

**6** If a reading is obtained or the test light does light up, yet the brake light still does not come on, check the wiring between the switch and the brake light bulb (see the *Wiring Diagrams* at the end of this Chapter).

### Switch renewal

#### Front brake switch

**7** The switch is mounted on the underside of the brake master cylinder. Disconnect the wiring connectors from the switch **(see illustration 14.2a)**.

**8** Undo the screw securing the switch to the bottom of the master cylinder and remove the switch.

**9** Installation is the reverse of removal. The switch isn't adjustable.

#### Rear brake switch

**10** The switch is mounted on the inside of the

right-hand heel plate **(see illustration 14.2b)**. Pull up the rubber boot and disconnect the wiring connector from the switch.

**11** Detach the lower end of the switch spring from the brake pedal, then hold the adjusting nut and unscrew and remove the switch.

**12** Installation is the reverse of removal. Make sure the brake light is activated just before the rear brake pedal takes effect. If adjustment is necessary, hold the switch and turn the adjusting nut until the brake light is activated as required.

## 15 Instrument cluster – removal and installation

### Removal

**1** Remove the fairing (see Chapter 8).

**2** Undo the screw securing the instrument cluster to the headlight assembly, then pull the cluster off. Note how the pegs on the back of the cluster engage the grommets in brackets on the headlight assembly (see Section 8). Pull back the boot on the instrument cluster wiring connector and disconnect the connector **(see illustration)**.

### Installation

**3** Installation is the reverse of removal. Check the condition of the grommets and fit new ones if they are damaged or deteriorated.

## 16 Instruments – check and renewal

**Note:** *The individual instruments and LEDs are integral with the instrument panel, separate components are not available.*

### Speedometer and speed sensor

#### Check

**1** If the speedometer, odometer or trip meter fail to work, take the motorcycle to a Suzuki dealer for assessment. Special equipment is needed to check the operation of the speedometer and the speed sensor.

#### Renewal

**2** Remove the instrument cluster (see Section 15). If required, undo the five screws on the back of the instrument cluster to separate the front cover, instrument panel and rear cover **(see illustration)**. Further dismantling is not possible.

**3** To remove the speed sensor, first remove the rider's seat (see Chapter 8). Trace the wiring from the sensor and disconnect it at the connector **(see illustration)**.

**4** Undo the screw securing the sensor to the sprocket cover and withdraw the sensor **(see illustration)**. If required, remove the sprocket cover and check the condition of the speed sensor rotor (see Chapter 6, Section 18).

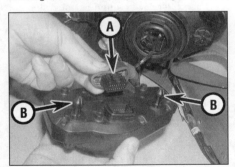

**15.2 Disconnect the instrument cluster wiring connector (A). Note the pegs (B)**

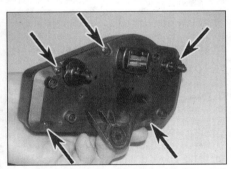

**16.2 Back of instrument cluster is secured by screws (arrowed)**

**16.3 Disconnect the speed sensor wiring connector**

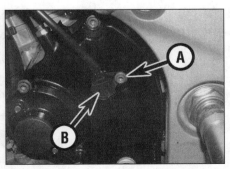

**16.4 Undo the screw (A) and withdraw the sensor (B)**

16.7 ADJ button location (arrowed)

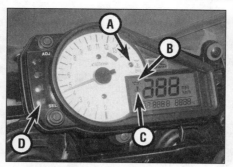

16.11 Warning LED (A), oil warning symbol (B), coolant temperature warning symbol (C) and fuel level warning LED (D)

16.18 Fuel level resistor (GSX-R600/1000 shown)

## Tachometer

### Check

5 Suzuki provides no data for testing the tachometer. If the tachometer fails to work, take the motorcycle to a Suzuki dealer for assessment.

6 In normal operation, when the ignition is first turned ON, the tachometer pointer will swing to full scale and then return to zero. This is part of the instrument's self checking procedure. If the tachometer pointer fails to return to zero it can be reset as follows.

7 Hold the ADJ button ON and turn the ignition ON (see illustration). Release the ADJ button three to five seconds after turning the ignition ON, then press the ADJ button twice within one second. If the tachometer is working correctly, the tachometer needle should now be at zero. This reset procedure should be completed with ten seconds. Turn the ignition OFF.

### Renewal

8 Remove the instrument cluster (see Section 15). If required, remove the instrument panel from the case (see Step 2).

## Coolant temperature LED and display

### Check

9 Ensure that the engine coolant temperature (ECT) sensor is working correctly (see Chapter 3, Section 5). Special equipment is needed to check the operation of the LED and LCD display circuits. If any of the circuits fail to work, take the motorcycle to a Suzuki dealer for assessment.

### Renewal

10 See Step 2.

## Oil pressure LED and symbol

### Check

11 When the ignition is first turned ON and before the engine is started, the oil warning symbol and the warning LED should come on (see illustration). When the engine is started they should extinguish. This is part of the instrument's self checking procedure.

12 If the display and light do not come on, turn the ignition OFF and disconnect the wiring connector from the oil pressure switch (see Section 17). Turn the ignition ON and earth (ground) the wiring connector on the crankcase – the warning LED should come on and the oil warning symbol should flicker. If the LED and warning symbol do not come on, the instrument panel should be renewed, although first check the wire between the oil pressure switch and instruments for continuity.

13 If the warning symbol and warning LED come on when the engine is running, and this is not due to low oil level or low oil pressure, disconnect the oil pressure switch wiring connector (see Section 17), then turn the ignition ON; the display and light should be out. If they are on, the wire between the switch and instrument cluster must be earthed (grounded) at some point.

### Renewal

14 See Step 2.

## Fuel level warning LED

### Check

15 When the ignition is first turned ON and before the engine is started, the fuel warning LED should come on for three seconds (see illustration 16.11). This is part of the instrument's self checking procedure. On GSX-R600K1, GSX-R750Y, K1 and GSX-R1000K1 models, the fuel warning light will flicker when the volume of fuel in the tank drops to 4 litres; when it drops to 2 litres the warning light will remain on. On all K2 models onwards, the fuel warning light will come on when the volume of fuel in the tank drops to 4 litres.

16 If the LED does not come on, check the wiring from the fuel level sensor to the instrument cluster for continuity (see Wiring Diagrams at the end of this Chapter). Also check the operation of the fuel level sensor (see Chapter 4, Section 7).

17 On GSX-R600K1, GSX-R750Y, K1 and GSX-R1000K1 models test the fuel level resistor. On GSX-R600 and GSX-R1000 models, the resistor is mounted on the frame underneath the rider's seat, on GSX-R750 models the resistor is mounted on the left-hand side of the sub-frame behind the seat cowling.

18 Remove the rider's seat or seat cowling (see Chapter 8) as applicable, then disconnect the fuel level resistor wiring connector (see illustration). Use an ohmmeter set to the ohms scale, measure the resistance between the red/black and orange/green wire terminals on the sensor side of the wiring connector, then measure the resistance between the black/light green and orange/green wire terminals. If the results are not as specified, the resistor is faulty and should be renewed.

19 If the wiring, level sensor, and where applicable the resistor, are in good order, the fuel level warning LED is faulty.

### Renewal

20 See Step 2.

## 17 Oil pressure switch – check, removal and installation

### Check

1 Remove the right-hand fairing side panel (see Chapter 8). The oil pressure switch is screwed into the right-hand side of the crankcase (see illustration).

2 Undo the nut and detach the wiring connector from the switch. Turn the ignition ON and check for voltage at the wiring connector. If there is voltage, earth (ground) the connector on the crankcase and check that the oil warning symbol and warning LED come on.

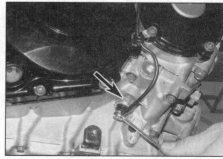

17.1 Location of the oil pressure switch

**18.5 Ignition switch is secured by two special Torx bolts**

3 Now touch the connector to the terminal on the switch and check that the oil warning symbol and warning LED come on. If the display and warning light do not come on, the switch must be assumed faulty and a new one must be fitted.

### Removal and installation

4 Drain the engine oil (see Chapter 1).
5 Detach the wiring connector from the switch, then unscrew the oil pressure switch and withdraw it from the crankcase.
6 Apply a suitable sealant (Suzuki-Bond 1207B or equivalent) to the threads near the switch body, then install it in the crankcase and tighten it to the torque setting specified at the beginning of this Chapter.
7 Attach the wiring connector and tighten the nut securely.
8 Fill the engine with the correct type and quantity of oil (see Chapter 1). Start the engine and check that there are no leaks around the switch.
9 Install the fairing side panel (see Chapter 8).

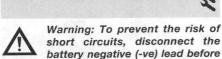

## 18 Ignition (main) switch –
check, removal and installation

⚠ *Warning: To prevent the risk of short circuits, disconnect the battery negative (-ve) lead before making any ignition (main) switch checks.*

### Check

1 Raise the fuel tank and remove the air filter housing (see Chapter 4). Trace the wiring from the ignition switch and disconnect it at the connector.
2 Using an ohmmeter or a continuity tester, check the continuity of the connector terminal pairs (see the *Wiring Diagrams* at the end of this Chapter). Continuity should exist between the terminals connected by a solid line in the switch box diagram when the switch is in the indicated position.
3 If the switch fails any of the tests, renew it.

### Removal and installation

**Note:** *The bolts used to secure the ignition switch to the top yoke are of a special Torx type which have a raised pip in their centre.*

*Ensure that you have the necessary Torx bit to undo them.*
4 Remove the fairing (see Chapter 8).
5 Raise the fuel tank and remove the air filter housing (see Chapter 4). Disconnect the ignition switch wiring connector, then free the wiring from its guide and feed it through to the switch **(see illustration)**. Undo the special Torx bolts used to mount the ignition switch to the underside of the top yoke and remove the switch.
6 Installation is the reverse of removal, noting the following:
● Apply a suitable non-permanent thread locking compound to the switch mounting bolts.
● Make sure the wiring is correctly routed and securely connected.

## 19 Handlebar switches –
check

1 Generally speaking, the switches are reliable and trouble-free. Most troubles, when they do occur, are caused by dirty or corroded contacts, but wear and breakage of internal parts is a possibility that should not be overlooked. If breakage does occur, the entire switch and related wiring harness will have to be renewed, since individual parts are not available.
2 The switches can be checked for continuity using an ohmmeter or a continuity test light. Always disconnect the battery negative (-ve) lead, which will prevent the possibility of a short circuit, before making the checks.
3 Remove the fairing right-hand side panel (see Chapter 8). Trace the wiring harness of the switch in question back to its connector and disconnect it.
4 Check for continuity between the terminals of the connector on the switch side, with the switch in the various positions (i.e. switch OFF – no continuity, switch ON – continuity) – see the switch boxes in the *Wiring Diagrams* at the end of this Chapter.
5 If the continuity check indicates a problem exists, remove the switch and spray the switch contacts with electrical contact cleaner (see Section 20). If they are accessible, the contacts can be scraped clean with a knife or polished with crocus cloth. If switch components are damaged or broken, it will be obvious when the switch is disassembled.

## 20 Handlebar switches –
removal and installation

### Right-hand switch

#### Removal

1 If the switch is to be removed from the bike, rather than just displaced from the handlebar, remove the fairing right-hand side panel (see

Chapter 8). Trace the wiring harness of the switch in question back to its connector and disconnect it. Work back along the harness, freeing it from its guide, noting its correct routing.
2 Disconnect the front brake light switch wiring connectors **(see illustration 14.2a)**.
3 Disconnect the throttle cables from the switch (see Chapter 4, Section 15) – this procedure includes switch removal.

#### Installation

4 Installation is the reverse of removal. Refer to Chapter 4 for installation of the throttle cables. Make sure the locating pin in the upper half of the switch fits into hole in the top of the handlebar.

### Left-hand switch

#### Removal

5 If the switch is to be removed from the bike, rather than just displaced from the handlebar, remove the fairing right-hand side panel. Trace the wiring harness of the switch in question back to its connector and disconnect it. Work back along the harness, freeing it from its guide, noting its correct routing.
6 Disconnect the clutch switch wiring connector **(see illustration 23.2)**.
7 Remove the fast idle cable from the switch (see Chapter 4, Section 16) – this procedure incorporates switch removal. **Note:** *Although no fast idle cable is fitted to GSX-R1000K2 models, follow the same procedure to remove the switch housing.*

#### Installation

8 Installation is the reverse of removal. Refer to Chapter 4 for installation of the fast idle cable. Make sure the locating pin in the upper half of the switch fits into hole in the top of the handlebar.

## 21 Gear position sensor
(neutral switch) –
check, removal and installation

**Note:** *The neutral LED in the instrument cluster is activated by the gear position (GP) sensor which is part of the fuel injection system. For full details of the GP sensor see Chapter 4, Section 11.*

### Check

1 Remove the rider's seat (see Chapter 8). Trace the wiring from the GP sensor on the lower left-hand side of the engine and disconnect it at the connector **(see illustration)**. Make sure the transmission is in neutral, then turn the ignition ON. With the connector disconnected, the neutral LED should be out. If not, the wire between the connector and instrument cluster must be earthed (grounded) at some point.
2 If the neutral LED doesn't come on with the transmission in neutral, refer to the *Wiring Diagrams* at the end of this Chapter and check

**21.1 Gear position sensor wiring connector**

**22.2 Sidestand switch wiring connector (arrowed)**

**22.4 Check the operation of the switch plunger (arrowed)**

the blue/black wire from the instrument cluster to the diode in the fusebox for continuity, then check the black wire from the diode to the gear position sensor for continuity. Check the diode as described in the next section.

**3** If the fuel injection system self-diagnostic function indicates a fault in the GP sensor, refer to Chapter 4 and check the sensor output voltage.

### Removal and installation

**4** Refer to Chapter 2, Section 17 to remove the sensor and check the condition of its contacts, plungers and springs.

### 22 Sidestand switch, relay and diode – check and renewal

#### Sidestand switch

**1** The sidestand switch is mounted on the sidestand bracket. The switch is part of the safety circuit which prevents or stops the engine running if the transmission is in gear whilst the sidestand is down, and prevents the engine from starting if the transmission is in gear unless the sidestand is up and the clutch lever is pulled in.

**2** Remove the rider's seat (see Chapter 8). Trace the wiring from the switch and disconnect it at the connector **(see illustration)**.

**3** Check the operation of the switch using an ohmmeter or continuity test light. Connect the meter between the terminals on the switch side of the connector. With the sidestand up there should be continuity (zero resistance) between the terminals, with the stand down there should be no continuity (infinite resistance).

**4** If the switch does not perform as expected, check that the fault is not caused by a sticking switch plunger due to the ingress of road dirt; spray the switch with a water dispersant aerosol **(see illustration)**. If the switch still does not work it is defective and must be renewed.

**5** If the switch is good, check the sidestand relay (Steps 11 to 13) and diode (Step 14). Also check the wiring between the various components (see *Wiring Diagrams* at the end of this Chapter).

**6** To renew the switch, first disconnect the switch wiring (see Step 2). Feed the wiring

back to the switch noting its routing and freeing it from any clips or ties.

**7** Unscrew the bolts securing the switch to the sidestand and remove the switch **(see illustration)**.

**8** Fit the new switch onto the bracket, then apply a suitable non-permanent thread locking compound to the bolt threads and tighten them securely.

**9** Make sure the wiring is correctly routed up to the connector and retained by clips and ties. Reconnect the wiring connector.

**10** Install the rider's seat (see Chapter 8).

#### Sidestand relay

**11** The integral turn signal/sidestand relay is located on the right-hand air duct in the fairing, next to the fusebox **(see illustration 5.1a)**.

**12** Pull the relay off its connector **(see illustration 13.4)**. Using an ohmmeter or continuity tester, check for continuity between the D and E terminals on the relay **(see illustration)**. There should be no continuity (infinite resistance).

**13** Now use jumper wires to connect the positive (+ve) terminal of a 12V battery to the D terminal on the relay and the negative (-ve) battery terminal to the C relay terminal, and again check for continuity between the D and E terminals. There should be continuity (zero resistance). If there is no continuity, fit a new relay.

#### Diode

**14** The diode is integral with the sidestand/turn signal relay. Pull the relay off its connector.

**15** Using an ohmmeter or continuity tester,

**22.7 Switch is secured by two bolts**

connect the positive (+ve) probe to C terminal of the diode and the negative (-ve) probe to A terminal **(see illustration 22.12)**. The diode should show continuity. Now reverse the probes. The diode should show no continuity. Repeat the tests between B terminal and A terminal. The same results should be achieved. If it doesn't behave as stated, install a new diode/turn signal relay/sidestand relay.

### 23 Clutch switch – check, removal and installation

#### Check

**1** The clutch switch is situated on the underside of the clutch lever bracket. The

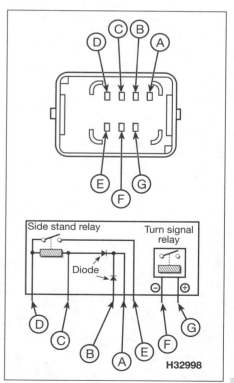

**22.12 Turn signal/sidestand relay and diode terminal identification**

**23.2 Clutch switch wiring connector (arrowed)**

**24.1a Horn location on GSX-R600 and GSX-R750 models**

**24.1b Horn location on GSX-R1000 models**

switch is part of the safety circuit and must be pulled in to allow the engine to be started.

**2** To check the switch, disconnect the wiring connector **(see illustration)**. Connect the probes of an ohmmeter or a continuity test light to the two switch terminals. With the clutch lever pulled in, there should be continuity (zero resistance). With the clutch lever out, there should be no continuity (infinite resistance).

**3** If the switch is good, check the other components in the starter circuit as described in the relevant sections of this Chapter. If all components are good, check the wiring between the various components (see the *Wiring Diagrams* at the end of this Chapter).

### Removal and installation

**4** Disconnect the wiring connector from the clutch switch **(see illustration 23.2)**. Undo the screw securing the switch to the clutch lever bracket and remove the switch.

**5** Installation is the reverse of removal. The switch isn't adjustable.

### 24 Horn –
check, removal and installation

### Check

**1** On GSX-R600 and GSX-R750 models, the horn is mounted on the top right-hand corner of the radiator **(see illustration)**. On GSX-R1000 models, the horn is mounted on the front of the frame below the steering head

**(see illustration)**. The horn is accessible without removing a fairing side panel, but access is improved if you do so (right-hand panel on GSX-R600 and GSX-R750 models, left-hand panel on GSX-R1000 models – see Chapter 8).

**2** Disconnect the wiring connectors from the horn. Using jumper wires, apply battery voltage directly to the terminals on the horn. If the horn sounds, check the switch (see Section 19) and the wiring between the switch and the horn (see the *Wiring Diagrams* at the end of this Chapter).

**3** If the horn doesn't sound, install a new one.

### Removal and installation

**4** If required, remove the right-hand fairing panel on GSX-R600 and GSX-R750 models, or the left-hand panel on GSX-R1000 models – see Chapter 8

**5** Disconnect the wiring connectors from the horn, then undo the mounting bolt and remove the horn from the bike.

**6** Install the horn and tighten the mounting bolt securely. Connect the wiring connectors and test the operation of the horn.

### 25 Starter relay –
check and renewal

### Check

**1** If the starter circuit is faulty, first check the main and ignition fuses (see Section 5).

**2** Remove the rider's seat (see Chapter 8) and

disconnect the battery negative (-ve) lead. Unclip the starter relay is from its location and remove the plastic cover **(see illustration 5.2b)**.

**3** Undo the bolt securing the starter motor lead to its terminal on the relay and disconnect the lead, then position the lead away from the terminal. Reconnect the battery negative (-ve) lead. With the ignition ON, the engine kill switch in the RUN position, the transmission in neutral and the clutch pulled in, press the starter switch. The relay should be heard to click. Turn the ignition OFF.

**4** If the relay doesn't click, disconnect the relay wiring connector and insert the positive (+ve) probe of a voltmeter into the yellow/green wire terminal in the connector and the negative (-ve) probe into the black/yellow wire terminal **(see illustrations)**. Check for battery voltage with the ignition ON, kill switch in the RUN position, clutch lever pulled in and starter switch pressed. If no voltage is present, check the terminals in the wiring connector, the wiring (see *Wiring Diagrams* at the end of this Chapter) and the other components in the starter circuit as described in the relevant sections of this Chapter.

**5** If there is voltage present, test the relay. Ensure the ignition is OFF and disconnect the battery negative (-ve) lead. Undo the bolts securing the starter motor and battery leads to the relay, noting where they fit, and remove the relay.

**6** Set a multimeter to the ohms scale and connect it across the relay's starter motor and battery lead terminals (A and B) **(see illustration)**. Use jumper wires to connect the

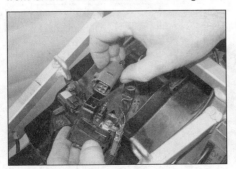

**25.4a Disconnect the starter relay wiring connector . . .**

**25.4b . . . and check for battery voltage as described**

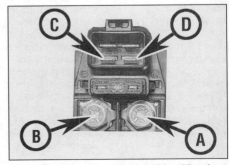

**25.6a Starter relay terminal identification**

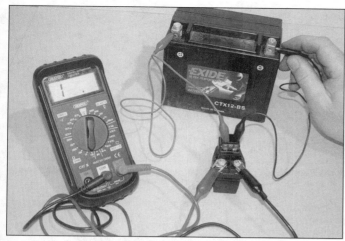

25.6b  Set-up for checking the starter relay for continuity

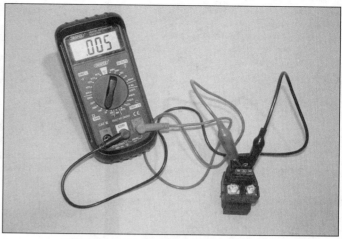

25.7  Measuring the starter relay resistance

positive (+ve) terminal of a 12V battery to the C terminal on the relay and the negative (-ve) battery terminal to the D relay terminal **(see illustration)**. The relay should be heard to click and there should be continuity (zero resistance) shown on the meter. Disconnect the battery. **Note:** *Do not apply battery voltage to the relay for more than 5 seconds to avoid damaging the relay coil.*

**7** Now use the multimeter set to the ohms scale to measure the resistance between the relay's C and D terminals and compare the result with the Specifications at the beginning of this Chapter **(see illustration)**. If the result of either test is not as specified, the relay is faulty and must be renewed.

### Renewal

**8** Remove the rider's seat (see Chapter 8) and disconnect the battery negative (-ve) lead.

**9** Unclip the starter relay is from its location and remove the plastic cover **(see illustration 5.2b)**. Undo the bolts securing the starter motor and battery leads to the relay, noting where they fit. Disconnect the relay wiring connector and remove the relay.

**10** Installation is the reverse of removal, ensuring the terminal bolts are securely tightened.

### 26  Starter motor –
removal and installation

### Removal

**1** Disconnect the battery negative (-ve) lead. Remove the fuel tank (see Chapter 4).

**2** Pull back the rubber boot on the starter motor terminal. On GSX-R600 and GSX-R750 models, undo the nut securing the lead to the motor and disconnect the lead; on GSX-R1000 models, undo the bolt securing the lead to the motor and disconnect the lead **(see illustration)**.

**3** Undo the two bolts securing the starter motor to the crankcase **(see illustration)**.

**4** Slide the starter motor out of the crankcase and remove it from the machine **(see illustration)**. Remove the O-ring on the end of the starter motor and discard it as a new one must be fitted on reassembly.

### Installation

**5** Install a new O-ring on the end of the starter motor and ensure it is seated in its groove **(see illustration)**. Apply a smear of engine oil or grease to the O-ring to aid installation.

**6** Manoeuvre the motor into position and slide it into the crankcase. Ensure that the starter motor teeth mesh correctly with those of the starter idle/reduction gear.

**7** Install the retaining bolts and tighten them securely.

**8** Connect the starter lead to the motor terminal and secure it with the nut or bolt as applicable (see Step 2). Install the rubber boot.

**9** Install the remaining components in the reverse order of removal.

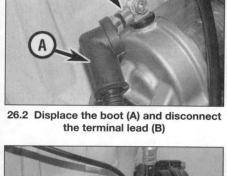

26.2  Displace the boot (A) and disconnect the terminal lead (B)

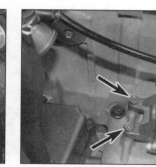

26.3  Starter motor is secured by two bolts (arrowed)

26.4  Withdraw the starter motor. Note the O-ring (arrowed)

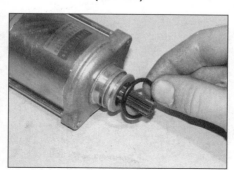

26.5  Fit a new O-ring

**27.2 Note the alignment marks . . .**

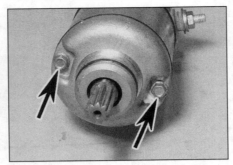

**27.3a . . . then unscrew the long bolts . . .**

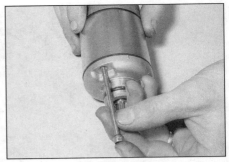

**27.3b . . . and withdraw them from the motor**

## 27 Starter motor –
disassembly, inspection and reassembly

### GSX-R600 and GSX-R750 models

#### Disassembly

**1** Remove the starter motor (see Section 26).
**2** Note the alignment marks between the main housing and the front and rear covers, or make your own if they aren't clear **(see illustration)**.
**3** Unscrew the two long bolts and withdraw them from the starter motor **(see illustrations)**. Discard their O-rings as new ones must be fitted on reassembly.
**4** Wrap some insulating tape around the teeth on the end of the starter motor shaft – this will protect the oil seal from damage as the front cover is removed. Remove the front cover from the motor along with its O-ring **(see illustrations)**. Remove the shim(s) from the front end of the armature shaft and the special washer from inside the front cover, noting how it fits **(see illustrations)**.
**5** Remove the main housing and O-ring from the armature, noting that it is held by the attraction of the magnets **(see illustration)**.
**6** Remove the rear cover from the armature along with the brushplate assembly **(see illustration)**. The brushes are under spring pressure and will probably pop out when the armature is removed. Remove the shims from the armature shaft **(see illustration)**.
**7** Noting the correct fitted location of each component, unscrew the terminal nut and remove it along with its washer, insulating washers and O-ring **(see illustration)**.

**27.4a Remove the front cover . . .**

Withdraw the terminal and brushplate assembly from the rear cover, noting how it fits **(see illustration)**.
**8** Lift the brush springs and slide the brushes out from their holders **(see illustrations)**.

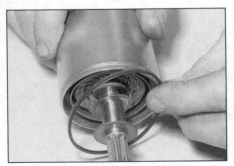

**27.4b . . . cover O-ring . . .**

**27.4c . . . and the shims from the armature shaft**

**27.4d Special washer is inside the front cover**

**27.5 Remove the main housing and O-ring**

**27.6a Remove the rear cover and brushplate assembly**

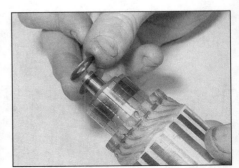

**27.6b Remove the shims from the armature shaft**

## Inspection

9 The parts of the starter motor that are most likely to require attention are the brushes. Suzuki give no specifications for the minimum length of the brushes, however if they are obviously worn, cracked, chipped, or otherwise damaged, a new brush plate should be installed. Ensure the brushes are firmly attached to their terminals.

10 Inspect the commutator bars on the armature for scoring, scratches and discoloration. The commutator can be cleaned and polished with crocus cloth, do not use sandpaper or emery paper. After cleaning, wipe away any residue with a cloth soaked in electrical system cleaner or denatured alcohol. Check that the insulation between each bar is below the level of the bars. If not, carefully scrape some away.

11 Using an ohmmeter or a continuity test light, check for continuity between the commutator bars (see illustration). Continuity (zero resistance) should exist between each bar and all of the others. Also, check for continuity between the commutator bars and the armature shaft (see illustration). There should be no continuity (infinite resistance) between the commutator and the shaft. If the checks indicate otherwise, the armature is defective.

12 Check for continuity between each brush and the terminal bolt. There should be continuity (zero resistance). Check for continuity between the terminal bolt and the housing (when assembled). There should be no continuity (infinite resistance).

13 Check the front end of the armature shaft for worn, cracked, chipped and broken teeth. If the shaft is damaged or worn, install a new armature.

14 Check the bearings in the end covers for wear and check the front cover oil seal (see illustration). Individual components are not available; fit new covers if necessary.

15 Check the terminal insulating washers, housing insulator and O-ring for signs of deterioration and renew them if necessary.

## Reassembly

16 Fit the brushes back into their holders and install the spring ends onto the brushes. Check that the brushes slide freely in the holders.

17 Ensure that the inner insulator is in place on the terminal, then fit the O-ring (see illustration). Insert the terminal through the rear cover and fit the brushplate assembly into the cover, making sure it is correctly located. Fit the insulating washers over the terminal, then fit the standard washer and the nut and tighten the nut securely (see illustration 27.7a).

18 Install the shims on the armature shaft. Apply a smear of molybdenum disulphide grease to the armature shaft and insert it carefully into the rear cover, locating the brushes on the commutator as you do. Check that each brush is securely pressed against the commutator by its spring.

27.7a Unscrew the terminal nut and remove the washer, insulating washers and O-ring

27.7b Withdraw the terminal and brushplate from the cover

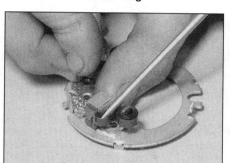
27.8a Lift the brush springs . . .

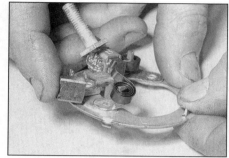
27.8b . . . and withdraw the brushes

19 If required, fit a new O-ring onto the main housing (see illustration), then fit the housing over the armature and onto the rear cover, aligning the marks made on removal. Note that the housing will be forcefully drawn onto

the armature by the magnets.

20 Install the shims onto the front of the armature shaft (see illustration 27.4c) and, if required, fit a new O-ring onto the front of the main housing. Apply a smear of grease to the

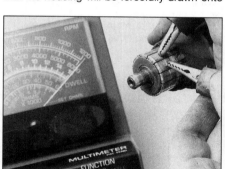
27.11a Checking for continuity between the commutator bars

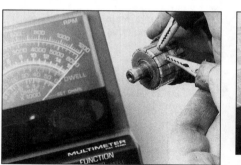
27.11b There should be no continuity between the commutator bars and the armature shaft

27.14 Check the seal and bearing in the front cover

27.17 Fit the terminal O-ring

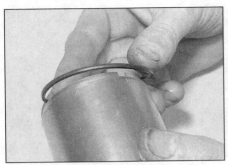

27.19 Fit a new O-ring onto the main housing

27.25 Unscrew the long bolts

27.26a Remove the front cover and cover O-ring

27.26b Remove the special washer from inside the front cover

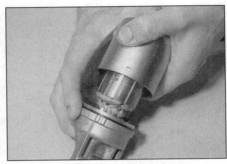

27.27a Remove the main housing . . .

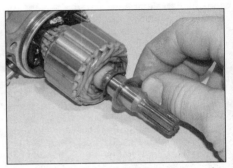

27.27b . . . and remove the shims from the armature shaft

lips of the front cover oil seal and fit the special washer into the cover, making sure its tabs locate correctly (see illustration 27.4d).
21 Install the cover, aligning the marks made on removal. Fit a new O-ring onto each of the long bolts, then install the bolts and tighten them securely. Remove the insulating tape from around the teeth on the shaft.
22 Install the starter motor (see Section 26).

### GSX-R1000 models

#### Disassembly

23 Remove the starter motor (see Section 26).
24 Note the alignment marks between the main housing and the front and rear covers, or make your own if they aren't clear.
25 Unscrew the two long bolts and withdraw them from the starter motor (see illustration).
26 Wrap some insulating tape around the teeth on the end of the starter motor shaft –

this will protect the oil seal from damage as the front cover is removed. Remove the front cover from the motor along with its O-ring (see illustration). Remove the special washer from inside the front cover, noting how it fits (see illustration).
27 Remove the main housing from the armature, noting that it is held by the attraction of the magnets (see illustration). Remove the shim(s) from the front end of the armature shaft (see illustration).
28 Remove the rear cover along with its O-ring and brushplate assembly from the armature (see illustration).

#### Inspection

29 The parts of the starter motor that are most likely to require attention are the brushes (see illustration). Suzuki give no specifications for the minimum length of the brushes, however if they are obviously worn, cracked, chipped, or

otherwise damaged, a new rear cover should be installed. Note: Although the brushplate assembly can be removed from the rear cover, Suzuki do not list it as a separate item. Ensure the brushes are firmly attached to their terminals.
30 Inspect the commutator bars on the armature for scoring, scratches and discoloration. The commutator can be cleaned and polished with crocus cloth, do not use sandpaper or emery paper. After cleaning, wipe away any residue with a cloth soaked in electrical system cleaner or denatured alcohol. Check that the insulation between each bar is below the level of the bars. If not, carefully scrape some away.
31 Using an ohmmeter or a continuity test light, check for continuity between the commutator bars (see illustration 27.11a). Continuity (zero resistance) should exist between each bar and all of the others. Also, check for continuity between the commutator bars and the armature shaft (see illustration 27.11b). There should be no continuity (infinite resistance) between the commutator and the shaft. If the checks indicate otherwise, the armature is defective.
32 Check for continuity between each brush and the terminal bolt. There should be continuity (zero resistance). Check for continuity between the terminal bolt and the housing. There should be no continuity (infinite resistance).
33 Check the front end of the armature shaft for worn, cracked, chipped and broken teeth. If the shaft is damaged or worn, install a new armature.

27.28 Remove the rear cover and brushplate assembly

27.29 Check the condition of the brushes and the brush springs

**34** Check the bearings in the end covers for wear and fit new covers if necessary. Check the front cover oil seal and fit a new seal if necessary (see illustration 27.14).

### Reassembly

**35** Check that the brushes slide freely in the holders. If required, fit a new O-ring onto the rear cover.

**36** Apply a smear of molybdenum disulphide grease to the armature shaft and insert it carefully into the rear cover, locating the brushes on the commutator as you do. Check that each brush is securely pressed against the commutator by its spring.

**37** Fit the main housing over the armature and onto the rear cover, aligning the marks made on removal. Note that the housing will be forcefully drawn onto the armature by the magnets.

**38** Install the shim(s) onto the front of the armature shaft (see illustration 27.27b). If required, fit a new O-ring onto the front cover. Apply a smear of grease to the lips of the front cover oil seal and fit the special washer into the cover, making sure its tabs locate correctly (see illustration 27.26b).

**39** Install the cover, aligning the marks made on removal. Install the long bolts and tighten them securely. Remove the insulating tape from around the teeth on the shaft.

**40** Install the starter motor (see Section 26).

## 28 Charging system testing –
### general information and precautions

**1** If the performance of the charging system is suspect, the system as a whole should be checked first, followed by testing of the individual components. **Note:** *Before beginning the checks, make sure the battery is fully charged and that all system connections are clean and tight.*

**2** Checking the output of the charging system and the performance of the various components within the charging system requires the use of a multimeter (with voltage, current, resistance checking facilities). If a multimeter is not available, the job of checking the charging system should be left to a Suzuki dealer.

**3** When making the checks, follow the procedures carefully to prevent incorrect connections or short circuits resulting in irreparable damage to electrical system components.

## 29 Charging system –
### leakage and output test

**1** If the charging system of the machine is thought to be faulty, remove the rider's seat (see Chapter 8) and perform the following checks.

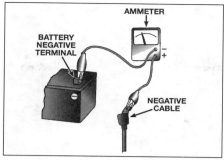

**29.3 Checking the charging system leakage rate. Connect the meter as shown**

### Leakage test

*Caution: Always connect an ammeter in series, never in parallel with the battery, otherwise it will be damaged. Do not turn the ignition ON or operate the starter motor when the ammeter is connected – a sudden surge in current will blow the meter's fuse.*

**2** Ensure the ignition is OFF, then remove the rider's seat and disconnect the battery negative (-ve) lead.

**3** Set the multimeter to the Amps function and connect its negative (-ve) probe to the battery negative (-ve) terminal, and positive (+ve) probe to the disconnected negative (-ve) lead (see illustration). Always set the meter to a high amps range initially and then bring it down to the mA (milli Amps) range; if there is a high current flow in the circuit it may blow the meter's fuse.

**4** Battery current leakage should not exceed the maximum limit (see Specifications). If a higher leakage rate is shown there is a short circuit in the wiring, although if an immobiliser or alarm is fitted, its current draw should be taken into account. Disconnect the meter and reconnect the battery negative (-ve) lead.

**5** If leakage is indicated, refer to *Wiring Diagrams* at the end of this Chapter to systematically disconnect individual electrical components and repeat the test until the source is identified.

### Output test

**6** Remove the rider's seat (see Chapter 8), then start the engine and warm it up to normal operating temperature.

**29.9a Alternator wiring connector (arrowed)**

**7** To check the regulated (DC) voltage output, allow the engine to idle with the headlight main beam (HI) turned ON. Connect a multimeter set to the 0-20 volts DC scale across the terminals of the battery. Connect the positive (+ve) meter probe to battery positive (+ve) terminal and the negative (-ve) meter probe to battery negative (-ve) terminal.

**8** Slowly increase the engine speed to 5000 rpm and note the reading obtained. Compare the result with the Specification at the beginning of this Chapter. If the regulated voltage output is outside the specification, check the alternator and the regulator (see Sections 30 and 31).

**9** To check the unregulated voltage output, first remove the fairing left-hand side panel (see Chapter 8). Trace the wiring back from the top of the alternator cover on the left-hand side of the engine to the wiring connector (see illustration). Start the engine and increase the engine speed to 5000 rpm, then using a multimeter set to 0-250 volts AC range, connect the meter probes to one pair of terminals at a time on the alternator side of the wiring connector (see illustration). Make a note of the three readings obtained.

**10** Compare the result with the Specification at the beginning of this Chapter. If the unregulated voltage output is outside the specification, check the alternator and the regulator (see Sections 30 and 31).

> **HAYNES HINT** *Clues to a faulty regulator are constantly blowing bulbs, with brightness varying considerably with engine speed, and battery overheating.*

## 30 Alternator –
### check, removal and installation

### Check

**1** Remove the rider's seat and the fairing left-hand side panel (see Chapter 8).

**2** Trace the wiring back from the top of the alternator cover on the left-hand side of the engine and disconnect it at the connector (see illustration).

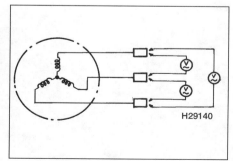

**29.9b Alternator no-load voltmeter test connections**

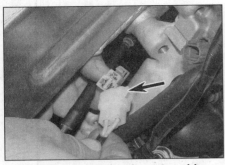

30.2 Disconnect the alternator wiring connector (arrowed)

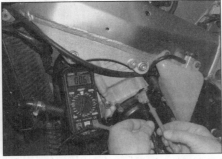

30.3 Checking the alternator stator coil resistance (GSX-R1000 shown)

3 Using a multimeter set to the ohms scale, connect the meter probes to one pair of terminals at a time on the alternator side of the wiring connector and measure the resistance between the terminals (see illustration). Make a note of the three readings obtained. Now check for continuity between each terminal and ground (earth).

4 If the stator coil windings are in good condition the three readings should be within the range shown in the Specifications at the beginning of this Chapter and there should be no continuity (infinite resistance) between any of the terminals and ground (earth). If not, the alternator stator coil assembly is faulty and

should be renewed. **Note:** *Before condemning the stator coils, check the fault is not due to damaged wiring between the connector and coils.*

## Removal

5 Remove the rider's seat and the fairing left-hand side panel (see Chapter 8). Disconnect the alternator wiring connector **(see illustration 30.2**. Free the wiring from any clips or ties and feed it through to the alternator cover.

6 Position a suitable receptacle underneath the alternator cover to catch any residual oil when the cover is removed.

7 Unscrew the alternator cover bolts, noting the position of the sealing washers and the bracket for the coolant hoses, and remove the cover **(see illustrations)**. Discard the gasket as a new one must be fitted on reassembly. Remove the dowels from either the cover or the crankcase if they are loose.

8 To remove the rotor bolt it is necessary to stop the crankshaft from turning. Suzuki produces a Service Tool (Pt. No. 09930-44520) to do this. If a rotor holding strap or tool is not available, and the engine is in the frame, place the transmission in gear and have an assistant apply the rear brake. Alternatively, a large spanner can be applied to the two flats machined into the boss in the rotor. Unscrew the bolt and remove the bolt and washer **(see illustrations)**.

9 To remove the rotor from the crankshaft taper it is necessary to use a rotor puller. Suzuki produces a service tool (Pt. No. 09930-34980) to do this. Thread a suitable bolt into the end of the crankshaft, then install the rotor puller fully onto the centre of the rotor. Hold the puller with a large spanner to stop it the crankshaft turning, then turn the puller centre bolt clockwise until the rotor is free of the crankshaft taper **(see illustrations)**. Remove the puller, then undo the bolt and remove the rotor.

10 To remove the stator from the cover,

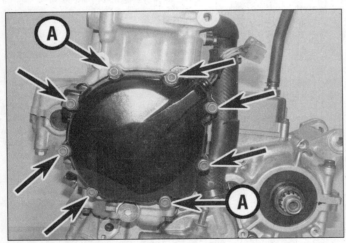

30.7a Unscrew the cover bolts, noting the sealing washers (A) . . .

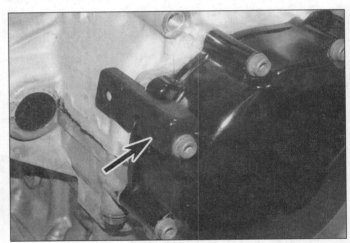

30.7b . . . and the bracket (arrowed) for the coolant hoses

30.8a Hold the rotor . . .

30.8b . . . and unscrew the bolt

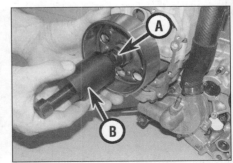

30.9a Install the bolt (A) and rotor puller (B) . . .

30.9b . . . then hold the puller and displace the rotor

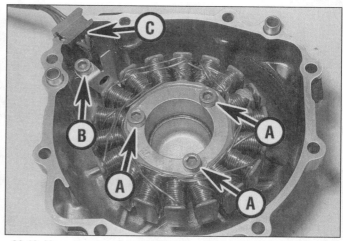

30.10 Unscrew the stator bolts (A) and the wiring clamp (B) and free the grommet (C)

unscrew the bolts securing the stator, and the bolt securing the wiring clamp, then remove the assembly, noting how the wiring grommet fits (see illustration).

## Installation

11 Apply a suitable sealant to the stator wiring grommet, then install the stator into the cover, aligning the grommet with the cut-out in the cover (see illustration). Install the stator and wiring clamp bolts and tighten them to the specified torque setting (see illustration 30.10).
12 Clean the tapered end of the crankshaft and the corresponding mating surface on the

inside of the rotor with a suitable solvent (see illustrations). Make sure that no metal objects have attached themselves to the magnet on the inside of the rotor, then slide the rotor onto the shaft.
13 Install the rotor bolt with its washer and tighten it to the torque setting specified at the beginning of this Chapter, using the method employed on removal to prevent the rotor from turning.
14 Apply a suitable sealant across the crankcase joints. If removed, fit the dowels into the crankcase and fit a new cover gasket, making sure it locates correctly onto the dowels (see illustration). Install the cover,

then install the cover bolts and the coolant hose bracket. Fit new sealing washers on the upper front and lower rear cover bolts (see illustration 30.7a). Tighten the bolts evenly in a criss-cross pattern.
15 Feed the alternator wiring back to its connector, making sure it is correctly routed and secured by any clips or ties, and reconnect it.
16 Check the engine oil level and top up if necessary (see Daily (pre-ride) checks).
17 Install the fairing side panel and the rider's seat (see Chapter 8).

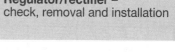

## 31 Regulator/rectifier – check, removal and installation

### Check

1 Remove the rider's seat and disconnect the battery negative (-ve) lead (see Section 3). Remove the seat cowling (see Chapter 8). The regulator/rectifier is mounted on the left-hand side of the rear sub-frame (see illustration). Disconnect the wiring connector.
2 Using a multimeter set to diode test, measure the voltage between the various terminals on the regulator/rectifier side of the

30.11 Apply sealant to the grommet and fit it into the cut-out in the cover

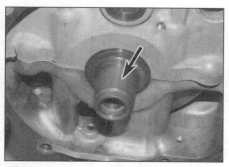

30.12a Clean the crankshaft (arrowed) . . .

30.12b . . . and the surface inside the rotor boss with solvent

30.14 Install the dowels (arrowed) and a new cover gasket

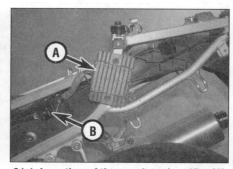

31.1 Location of the regulator/rectifier (A) and its wiring connector (B)

**9**

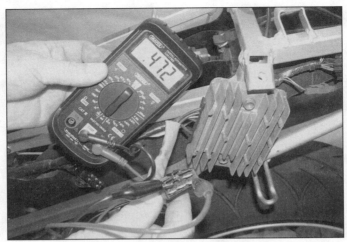

31.2a  Measuring the voltage between the regulator/rectifier wiring terminals

wiring connector as shown in the table **(see illustrations)**. **Note:** *Depending on the multimeter used for the test, the results may vary from the specified figures. However, as long as the variance is constant, the test will give an indication of the condition of the regulator/rectifier. If the readings do not compare closely with those shown in the table, have the regulator/rectifier tested by a Suzuki dealer.*

3  If the regulator/rectifier appears to be good, check the wiring between the battery, regulator/rectifier and alternator, and the wiring connectors (see *Wiring Diagrams* at the end of this Chapter).

### Removal and installation

4  Remove the rider's seat and disconnect the battery negative (-ve) lead (see Section 3). Remove the seat cowling (see Chapter 8). Disconnect the regulator/rectifier wiring connector.

5  Undo the two bolts securing the regulator/rectifier and remove it, noting the spacers between the unit and the frame.

6  Install the new unit, bolts and spacers, then tighten the bolts securely. Connect the wiring connector.

7  Install the seat cowling (see Chapter 8). Reconnect the battery negative lead (-ve) and install the rpider's seat.

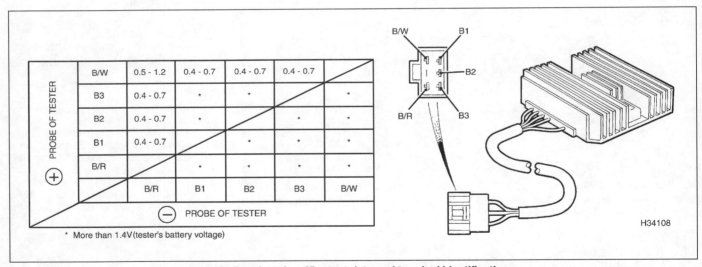

| PROBE OF TESTER (+) | B/W | 0.5 - 1.2 | 0.4 - 0.7 | 0.4 - 0.7 | 0.4 - 0.7 | |
|---|---|---|---|---|---|---|
| | B3 | 0.4 - 0.7 | * | * | | * |
| | B2 | 0.4 - 0.7 | * | | * | * |
| | B1 | 0.4 - 0.7 | | * | * | * |
| | B/R | | * | * | * | * |
| | | B/R | B1 | B2 | B3 | B/W |
| | | | (-) PROBE OF TESTER | | | |

* More than 1.4V (tester's battery voltage)

H34108

31.2b  Regulator/rectifier test data and terminal identification

B  Black                    B/R  Black/red                    B/W  Black/white

H32629

**Mode select switch connector**

**Engine management ECM**

**Ignition coil/spark plugs**
- 4
- 3
- 2
- 1

**Secondary throttle control unit**

**Rear brake switch**

**Side stand switch**

**Ignition switch**
| ON |
| OFF |
| Lock |
| P |

**Starter switch**

**Front brake switch**

**Speed sensor**

**Lighting switch**
| OFF |
| S |
| On |

**Engine stop switch**

**Speedometer**
1 Neutral indicator LED
2 High beam indicator LED
3 Turn signal indicatator LED
4 Fuel indicator LED
5 Oil pressure/engine coolant temp./fuel indicator LED

- 5
- 4
- 3
- 2
- 1

**Rear right turn signal**

**Brake light /tail light**

**Brake light /tail light**

**Licence plate light**

**Rear left turn signal**

**Starter relay & main fuse**

30A

**Starter motor**

**Battery**

**Alternator**

**Regulator/ rectifier**

**Tip-over sensor**

**Crank position sensor**

**Cam position sensor**

**Gear position sensor**

**Oil pressure switch**

**Fuel pump /fuel level switch**

**Fuel pump relay**

**Injectors**
- 1
- 2
- 3
- 4

**Secondary throttle valve servo**

**Throttle position sensor**

**Intake air pressure sensor**

**Intake air temp. sensor**

**Coolant temp. sensor**

**Atmo. pressure sensor**

**Cooling fan and switch**

**GSX-R600K1 Europe**

**Fuel level light resistor**

**Fuse box**
1 Headlight high 15A
2 Headlight low 10A
3 Fuel pump 10A
4 Ignition 15A
5 Signal 15A
6 Fan 10A
7 Turn signal/ side stand relay

- 1 2 3 4 5 6
- 7

**Clutch lever switch**

**Turn signal switch**
| L | Push | R |

**Front right turn signal**

**Headlight (low)**

**Headlight (high)**

**Position light**

**Front left turn signal**

**Horn**

**Horn switch**

**Passing light switch**

**Dimmer switch**
| High |
| Low |

9

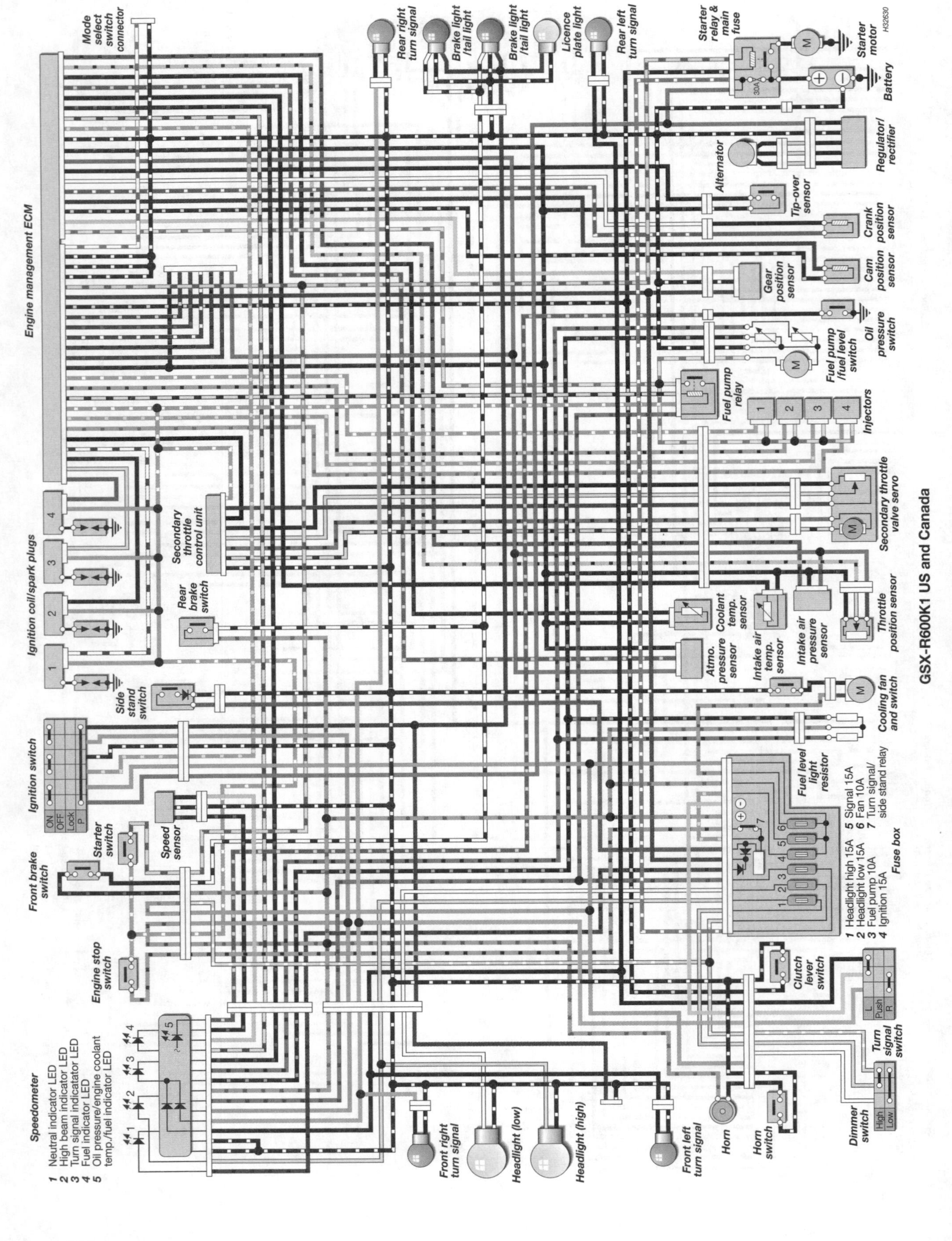

Mode select switch connector

Rear right turn signal

Brake light /tail light

Brake light /tail light

Licence plate light

Rear left turn signal

Starter relay & main fuse

Starter motor

Battery

Regulator/ rectifier

Alternator

Tip-over sensor

Crank position sensor

Cam position sensor

Gear position sensor

Oil pressure switch

Fuel pump /fuel level switch

Fuel pump relay

Injectors
1 2 3 4

Engine management ECM

Ignition coil/spark plugs

Secondary throttle control unit

Rear brake switch

Side stand switch

Secondary throttle valve servo

Throttle position sensor

Coolant temp. sensor

Intake air temp. sensor

Intake air pressure sensor

Atmo. pressure sensor

Cooling fan and switch

Fuel level light resistor

Ignition switch
ON
OFF
Lock
P

Front brake switch

Starter switch

Speed sensor

Engine stop switch

**GSX-R600K1 US and Canada**

Fuse box
1 Headlight high 15A    5 Signal 15A
2 Headlight low 15A     6 Fan 10A
3 Fuel pump 10A         7 Turn signal/
4 Ignition 15A            side stand relay

Clutch lever switch

L Push R

Turn signal switch

Speedometer
1 Neutral indicator LED
2 High beam indicator LED
3 Turn signal indicator LED
4 Fuel indicator LED
5 Oil pressure/engine coolant temp./fuel indicator LED

Front right turn signal

Headlight (low)

Headlight (high)

Front left turn signal

Horn

Horn switch

Dimmer switch
High
Low

H32630

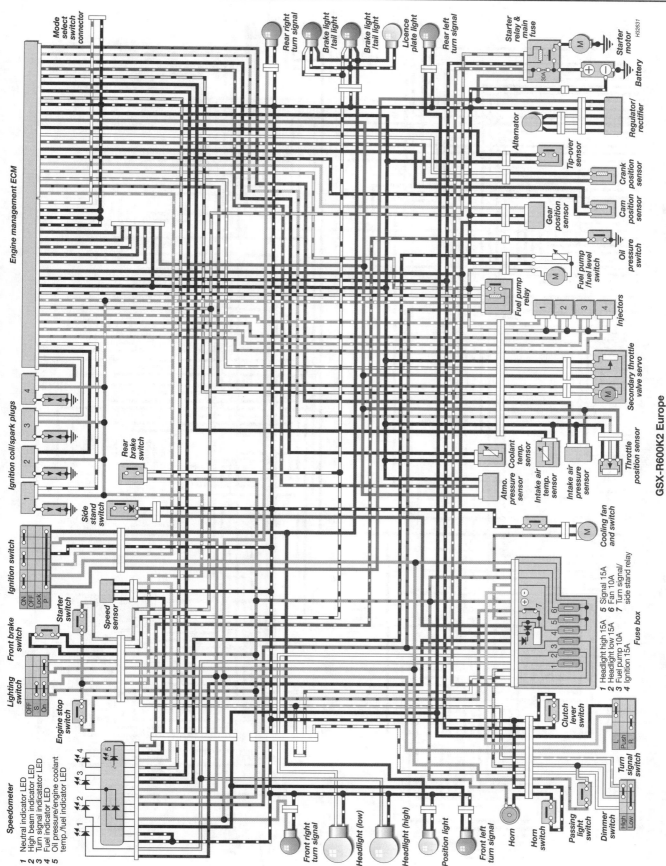

**Speedometer**
1 Neutral indicator LED
2 High beam indicator LED
3 Turn signal indicatator LED
4 Fuel indicator LED
5 Oil pressure/engine coolant
temp./fuel indicator LED

GSX-R600K2 Europe

**Fuse box**
1 Headlight high 15A
2 Headlight low 10A
3 Fuel pump 10A
4 Ignition 15A
5 Signal 15A
6 Fan 10A
7 Turn signal/
side stand relay

H32631

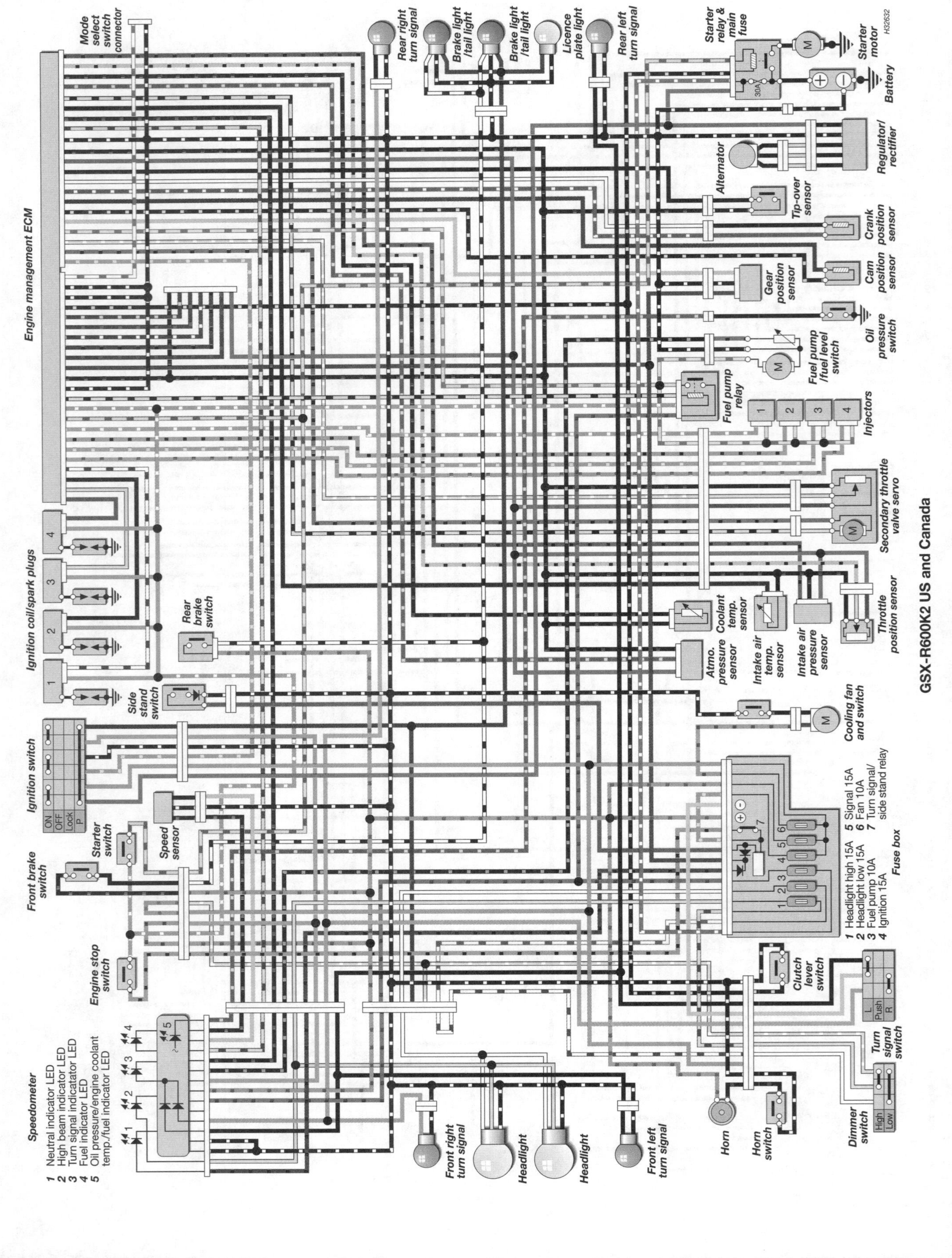

Mode select switch connector

Engine management ECM

Rear right turn signal

Brake light /tail light

Brake light /tail light

Licence plate light

Rear left turn signal

Starter relay & main fuse

30A

Starter motor

Battery

Regulator/ rectifier

Alternator

Tip-over sensor

Crank position sensor

Cam position sensor

Gear position sensor

Oil pressure switch

Fuel pump /fuel level switch

Fuel pump relay

Injectors

1 2 3 4

Secondary throttle valve servo

Throttle position sensor

Intake air pressure sensor

Intake air temp. sensor

Coolant temp. sensor

Atmo. pressure sensor

Cooling fan and switch

Ignition coil/spark plugs

4 3 2 1

Rear brake switch

Side stand switch

Ignition switch

ON OFF LOCK P

Starter switch

Speed sensor

Front brake switch

Engine stop switch

Fuse box

1 Headlight high 15A    5 Signal 15A
2 Headlight low 15A     6 Fan 10A
3 Fuel pump 10A         7 Turn signal/
4 Ignition 15A            side stand relay

Clutch lever switch

L Push R

Turn signal switch

Dimmer switch
High Low

Horn

Horn switch

Speedometer

1 Neutral indicator LED
2 High beam indicator LED
3 Turn signal indicator LED
4 Fuel indicator LED
5 Oil pressure/engine coolant temp./fuel indicator LED

5 4 3 2 1

Front right turn signal

Headlight

Headlight

Front left turn signal

GSX-R600K2 US and Canada

H32632

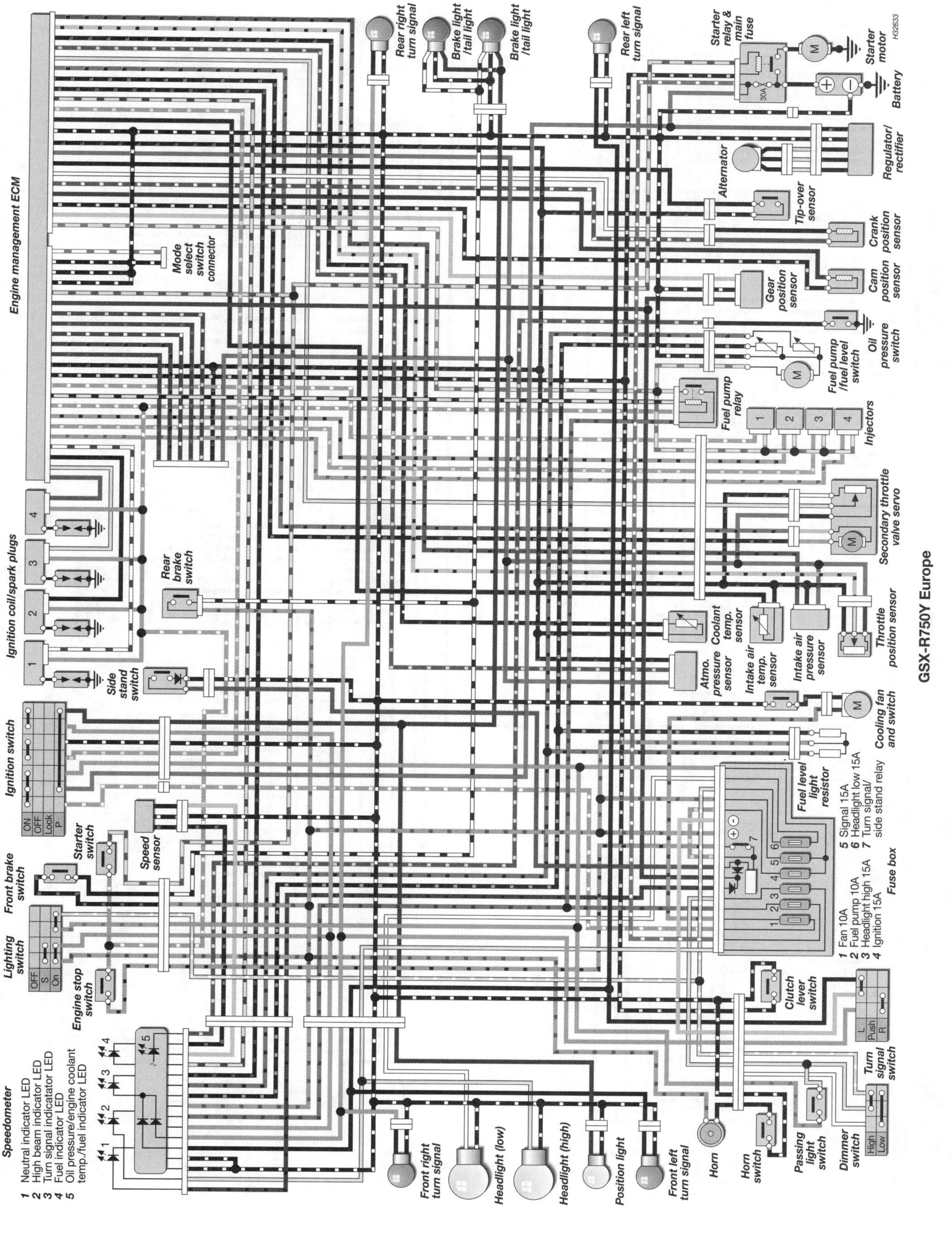

Engine management ECM

Mode select switch connector

Ignition coil/spark plugs

4
3
2
1

Rear brake switch

Side stand switch

Ignition switch

ON
OFF
Lock
P

Front brake switch

Starter switch

Speed sensor

Lighting switch

OFF
S
On

Engine stop switch

Speedometer
1 Neutral indicator LED
2 High beam indicator LED
3 Turn signal indicatator LED
4 Fuel indicator LED
5 Oil pressure/engine coolant temp./fuel indicator LED

Rear right turn signal
Brake light /tail light
Brake light /tail light
Rear left turn signal

Starter relay & main fuse
30A
M
Starter motor
Battery

Regulator/ rectifier

Alternator

Tip-over sensor

Crank position sensor

Gear position sensor

Cam position sensor

Oil pressure switch

Fuel pump /fuel switch

Fuel pump relay

Injectors
1 2 3 4

Secondary throttle valve servo

Throttle position sensor

Coolant temp. sensor

Intake air temp. sensor

Intake air pressure sensor

Atmo. pressure sensor

Cooling fan and switch

Fuel level light resistor

Fuse box
1 Fan 10A
2 Fuel pump 10A
3 Headlight high 15A
4 Ignition 15A
5 Signal 15A
6 Headlight low 15A
7 Turn signal/ side stand relay

Clutch lever switch

Turn signal switch

Front right turn signal
Headlight (low)
Headlight (high)
Position light
Front left turn signal
Horn
Horn switch
Passing light switch
Dimmer switch

GSX-R750Y Europe

9

H32634

Rear right turn signal

Brake light /tail light

Brake light /tail light

Rear left turn signal

Starter relay & main fuse

Starter motor

Battery

Regulator/ rectifier

Alternator

Tip-over sensor

Crank position sensor

Cam position sensor

Gear position sensor

Oil pressure switch

Fuel pump /fuel level switch

Fuel pump relay

Injectors

1 2 3 4

Engine management ECM

Mode select switch connector

Secondary throttle valve servo

Throttle position sensor

Coolant temp. sensor

Intake air temp. sensor

Intake air pressure sensor

Atmo. pressure sensor

Cooling fan and switch

Ignition coil/spark plugs

4 3 2 1

Rear brake switch

Side stand switch

Ignition switch

| | |
|---|---|
| ON | |
| OFF | |
| Lock | |
| P | |

Starter switch

Speed sensor

Front brake switch

Lighting switch

| |
|---|
| OFF |
| S |
| On |

Engine stop switch

Fuel level light resistor

Fuse box

5 Signal 15A
6 Headlight low 15A
7 Turn signal/ side stand relay

1 Fan 10A
2 Fuel pump 10A
3 Headlight high 15A
4 Ignition 15A

GSX-R750K1 Europe

Clutch lever switch

Turn signal switch

| |
|---|
| L |
| Push |
| R |

Passing light switch

Dimmer switch

| | |
|---|---|
| High | |
| Low | |

Speedometer

1 Neutral indicator LED
2 High beam indicator LED
3 Turn signal indicatator LED
4 Fuel indicator LED
5 Oil pressure/engine coolant temp./fuel indicator LED

5 4 3 2 1

Front right turn signal

Headlight (low)

Headlight (high)

Position light

Front left turn signal

Horn

Horn switch

H32635

**Engine management ECM**

**Ignition coil/spark plugs**

4
3
2
1

**Mode select switch connector**

**Rear brake switch**

**Side stand switch**

**Speedometer**

1  Neutral indicator LED
2  High beam indicator LED
3  Turn signal indicator LED
4  Fuel indicator LED
5  Oil pressure/engine coolant
   temp./fuel indicator LED

**Ignition switch**

ON
OFF
Lock
P

**Starter switch**

**Speed sensor**

**Front brake switch**

**Engine stop switch**

Rear right turn signal

Brake light /tail light

Brake light /tail light

Rear left turn signal

Front right turn signal

Headlight (low)

Headlight (high)

Front left turn signal

**Starter relay & main fuse**

30A

M
**Starter motor**

**Battery**

**Regulator/ rectifier**

**Alternator**

**Tip-over sensor**

**Crank position sensor**

**Cam position sensor**

**Gear position sensor**

**Oil pressure switch**

**Fuel pump /fuel level switch**

M

**Fuel pump relay**

**Injectors**

1  2  3  4

**Secondary throttle valve servo**

M

**Coolant temp. sensor**

**Intake air temp. sensor**

**Throttle position sensor**

**Intake air pressure sensor**

**Atmo. pressure sensor**

**Cooling fan and switch**

M

**Fuel level light resistor**

+
7

5  4  3  2  1  6  7

1  2  3  4  5  6

1  2  3  4

1  Fan 10A
2  Fuel pump 10A
3  Headlight high 15A
4  Ignition 15A

5  Signal 15A
6  Headlight low 15A
7  Turn signal/
   side stand relay

**Fuse box**

**Clutch lever switch**

L
Push
R

**Turn signal switch**

**Horn**

**Horn switch**

**Dimmer switch**

High
Low

**GSX-R750Y US and Canada**

9

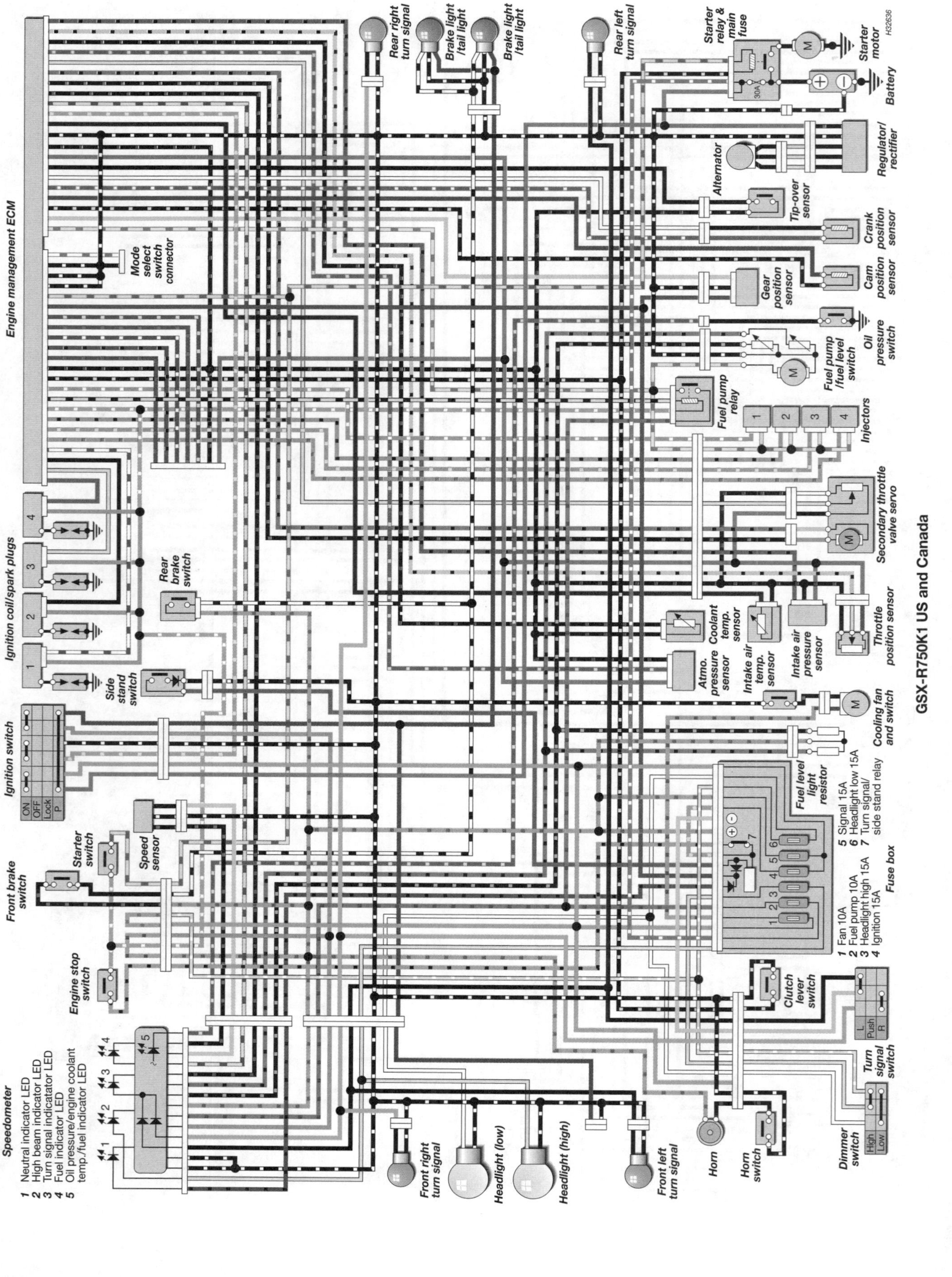

GSX-R750K1 US and Canada

H32636

**Speedometer**
1 Neutral indicator LED
2 High beam indicator LED
3 Turn signal indicatator LED
4 Fuel indicator LED
5 Oil pressure/engine coolant temp./fuel indicator LED

**Fuse box**
1 Fan 10A
2 Fuel pump 10A
3 Headlight high 15A
4 Ignition 15A
5 Signal 15A
6 Headlight low 15A
7 Turn signal/ side stand relay

Engine management ECM

Rear right turn signal

Brake light /tail light

Brake light /tail light

Licence plate light

Rear left turn signal

Starter relay & main fuse

Starter motor

Battery

Alternator

Regulator/ rectifier

Tip-over sensor

Crank position sensor

Mode select switch connector

Gear position sensor

Cam position sensor

Oil pressure switch

Fuel pump /fuel level switch

Fuel pump relay

Injectors

1 2 3 4

Ignition coil/spark plugs

4

3

2

1

Rear brake switch

Secondary throttle valve servo

Throttle position sensor

Coolant temp. sensor

Intake air temp. sensor

Intake air pressure sensor

Side stand switch

Atmo. pressure sensor

GSX-R750K2 Europe

Cooling fan and switch

Ignition switch

| | ON | OFF | Lock | P |

Starter switch

Speed sensor

Front brake switch

Lighting switch

| | OFF | S | On |

Engine stop switch

Clutch lever switch

Fuse box

1 Headlight high 15A
2 Headlight low 15A
3 Fuel pump 10A
4 Ignition 15A
5 Signal 15A
6 Fan 10A
7 Turn signal/ side stand relay

1 2 3 4 5 6 7

Turn signal switch

| | L | Push | R |

Speedometer

1 Neutral indicator LED
2 High beam indicator LED
3 Turn signal indicatator LED
4 Fuel indicator LED
5 Oil pressure/engine coolant temp./fuel indicator LED

5

4 4

3

2

1

Front right turn signal

Headlight (low)

Headlight (high)

Position light

Front left turn signal

Horn

Horn switch

Passing light switch

Dimmer switch

| | High | Low |

H32637

9

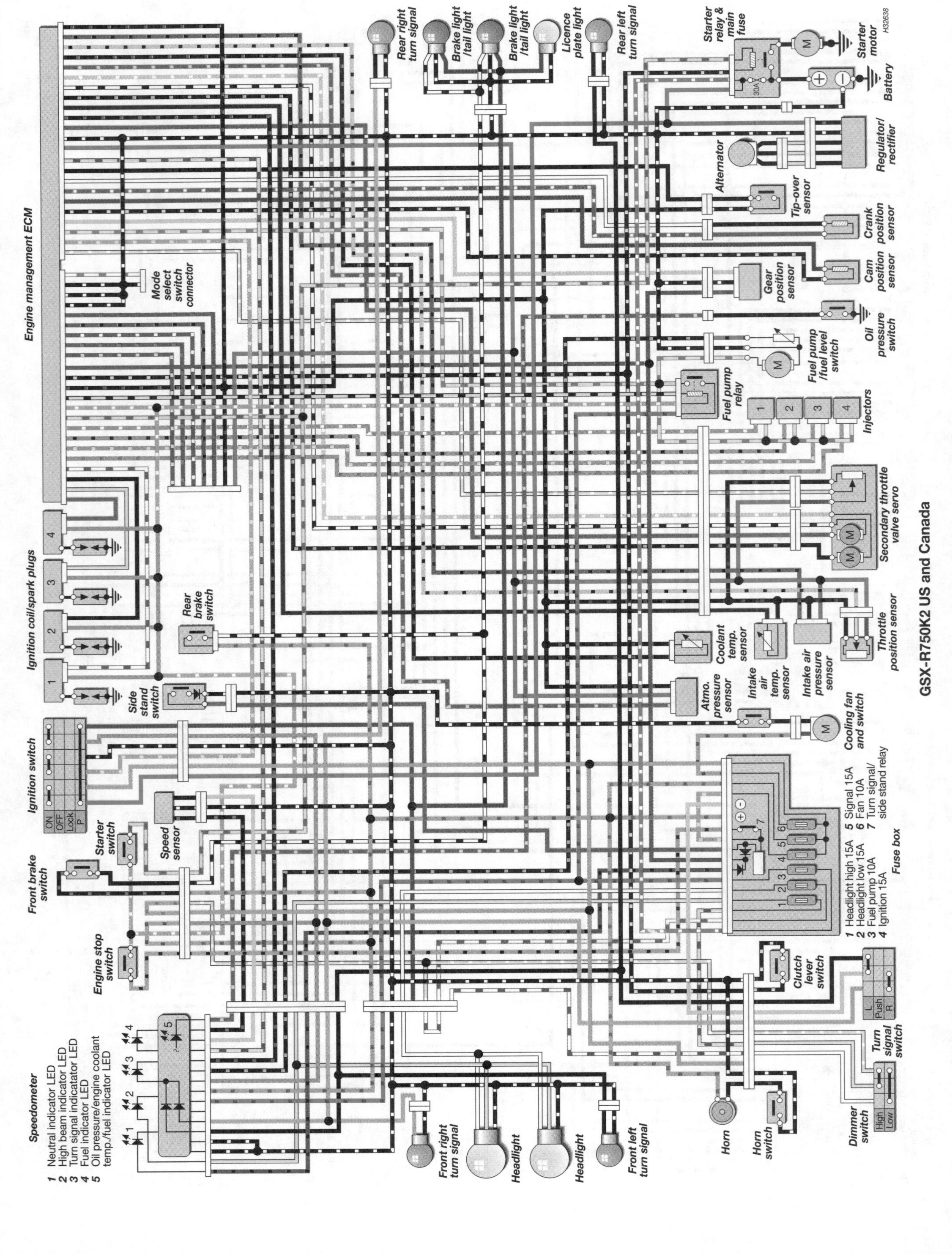
Engine management ECM
Mode select switch connector
Ignition coil/spark plugs
1
2
3
4
Ignition switch
ON
OFF
Lock
P
Front brake switch
Starter switch
Speed sensor
Rear brake switch
Side stand switch
Engine stop switch
Speedometer
1 Neutral indicator LED
2 High beam indicator LED
3 Turn signal indicatator LED
4 Fuel indicator LED
5 Oil pressure/engine coolant temp./fuel indicator LED
Front right turn signal
Headlight
Headlight
Front left turn signal
Horn
Horn switch
Dimmer switch
High
Low
Turn signal switch
L
Push
R
Clutch lever switch
Fuse box
1 Headlight high 15A
2 Headlight low 15A
3 Fuel pump 10A
4 Ignition 15A
5 Signal 15A
6 Fan 10A
7 Turn signal/ side stand relay
Cooling fan and switch
Atmo. pressure sensor
Intake air temp. sensor
Intake air pressure sensor
Coolant temp. sensor
Throttle position sensor
Secondary throttle valve servo
Injectors
Fuel pump relay
Fuel pump /fuel level switch
Oil pressure switch
Gear position sensor
Cam position sensor
Crank position sensor
Tip-over sensor
Alternator
Regulator/ rectifier
Battery
Starter motor
Starter relay & main fuse
30A
Rear right turn signal
Brake light /tail light
Brake light /tail light
Licence plate light
Rear left turn signal
H32638

GSX-R750K2 US and Canada

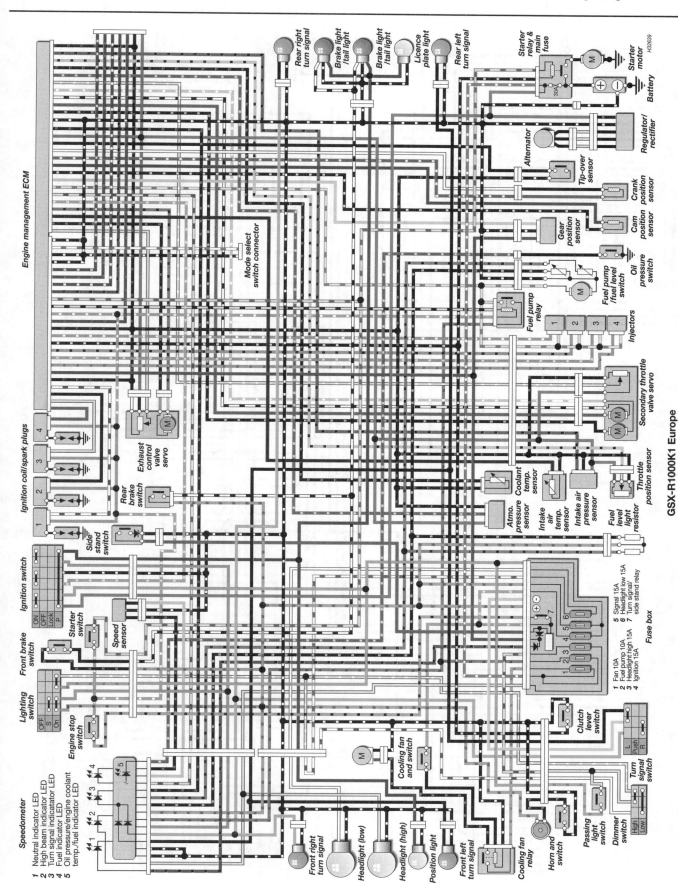

**GSX-R1000K1 Europe**

**Speedometer**
1 Neutral indicator LED
2 High beam indicator LED
3 Turn signal indicator LED
4 Fuel indicator LED
5 Oil pressure/engine coolant temp./fuel indicator LED

**Fuse box**
1 Fan 10A
2 Fuel pump 10A
3 Headlight high 15A
4 Ignition 15A
5 Signal 15A
6 Headlight low 15A
7 Turn signal/side stand relay

9

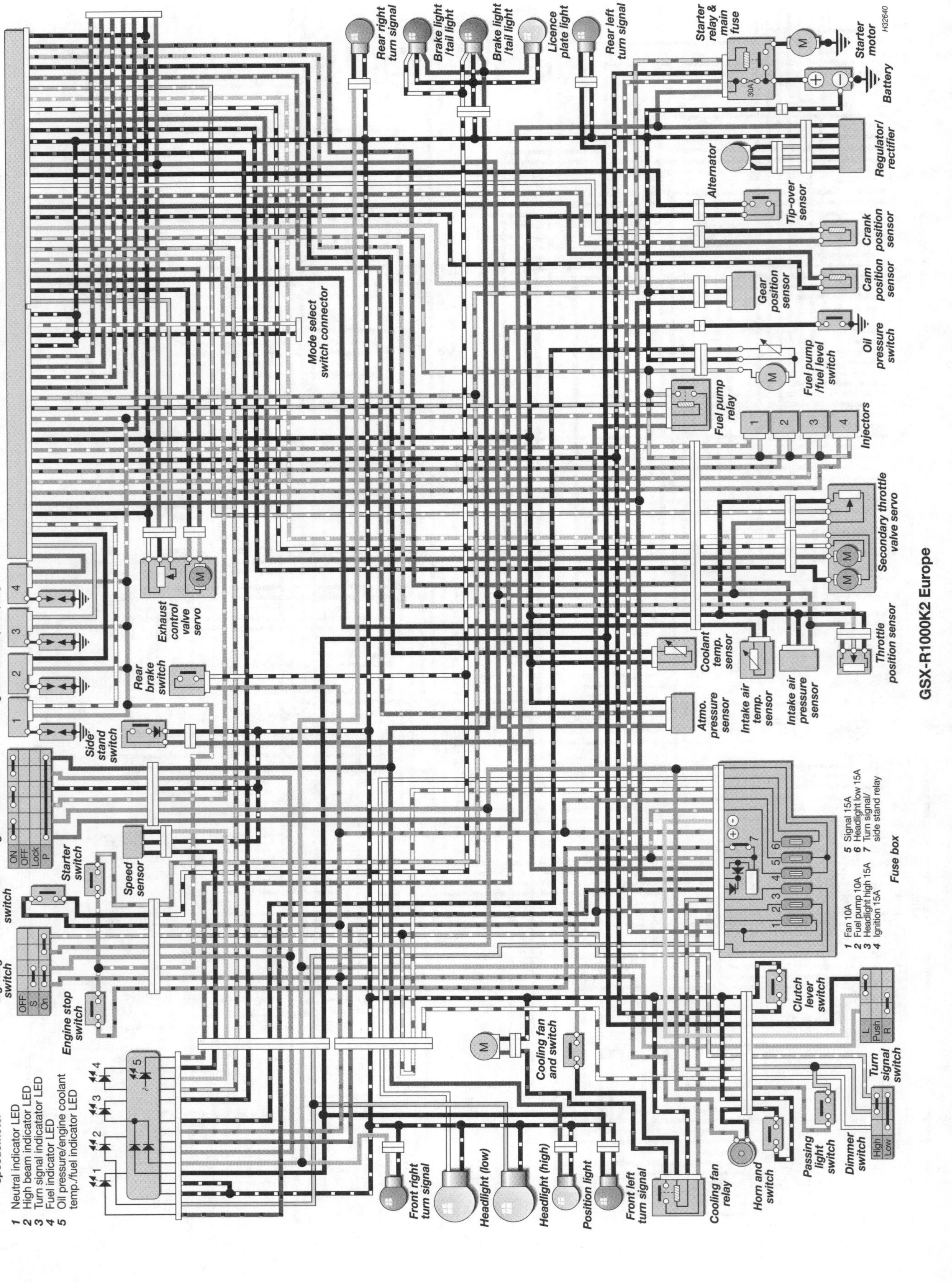

GSX-R1000K2 Europe

**Speedometer**
1 Neutral indicator LED
2 High beam indicator LED
3 Turn signal indicatator LED
4 Fuel indicator LED
5 Oil pressure/engine coolant temp./fuel indicator LED

**Fuse box**
1 Fan 10A
2 Fuel pump 10A
3 Headlight high 15A
4 Ignition 15A
5 Signal 15A
6 Headlight low 15A
7 Turn signal/side stand relay

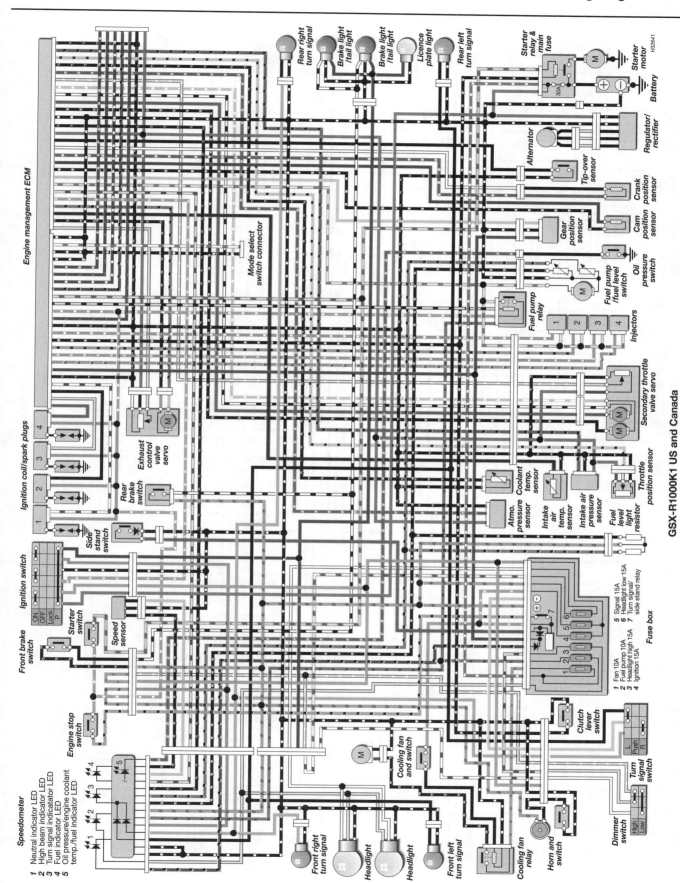

GSX-R1000K1 US and Canada

**Speedometer**
1 Neutral indicator LED
2 High beam indicator LED
3 Turn signal indicatior LED
4 Fuel indicator LED
5 Oil pressure/engine coolant temp./fuel indicator LED

**Fuse box**
1 Fan 10A
2 Fuel pump 10A
3 Headlight high 15A
4 Ignition 15A
5 Signal 15A
6 Headlight low 15A
7 Turn signal/ side stand relay

9

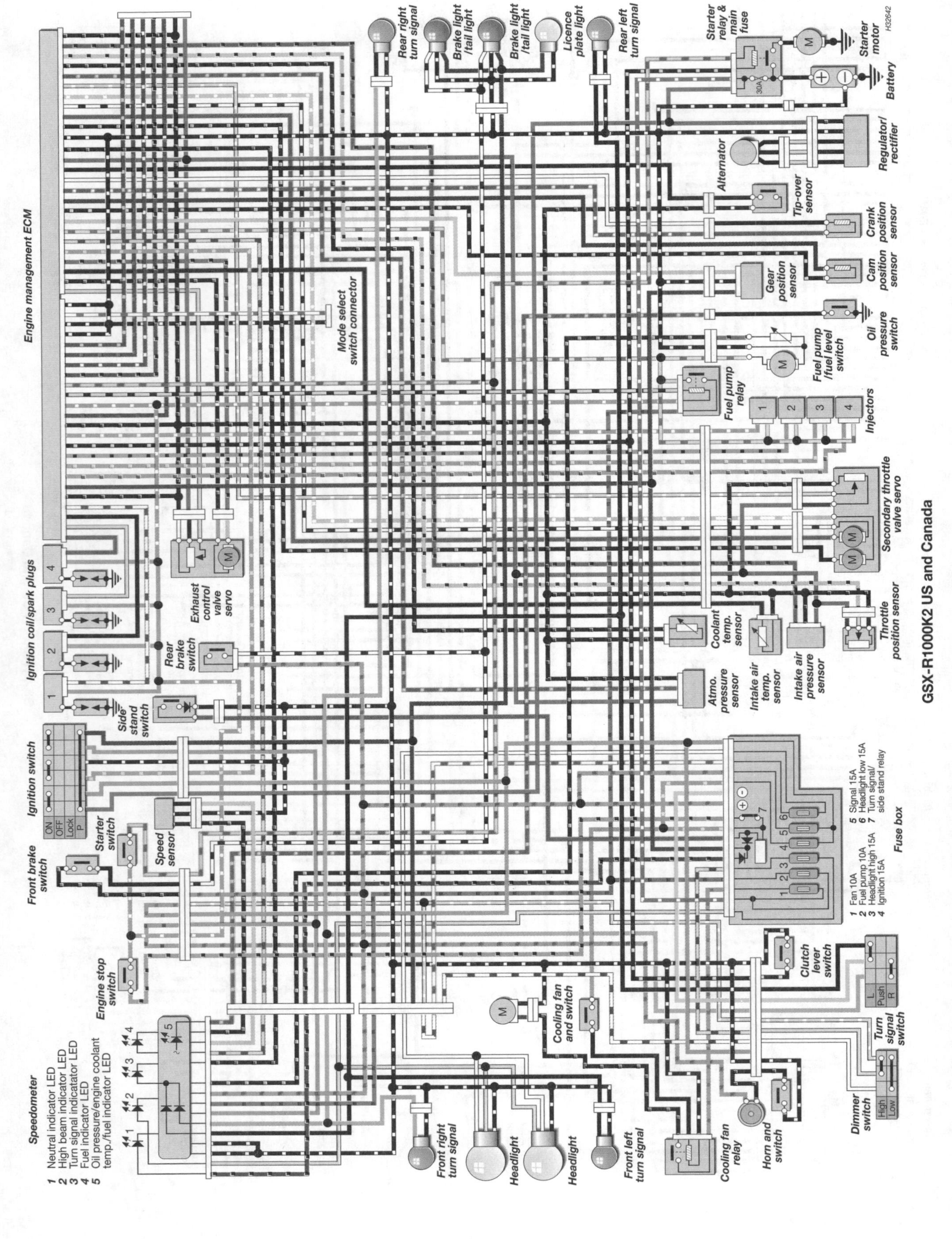

GSX-R1000K2 US and Canada

H32642

Engine management ECM

Mode select switch connector

Ignition coil/spark plugs
4
3
2
1

Exhaust control valve servo

Rear brake switch

Side stand switch

Speedometer
1 Neutral indicator LED
2 High beam indicator LED
3 Turn signal indicator LED
4 Fuel indicator LED
5 Oil pressure/engine coolant temp./fuel indicator LED
1
2
3
4
5

Ignition switch
ON
OFF
Lock
P

Front brake switch

Starter switch

Speed sensor

Engine stop switch

Front right turn signal

Headlight

Headlight

Front left turn signal

Cooling fan relay

Horn and switch

Rear right turn signal

Brake light /tail light

Brake light /tail light

Licence plate light

Rear left turn signal

Starter relay & main fuse

Starter motor

Battery

Regulator/ rectifier

Alternator

Tip-over sensor

Crank position sensor

Cam position sensor

Gear position sensor

Oil pressure switch

Fuel pump /fuel level switch

Fuel pump relay

Injectors
1
2
3
4

Secondary throttle valve servo

Throttle position sensor

Coolant temp. sensor

Intake air temp. sensor

Intake air pressure sensor

Atmo. pressure sensor

Fuse box
1 Fan 10A
2 Fuel pump 10A
3 Headlight high 15A
4 Ignition 15A
5 Signal 15A
6 Headlight low 15A
7 Turn signal/ side stand relay

Clutch lever switch
L
Push
R

Turn signal switch

Dimmer switch
High
Low

Cooling fan and switch

# Reference

## Tools and Workshop Tips

● Building up a tool kit and equipping your workshop ● Using tools ● Understanding bearing, seal, fastener and chain sizes and markings ● Repair techniques

## Security

● Locks and chains ● U-locks ● Disc locks ● Alarms and immobilisers ● Security marking systems ● Tips on how to prevent bike theft

## Lubricants and fluids

● Engine oils ● Transmission (gear) oils ● Coolant/anti-freeze ● Fork oils and suspension fluids ● Brake/clutch fluids ● Spray lubes, degreasers and solvents

## Conversion Factors

34 Nm x 0.738
= 25 lbf ft

● Formulae for conversion of the metric (SI) units used throughout the manual into Imperial measures

## MOT Test Checks

● A guide to the UK MOT test ● Which items are tested ● How to prepare your motorcycle for the test and perform a pre-test check

## Storage

● How to prepare your motorcycle for going into storage and protect essential systems ● How to get the motorcycle back on the road

## Fault Finding

● Common faults and their likely causes ● How to check engine cylinder compression ● How to make electrical tests and use test meters

## Technical Terms Explained

● Component names, technical terms and common abbreviations explained

## Index

## Buying tools

A toolkit is a fundamental requirement for servicing and repairing a motorcycle. Although there will be an initial expense in building up enough tools for servicing, this will soon be offset by the savings made by doing the job yourself. As experience and confidence grow, additional tools can be added to enable the repair and overhaul of the motorcycle. Many of the specialist tools are expensive and not often used so it may be preferable to hire them, or for a group of friends or motorcycle club to join in the purchase.

As a rule, it is better to buy more expensive, good quality tools. Cheaper tools are likely to wear out faster and need to be renewed more often, nullifying the original saving.

*Warning: To avoid the risk of a poor quality tool breaking in use, causing injury or damage to the component being worked on, always aim to purchase tools which meet the relevant national safety standards.*

The following lists of tools do not represent the manufacturer's service tools, but serve as a guide to help the owner decide which tools are needed for this level of work. In addition, items such as an electric drill, hacksaw, files, soldering iron and a workbench equipped with a vice, may be needed. Although not classed as tools, a selection of bolts, screws, nuts, washers and pieces of tubing always come in useful.

For more information about tools, refer to the Haynes *Motorcycle Workshop Practice TechBook* (Bk. No. 3470).

## Manufacturer's service tools

Inevitably certain tasks require the use of a service tool. Where possible an alternative tool or method of approach is recommended, but sometimes there is no option if personal injury or damage to the component is to be avoided. Where required, service tools are referred to in the relevant procedure.

Service tools can usually only be purchased from a motorcycle dealer and are identified by a part number. Some of the commonly-used tools, such as rotor pullers, are available in aftermarket form from mail-order motorcycle tool and accessory suppliers.

# Maintenance and minor repair tools

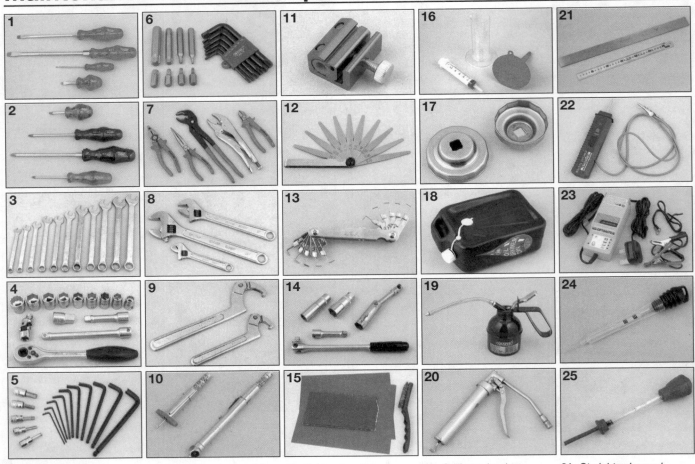

1 Set of flat-bladed screwdrivers
2 Set of Phillips head screwdrivers
3 Combination open-end and ring spanners
4 Socket set (3/8 inch or 1/2 inch drive)
5 Set of Allen keys or bits

6 Set of Torx keys or bits
7 Pliers, cutters and self-locking grips (Mole grips)
8 Adjustable spanners
9 C-spanners
10 Tread depth gauge and tyre pressure gauge

11 Cable oiler clamp
12 Feeler gauges
13 Spark plug gap measuring tool
14 Spark plug spanner or deep plug sockets
15 Wire brush and emery paper

16 Calibrated syringe, measuring vessel and funnel
17 Oil filter adapters
18 Oil drainer can or tray
19 Pump type oil can
20 Grease gun

21 Straight-edge and steel rule
22 Continuity tester
23 Battery charger
24 Hydrometer (for battery specific gravity check)
25 Anti-freeze tester (for liquid-cooled engines)

# Repair and overhaul tools

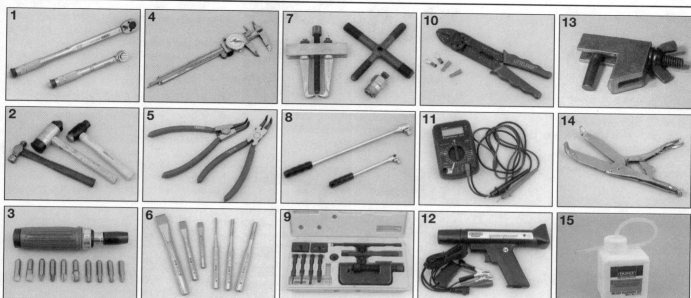

1  Torque wrench
   (small and mid-ranges)
2  Conventional, plastic or
   soft-faced hammers
3  Impact driver set

4  Vernier gauge
5  Circlip pliers (internal and
   external, or combination)
6  Set of cold chisels
   and punches

7  Selection of pullers
8  Breaker bars
9  Chain breaking/
   riveting tool set

10 Wire stripper and
   crimper tool
11 Multimeter (measures
   amps, volts and ohms)
12 Stroboscope (for
   dynamic timing checks)

13 Hose clamp
   (wingnut type shown)
14 Clutch holding tool
15 One-man brake/clutch
   bleeder kit

# Specialist tools

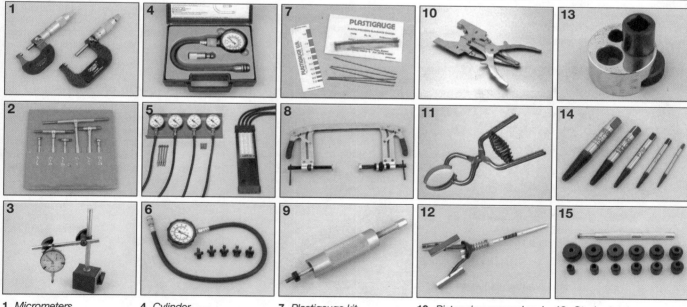

1  Micrometers
   (external type)
2  Telescoping gauges
3  Dial gauge

4  Cylinder
   compression gauge
5  Vacuum gauges (left) or
   manometer (right)
6  Oil pressure gauge

7  Plastigauge kit
8  Valve spring compressor
   (4-stroke engines)
9  Piston pin drawbolt tool

10 Piston ring removal and
   installation tool
11 Piston ring clamp
12 Cylinder bore hone
   (stone type shown)

13 Stud extractor
14 Screw extractor set
15 Bearing driver set

## 1  Workshop equipment and facilities

### The workbench

● Work is made much easier by raising the bike up on a ramp - components are much more accessible if raised to waist level. The hydraulic or pneumatic types seen in the dealer's workshop are a sound investment if you undertake a lot of repairs or overhauls (see illustration 1.1).

1.1  Hydraulic motorcycle ramp

● If raised off ground level, the bike must be supported on the ramp to avoid it falling. Most ramps incorporate a front wheel locating clamp which can be adjusted to suit different diameter wheels. When tightening the clamp, take care not to mark the wheel rim or damage the tyre - use wood blocks on each side to prevent this.
● Secure the bike to the ramp using tie-downs (see illustration 1.2). If the bike has only a sidestand, and hence leans at a dangerous angle when raised, support the bike on an auxiliary stand.

1.2  Tie-downs are used around the passenger footrests to secure the bike

● Auxiliary (paddock) stands are widely available from mail order companies or motorcycle dealers and attach either to the wheel axle or swingarm pivot (see illustration 1.3). If the motorcycle has a centrestand, you can support it under the crankcase to prevent it toppling whilst either wheel is removed (see illustration 1.4).

1.3  This auxiliary stand attaches to the swingarm pivot

1.4  Always use a block of wood between the engine and jack head when supporting the engine in this way

### Fumes and fire

● Refer to the Safety first! page at the beginning of the manual for full details. Make sure your workshop is equipped with a fire extinguisher suitable for fuel-related fires (Class B fire - flammable liquids) - it is not sufficient to have a water-filled extinguisher.
● Always ensure adequate ventilation is available. Unless an exhaust gas extraction system is available for use, ensure that the engine is run outside of the workshop.
● If working on the fuel system, make sure the workshop is ventilated to avoid a build-up of fumes. This applies equally to fume build-up when charging a battery. Do not smoke or allow anyone else to smoke in the workshop.

### Fluids

● If you need to drain fuel from the tank, store it in an approved container marked as suitable for the storage of petrol (gasoline) (see illustration 1.5). Do not store fuel in glass jars or bottles.

1.5  Use an approved can only for storing petrol (gasoline)

● Use proprietary engine degreasers or solvents which have a high flash-point, such as paraffin (kerosene), for cleaning off oil, grease and dirt - never use petrol (gasoline) for cleaning. Wear rubber gloves when handling solvent and engine degreaser. The fumes from certain solvents can be dangerous - always work in a well-ventilated area.

### Dust, eye and hand protection

● Protect your lungs from inhalation of dust particles by wearing a filtering mask over the nose and mouth. Many frictional materials still contain asbestos which is dangerous to your health. Protect your eyes from spouts of liquid and sprung components by wearing a pair of protective goggles (see illustration 1.6).

1.6  A fire extinguisher, goggles, mask and protective gloves should be at hand in the workshop

● Protect your hands from contact with solvents, fuel and oils by wearing rubber gloves. Alternatively apply a barrier cream to your hands before starting work. If handling hot components or fluids, wear suitable gloves to protect your hands from scalding and burns.

### What to do with old fluids

● Old cleaning solvent, fuel, coolant and oils should not be poured down domestic drains or onto the ground. Package the fluid up in old oil containers, label it accordingly, and take it to a garage or disposal facility. Contact your local authority for location of such sites or ring the oil care hotline.

OIL CARE
FOLLOW THE CODE
OIL BANK LINE
0800 66 33 66
www.oilbankline.org.uk

*Note: It is antisocial and illegal to dump oil down the drain. To find the location of your local oil recycling bank, call this number free.*

*In the USA, note that any oil supplier must accept used oil for recycling.*

## 2 Fasteners -
### screws, bolts and nuts

### *Fastener types and applications*

#### Bolts and screws

● Fastener head types are either of hexagonal, Torx or splined design, with internal and external versions of each type **(see illustrations 2.1 and 2.2)**; splined head fasteners are not in common use on motorcycles. The conventional slotted or Phillips head design is used for certain screws. Bolt or screw length is always measured from the underside of the head to the end of the item **(see illustration 2.11)**.

**2.1 Internal hexagon/Allen (A), Torx (B) and splined (C) fasteners, with corresponding bits**

**2.2 External Torx (A), splined (B) and hexagon (C) fasteners, with corresponding sockets**

● Certain fasteners on the motorcycle have a tensile marking on their heads, the higher the marking the stronger the fastener. High tensile fasteners generally carry a 10 or higher marking. Never replace a high tensile fastener with one of a lower tensile strength.

#### Washers **(see illustration 2.3)**

● Plain washers are used between a fastener head and a component to prevent damage to the component or to spread the load when torque is applied. Plain washers can also be used as spacers or shims in certain assemblies. Copper or aluminium plain washers are often used as sealing washers on drain plugs.

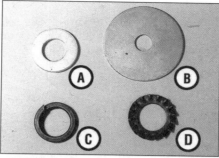

**2.3 Plain washer (A), penny washer (B), spring washer (C) and serrated washer (D)**

● The split-ring spring washer works by applying axial tension between the fastener head and component. If flattened, it is fatigued and must be renewed. If a plain (flat) washer is used on the fastener, position the spring washer between the fastener and the plain washer.

● Serrated star type washers dig into the fastener and component faces, preventing loosening. They are often used on electrical earth (ground) connections to the frame.

● Cone type washers (sometimes called Belleville) are conical and when tightened apply axial tension between the fastener head and component. They must be installed with the dished side against the component and often carry an OUTSIDE marking on their outer face. If flattened, they are fatigued and must be renewed.

● Tab washers are used to lock plain nuts or bolts on a shaft. A portion of the tab washer is bent up hard against one flat of the nut or bolt to prevent it loosening. Due to the tab washer being deformed in use, a new tab washer should be used every time it is disturbed.

● Wave washers are used to take up endfloat on a shaft. They provide light springing and prevent excessive side-to-side play of a component. Can be found on rocker arm shafts.

#### Nuts and split pins

● Conventional plain nuts are usually six-sided **(see illustration 2.4)**. They are sized by thread diameter and pitch. High tensile nuts carry a number on one end to denote their tensile strength.

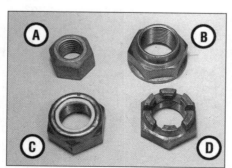

**2.4 Plain nut (A), shouldered locknut (B), nylon insert nut (C) and castellated nut (D)**

● Self-locking nuts either have a nylon insert, or two spring metal tabs, or a shoulder which is staked into a groove in the shaft - their advantage over conventional plain nuts is a resistance to loosening due to vibration. The nylon insert type can be used a number of times, but must be renewed when the friction of the nylon insert is reduced, ie when the nut spins freely on the shaft. The spring tab type can be reused unless the tabs are damaged. The shouldered type must be renewed every time it is disturbed.

● Split pins (cotter pins) are used to lock a castellated nut to a shaft or to prevent slackening of a plain nut. Common applications are wheel axles and brake torque arms. Because the split pin arms are deformed to lock around the nut a new split pin must always be used on installation - always fit the correct size split pin which will fit snugly in the shaft hole. Make sure the split pin arms are correctly located around the nut **(see illustrations 2.5 and 2.6)**.

**2.5 Bend split pin (cotter pin) arms as shown (arrows) to secure a castellated nut**

**2.6 Bend split pin (cotter pin) arms as shown to secure a plain nut**

*Caution: If the castellated nut slots do not align with the shaft hole after tightening to the torque setting, tighten the nut until the next slot aligns with the hole - never slacken the nut to align its slot.*

● R-pins (shaped like the letter R), or slip pins as they are sometimes called, are sprung and can be reused if they are otherwise in good condition. Always install R-pins with their closed end facing forwards **(see illustration 2.7)**.

**2.7 Correct fitting of R-pin. Arrow indicates forward direction**

### Circlips (see illustration 2.8)

● Circlips (sometimes called snap-rings) are used to retain components on a shaft or in a housing and have corresponding external or internal ears to permit removal. Parallel-sided (machined) circlips can be installed either way round in their groove, whereas stamped circlips (which have a chamfered edge on one face) must be installed with the chamfer facing away from the direction of thrust load (see illustration 2.9).

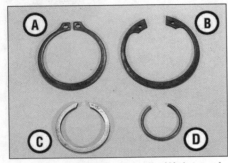

**2.8 External stamped circlip (A), internal stamped circlip (B), machined circlip (C) and wire circlip (D)**

● Always use circlip pliers to remove and install circlips; expand or compress them just enough to remove them. After installation, rotate the circlip in its groove to ensure it is securely seated. If installing a circlip on a splined shaft, always align its opening with a shaft channel to ensure the circlip ends are well supported and unlikely to catch (see illustration 2.10).

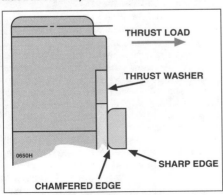

THRUST LOAD

THRUST WASHER

SHARP EDGE

CHAMFERED EDGE

0650H

**2.9 Correct fitting of a stamped circlip**

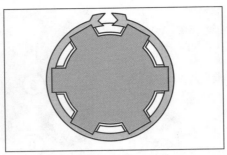

**2.10 Align circlip opening with shaft channel**

● Circlips can wear due to the thrust of components and become loose in their grooves, with the subsequent danger of becoming dislodged in operation. For this reason, renewal is advised every time a circlip is disturbed.
● Wire circlips are commonly used as piston pin retaining clips. If a removal tang is provided, long-nosed pliers can be used to dislodge them, otherwise careful use of a small flat-bladed screwdriver is necessary. Wire circlips should be renewed every time they are disturbed.

### Thread diameter and pitch

● Diameter of a male thread (screw, bolt or stud) is the outside diameter of the threaded portion (see illustration 2.11). Most motorcycle manufacturers use the ISO (International Standards Organisation) metric system expressed in millimetres, eg M6 refers to a 6 mm diameter thread. Sizing is the same for nuts, except that the thread diameter is measured across the valleys of the nut.
● Pitch is the distance between the peaks of the thread (see illustration 2.11). It is expressed in millimetres, thus a common bolt size may be expressed as 6.0 x 1.0 mm (6 mm thread diameter and 1 mm pitch). Generally pitch increases in proportion to thread diameter, although there are always exceptions.
● Thread diameter and pitch are related for conventional fastener applications and the accompanying table can be used as a guide. Additionally, the AF (Across Flats), spanner or socket size dimension of the bolt or nut (see illustration 2.11) is linked to thread and pitch specification. Thread pitch can be measured with a thread gauge (see illustration 2.12).

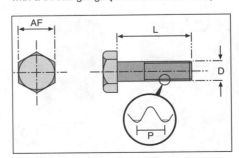

AF

L

D

P

**2.11 Fastener length (L), thread diameter (D), thread pitch (P) and head size (AF)**

**2.12 Using a thread gauge to measure pitch**

| AF size | Thread diameter x pitch (mm) |
|---------|------------------------------|
| 8 mm    | M5 x 0.8                     |
| 8 mm    | M6 x 1.0                     |
| 10 mm   | M6 x 1.0                     |
| 12 mm   | M8 x 1.25                    |
| 14 mm   | M10 x 1.25                   |
| 17 mm   | M12 x 1.25                   |

● The threads of most fasteners are of the right-hand type, ie they are turned clockwise to tighten and anti-clockwise to loosen. The reverse situation applies to left-hand thread fasteners, which are turned anti-clockwise to tighten and clockwise to loosen. Left-hand threads are used where rotation of a component might loosen a conventional right-hand thread fastener.

### Seized fasteners

● Corrosion of external fasteners due to water or reaction between two dissimilar metals can occur over a period of time. It will build up sooner in wet conditions or in countries where salt is used on the roads during the winter. If a fastener is severely corroded it is likely that normal methods of removal will fail and result in its head being ruined. When you attempt removal, the fastener thread should be heard to crack free and unscrew easily - if it doesn't, stop there before damaging something.
● A smart tap on the head of the fastener will often succeed in breaking free corrosion which has occurred in the threads (see illustration 2.13).
● An aerosol penetrating fluid (such as WD-40) applied the night beforehand may work its way down into the thread and ease removal. Depending on the location, you may be able to make up a Plasticine well around the fastener head and fill it with penetrating fluid.

**2.13 A sharp tap on the head of a fastener will often break free a corroded thread**

● If you are working on an engine internal component, corrosion will most likely not be a problem due to the well lubricated environment. However, components can be very tight and an impact driver is a useful tool in freeing them (see illustration 2.14).

**2.14 Using an impact driver to free a fastener**

● Where corrosion has occurred between dissimilar metals (eg steel and aluminium alloy), the application of heat to the fastener head will create a disproportionate expansion rate between the two metals and break the seizure caused by the corrosion. Whether heat can be applied depends on the location of the fastener - any surrounding components likely to be damaged must first be removed (see illustration 2.15). Heat can be applied using a paint stripper heat gun or clothes iron, or by immersing the component in boiling water - wear protective gloves to prevent scalding or burns to the hands.

**2.15 Using heat to free a seized fastener**

● As a last resort, it is possible to use a hammer and cold chisel to work the fastener head unscrewed (see illustration 2.16). This will damage the fastener, but more importantly extreme care must be taken not to damage the surrounding component.

*Caution: Remember that the component being secured is generally of more value than the bolt, nut or screw - when the fastener is freed, do not unscrew it with force, instead work the fastener back and forth when resistance is felt to prevent thread damage.*

**2.16 Using a hammer and chisel to free a seized fastener**

### Broken fasteners and damaged heads

● If the shank of a broken bolt or screw is accessible you can grip it with self-locking grips. The knurled wheel type stud extractor tool or self-gripping stud puller tool is particularly useful for removing the long studs which screw into the cylinder mouth surface of the crankcase or bolts and screws from which the head has broken off (see illustration 2.17). Studs can also be removed by locking two nuts together on the threaded end of the stud and using a spanner on the lower nut (see illustration 2.18).

**2.17 Using a stud extractor tool to remove a broken crankcase stud**

**2.18 Two nuts can be locked together to unscrew a stud from a component**

● A bolt or screw which has broken off below or level with the casing must be extracted using a screw extractor set. Centre punch the fastener to centralise the drill bit, then drill a hole in the fastener (see illustration 2.19). Select a drill bit which is approximately half to three-quarters the

**2.19 When using a screw extractor, first drill a hole in the fastener . . .**

diameter of the fastener and drill to a depth which will accommodate the extractor. Use the largest size extractor possible, but avoid leaving too small a wall thickness otherwise the extractor will merely force the fastener walls outwards wedging it in the casing thread.

● If a spiral type extractor is used, thread it anti-clockwise into the fastener. As it is screwed in, it will grip the fastener and unscrew it from the casing (see illustration 2.20).

**2.20 . . . then thread the extractor anti-clockwise into the fastener**

● If a taper type extractor is used, tap it into the fastener so that it is firmly wedged in place. Unscrew the extractor (anti-clockwise) to draw the fastener out.

> ⚠ *Warning: Stud extractors are very hard and may break off in the fastener if care is not taken - ask an engineer about spark erosion if this happens.*

● Alternatively, the broken bolt/screw can be drilled out and the hole retapped for an oversize bolt/screw or a diamond-section thread insert. It is essential that the drilling is carried out squarely and to the correct depth, otherwise the casing may be ruined - if in doubt, entrust the work to an engineer.

● Bolts and nuts with rounded corners cause the correct size spanner or socket to slip when force is applied. Of the types of spanner/socket available always use a six-point type rather than an eight or twelve-point type - better grip

**2.21 Comparison of surface drive ring spanner (left) with 12-point type (right)**

is obtained. Surface drive spanners grip the middle of the hex flats, rather than the corners, and are thus good in cases of damaged heads **(see illustration 2.21)**.

● Slotted-head or Phillips-head screws are often damaged by the use of the wrong size screwdriver. Allen-head and Torx-head screws are much less likely to sustain damage. If enough of the screw head is exposed you can use a hacksaw to cut a slot in its head and then use a conventional flat-bladed screwdriver to remove it. Alternatively use a hammer and cold chisel to tap the head of the fastener around to slacken it. Always replace damaged fasteners with new ones, preferably Torx or Allen-head type.

HAYNES
HiNT

*A dab of valve grinding compound between the screw head and screw-driver tip will often give a good grip.*

### Thread repair

● Threads (particularly those in aluminium alloy components) can be damaged by overtightening, being assembled with dirt in the threads, or from a component working loose and vibrating. Eventually the thread will fail completely, and it will be impossible to tighten the fastener.

● If a thread is damaged or clogged with old locking compound it can be renovated with a thread repair tool (thread chaser) **(see illustrations 2.22 and 2.23)**; special thread

**2.22 A thread repair tool being used to correct an internal thread**

**2.23 A thread repair tool being used to correct an external thread**

chasers are available for spark plug hole threads. The tool will not cut a new thread, but clean and true the original thread. Make sure that you use the correct diameter and pitch tool. Similarly, external threads can be cleaned up with a die or a thread restorer file **(see illustration 2.24)**.

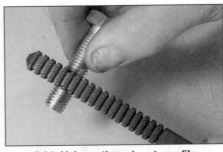

**2.24 Using a thread restorer file**

● It is possible to drill out the old thread and retap the component to the next thread size. This will work where there is enough surrounding material and a new bolt or screw can be obtained. Sometimes, however, this is not possible - such as where the bolt/screw passes through another component which must also be suitably modified, also in cases where a spark plug or oil drain plug cannot be obtained in a larger diameter thread size.

● The diamond-section thread insert (often known by its popular trade name of Heli-Coil) is a simple and effective method of renewing the thread and retaining the original size. A kit can be purchased which contains the tap, insert and installing tool **(see illustration 2.25)**. Drill out the damaged thread with the size drill specified **(see illustration 2.26)**. Carefully retap the thread **(see illustration 2.27)**. Install the

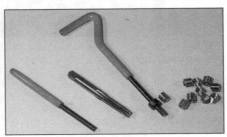

**2.25 Obtain a thread insert kit to suit the thread diameter and pitch required**

**2.26 To install a thread insert, first drill out the original thread . . .**

**2.27 . . . tap a new thread . . .**

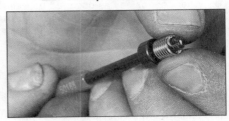

**2.28 . . . fit insert on the installing tool . . .**

**2.29 . . . and thread into the component . . .**

**2.30 . . . break off the tang when complete**

insert on the installing tool and thread it slowly into place using a light downward pressure **(see illustrations 2.28 and 2.29)**. When positioned between a 1/4 and 1/2 turn below the surface withdraw the installing tool and use the break-off tool to press down on the tang, breaking it off **(see illustration 2.30)**.

● There are epoxy thread repair kits on the market which can rebuild stripped internal threads, although this repair should not be used on high load-bearing components.

## Thread locking and sealing compounds

● Locking compounds are used in locations where the fastener is prone to loosening due to vibration or on important safety-related items which might cause loss of control of the motorcycle if they fail. It is also used where important fasteners cannot be secured by other means such as lockwashers or split pins.

● Before applying locking compound, make sure that the threads (internal and external) are clean and dry with all old compound removed. Select a compound to suit the component being secured - a non-permanent general locking and sealing type is suitable for most applications, but a high strength type is needed for permanent fixing of studs in castings. Apply a drop or two of the compound to the first few threads of the fastener, then thread it into place and tighten to the specified torque. Do not apply excessive thread locking compound otherwise the thread may be damaged on subsequent removal.

● Certain fasteners are impregnated with a dry film type coating of locking compound on their threads. Always renew this type of fastener if disturbed.

● Anti-seize compounds, such as copper-based greases, can be applied to protect threads from seizure due to extreme heat and corrosion. A common instance is spark plug threads and exhaust system fasteners.

## 3 Measuring tools and gauges

## Feeler gauges

● Feeler gauges (or blades) are used for measuring small gaps and clearances (see illustration 3.1). They can also be used to measure endfloat (sideplay) of a component on a shaft where access is not possible with a dial gauge.

● Feeler gauge sets should be treated with care and not bent or damaged. They are etched with their size on one face. Keep them clean and very lightly oiled to prevent corrosion build-up.

**3.1 Feeler gauges are used for measuring small gaps and clearances - thickness is marked on one face of gauge**

● When measuring a clearance, select a gauge which is a light sliding fit between the two components. You may need to use two gauges together to measure the clearance accurately.

## Micrometers

● A micrometer is a precision tool capable of measuring to 0.01 or 0.001 of a millimetre. It should always be stored in its case and not in the general toolbox. It must be kept clean and never dropped, otherwise its frame or measuring anvils could be distorted resulting in inaccurate readings.

● External micrometers are used for measuring outside diameters of components and have many more applications than internal micrometers. Micrometers are available in different size ranges, eg 0 to 25 mm, 25 to 50 mm, and upwards in 25 mm steps; some large micrometers have interchangeable anvils to allow a range of measurements to be taken. Generally the largest precision measurement you are likely to take on a motorcycle is the piston diameter.

● Internal micrometers (or bore micrometers) are used for measuring inside diameters, such as valve guides and cylinder bores. Telescoping gauges and small hole gauges are used in conjunction with an external micrometer, whereas the more expensive internal micrometers have their own measuring device.

### External micrometer

**Note:** *The conventional analogue type instrument is described. Although much easier to read, digital micrometers are considerably more expensive.*

● Always check the calibration of the micrometer before use. With the anvils closed (0 to 25 mm type) or set over a test gauge (for

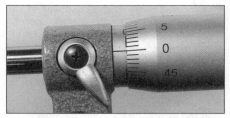

**3.2 Check micrometer calibration before use**

the larger types) the scale should read zero (see illustration 3.2); make sure that the anvils (and test piece) are clean first. Any discrepancy can be adjusted by referring to the instructions supplied with the tool. Remember that the micrometer is a precision measuring tool - don't force the anvils closed, use the ratchet (4) on the end of the micrometer to close it. In this way, a measured force is always applied.

● To use, first make sure that the item being measured is clean. Place the anvil of the micrometer (1) against the item and use the thimble (2) to bring the spindle (3) lightly into contact with the other side of the item (see illustration 3.3). Don't tighten the thimble down because this will damage the micrometer - instead use the ratchet (4) on the end of the micrometer. The ratchet mechanism applies a measured force preventing damage to the instrument.

● The micrometer is read by referring to the linear scale on the sleeve and the annular scale on the thimble. Read off the sleeve first to obtain the base measurement, then add the fine measurement from the thimble to obtain the overall reading. The linear scale on the sleeve represents the measuring range of the micrometer (eg 0 to 25 mm). The annular scale

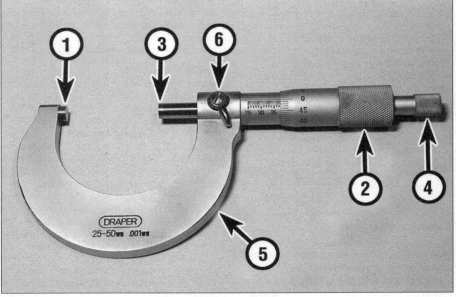

**3.3 Micrometer component parts**

| | | |
|---|---|---|
| 1 Anvil | 3 Spindle | 5 Frame |
| 2 Thimble | 4 Ratchet | 6 Locking lever |

on the thimble will be in graduations of 0.01 mm (or as marked on the frame) - one full revolution of the thimble will move 0.5 mm on the linear scale. Take the reading where the datum line on the sleeve intersects the thimble's scale. Always position the eye directly above the scale otherwise an inaccurate reading will result.

In the example shown the item measures 2.95 mm (see illustration 3.4):

| | |
|---|---|
| Linear scale | 2.00 mm |
| Linear scale | 0.50 mm |
| Annular scale | 0.45 mm |
| Total figure | 2.95 mm |

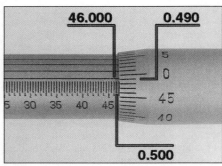

**3.5 Micrometer reading of 46.99 mm on linear and annular scales . . .**

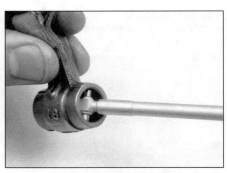

**3.7 Expand the telescoping gauge in the bore, lock its position . . .**

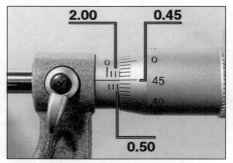

**3.4 Micrometer reading of 2.95 mm**

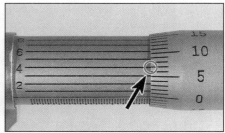

**3.6 . . . and 0.004 mm on vernier scale**

**3.8 . . . then measure the gauge with a micrometer**

Most micrometers have a locking lever (6) on the frame to hold the setting in place, allowing the item to be removed from the micrometer.
● Some micrometers have a vernier scale on their sleeve, providing an even finer measurement to be taken, in 0.001 increments of a millimetre. Take the sleeve and thimble measurement as described above, then check which graduation on the vernier scale aligns with that of the annular scale on the thimble **Note:** *The eye must be perpendicular to the scale when taking the vernier reading - if necessary rotate the body of the micrometer to ensure this.* Multiply the vernier scale figure by 0.001 and add it to the base and fine measurement figures.

In the example shown the item measures 46.994 mm (see illustrations 3.5 and 3.6):

| | |
|---|---|
| Linear scale (base) | 46.000 mm |
| Linear scale (base) | 00.500 mm |
| Annular scale (fine) | 00.490 mm |
| Vernier scale | 00.004 mm |
| Total figure | 46.994 mm |

### Internal micrometer

● Internal micrometers are available for measuring bore diameters, but are expensive and unlikely to be available for home use. It is suggested that a set of telescoping gauges and small hole gauges, both of which must be used with an external micrometer, will suffice for taking internal measurements on a motorcycle.
● Telescoping gauges can be used to

measure internal diameters of components. Select a gauge with the correct size range, make sure its ends are clean and insert it into the bore. Expand the gauge, then lock its position and withdraw it from the bore (see illustration 3.7). Measure across the gauge ends with a micrometer (see illustration 3.8).
● Very small diameter bores (such as valve guides) are measured with a small hole gauge. Once adjusted to a slip-fit inside the component, its position is locked and the gauge withdrawn for measurement with a micrometer (see illustrations 3.9 and 3.10).

### Vernier caliper

**Note:** *The conventional linear and dial gauge type instruments are described. Digital types are easier to read, but are far more expensive.*
● The vernier caliper does not provide the precision of a micrometer, but is versatile in being able to measure internal and external diameters. Some types also incorporate a depth gauge. It is ideal for measuring clutch plate friction material and spring free lengths.
● To use the conventional linear scale vernier, slacken off the vernier clamp screws (1) and set its jaws over (2), or inside (3), the item to be measured (see illustration 3.11). Slide the jaw into contact, using the thumb-wheel (4) for fine movement of the sliding scale (5) then tighten the clamp screws (1). Read off the main scale (6) where the zero on the sliding scale (5) intersects it, taking the whole number to the left of the zero; this provides the base measurement. View along the sliding scale and select the division which

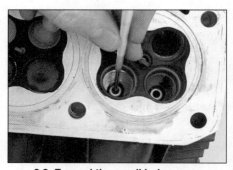

**3.9 Expand the small hole gauge in the bore, lock its position . . .**

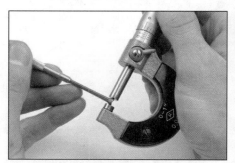

**3.10 . . . then measure the gauge with a micrometer**

lines up exactly with any of the divisions on the main scale, noting that the divisions usually represents 0.02 of a millimetre. Add this fine measurement to the base measurement to obtain the total reading.

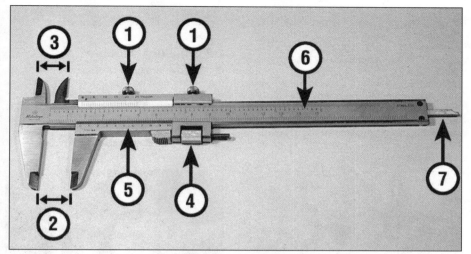

**3.11 Vernier component parts (linear gauge)**

| | | | |
|---|---|---|---|
| 1 | Clamp screws | 3 | Internal jaws |
| 2 | External jaws | 4 | Thumbwheel |
| 5 | Sliding scale | 7 | Depth gauge |
| 6 | Main scale | | |

In the example shown the item measures 55.92 mm **(see illustration 3.12)**:

**3.12 Vernier gauge reading of 55.92 mm**

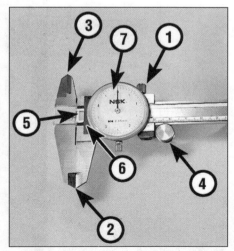

**3.13 Vernier component parts (dial gauge)**

| | | | |
|---|---|---|---|
| 1 | Clamp screw | 5 | Main scale |
| 2 | External jaws | 6 | Sliding scale |
| 3 | Internal jaws | 7 | Dial gauge |
| 4 | Thumbwheel | | |

| Base measurement | 55.00 mm |
|---|---|
| Fine measurement | 00.92 mm |
| **Total figure** | **55.92 mm** |

● Some vernier calipers are equipped with a dial gauge for fine measurement. Before use, check that the jaws are clean, then close them fully and check that the dial gauge reads zero. If necessary adjust the gauge ring accordingly. Slacken the vernier clamp screw (1) and set its jaws over (2), or inside (3), the item to be measured **(see illustration 3.13)**. Slide the jaws into contact, using the thumbwheel (4) for fine movement. Read off the main scale (5) where the edge of the sliding scale (6) intersects it, taking the whole number to the left of the zero; this provides the base measurement. Read off the needle position on the dial gauge (7) scale to provide the fine measurement; each division represents 0.05 of a millimetre. Add this fine measurement to the base measurement to obtain the total reading.

In the example shown the item measures 55.95 mm **(see illustration 3.14)**:

| Base measurement | 55.00 mm |
|---|---|
| Fine measurement | 00.95 mm |
| **Total figure** | **55.95 mm** |

**3.14 Vernier gauge reading of 55.95 mm**

## Plastigauge

● Plastigauge is a plastic material which can be compressed between two surfaces to measure the oil clearance between them. The width of the compressed Plastigauge is measured against a calibrated scale to determine the clearance.

● Common uses of Plastigauge are for measuring the clearance between crankshaft journal and main bearing inserts, between crankshaft journal and big-end bearing inserts, and between camshaft and bearing surfaces. The following example describes big-end oil clearance measurement.

● Handle the Plastigauge material carefully to prevent distortion. Using a sharp knife, cut a length which corresponds with the width of the bearing being measured and place it carefully across the journal so that it is parallel with the shaft **(see illustration 3.15)**. Carefully install both bearing shells and the connecting rod. Without rotating the rod on the journal tighten its bolts or nuts (as applicable) to the specified torque. The connecting rod and bearings are then disassembled and the crushed Plastigauge examined.

**3.15 Plastigauge placed across shaft journal**

● Using the scale provided in the Plastigauge kit, measure the width of the material to determine the oil clearance **(see illustration 3.16)**. Always remove all traces of Plastigauge after use using your fingernails.

*Caution: Arriving at the correct clearance demands that the assembly is torqued correctly, according to the settings and sequence (where applicable) provided by the motorcycle manufacturer.*

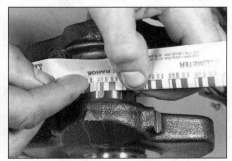

**3.16 Measuring the width of the crushed Plastigauge**

## Dial gauge or DTI (Dial Test Indicator)

● A dial gauge can be used to accurately measure small amounts of movement. Typical uses are measuring shaft runout or shaft endfloat (sideplay) and setting piston position for ignition timing on two-strokes. A dial gauge set usually comes with a range of different probes and adapters and mounting equipment.

● The gauge needle must point to zero when at rest. Rotate the ring around its periphery to zero the gauge.

● Check that the gauge is capable of reading the extent of movement in the work. Most gauges have a small dial set in the face which records whole millimetres of movement as well as the fine scale around the face periphery which is calibrated in 0.01 mm divisions. Read off the small dial first to obtain the base measurement, then add the measurement from the fine scale to obtain the total reading.

In the example shown the gauge reads 1.48 mm **(see illustration 3.17)**:

| | |
|---|---|
| Base measurement | 1.00 mm |
| Fine measurement | 0.48 mm |
| Total figure | **1.48 mm** |

**3.17  Dial gauge reading of 1.48 mm**

● If measuring shaft runout, the shaft must be supported in vee-blocks and the gauge mounted on a stand perpendicular to the shaft. Rest the tip of the gauge against the centre of the shaft and rotate the shaft slowly whilst watching the gauge reading **(see illustration 3.18)**. Take several measurements along the length of the shaft and record the

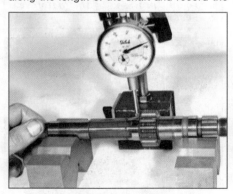

**3.18  Using a dial gauge to measure shaft runout**

maximum gauge reading as the amount of runout in the shaft. **Note:** *The reading obtained will be total runout at that point - some manufacturers specify that the runout figure is halved to compare with their specified runout limit.*

● Endfloat (sideplay) measurement requires that the gauge is mounted securely to the surrounding component with its probe touching the end of the shaft. Using hand pressure, push and pull on the shaft noting the maximum endfloat recorded on the gauge **(see illustration 3.19)**.

**3.19  Using a dial gauge to measure shaft endfloat**

● A dial gauge with suitable adapters can be used to determine piston position BTDC on two-stroke engines for the purposes of ignition timing. The gauge, adapter and suitable length probe are installed in the place of the spark plug and the gauge zeroed at TDC. If the piston position is specified as 1.14 mm BTDC, rotate the engine back to 2.00 mm BTDC, then slowly forwards to 1.14 mm BTDC.

## Cylinder compression gauges

● A compression gauge is used for measuring cylinder compression. Either the rubber-cone type or the threaded adapter type can be used. The latter is preferred to ensure a perfect seal against the cylinder head. A 0 to 300 psi (0 to 20 Bar) type gauge (for petrol/gasoline engines) will be suitable for motorcycles.

● The spark plug is removed and the gauge either held hard against the cylinder head (cone type) or the gauge adapter screwed into the cylinder head (threaded type) **(see illustration 3.20)**. Cylinder compression is measured with the engine turning over, but not running - carry out the compression test as described in

**3.20  Using a rubber-cone type cylinder compression gauge**

*Fault Finding Equipment.* The gauge will hold the reading until manually released.

## Oil pressure gauge

● An oil pressure gauge is used for measuring engine oil pressure. Most gauges come with a set of adapters to fit the thread of the take-off point **(see illustration 3.21)**. If the take-off point specified by the motorcycle manufacturer is an external oil pipe union, make sure that the specified replacement union is used to prevent oil starvation.

**3.21  Oil pressure gauge and take-off point adapter (arrow)**

● Oil pressure is measured with the engine running (at a specific rpm) and often the manufacturer will specify pressure limits for a cold and hot engine.

## Straight-edge and surface plate

● If checking the gasket face of a component for warpage, place a steel rule or precision straight-edge across the gasket face and measure any gap between the straight-edge and component with feeler gauges **(see illustration 3.22)**. Check diagonally across the component and between mounting holes **(see illustration 3.23)**.

**3.22  Use a straight-edge and feeler gauges to check for warpage**

**3.23  Check for warpage in these directions**

● Checking individual components for warpage, such as clutch plain (metal) plates, requires a perfectly flat plate or piece or plate glass and feeler gauges.

## 4  Torque and leverage

### What is torque?

● Torque describes the twisting force about a shaft. The amount of torque applied is determined by the distance from the centre of the shaft to the end of the lever and the amount of force being applied to the end of the lever; distance multiplied by force equals torque.

● The manufacturer applies a measured torque to a bolt or nut to ensure that it will not slacken in use and to hold two components securely together without movement in the joint. The actual torque setting depends on the thread size, bolt or nut material and the composition of the components being held.

● Too little torque may cause the fastener to loosen due to vibration, whereas too much torque will distort the joint faces of the component or cause the fastener to shear off. Always stick to the specified torque setting.

### Using a torque wrench

● Check the calibration of the torque wrench and make sure it has a suitable range for the job. Torque wrenches are available in Nm (Newton-metres), kgf m (kilograms-force metre), lbf ft (pounds-feet), lbf in (inch-pounds). Do not confuse lbf ft with lbf in.

● Adjust the tool to the desired torque on the scale (see illustration 4.1). If your torque wrench is not calibrated in the units specified, carefully convert the figure (see Conversion Factors). A manufacturer sometimes gives a torque setting as a range (8 to 10 Nm) rather than a single figure - in this case set the tool midway between the two settings. The same torque may be expressed as 9 Nm ± 1 Nm. Some torque wrenches have a method of locking the setting so that it isn't inadvertently altered during use.

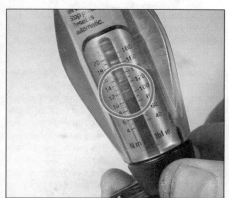

**4.1  Set the torque wrench index mark to the setting required, in this case 12 Nm**

● Install the bolts/nuts in their correct location and secure them lightly. Their threads must be clean and free of any old locking compound. Unless specified the threads and flange should be dry - oiled threads are necessary in certain circumstances and the manufacturer will take this into account in the specified torque figure. Similarly, the manufacturer may also specify the application of thread-locking compound.

● Tighten the fasteners in the specified sequence until the torque wrench clicks, indicating that the torque setting has been reached. Apply the torque again to double-check the setting. Where different thread diameter fasteners secure the component, as a rule tighten the larger diameter ones first.

● When the torque wrench has been finished with, release the lock (where applicable) and fully back off its setting to zero - do not leave the torque wrench tensioned. Also, do not use a torque wrench for slackening a fastener.

### Angle-tightening

● Manufacturers often specify a figure in degrees for final tightening of a fastener. This usually follows tightening to a specific torque setting.

● A degree disc can be set and attached to the socket (see illustration 4.2) or a protractor can be used to mark the angle of movement on the bolt/nut head and the surrounding casting (see illustration 4.3).

**4.2  Angle tightening can be accomplished with a torque-angle gauge . . .**

**4.3  . . . or by marking the angle on the surrounding component**

### Loosening sequences

● Where more than one bolt/nut secures a component, loosen each fastener evenly a little at a time. In this way, not all the stress of the joint is held by one fastener and the components are not likely to distort.

● If a tightening sequence is provided, work in the REVERSE of this, but if not, work from the outside in, in a criss-cross sequence (see illustration 4.4).

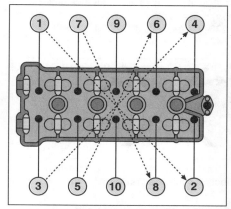

**4.4  When slackening, work from the outside inwards**

### Tightening sequences

● If a component is held by more than one fastener it is important that the retaining bolts/nuts are tightened evenly to prevent uneven stress build-up and distortion of sealing faces. This is especially important on high-compression joints such as the cylinder head.

● A sequence is usually provided by the manufacturer, either in a diagram or actually marked in the casting. If not, always start in the centre and work outwards in a criss-cross pattern (see illustration 4.5). Start off by securing all bolts/nuts finger-tight, then set the torque wrench and tighten each fastener by a small amount in sequence until the final torque is reached. By following this practice,

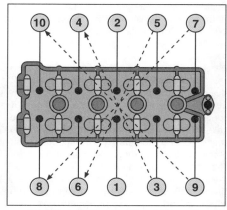

**4.5  When tightening, work from the inside outwards**

the joint will be held evenly and will not be distorted. Important joints, such as the cylinder head and big-end fasteners often have two- or three-stage torque settings.

## Applying leverage

● Use tools at the correct angle. Position a socket wrench or spanner on the bolt/nut so that you pull it towards you when loosening. If this can't be done, push the spanner without curling your fingers around it **(see illustration 4.6)** - the spanner may slip or the fastener loosen suddenly, resulting in your fingers being crushed against a component.

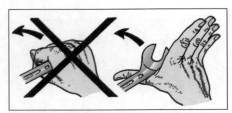

**4.6 If you can't pull on the spanner to loosen a fastener, push with your hand open**

● Additional leverage is gained by extending the length of the lever. The best way to do this is to use a breaker bar instead of the regular length tool, or to slip a length of tubing over the end of the spanner or socket wrench.
● If additional leverage will not work, the fastener head is either damaged or firmly corroded in place (see *Fasteners*).

## 5 Bearings

## Bearing removal and installation

### Drivers and sockets

● Before removing a bearing, always inspect the casing to see which way it must be driven out - some casings will have retaining plates or a cast step. Also check for any identifying markings on the bearing and if installed to a certain depth, measure this at this stage. Some roller bearings are sealed on one side - take note of the original fitted position.
● Bearings can be driven out of a casing using a bearing driver tool (with the correct size head) or a socket of the correct diameter. Select the driver head or socket so that it contacts the outer race of the bearing, not the balls/rollers or inner race. Always support the casing around the bearing housing with wood blocks, otherwise there is a risk of fracture. The bearing is driven out with a few blows on the driver or socket from a heavy mallet. Unless access is severely restricted (as with wheel bearings), a pin-punch is not recommended unless it is moved around the bearing to keep it square in its housing.

● The same equipment can be used to install bearings. Make sure the bearing housing is supported on wood blocks and line up the bearing in its housing. Fit the bearing as noted on removal - generally they are installed with their marked side facing outwards. Tap the bearing squarely into its housing using a driver or socket which bears only on the bearing's outer race - contact with the bearing balls/rollers or inner race will destroy it **(see illustrations 5.1 and 5.2)**.
● Check that the bearing inner race and balls/rollers rotate freely.

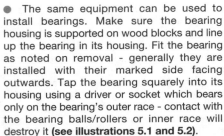

**5.1 Using a bearing driver against the bearing's outer race**

**5.2 Using a large socket against the bearing's outer race**

### Pullers and slide-hammers

● Where a bearing is pressed on a shaft a puller will be required to extract it **(see illustration 5.3)**. Make sure that the puller clamp or legs fit securely behind the bearing and are unlikely to slip out. If pulling a bearing

**5.3 This bearing puller clamps behind the bearing and pressure is applied to the shaft end to draw the bearing off**

off a gear shaft for example, you may have to locate the puller behind a gear pinion if there is no access to the race and draw the gear pinion off the shaft as well **(see illustration 5.4)**.

*Caution: Ensure that the puller's centre bolt locates securely against the end of the shaft and will not slip when pressure is applied. Also ensure that puller does not damage the shaft end.*

**5.4 Where no access is available to the rear of the bearing, it is sometimes possible to draw off the adjacent component**

● Operate the puller so that its centre bolt exerts pressure on the shaft end and draws the bearing off the shaft.
● When installing the bearing on the shaft, tap only on the bearing's inner race - contact with the balls/rollers or outer race with destroy the bearing. Use a socket or length of tubing as a drift which fits over the shaft end **(see illustration 5.5)**.

**5.5 When installing a bearing on a shaft use a piece of tubing which bears only on the bearing's inner race**

● Where a bearing locates in a blind hole in a casing, it cannot be driven or pulled out as described above. A slide-hammer with knife-edged bearing puller attachment will be required. The puller attachment passes through the bearing and when tightened expands to fit firmly behind the bearing **(see illustration 5.6)**. By operating the slide-hammer part of the tool the bearing is jarred out of its housing **(see illustration 5.7)**.
● It is possible, if the bearing is of reasonable weight, for it to drop out of its housing if the casing is heated as described opposite. If this

**5.6 Expand the bearing puller so that it locks behind the bearing . . .**

**5.7 . . . attach the slide hammer to the bearing puller**

method is attempted, first prepare a work surface which will enable the casing to be tapped face down to help dislodge the bearing - a wood surface is ideal since it will not damage the casing's gasket surface. Wearing protective gloves, tap the heated casing several times against the work surface to dislodge the bearing under its own weight **(see illustration 5.8)**.

**5.8 Tapping a casing face down on wood blocks can often dislodge a bearing**

● Bearings can be installed in blind holes using the driver or socket method described above.

## Drawbolts

● Where a bearing or bush is set in the eye of a component, such as a suspension linkage arm or connecting rod small-end, removal by drift may damage the component. Furthermore, a rubber bushing in a shock absorber eye cannot successfully be driven out of position. If access is available to a engineering press, the task is straightforward. If not, a drawbolt can be fabricated to extract the bearing or bush.

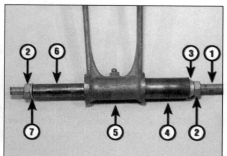

**5.9 Drawbolt component parts assembled on a suspension arm**

1 Bolt or length of threaded bar
2 Nuts
3 Washer (external diameter greater than tubing internal diameter)
4 Tubing (internal diameter sufficient to accommodate bearing)
5 Suspension arm with bearing
6 Tubing (external diameter slightly smaller than bearing)
7 Washer (external diameter slightly smaller than bearing)

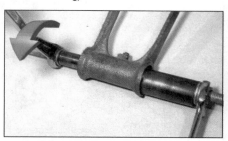

**5.10 Drawing the bearing out of the suspension arm**

● To extract the bearing/bush you will need a long bolt with nut (or piece of threaded bar with two nuts), a piece of tubing which has an internal diameter larger than the bearing/bush, another piece of tubing which has an external diameter slightly smaller than the bearing/bush, and a selection of washers **(see illustrations 5.9 and 5.10)**. Note that the pieces of tubing must be of the same length, or longer, than the bearing/bush.
● The same kit (without the pieces of tubing) can be used to draw the new bearing/bush back into place **(see illustration 5.11)**.

**5.11 Installing a new bearing (1) in the suspension arm**

### Temperature change

● If the bearing's outer race is a tight fit in the casing, the aluminium casing can be heated to release its grip on the bearing. Aluminium will expand at a greater rate than the steel bearing outer race. There are several ways to do this, but avoid any localised extreme heat (such as a blow torch) - aluminium alloy has a low melting point.
● Approved methods of heating a casing are using a domestic oven (heated to 100°C) or immersing the casing in boiling water **(see illustration 5.12)**. Low temperature range localised heat sources such as a paint stripper heat gun or clothes iron can also be used **(see illustration 5.13)**. Alternatively, soak a rag in boiling water, wring it out and wrap it around the bearing housing.

> ⚠️ **Warning: All of these methods require care in use to prevent scalding and burns to the hands. Wear protective gloves when handling hot components.**

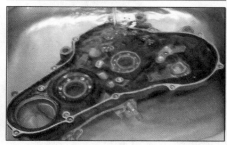

**5.12 A casing can be immersed in a sink of boiling water to aid bearing removal**

**5.13 Using a localised heat source to aid bearing removal**

● If heating the whole casing note that plastic components, such as the neutral switch, may suffer - remove them beforehand.
● After heating, remove the bearing as described above. You may find that the expansion is sufficient for the bearing to fall out of the casing under its own weight or with a light tap on the driver or socket.
● If necessary, the casing can be heated to aid bearing installation, and this is sometimes the recommended procedure if the motorcycle manufacturer has designed the housing and bearing fit with this intention.

Installation of bearings can be eased by placing them in a freezer the night before installation. The steel bearing will contract slightly, allowing easy insertion in its housing. This is often useful when installing steering head outer races in the frame.

## Bearing types and markings

Plain shell bearings, ball bearings, needle roller bearings and tapered roller bearings will all be found on motorcycles (see illustrations 5.14 and 5.15). The ball and roller types are usually caged between an inner and outer race, but uncaged variations may be found.

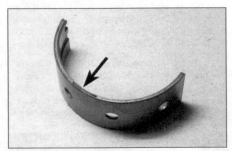

5.14 Shell bearings are either plain or grooved. They are usually identified by colour code (arrow)

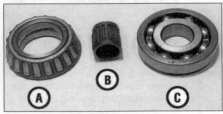

5.15 Tapered roller bearing (A), needle roller bearing (B) and ball journal bearing (C)

Shell bearings (often called inserts) are usually found at the crankshaft main and connecting rod big-end where they are good at coping with high loads. They are made of a phosphor-bronze material and are impregnated with self-lubricating properties.

Ball bearings and needle roller bearings consist of a steel inner and outer race with the balls or rollers between the races. They require constant lubrication by oil or grease and are good at coping with axial loads. Taper roller bearings consist of rollers set in a tapered cage set on the inner race; the outer race is separate. They are good at coping with axial loads and prevent movement along the shaft - a typical application is in the steering head.

Bearing manufacturers produce bearings to ISO size standards and stamp one face of the bearing to indicate its internal and external diameter, load capacity and type (see illustration 5.16).

Metal bushes are usually of phosphor-bronze material. Rubber bushes are used in suspension mounting eyes. Fibre bushes have also been used in suspension pivots.

5.16 Typical bearing marking

## Bearing fault finding

If a bearing outer race has spun in its housing, the housing material will be damaged. You can use a bearing locking compound to bond the outer race in place if damage is not too severe.

Shell bearings will fail due to damage of their working surface, as a result of lack of lubrication, corrosion or abrasive particles in the oil (see illustration 5.17). Small particles of dirt in the oil may embed in the bearing material whereas larger particles will score the bearing and shaft journal. If a number of short journeys are made, insufficient heat will be generated to drive off condensation which has built up on the bearings.

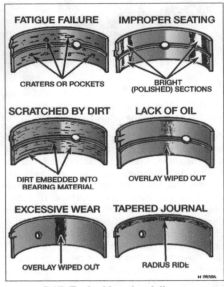

5.17 Typical bearing failures

Ball and roller bearings will fail due to lack of lubrication or damage to the balls or rollers. Tapered-roller bearings can be damaged by overloading them. Unless the bearing is sealed on both sides, wash it in paraffin (kerosene) to remove all old grease then allow it to dry. Make a visual inspection looking to dented balls or rollers, damaged cages and worn or pitted races (see illustration 5.18).

A ball bearing can be checked for wear by listening to it when spun. Apply a film of light oil to the bearing and hold it close to the ear - hold the outer race with one hand and spin the inner

5.18 Example of ball journal bearing with damaged balls and cages

5.19 Hold outer race and listen to inner race when spun

race with the other hand (see illustration 5.19). The bearing should be almost silent when spun; if it grates or rattles it is worn.

## 6  Oil seals

## Oil seal removal and installation

Oil seals should be renewed every time a component is dismantled. This is because the seal lips will become set to the sealing surface and will not necessarily reseal.

Oil seals can be prised out of position using a large flat-bladed screwdriver (see illustration 6.1). In the case of crankcase seals, check first that the seal is not lipped on the inside, preventing its removal with the crankcases joined.

6.1 Prise out oil seals with a large flat-bladed screwdriver

New seals are usually installed with their marked face (containing the seal reference code) outwards and the spring side towards the fluid being retained. In certain cases, such as a two-stroke engine crankshaft seal, a double lipped seal may be used due to there being fluid or gas on each side of the joint.

● Use a bearing driver or socket which bears only on the outer hard edge of the seal to install it in the casing - tapping on the inner edge will damage the sealing lip.

## Oil seal types and markings

● Oil seals are usually of the single-lipped type. Double-lipped seals are found where a liquid or gas is on both sides of the joint.
● Oil seals can harden and lose their sealing ability if the motorcycle has been in storage for a long period - renewal is the only solution.
● Oil seal manufacturers also conform to the ISO markings for seal size - these are moulded into the outer face of the seal (**see illustration 6.2**).

**6.2 These oil seal markings indicate inside diameter, outside diameter and seal thickness**

## 7  Gaskets and sealants

## Types of gasket and sealant

● Gaskets are used to seal the mating surfaces between components and keep lubricants, fluids, vacuum or pressure contained within the assembly. Aluminium gaskets are sometimes found at the cylinder joints, but most gaskets are paper-based. If the mating surfaces of the components being joined are undamaged the gasket can be installed dry, although a dab of sealant or grease will be useful to hold it in place during assembly.
● RTV (Room Temperature Vulcanising) silicone rubber sealants cure when exposed to moisture in the atmosphere. These sealants are good at filling pits or irregular gasket faces, but will tend to be forced out of the joint under very high torque. They can be used to replace a paper gasket, but first make sure that the width of the paper gasket is not essential to the shimming of internal components. RTV sealants should not be used on components containing petrol (gasoline).
● Non-hardening, semi-hardening and hard setting liquid gasket compounds can be used with a gasket or between a metal-to-metal joint. Select the sealant to suit the application: universal non-hardening sealant can be used on virtually all joints; semi-hardening on joint faces which are rough or damaged; hard setting sealant on joints which require a permanent bond and are subjected to high temperature and pressure. **Note:** *Check first if the paper gasket has a bead of sealant*

*impregnated in its surface before applying additional sealant.*
● When choosing a sealant, make sure it is suitable for the application, particularly if being applied in a high-temperature area or in the vicinity of fuel. Certain manufacturers produce sealants in either clear, silver or black colours to match the finish of the engine. This has a particular application on motorcycles where much of the engine is exposed.
● Do not over-apply sealant. That which is squeezed out on the outside of the joint can be wiped off, whereas an excess of sealant on the inside can break off and clog oilways.

## Breaking a sealed joint

● Age, heat, pressure and the use of hard setting sealant can cause two components to stick together so tightly that they are difficult to separate using finger pressure alone. Do not resort to using levers unless there is a pry point provided for this purpose (**see illustration 7.1**) or else the gasket surfaces will be damaged.
● Use a soft-faced hammer (**see illustration 7.2**) or a wood block and conventional hammer to strike the component near the mating surface. Avoid hammering against cast extremities since they may break off. If this method fails, try using a wood wedge between the two components.

> **Caution: If the joint will not separate, double-check that you have removed all the fasteners.**

**7.1 If a pry point is provided, apply gently pressure with a flat-bladed screwdriver**

**7.2 Tap around the joint with a soft-faced mallet if necessary - don't strike cooling fins**

## Removal of old gasket and sealant

● Paper gaskets will most likely come away complete, leaving only a few traces stuck on

**HAYNES HINT**

*Most components have one or two hollow locating dowels between the two gasket faces. If a dowel cannot be removed, do not resort to gripping it with pliers - it will almost certainly be distorted. Install a close-fitting socket or Phillips screwdriver into the dowel and then grip the outer edge of the dowel to free it.*

the sealing faces of the components. It is imperative that all traces are removed to ensure correct sealing of the new gasket.
● Very carefully scrape all traces of gasket away making sure that the sealing surfaces are not gouged or scored by the scraper (**see illustrations 7.3, 7.4 and 7.5**). Stubborn deposits can be removed by spraying with an aerosol gasket remover. Final preparation of

**7.3 Paper gaskets can be scraped off with a gasket scraper tool . . .**

**7.4 . . . a knife blade . . .**

**7.5 . . . or a household scraper**

7.6 Fine abrasive paper is wrapped around a flat file to clean up the gasket face

7.7 A kitchen scourer can be used on stubborn deposits

the gasket surface can be made with very fine abrasive paper or a plastic kitchen scourer **(see illustrations 7.6 and 7.7)**.

● Old sealant can be scraped or peeled off components, depending on the type originally used. Note that gasket removal compounds are available to avoid scraping the components clean; make sure the gasket remover suits the type of sealant used.

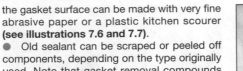

## 8  Chains

### *Breaking and joining final drive chains*

● Drive chains for all but small bikes are continuous and do not have a clip-type connecting link. The chain must be broken using a chain breaker tool and the new chain securely riveted together using a new soft rivet-type link. Never use a clip-type connecting link instead of a rivet-type link, except in an emergency. Various chain breaking and riveting tools are available, either as separate tools or combined as illustrated in the accompanying photographs - read the instructions supplied with the tool carefully.

> ⚠ *Warning: The need to rivet the new link pins correctly cannot be overstressed - loss of control of the motorcycle is very likely to result if the chain breaks in use.*

● Rotate the chain and look for the soft link. The soft link pins look like they have been

8.1 Tighten the chain breaker to push the pin out of the link . . .

8.2 . . . withdraw the pin, remove the tool . . .

8.3 . . . and separate the chain link

deeply centre-punched instead of peened over like all the other pins **(see illustration 8.9)** and its sideplate may be a different colour. Position the soft link midway between the sprockets and assemble the chain breaker tool over one of the soft link pins **(see illustration 8.1)**. Operate the tool to push the pin out through the chain **(see illustration 8.2)**. On an O-ring chain, remove the O-rings **(see illustration 8.3)**. Carry out the same procedure on the other soft link pin.

> *Caution: Certain soft link pins (particularly on the larger chains) may require their ends to be filed or ground off before they can be pressed out using the tool.*

● Check that you have the correct size and strength (standard or heavy duty) new soft link - do not reuse the old link. Look for the size marking on the chain sideplates **(see illustration 8.10)**.

● Position the chain ends so that they are engaged over the rear sprocket. On an O-ring

8.4 Insert the new soft link, with O-rings, through the chain ends . . .

8.5 . . . install the O-rings over the pin ends . . .

8.6 . . . followed by the sideplate

chain, install a new O-ring over each pin of the link and insert the link through the two chain ends **(see illustration 8.4)**. Install a new O-ring over the end of each pin, followed by the sideplate (with the chain manufacturer's marking facing outwards) **(see illustrations 8.5 and 8.6)**. On an unsealed chain, insert the link through the two chain ends, then install the sideplate with the chain manufacturer's marking facing outwards.

● Note that it may not be possible to install the sideplate using finger pressure alone. If using a joining tool, assemble it so that the plates of the tool clamp the link and press the sideplate over the pins **(see illustration 8.7)**. Otherwise, use two small sockets placed over

8.7 Push the sideplate into position using a clamp

**8.8 Assemble the chain riveting tool over one pin at a time and tighten it fully**

**8.9 Pin end correctly riveted (A), pin end unriveted (B)**

the rivet ends and two pieces of the wood between a G-clamp. Operate the clamp to press the sideplate over the pins.
● Assemble the joining tool over one pin (following the maker's instructions) and tighten the tool down to spread the pin end securely **(see illustrations 8.8 and 8.9)**. Do the same on the other pin.

> **Warning: Check that the pin ends are secure and that there is no danger of the sideplate coming loose. If the pin ends are cracked the soft link must be renewed.**

## Final drive chain sizing

● Chains are sized using a three digit number, followed by a suffix to denote the chain type **(see illustration 8.10)**. Chain type is either standard or heavy duty (thicker sideplates), and also unsealed or O-ring/X-ring type.
● The first digit of the number relates to the pitch of the chain, ie the distance from the centre of one pin to the centre of the next pin **(see illustration 8.11)**. Pitch is expressed in eighths of an inch, as follows:

**8.10 Typical chain size and type marking**

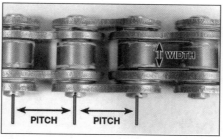

**8.11 Chain dimensions**

Sizes commencing with a 4 (eg 428) have a pitch of 1/2 inch (12.7 mm)

Sizes commencing with a 5 (eg 520) have a pitch of 5/8 inch (15.9 mm)

Sizes commencing with a 6 (eg 630) have a pitch of 3/4 inch (19.1 mm)

● The second and third digits of the chain size relate to the width of the rollers, again in imperial units, eg the 525 shown has 5/16 inch (7.94 mm) rollers **(see illustration 8.11)**.

## 9 Hoses

### Clamping to prevent flow

● Small-bore flexible hoses can be clamped to prevent fluid flow whilst a component is worked on. Whichever method is used, ensure that the hose material is not permanently distorted or damaged by the clamp.
a) A brake hose clamp available from auto accessory shops **(see illustration 9.1)**.
b) A wingnut type hose clamp **(see illustration 9.2)**.

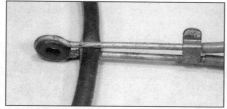

**9.1 Hoses can be clamped with an automotive brake hose clamp . . .**

**9.2 . . . a wingnut type hose clamp . . .**

c) Two sockets placed each side of the hose and held with straight-jawed self-locking grips **(see illustration 9.3)**.
d) Thick card each side of the hose held between straight-jawed self-locking grips **(see illustration 9.4)**.

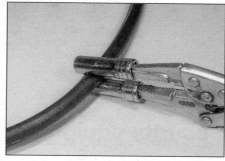

**9.3 . . . two sockets and a pair of self-locking grips . . .**

**9.4 . . . or thick card and self-locking grips**

### Freeing and fitting hoses

● Always make sure the hose clamp is moved well clear of the hose end. Grip the hose with your hand and rotate it whilst pulling it off the union. If the hose has hardened due to age and will not move, slit it with a sharp knife and peel its ends off the union **(see illustration 9.5)**.
● Resist the temptation to use grease or soap on the unions to aid installation; although it helps the hose slip over the union it will equally aid the escape of fluid from the joint. It is preferable to soften the hose ends in hot water and wet the inside surface of the hose with water or a fluid which will evaporate.

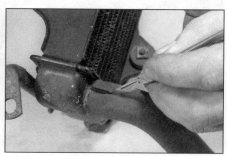

**9.5 Cutting a coolant hose free with a sharp knife**

## Introduction

In less time than it takes to read this introduction, a thief could steal your motorcycle. Returning only to find your bike has gone is one of the worst feelings in the world. Even if the motorcycle is insured against theft, once you've got over the initial shock, you will have the inconvenience of dealing with the police and your insurance company.

The motorcycle is an easy target for the professional thief and the joyrider alike and the official figures on motorcycle theft make for depressing reading; on average a motorcycle is stolen every 16 minutes in the UK!

Motorcycle thefts fall into two categories, those stolen 'to order' and those taken by opportunists. The thief stealing to order will be on the look out for a specific make and model and will go to extraordinary lengths to obtain that motorcycle. The opportunist thief on the other hand will look for easy targets which can be stolen with the minimum of effort and risk.

Whilst it is never going to be possible to make your machine 100% secure, it is estimated that around half of all stolen motorcycles are taken by opportunist thieves. Remember that the opportunist thief is always on the look out for the easy option: if there are two similar motorcycles parked side-by-side, they will target the one with the lowest level of security. By taking a few precautions, you can reduce the chances of your motorcycle being stolen.

# Security equipment

There are many specialised motorcycle security devices available and the following text summarises their applications and their good and bad points.

Once you have decided on the type of security equipment which best suits your needs, we recommended that you read one of the many equipment tests regularly carried out by the motorcycle press. These tests compare the products from all the major manufacturers and give impartial ratings on their effectiveness, value-for-money and ease of use.

No one item of security equipment can provide complete protection. It is highly recommended that two or more of the items described below are combined to increase the security of your motorcycle (a lock and chain plus an alarm system is just about ideal). The more security measures fitted to the bike, the less likely it is to be stolen.

### Lock and chain

**Pros:** *Very flexible to use; can be used to secure the motorcycle to almost any immovable object. On some locks and chains, the lock can be used on its own as a disc lock (see below).*

**Cons:** *Can be very heavy and awkward to carry on the motorcycle, although some types will be supplied with a carry bag which can be strapped to the pillion seat.*

● Heavy-duty chains and locks are an excellent security measure **(see illustration 1)**. Whenever the motorcycle is parked, use the lock and chain to secure the machine to a solid, immovable object such as a post or railings. This will prevent the machine from being ridden away or being lifted into the back of a van.

● When fitting the chain, always ensure the chain is routed around the motorcycle frame or swingarm **(see illustrations 2 and 3)**. Never merely pass the chain around one of the wheel rims; a thief may unbolt the wheel and lift the rest of the machine into a van, leaving you with just the wheel! Try to avoid having excess chain free, thus making it difficult to use cutting tools, and keep the chain and lock off the ground to prevent thieves attacking it with a cold chisel. Position the lock so that its lock barrel is facing downwards; this will make it harder for the thief to attack the lock mechanism.

Ensure the lock and chain you buy is of good quality and long enough to shackle your bike to a solid object

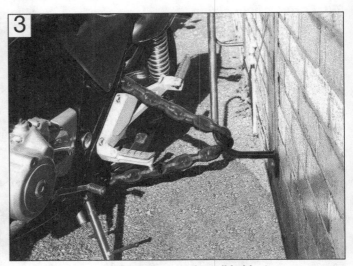

Pass the chain through the bike's frame, rather than just through a wheel . . .

. . . and loop it around a solid object

## U-locks

**Pros:** *Highly effective deterrent which can be used to secure the bike to a post or railings. Most U-locks come with a carrier which allows the lock to be easily carried on the bike.*

**Cons:** *Not as flexible to use as a lock and chain.*

● These are solid locks which are similar in use to a lock and chain. U-locks are lighter than a lock and chain but not so flexible to use. The length and shape of the lock shackle limit the objects to which the bike can be secured **(see illustration 4)**.

## Disc locks

**Pros:** *Small, light and very easy to carry; most can be stored underneath the seat.*

**Cons:** *Does not prevent the motorcycle being lifted into a van. Can be very embarrassing if you*

**U-locks can be used to secure the bike to a solid object – ensure you purchase one which is long enough**

forget to remove the lock before attempting to ride off!

● Disc locks are designed to be attached to the front brake disc. The lock passes through one of the holes in the disc and prevents the wheel rotating by jamming against the fork/brake caliper **(see illustration 5)**. Some are equipped with an alarm siren which sounds if the disc lock is moved; this not only acts as a theft deterrent but also as a handy reminder if you try to move the bike with the lock still fitted.

● Combining the disc lock with a length of cable which can be looped around a post or railings provides an additional measure of security **(see illustration 6)**.

## Alarms and immobilisers

**Pros:** *Once installed it is completely hassle-free to use. If the system is 'Thatcham' or 'Sold Secure-approved', insurance companies may give you a discount.*

**Cons:** *Can be expensive to buy and complex to install. No system will prevent the motorcycle from being lifted into a van and taken away.*

● Electronic alarms and immobilisers are available to suit a variety of budgets. There are three different types of system available: pure alarms, pure immobilisers, and the more expensive systems which are combined alarm/immobilisers **(see illustration 7)**.
● An alarm system is designed to emit an audible warning if the motorcycle is being tampered with.
● An immobiliser prevents the motorcycle being started and ridden away by disabling its electrical systems.
● When purchasing an alarm/immobiliser system, check the cost of installing the system unless you are able to do it yourself. If the motorcycle is not used regularly, another consideration is the current drain of the system. All alarm/immobiliser systems are powered by the motorcycle's battery; purchasing a system with a very low current drain could prevent the battery losing its charge whilst the motorcycle is not being used.

**A typical disc lock attached through one of the holes in the disc**

**A disc lock combined with a security cable provides additional protection**

**A typical alarm/immobiliser system**

Indelible markings can be applied to most areas of the bike – always apply the manufacturer's sticker to warn off thieves

Chemically-etched code numbers can be applied to main body panels . . .

. . . again, always ensure that the kit manufacturer's sticker is applied in a prominent position

### Security marking kits

**Pros:** *Very cheap and effective deterrent. Many insurance companies will give you a discount on your insurance premium if a recognised security marking kit is used on your motorcycle.*

**Cons:** *Does not prevent the motorcycle being stolen by joyriders.*

● There are many different types of security marking kits available. The idea is to mark as many parts of the motorcycle as possible with a unique security number **(see illustrations 8, 9 and 10)**. A form will be included with the kit to register your personal details and those of the motorcycle with the kit manufacturer. This register is made available to the police to help them trace the rightful owner of any motorcycle or components which they recover should all other forms of identification have been removed. Always apply the warning stickers provided with the kit to deter thieves.

### Ground anchors, wheel clamps and security posts

**Pros:** *An excellent form of security which will deter all but the most determined of thieves.*

**Cons:** *Awkward to install and can be expensive.*

● Whilst the motorcycle is at home, it is a good idea to attach it securely to the floor or a solid wall, even if it is kept in a securely locked garage. Various types of ground anchors, security posts and wheel clamps are available for this purpose **(see illustration 11)**. These security devices are either bolted to a solid concrete or brick structure or can be cemented into the ground.

Permanent ground anchors provide an excellent level of security when the bike is at home

# Security at home

A high percentage of motorcycle thefts are from the owner's home. Here are some things to consider whenever your motorcycle is at home:

✔ Where possible, always keep the motorcycle in a securely locked garage. Never rely solely on the standard lock on the garage door, these are usual hopelessly inadequate. Fit an additional locking mechanism to the door and consider having the garage alarmed. A security light, activated by a movement sensor, is also a good investment.

✔ Always secure the motorcycle to the ground or a wall, even if it is inside a securely locked garage.

✔ Do not regularly leave the motorcycle outside your home, try to keep it out of sight wherever possible. If a garage is not available, fit a motorcycle cover over the bike to disguise its true identity.

✔ It is not uncommon for thieves to follow a motorcyclist home to find out where the bike is kept. They will then return at a later date. Be aware of this whenever you are returning

home on your motorcycle. If you suspect you are being followed, do not return home, instead ride to a garage or shop and stop as a precaution.

✔ When selling a motorcycle, do not provide your home address or the location where the bike is normally kept. Arrange to meet the buyer at a location away from your home. Thieves have been known to pose as potential buyers to find out where motorcycles are kept and then return later to steal them.

# Security away from the home

As well as fitting security equipment to your motorcycle here are a few general rules to follow whenever you park your motorcycle.

✔ Park in a busy, public place.

✔ Use car parks which incorporate security features, such as CCTV.

✔ At night, park in a well-lit area, preferably directly underneath a street light.

✔ Engage the steering lock.

✔ Secure the motorcycle to a solid, immovable object such as a post or railings with an additional lock. If this is not possible,

secure the bike to a friend's motorcycle. Some public parking places provide security loops for motorcycles.

✔ Never leave your helmet or luggage attached to the motorcycle. Take them with you at all times.

# Lubricants and fluids

A wide range of lubricants, fluids and cleaning agents is available for motor-cycles. This is a guide as to what is available, its applications and properties.

## Four-stroke engine oil

● Engine oil is without doubt the most important component of any four-stroke engine. Modern motorcycle engines place a lot of demands on their oil and choosing the right type is essential. Using an unsuitable oil will lead to an increased rate of engine wear and could result in serious engine damage. Before purchasing oil, always check the recommended oil specification given by the manufacturer. The manufacturer will state a recommended 'type or classification' and also a specific 'viscosity' range for engine oil.

● The oil 'type or classification' is identified by its API (American Petroleum Institute) rating. The API rating will be in the form of two letters, e.g. SG. The S identifies the oil as being suitable for use in a petrol (gasoline) engine (S stands for spark ignition) and the second letter, ranging from A to J, identifies the oil's performance rating. The later this letter, the higher the specification of the oil; for example API SG oil exceeds the requirements of API SF oil. Note: *On some oils there may also be a second rating consisting of another two letters, the first letter being C, e.g. API SF/CD. This rating indicates the oil is also suitable for use in a diesel engines (the C stands for compression ignition) and is thus of no relevance for motorcycle use.*

● The 'viscosity' of the oil is identified by its SAE (Society of Automotive Engineers) rating. All modern engines require multigrade oils and the SAE rating will consist of two numbers, the first followed by a W, e.g.

10W/40. The first number indicates the viscosity rating of the oil at low temperatures (W stands for winter – tested at –20ºC) and the second number represents the viscosity of the oil at high temperatures (tested at 100ºC). The lower the number, the thinner the oil. For example an oil with an SAE 10W/40 rating will give better cold starting and running than an SAE 15W/40 oil.

● As well as ensuring the 'type' and 'viscosity' of the oil match the recommendations, another consideration to make when buying engine oil is whether to purchase a standard mineral-based oil, a semi-synthetic oil (also known as a synthetic blend or synthetic-based oil) or a fully-synthetic oil. Although all oils will have a similar rating and viscosity, their cost will vary considerably; mineral-based oils are the cheapest, the fully-synthetic oils the most expensive with the semi-synthetic oils falling somewhere in-between. This decision is very much up to the owner, but it should be noted that modern synthetic oils have far better lubricating and cleaning qualities than traditional mineral-based oils and tend to retain these properties for far longer. Bearing in mind the operating conditions inside a modern, high-revving motorcycle engine it is highly recommended that a fully synthetic oil is used. The extra expense at each service could save you money in the long term by preventing premature engine wear.

● As a final note always ensure that the oil is specifically designed for use in motorcycle engines. Engine oils designed primarily for use in car engines sometimes contain additives or friction modifiers which could cause clutch slip on a motorcycle fitted with a wet-clutch.

## Two-stroke engine oil

● Modern two-stroke engines, with their high power outputs, place high demands on their oil. If engine seizure is to be avoided it is essential that a high-quality oil is used. Two-stroke oils differ hugely from four-stroke oils. The oil lubricates only the crankshaft and piston(s) (the transmission has its own lubricating oil) and is used on a total-loss basis where it is burnt completely during the combustion process.

● The Japanese have recently introduced a classification system for two-stroke oils, the JASO rating. This rating is in the form of two letters, either FA, FB or FC – FA is the lowest classification and FC the highest. Ensure the oil being used meets or exceeds the recommended rating specified by the manufacturer.

● As well as ensuring the oil rating matches the recommendation, another consideration to make when buying engine oil is whether to purchase a standard mineral-based oil, a semi-synthetic oil (also known as a synthetic blend or synthetic-based oil) or a fully-synthetic oil. The cost of each type of oil varies considerably; mineral-based oils are the cheapest, the fully-synthetic oils the most expensive with the semi-synthetic oils falling somewhere in-between. This decision is very much up to the owner, but it should be noted that modern synthetic oils have far better lubricating properties and burn cleaner than traditional mineral-based oils. It is therefore recommended that a fully synthetic oil is used. The extra expense could save you money in the long term by preventing premature engine wear, engine performance will be improved, carbon deposits and exhaust smoke will be reduced.

● Always ensure that the oil is specifically designed for use in an injector system. Many high quality two-stroke oils are designed for competition use and need to be pre-mixed with fuel. These oils are of a much higher viscosity and are not designed to flow through the injector pumps used on road-going two-stroke motorcycles.

## Transmission (gear) oil

● On a two-stroke engine, the transmission and clutch are lubricated by their own separate oil bath which must be changed in accordance with the Maintenance Schedule.
● Although the engine and transmission units of most four-strokes use a common lubrication supply, there are some exceptions where the engine and gearbox have separate oil reservoirs and a dry clutch is used.
● Motorcycle manufacturers will either recommend a monograde transmission oil or a four-stroke multigrade engine oil to lubricate the transmission.
● Transmission oils, or gear oils as they are often called, are designed specifically for use in transmission systems. The viscosity of these oils is represented by an SAE number, but the scale of measurement applied is different to that used to grade engine oils. As a rough guide a SAE90 gear oil will be of the same viscosity as an SAE50 engine oil.

## Shaft drive oil

● On models equipped with shaft final drive, the shaft drive gears are will have their own oil supply. The manufacturer will state a recommended 'type or classification' and also a specific 'viscosity' range in the same manner as for four-stroke engine oil.
● Gear oil classification is given by the number which follows the API GL (GL standing for gear lubricant) rating, the higher the number, the higher the specification of the oil, e.g. API GL5 oil is a higher specification than API GL4 oil. Ensure the oil meets or

exceeds the classification specified and is of the correct viscosity. The viscosity of gear oils is also represented by an SAE number but the scale of measurement used is different to that used to grade engine oils. As a rough guide an SAE90 gear oil will be of the same viscosity as an SAE50 engine oil.
● If the use of an EP (Extreme Pressure) gear oil is specified, ensure the oil purchased is suitable.

## Fork oil and suspension fluid

● Conventional telescopic front forks are hydraulic and require fork oil to work. To ensure the forks function correctly, the fork oil must be changed in accordance with the Maintenance Schedule.
● Fork oil is available in a variety of viscosities, identified by their SAE rating; fork oil ratings vary from light (SAE 5) to heavy (SAE 30). When purchasing fork oil, ensure the viscosity rating matches that specified by the manufacturer.
● Some lubricant manufacturers also produce a range of high-quality suspension fluids which are very similar to fork oil but are designed mainly for competition use. These fluids may have a different viscosity rating system which is not to be confused with the SAE rating of normal fork oil. Refer to the manufacturer's instructions if in any doubt.

## Brake and clutch fluid

● All disc brake systems and some clutch systems are hydraulically operated. To ensure correct operation, the hydraulic fluid must be changed in accordance with the Maintenance Schedule.
● Brake and clutch fluid is classified by its DOT rating with most motorcycle manufacturers specifying DOT 3 or 4 fluid. Both fluid types are glycol-based and can be mixed together without adverse effect; DOT 4 fluid exceeds the requirements of DOT 3

fluid. Although it is safe to use DOT 4 fluid in a system designed for use with DOT 3 fluid, never use DOT 3 fluid in a system which specifies the use of DOT 4 as this will adversely affect the system's performance. The type required for the system will be marked on the fluid reservoir cap.
● Some manufacturers also produce a DOT 5 hydraulic fluid. DOT 5 hydraulic fluid is silicone-based and is not compatible with the glycol-based DOT 3 and 4 fluids. Never mix DOT 5 fluid with DOT 3 or 4 fluid as this will seriously affect the performance of the hydraulic system.

## Coolant/antifreeze

● When purchasing coolant/antifreeze, always ensure it is suitable for use in an aluminium engine and contains corrosion inhibitors to prevent possible blockages of the internal coolant passages of the system. As a general rule, most coolants are designed to be used neat and should not be diluted whereas antifreeze can be mixed with distilled water to provide a coolant solution of the required strength. Refer to the manufacturer's instructions on the bottle.
● Ensure the coolant is changed in accordance with the Maintenance Schedule.

## Chain lube

● Chain lube is an aerosol-type spray lubricant specifically designed for use on motorcycle final drive chains. Chain lube has two functions, to minimise friction between the final drive chain and sprockets and to prevent corrosion of the chain. Regular use of a good-quality chain lube will extend the life of the drive chain and sprockets and thus maximise the power being transmitted from the transmission to the rear wheel.
● When using chain lube, always allow some time for the solvents in the lube to evaporate before riding the motorcycle. This will minimise the amount of lube which will

'fling' off from the chain when the motorcycle is used. If the motorcycle is equipped with an 'O-ring' chain, ensure the chain lube is labelled as being suitable for use on 'O-ring' chains.

## Degreasers and solvents

● There are many different types of solvents and degreasers available to remove the grime and grease which accumulate around the motorcycle during normal use. Degreasers and solvents are usually available as an aerosol-type spray or as a liquid which you apply with a brush. Always closely follow the manufacturer's instructions and wear eye protection during use. Be aware that many solvents are flammable and may give off noxious fumes; take adequate precautions when using them (see *Safety First!*).
● For general cleaning, use one of the many solvents or degreasers available from most motorcycle accessory shops. These solvents are usually applied then left for a certain time before being washed off with water.

**Brake cleaner** is a solvent specifically designed to remove all traces of oil, grease and dust from braking system components. Brake cleaner is designed to evaporate quickly and leaves behind no residue.

**Carburettor cleaner** is an aerosol-type solvent specifically designed to clear carburettor blockages and break down the hard deposits and gum often found inside carburettors during overhaul.

**Contact cleaner** is an aerosol-type solvent designed for cleaning electrical components. The cleaner will remove all traces of oil and dirt from components such as switch contacts or fouled spark plugs and then dry, leaving behind no residue.

**Gasket remover** is an aerosol-type solvent designed for removing stubborn gaskets from engine components during overhaul. Gasket remover will minimise the amount of scraping required to remove the gasket and therefore reduce the risk of damage to the mating surface.

## Spray lubricants

● Aerosol-based spray lubricants are widely available and are excellent for lubricating lever pivots and exposed cables and switches. Try to use a lubricant which is of the dry-film type as the fluid evaporates, leaving behind a dry-film of lubricant. Lubricants which leave behind an oily residue will attract dust and dirt which will increase the rate of wear of the cable/lever.

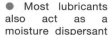
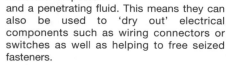

● Most lubricants also act as a moisture dispersant and a penetrating fluid. This means they can also be used to 'dry out' electrical components such as wiring connectors or switches as well as helping to free seized fasteners.

## Greases

● Grease is used to lubricate many of the pivot-points. A good-quality multi-purpose grease is suitable for most applications but some manufacturers will specify the use of specialist greases for use on components such as swingarm and suspension linkage bushes. These specialist greases can be purchased from most motorcycle (or car) accessory shops; commonly specified types include molybdenum disulphide grease, lithium-based grease, graphite-based grease, silicone-based grease and high-temperature copper-based grease.

## Gasket sealing compounds

● Gasket sealing compounds can be used in conjunction with gaskets, to improve their sealing capabilities, or on their own to seal metal-to-metal joints. Depending on their type, sealing compounds either set hard or stay relatively soft and pliable.

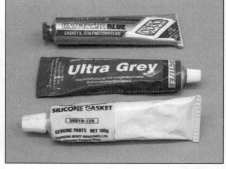

● When purchasing a gasket sealing compound, ensure that it is designed specifically for use on an internal combustion engine. General multi-purpose sealants available from DIY stores may appear visibly similar but they are not designed to withstand the extreme heat or contact with fuel and oil encountered when used on an engine (see *Tools and Workshop Tips* for further information).

## Thread locking compound

● Thread locking compounds are used to secure certain threaded fasteners in position to prevent them from loosening due to vibration. Thread locking compounds can be purchased from most motorcycle (and car) accessory shops. Ensure the threads of the both components are completely clean and dry before sparingly applying the locking compound (see *Tools and Workshop Tips* for further information).

## Fuel additives

● Fuel additives which protect and clean the fuel system components are widely available. These additives are designed to remove all traces of deposits that build up on the carburettors/injectors and prevent wear, helping the fuel system to operate more efficiently. If a fuel additive is being used, check that it is suitable for use with your motorcycle, especially if your motorcycle is equipped with a catalytic converter.

● Octane boosters are also available. These additives are designed to improve the performance of highly-tuned engines being run on normal pump-fuel and are of no real use on standard motorcycles.

# Conversion Factors

## Length (distance)

| | | | | | |
|---|---|---|---|---|---|
| Inches (in) | x 25.4 | = Millimetres (mm) | x 0.0394 | = Inches (in) |
| Feet (ft) | x 0.305 | = Metres (m) | x 3.281 | = Feet (ft) |
| Miles | x 1.609 | = Kilometres (km) | x 0.621 | = Miles |

## Volume (capacity)

| | | | | | |
|---|---|---|---|---|---|
| Cubic inches (cu in; in³) | x 16.387 | = Cubic centimetres (cc; cm³) | x 0.061 | = Cubic inches (cu in; in³) |
| Imperial pints (Imp pt) | x 0.568 | = Litres (l) | x 1.76 | = Imperial pints (Imp pt) |
| Imperial quarts (Imp qt) | x 1.137 | = Litres (l) | x 0.88 | = Imperial quarts (Imp qt) |
| Imperial quarts (Imp qt) | x 1.201 | = US quarts (US qt) | x 0.833 | = Imperial quarts (Imp qt) |
| US quarts (US qt) | x 0.946 | = Litres (l) | x 1.057 | = US quarts (US qt) |
| Imperial gallons (Imp gal) | x 4.546 | = Litres (l) | x 0.22 | = Imperial gallons (Imp gal) |
| Imperial gallons (Imp gal) | x 1.201 | = US gallons (US gal) | x 0.833 | = Imperial gallons (Imp gal) |
| US gallons (US gal) | x 3.785 | = Litres (l) | x 0.264 | = US gallons (US gal) |

## Mass (weight)

| | | | | | |
|---|---|---|---|---|---|
| Ounces (oz) | x 28.35 | = Grams (g) | x 0.035 | = Ounces (oz) |
| Pounds (lb) | x 0.454 | = Kilograms (kg) | x 2.205 | = Pounds (lb) |

## Force

| | | | | | |
|---|---|---|---|---|---|
| Ounces-force (ozf; oz) | x 0.278 | = Newtons (N) | x 3.6 | = Ounces-force (ozf; oz) |
| Pounds-force (lbf; lb) | x 4.448 | = Newtons (N) | x 0.225 | = Pounds-force (lbf; lb) |
| Newtons (N) | x 0.1 | = Kilograms-force (kgf; kg) | x 9.81 | = Newtons (N) |

## Pressure

| | | | | | |
|---|---|---|---|---|---|
| Pounds-force per square inch (psi; lbf/in²; lb/in²) | x 0.070 | = Kilograms-force per square centimetre (kgf/cm²; kg/cm²) | x 14.223 | = Pounds-force per square inch (psi; lbf/in²; lb/in²) |
| Pounds-force per square inch (psi; lbf/in²; lb/in²) | x 0.068 | = Atmospheres (atm) | x 14.696 | = Pounds-force per square inch (psi; lbf/in²; lb/in²) |
| Pounds-force per square inch (psi; lbf/in²; lb/in²) | x 0.069 | = Bars | x 14.5 | = Pounds-force per square inch (psi; lbf/in²; lb/in²) |
| Pounds-force per square inch (psi; lbf/in²; lb/in²) | x 6.895 | = Kilopascals (kPa) | x 0.145 | = Pounds-force per square inch (psi; lbf/in²; lb/in²) |
| Kilopascals (kPa) | x 0.01 | = Kilograms-force per square centimetre (kgf/cm²; kg/cm²) | x 98.1 | = Kilopascals (kPa) |
| Millibar (mbar) | x 100 | = Pascals (Pa) | x 0.01 | = Millibar (mbar) |
| Millibar (mbar) | x 0.0145 | = Pounds-force per square inch (psi; lbf/in²; lb/in²) | x 68.947 | = Millibar (mbar) |
| Millibar (mbar) | x 0.75 | = Millimetres of mercury (mmHg) | x 1.333 | = Millibar (mbar) |
| Millibar (mbar) | x 0.401 | = Inches of water (inH₂O) | x 2.491 | = Millibar (mbar) |
| Millimetres of mercury (mmHg) | x 0.535 | = Inches of water (inH₂O) | x 1.868 | = Millimetres of mercury (mmHg) |
| Inches of water (inH₂O) | x 0.036 | = Pounds-force per square inch (psi; lbf/in²; lb/in²) | x 27.68 | = Inches of water (inH₂O) |

## Torque (moment of force)

| | | | | | |
|---|---|---|---|---|---|
| Pounds-force inches (lbf in; lb in) | x 1.152 | = Kilograms-force centimetre (kgf cm; kg cm) | x 0.868 | = Pounds-force inches (lbf in; lb in) |
| Pounds-force inches (lbf in; lb in) | x 0.113 | = Newton metres (Nm) | x 8.85 | = Pounds-force inches (lbf in; lb in) |
| Pounds-force inches (lbf in; lb in) | x 0.083 | = Pounds-force feet (lbf ft; lb ft) | x 12 | = Pounds-force inches (lbf in; lb in) |
| Pounds-force feet (lbf ft; lb ft) | x 0.138 | = Kilograms-force metres (kgf m; kg m) | x 7.233 | = Pounds-force feet (lbf ft; lb ft) |
| Pounds-force feet (lbf ft; lb ft) | x 1.356 | = Newton metres (Nm) | x 0.738 | = Pounds-force feet (lbf ft; lb ft) |
| Newton metres (Nm) | x 0.102 | = Kilograms-force metres (kgf m; kg m) | x 9.804 | = Newton metres (Nm) |

## Power

| | | | | | |
|---|---|---|---|---|---|
| Horsepower (hp) | x 745.7 | = Watts (W) | x 0.0013 | = Horsepower (hp) |

## Velocity (speed)

| | | | | | |
|---|---|---|---|---|---|
| Miles per hour (miles/hr; mph) | x 1.609 | = Kilometres per hour (km/hr; kph) | x 0.621 | = Miles per hour (miles/hr; mph) |

## Fuel consumption*

| | | | | | |
|---|---|---|---|---|---|
| Miles per gallon (mpg) | x 0.354 | = Kilometres per litre (km/l) | x 2.825 | = Miles per gallon (mpg) |

## Temperature

Degrees Fahrenheit = (°C x 1.8) + 32          Degrees Celsius (Degrees Centigrade; °C) = (°F - 32) x 0.56

*It is common practice to convert from miles per gallon (mpg) to litres/100 kilometres (l/100km), where mpg x l/100 km = 282*

## About the MOT Test

In the UK, all vehicles more than three years old are subject to an annual test to ensure that they meet minimum safety requirements. A current test certificate must be issued before a machine can be used on public roads, and is required before a road fund licence can be issued. Riding without a current test certificate will also invalidate your insurance.

For most owners, the MOT test is an annual cause for anxiety, and this is largely due to owners not being sure what needs to be checked prior to submitting the motorcycle for testing. The simple answer is that a fully roadworthy motorcycle will have no difficulty in passing the test.

This is a guide to getting your motorcycle through the MOT test. Obviously it will not be possible to examine the motorcycle to the same standard as the professional MOT tester, particularly in view of the equipment required for some of the checks. However, working through the following procedures will enable you to identify any problem areas before submitting the motorcycle for the test.

It has only been possible to summarise the test requirements here, based on the regulations in force at the time of printing. Test standards are becoming increasingly stringent, although there are some exemptions for older vehicles. More information about the MOT test can be obtained from the TSO publications, *How Safe is your Motorcycle* and *The MOT Inspection Manual for Motorcycle Testing*.

Many of the checks require that one of the wheels is raised off the ground. If the motorcycle doesn't have a centre stand, note that an auxiliary stand will be required. Additionally, the help of an assistant may prove useful.

Certain exceptions apply to machines under 50 cc, machines without a lighting system, and Classic bikes - if in doubt about any of the requirements listed below seek confirmation from an MOT tester prior to submitting the motorcycle for the test.

Check that the frame number is clearly visible.

> **HAYNES HiNT**
>
> *If a component is in borderline condition, the tester has discretion in deciding whether to pass or fail it. If the motorcycle presented is clean and evidently well cared for, the tester may be more inclined to pass a borderline component than if the motorcycle is scruffy and apparently neglected.*

# Electrical System

### Lights, turn signals, horn and reflector

✔ With the ignition on, check the operation of the following electrical components. **Note:** *The electrical components on certain small-capacity machines are powered by the generator, requiring that the engine is run for this check.*

a) *Headlight and tail light. Check that both illuminate in the low and high beam switch positions.*

b) *Position lights. Check that the front position (or sidelight) and tail light illuminate in this switch position.*

c) *Turn signals. Check that all flash at the correct rate, and that the warning light(s) function correctly. Check that the turn signal switch works correctly.*

d) *Hazard warning system (where fitted). Check that all four turn signals flash in this switch position.*

e) *Brake stop light. Check that the light comes on when the front and rear brakes are independently applied. Models first used on or after 1st April 1986 must have a brake light switch on each brake.*

f) *Horn. Check that the sound is continuous and of reasonable volume.*

✔ Check that there is a red reflector on the rear of the machine, either mounted separately or as part of the tail light lens.

✔ Check the condition of the headlight, tail light and turn signal lenses.

### Headlight beam height

✔ The MOT tester will perform a headlight beam height check using specialised beam setting equipment **(see illustration 1)**. This equipment will not be available to the home mechanic, but if you suspect that the headlight is incorrectly set or may have been maladjusted in the past, you can perform a rough test as follows.

✔ Position the bike in a straight line facing a brick wall. The bike must be off its stand, upright and with a rider seated. Measure the height from the ground to the centre of the headlight and mark a horizontal line on the wall at this height. Position the motorcycle 3.8 metres from the wall and draw a vertical

**Headlight beam height checking equipment**

line up the wall central to the centreline of the motorcycle. Switch to dipped beam and check that the beam pattern falls slightly lower than the horizontal line and to the left of the vertical line **(see illustration 2)**.

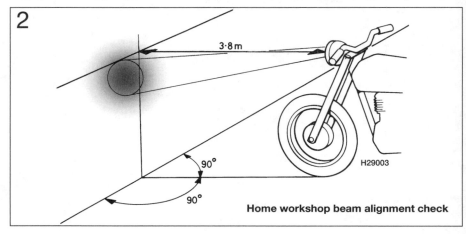

3·8 m

90°

90°

H29003

**Home workshop beam alignment check**

# Exhaust System and Final Drive

### Exhaust

✔ Check that the exhaust mountings are secure and that the system does not foul any of the rear suspension components.

✔ Start the motorcycle. When the revs are increased, check that the exhaust is neither holed nor leaking from any of its joints. On a linked system, check that the collector box is not leaking due to corrosion.

✔ Note that the exhaust decibel level ("loudness" of the exhaust) is assessed at the discretion of the tester. If the motorcycle was first used on or after 1st January 1985 the silencer must carry the BSAU 193 stamp, or a marking relating to its make and model, or be of OE (original equipment) manufacture. If the silencer is marked NOT FOR ROAD USE, RACING USE ONLY or similar, it will fail the MOT.

### Final drive

✔ On chain or belt drive machines, check that the chain/belt is in good condition and does not have excessive slack. Also check that the sprocket is securely mounted on the rear wheel hub. Check that the chain/belt guard is in place.

✔ On shaft drive bikes, check for oil leaking from the drive unit and fouling the rear tyre.

# Steering and Suspension

### Steering

✔ With the front wheel raised off the ground, rotate the steering from lock to lock. The handlebar or switches must not contact the fuel tank or be close enough to trap the rider's hand. Problems can be caused by damaged lock stops on the lower yoke and frame, or by the fitting of non-standard handlebars.

✔ When performing the lock to lock check, also ensure that the steering moves freely without drag or notchiness. Steering movement can be impaired by poorly routed cables, or by overtight head bearings or worn bearings. The tester will perform a check of the steering head bearing lower race by mounting the front wheel on a surface plate, then performing a lock to lock check with the weight of the machine on the lower bearing (see illustration 3).

✔ Grasp the fork sliders (lower legs) and attempt to push and pull on the forks (see

**Front wheel mounted on a surface plate for steering head bearing lower race check**

illustration 4). Any play in the steering head bearings will be felt. Note that in extreme cases, wear of the front fork bushes can be misinterpreted for head bearing play.

✔ Check that the handlebars are securely mounted.

✔ Check that the handlebar grip rubbers are secure. They should by bonded to the bar left end and to the throttle cable pulley on the right end.

### Front suspension

✔ With the motorcycle off the stand, hold the front brake on and pump the front forks up and down (see illustration 5). Check that they are adequately damped.

**Checking the steering head bearings for freeplay**

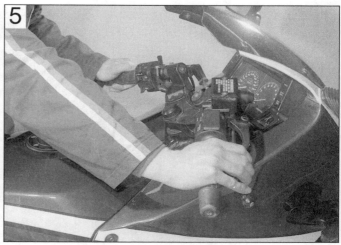

**Hold the front brake on and pump the front forks up and down to check operation**

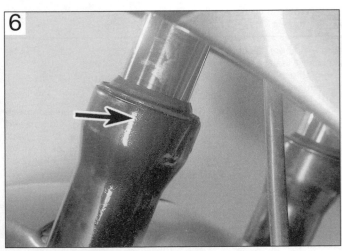

Inspect the area around the fork dust seal for oil leakage (arrow)

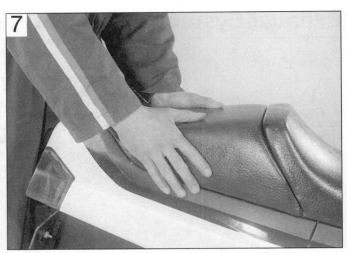

Bounce the rear of the motorcycle to check rear suspension operation

Checking for rear suspension linkage play

✔ Inspect the area above and around the front fork oil seals **(see illustration 6)**. There should be no sign of oil on the fork tube (stanchion) nor leaking down the slider (lower leg). On models so equipped, check that there is no oil leaking from the anti-dive units.

✔ On models with swingarm front suspension, check that there is no freeplay in the linkage when moved from side to side.

## Rear suspension

✔ With the motorcycle off the stand and an assistant supporting the motorcycle by its handlebars, bounce the rear suspension **(see illustration 7)**. Check that the suspension components do not foul on any of the cycle parts and check that the shock absorber(s) provide adequate damping.

✔ Visually inspect the shock absorber(s) and check that there is no sign of oil leakage from its damper. This is somewhat restricted on certain single shock models due to the location of the shock absorber.

✔ With the rear wheel raised off the ground, grasp the wheel at the highest point and attempt to pull it up **(see illustration 8)**. Any play in the swingarm pivot or suspension linkage bearings will be felt as movement. **Note:** *Do not confuse play with actual suspension movement.* Failure to lubricate suspension linkage bearings can lead to bearing failure **(see illustration 9)**.

✔ With the rear wheel raised off the ground, grasp the swingarm ends and attempt to move the swingarm from side to side and forwards and backwards - any play indicates wear of the swingarm pivot bearings **(see illustration 10)**.

Worn suspension linkage pivots (arrows) are usually the cause of play in the rear suspension

Grasp the swingarm at the ends to check for play in its pivot bearings

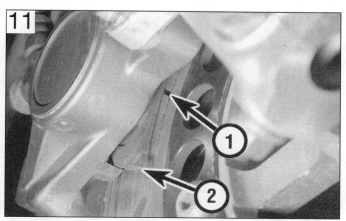

**Brake pad wear can usually be viewed without removing the caliper. Most pads have wear indicator grooves (1) and some also have indicator tangs (2)**

**On drum brakes, check the angle of the operating lever with the brake fully applied. Most drum brakes have a wear indicator pointer and scale.**

# Brakes, Wheels and Tyres

## Brakes

✔ With the wheel raised off the ground, apply the brake then free it off, and check that the wheel is about to revolve freely without brake drag.

✔ On disc brakes, examine the disc itself. Check that it is securely mounted and not cracked.

✔ On disc brakes, view the pad material through the caliper mouth and check that the pads are not worn down beyond the limit **(see illustration 11)**.

✔ On drum brakes, check that when the brake is applied the angle between the operating lever and cable or rod is not too great **(see illustration 12)**. Check also that the operating lever doesn't foul any other components.

✔ On disc brakes, examine the flexible hoses from top to bottom. Have an assistant hold the brake on so that the fluid in the hose is under pressure, and check that there is no sign of fluid leakage, bulges or cracking. If there are any metal brake pipes or unions, check that these are free from corrosion and damage. Where a brake-linked anti-dive system is fitted, check the hoses to the anti-dive in a similar manner.

✔ Check that the rear brake torque arm is secure and that its fasteners are secured by self-locking nuts or castellated nuts with split-pins or R-pins **(see illustration 13)**.

✔ On models with ABS, check that the self-check warning light in the instrument panel works.

✔ The MOT tester will perform a test of the motorcycle's braking efficiency based on a calculation of rider and motorcycle weight. Although this cannot be carried out at home, you can at least ensure that the braking systems are properly maintained. For hydraulic disc brakes, check the fluid level, lever/pedal feel (bleed of air if its spongy) and pad material. For drum brakes, check adjustment, cable or rod operation and shoe lining thickness.

## Wheels and tyres

✔ Check the wheel condition. Cast wheels should be free from cracks and if of the built-up design, all fasteners should be secure. Spoked wheels should be checked for broken, corroded, loose or bent spokes.

✔ With the wheel raised off the ground, spin the wheel and visually check that the tyre and wheel run true. Check that the tyre does not foul the suspension or mudguards.

✔ With the wheel raised off the ground, grasp the wheel and attempt to move it about the axle (spindle) **(see illustration 14)**. Any play felt here indicates wheel bearing failure.

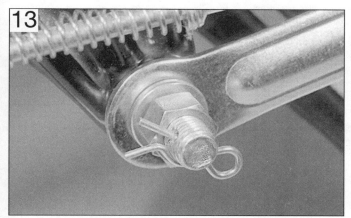

**Brake torque arm must be properly secured at both ends**

**Check for wheel bearing play by trying to move the wheel about the axle (spindle)**

Checking the tyre tread depth

Tyre direction of rotation arrow can be found on tyre sidewall

Castellated type wheel axle (spindle) nut must be secured by a split pin or R-pin

Two straightedges are used to check wheel alignment

✔ Check the tyre tread depth, tread condition and sidewall condition (see illustration 15).
✔ Check the tyre type. Front and rear tyre types must be compatible and be suitable for road use. Tyres marked NOT FOR ROAD USE, COMPETITION USE ONLY or similar, will fail the MOT.

✔ If the tyre sidewall carries a direction of rotation arrow, this must be pointing in the direction of normal wheel rotation (see illustration 16).
✔ Check that the wheel axle (spindle) nuts (where applicable) are properly secured. A self-locking nut or castellated nut with a split-pin or R-pin can be used (see illustration 17).
✔ Wheel alignment is checked with the motorcycle off the stand and a rider seated. With the front wheel pointing straight ahead, two perfectly straight lengths of metal or wood and placed against the sidewalls of both tyres (see illustration 18). The gap each side of the front tyre must be equidistant on both sides. Incorrect wheel alignment may be due to a cocked rear wheel (often as the result of poor chain adjustment) or in extreme cases, a bent frame.

# General checks and condition

✔ Check the security of all major fasteners, bodypanels, seat, fairings (where fitted) and mudguards.

✔ Check that the rider and pillion footrests, handlebar levers and brake pedal are securely mounted.

✔ Check for corrosion on the frame or any load-bearing components. If severe, this may affect the structure, particularly under stress.

# Sidecars

A motorcycle fitted with a sidecar requires additional checks relating to the stability of the machine and security of attachment and swivel joints, plus specific wheel alignment (toe-in) requirements. Additionally, tyre and lighting requirements differ from conventional motorcycle use. Owners are advised to check MOT test requirements with an official test centre.

# Preparing for storage

## Before you start

If repairs or an overhaul is needed, see that this is carried out now rather than left until you want to ride the bike again.

Give the bike a good wash and scrub all dirt from its underside. Make sure the bike dries completely before preparing for storage.

## Engine

● Remove the spark plug(s) and lubricate the cylinder bores with approximately a teaspoon of motor oil using a spout-type oil can **(see illustration 1)**. Reinstall the spark plug(s). Crank the engine over a couple of times to coat the piston rings and bores with oil. If the bike has a kickstart, use this to turn the engine over. If not, flick the kill switch to the OFF position and crank the engine over on the starter **(see illustration 2)**. If the nature on the ignition system prevents the starter operating with the kill switch in the OFF position,

remove the spark plugs and fit them back in their caps; ensure that the plugs are earthed (grounded) against the cylinder head when the starter is operated **(see illustration 3)**.

⚠ *Warning: It is important that the plugs are earthed (grounded) away from the spark plug holes otherwise there is a risk of atomised fuel from the cylinders igniting.*

**HAYNES HiNT** *On a single cylinder four-stroke engine, you can seal the combustion chamber completely by positioning the piston at TDC on the compression stroke.*

● Drain the carburettor(s) otherwise there is a risk of jets becoming blocked by gum deposits from the fuel **(see illustration 4)**.

● If the bike is going into long-term storage, consider adding a fuel stabiliser to the fuel in the tank. If the tank is drained completely, corrosion of its internal surfaces may occur if left unprotected for a long period. The tank can be treated with a rust preventative especially for this purpose. Alternatively, remove the tank and pour half a litre of motor oil into it, install the filler cap and shake the tank to coat its internals with oil before draining off the excess. The same effect can also be achieved by spraying WD40 or a similar water-dispersant around the inside of the tank via its flexible nozzle.

● Make sure the cooling system contains the correct mix of antifreeze. Antifreeze also contains important corrosion inhibitors.

● The air intakes and exhaust can be sealed off by covering or plugging the openings. Ensure that you do not seal in any condensation; run the engine until it is hot,

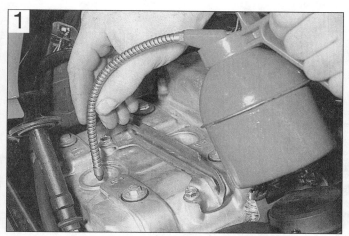

Squirt a drop of motor oil into each cylinder

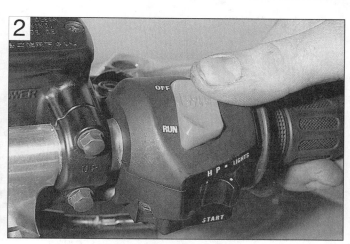

Flick the kill switch to OFF . . .

. . . and ensure that the metal bodies of the plugs (arrows) are earthed against the cylinder head

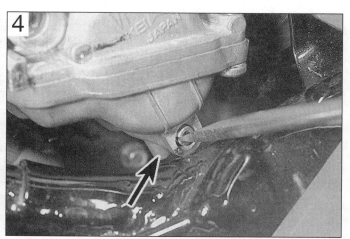

Connect a hose to the carburettor float chamber drain stub (arrow) and unscrew the drain screw

Exhausts can be sealed off with a plastic bag

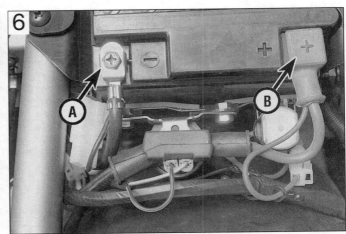

Disconnect the negative lead (A) first, followed by the positive lead (B)

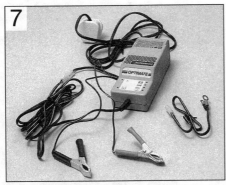

Use a suitable battery charger - this kit also assess battery condition

then switch off and allow to cool. Tape a piece of thick plastic over the silencer end(s) **(see illustration 5)**. Note that some advocate pouring a tablespoon of motor oil into the silencer(s) before sealing them off.

## Battery

● Remove it from the bike - in extreme cases of cold the battery may freeze and crack its case **(see illustration 6)**.

● Check the electrolyte level and top up if necessary (conventional refillable batteries). Clean the terminals.
● Store the battery off the motorcycle and away from any sources of fire. Position a wooden block under the battery if it is to sit on the ground.
● Give the battery a trickle charge for a few hours every month **(see illustration 7)**.

## Tyres

● Place the bike on its centrestand or an auxiliary stand which will support the motorcycle in an upright position. Position wood blocks under the tyres to keep them off the ground and to provide insulation from damp. If the bike is being put into long-term storage, ideally both tyres should be off the ground; not only will this protect the tyres, but will also ensure that no load is placed on the steering head or wheel bearings.
● Deflate each tyre by 5 to 10 psi, no more or the beads may unseat from the rim, making subsequent inflation difficult on tubeless tyres.

## Pivots and controls

● Lubricate all lever, pedal, stand and

footrest pivot points. If grease nipples are fitted to the rear suspension components, apply lubricant to the pivots.
● Lubricate all control cables.

## Cycle components

● Apply a wax protectant to all painted and plastic components. Wipe off any excess, but don't polish to a shine. Where fitted, clean the screen with soap and water.
● Coat metal parts with Vaseline (petroleum jelly). When applying this to the fork tubes, do not compress the forks otherwise the seals will rot from contact with the Vaseline.
● Apply a vinyl cleaner to the seat.

## Storage conditions

● Aim to store the bike in a shed or garage which does not leak and is free from damp.
● Drape an old blanket or bedspread over the bike to protect it from dust and direct contact with sunlight (which will fade paint). This also hides the bike from prying eyes. Beware of tight-fitting plastic covers which may allow condensation to form and settle on the bike.

# Getting back on the road

## Engine and transmission

● Change the oil and replace the oil filter. If this was done prior to storage, check that the oil hasn't emulsified - a thick whitish substance which occurs through condensation.
● Remove the spark plugs. Using a spout-type oil can, squirt a few drops of oil into the cylinder(s). This will provide initial lubrication as the piston rings and bores comes back into contact. Service the spark plugs, or fit new ones, and install them in the engine.

● Check that the clutch isn't stuck on. The plates can stick together if left standing for some time, preventing clutch operation. Engage a gear and try rocking the bike back and forth with the clutch lever held against the handlebar. If this doesn't work on cable-operated clutches, hold the clutch lever back against the handlebar with a strong elastic band or cable tie for a couple of hours **(see illustration 8)**.
● If the air intakes or silencer end(s) were blocked off, remove the bung or cover used.
● If the fuel tank was coated with a rust

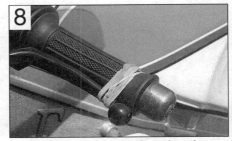

Hold clutch lever back against the handlebar with elastic bands or a cable tie

preventative, oil or a stabiliser added to the fuel, drain and flush the tank and dispose of the fuel sensibly. If no action was taken with the fuel tank prior to storage, it is advised that the old fuel is disposed of since it will go off over a period of time. Refill the fuel tank with fresh fuel.

## Frame and running gear

● Oil all pivot points and cables.
● Check the tyre pressures. They will definitely need inflating if pressures were reduced for storage.
● Lubricate the final drive chain (where applicable).
● Remove any protective coating applied to the fork tubes (stanchions) since this may well destroy the fork seals. If the fork tubes weren't protected and have picked up rust spots, remove them with very fine abrasive paper and refinish with metal polish.
● Check that both brakes operate correctly. Apply each brake hard and check that it's not possible to move the motorcycle forwards, then check that the brake frees off again once released. Brake caliper pistons can stick due to corrosion around the piston head, or on the sliding caliper types, due to corrosion of the slider pins. If the brake doesn't free off after repeated operation, take the caliper off for examination. Similarly drum brakes can stick

due to a seized operating cam, cable or rod linkage.
● If the motorcycle has been in long-term storage, renew the brake fluid and clutch fluid (where applicable).
● Depending on where the bike has been stored, the wiring, cables and hoses may have been nibbled by rodents. Make a visual check and investigate disturbed wiring loom tape.

## Battery

● If the battery has been previously removal and given top up charges it can simply be reconnected. Remember to connect the positive cable first and the negative cable last.
● On conventional refillable batteries, if the battery has not received any attention, remove it from the motorcycle and check its electrolyte level. Top up if necessary then charge the battery. If the battery fails to hold a charge and a visual checks show heavy white sulphation of the plates, the battery is probably defective and must be renewed. This is particularly likely if the battery is old. Confirm battery condition with a specific gravity check.
● On sealed (MF) batteries, if the battery has not received any attention, remove it from the motorcycle and charge it according to the information on the battery case - if the battery fails to hold a charge it must be renewed.

## Starting procedure

● If a kickstart is fitted, turn the engine over a couple of times with the ignition OFF to distribute oil around the engine. If no kickstart is fitted, flick the engine kill switch OFF and the ignition ON and crank the engine over a couple of times to work oil around the upper cylinder components. If the nature of the ignition system is such that the starter won't work with the kill switch OFF, remove the spark plugs, fit them back into their caps and earth (ground) their bodies on the cylinder head. Reinstall the spark plugs afterwards.
● Switch the kill switch to RUN, operate the choke and start the engine. If the engine won't start don't continue cranking the engine - not only will this flatten the battery, but the starter motor will overheat. Switch the ignition off and try again later. If the engine refuses to start, go through the fault finding procedures in this manual. **Note:** *If the bike has been in storage for a long time, old fuel or a carburettor blockage may be the problem. Gum deposits in carburettors can block jets - if a carburettor cleaner doesn't prove successful the carburettors must be dismantled for cleaning.*
● Once the engine has started, check that the lights, turn signals and horn work properly.
● Treat the bike gently for the first ride and check all fluid levels on completion. Settle the bike back into the maintenance schedule.

This Section provides an easy reference-guide to the more common faults that are likely to afflict your machine. Obviously, the opportunities are almost limitless for faults to occur as a result of obscure failures, and to try and cover all eventualities would require a book. Indeed, a number have been written on the subject.

Successful troubleshooting is not a mysterious 'black art' but the application of a bit of knowledge combined with a systematic and logical approach to the problem. Approach any troubleshooting by first accurately identifying the symptom and then checking through the list of possible causes, starting with the simplest or most obvious and progressing in stages to the most complex.

Take nothing for granted, but above all apply liberal quantities of common sense.

The main symptom of a fault is given in the text as a major heading below which are listed the various systems or areas which may contain the fault. Details of each possible cause for a fault and the remedial action to be taken are given, in brief, in the paragraphs below each heading. Further information should be sought in the relevant Chapter.

## 1 Engine doesn't start or is difficult to start

- ☐ Starter motor doesn't rotate
- ☐ Starter motor rotates but engine does not turn over
- ☐ Starter works but engine won't turn over (seized)
- ☐ No fuel flow
- ☐ Engine flooded
- ☐ No spark or weak spark
- ☐ Compression low
- ☐ Stalls after starting
- ☐ Rough idle

## 2 Poor running at low speed

- ☐ Spark weak
- ☐ Fuel/air mixture incorrect
- ☐ Compression low
- ☐ Poor acceleration

## 3 Poor running or no power at high speed

- ☐ Firing incorrect
- ☐ Fuel/air mixture incorrect
- ☐ Compression low
- ☐ Knocking or pinking
- ☐ Miscellaneous causes

## 4 Overheating

- ☐ Engine overheats
- ☐ Firing incorrect
- ☐ Fuel/air mixture incorrect
- ☐ Compression too high
- ☐ Engine load excessive
- ☐ Lubrication inadequate
- ☐ Miscellaneous causes

## 5 Clutch problems

- ☐ Clutch slipping
- ☐ Clutch not disengaging completely

## 6 Gearchanging problems

- ☐ Doesn't go into gear, or lever doesn't return
- ☐ Jumps out of gear
- ☐ Overselects

## 7 Abnormal engine noise

- ☐ Knocking or pinking
- ☐ Piston slap or rattling
- ☐ Valve noise
- ☐ Other noise

## 8 Abnormal driveline noise

- ☐ Clutch noise
- ☐ Transmission noise
- ☐ Final drive noise

## 9 Abnormal frame and suspension noise

- ☐ Front end noise
- ☐ Shock absorber noise
- ☐ Brake noise

## 10 Oil pressure warning light comes on

- ☐ Engine lubrication system
- ☐ Electrical system

## 11 Excessive exhaust smoke

- ☐ White smoke
- ☐ Black smoke
- ☐ Brown smoke

## 12 Poor handling or stability

- ☐ Handlebar hard to turn
- ☐ Handlebar shakes or vibrates excessively
- ☐ Handlebar pulls to one side
- ☐ Poor shock absorbing qualities

## 13 Braking problems

- ☐ Brakes are spongy, don't hold
- ☐ Brake lever or pedal pulsates
- ☐ Brakes drag

## 14 Electrical problems

- ☐ Battery dead or weak
- ☐ Battery overcharged

# 1 Engine doesn't start or is difficult to start

## Starter motor doesn't rotate

☐ Engine kill switch OFF.
☐ Fuse blown. Check main fuse and ignition circuit fuse (Chapter 9).
☐ Battery voltage low. Check and recharge battery (Chapter 9).
☐ Starter motor defective. Make sure the wiring to the starter is secure. Make sure the starter relay clicks when the start button is pushed. If the relay clicks, then the fault is in the wiring or motor (see Chapter 9).
☐ Starter switch not contacting. The contacts could be wet, corroded or dirty. Disassemble and clean the switch (Chapter 9).
☐ Wiring open or shorted. Check all wiring connections and harnesses to make sure that they are dry, tight and not corroded. Also check for broken or frayed wires that can cause a short to ground (earth) (see *Wiring diagrams*, Chapter 9).
☐ Ignition (main) switch defective. Check the switch and renew it if it is defective (see Chapter 9).
☐ Engine kill switch defective. Check for wet, dirty or corroded contacts. Clean or renew the switch as necessary (see Chapter 9).
☐ Faulty gear position sensor, sidestand switch or clutch switch. Check the wiring to each switch and the switch itself (see Chapter 9).
☐ Faulty sidestand relay or diode (Chapter 9).
☐ Fuel injection system shutdown due to system fault (Chapter 4).

## Starter motor rotates but engine does not turn over

☐ Starter motor clutch defective. Inspect and repair or renew (see Chapter 2).
☐ Damaged idler or starter gears. Inspect and renew the damaged parts (see Chapter 2).

## Starter works but engine won't turn over (seized)

☐ Seized engine caused by one or more internally damaged components. Failure due to wear, abuse or lack of lubrication. Damage can include seized valves, followers, camshafts, pistons, crankshaft, connecting rod bearings, or transmission gears or bearings. Refer to Chapter 2 for engine disassembly.

## No fuel flow

☐ No fuel in tank.
☐ Fuel tank breather hose obstructed.
☐ Fuel pump faulty, or the fuel filter is blocked (see Chapter 4).
☐ Fuel hose clogged. Remove the fuel hose and carefully blow through it. Check the fuel filter for damage.
☐ Fuel rail or injector clogged. For all of the injectors to be clogged, either a very bad batch of fuel with an unusual additive has been used, or some other foreign material has entered the tank. Check the fuel filter. In some cases, if a machine has been unused for several months, the fuel turns to a varnish-like liquid which can cause an injector needle to stick to its seat. Drain the tank and fuel system (Chapter 4).

## Engine flooded

☐ Injector needle valve worn or stuck open. A piece of dirt, rust or other debris can cause the needle to seat improperly, causing excess fuel to be admitted to the throttle body. In this case, the injector should be cleaned and the needle and seat inspected (see Chapter 4). If the needle and seat are worn, then the leaking will persist and the parts should be renewed.
☐ Starting technique incorrect. Under normal circumstances (i.e. if all the components of the fuel injection system are good) the machine should start with the throttle closed. On GSX-R600/750 and GSX-R1000K1 models, when the engine is cold the fast idle (choke) should be operated and the engine started with the thottle opened slightly.

## No spark or weak spark

☐ Ignition switch OFF.
☐ Engine kill switch turned to the OFF position.
☐ Ignition or kill switch shorted. This is usually caused by water, corrosion, damage or excessive wear. The switches can be disassembled and cleaned with electrical contact cleaner. If cleaning does not help, renew the switches (see Chapter 9).
☐ Battery voltage low. Check and recharge the battery as necessary (Chapter 9).
☐ Ignition coil/spark plug caps not making good contact. Make sure that the caps fit snugly over the plug ends.
☐ Spark plugs dirty, defective or worn out. Locate reason for fouled plugs using spark plug condition chart on the inside back cover and follow the plug maintenance procedures (see Chapter 1).
☐ Incorrect spark plugs. Wrong type or heat range. Check and install correct plugs (see Chapter 1).
☐ Ignition coil/spark plug cap defective. Test and renew if necessary (Chapter 5).
☐ Fuel injection system shutdown due to system fault (Chapter 4).
☐ Camshaft position (CMP) sensor defective (see Chapter 4).
☐ Crankshaft position (CKP) sensor defective (see Chapter 4).
☐ Engine control module (ECM) defective (see Chapter 5).
☐ Wiring shorted or broken between:
   a) Ignition (main) switch and engine kill switch (or blown fuse)
   b) ECM and engine kill switch
   c) ECM and ignition coil/caps
   e) ECM and CKP
☐ Make sure that all wiring connections are clean, dry and tight. Look for chafed and broken wires (see Chapters 5 and 9).

# 1 Engine doesn't start or is difficult to start (continued)

## *Compression low*

☐ Spark plugs loose. Remove the plugs and inspect their threads. Reinstall and tighten securely (see Chapter 1).

☐ Cylinder head not sufficiently tightened down. If a cylinder head is suspected of being loose, then there's a chance that the gasket or head is damaged if the problem has persisted for any length of time. The head bolts should be tightened to the proper torque and in the correct sequence (Chapter 2).

☐ Improper valve clearance. This means that the valve is not closing completely and compression pressure is leaking past the valve. Check and adjust the valve clearances (Chapter 1).

☐ Cylinder and/or piston worn. Excessive wear will cause compression pressure to leak past the rings. This is usually accompanied by worn rings as well. A top-end overhaul is necessary (Chapter 2).

☐ Piston rings worn, weak, broken, or sticking. Broken or sticking piston rings usually indicate a lubrication or carburation problem that causes excess carbon deposits to form on the pistons and rings. Top-end overhaul is necessary (Chapter 2).

☐ Piston ring-to-groove clearance excessive. This is caused by excessive wear of the piston ring lands. Piston renewal is necessary (Chapter 2).

☐ Cylinder head gasket damaged. If a head is allowed to become loose, or if excessive carbon build-up on the piston crown and combustion chamber causes extremely high compression, the head gasket may leak. Retorquing the head is not always sufficient to restore the seal, so gasket renewal is necessary (Chapter 2).

☐ Cylinder head warped. This is caused by overheating or improperly tightened head bolts. Machine shop resurfacing or head renewal is necessary (Chapter 2).

☐ Valve spring broken or weak. Caused by component failure or wear; the springs must be renewed (Chapter 2).

☐ Valve not seating properly. This is caused by a bent valve (from over-revving or improper valve adjustment), burned valve or seat (improper carburation) or an accumulation of carbon deposits on the seat. The valves must be cleaned and/or renewed and the seats serviced (Chapter 2).

## *Stalls after starting*

☐ Faulty fast idle (choke) action. Check the operation of the fast idle mechanism (see Chapter 4).

☐ Engine idle speed incorrect. Turn idle adjusting screw until the engine idles at the specified rpm (Chapter 1).

☐ Ignition malfunction (see Chapter 5).

☐ Fuel injection system malfunction (see Chapter 4).

☐ Fuel contaminated. The fuel can be contaminated with either dirt or water, or can change chemically if the machine has been unused for several months. Drain the tank and fuel system (Chapter 4).

☐ Intake air leak. Check for loose throttle body-to-inlet manifold connections, loose or damaged PAIR vacuum hose or missing vacuum gauge blanking caps (Chapter 4).

## *Rough idle*

☐ Idle speed incorrect (see Chapter 1).

☐ Ignition fault (see Chapter 5).

☐ Throttle valves not synchronised. Adjust them with vacuum gauge or manometer set as described in Chapter 1.

☐ Fuel injection system malfunction (see Chapter 4).

☐ Fuel contaminated. The fuel can be contaminated with either dirt or water, or can change chemically if the machine has been unused for several months. Drain the tank and the fuel system (Chapter 4).

☐ Intake air leak. Check for loose throttle body-to-inlet manifold connections, loose or damaged PAIR vacuum hose or missing vacuum gauge blanking caps (Chapter 4).

☐ Air filter clogged. Clean or renew the air filter element (Chapter 1).

# 2 Poor running at low speeds

## Spark weak

- [ ] Battery voltage low. Check and recharge battery (see Chapter 9).
- [ ] Ignition coil/spark plug caps not making good contact. Make sure that the caps fit snugly over the plug ends.
- [ ] Spark plugs dirty, defective or worn out. Locate reason for fouled plugs using spark plug condition chart on the inside back cover and follow the plug maintenance procedures (see Chapter 1).
- [ ] Incorrect spark plugs. Wrong type or heat range. Check and install correct plugs (see Chapter 1).
- [ ] Ignition coil/spark plug cap defective. Test and renew if necessary (see Chapter 5).

## Fuel/air mixture incorrect

- [ ] Fuel tank breather hose obstructed.
- [ ] Fuel pump faulty, or the fuel filter is blocked (see Chapter 4).
- [ ] Fuel hose clogged. Remove the fuel hose and carefully blow through it. Check the fuel filter for damage.
- [ ] Fuel rail or injector clogged. For all of the injectors to be clogged, either a very bad batch of fuel with an unusual additive has been used, or some other foreign material has entered the tank. Check the fuel filter. In some cases, if a machine has been unused for several months, the fuel turns to a varnish-like liquid which can cause an injector needle to stick to its seat. Drain the tank and fuel system (Chapter 4).
- [ ] Intake air leak. Check for loose throttle body-to-inlet manifold connections, loose or damaged PAIR vacuum hose or missing vacuum gauge blanking caps (Chapter 4).
- [ ] Air filter clogged. Renew the air filter element (Chapter 1).

## Compression low

- [ ] Spark plugs loose. Remove the plugs and inspect their threads. Reinstall and tighten securely (see Chapter 1).
- [ ] Cylinder head not sufficiently tightened down. If a cylinder head is suspected of being loose, then there's a chance that the gasket or head is damaged if the problem has persisted for any length of time. The head bolts should be tightened to the proper torque and in the correct sequence (Chapter 2).
- [ ] Improper valve clearance. This means that the valve is not closing completely and compression pressure is leaking past the valve. Check and adjust the valve clearances (Chapter 1).
- [ ] Cylinder and/or piston worn. Excessive wear will cause compression pressure to leak past the rings. This is usually accompanied by worn rings as well. A top-end overhaul is necessary (Chapter 2).
- [ ] Piston rings worn, weak, broken, or sticking. Broken or sticking piston rings usually indicate a lubrication or carburation problem that causes excess carbon deposits to form on the pistons and rings. Top-end overhaul is necessary (Chapter 2).
- [ ] Piston ring-to-groove clearance excessive. This is caused by excessive wear of the piston ring lands. Piston renewal is necessary (Chapter 2).
- [ ] Cylinder head gasket damaged. If a head is allowed to become loose, or if excessive carbon build-up on the piston crown and combustion chamber causes extremely high compression, the head gasket may leak. Retorquing the head is not always sufficient to restore the seal, so gasket renewal is necessary (Chapter 2).
- [ ] Cylinder head warped. This is caused by overheating or improperly tightened head bolts. Machine shop resurfacing or head renewal is necessary (Chapter 2).
- [ ] Valve spring broken or weak. Caused by component failure or wear; the springs must be renewed (Chapter 2).
- [ ] Valve not seating properly. This is caused by a bent valve (from over-revving or improper valve adjustment), burned valve or seat (improper carburation) or an accumulation of carbon deposits on the seat (from carburation or lubrication problems). The valves must be cleaned and/or renewed and the seats serviced (Chapter 2).

## Poor acceleration

- [ ] Timing not advancing. The crankshaft position sensor (CKP) or the engine control module (ECM) may be defective (see Chapters 4 and 5). If so, they must be renewed.
- [ ] Throttle valves not synchronised. Adjust them with a vacuum gauge set or manometer (see Chapter 1).
- [ ] Engine oil viscosity too high. Using a heavier oil than that recommended in Chapter 1 can damage the oil pump or lubrication system and cause drag on the engine.
- [ ] Brakes dragging. Usually caused by debris which has entered the brake caliper piston seals, or from a warped disc or bent axle (see Chapter 7).

# 3 Poor running or no power at high speed

## Firing incorrect

- [ ] Ignition coil/spark plug caps not making good contact. Make sure that the caps fit snugly over the plug ends and that the wiring is secure.
- [ ] Spark plugs dirty, defective or worn out. Locate reason for fouled plugs using spark plug condition chart on the inside back cover and follow the plug maintenance procedures (see Chapter 1).
- [ ] Incorrect spark plugs. Wrong type or heat range. Check and install correct plugs (see Chapter 1).
- [ ] Ignition coil/spark plug cap defective. Test and renew if necessary (see Chapter 5).
- [ ] Faulty ECM (engine control module) (see Chapter 5).

## Fuel/air mixture incorrect

- [ ] Fuel tank breather hose obstructed.
- [ ] Fuel pump faulty, or the fuel filter is blocked (see Chapter 4).
- [ ] Fuel hose clogged. Remove the fuel hose and carefully blow through it. Check the fuel filter for damage.
- [ ] Fuel rail or injector clogged. For all of the injectors to be clogged, either a very bad batch of fuel with an unusual additive has been used, or some other foreign material has entered the tank. Check the fuel filter. In some cases, if a machine has been unused for several months, the fuel turns to a varnish-like liquid which can cause an injector needle to stick to its seat. Drain the tank and fuel system (Chapter 4).
- [ ] Intake air leak. Check for loose throttle body-to-inlet manifold connections, loose or damaged PAIR vacuum hose or missing vacuum gauge blanking caps (Chapter 4).
- [ ] Air filter clogged. Renew the air filter element (Chapter 1).

## Compression low

- [ ] Spark plugs loose. Remove the plugs and inspect their threads. Reinstall and tighten securely (see Chapter 1).
- [ ] Cylinder head not sufficiently tightened down. If a cylinder head is suspected of being loose, then there's a chance that the gasket or head is damaged if the problem has persisted for any length of time. The head bolts should be tightened to the proper torque and in the correct sequence (Chapter 2).
- [ ] Improper valve clearance. This means that the valve is not closing completely and compression pressure is leaking past the valve. Check and adjust the valve clearances (Chapter 1).
- [ ] Cylinder and/or piston worn. Excessive wear will cause compression pressure to leak past the rings. This is usually accompanied by worn rings as well. A top-end overhaul is necessary (Chapter 2).
- [ ] Piston rings worn, weak, broken, or sticking. Broken or sticking piston rings usually indicate a lubrication or carburation problem that causes excess carbon deposits to form on the pistons and rings. Top-end overhaul is necessary (Chapter 2).
- [ ] Piston ring-to-groove clearance excessive. This is caused by excessive wear of the piston ring lands. Piston renewal is necessary (Chapter 2).
- [ ] Cylinder head gasket damaged. If a head is allowed to become loose, or if excessive carbon build-up on the piston crown and combustion chamber causes extremely high compression, the head gasket may leak. Retorquing the head is not always sufficient to restore the seal, so gasket renewal is necessary (Chapter 2).
- [ ] Cylinder head warped. This is caused by overheating or improperly tightened head bolts. Machine shop resurfacing or head renewal is necessary (Chapter 2).
- [ ] Valve spring broken or weak. Caused by component failure or wear; the springs must be renewed (Chapter 2).
- [ ] Valve not seating properly. This is caused by a bent valve (from over-revving or improper valve adjustment), burned valve or seat (improper carburation) or an accumulation of carbon deposits on the seat (from carburation or lubrication problems). The valves must be cleaned and/or renewed and the seats serviced (Chapter 2).

## Knocking or pinking

- [ ] Carbon build-up in combustion chamber. Use of a fuel additive that will dissolve the adhesive bonding the carbon particles to the piston crown and chamber is the easiest way to remove the build-up. Otherwise, the cylinder head will have to be removed and decarbonised (Chapter 2).
- [ ] Incorrect or poor quality fuel. Old or improper grades of fuel can cause detonation. This causes the piston to rattle, thus the knocking or pinking sound. Drain old fuel and always use the recommended fuel grade.
- [ ] Spark plug heat range incorrect. Uncontrolled detonation indicates the plug heat range is too hot. The plug in effect becomes a glow plug, raising cylinder temperatures. Install the proper heat range plug (Chapter 1).
- [ ] Improper air/fuel mixture. This will cause the cylinders to run hot, which leads to detonation. A blockage in the fuel system or an air leak can cause this imbalance (see Chapter 4).

## Miscellaneous causes

- [ ] Throttle valve doesn't open fully. Adjust the throttle twistgrip freeplay (see Chapter 1).
- [ ] Clutch slipping due loose or worn clutch components (see Chapter 2).
- [ ] Timing not advancing. The crankshaft position sensor (CKP) or the engine control module (ECM) may be defective (see Chapters 4 and 5). If so, they must be renewed.
- [ ] Engine oil viscosity too high. Using a heavier oil than the one recommended in Chapter 1 can damage the oil pump or lubrication system and cause drag on the engine.
- [ ] Brakes dragging. Usually caused by debris which has entered the brake caliper piston seals, or from a warped disc or bent axle (see Chapter 7).

# 4 Overheating

## Engine overheats

☐ Coolant level low. Check and add coolant (see Chapter 1).
☐ Leak in cooling system. Check cooling system hoses and radiator for leaks and other damage. Repair or renew parts as necessary (see Chapter 3).
☐ Faulty thermostat. Check and renew as described in Chapter 3.
☐ Faulty radiator cap. Remove the cap and have it pressure tested.
☐ Coolant passages clogged. Have the entire system drained and flushed, then refill with fresh coolant.
☐ Water pump defective. Remove the pump and check the components (see Chapter 3).
☐ Clogged or damaged radiator fins (see Chapter 3).
☐ Faulty cooling fan or fan switch (see Chapter 3).

## Firing incorrect

☐ Wrongly connected ignition coil/spark plug cap wiring.
☐ Spark plugs dirty, defective or worn out. Locate reason for fouled plugs using spark plug condition chart on the inside back cover and follow the plug maintenance procedures (see Chapter 1).
☐ Incorrect spark plugs. Wrong type or heat range. Check and install correct plugs (see Chapter 1).
☐ Ignition coil/spark plug cap defective. Test and renew if necessary (see Chapter 5).
☐ Faulty ECM (engine control module) (see Chapter 5).

## Fuel/air mixture incorrect

☐ Fuel tank breather hose obstructed.
☐ Fuel pump faulty, or the fuel filter is blocked (see Chapter 4).
☐ Fuel hose clogged. Remove the fuel hose and carefully blow through it. Check the fuel filter for damage.
☐ Fuel rail or injector clogged. For all of the injectors to be clogged, either a very bad batch of fuel with an unusual additive has been used, or some other foreign material has entered the tank. Check the fuel filter. In some cases, if a machine has been unused for several months, the fuel turns to a varnish-like liquid which can cause an injector needle to stick to its seat. Drain the tank and fuel system (Chapter 4).
☐ Intake air leak. Check for loose throttle body-to-intake manifold connections, loose or damaged PAIR vacuum hose or missing vacuum gauge blanking caps (Chapter 4).
☐ Air filter clogged. Renew the air filter element (Chapter 1).

## Compression too high

☐ Carbon build-up in combustion chamber. Use of a fuel additive that will dissolve the adhesive bonding the carbon particles to the piston crown and chamber is the easiest way to remove the build-up. Otherwise, the cylinder head will have to be removed and decarbonised (Chapter 2).
☐ Improperly machined head surface or installation of incorrect gasket during engine assembly.

## Engine load excessive

☐ Clutch slipping due loose or worn clutch components (see Chapter 2).
☐ Engine oil level too high. Too much oil will cause pressurisation of the crankcase and inefficient engine operation. Check Specifications and drain to proper level (Chapter 1).
☐ Engine oil viscosity too high. Using a heavier oil than the one recommended in Chapter 1 can damage the oil pump or lubrication system as well as cause drag on the engine.
☐ Brakes dragging. Usually caused by debris which has entered the brake caliper piston seals, or from a warped disc or bent axle (see Chapter 7).

## Lubrication inadequate

☐ Engine oil level too low. Friction caused by intermittent lack of lubrication or from oil that is overworked can cause overheating. The oil provides a definite cooling function in the engine. Check the oil level (see Daily (pre-ride) checks).
☐ Low engine oil pressure. Check the pressure (see Chapter 1).
☐ Blocked oil filter or oil cooler (see Chapter 2).
☐ Poor quality engine oil or incorrect viscosity or type. Oil is rated not only according to viscosity but also according to type. Some oils are not rated high enough for use in this engine. Check the Specifications section and change to the correct oil (Chapter 1).

## Miscellaneous causes

☐ Modification to exhaust system. Most aftermarket exhaust systems cause the engine to run leaner, which make them run hotter. When installing an accessory exhaust system, always check with the manufacturer/supplier as to whether the ECM requires re-mapping.

# 5 Clutch problems

## Clutch slipping

☐ Insufficient clutch cable freeplay. Check and adjust (see Chapter 1).
☐ Clutch plates worn or warped. Overhaul the clutch assembly (see Chapter 2).
☐ Clutch springs broken or weak. Old or heat-damaged (from slipping clutch) springs should be renewed (Chapter 2).
☐ Faulty clutch release mechanism. Renew any defective parts (see Chapter 2).
☐ Clutch centre or housing unevenly worn. This causes improper engagement of the plates. Renew the damaged or worn parts (see Chapter 2).

## Clutch not disengaging completely

☐ Excessive clutch cable freeplay. Check and adjust (see Chapter 1).
☐ Clutch plates warped or damaged. This will cause clutch drag, which in turn will cause the machine to creep. Overhaul the clutch assembly (see Chapter 2).

☐ Clutch springs fatigued or broken. Check and renew the springs (see Chapter 2).
☐ Engine oil deteriorated. Old, thin oil will not provide proper lubrication for the plates, causing the clutch to drag. Renew the oil and filter (see Chapter 1).
☐ Engine oil viscosity too high. Using a heavier oil than recommended in Chapter 1 can cause the plates to stick together. Change to the correct weight oil.
☐ Clutch housing bearing seized on the transmission input shaft. Lack of lubrication, severe wear or damage can cause the bearing to seize. Overhaul of the clutch, and perhaps transmission, may be necessary to repair the damage (see Chapter 2).
☐ Faulty clutch release mechanism. Renew any defective parts (see Chapter 2).
☐ Loose clutch centre nut. Causes housing and centre misalignment putting a drag on the engine. Engagement adjustment continually varies. Overhaul the clutch assembly (see Chapter 2).

# 6 Gearchanging problems

## Doesn't go into gear or lever doesn't return

☐ Clutch not disengaging (see above).
☐ Gearchange mechanism stopper arm spring weak or broken, or arm roller broken or worn. Renew the spring or arm (see Chapter 2).
☐ Selector fork(s) bent, worn or seized. Overhaul the transmission (see Chapter 2).
☐ Gear(s) stuck on shaft. Most often caused by a lack of lubrication or excessive wear in transmission bearings and bushes. Overhaul the transmission (see Chapter 2).
☐ Selector drum binding. Caused by lubrication failure or excessive wear. Renew the drum and bearing (see Chapter 2).
☐ Gearchange mechanism return spring weak or broken (see Chapter 2).
☐ Gearchange linkage arm broken. Splines stripped out of arm or shaft, caused by a loose linkage arm pinch bolt or from dropping the machine (see Chapter 2).

## Jumps out of gear

☐ Selector fork(s) worn (see Chapter 2).
☐ Selector fork groove(s) in selector drum worn (see Chapter 2).
☐ Gear pinion dogs or dog slots worn or damaged. The gear pinions should be inspected and renewed. No attempt should be made to repair the worn parts.

## Overselects

☐ Gearchange mechanism stopper arm spring weak or broken, or arm roller broken or worn. Renew the spring or arm (see Chapter 2).
☐ Gearchange mechanism return spring weak or broken (see Chapter 2).

# 7 Abnormal engine noise

### Knocking or pinking

☐ Carbon build-up in combustion chamber. Use of a fuel additive that will dissolve the adhesive bonding the carbon particles to the piston crown and chamber is the easiest way to remove the build-up. Otherwise, the cylinder head will have to be removed and decarbonised (Chapter 2).

☐ Incorrect or poor quality fuel. Old or improper grades of fuel can cause detonation. This causes the piston to rattle, thus the knocking or pinking sound. Drain old fuel and always use the recommended fuel grade.

☐ Spark plug heat range incorrect. Uncontrolled detonation indicates the plug heat range is too hot. The plug in effect becomes a glow plug, raising cylinder temperatures. Install the proper heat range plug (Chapter 1).

☐ Improper air/fuel mixture. This will cause the cylinders to run hot, which leads to detonation. A blockage in the fuel system or an air leak can cause this imbalance (see Chapter 4).

### Piston slap or rattling

☐ Cylinder-to-piston clearance excessive. Cylinder and/or piston worn, usually accompanied by worn rings as well. A top-end overhaul is necessary (see Chapter 2).

☐ Piston ring(s) worn, broken or sticking. Overhaul the top-end (see Chapter 2).

☐ Piston pin, piston pin bore or connecting rod small-end worn from high mileage or seized due to lack of lubrication (see Chapter 2).

☐ Piston seizure damage. Usually from lack of lubrication or overheating. Renew the pistons and upper crankcase, as necessary (see Chapter 2).

☐ Connecting rod big-end clearance excessive. Caused by excessive wear or lack of lubrication. Renew worn parts.

☐ Connecting rod bent. Caused by over-revving, trying to start a badly flooded engine or from ingesting a foreign object into the combustion chamber. Renew the damaged parts (Chapter 2).

### Valve noise

☐ Incorrect valve clearances – check and adjust (see Chapter 1).

☐ Valve spring broken or weak. Check and renew weak valve springs (see Chapter 2).

☐ Camshaft or camshaft journals in the cylinder head worn or damaged. Lubrication failure at high rpm is usually the cause of damage due to insufficient oil or failure to change the oil at the recommended intervals. Since there are no replaceable bearings in the head, the head itself will have to be renewed (see Chapter 2).

### Other noise

☐ Cylinder head gasket leaking. Check around the joint for blowing with the engine running.

☐ Exhaust pipe leaking at cylinder head connection. Caused by incorrect fit of pipe(s), loose exhaust flange or damaged gasket. All exhaust system fasteners should be tightened evenly and carefully to avoid leaks (see Chapter 4).

☐ Crankshaft runout excessive. Caused by a bent crankshaft (from over-revving) or damage from an upper cylinder component failure. Can also be attributed to dropping the machine on either of the crankshaft ends.

☐ Engine mounting bolts loose – ensure all the bolts are tightened to the specified torque settings (see Chapter 2).

☐ Crankshaft bearings worn (see Chapter 2).

☐ Cam chain rattle, due to worn chain or defective tensioner. Also worn chain tensioner/guide blades (see Chapter 2).

# 8 Abnormal driveline noise

### Clutch noise

☐ Clutch housing/friction plate clearance excessive (Chapter 2).
☐ Wear between the clutch housing splines and input shaft splines (Chapter 2).
☐ Worn release bearing (Chapter 2).

### Transmission noise

☐ Bearings worn. Also includes the possibility that the shafts are worn. Overhaul the transmission (Chapter 2).
☐ Gears worn or chipped (Chapter 2).
☐ Metal chips jammed in gear teeth. Probably pieces from a broken clutch, gear or selector mechanism that were picked up by the gears. This will cause early bearing failure (Chapter 2).

☐ Engine oil level too low. Causes a howl from transmission. Also affects engine power and clutch operation (Chapter 1).

### Final drive noise

☐ Chain not adjusted properly (Chapter 1).
☐ Front or rear sprocket loose. Tighten fasteners (Chapter 6).
☐ Sprockets and/or chain worn. Renew sprockets and chain (Chapter 6).
☐ Rear sprocket warped. Renew sprocket (Chapter 6).
☐ Rubber dampers in rear wheel worn (Chapter 6).

# 9 Abnormal frame and suspension noise

### Front end noise

☐ Low fluid level or improper viscosity oil in forks. This can sound like spurting and is usually accompanied by irregular fork action (Chapter 6).
☐ Spring weak or broken. Makes a clicking or scraping sound. Fork oil, when drained, will have a lot of metal particles in it (Chapter 6).
☐ Steering head bearings loose or damaged. Clicks when braking. Check and adjust or renew as necessary (Chapters 1 and 6).
☐ Fork yoke clamp bolts loose – ensure all the bolts are tightened to the specified torque (Chapter 6).
☐ Forks bent. Good possibility if machine has been dropped. Renew forks (Chapter 6).
☐ Front axle or axle pinch bolts loose. Tighten them to the specified torque (Chapter 7).
☐ Loose or worn wheel bearings. Check and renew as needed (Chapters 1 and 7).

### Shock absorber noise

☐ Fluid level incorrect. Indicates a leak caused by defective seal. Shock will be covered with oil. Renew shock or seek advice on repair from a suspension specialist (Chapter 6).
☐ Defective shock absorber with internal damage. This is in the body of the shock and can't be remedied. The shock must be renewed or rebuilt (Chapter 6).

☐ Bent or damaged shock body. Renew the shock (Chapter 6).
☐ Loose or worn suspension linkage components. Check and renew as necessary (Chapter 6).

### Brake noise

☐ Squeal caused by pad shim not installed or positioned correctly (where fitted) (Chapter 7).
☐ Squeal caused by dust on brake pads. Usually found in combination with glazed pads. Clean using brake cleaning solvent (Chapter 7).
☐ Pads glazed. Caused by excessive heat from prolonged hard use or from contamination. DO NOT use sandpaper, emery cloth, carborundum cloth or any other abrasive to roughen the pad surfaces as abrasives will stay in the pad material and damage the disc. A very fine flat file can be used, but pad renewal is suggested as a cure (Chapter 7).
☐ Contamination of brake pads. Oil or brake fluid can cause the brake pads to chatter or squeal. Fit new pads. Identify the cause of the contamination, especially check the caliper piston seals for leaking fluid. Clean disc thoroughly with brake system cleaner (Chapter 7).
☐ Disc warped. Can cause a chattering, clicking or intermittent squeal. Usually accompanied by a pulsating lever and uneven braking. Renew the disc (Chapter 7).
☐ Loose or worn wheel bearings. Check and renew as needed (Chapters 1 and 7).

# 10 Oil pressure warning light comes on

### Engine lubrication system

☐ Engine oil level low. Inspect for leak or other problem causing low oil level and add recommended oil (see *Daily (pre-ride) checks*).

☐ Engine oil pump defective, blocked oil strainer gauze or failed pressure regulator. Carry out an oil pressure check (Chapter 1).

☐ Engine oil viscosity too low. Very old, thin oil or an improper weight of oil used in the engine. Change to correct oil (Chapter 1).

☐ Camshaft or crankshaft journals worn. Excessive wear causing drop in oil pressure. Abnormal wear could be caused by oil starvation at high rpm from low oil level or improper weight or type of oil (Chapter 1).

### Electrical system

☐ Oil pressure switch defective. Check the switch according to the procedure in Chapter 9. Renew it if it is defective.

☐ Oil pressure warning LED or symbol defective. Check for pinched, shorted, disconnected or damaged wiring (Chapter 9).

# 11 Excessive exhaust smoke

### White smoke

☐ Piston rings worn or broken, causing oil from the crankcase to be pulled past the piston into the combustion chamber. Renew the rings (Chapter 2).

☐ Cylinders worn or scored. Caused by overheating or oil starvation. Install a new upper crankcase (Chapter 2).

☐ Valve oil seal damaged or worn. Renew oil seals (Chapter 2).

☐ Valve guide worn. Perform a complete valve job (Chapter 2).

☐ Engine oil level too high, which causes the oil to be forced past the rings. Drain oil to the proper level (see Daily (pre-ride) checks).

☐ Head gasket broken between oil return and cylinder. Causes oil to be pulled into the combustion chamber. Renew the head gasket and check the head for warpage (Chapter 2).

☐ Abnormal crankcase pressurisation which forces oil past the rings, usually caused by a clogged breather.

### Black smoke

☐ Air filter clogged. Clean or renew the element (Chapter 1).

☐ Fuel injection system malfunction (Chapter 4).

### Brown smoke

☐ Air filter poorly sealed or not installed (Chapter 1).

☐ Fuel injection system malfunction (Chapter 4).

# 12 Poor handling or stability

### Handlebar hard to turn

☐ Steering head bearing adjuster nut too tight. Check adjustment as described in Chapter 1.

☐ Bearings damaged. Roughness can be felt as the bars are turned from side-to-side. Renew bearings (Chapter 6).

☐ Races dented or worn. Denting results from wear in only one position (e.g., straight ahead), from a collision or hitting a pothole or from dropping the machine. Renew bearings (Chapter 6).

☐ Steering stem lubrication inadequate. Causes are grease getting hard from age or being washed out by high pressure car washes. Disassemble steering head and repack bearings (Chapter 6).

☐ Steering stem bent. Caused by a collision, hitting a pothole or by dropping the machine. Renew damaged part. Don't try to straighten the steering stem (Chapter 6).

☐ Front tyre air pressure too low (Chapter 1).

### Handlebar shakes or vibrates excessively

☐ Tyres worn or out of balance (Chapter 7).

☐ Swingarm bearings worn. Renew worn bearings (Chapter 6).

☐ Failed steering damper.

☐ Wheel rim(s) warped or damaged. Inspect wheels for runout (Chapter 7).

☐ Wheel bearings worn. Worn front or rear wheel bearings can cause poor tracking. Worn front bearings will cause wobble (Chapters 1 and 7).

☐ Fork yoke clamp bolts or handlebar clamp bolts loose. Tighten them to the specified torque (Chapter 6).

☐ Engine mounting bolts loose. Will cause excessive vibration with increased engine rpm – ensure all the bolts are tightened to the specified torque settings (see Chapter 2).

### Machine pulls to one side

☐ Frame bent. Definitely suspect this if the machine has been dropped. May or may not be accompanied by cracking near the steering head, swingarm mountings or engine mountings. Renew the frame (Chapter 6).

☐ Wheels out of alignment. Caused by improper location of axle spacers or from bent steering stem or frame (Chapter 6).

☐ Forks bent. Disassemble the forks and renew the damaged parts (Chapter 6).

☐ Swingarm bent or twisted. Renew the arm (Chapter 6).

☐ Fork oil level uneven. Check and add or drain as necessary (Chapter 6).

### Poor shock absorbing qualities

☐ Too hard:
   a)   Suspension settings incorrect.
   b)   Fork oil level excessive (Chapter 6).
   c)   Fork oil viscosity too high. Use a lighter oil (see the Specifications in Chapter 6).
   d)   Fork tube bent. Causes a harsh, sticking feeling (Chapter 6).
   e)   Fork internal damage (Chapter 6).
   f)   Shock shaft or body bent or damaged (Chapter 6).
   g)   Shock internal damage.
   h)   Tyre pressure too high (Chapter 1).

☐ Too soft:
   a)   Suspension settings incorrect.
   b)   Fork oil level too low (Chapter 6).
   c)   Fork oil viscosity too light (Chapter 6).
   d)   Fork springs weak or broken (Chapter 6).
   e)   Fork or shock oil leaking (Chapter 6).
   f)   Shock internal damage (Chapter 6).

## 13 Braking problems

### Brakes are spongy, don't hold

- ☐ Low brake fluid level (see *Daily (pre-ride) checks*).
- ☐ Air in hydraulic system. Caused by inattention to master cylinder fluid level or by leakage. Locate problem and bleed brakes (Chapter 7).
- ☐ Pad or disc worn (Chapters 1 and 7).
- ☐ Contaminated pads. Caused by contamination with oil, grease, brake fluid, etc. Fit new pads. Identify the cause of the contamination, especially check the caliper piston seals for leaking fluid. Clean disc thoroughly with brake system cleaner (Chapter 7).
- ☐ Brake fluid deteriorated. Fluid is old or contaminated. Drain system, replenish with new fluid and bleed the system (Chapter 7).
- ☐ Master cylinder internal seals worn or damaged causing fluid to bypass (Chapter 7).
- ☐ Master cylinder bore scratched by foreign material or broken spring. Repair or renew master cylinder (Chapter 7).
- ☐ Disc warped. Renew disc (Chapter 7).

### Brake lever or pedal pulsates

- ☐ Disc warped. Renew disc (Chapter 7).
- ☐ Axle bent. Renew axle (Chapter 7).
- ☐ Brake caliper bolts loose – tighten the bolts to the specified torque (Chapter 7).
- ☐ Wheel warped or otherwise damaged (Chapter 7).
- ☐ Wheel bearings damaged or worn (Chapters 1 and 7).

### Brakes drag

- ☐ Master cylinder piston seized. Caused by wear or damage to piston or cylinder bore (Chapter 7).
- ☐ Lever balky or stuck. Check pivot and lubricate (Chapter 7).
- ☐ Brake caliper piston seized in bore. Caused by corrosion or ingestion of dirt past deteriorated seal (Chapter 7).
- ☐ Brake pad damaged. Pad material separated from backing plate. Usually caused by faulty manufacturing process or from contact with chemicals. Renew pads (Chapter 7).
- ☐ Pads improperly installed (Chapter 7).
- ☐ Brake caliper incorrectly installed (Chapter 7).

# 14 Electrical problems

### Battery dead or weak

- [ ] Battery faulty. Caused by sulphated plates which are shorted through sedimentation. Confirm with battery condition check (Chapter 9).
- [ ] Broken battery terminal making only occasional contact.
- [ ] Battery leads making poor contact (Chapter 9).
- [ ] Load excessive. Caused by addition of high wattage lights or other electrical accessories.
- [ ] Ignition (main) switch defective. Switch either grounds (earths) internally or fails to shut off system. Renew the switch (Chapter 9).
- [ ] Regulator/rectifier defective (Chapter 9).
- [ ] Alternator stator coil open or shorted (Chapter 9).
- [ ] Charging system fault. Check for excessive current leakage (Chapter 9).
- [ ] Wiring faulty. Wiring grounded (earthed) or connections loose in ignition, charging or lighting circuits (Chapter 9).

### Battery overcharged

- [ ] Regulator/rectifier defective. Overcharging is noticed when battery gets excessively warm (Chapter 9).
- [ ] Battery faulty. Confirm with battery condition check (Chapter 9).
- [ ] Battery amperage too low, wrong type or size of battery. Install manufacturer's specified amp-hour battery to handle charging load (Chapter 9).

## Checking engine compression

● Low compression will result in exhaust smoke, heavy oil consumption, poor starting and poor performance. A compression test will provide useful information about an engine's condition and if performed regularly, can give warning of trouble before any other symptoms become apparent.

● A compression gauge will be required, along with an adapter to suit the spark plug hole thread size. Note that the screw-in type gauge/adapter set up is preferable to the rubber cone type.

● Before carrying out the test, first check the valve clearances as described in Chapter 1.

1 Run the engine until it reaches normal operating temperature, then stop it and remove the spark plug(s), taking care not to scald your hands on the hot components.

2 Install the gauge adapter and compression gauge in No. 1 cylinder spark plug hole (see illustration 1).

Screw the compression gauge adapter into the spark plug hole, then screw the gauge into the adapter

3 On kickstart-equipped motorcycles, make sure the ignition switch is OFF, then open the throttle fully and kick the engine over a couple of times until the gauge reading stabilises.

4 On motorcycles with electric start only, the procedure will differ depending on the nature of the ignition system. Flick the engine kill switch (engine stop switch) to OFF and turn the ignition switch ON; open the throttle fully and crank the engine over on the starter motor for a couple of revolutions until the gauge reading stabilises. If the starter will not operate with the kill switch OFF, turn the ignition switch OFF and refer to the next paragraph.

5 Install the plugs back in their caps and arrange the plug electrodes so that their metal bodies are earthed (grounded) against the cylinder heads; this is essential to prevent damage to the ignition system (see illustration 2). Position the plugs well away

All spark plugs must be earthed (grounded) against the cylinder head

from the plug holes otherwise there is a risk of atomised fuel escaping from the plug holes and igniting. As a safety precaution, cover the cylinder head with rag. Turn the ignition switch and kill switch ON, pull in the clutch lever, open the throttle fully and crank the engine over on the starter motor for a couple of revolutions until the gauge reading stabilises.

6 After one or two revolutions the pressure should build up to a maximum figure and then stabilise. Take a note of this reading and on multi-cylinder engines repeat the test on the remaining cylinders.

7 The correct pressures are given in Chapter 1 Specifications. If the results fall within the specified range and on multi-cylinder engines all are relatively equal, the engine is in good condition. If there is a marked difference between the readings, or if the readings are lower than specified, inspection of the top-end components will be required.

8 Low compression pressure may be due to worn cylinder bores, pistons or rings, failure of the cylinder head gasket, worn valve seals, or poor valve seating.

9 To distinguish between cylinder/piston wear and valve leakage, pour a small quantity of oil into the bore to temporarily seal the piston rings, then repeat the compression tests (see illustration 3). If the readings show

Bores can be temporarily sealed with a squirt of motor oil

a noticeable increase in pressure this confirms that the cylinder bore, piston, or rings are worn. If, however, no change is indicated, the cylinder head gasket or valves should be examined.

10 High compression pressure indicates excessive carbon build-up in the combustion chamber and on the piston crown. If this is the case the cylinder head should be removed and the deposits removed. Note that excessive carbon build-up is less likely with the used on modern fuels.

## Checking battery open-circuit voltage

 *Warning: The gases produced by the battery are explosive - never smoke or create any sparks in the vicinity of the battery. Never allow the electrolyte to contact your skin or clothing - if it does, wash it off and seek immediate medical attention.*

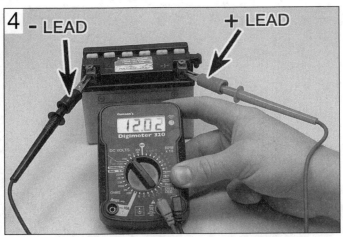

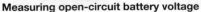

Measuring open-circuit battery voltage

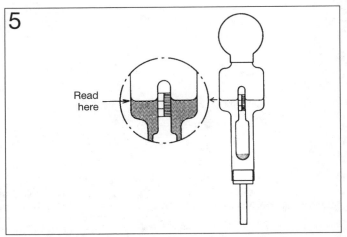

Float-type hydrometer for measuring battery specific gravity

● Before any electrical fault is investigated the battery should be checked.

● You'll need a dc voltmeter or multimeter to check battery voltage. Check that the leads are inserted in the correct terminals on the meter, red lead to positive (+ve), black lead to negative (-ve). Incorrect connections can damage the meter.

● A sound fully-charged 12 volt battery should produce between 12.3 and 12.6 volts across its terminals (12.8 volts for a maintenance-free battery). On machines with a 6 volt battery, voltage should be between 6.1 and 6.3 volts.

**1** Set a multimeter to the 0 to 20 volts dc range and connect its probes across the battery terminals. Connect the meter's positive (+ve) probe, usually red, to the battery positive (+ve) terminal, followed by the meter's negative (-ve) probe, usually black, to the battery negative terminal (-ve) **(see illustration 4)**.

**2** If battery voltage is low (below 10 volts on a 12 volt battery or below 4 volts on a six volt battery), charge the battery and test the voltage again. If the battery repeatedly goes flat, investigate the motorcycle's charging system.

## Checking battery specific gravity (SG)

⚠️ **Warning: The gases produced by the battery are explosive - never smoke or create any sparks in the vicinity of the battery. Never allow the electrolyte to contact your skin or clothing - if it does, wash it off and seek immediate medical attention.**

● The specific gravity check gives an indication of a battery's state of charge.

● A hydrometer is used for measuring specific gravity. Make sure you purchase one which has a small enough hose to insert in the aperture of a motorcycle battery.

● Specific gravity is simply a measure of the electrolyte's density compared with that of water. Water has an SG of 1.000 and fully-charged battery electrolyte is about 26% heavier, at 1.260.

● Specific gravity checks are not possible on maintenance-free batteries. Testing the open-circuit voltage is the only means of determining their state of charge.

**1** To measure SG, remove the battery from the motorcycle and remove the first cell cap. Draw

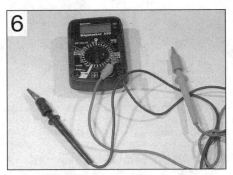

Digital multimeter can be used for all electrical tests

some electrolyte into the hydrometer and note the reading **(see illustration 5)**. Return the electrolyte to the cell and install the cap.

**2** The reading should be in the region of 1.260 to 1.280. If SG is below 1.200 the battery needs charging. Note that SG will vary with temperature; it should be measured at 20°C (68°F). Add 0.007 to the reading for every 10°C above 20°C, and subtract 0.007 from the reading for every 10°C below 20°C. Add 0.004 to the reading for every 10°F above 68°F, and subtract 0.004 from the reading for every 10°F below 68°F.

**3** When the check is complete, rinse the hydrometer thoroughly with clean water.

## Checking for continuity

● The term continuity describes the uninterrupted flow of electricity through an electrical circuit. A continuity check will determine whether an **open-circuit** situation exists.

● Continuity can be checked with an ohmmeter, multimeter, continuity tester or battery and bulb test circuit **(see illustrations 6, 7 and 8)**.

Battery-powered continuity tester

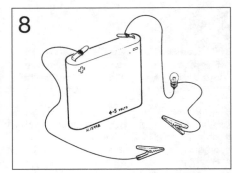

Battery and bulb test circuit

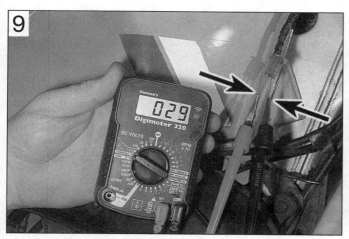

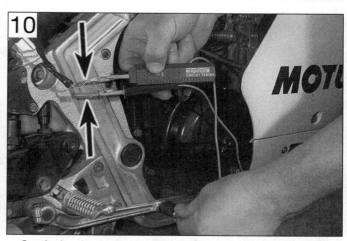

Continuity check of front brake light switch using a meter - note split pins used to access connector terminals

Continuity check of rear brake light switch using a continuity tester

● All of these instruments are self-powered by a battery, therefore the checks are made with the ignition OFF.

● As a safety precaution, always disconnect the battery negative (-ve) lead before making checks, particularly if ignition switch checks are being made.

● If using a meter, select the appropriate ohms scale and check that the meter reads infinity (∞). Touch the meter probes together and check that meter reads zero; where necessary adjust the meter so that it reads zero.

● After using a meter, always switch it OFF to conserve its battery.

## Switch checks

1 If a switch is at fault, trace its wiring up to the wiring connectors. Separate the wire connectors and inspect them for security and condition. A build-up of dirt or corrosion here will most likely be the cause of the problem - clean up and apply a water dispersant such as WD40.

2 If using a test meter, set the meter to the ohms x 10 scale and connect its probes across the wires from the switch **(see illustration 9)**. Simple ON/OFF type switches, such as brake light switches, only have two

wires whereas combination switches, like the ignition switch, have many internal links. Study the wiring diagram to ensure that you are connecting across the correct pair of wires. Continuity (low or no measurable resistance - 0 ohms) should be indicated with the switch ON and no continuity (high resistance) with it OFF.

3 Note that the polarity of the test probes doesn't matter for continuity checks, although care should be taken to follow specific test procedures if a diode or solid-state component is being checked.

4 A continuity tester or battery and bulb circuit can be used in the same way. Connect its probes as described above **(see illustration 10)**. The light should come on to indicate continuity in the ON switch position, but should extinguish in the OFF position.

## Wiring checks

● Many electrical faults are caused by damaged wiring, often due to incorrect routing or chaffing on frame components.

● Loose, wet or corroded wire connectors can also be the cause of electrical problems, especially in exposed locations.

1 A continuity check can be made on a single length of wire by disconnecting it at each end

and connecting a meter or continuity tester across both ends of the wire **(see illustration 11)**.

2 Continuity (low or no resistance - 0 ohms) should be indicated if the wire is good. If no continuity (high resistance) is shown, suspect a broken wire.

### Checking for voltage

● A voltage check can determine whether current is reaching a component.

● Voltage can be checked with a dc voltmeter, multimeter set on the dc volts scale, test light or buzzer **(see illustrations 12 and 13)**. A meter has the advantage of being able to measure actual voltage.

● When using a meter, check that its leads are inserted in the correct terminals on the meter, red to positive (+ve), black to negative (-ve). Incorrect connections can damage the meter.

● A voltmeter (or multimeter set to the dc volts scale) should always be connected in parallel (across the load). Connecting it in series will destroy the meter.

● Voltage checks are made with the ignition ON.

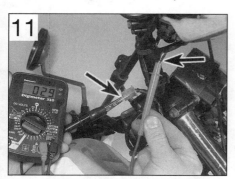

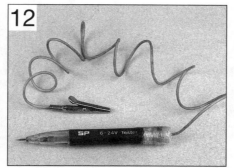

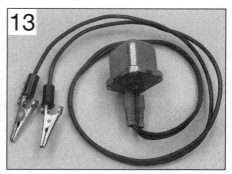

Continuity check of front brake light switch sub-harness

A simple test light can be used for voltage checks

A buzzer is useful for voltage checks

**Checking for voltage at the rear brake light power supply wire using a meter . . .**

**1** First identify the relevant wiring circuit by referring to the wiring diagram at the end of this manual. If other electrical components share the same power supply (ie are fed from the same fuse), take note whether they are working correctly - this is useful information in deciding where to start checking the circuit.

**2** If using a meter, check first that the meter leads are plugged into the correct terminals on the meter (see above). Set the meter to the dc volts function, at a range suitable for the battery voltage. Connect the meter red probe (+ve) to the power supply wire and the black probe to a good metal earth (ground) on the motorcycle's frame or directly to the battery negative (-ve) terminal **(see illustration 14)**. Battery voltage should be shown on the meter

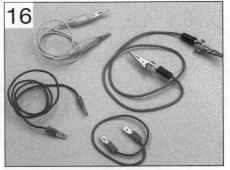

**A selection of jumper wires for making earth (ground) checks**

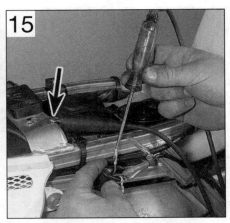

**. . . or a test light - note the earth connection to the frame (arrow)**

with the ignition switched ON.

**3** If using a test light or buzzer, connect its positive (+ve) probe to the power supply terminal and its negative (-ve) probe to a good earth (ground) on the motorcycle's frame or directly to the battery negative (-ve) terminal **(see illustration 15)**. With the ignition ON, the test light should illuminate or the buzzer sound.

**4** If no voltage is indicated, work back towards the fuse continuing to check for voltage. When you reach a point where there is voltage, you know the problem lies between that point and your last check point.

## Checking the earth (ground)

● Earth connections are made either directly to the engine or frame (such as sensors, neutral switch etc. which only have a positive feed) or by a separate wire into the earth circuit of the wiring harness. Alternatively a short earth wire is sometimes run directly from the component to the motorcycle's frame.

● Corrosion is often the cause of a poor earth connection.

● If total failure is experienced, check the security of the main earth lead from the

negative (-ve) terminal of the battery and also the main earth (ground) point on the wiring harness. If corroded, dismantle the connection and clean all surfaces back to bare metal.

**1** To check the earth on a component, use an insulated jumper wire to temporarily bypass its earth connection **(see illustration 16)**. Connect one end of the jumper wire between the earth terminal or metal body of the component and the other end to the motorcycle's frame.

**2** If the circuit works with the jumper wire installed, the original earth circuit is faulty. Check the wiring for open-circuits or poor connections. Clean up direct earth connections, removing all traces of corrosion and remake the joint. Apply petroleum jelly to the joint to prevent future corrosion.

## Tracing a short-circuit

● A short-circuit occurs where current shorts to earth (ground) bypassing the circuit components. This usually results in a blown fuse.

● A short-circuit is most likely to occur where the insulation has worn through due to wiring chafing on a component, allowing a direct path to earth (ground) on the frame.

**1** Remove any bodypanels necessary to access the circuit wiring.

**2** Check that all electrical switches in the circuit are OFF, then remove the circuit fuse and connect a test light, buzzer or voltmeter (set to the dc scale) across the fuse terminals. No voltage should be shown.

**3** Move the wiring from side to side whilst observing the test light or meter. When the test light comes on, buzzer sounds or meter shows voltage, you have found the cause of the short. It will usually shown up as damaged or burned insulation.

**4** Note that the same test can be performed on each component in the circuit, even the switch.

# A

**ABS (Anti-lock braking system)** A system, usually electronically controlled, that senses incipient wheel lockup during braking and relieves hydraulic pressure at wheel which is about to skid.
**Aftermarket** Components suitable for the motorcycle, but not produced by the motorcycle manufacturer.
**Allen key** A hexagonal wrench which fits into a recessed hexagonal hole.
**Alternating current (ac)** Current produced by an alternator. Requires converting to direct current by a rectifier for charging purposes.
**Alternator** Converts mechanical energy from the engine into electrical energy to charge the battery and power the electrical system.
**Ampere (amp)** A unit of measurement for the flow of electrical current. Current = Volts ÷ Ohms.
**Ampere-hour (Ah)** Measure of battery capacity.
**Angle-tightening** A torque expressed in degrees. Often follows a conventional tightening torque for cylinder head or main bearing fasteners **(see illustration)**.

**Angle-tightening cylinder head bolts**

**Antifreeze** A substance (usually ethylene glycol) mixed with water, and added to the cooling system, to prevent freezing of the coolant in winter. Antifreeze also contains chemicals to inhibit corrosion and the formation of rust and other deposits that would tend to clog the radiator and coolant passages and reduce cooling efficiency.
**Anti-dive** System attached to the fork lower leg (slider) to prevent fork dive when braking hard.
**Anti-seize compound** A coating that reduces the risk of seizing on fasteners that are subjected to high temperatures, such as exhaust clamp bolts and nuts.
**API** American Petroleum Institute. A quality standard for 4-stroke motor oils.
**Asbestos** A natural fibrous mineral with great heat resistance, commonly used in the composition of brake friction materials. Asbestos is a health hazard and the dust created by brake systems should never be inhaled or ingested.
**ATF** Automatic Transmission Fluid. Often used in front forks.
**ATU** Automatic Timing Unit. Mechanical device for advancing the ignition timing on early engines.
**ATV** All Terrain Vehicle. Often called a Quad.
**Axial play** Side-to-side movement.
**Axle** A shaft on which a wheel revolves. Also known as a spindle.

# B

**Backlash** The amount of movement between meshed components when one component is held still. Usually applies to gear teeth.
**Ball bearing** A bearing consisting of a hardened inner and outer race with hardened steel balls between the two races.
**Bearings** Used between two working surfaces to prevent wear of the components and a build-up of heat. Four types of bearing are commonly used on motorcycles: plain shell bearings, ball bearings, tapered roller bearings and needle roller bearings.
**Bevel gears** Used to turn the drive through 90°. Typical applications are shaft final drive and camshaft drive **(see illustration)**.

**Bevel gears are used to turn the drive through 90°**

**BHP** Brake Horsepower. The British measurement for engine power output. Power output is now usually expressed in kilowatts (kW).
**Bias-belted tyre** Similar construction to radial tyre, but with outer belt running at an angle to the wheel rim.
**Big-end bearing** The bearing in the end of the connecting rod that's attached to the crankshaft.
**Bleeding** The process of removing air from an hydraulic system via a bleed nipple or bleed screw.
**Bottom-end** A description of an engine's crankcase components and all components contained there-in.
**BTDC** Before Top Dead Centre in terms of piston position. Ignition timing is often expressed in terms of degrees or millimetres BTDC.
**Bush** A cylindrical metal or rubber component used between two moving parts.
**Burr** Rough edge left on a component after machining or as a result of excessive wear.

# C

**Cam chain** The chain which takes drive from the crankshaft to the camshaft(s).
**Canister** The main component in an evaporative emission control system (California market only); contains activated charcoal granules to trap vapours from the fuel system rather than allowing them to vent to the atmosphere.
**Castellated** Resembling the parapets along the top of a castle wall. For example, a castellated wheel axle or spindle nut.
**Catalytic converter** A device in the exhaust system of some machines which converts certain pollutants in the exhaust gases into less harmful substances.
**Charging system** Description of the components which charge the battery, ie the alternator, rectifer and regulator.
**Circlip** A ring-shaped clip used to prevent endwise movement of cylindrical parts and shafts. An internal circlip is installed in a groove in a housing; an external circlip fits into a groove on the outside of a cylindrical piece such as a shaft. Also known as a snap-ring.
**Clearance** The amount of space between two parts. For example, between a piston and a cylinder, between a bearing and a journal, etc.
**Coil spring** A spiral of elastic steel found in various sizes throughout a vehicle, for example as a springing medium in the suspension and in the valve train.
**Compression** Reduction in volume, and increase in pressure and temperature, of a gas, caused by squeezing it into a smaller space.
**Compression damping** Controls the speed the suspension compresses when hitting a bump.
**Compression ratio** The relationship between cylinder volume when the piston is at top dead centre and cylinder volume when the piston is at bottom dead centre.
**Continuity** The uninterrupted path in the flow of electricity. Little or no measurable resistance.
**Continuity tester** Self-powered bleeper or test light which indicates continuity.
**Cp** Candlepower. Bulb rating commonly found on US motorcycles.
**Crossply tyre** Tyre plies arranged in a criss-cross pattern. Usually four or six plies used, hence 4PR or 6PR in tyre size codes.
**Cush drive** Rubber damper segments fitted between the rear wheel and final drive sprocket to absorb transmission shocks **(see illustration)**.

**Cush drive rubbers dampen out transmission shocks**

# D

**Degree disc** Calibrated disc for measuring piston position. Expressed in degrees.
**Dial gauge** Clock-type gauge with adapters for measuring runout and piston position. Expressed in mm or inches.
**Diaphragm** The rubber membrane in a master cylinder or carburettor which seals the upper chamber.
**Diaphragm spring** A single sprung plate often used in clutches.
**Direct current (dc)** Current produced by a dc generator.

**Decarbonisation** The process of removing carbon deposits - typically from the combustion chamber, valves and exhaust port/system.

**Detonation** Destructive and damaging explosion of fuel/air mixture in combustion chamber instead of controlled burning.

**Diode** An electrical valve which only allows current to flow in one direction. Commonly used in rectifiers and starter interlock systems.

**Disc valve (or rotary valve)** A induction system used on some two-stroke engines.

**Double-overhead camshaft (DOHC)** An engine that uses two overhead camshafts, one for the intake valves and one for the exhaust valves.

**Drivebelt** A toothed belt used to transmit drive to the rear wheel on some motorcycles. A drivebelt has also been used to drive the camshafts. Drivebelts are usually made of Kevlar.

**Driveshaft** Any shaft used to transmit motion. Commonly used when referring to the final driveshaft on shaft drive motorcycles.

# E

**Earth return** The return path of an electrical circuit, utilising the motorcycle's frame.

**ECU (Electronic Control Unit)** A computer which controls (for instance) an ignition system, or an anti-lock braking system.

**EGO** Exhaust Gas Oxygen sensor. Sometimes called a Lambda sensor.

**Electrolyte** The fluid in a lead-acid battery.

**EMS (Engine Management System)** A computer controlled system which manages the fuel injection and the ignition systems in an integrated fashion.

**Endfloat** The amount of lengthways movement between two parts. As applied to a crankshaft, the distance that the crankshaft can move side-to-side in the crankcase.

**Endless chain** A chain having no joining link. Common use for cam chains and final drive chains.

**EP (Extreme Pressure)** Oil type used in locations where high loads are applied, such as between gear teeth.

**Evaporative emission control system** Describes a charcoal filled canister which stores fuel vapours from the tank rather than allowing them to vent to the atmosphere. Usually only fitted to California models and referred to as an EVAP system.

**Expansion chamber** Section of two-stroke engine exhaust system so designed to improve engine efficiency and boost power.

# F

**Feeler blade or gauge** A thin strip or blade of hardened steel, ground to an exact thickness, used to check or measure clearances between parts.

**Final drive** Description of the drive from the transmission to the rear wheel. Usually by chain or shaft, but sometimes by belt.

**Firing order** The order in which the engine cylinders fire, or deliver their power strokes, beginning with the number one cylinder.

**Flooding** Term used to describe a high fuel level in the carburettor float chambers, leading to fuel overflow. Also refers to excess fuel in the combustion chamber due to incorrect starting technique.

**Free length** The no-load state of a component when measured. Clutch, valve and fork spring lengths are measured at rest, without any preload.

**Freeplay** The amount of travel before any action takes place. The looseness in a linkage, or an assembly of parts, between the initial application of force and actual movement. For example, the distance the rear brake pedal moves before the rear brake is actuated.

**Fuel injection** The fuel/air mixture is metered electronically and directed into the engine intake ports (indirect injection) or into the cylinders (direct injection). Sensors supply information on engine speed and conditions.

**Fuel/air mixture** The charge of fuel and air going into the engine. See **Stoichiometric ratio**.

**Fuse** An electrical device which protects a circuit against accidental overload. The typical fuse contains a soft piece of metal which is calibrated to melt at a predetermined current flow (expressed as amps) and break the circuit.

# G

**Gap** The distance the spark must travel in jumping from the centre electrode to the side electrode in a spark plug. Also refers to the distance between the ignition rotor and the pickup coil in an electronic ignition system.

**Gasket** Any thin, soft material - usually cork, cardboard, asbestos or soft metal - installed between two metal surfaces to ensure a good seal. For instance, the cylinder head gasket seals the joint between the block and the cylinder head.

**Gauge** An instrument panel display used to monitor engine conditions. A gauge with a movable pointer on a dial or a fixed scale is an analogue gauge. A gauge with a numerical readout is called a digital gauge.

**Gear ratios** The drive ratio of a pair of gears in a gearbox, calculated on their number of teeth.

**Glaze-busting** see **Honing**

**Grinding** Process for renovating the valve face and valve seat contact area in the cylinder head.

**Gudgeon pin** The shaft which connects the connecting rod small-end with the piston. Often called a piston pin or wrist pin.

# H

**Helical gears** Gear teeth are slightly curved and produce less gear noise that straight-cut gears. Often used for primary drives.

**Installing a Helicoil thread insert in a cylinder head**

**Helicoil** A thread insert repair system. Commonly used as a repair for stripped spark plug threads **(see illustration)**.

**Honing** A process used to break down the glaze on a cylinder bore (also called glaze-busting). Can also be carried out to roughen a rebored cylinder to aid ring bedding-in.

**HT (High Tension)** Description of the electrical circuit from the secondary winding of the ignition coil to the spark plug.

**Hydraulic** A liquid filled system used to transmit pressure from one component to another. Common uses on motorcycles are brakes and clutches.

**Hydrometer** An instrument for measuring the specific gravity of a lead-acid battery.

**Hygroscopic** Water absorbing. In motorcycle applications, braking efficiency will be reduced if DOT 3 or 4 hydraulic fluid absorbs water from the air - care must be taken to keep new brake fluid in tightly sealed containers.

# I

**lbf ft** Pounds-force feet. An imperial unit of torque. Sometimes written as ft-lbs.

**lbf in** Pound-force inch. An imperial unit of torque, applied to components where a very low torque is required. Sometimes written as in-lbs.

**IC** Abbreviation for Integrated Circuit.

**Ignition advance** Means of increasing the timing of the spark at higher engine speeds. Done by mechanical means (ATU) on early engines or electronically by the ignition control unit on later engines.

**Ignition timing** The moment at which the spark plug fires, expressed in the number of crankshaft degrees before the piston reaches the top of its stroke, or in the number of millimetres before the piston reaches the top of its stroke.

**Infinity (∞)** Description of an open-circuit electrical state, where no continuity exists.

**Inverted forks (upside down forks)** The sliders or lower legs are held in the yokes and the fork tubes or stanchions are connected to the wheel axle (spindle). Less unsprung weight and stiffer construction than conventional forks.

# J

**JASO** Quality standard for 2-stroke oils.

**Joule** The unit of electrical energy.

**Journal** The bearing surface of a shaft.

# K

**Kickstart** Mechanical means of turning the engine over for starting purposes. Only usually fitted to mopeds, small capacity motorcycles and off-road motorcycles.

**Kill switch** Handebar-mounted switch for emergency ignition cut-out. Cuts the ignition circuit on all models, and additionally prevent starter motor operation on others.

**km** Symbol for kilometre.

**kmh** Abbreviation for kilometres per hour.

# L

**Lambda (λ) sensor** A sensor fitted in the exhaust system to measure the exhaust gas oxygen content (excess air factor).

**Lapping** see **Grinding**.
**LCD** Abbreviation for Liquid Crystal Display.
**LED** Abbreviation for Light Emitting Diode.
**Liner** A steel cylinder liner inserted in a aluminium alloy cylinder block.
**Locknut** A nut used to lock an adjustment nut, or other threaded component, in place.
**Lockstops** The lugs on the lower triple clamp (yoke) which abut those on the frame, preventing handlebar-to-fuel tank contact.
**Lockwasher** A form of washer designed to prevent an attaching nut from working loose.
**LT Low Tension** Description of the electrical circuit from the power supply to the primary winding of the ignition coil.

## M

**Main bearings** The bearings between the crankshaft and crankcase.
**Maintenance-free (MF) battery** A sealed battery which cannot be topped up.
**Manometer** Mercury-filled calibrated tubes used to measure intake tract vacuum. Used to synchronise carburettors on multi-cylinder engines.
**Micrometer** A precision measuring instrument that measures component outside diameters **(see illustration)**.

**Tappet shims are measured with a micrometer**

**MON (Motor Octane Number)** A measure of a fuel's resistance to knock.
**Monograde oil** An oil with a single viscosity, eg SAE80W.
**Monoshock** A single suspension unit linking the swingarm or suspension linkage to the frame.
**mph** Abbreviation for miles per hour.
**Multigrade oil** Having a wide viscosity range (eg 10W40). The W stands for Winter, thus the viscosity ranges from SAE10 when cold to SAE40 when hot.
**Multimeter** An electrical test instrument with the capability to measure voltage, current and resistance. Some meters also incorporate a continuity tester and buzzer.

## N

**Needle roller bearing** Inner race of caged needle rollers and hardened outer race. Examples of uncaged needle rollers can be found on some engines. Commonly used in rear suspension applications and in two-stroke engines.
**Nm** Newton metres.
**NOx** Oxides of Nitrogen. A common toxic pollutant emitted by petrol engines at higher temperatures.

## O

**Octane** The measure of a fuel's resistance to knock.
**OE (Original Equipment)** Relates to components fitted to a motorcycle as standard or replacement parts supplied by the motorcycle manufacturer.
**Ohm** The unit of electrical resistance. Ohms = Volts ÷ Current.
**Ohmmeter** An instrument for measuring electrical resistance.
**Oil cooler** System for diverting engine oil outside of the engine to a radiator for cooling purposes.
**Oil injection** A system of two-stroke engine lubrication where oil is pump-fed to the engine in accordance with throttle position.
**Open-circuit** An electrical condition where there is a break in the flow of electricity - no continuity (high resistance).
**O-ring** A type of sealing ring made of a special rubber-like material; in use, the O-ring is compressed into a groove to provide the sealing action.
**Oversize (OS)** Term used for piston and ring size options fitted to a rebored cylinder.
**Overhead cam (sohc) engine** An engine with single camshaft located on top of the cylinder head.
**Overhead valve (ohv) engine** An engine with the valves located in the cylinder head, but with the camshaft located in the engine block or crankcase.
**Oxygen sensor** A device installed in the exhaust system which senses the oxygen content in the exhaust and converts this information into an electric current. Also called a Lambda sensor.

## P

**Plastigauge** A thin strip of plastic thread, available in different sizes, used for measuring clearances. For example, a strip of Plastigauge is laid across a bearing journal. The parts are assembled and dismantled; the width of the crushed strip indicates the clearance between journal and bearing.
**Polarity** Either negative or positive earth (ground), determined by which battery lead is connected to the frame (earth return). Modern motorcycles are usually negative earth.
**Pre-ignition** A situation where the fuel/air mixture ignites before the spark plug fires. Often due to a hot spot in the combustion chamber caused by carbon build-up. Engine has a tendency to 'run-on'.
**Pre-load (suspension)** The amount a spring is compressed when in the unloaded state. Preload can be applied by gas, spacer or mechanical adjuster.
**Premix** The method of engine lubrication on older two-stroke engines. Engine oil is mixed with the petrol in the fuel tank in a specific ratio. The fuel/oil mix is sometimes referred to as "petroil".
**Primary drive** Description of the drive from the crankshaft to the clutch. Usually by gear or chain.
**PS** Pfedestärke - a German interpretation of BHP.
**PSI** Pounds-force per square inch. Imperial measurement of tyre pressure and cylinder pressure measurement.
**PTFE** Polytetrafluoroethylene. A low friction substance.

**Pulse secondary air injection system** A process of promoting the burning of excess fuel present in the exhaust gases by routing fresh air into the exhaust ports.

## Q

**Quartz halogen bulb** Tungsten filament surrounded by a halogen gas. Typically used for the headlight **(see illustration)**.

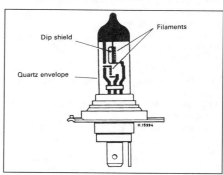

**Quartz halogen headlight bulb construction**

## R

**Rack-and-pinion** A pinion gear on the end of a shaft that mates with a rack (think of a geared wheel opened up and laid flat). Sometimes used in clutch operating systems.
**Radial play** Up and down movement about a shaft.
**Radial ply tyres** Tyre plies run across the tyre (from bead to bead) and around the circumference of the tyre. Less resistant to tread distortion than other tyre types.
**Radiator** A liquid-to-air heat transfer device designed to reduce the temperature of the coolant in a liquid cooled engine.
**Rake** A feature of steering geometry - the angle of the steering head in relation to the vertical **(see illustration)**.

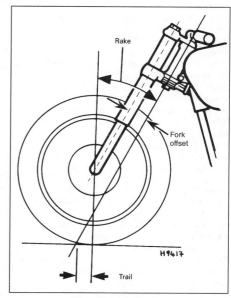

**Steering geometry**

**Rebore** Providing a new working surface to the cylinder bore by boring out the old surface. Necessitates the use of oversize piston and rings.

**Rebound damping** A means of controlling the oscillation of a suspension unit spring after it has been compressed. Resists the spring's natural tendency to bounce back after being compressed.

**Rectifier** Device for converting the ac output of an alternator into dc for battery charging.

**Reed valve** An induction system commonly used on two-stroke engines.

**Regulator** Device for maintaining the charging voltage from the generator or alternator within a specified range.

**Relay** A electrical device used to switch heavy current on and off by using a low current auxiliary circuit.

**Resistance** Measured in ohms. An electrical component's ability to pass electrical current.

**RON (Research Octane Number)** A measure of a fuel's resistance to knock.

**rpm** revolutions per minute.

**Runout** The amount of wobble (in-and-out movement) of a wheel or shaft as it's rotated. The amount a shaft rotates 'out-of-true'. The out-of-round condition of a rotating part.

# S

**SAE (Society of Automotive Engineers)** A standard for the viscosity of a fluid.

**Sealant** A liquid or paste used to prevent leakage at a joint. Sometimes used in conjunction with a gasket.

**Service limit** Term for the point where a component is no longer useable and must be renewed.

**Shaft drive** A method of transmitting drive from the transmission to the rear wheel.

**Shell bearings** Plain bearings consisting of two shell halves. Most often used as big-end and main bearings in a four-stroke engine. Often called bearing inserts.

**Shim** Thin spacer, commonly used to adjust the clearance or relative positions between two parts. For example, shims inserted into or under tappets or followers to control valve clearances. Clearance is adjusted by changing the thickness of the shim.

**Short-circuit** An electrical condition where current shorts to earth (ground) bypassing the circuit components.

**Skimming** Process to correct warpage or repair a damaged surface, eg on brake discs or drums.

**Slide-hammer** A special puller that screws into or hooks onto a component such as a shaft or bearing; a heavy sliding handle on the shaft bottoms against the end of the shaft to knock the component free.

**Small-end bearing** The bearing in the upper end of the connecting rod at its joint with the gudgeon pin.

**Spalling** Damage to camshaft lobes or bearing journals shown as pitting of the working surface.

**Specific gravity (SG)** The state of charge of the electrolyte in a lead-acid battery. A measure of the electrolyte's density compared with water.

**Straight-cut gears** Common type gear used on gearbox shafts and for oil pump and water pump drives.

**Stanchion** The inner sliding part of the front forks, held by the yokes. Often called a fork tube.

**Stoichiometric ratio** The optimum chemical air/fuel ratio for a petrol engine, said to be 14.7 parts of air to 1 part of fuel.

**Sulphuric acid** The liquid (electrolyte) used in a lead-acid battery. Poisonous and extremely corrosive.

**Surface grinding (lapping)** Process to correct a warped gasket face, commonly used on cylinder heads.

# T

**Tapered-roller bearing** Tapered inner race of caged needle rollers and separate tapered outer race. Examples of taper roller bearings can be found on steering heads.

**Tappet** A cylindrical component which transmits motion from the cam to the valve stem, either directly or via a pushrod and rocker arm. Also called a cam follower.

**TCS** Traction Control System. An electronically-controlled system which senses wheel spin and reduces engine speed accordingly.

**TDC** Top Dead Centre denotes that the piston is at its highest point in the cylinder.

**Thread-locking compound** Solution applied to fastener threads to prevent slackening. Select type to suit application.

**Thrust washer** A washer positioned between two moving components on a shaft. For example, between gear pinions on gearshaft.

**Timing chain** See **Cam Chain.**

**Timing light** Stroboscopic lamp for carrying out ignition timing checks with the engine running.

**Top-end** A description of an engine's cylinder block, head and valve gear components.

**Torque** Turning or twisting force about a shaft.

**Torque setting** A prescribed tightness specified by the motorcycle manufacturer to ensure that the bolt or nut is secured correctly. Undertightening can result in the bolt or nut coming loose or a surface not being sealed. Overtightening can result in stripped threads, distortion or damage to the component being retained.

**Torx key** A six-point wrench.

**Tracer** A stripe of a second colour applied to a wire insulator to distinguish that wire from another one with the same colour insulator. For example, Br/W is often used to denote a brown insulator with a white tracer.

**Trail** A feature of steering geometry. Distance from the steering head axis to the tyre's central contact point.

**Triple clamps** The cast components which extend from the steering head and support the fork stanchions or tubes. Often called fork yokes.

**Turbocharger** A centrifugal device, driven by exhaust gases, that pressurises the intake air. Normally used to increase the power output from a given engine displacement.

**TWI** Abbreviation for Tyre Wear Indicator. Indicates the location of the tread depth indicator bars on tyres.

# U

**Universal joint or U-joint (UJ)** A double-pivoted connection for transmitting power from a driving to a driven shaft through an angle. Typically found in shaft drive assemblies.

**Unsprung weight** Anything not supported by the bike's suspension (ie the wheel, tyres, brakes, final drive and bottom (moving) part of the suspension).

# V

**Vacuum gauges** Clock-type gauges for measuring intake tract vacuum. Used for carburettor synchronisation on multi-cylinder engines.

**Valve** A device through which the flow of liquid, gas or vacuum may be stopped, started or regulated by a moveable part that opens, shuts or partially obstructs one or more ports or passageways. The intake and exhaust valves in the cylinder head are of the poppet type.

**Valve clearance** The clearance between the valve tip (the end of the valve stem) and the rocker arm or tappet/follower. The valve clearance is measured when the valve is closed. The correct clearance is important - if too small the valve won't close fully and will burn out, whereas if too large noisy operation will result.

**Valve lift** The amount a valve is lifted off its seat by the camshaft lobe.

**Valve timing** The exact setting for the opening and closing of the valves in relation to piston position.

**Vernier caliper** A precision measuring instrument that measures inside and outside dimensions. Not quite as accurate as a micrometer, but more convenient.

**VIN** Vehicle Identification Number. Term for the bike's engine and frame numbers.

**Viscosity** The thickness of a liquid or its resistance to flow.

**Volt** A unit for expressing electrical "pressure" in a circuit. Volts = current x ohms.

# W

**Water pump** A mechanically-driven device for moving coolant around the engine.

**Watt** A unit for expressing electrical power. Watts = volts x current.

**Wear limit** see **Service limit**

**Wet liner** A liquid-cooled engine design where the pistons run in liners which are directly surrounded by coolant (**see illustration**).

**Wet liner arrangement**

**Wheelbase** Distance from the centre of the front wheel to the centre of the rear wheel.

**Wiring harness or loom** Describes the electrical wires running the length of the motorcycle and enclosed in tape or plastic sheathing. Wiring coming off the main harness is usually referred to as a sub harness.

**Woodruff key** A key of semi-circular or square section used to locate a gear to a shaft. Often used to locate the alternator rotor on the crankshaft.

**Wrist pin** Another name for gudgeon or piston pin.

**Notes**

# Haynes Motorcycle Manuals – The Complete List

| Title | Book No |
|---|---|
| **BMW** | |
| **BMW 2-valve Twins (70 - 96)** | 0249 |
| **BMW K100 & 75 2-valve Models (83 - 96)** | 1373 |
| **BMW R850 & R1100 4-valve Twins (93 - 97)** | 3466 |
| **BSA** | |
| BSA Bantam (48 - 71) | 0117 |
| BSA Unit Singles (58 - 72) | 0127 |
| BSA Pre-unit Singles (54 - 61) | 0326 |
| BSA A7 & A10 Twins (47 - 62) | 0121 |
| BSA A50 & A65 Twins (62 - 73) | 0155 |
| **DUCATI** | |
| **Ducati 600, 750 & 900 2-valve V-Twins (91 - 96)** | 3290 |
| **Ducati 748, 916 & 996 4-valve V-Twins (94 - 01)** | 3756 |
| **HARLEY-DAVIDSON** | |
| **Harley-Davidson Sportsters (70 - 01)** | 0702 |
| **Harley-Davidson Big Twins (70 - 99)** | 0703 |
| **HONDA** | |
| Honda NB, ND, NP & NS50 Melody (81 - 85) | ◊ 0622 |
| Honda NE/NB50 Vision & SA50 Vision Met-in (85 - 95) | ◊ 1278 |
| Honda MB, MBX, MT & MTX50 (80 - 93) | 0731 |
| Honda C50, C70 & C90 (67 - 99) | 0324 |
| Honda XR80R & XR100R (85 - 96) | 2218 |
| Honda XL/XR 80, 100, 125, 185 & 200 2-valve Models (78 - 87) | 0566 |
| Honda H100 & H100S Singles (80 - 92) | ◊ 0734 |
| Honda CB/CD125T & CM125C Twins (77 - 88) | ◊ 0571 |
| Honda CG125 (76 - 00) | ◊ 0433 |
| Honda NS125 (86 - 93) | ◊ 3056 |
| Honda MBX/MTX125 & MTX200 (83 - 93) | ◊ 1132 |
| Honda CD/CM185 200T & CM250C 2-valve Twins (77 - 85) | 0572 |
| Honda XL/XR 250 & 500 (78 - 84) | 0567 |
| Honda XR250L, XR250R & XR400R (86 - 01) | 2219 |
| Honda CB250 & CB400N Super Dreams (78 - 84) | ◊ 0540 |
| Honda CR Motocross Bikes (86 - 01) | 2222 |
| Honda Elsinore 250 (73 - 75) | 0217 |
| **Honda CBR400RR Fours (88 - 99)** | 3552 |
| **Honda VFR400 (NC30) & RVF400 (NC35) V-Fours (89 - 98)** | 3496 |
| **Honda CB500 (93 - 01)** | 3753 |
| Honda CB400 & CB550 Fours (73 - 77) | 0262 |
| Honda CX/GL500 & 650 V-Twins (78 - 86) | 0442 |
| Honda CBX550 Four (82 - 86) | ◊ 0940 |
| Honda XL600R & XR600R (83 - 00) | 2183 |
| **Honda XL600/650V Transalp & XRV750 Africa Twin (87 - 02)** | 3919 |
| **Honda CBR600F1 & 1000F Fours (87 - 96)** | 1730 |
| **Honda CBR600F2 & F3 Fours (91 - 98)** | 2070 |
| **Honda CBR600F4 (99 - 02)** | 3911 |
| **Honda CB600F Hornet (98 - 02)** | 3915 |
| Honda CB650 sohc Fours (78 - 84) | 0665 |
| **Honda NTV600/650/Deauville V-Twins (88 - 01)** | 3243 |
| Honda Shadow VT600 & 750 (USA) (88 - 99) | 2312 |
| Honda CB750 sohc Four (69 - 79) | 0131 |
| Honda V45/65 Sabre & Magna (82 - 88) | 0820 |
| **Honda VFR750 & 700 V-Fours (86 - 97)** | 2101 |
| **Honda VFR800 V-Fours (97 - 99)** | 3703 |
| **Honda VTR1000 (FireStorm, Super Hawk) & XL1000V (Varadero) (97 - 00)** | 3744 |
| Honda CB750 & CB900 dohc Fours (78 - 84) | 0535 |
| **Honda CBR900RR FireBlade (92 - 99)** | 2161 |
| **Honda CBR1100XX Super Blackbird (97 - 02)** | 3901 |
| **Honda ST1100 Pan European V-Fours (90 - 01)** | 3384 |

| Title | Book No |
|---|---|
| Honda Shadow VT1100 (USA) (85 - 98) | 2313 |
| Honda GL1000 Gold Wing (75 - 79) | 0309 |
| Honda GL1100 Gold Wing (79 - 81) | 0669 |
| Honda Gold Wing 1200 (USA) (84 - 87) | 2199 |
| Honda Gold Wing 1500 (USA) (88 - 00) | 2225 |
| **KAWASAKI** | |
| Kawasaki AE/AR 50 & 80 (81 - 95) | 1007 |
| Kawasaki KC, KE & KH100 (75 - 99) | 1371 |
| Kawasaki KMX125 & 200 (86 - 96) | ◊ 3046 |
| Kawasaki 250, 350 & 400 Triples (72 - 79) | 0134 |
| Kawasaki 400 & 440 Twins (74 - 81) | 0281 |
| Kawasaki 400, 500 & 550 Fours (79 - 91) | 0910 |
| Kawasaki EN450 & 500 Twins (Ltd/Vulcan) (85 - 93) | 2053 |
| **Kawasaki EX & ER500 (GPZ500S & ER-5) Twins (87 - 99)** | 2052 |
| **Kawasaki ZX600 (Ninja ZX-6, ZZ-R600) Fours (90 - 00)** | 2146 |
| **Kawasaki ZX-6R Ninja Fours (95 - 98)** | 3541 |
| **Kawasaki ZX600 (GPZ600R, GPX600R, Ninja 600R & RX) & ZX750 (GPX750R, Ninja 750R) Fours (85 - 97)** | 1780 |
| Kawasaki 650 Four (76 - 78) | 0373 |
| Kawasaki 750 Air-cooled Fours (80 - 91) | 0574 |
| **Kawasaki ZR550 & 750 Zephyr Fours (90 - 97)** | 3382 |
| **Kawasaki ZX750 (Ninja ZX-7 & ZXR750) Fours (89 - 96)** | 2054 |
| **Kawasaki Ninja ZX-7R & ZX-9R (ZX750P, ZX900B/C/D/E) (94 - 00)** | 3721 |
| Kawasaki 900 & 1000 Fours (73 - 77) | 0222 |
| **Kawasaki ZX900, 1000 & 1100 Liquid-cooled Fours (83 - 97)** | 1681 |
| **MOTO GUZZI** | |
| Moto Guzzi 750, 850 & 1000 V-Twins (74 - 78) | 0339 |
| **MZ** | |
| MZ ETZ Models (81 - 95) | ◊ 1680 |
| **NORTON** | |
| Norton 500, 600, 650 & 750 Twins (57 - 70) | 0187 |
| Norton Commando (68 - 77) | 0125 |
| **PIAGGIO** | |
| Piaggio (Vespa) Scooters (91 - 98) | 3492 |
| **SUZUKI** | |
| Suzuki GT, ZR & TS50 (77 - 90) | ◊ 0799 |
| Suzuki TS50X (84 - 00) | ◊ 1599 |
| Suzuki 100, 125, 185 & 250 Air-cooled Trail bikes (79 - 89) | 0797 |
| Suzuki GP100 & 125 Singles (78 - 93) | ◊ 0576 |
| Suzuki GS, GN, GZ & DR125 Singles (82 - 99) | ◊ 0888 |
| Suzuki GT250X7, GT200X5 & SB200 Twins (78 - 83) | ◊ 0469 |
| Suzuki GS/GSX250, 400 & 450 Twins (79 - 85) | 0736 |
| **Suzuki GS500E Twin (89 - 97)** | 3238 |
| Suzuki GS550 (77 - 82) & GS750 Fours (76 - 79) | 0363 |
| Suzuki GS/GSX550 4-valve Fours (83 - 88) | 1133 |
| **Suzuki GSX-R600 & 750 (96 - 99)** | 3553 |
| **Suzuki GSF600 & 1200 Bandit Fours (95 - 01)** | 3367 |
| Suzuki GS850 Fours (78 - 88) | 0536 |
| Suzuki GS1000 Four (77 - 79) | 0484 |
| **Suzuki GSX-R750, GSX-R1100 (85 - 92), GSX600F, GSX750F, GSX1100F (Katana) Fours (88 - 96)** | 2055 |
| Suzuki GS/GSX1000, 1100 & 1150 4-valve Fours (79 - 88) | 0737 |
| **TRIUMPH** | |
| Triumph 350 & 500 Unit Twins (58 - 73) | 0137 |
| Triumph Pre-Unit Twins (47 - 62) | 0251 |
| Triumph 650 & 750 2-valve Unit Twins (63 - 83) | 0122 |
| Triumph Trident & BSA Rocket 3 (69 - 75) | 0136 |
| **Triumph Fuel Injected Triples (97 - 00)** | 3755 |
| Triumph Triples & Fours (carburettor engines) (91 - 99) | 2162 |

| Title | Book No |
|---|---|
| **VESPA** | |
| Vespa P/PX125, 150 & 200 Scooters (78 - 95) | 0707 |
| Vespa Scooters (59 - 78) | 0126 |
| **YAMAHA** | |
| Yamaha DT50 & 80 Trail Bikes (78 - 95) | ◊ 0800 |
| Yamaha T50 & 80 Townmate (83 - 95) | ◊ 1247 |
| Yamaha YB100 Singles (73 - 91) | ◊ 0474 |
| Yamaha RS/RXS100 & 125 Singles (74 - 95) | 0331 |
| Yamaha RD & DT125LC (82 - 87) | ◊ 0887 |
| Yamaha TZR125 (87 - 93) & DT125R (88 - 95) | ◊ 1655 |
| Yamaha TY50, 80, 125 & 175 (74 - 84) | ◊ 0464 |
| Yamaha XT & SR125 (82 - 96) | 1021 |
| Yamaha Trail Bikes (81 - 00) | 2350 |
| Yamaha 250 & 350 Twins (70 - 79) | 0040 |
| Yamaha XS250, 360 & 400 sohc Twins (75 - 84) | 0378 |
| Yamaha RD250 & 350LC Twins (80 - 82) | 0803 |
| Yamaha RD350 YPVS Twins (83 - 95) | 1158 |
| Yamaha RD400 Twin (75 - 79) | 0333 |
| Yamaha XT, TT & SR500 Singles (75 - 83) | 0342 |
| Yamaha XZ550 Vision V-Twins (82 - 85) | 0821 |
| Yamaha FJ, FZ, XJ & YX600 Radian (84 - 92) | 2100 |
| Yamaha XJ600S (Diversion, Seca II) & XJ600N Fours (92 - 99) | 2145 |
| **Yamaha YZF600R Thundercat & FZS600 Fazer (96 - 00)** | 3702 |
| **Yamaha YZF-R6 (98 - 02)** | 3900 |
| Yamaha 650 Twins (70 - 83) | 0341 |
| Yamaha XJ650 & 750 Fours (80 - 84) | 0738 |
| Yamaha XS750 & 850 Triples (76 - 85) | 0340 |
| **Yamaha TDM850, TRX850 & XTZ750 (89 - 99)** | 3540 |
| **Yamaha YZF750R & YZF1000R Thunderace (93 - 00)** | 3720 |
| **Yamaha FZR600, 750 & 1000 Fours (87 - 96)** | 2056 |
| **Yamaha XV V-Twins (81 - 96)** | 0802 |
| **Yamaha XJ900F Fours (83 - 94)** | 3239 |
| **Yamaha XJ900S Diversion (94 - 01)** | 3739 |
| **Yamaha YZF-R1 (98 - 01)** | 3754 |
| **Yamaha FJ1100 & 1200 Fours (84 - 96)** | 2057 |
| **ATVs** | |
| Honda ATC70, 90, 110, 185 & 200 (71 - 85) | 0565 |
| Honda TRX300 Shaft Drive ATVs (88 - 00) | 2125 |
| Honda TRX300EX & TRX400EX ATVs (93 - 99) | 2318 |
| Kawasaki Bayou 220/300 & Prairie 300 ATVs (86 - 01) | 2351 |
| Polaris ATVs (85 to 97) | 2302 |
| Yamaha YT, YFM, YTM & YTZ ATVs (80 - 85) | 1154 |
| Yamaha YFS200 Blaster ATV (88 - 98) | 2317 |
| Yamaha YFB250 Timberwolf ATV (92 - 96) | 2217 |
| Yamaha YFM350 (ER and Big Bear) ATVs (87 - 99) | 2126 |
| Yamaha Warrior and Banshee ATVs (87 - 99) | 2314 |
| ATV Basics | 10450 |
| **MOTORCYCLE TECHBOOKS** | |
| Motorcycle Basics TechBook (2nd Edition) | 3515 |
| Motorcycle Electrical TechBook (3rd Edition) | 3471 |
| Motorcycle Fuel Systems TechBook | 3514 |
| Motorcycle Workshop Practice TechBook (2nd Edition) | 3470 |

◊ = not available in the USA    **Bold type** = Superbike

The manuals on this page are available through good motorcycle dealers and accessory shops.
In case of difficulty, contact: **Haynes Publishing**
(UK) **+44 1963 442030**    (USA) **+1 805 4986703**
(FR) **+33 1 47 78 50 50**    (SV) **+46 18 124016**
(Australia/New Zealand) **+61 3 9763 8100**

# Preserving Our Motoring Heritage

<
*The Model J Duesenberg Derham Tourster. Only eight of these magnificent cars were ever built – this is the only example to be found outside the United States of America*

Almost every car you've ever loved, loathed or desired is gathered under one roof at the Haynes Motor Museum. Over 300 immaculately presented cars and motorbikes represent every aspect of our motoring heritage, from elegant reminders of bygone days, such as the superb Model J Duesenberg to curiosities like the bug-eyed BMW Isetta. There are also many old friends and flames. Perhaps you remember the 1959 Ford Popular that you did your courting in? The magnificent 'Red Collection' is a spectacle of classic sports cars including AC, Alfa Romeo, Austin Healey, Ferrari, Lamborghini, Maserati, MG, Riley, Porsche and Triumph.

## A Perfect Day Out

Each and every vehicle at the Haynes Motor Museum has played its part in the history and culture of Motoring. Today, they make a wonderful spectacle and a great day out for all the family. Bring the kids, bring Mum and Dad, but above all bring your camera to capture those golden memories for ever. You will also find an impressive array of motoring memorabilia, a comfortable 70 seat video cinema and one of the most extensive transport book shops in Britain. The Pit Stop Cafe serves everything from a cup of tea to wholesome, home-made meals or, if you prefer, you can enjoy the large picnic area nestled in the beautiful rural surroundings of Somerset.

>
*John Haynes O.B.E., Founder and Chairman of the museum at the wheel of a Haynes Light 12.*

<
*The 1936 490cc sohc-engined International Norton – well known for its racing success*

The Museum is situated on the A359 Yeovil to Frome road at Sparkford, just off the A303 in Somerset. It is about 40 miles south of Bristol, and 25 minutes drive from the M5 intersection at Taunton.

Open 9.30am - 5.30pm (10.00am - 4.00pm Winter) 7 days a week, *except Christmas Day, Boxing Day and New Years Day*
Special rates available for schools, coach parties and outings  Charitable Trust No. 292048